C. Vann Woodward

C. Vann Woodward

America's Historian

JAMES C. COBB

THE UNIVERSITY OF NORTH CAROLINA PRESS

Chapel Hill

This book was published with the assistance of the
Fred W. Morrison Fund of the University of North Carolina Press.

Designed by Jamison Cockerham
Set in Arno and Scala Sans
by codeMantra

Manufactured in the United States of America

The University of North Carolina Press has been a member
of the Green Press Initiative since 2003.

Cover illustration derived from a sketch of
C. Vann Woodward by Charles W. Joyner, 1998.

LIBRARY OF CONGRESS CATALOGING-IN-PUBLICATION DATA
Names: Cobb, James C. (James Charles), 1947– author.
Title: C. Vann Woodward : America's historian / James C. Cobb.
Description: Chapel Hill : The University of North Carolina Press,
[2022] | Includes bibliographical references and index.
Identifiers: LCCN 2022015177 | ISBN 9781469670218
(cloth ; alk. paper) | ISBN 9781469670225 (ebook)
Subjects: LCSH: Woodward, C. Vann (Comer Vann), 1908–1999. |
Historians—United States—Biography. | Southern States—Historiography.
Classification: LCC E175.5.W653 C63 2022 |
DDC 973.07202 [B]—dc23/eng/20220525
LC record available at https://lccn.loc.gov/2022015177

TO MY STUDENTS

who gave me the best years of my life

Contents

Preface & Acknowledgments ix

Introduction: The Legendary Historian 1

1 Another Mark Twain If He Applied Himself:
The Superintendent's Son Spreads His Wings 9

2 A Southern Historian I Must Be—Or Somehow Become:
A Budding Biographer Makes Hard Choices 17

3 History, I Find, Is a Collection of Facts: Pursuing
the "Cursed Degree" in Chapel Hill 39

4 A Better Read Than Huxley's New Novel:
Telling the Tom Watson Story 58

5 A Chance to Have My Say about the Period:
The Origins of *Origins* 83

6 Juleps for the Few and Pellagra for the Crew: Reckoning
with the Redeemer–New South Legacy 105

7 Cordially Invited to Be Absent: Integrating
the Southern Historical Association 128

8 A Fundamental Attack upon the Prevailing View:
Launching *The Strange Career of Jim Crow* 154

9 Wrong in All Its Major Parts: *Strange Career* Returns to Earth 184

10 A Basis for Criticizing the American Legend:
Southern History as Both Asset and Burden 207

11 Tortured for Months: The Agony of Moving to Yale 230

12 Therapist of the Public Mind: The Strange
Career of C. Vann Woodward 254

13 I Mean to Do All I Can: The Mentor Flexes His Muscles 276

14 An Ever More Conservative Old Liberal:
Moving to the Right or Standing Fast? 298

15 I Do Not See How I Could Have Been Misunderstood:
Sorting Out the Aptheker Debacle 319

16 The Masterpiece That Became a Hoax (and Won a
Pulitzer): Rewriting Mary Chesnut's Diary 342

17 Still More That I Can Do: The Satisfactions
of Staying the Course 369

Conclusion: America's Historian 395

Notes 423

Index 473

A section of illustrations begins on page 407

Preface & Acknowledgments

My first live sighting of C. Vann Woodward came in November 1973, when I attended my first meeting of the Southern Historical Association right after passing my comprehensive PhD exams at the University of Georgia. My acquaintance with Woodward's writing dated back to my undergraduate encounter with "The Search for a Central Theme," his famed essay on the true essence of southern identity. His near ubiquitous presence in the literature in southern history that I was obliged to devour in completing my PhD coursework and prepping for my exams had left no doubt that his work had made an extraordinarily pronounced and pervasive imprint, not only on his particular field, but on the entire profession. Nothing about his appearance struck me as particularly noteworthy when I laid eyes on him nearly half a century ago. With his thick-rimmed glasses and trademark tweed jacket (from which he exacted enormous mileage over the years), he hardly stood out at a gathering of historians. His appearance belied the formidable singularity of his presence, however. It was clear to me that many in attendance for the session on the civil rights movement that he chaired were there, not for further enlightenment on the topic, but for the opportunity to get a closer look at the man presiding over the discussion. Elsewhere during the meeting, his movements could easily be tracked by the abrupt decrease in the decibel level, even amid the din of the book exhibit, as well as the cocked eyes and subtle nudges employed by the hangers-on to alert those around him to his presence. I would observe this ritual again and again over the next twenty-five years, including his final SHA meeting appearance at the age of ninety in 1998. I found myself in Woodward's company on several occasions over that span.

Beyond repeated references to how much my work had benefited from his, something he had surely heard hundreds of times from others, my MO was to respect his characteristically polite reserve. Not the least of my reasons for doing so was seeing him so often beset by people whom he clearly did not recognize but insisted nonetheless on slapping him on the back and calling him "Vann" with sufficient volume and gusto to suggest that the two had once been inseparable childhood chums.

Recollections of these occasions gradually merged with my continuing reflections on how much and for how long Woodward had influenced not only my individual scholarly endeavors but the study of American history in general. The catalyst for action on these reflections came in the form of an invitation to speak at a conference at Rice University in 2001 commemorating the fiftieth anniversary of the publication of Woodward's *Origins of the New South*. This commitment led me to make my first foray into Woodward's papers at Yale University, which at that point had only recently become accessible to researchers. The richness of what I found on a brief visit sealed the deal for me. If I lived long enough to dispatch all the commitments hanging over me at that point, I meant to write a book about C. Vann Woodward.

There were to be many return visits to New Haven in the years to come as I made my way through the ninety-six boxes containing Woodward's voluminous correspondence, as well as scattered notes and drafts of his published and unpublished writings, all dating from the late 1920s to a few months before his death in December 1999. There would also be a number of excursions to other archives, as well as countless hours devoted to getting so long and richly complex a story straight in a manuscript of manageable size. All of this is to say that, while I began this project thinking myself fully aware of the challenge of doing justice to so singularly rich, expansive, and important a career as Woodward's, I sorely underestimated the investment of time and energy that such an effort would ultimately entail. I hasten to acknowledge that by no means all of the hours and efforts dedicated to bringing this book to fruition were my own.

I am particularly grateful to the two anonymous readers who reviewed this book in manuscript for UNC Press and provided invaluable guidance in making the final product clearer, tighter, and better organized. Charles Eagles, Will Holmes, and Larry Powell also read key portions of the text and provided suggestions that made all of them better. I benefited a great deal from the generosity of John Herbert Roper in making the transcripts of the interviews he conducted for his 1987 book, *C. Vann Woodward, Southerner*, available to other scholars in the Southern Historical Collections at the University of North Carolina. We should all be grateful for the wonderful resource my late friend Michael O'Brien provided in his 2013 collection, *The Letters of C. Vann Woodward*. (When I was asked to read the book in manuscript for Yale University Press, I quickly realized that had Michael and I had not only worked in the same collection but spent our time reading a lot of the same correspondence. In the end, I ran across no more than a handful letters that I had not seen. The two on which I drew for this book are credited herein.)

It is simply a given that every historian who finishes a thoroughly researched book bears a profound indebtedness to some knowledgeable and cooperative archivists. The greatest of my debts in this particular category is to Christine Weideman and her consistently proficient and supportive staff in the Manuscripts and Special Collections Division of Yale's Sterling Memorial Library, where Genevieve Coyle was particularly helpful. I have ventured into my share of archives over the years, but I have yet to find a better place to work than the one afforded me at Yale. Though I spent less time in Emory's Stuart A. Rose Manuscript, Archives, and Rare Book Library, I could not have asked for more helpful and efficient assistance than I received, most notably from Carrie Hintz and Rachel Detzler. The staff at UNC's Southern Historical Collection did their usual jam-up job of helping me to locate and examine materials efficiently. I am deeply grateful to members of the staff in the Special and Area Studies Collections of the George A. Smathers Library at the University of Florida for providing me with copies of all the letters to and from C. Vann Woodward in the William G. Carleton Papers. I am likewise indebted to Scott Glassman, Jonathan Haws, Patrick Hayes, Tore Olsson, and Ben Parten for their archival digging in my stead and to Ashton Ellett and Matthew Burkhalter for imposing a semblance of organization on the materials I accumulated over the course of my research meanderings. I am grateful to Andre Bernard, William Ferris, Jennifer Julier, Hal Rainey, and Randall Stephens for their cooperation in gathering the illustrations for the book. I owe special thanks to the family of the late Charles Joyner for allowing me to use Chaz's sketch of Woodward for the cover and to Wingate Downs for having the courage to photograph the author. Glenda Gilmore offered invaluable guidance and information, as well as unfailing empathy. Deepest personal and professional thanks are also due to Mark Simpson-Vos and his associates at UNC Press. Mark's patient, sensitive guidance and support were absolutely vital to my efforts to complete this book despite the challenges posed over the past twelve months by my wife Lyra's severe illness. As to Lyra herself, I lack both the vocabulary and the emotional discipline to convey the full measure of my gratitude and pleasure at seeing her at first survive an ordeal that would have killed most people and then power back to resume her vital role as not only my go-to editor but the long-suffering soul mate whose love and companionship I cherish more than anything in my life.

My wife and family have been the greatest of my blessings, but not the least of them, surely, has been the opportunity to make a living doing something that I would have gladly done for free, absent such necessities as housing, groceries, and, needless to say, beer. Though I have found genuine satisfaction in the writing I have managed to do over the years, I take greatest pride in the number of my former PhD students whose dissertations are now represented in the still-swelling stack of books strategically positioned to catch the eye of anyone entering our front door. I have reaped untold benefits from my interactions with these and scores of other former graduate students who have enriched my classes and worn my office carpet threadbare over the past forty-five years. Their reactions to my efforts to guide and instruct them have consistently pushed me toward what my very wise mother would have called a much deeper understanding of what I knew. More important still are the enduring personal bonds forged in these countless interactions. These alone would more than justify dedicating this book to the people who have given so much warmth and meaning to my life.

Athens, Georgia
December 2021

C. Vann Woodward

Introduction

The Legendary Historian

C. Vann Woodward was scarcely two weeks shy of his ninetieth birthday on October 28, 1998, when he joined Arthur Schlesinger Jr. and Sean Wilentz for a C-SPAN press conference aimed at publicizing their cosponsored petition, signed by more than 400 fellow historians, opposing the move by congressional Republicans to impeach President Bill Clinton. Although Schlesinger was the best known of the three, he went out of his way to defer to Woodward as not only "the Dean of the historical profession in the United States" but its long-acknowledged "conscience" and principal source of "moral leadership." Wilentz echoed Schlesinger's reference to Woodward as the "conscience of the profession," which explained why the first call he made seeking guidance and support for this effort went to his former teacher at Yale.[1]

From the press conference, it was on to an appearance on the Public Broadcasting System's *Charlie Rose Show*, where Woodward seemed to struggle with making himself clear and Schlesinger and Wilentz wound up doing most of the talking. In truth, both historians were likely less concerned about the substance of anything Woodward said than the statement he made simply by appearing with them. Each recognized that the imprimatur of someone so widely respected, not simply for his scholarship, but for his integrity and moral vision, lent critical legitimacy to what some had disparaged as a fundamentally partisan effort. For his part, Rose appeared humbled by

Woodward's mere presence, assuring him that he would have "invited you on this program even if I hadn't read this statement. . . . It's a great pleasure to have you here today."[2]

Scarcely a year later, Woodward would command even greater reverence from a chorus of distinguished eulogists, including Harvard historian and future president Drew Gilpin Faust, who pronounced him "the twentieth century's greatest American historian." Grand as such an assessment seems simply on its face, however, it might not even do full justice to the scope or scale of Woodward's accomplishments. He was scarcely the only twentieth-century American historian to enhance or expand our understanding of key aspects of the nation's past. Yet we would be hard-pressed indeed to find any among them—or, for that matter, among scholars of any other disciplinary stripe—who earned such deference and respect within the academic sphere while achieving such prominence outside it, much less maintained both for nearly so long. Nor did Woodward acquire or retain his lofty stature, as either a professional historian or a public intellectual, by resolutely steering clear of crises and controversies. A tireless advocate for social justice, from his twenties until his nineties, he compiled an astonishing record of direct involvement in crusading for racial integration, defending civil liberties and academic freedom, and combating abuses of power in the highest echelons of government. In this, he revealed a personal commitment to changing the present that his writings about the past often seemed calculated to inspire in others.[3]

Such an expansive record of social and intellectual achievement seemed, to say the least, unlikely for someone born in rural Arkansas during the first decade of the twentieth century, raised in its Klan-infested communities, and educated in its public schools. His friend and admirer Arthur Schlesinger prepped at Phillips Exeter Academy before going on to graduate summa cum laude from Harvard. Woodward was fresh out Morrilton High School in the fall of 1926 when he ventured roughly 100 miles south to Henderson-Brown College, a tiny, conservative Methodist college in Arkadelphia. Two years later, he moved on to Emory University in Atlanta, another Methodist institution, larger and less insular, but still conservative, and hardly anyone's idea of a breeding ground for radical ideas in the 1920s.

Appropriately enough for someone whose keen sense of irony would suffuse and enrich much of his most influential writing, Woodward's career was a story rich in unexpected twists, abrupt turns, and unforeseen outcomes. Perhaps the most surprising of these was that he became a historian at all. His brief exposure to the discipline at Emory had persuaded him that he wanted no part of it as a profession. His overriding passion was literature at that point, and so it remained, even after he enrolled in the history PhD program at the University of North Carolina in 1934 purely as a means of securing the funding he needed to complete his biography of Georgia Populist firebrand Tom Watson. He would complain incessantly over the next three years about the excruciatingly ponderous and uninspiring reading and coursework required of him in pursuing a "cursed degree" he had no intention of putting to use. He invested minimal effort in meeting these requirements, focusing instead on completing his Watson manuscript, but his single-mindedness paid off in a dissertation that was submitted to Macmillan in May 1937 and published less than a year later with scarcely a trace of revision.[4]

Despite the favorable response to *Tom Watson: Agrarian Rebel* in academic circles, his indifferently acquired PhD in history remained largely an afterthought until its dismal sales figures finally forced him to admit that he could not make a living strictly as a biographer. With that, the stage was set for arguably the most pivotal of all the timely and fortuitous twists that were to become the hallmark of his long career. The invitation to write volume 9 of the new History of the South series, encompassing the period 1877–1913, came in March 1939 after the author originally chosen for the book abruptly withdrew from the project. Owing to the onset of World War II and other delays, the volume would not appear until 1951, though it would soon prove itself worth the wait. The research effort behind *Origins of the New South* was massive enough to produce another book, *Reunion and Reaction*, a boldly revisionist take on the Compromise of 1877, which ostensibly brought down the curtain on Reconstruction. Yet it was *Origins*, a commanding synthesis of a little-explored period, that shredded the dominant, wholly sanitized New South historical account of the era, which would quickly establish its author as the leading authority on southern history since the Civil War.[5]

Meanwhile, the book that would fuel Woodward's meteoric ascent to prominence beyond the academy grew out of a series of lectures, delivered in September 1954, scarcely four months after the Supreme Court's landmark school desegregation ruling in *Brown v. Board of Education*. They were rushed into print essentially verbatim by Oxford University Press in April 1955 as *The Strange Career of Jim Crow*. Looking to rally active support for enforcing the Brown decree, Woodward took issue with the widespread perception that rigid racial segregation had been an elemental fixture in southern life far too long to be eradicated by a mere Supreme Court decree. Contending that segregation dated back little more than fifty years, to the Jim Crow statutes of the 1890s, he encouraged readers to believe that, as a creation of law in its own right—and a fairly recent one at that—the practice could surely be eliminated by the same means. Regardless of whether they bought his argument, a great many Americans bought his book (which would appear in three revised editions and go on to sell in the neighborhood of a million copies) simply because it offered the best—and for quite some time, the only—brief overall narrative of the origins and development of segregation at a time when it could hardly have been more relevant.[6]

Well into the twentieth century, southerners writing about their region's past in any genre were expected to hew tightly to the tenets of a highly orthodox historical creed aimed at rationalizing the South's current racial, political, and economic system as the most logical and feasible extension of strategies devised to help it overcome the devastation and havoc wrought by the Civil War and Reconstruction. Between 1938 and 1955, Woodward had challenged this narrative—and the sense of legitimacy it conveyed on the present order—in four books, which, as historian Richard H. King claimed with little exaggeration, collectively "revolutionized the established views of Southern history from the end of the Civil War to World War I." This was no small achievement for someone who had once steadfastly rejected even the notion of becoming a historian. Yet, in another striking twist, at age forty-six, with nearly half his life and two-thirds of what proved to be an exceptionally long and productive career before him, the man on the cusp of becoming the reigning eminence in his field had published his last book-length, originally researched work of history.[7]

There would be an abortive attempt to write a book on Reconstruction and a handful of important articles for major professional journals, to be sure. Going forward, however, Woodward's written contributions as a historian, arguably some of the greatest he would render, were to come elsewhere, in scores of essays, commentaries, and opinion pieces appearing in widely read publications ranging from the *New York Times* to the *New York Review of Books* and to *Harper's*, *Newsweek*, and *Time*.

A number of these would resurface in published collections of his writings, the best known being the enormously engaging *Burden of Southern History*, where he deftly explored the nature of both southern and national identity and the vital importance of each to the other. Though never hesitant to address the South's historic wrongs and enduring flaws, as several essays in this collection revealed, he maintained a powerful and unapologetic emotional attachment to his downtrodden native region and frequently reminded its self-righteous northern critics that their own backyards could use a bit of work as well. Despite the book's title, its contents offered as many lessons for Americans outside the South as within it, including his precocious warnings about the inherently dangerous presumptions of national innocence and invincibility that sustained the mythology of American exceptionalism. These were borne out repeatedly as the nation endured the tragedy and folly of intervention and escalation in Vietnam, the explosion of wanton violence and rage in its central cities, and the humiliation and disillusionment of the Watergate scandal. A comprehensive tally of Woodward's writing aimed at readers outside the traditional academic realm would offer a veritable laundry list of the critical national and international issues that concerned Americans in general at one point or another over the better part of his ninety-one years.

One might have predicted that, at some point, his growing popular appeal would either undermine his lofty standing among his academic colleagues or, as it seemed to do with Schlesinger, encourage Woodward to abandon that calling altogether. Yet, if anything, the effect was just the opposite. After securing a position at Johns Hopkins immediately after the war, he had politely resisted the advances of a formidable procession of ardent academic suitors before Yale came calling with the offer of a prestigious Sterling Professorship in 1960. Between Hopkins and Yale, he would direct more than forty PhD dissertations to completion. Among their authors were three future Pulitzer laureates, not to mention many more who garnered other prestigious awards too numerous to cite. Others have directed more dissertations, certainly, but surely no American historian has managed over a three-decade span to attract and train a collection of graduate students who, as a group, registered a more substantial impact on their field. His noted generosity in reading and commenting on the work of dozens of others at various stages in their careers and his nearly four-decade tenure as the editor of the multivolume Oxford History of the United States make it even more difficult to exaggerate Woodward's importance to scholarship in American history during the last half of the twentieth century.

Woodward's contributions to the profession earned him an extended tenure as an unrivaled power broker and influencer in historical circles and beyond. His word carried enormous weight in decisions about who was hired and promoted, and whose book was published, reviewed in the right places, and garnered major awards, particularly the Pulitzer. In this, his career offers a rare glimpse into the intricacies and subtleties of high-altitude academic politics, and how academic elites function and retain their status, even as rapidly shifting ideological and methodological currents seem to shake the foundations of their respective disciplines.

Extraordinary as the stature he achieved within his own grudgingly chosen profession might be, the broader importance of Woodward's story lies in the insights it offers into major developments and trends in American intellectual life and public affairs during the better part of the twentieth century. At the outset of his career, his readiness to buck the established narrative in southern history set him apart from the overwhelming majority of the white historians who preceded him. Yet in his mind, surely, it put him in the infinitely preferable company of William Faulkner, Thomas Wolfe, and Robert Penn Warren, as part of the so-called Generation of 1900, a cadre of gifted and independent-minded southern writers born primarily between 1890 and 1910. This literary cohort had emerged near the end of the 1920s as Modernist challengers to what was, at heart, a tightly scripted Victorian vision of past and present grounded in the conjoined myths of Old South gentility and New South progress. Woodward would step forward a decade later as a historian bent on doing much the same thing, and he readily acknowledged his profound indebtedness to Faulkner, Wolfe, and Warren for illustrating "the presence of the past in the present" so vividly and thus setting a standard to which he believed all historians should aspire. Meanwhile, Woodward's appreciation of the clarity and grace vital to an effective literary style became a hallmark of his writing. Flannery O'Connor was hardly given to praising other southern writers not named Faulkner, but after devouring *The Burden of Southern History*, she reported to a friend that she had "taken up reading C. Vann Woodward.... Southern history usually gives me a pain, but this man knows how to write English."[8]

His dedication to clear and accessible writing surely served Woodward well as he led the way, along with Schlesinger and Richard Hofstadter, in reinvigorating public interest in history by harnessing it to new, more socially purposeful ends. In this regard, no aspect of Woodward's career looms larger than what it says about the importance of how historians perceive the very nature and purpose of their craft, particularly with respect to making their treatments of the past usable for their contemporary readers.

Even in his earlier scholarly writing, Woodward's zeal for reshaping history into a potential catalyst for social betterment in the present led him more than once to claim too much for the relatively slender share of supporting evidence at his disposal and even to distort it to better suit his purpose. It would take a while, but his willingness to allow what he saw as the needs of the present to color his interpretations of the past finally caught up with him. Succeeding generations of historians unearthed mounds of evidence running contrary to many of his interpretations and suggested that he had passed too lightly over the realities of historical context in his search for some more hopeful lesson applicable to his own day. Though Woodward was not about to admit it, many of the principal arguments offered in the four books written in the first twenty years of his career (and later credited with transforming the study of southern history) had been effectively taken to the historiographical woodshed well before his death in 1999. Yet the critical scrutiny devoted to Woodward's historical monographs over the last half of the twentieth century was, in a real sense, a tribute to the seminal importance of his contributions to scholarship during the first phase of his career. Indeed, the powerful and widespread impulse to test his arguments, evaluate his aims, methods, and assumptions, and follow up on the questions he raised was very nearly sufficient in and of itself to dynamize the study of southern history since the Civil War for the better part of two generations.

Even so, Woodward's story is no thoroughly heroic and triumphal narrative from beginning to end. Heavily invested through word and deed in the long battle for racial integration, he was sorely angered in the mid-1960s to see many younger blacks suddenly renouncing the aims and belittling, even undermining, the hard-won achievements of the civil rights movement while embracing the ideal of black separatism. This anger, in turn, fueled his steadfast opposition to separate black studies programs, while he saw "multiculturalism" and its various outcroppings running counter to America's historic commitment to "E Pluribus Unum." Woodward's steadfast late-career resistance to such developments arising on the left tempted some to stereotype him as yet another young liberal firebrand whose views shifted markedly to the right as he grew older. In reality, though, his fundamental stance on race, race relations, and cultural assimilation had remained remarkably consistent throughout his adult life. Beginning in the 1960s, what he saw on campus and beyond amounted to an outright rejection of some of his most deeply felt beliefs. His bitterness at this disillusioning turn of events mounted in the face of the sustained emotional pounding he suffered between 1969 and 1982, when he lost his only child, his three closest friends, and his wife.

Woodward was never much given to sharing his inner feelings. What he admitted as a young man—that he was "prone to conceal a good deal"—was true throughout his life, leaving even those who knew him best to acknowledge their difficulties in reading his thoughts and emotions. He generally managed to keep his enduring grief over the personal losses he suffered at bay by committing himself to a work regimen more befitting an anxious assistant professor coming up for tenure. He was less successful in bottling up his anger over the direction of his profession and higher education in general and his frustration at being unable to do much about it. His bruised ego got the better of him in his over-the-top campaign to prevent historian and high-profile Communist Party spokesman Herbert Aptheker from teaching an undergraduate seminar at Yale. Meanwhile, his righteous anger at what he saw as a tidal wave of political correctness engulfing college campuses also seemed to blur his judgment, as it did in his largely uncritical endorsement of right-wing provocateur Dinesh D'Souza's sensationalized account of multiculturalism run amok in American universities.[9]

Still, signs that such lapses in judgement, discretion, and self-control as marked the final decades of his long life and career had significantly blemished his reputation or diminished his standing were not readily detectable. His appearances at the Southern Historical Association still brought something of a hush over the proceedings, and on the very last of those visits, in November 1998, those proceedings featured a celebration of his ninetieth birthday. Scarcely a year later, the torrent of superlatives unloosed in eulogies, obituaries, and tributes from former students as well as many who knew him only through his writing marked the passing of a person of truly monumental stature. Nor has that stature grown perceptibly stooped with the passage of time. Woodward's visage eventually became so familiar that it was immortalized in the caricature of a kindly old professor squinting out through his thick glasses and clad in his signature tweed. And, suffice it to say, few historians have approached the widespread name recognition he achieved in his lifetime, let alone maintained it in death. In the twentieth year after his passing, a Google Scholar search for his name yields roughly a thousand hits, and that name is often prefaced by "legendary historian" when it appears in pieces written for public audiences. This book explores the making of that legend and the brilliant, complicated, and sometimes perplexing figure it both exalts and obscures.

1

Another Mark Twain
If He Applied Himself

The Superintendent's Son Spreads His Wings

Comer Vann Woodward was born in Vanndale, Cross County, Arkansas, on November 13, 1908. The county was named for David C. Cross, a native of Gates County, North Carolina, who had moved into the area, amassed a fortune in land speculation, and owned as much as 83,000 acres in 1860. Cross was also the nephew of Woodward's great-great-grandmother Nancy Cross, who had married John Vann, a legislator and leading citizen of Hertford County, North Carolina, in 1806. Their son Renselear Vann had moved first to Fayette County, Tennessee, where he had married Emily Maget in 1843, and then on to northeastern Arkansas in 1850. Renselear and Emily reportedly owned twenty-six slaves and some 600 acres of land when they built the post office and general store that would become the heart of Vanndale.[1]

Woodward's grandfather John Maget Vann had served four years in the Confederate army but was still a teenager when Lee surrendered. He returned from the war to establish himself as a successful merchant and agricultural landlord. His marriage to Ida Hare, whose family was prominent in both local Methodist and business circles, produced three children, among them Emily "Bess" Branch Vann. Whatever concerns there might have been about the young man who would grow up to be Vanndale's favorite son, the adequacy of his exposure to Methodism should never have been in doubt, for his father, Hugh Alison "Jack" Woodward, was the son of William Benjamin Woodward, a circuit-riding Tennessee Methodist preacher, and maintained his strong allegiance to the church throughout his career as an educator and administrator. The same was true for Hugh's older brother Comer. W. B. Woodward had married Elizabeth Lockhart in 1870, only to die of tuberculosis in 1879, consigning his widow and her four children to what Comer recalled as a constant "struggle against poverty." With their mother's death nine years later, the children were fortunate to come under the supervision and enjoy the support of a kindly Methodist minister who imbued them with a sense of the importance of education, leaving both Comer and Jack to pursue careers in that field.[2]

The Woodward family's ties to the clergy had accorded a higher social standing than their actual economic standing would suggest. Though Vann would steadfastly deny any interest in his family's ancestral status and rank, he suggested otherwise when he shared his rather fanciful notion that his paternal grandmother was quite possibly the illegitimate great-granddaughter of the famous novelist Sir Walter Scott. While visiting Scotland, he had visited the grave of Sir John Lockhart, who was both Scott's biographer and his son-in-law. One of Lockhart's sons, Walter, had reputedly been a rounder and wastrel who came to an untimely and undignified end at the hands of persons unknown. Woodward's notion that the no-good Walter Lockhart had sired his grandmother Elizabeth Lockhart out of wedlock stemmed from an incident he recalled from childhood in which his father had been contacted by a British barrister who felt that Jack Woodward might well be a beneficiary of a substantial estate he was trying to settle. At the time, Woodward remembered, despite the urgings of his mother, his "impecunious schoolmaster" father had refused to pursue the matter. Yet, intrigued as Woodward was by the possibility that his grandmother "came from Scotland," the notion runs contrary to census records suggesting that she was born in Franklin County, Tennessee, in 1852.[3]

As the son of an educator, Woodward was certainly exposed to the importance of learning at an early age. Both Comer and Jack Woodward had attended Emory College before its campus was moved from the tiny town of Oxford, Georgia, into the shadow of Atlanta in Decatur. After further study at the University of Tennessee and the University of Chicago, followed by a brief teaching stint in Georgia, Jack took a job at Pine Bluff, Arkansas, south of Little Rock, in 1903. Two years later, Jack Woodward moved 120 miles to the northeast to become the superintendent at Wynne, in Cross County, where he met and married Bess Vann. After eleven years and two children, the family moved first to Arkadelphia, southwest of Little Rock, where Jack was superintendent for two years before heading north to assume the same post at Morrilton in 1918 when Vann was ten. In Morrilton, Vann was subject to all the adolescent taunting and even ostracism that came with spending his school years with "the label 'Superintendent's Son' stamped on my back." Not surprisingly in this circumstance, he committed himself to a pattern of rambunctious behavior, designed to prove himself simply "one of the boys." At the prodding of his father, Vann also tried out for football and played center on the Morrilton High team. He protested later that, despite "thoroughly detesting the game," he knew that had he not at least "come out" for football, "the girls would pay me no mind." Woodward was more athletic and athletically inclined than he chose to admit, and he went on to earn varsity letters in the sport.[4]

In fact, being singled out as the son of the school superintendent seemed to make the young man all the more sensitive to the way his male peers perceived his masculinity. Though he enjoyed a much closer bond with his mother than his father, Bess Woodward's earnest efforts to persuade him to learn the piano came to naught because the idea struck him as too "sissy." Even so, Bess, an excellent pianist, had delighted in playing classical music for him when he was a child because, he later recalled, "she knew I loved it." As an adult, he would remain fully sensitive to her love of music. With the family living in Georgia in 1930, the financial boost promised by a teaching position at Georgia Tech was reason enough, he thought, to "start making plans now for getting the 'Mater' off to Atlanta [from nearby Oxford] for every one of the Grand Opera performances. We can't afford to let her miss a one."[5]

Though he had no desire to be tagged as the stereotypical "bookworm," Vann quietly spent many an hour at the Carnegie Library in Morrilton, where he not only read "the usual boys [sic] books," but discovered Henry James's *Portrait of a Lady* and, at age fourteen, "became something of a James addict." (Woodward's appetite for reading would not dissipate as he aged or pursued his own writing. When he was called to active service in World War II, the list of books stored in his Library of Congress cupboard for the duration of the war included more than 250 titles. Predictably enough, most focused on U.S. and European history, but authors ranging from Plato and Aristotle to Goethe to John Keats to James Joyce accounted for a substantial share.) Of his formal secondary education, Woodward would later admit that "the only thing of lasting value" was "the years of Latin I took under my father." Yet he had "learned to treasure" his schooling in Morillton, for it had allowed him to spend "the crucial and impressionable years of adolescence with boys and girls from both sides of the railroad tracks and all levels of the small social heap—bottom to top (so long as they were white)."[6]

Upon graduating from Morrilton High in 1926, it was back to Arkadelphia for Vann, who enrolled in Henderson-Brown College, then a small, struggling Methodist liberal arts school, where he soon made a mark for himself among both students and faculty. Though he was not averse to some illicit partying fueled by some Prohibition-era bootleg spirits, known otherwise as "Virginia Dare Tonic," Woodward's interest in books soon led him to become a fixture in the Garland Literary Society. This affiliation came perhaps in spite of rather than because of its rather gung-ho motto, "Let Us Work Upward," for it was quickly apparent that he took particular satisfaction in puncturing romantic illusions about history and public affairs. His first speech to the group addressed the very issue of the difference between historical "Romance and Realities." He also excelled as a debater, even leading the Henderson-Brown team to a victory over Ole Miss in 1928. Although Woodward's address on "The Outlawry of War" garnered first place in a statewide oratorical competition, faculty and fellow students picked up on a trait that would mark him throughout his career—he was notably less effective as a speaker than as a writer. As a friend and classmate put it, "If he'd only pass out copies of his addresses, and let people who are interested read them, everything would be better." Many who would hear Woodward at the lectern in years to come would have agreed. His soft voice and halting and mumbled delivery so frustrated his graduate adviser, Howard K. Beale, that several years after he received his PhD, Beale had admonished him to "even yet go out behind the barn and practice so that you won't talk as if you had mush in your mouth." These proclivities were all the more unfortunate in light of the young man's precocious erudition. Reporting on Woodward's talk to the Garland Literary Society, a writer for the school paper, the *Oracle*, deemed the address "of such a deep nature, we fear, that some of his listeners did not catch the fullest significance of his words," adding that "lack of space forbids our doing them justice here."[7]

Woodward's approach to his course assignments was no less ambitious. In an essay on "Impressionistic Prose," he observed that "the very lifeblood of Impressionism is its suggestiveness. If it fails to suggest the proper images, is the most dismal example of pedantry in literature. . . . But that rare jewel of pure Impressionism is worth the price of digging for. It is the highest priced gem of literature, in that it is infinitely more highly polished, it is possessed of innumerable facets and finally it does not depend upon reflected light for its beauty, but is brilliant because it seems to contain its own source of light."[8]

The young writer may have seen himself spreading his own literary wings just a bit when he fancied himself astride the mythic "winged Pegasus," his senses suddenly so acute that everything in the town seemed different: "The streetlights glow with a new meaning and the missing ones are dark for a reason. . . . Familiar faces flow by, each casts a warning, gives a hint, smiles at some hidden meaning. . . . The pavement is a dark strain flowing with occult obscurities."[9]

As he would so frequently throughout his later career, at Henderson-Brown Woodward put his skills as a writer to good use in support of the causes he embraced. As part of a small but determined and self-confident student cohort, he defended the school against efforts to reduce it to two-year status or shut it down altogether. (In the end the Methodist church effectively ceded it to the State of Arkansas, which maintained it as a teacher's college.) He also championed numerous reforms on a campus where both the academic and extracurricular opportunities for women were more reminiscent of the nineteenth century than the twentieth. There was also the woefully underfinanced library, a particularly critical concern for a bibliophile like Woodward, and other campus services and activities that suffered under the inept and impetuous oversight of soon-to-be-deposed president Clifford L. Hornaday. Not all his energies were dedicated to rabble-rousing, however. Woodward was thoroughly immersed in all sorts of campus activities, serving as class treasurer and the first president of the college's International Relations Club, and his yearbook photo caption, "a true friend, a good student, and a loyal classmate," suggested a fairly well-rounded young man.[10]

Woodward attracted no more avowed champion at Henderson-Brown than his English instructor, Boulware Martin, who nurtured his literary aspirations and maintained that he was not a stirring speaker because he knew he had something important to say and saw no need to resort to "pyrotechnics to get people to listen." Based on the writing he did in her courses and what she had seen of his writing in the *Oracle*, Martin thought that this young man, who seemed to have read practically every book in the college library, truly had the makings of a great satirical writer, and a classmate suggested that he could have been "another Mark Twain, if he applied himself." Certainly, Martin recalled, "although he liked history, he was much more interested in English and writing."[11]

To say the least, Woodward's relationship with the young and quite attractive Boulware Martin was intense and would remain so well after he left Arkadelphia. As she struggled with a personal crisis in 1930, he reminded her, "I love you and would do all I could to help you. You believe that don't you?

. . . My heart is full for you, even if it does not run into words." He also pled for a photograph, expressing his pleasure with "your habit of parting your teeth in the middle" and assuring her that he would be "charmed by your reflective mood."[12]

As he matured, Woodward seemed to become less passionate in his feelings toward his former teacher, although the opposite proved true for her. The two had spent a memorable evening together in New Orleans in 1929 while she was working on her master's degree at H. Sophie Newcomb Memorial College. After he returned to Henderson-Brown some twenty years later (as an accomplished scholar and a married man), she confessed her disappointment that he had "quite properly" left her at the front door of the residence hall "in that sweet-scented New Orleans midnight." Beyond assuring him that she had "always loved" him and carried him "in my heart all these years," she likely left him a bit nonplussed when she confided that, even after so long a time, she had felt a "sudden pain and choking" when he bid her goodnight at the end of his recent visit with her.[13]

Though Woodward had moved on emotionally, he never forgot his intellectual indebtedness to Boulware Martin or his experience at Henderson-Brown in general. His curiosity had always extended well beyond the confines of the tiny college, however. At the end of his freshman year in 1927, he somehow managed to persuade his parents to let him go to Europe. Starting out with only twenty dollars in his pocket, he first hitchhiked to New York City and then down to Norfolk, Virginia. There, much to his mother's consternation, he was jailed briefly as a vagrant after he was found sleeping in a bed of pansies before signing on to work on the S.S. *Westerner*, a freighter bound for Rotterdam. The time he spent with crewmates from southern and eastern Europe proved educational, and he was indebted especially to the tyrannical "bos'n," whose facility with "Russian cuss words" enriched the already extensive vocabulary of the young "landlubber" who recalled mastering the man's native tongue "with surprising alacrity."[14]

This great adventure may well have figured in his decision the following year to broaden his horizons by leaving Henderson-Brown for Emory University, which he admitted to choosing "mainly [out of] admiration" for his uncle and namesake, Comer McDonald Woodward, a sociologist who also served as dean of men at Emory. Like his brother Jack, "Uncle Comer" had received an undergraduate degree from Emory College in 1900 before earning an MA and Bachelor of Divinity at the University of Chicago. An ordained minister, he had taught at Southern Methodist University before coming to Emory and had earned a reputation as a socially conscious scholar deeply committed to the Methodist faith.[15]

Comer M. Woodward ultimately influenced his nephew profoundly, not simply in the critical assistance he offered the young man in opening doors and pursuing opportunities, but in the scholar-activist role model that he provided. In this latter capacity, he may have, however unwittingly, made it harder for young Vann to relate to his own father. Not only did he later re-call seeing what he took to be a lynch mob in Morrilton as a youth, but he remembered vividly a Sunday morning when a local Klan representative in full regalia strode into the Methodist church and delivered a contribution, which the minister readily accepted. When his uncle Comer, who was active in various interracially cooperative initiatives in Atlanta, came to visit shortly thereafter and offered a spirited denunciation of the Klan at the dinner table, the teenager was struck by his father's taut silence on the matter, and he re-called "turning against him" at that point. As he grew older, Woodward came to realize that, as superintendent of the public schools, "the poor man," would surely "have risked his whole job [and] the livelihood if not the actual lives of our whole family" had he spoken out openly against the Klan. This admission came rather late in Woodward's life, however, and well after his father's death.[16]

Comer Woodward's readiness to condemn persecution and injustice, al-beit only within the confines of his brother and sister-in-law's home in this case, was not the only way in which Vann found his uncle more appealing than his father. Where Jack Woodward had shuffled his family back and forth across the state searching for a more remunerative but still safe position as a public-school administrator, Comer had ventured out into the world, seized the opportunities, and made things happen. He also made things happen, not just for his nephew, but for his brother as well. Sensing that Jack was entertaining thoughts of moving into higher education, possibly at Emory, Comer drew on his extensive local contacts to push his brother as a candidate for superintendent of the local Decatur, Georgia, public schools. Picking up on inside information indicating that the school board was hesitant to ask Jack to come all the way from Arkansas at his own expense for an interview, he also surmised that they were unlikely to "hire anyone they haven't talked to" and urged Jack to "pull yourself together. Forget about the expense of the trip for the present and come on down here. We may blow up in our plans but I believe you are going to carry through." Lest his brother drag his feet on making travel arrangements, Comer even provided information about train connections.[17]

When Jack's somewhat reluctant candidacy did not "carry through," Comer reasoned that "if you want to transfer to college teaching, your best chance would be getting your master's degree." Doing so, he thought, would be much easier if his brother were principal of Decatur High School, as opposed to holding the more demanding post of superintendent of the entire system. Knowing that the principal's position would be filled shortly, Comer advised Jack that "whatever is to be done must be done soon."[18]

Jack Woodward seemed resigned to having missed out on the superintendent's job because "the Lord didn't see it that way, and I think he knows best." He resisted his brother's prodding about the principal's job because he felt that he should simply "cut loose" if he decided to do his graduate work at Emory and that "to accept the principalship would not help the situation." He expressed enthusiasm about coming to Emory to get his master's degree and peppered Comer with questions about places to live and whether he should attempt to do the first portion of his coursework by correspondence. He did, however, caution his brother against being disappointed "if we back out."[19]

Fearful of just such an outcome, Comer responded with a brief lecture that might well have been boiled down to "Carpe diem": "The whole thing turns on the will to get up and do it. The timid and fearful cannot risk large adventures. But the chance and the game are worth the try. . . . 'Come on in, the water[']s fine.' Remember also that the achievers do not stay always close to the shore." Apparently, Jack and Bess Woodward clung to the shore just a bit longer before making the big move, for they did not make it to Emory until the fall of 1928, a few months after Vann. With Bess taking courses at the same time as Jack and Vann, the Woodwards seemed to have made a family affair of it at Emory. A year later, his master's degree in hand, Jack moved, no doubt with Comer's deft assistance, into a position as an associate dean responsible for Emory Junior College and an attached preparatory academy. Both schools were in Oxford, Georgia, some thirty-five miles southeast of Atlanta, which had been home to the entire school until the main campus was relocated to Decatur, beginning in 1915.[20]

As near to ideal as Jack's situation seemed at this point, adjusting to the move and his new career proved difficult. He resigned his post at the junior college in 1934 for undisclosed reasons and spent the bulk of the next twenty years teaching part-time at various local colleges before having a brief and unsuccessful try at selling insurance. His son, on the other hand, would thrive from the start after the move, not just to Emory, but to a dynamic, restive Atlanta, where he would seize on the opportunity, not simply to witness firsthand, but to actively immerse himself in the major social and ideological conflicts of the day.

2

A Southern Historian I Must Be—
Or Somehow Become

A Budding Biographer Makes Hard Choices

Perhaps because Vann Woodward had seen a great deal more of the world than any but few nineteen-year-olds of his day when he arrived at Emory in 1928, his transition to a much bigger school in a much bigger city proved remarkably smooth. Although Emory had been around for ninety years, the school had been in its current location for less than a decade. Its relatively isolated original location and austere Methodist governance did not work in its favor, and in 1914 the school was still languishing in Oxford as Emory College when the bishops of the Methodist Episcopal Church, South, announced plans to establish a new Methodist university in the South. The decision to locate that university in Atlanta came after Asa Candler, the brother of former Emory president Warren Candler and, more important, the founder of the Coca-Cola Corporation, offered the Methodist Church a gift of $1 million and seventy-two acres of lush woods and pastureland in the Druid Hills area six miles northeast of downtown. Church officials quickly saw the wisdom then of relocating Emory College's liberal arts programs to this new campus, where, in September 1919, they joined the newly created schools of theology, law, medicine, business, and graduate studies.[1]

Though the institutional climate remained conservative, Emory boasted a respectable academic reputation by the time the entering junior from Arkansas made it to campus. Woodward had "reluctantly" joined Alpha Tau Omega fraternity, but he quickly rejected the superficiality and coerced camaraderie of Greek life. Taking up where he had left off at Henderson-Brown, he was soon writing essays for a variety of student publications, including the campus literary magazine, the *Phoenix*, while holding down a spot on the debate team. In a time when, even at a private school, students' grades were by no means a private matter, the *Atlanta Constitution* noted that while a "large percentage" of Emory freshman had been "barred" for the winter quarter in 1930 because of "scholarship deficiencies" during the previous term, a strong performance by upperclassmen boosted honor roll percentages in comparison to the previous year. Only two students had earned As in all four of their courses. The trio who had managed three As and a B included none other than Vann Woodward, who outpaced his friend and future fellow southern historian David Potter, who had made two As that were unfortunately accompanied by a lowly C.[2]

At the end of spring quarter 1930, Vann would graduate cum laude as one of the first recipients of Emory's new Bachelor of Philosophy degree. Though he seemed to have more interest in literary pursuits than anything else, Woodward had come in as "a totally confused undergraduate looking for something to call my major." Perhaps feeling a certain obligation to his uncle, he took a stab at sociology, but although a semester in Comer's course left his affection for his uncle "undiminished," it also left his interest in sociology "unstimulated." By his senior year, he had gravitated toward philosophy, drawn in part by the classes offered by an enthusiastic young newcomer to the faculty, Leroy Loemker. Although Loemker did not strike the young man as an activist, he had been instrumental in establishing a speaker series featuring racially integrated audiences and had supported efforts to introduce Marxist writings to the library's collection. Woodward remembered Loemker as somewhat "old-fashioned," yet the philosopher did seem to press upon the young intellectual what John Herbert Roper described as a certain "pragmatic activism," somewhat after the fashion of a William James, who envisioned a personal philosophy as something not simply espoused but acted upon in light of one's own experience.[3]

For his part Loemker recalled that his very first bachelor of philosophy student showed a real fascination with German. Feeling mightily put upon as a senior by having to sit through a required introductory course in logic, instead of answering what he considered to be trivial and mundane questions on the final examination, Woodward had simply quoted Mephistopheles's admonition to a medical student in Goethe's *Faust*: "Grau, teurer Freund, ist alle Theorie, und grün des Lebens goldner Baum" (Dear friend, all theory is gray, and green the golden tree of life). Although the professor apparently wrote off this flippant gesture to the impetuosity of youth, this would hardly be the last time that Woodward failed to conceal his impatience with having to master material that he deemed less than germane to his current interest or purpose.[4]

More than thirty years after he graduated from Emory, Woodward professed few fond memories of the school: "I remember to this day the depressing effect the place had on me, particularly the cloying politeness and vacuous gentility of the place.... And I remember that everybody seemed to be running for some elective office, being more than anything else careful not to offend anybody." In reality, the most significant influences on Woodward at Emory came, not from faculty, but from two of his contemporaries and closest friends, Glenn Rainey and Ernest Hartsock. Rainey, a native Atlantan, earned an AB and an MA from Emory. Although his undergraduate concentration was literature, his master's thesis on the Atlanta race riot of 1906 was directed by historian Theodore Jack. Rainey was an avid and effective debater who wound up coaching the Emory team (where he encountered Woodward) before departing for a job in the English department at Georgia Tech in 1929. The following year, he headed off to Northwestern, completing the coursework for his PhD in political science before returning to Georgia Tech, where he taught English until his retirement in 1974. Although he returned repeatedly to his dissertation on "The Independent Movement in Georgia," a study of political insurgency in the late nineteenth century, he never submitted it for approval.[5]

Rainey devoted considerable energy to social activism and was known for his outspoken assaults on the poll tax, lynching, and other forms of racial discrimination and persecution. This inclination would make him a friend and confidant of Lillian Smith and bring him into the orbit of such liberal organizations as the Southern Conference for Human Welfare. For all his interest in current affairs, Rainey retained a powerful fascination with literature. He would go on to translate a volume of Chaucer, and as an aspiring poet, he would see his verse published in several outlets, including Emory's *Phoenix*, where he worked as business manager with editor Ernest Hartsock, who would make the Woodward-Rainey duo into a distinctly literary-minded trio.[6]

Also a native Atlantan, Hartsock was an Emory undergraduate who stayed on for graduate work, and by the mid-1920s he was already widely recognized as a poet of great talent and promise. In fact, he would publish three volumes of verse, and his individual poems appeared in many of the leading journals of the day. Hartsock's "Strange Splendor" would win first honors from the American Poetry Society in 1929. Like many other young writers and artists of his generation, he was in open rebellion against the old, sterile, romantic tradition in southern letters. Stung by the ring of truth in H. L. Mencken's caustic dismissal of the intellectually sterile South as "The Sahara of the Bozart [Beaux-Arts]" and determined to address this criticism with fresh, innovative writing, Hartsock revamped the masthead of the *Phoenix* by designating it as "an oasis in the Sahara of the Bozart." He proceeded shortly thereafter to launch his own magazine of verse and name it *Bozart* as well, along with the small independent press that he opened to defray the costs of producing the magazine.

Hartsock epitomized the stereotypical "struggling poet" in several respects. His once comfortably situated family had met with financial disaster thanks to his father's involvement in a failed Florida real estate venture. He managed to supplement his meager earnings as an instructor in English, first at Emory and then at Georgia Tech, by playing the organ at a local church, but even after he accepted a specially created position as professor of poetics at Oglethorpe University, his parents' all but total dependence on him remained a severe strain on both his finances and his nerves. The stress did nothing to improve the health of a frail and sickly young man who seemed to carry a sense of resignation to his impending doom wherever he went. The feeling was pervasive in Hartsock's verse, which, though not exclusively mordant in tone, tended to underscore both the evanescence of human pleasure and joy and the looming certainty of death. In his "Brief Abandon" the narrator proclaims, "This is the day for daisies; let us go. . . . Do not delay. We are not long together. . . . Days of brief abandon will not come when we are under ground. . . . There will be days for tears and dust hereafter: this is the day for daisies, and for laughter."[7]

Hartsock's trials as an unlikely provider for his family were compounded by the stress of living as a closeted gay man in a city scarcely known for its tolerance in that era. Keenly aware of Hartsock's tortured personal life and physical and emotionally frailty, both Woodward and Rainey felt an intense obligation to take care of their brilliant but erratic and unstable mentor and friend. Both men spent a great deal of time with Hartsock, and the influence of his highly developed skills as a writer and editor of text shone through in the strikingly elegant prose in their correspondence. Yet for all their genuine sense of indebtedness to him, in the end, their determined efforts to keep Ernest afloat both financially and emotionally came to naught.

Woodward and Rainey grew alternately frustrated and alarmed as Hartsock complained constantly of a variety of pain and suffering. He was tormented by insomnia and crippling headaches, which, his physician warned, could foretell a rupture in a blood vessel in his forehead already so severely swollen that it "stands out like a cord." If this condition was induced by stress, there seemed to be little hope of relieving it in the foreseeable future, for Hartsock's father's steadily deteriorating financial situation simply underscored his obligation to contribute to his parents' upkeep.[8]

This obligation was all the more burdensome in the early months of the Great Depression. Though his own father was still employed by Emory, Woodward seemed overjoyed when he wrote his "Mater" and "Pater" in the spring of 1930 to let them know that, with his undergraduate degree from Emory just freshly in hand, he had received a most opportune invitation to teach English at Georgia Tech during the next academic year. This meant that he would "not have to call upon you or the Salvation Army either for my support." It also promised a more relaxed lifestyle for a young man of his independent temperament.[9]

Still, though he was only twenty-two, Woodward's continuing concern about Hartsock weighed heavily on him as he and Rainey agonized over what could be done to lighten their friend's emotional burden. He spoke with Hartsock virtually every day, either in person or by phone. Though they sometimes suspected their poet friend might be taking a certain poetic license in dramatizing his ailments, when Rainey wrote from Northwestern in early November 1930 to express his genuine distress over what he sensed was Hartsock's rapidly deteriorating condition, Woodward could only confirm his fears. "Your alarm over Ernest's condition is all too well justified," he reported. "It is no poetic vapor rings this time, I am afraid. . . . He is struggling under a stupendous load that would floor many better-balanced people than he is."[10]

If their friend were not suffering under a terrific emotional burden already, as Woodward and Rainey had feared, Hartsock's new volume of poetry, *Strange Splendor*, was selling "wretchedly," Woodward reported. "It infuriates me," and he added, "The newspapers have all but ignored him while the New York reviews have so far maintained a damning silence." Scarcely a month later, Woodward's assessment of the severity of Hartsock's tragic condition would be borne out when, despite the fervent efforts of doctors to save him, the brilliant young poet died at age twenty-seven of complications related to "pernicious anemia." When Hartsock expired at 4:30 A.M. on December 14, 1930, Woodward was at his bedside.[11]

Losing Hartsock clearly wounded both men emotionally, and his death left them feeling obligated to safeguard his reputation and legacy. Woodward did his best to stay involved in several planned efforts to honor Ernest. One of Hartsock's benefactors, Benjamin Musser, was supposedly working on a biography. Woodward had full confidence in Musser's "poetic ability and appreciation of Ernest's work," but he confessed to "concerns in another direction" without explicitly mentioning that Musser might also be gay and far less discreet about it than Ernest had been. Though his misgivings about Musser proved to be unfounded, Woodward and Rainey understood full well that, although Hartsock joked about the society women he encountered at tea parties and poetry readings, he would not have welcomed their disapproval, even in death.[12]

This was Woodward's first experience with losing someone truly close to him and being powerless to stop it, and he admitted that there would "always be pictures that I associate with the death." Though he maintained his air of youthful insouciance, Ernest Hartsock's passing left a distinct void in both his and Rainey's lives. Their interactions with their ill-fated mentor had affected both men profoundly, and their intense discussions, both before and after his death, about the work of various writers and the best means of developing their own literary "style" were a testament to Hartsock's influence. Although given to the occasional posturing and affected manner of the dilettante, on their own, they had dutifully immersed themselves in literature of all sorts, ranging from Laurence Sterne's *Tristram Shandy* to the works of James Joyce and Marcel Proust. The latter had supposedly influenced some up-and-coming novelists, and Rainey thought he owed it to himself to give Proust's writing "a chance to influence me while I am in the process of becoming a novelist." A few pages into Proust, Woodward exuberantly pronounced him "infallible" and "god like," his every sentence a "*tour de force*," before further reading led to Proust's unceremonious demotion to "dull, damned dull."[13]

This is not to say that keeping up with the literary Joneses was Woodward's or Rainey's sole concern. The rabid racial hatred that Rainey had documented in his master's thesis about the Atlanta race riot of 1906 was still much in evidence a quarter century later. He and his socially conscious friend from Arkansas were not self-styled visionaries dreaming of "a perfect world," Rainey later explained. Rather, they simply "didn't want black people burned." The two young men simply found it impossible to tolerate a society where "black people were being torn apart just as a part of life." Woodward was still at Emory when, thanks to his socially involved and superbly connected uncle Comer, he would meet John Hope, the strong and determined black leader who served as president of Atlanta University. Comer also introduced him to Will Alexander. Alexander was then head of the Commission on Interracial Cooperation, a group formed in the hope of easing racial tensions after World War I whose members included both John Hope and Comer Woodward.[14]

Making Alexander's acquaintance was fortunate indeed for young Vann because "Dr. Will" oversaw the Rosenwald Fund's scholarships for promising young southerners interested in solving their region's manifold problems. Woodward applied for a Rosenwald scholarship at the prodding of Alexander, and though he had spoken to him "pretty frankly about my lack of direction and my hesitancy of obligating myself," he quickly surmised that his chances of getting one were still pretty good. Even so, he confided to Rainey in February 1931, "I don't know whether I shall accept it. As the Germans so picturesquely put it, *Ich habe kein sitzfleisch* [I have no staying power]." He could always continue teaching English at Georgia Tech, after all. Now that he had his class preparation down, his teaching duties were requiring less of his time, freeing him up "for a rather prodigious amount of reading that I'm doing." If he did remain in Atlanta for another year, he supposed that he might pass the summer in New York or studying in Germany.[15]

When the official scholarship offer came through, Woodward came close to declining it. The stipend was restricted to the social sciences, he explained to Rainey, and he was "more interested in disinterested subjects, E. G., Philosophy, language, literature etc." and "rather in love with the easily gleaned satisfaction [that] is to be had at Tech." He changed his mind about accepting the scholarship only after his friend Charles Ferguson, a "literary go-getter" from New York, paid him a visit and suggested that he "take the scholarship as a sign from the gods and work at it only as I would've at a job that paid me $750. Do it in halftime. On the side accomplish more personal ends," such as, Ferguson suggested, "a graphic and rather panoramic picture of the Negro in America since the Civil War from all angles—economic, religious, aesthetic, social, etc."[16]

Such an undertaking, Woodward conceded, would "absolutely necessitate a complete reorganization of my way of living," requiring a much faster "tempo" and greater "intensity" than he had thus far been able to generate. His uncle Comer had been less than encouraging in response to the idea, primarily because of the problem of gathering the data for such a broad study. Yet although the work he envisioned would certainly "make pretenses at authenticity, even careful documentation . . . that would not be the primary aim. Rather it would be [its] attractiveness and wide appeal to people of my own interest, such as you. Something that would be bought and read and commented upon—in other words as offensive as the odor is to your environs, a book that would sell." Despite his uncle's skepticism, Woodward noted that Will Alexander was "all for the idea," raising the prospect that he might even secure "Rosenwald backing for a stipend."[17]

Woodward's response to Ferguson's suggestion revealed the exuberant self-assurance and enthusiasm of youth, but his ardor for such a major, long-term project seemed to cool quickly over the next few months, and by the time he headed off to Columbia, he admitted to having "little but the vaguest idea" of what he was going to do once he got there. Putting his experience at Emory aside briefly, he signed up for a sociology course whose instructor proved to be "a hopelessly doddering sentimentalist" who "read us Kipling's 'If'" the first day and recommended that we ponder these chastening lines." Dismayed by his uninspiring early encounters with professors at Columbia, Woodward confided to Rainey that he had very nearly "decided that unless I hit upon a field that really challenges my interest, something that I can be happy in studying, that I shall turn to something else besides teaching— anything. Anything would be better than becoming something that I despise when I see it in another person."[18]

Frustrated by his difficulties in finding a concentration of study that would at least prove less offensive than sociology, Woodward soon grew "heartily disgusted with myself and the school" and binged on Broadway shows. While he was pounding the pavement pondering his future, good fortune smiled yet again on the young scholar when he encountered Charles W. Pipkin, an acquaintance from Morrilton, who was teaching at Columbia as a visiting professor of political science. Pipkin first persuaded Woodward to concentrate in "Public Law," which amounted to something akin to political theory, and then convinced his fellow Arkansan to share his large, swanky apartment. It was fair to say that, initially at least, Woodward was far more pleased with the latter decision than the former, which condemned him to wade through many a "ponderous volume of Constitutional law." Yet as he explained to his uncle Comer, his rather unfocused undergraduate background had left him poorly prepared to meet the graduate requirements in any field, and so, public law it was to be even though he knew "nothing of the field and others are more attractive." As it was, he could only "plug along and forget, for the while, my other interests" while taking on courses in unfamiliar areas, "each requiring elementary groundwork on the side."[19]

Woodward did find a welcome distraction in the suggestion of Pipkin, a former Rhodes scholar, that he pursue one of these highly competitive awards himself, and though the application deadline was practically at hand, he showed no hesitation in enlisting his uncle's assistance in securing Emory's endorsement for the scholarship. With dutiful Uncle Comer shepherding his application, Woodward won one of Georgia's nominations for the Rhodes, though he failed to garner the coveted prize that he felt would have meant "a world to my development."[20]

Woodward explained to Rainey that he had serious doubts about applying for the Rhodes scholarship because he had never "conceived of myself as the type of rah rah Ubermensch they seem to admire," and he realized that he was struggling to "create the fiction that I am an intellectual giant in embryo that only requires three years of Oxford atmosphere to hatch me out." He had just turned twenty-three when he met with the Georgia Rhodes Committee for his interview in early December 1931. He must surely have found it a bit of a shock when one of the interviewers told him later that his "personal attainments and promise" would surely have gained him one of the scholarships, but the fact that he would be twenty-four when he came to Oxford ran counter to the preference of "those higher up" for younger, "less fully matured" candidates who were presumably "more open to new impressions" and likely to "fit into the Oxford system more easily than those whose opinions and habits are more firmly fixed."[21]

Woodward had entered the Rhodes competition largely as an afterthought, though, and had little difficulty putting the affair behind him. However grudgingly, he made his peace with the academic routine at Columbia and began a master's thesis on the notorious Alabama demagogue Senator J. Thomas Heflin. After completing a couple of chapters of what he insisted began as "an academic joke," he reported that, after his thesis director saw them, he "practically offered me his place" and said he thought Woodward "could get a fellowship" on the basis of the work. The final document turned out to be "remarkably good," Woodward thought, and he had to admit that he "had a good deal of fun with it." In reality, the literary merit of his work notably outshone the scholarly, for as much as anything, the thesis was a showcase for Woodward's budding talents as a writer, not to mention his flair for sarcasm. Noting that the key to Heflin's meteoric political ascent was his "magic tongue," he described "Tom," as he referred to him throughout the text, turning his highly developed demagogic skills to the task of dissuading white voters from deserting the Democratic Party for the Populists: "With Tom baying upon the bloody trail of black devils, scalawags, alien influences, and other horrendous monsters or exhorting the impoverished to rally to the support of the glorious agrarian aristocracy of the Old South, to save their daughters from the clutches of Negro bucks and to assert their God-given superiority over a damned race—of what trifling importance seemed such obscure matters as taxation, currency, representation and ballot box corruption?"[22]

Woodward also seemed a mite casual about his project when he allowed that "since it is available, we might as well hear Heflin's own account of his part in the [1924 Democratic] Convention." He seemed more engaged when describing an evening, as if he had witnessed it personally, when young Tom was first smitten by the idea of a political career while listening to his father and the local congressman discuss the sad fate of the postbellum South. He provided no documentation here or in numerous other lengthy stretches of his narrative. When Woodward claimed that Heflin had acted at the behest of the Klan in 1924 in launching a crusade against Roman Catholics, aliens, and their champions in New York's Tammany Democratic machine, his source was "journalists in close touch with Alabama affairs," although he had neither interviewed any nor cited their writings to this effect. Heflin's anti-Catholic, anti-Tammany stance carried over into the 1928 presidential election, in which he encouraged his fellow Democrats in Alabama to desert the party of their fathers rather than support New Yorker Al Smith. This apostasy cost Heflin his Senate seat two years later, but Woodward had offered no rationale for his thesis at the beginning, and rather than providing a closing assessment of the significance or meaning of Heflin's career, he simply devoted most of the last page of his text to Tom's farewell speech on his final day in office.[23]

Although it hardly ranked as a pathbreaking contribution to scholarship, the thesis at least provided the germ of inspiration for a book project. Woodward provisionally titled it "Seven for Demos," because he envisioned it covering seven of the South's most colorful political demagogues, including Heflin, as well as Huey P. Long of Louisiana, Benjamin R. Tillman of South Carolina, James K. Vardaman of Mississippi, and Thomas E. Watson of Georgia. He was not immediately off and running down that path when he left Columbia in the spring of 1932, however. There was first a brief flirtation with Rainey's idea of a topically current magazine based in Georgia and perhaps modeled to some extent on Howard Odum's *Social Forces*. "It will simply be a matter of determination," Woodward thought, "and the will to do it at any cost. I feel most the need of something that will challenge every ounce of the energy and resources in me, and there's no doubt but that the magazine task is the thing." He had also inquired about teaching at MIT and

possibly taking additional courses at Harvard, but he could not even entertain the prospect of at least two more years of sustained graduate study. "If
I did it," Woodward observed, prophetically as it turned out, "it would have
to be under a drunken stupor or the logic of daily bread." For the time being,
at least, he would simply "trust to an indulgent mistress of good fortune to
send me where she will."[24]

Self-confident, widely read, with a trip to Europe already under his belt,
Woodward had hardly been a country bumpkin when he arrived in New York,
but his experience there clearly expanded his horizons nonetheless. Shortly
after his arrival, one of his old friends invited him to a party where he rubbed
shoulders with Langston Hughes "and other Harlem celebrities." He had
met writer J. Saunders Redding, who taught at Morehouse, and socialized a
bit with students at Atlanta's black colleges. In New York, he enjoyed a great
deal more interaction with blacks, not to mention émigrés, communists, and
political radicals of all stripes. His friend and host Pipkin was also quite well
connected in the city, and Woodward benefited from his associations, even
though he experienced a few awkward moments in politely making it clear
to Pipkin, who apparently was gay, that his houseguest was not.[25]

Before Woodward completed his stay in the big city, he had even made
his stage debut in a production of the Harlem Experimental Theater, which
had evolved from a group formed originally by W. E. B. Du Bois and others. The play was the work of a friend whom a rather tipsy Woodward had
assured that "she had no living rival outside of William Shakespeare." This
had obliged him to "take a part—the only white one" in *Underground*, a play
drawn from *Uncle Tom's Cabin*, "minus the blocks of ice and the bloodhounds
and Little Eva. I was Simon Legree turned wrong-side out to prove with
flesh and blood, a goatee and a broad 'a' that after all slave owners were not
all bad, but slavery was a degrading institution and the emancipated people
should forgive the people of the South and that democracy is the best of all
possible forms of government provided the Negro is not disfranchised and
he must be given the vote or something terrible is likely to happen." He had
"accomplished the entire interpretation," Woodward bragged, "with a few
well-chosen gestures, a subtle inflection of my A's, and some intricate pan-
tomime while twirling my cane and mixing a mint julep—there was also a
big black cigar."[26]

Leaving Columbia in high spirits, Woodward reported that he had also
taken part in a student strike, assuming "the minor role of first soap-box
speaker, who was used as a decoy to draw all the eggs before the main speakers were introduced." Triggered by the expulsion of the editor of the school

newspaper for a scathing piece about standards in the dining halls, the uprising, he boasted, had "put [Columbia president] Nicholas Murray Butler in his place, brought him to his knees, and extracted a recantation."[27]

Woodward knew when he left Columbia in early summer 1932 that his teaching position in the English Department at Georgia Tech would be waiting for him in the fall. The first order of business for him was a much-anticipated trip to Europe and the Soviet Union, where he would get his first impressions of life under communist rule. Although the tone of his recollections of the experience changed noticeably as he grew older, at age twenty-three he clearly saw much that fascinated and intrigued him. Fresh from his Soviet excursion, he wrote Rainey from Vienna in August 1932, acknowledging that he had not been allowed to spend his time "brushing elbows with the proletariat," because he had been watched constantly and had gone only where his guide had been allowed to take him. Even in correspondence with his closest friend, Woodward was circumspect about what he had managed to see, urging Rainey "and the rest of the Blessed to adopt the attitude of three philosophic monkeys toward anything about Russia good or evil till I come bringing the word and the light." He admitted, however, that had his finances allowed, he would have extended his stay and revealed that he had been "offered an attractive place in Moscow teaching English and might go back next year. No place in the world could be as interesting." In the end, he urged Rainey to "use your discretion about annunciating my Soviet enthusiasm." Ironically, in a series of pieces written for the *Atlanta Journal* after his return, Woodward himself let some of that enthusiasm come through in his account of a late-night conversation with "Russian friends" in the prow of a boat on the Volga: "Their talk, as always, was about their work, the revolution, the five-year plan, tractors, factories, farms, power plants. . . . I felt an exhilaration and wonder at the impetuous optimism and fervor of these new people of the new world."[28]

Woodward would encounter not just communism but Nazism in 1932: his final stop before returning to his teaching duties at Georgia Tech was in Berlin, where he stayed with a Jewish family who manifested little apparent anxiety about their fate at that point. He did witness some abusive anti-Semitic behavior by some of Hitler's Brownshirts and take in some parades and rallies, but most of the Germans he met had assured him that "Nazis were mad people who would never come to power."[29]

Throughout his journey and especially during his monthlong stay in the USSR, Woodward faced interrogation and criticism about the "Scottsboro case," involving nine young Alabama black men falsely accused of rape in 1931, which had quickly become an international cause célèbre. This experience was enough, as he put it later, to spur him "to do something about such incidents when I got back," and within months of his return, he would embark on a long career of public activism in pursuit of social justice. There were active fascist groups back in Atlanta as well, not to mention communists, whom Woodward would encounter on a very different level as he made good on his vow to become more involved on the side of racial justice in the South. He had joined both Rainey and his uncle Comer in signing a statement protesting the arbitrary arrests and harassment of Communist Party spokesmen in Atlanta in the summer of 1930. The sixty-two signatories, including ministers, professional men, and some of the city's socially prominent women, pointedly rejected "the revolutionary philosophy and tactics of the Communist Party" but insisted that party members "should be protected in their constitutional rights of free speech and assemblage."[30]

Nearly two years later, after helping to organize a rally at the Fulton County courthouse that drew a thousand jobless Atlantans demanding "immediate" public relief, Angelo Herndon, a young black Communist Party organizer, was arrested on July 11, 1932, and charged with "inciting insurrection." His arrest was based on an ancient statute of dubious constitutionality, enacted in the hope of preventing slave uprisings. His three-day trial nonetheless ended in a conviction in January 1933, albeit with a recommendation for "mercy," which, in the Georgia of that era, would have spared him the electric chair but consigned him to prison for eighteen to twenty years. The affair struck Woodward as "another thing that is going to disgrace us abroad . . . like the Scottsboro case," and calls for a local defense committee drew him, along with a number of local Communist Party members, to an organizational meeting.[31]

The group was casting about, as Woodward put it, "for people with reputable credentials," and they seized not only on the young professor from Georgia Tech but on Mary Raoul Millis, a wealthy and prominent Atlantan who also happened to be an active and outspoken socialist. Though Millis was chosen initially to chair the Herndon defense committee, she abruptly resigned when one of the communists in the group rose to denounce "social fascists" such as she. This "catapulted" Woodward into the committee chairmanship, a post he had not sought and one in which he was quickly outdone by the communists, who effectively "took over" the group and sought to manipulate it for their own ends. Responding to suggestions that they might enlist the assistance of Woodward's benefactor, Will Alexander, he thoughtlessly wrote one of Herndon's lawyers that Alexander was "so conservative that he's hopeless in this case." To his great chagrin, Woodward found himself quoted to that effect in a subsequent edition of the *Daily Worker*, only to receive a clipping of the story from Alexander with a note appended: "The cut of a friend is the unkindest cut of all."[32]

Luckily for Woodward, Alexander was an extraordinarily understanding and forgiving person, and he would continue to play a critical role in advancing the young man's career. As that career blossomed, it became a popular bit of Woodwardiana that his involvement in the Angelo Herndon case had cost him his teaching job at Georgia Tech, a position in which, by all accounts, including his own, he was quite content. Woodward's involvement in the Herndon case had surely won him no points with the school's administration. In reality, though, his dismissal arose from fiscal rather than ideological concerns, as the State of Georgia struggled to stay afloat in some of the darkest days of the Great Depression. A $30,000 budget cut in 1933 clearly meant that some faculty had to go, and as the English Department's most recent hire, he was one of them. (Rainey would later point out that he had survived the cuts despite boasting a much more imposing reputation as a troublemaker than his younger friend.) The feisty Woodward did gain a measure of deferred satisfaction in the affair, however, when he filed an ultimately successful suit against the state, which had arbitrarily and retroactively revised its pay schedules and sought to deny the fired instructors some of what they were due for services rendered prior to their dismissal.[33]

In the short run, however, there was nothing for the suddenly jobless young instructor to do but pack up and head down the road to take up residence in Oxford with his parents. Save for the shortage of funds, Woodward seemed to welcome the time off, primarily because he was eager to get back to his planned book on seven southern demagogues, although, in the interim since leaving Columbia, he had grown increasingly concerned about the feasibility of writing about so many flamboyant and ultimately complex characters. At the same time, his personal interest in Tom Watson had grown steadily more compelling. A fiery orator and editorialist, Watson had emerged as a force in Georgia politics toward the end of the nineteenth century. As a champion of the state's downtrodden dirt farmers, he left little doubt of his empathy with their struggle against steadily declining cotton prices and their seemingly irreversible descent into the quagmire of debt and dependence that marked the system of farm tenancy. Most notably, representing first the Farmers' Alliance and then the Populist Party, Watson had openly and repeatedly encouraged political cooperation between oppressed white and black farmers, thereby alarming and outraging the conservative, post-Redeemer Democrats who represented the powerful coalition of large landholders and industrial interests that had seized control of Georgia politics in the aftermath of Reconstruction.

Running as a Democrat with the enthusiastic endorsement of the Farmers' Alliance, Watson won Georgia's Tenth District congressional seat in 1890, only to be defeated for reelection in 1892 and again in 1894 by blatantly fraudulent means both times. Yet the enormous support he enjoyed among Populists nationwide by that point placed him at the center of an agonized debate over whether the party should enter into a fusion arrangement in 1896 by endorsing the presidential candidacy of the ostensibly Populist-leaning Democratic presidential nominee, William Jennings Bryan of Nebraska. In exchange, the Democrats purportedly promised to drop their vice-presidential nominee, Arthur Sewall of Maine, a wealthy and decidedly anti-Populist banking and shipping magnate, in favor of Watson. Personally opposed to fusion but hoping to maintain harmony in his own party, Watson grimly agreed to become the Populist vice-presidential candidate, only to see the Democrats not only renege on dropping Sewall but largely ignore him and his fellow Populists throughout the campaign. Emotionally and financially devastated after the debacle of 1896, Watson withdrew from direct political involvement for nearly eight years before again answering the call of what remained of his old party, accepting its nomination for the presidency in both 1904 and 1908.[34]

Watson continued to employ much of the rhetoric and maintain many of the stances that marked his agrarian insurgency. Yet during his roughly eight years of relative seclusion, he seemed to have undergone an altogether tragic Dr. Jekyll–to–Mr. Hyde reversal of character, reemerging as a rabid, even bloodthirsty, purveyor of racial and religious bigotry. Defending and often all but encouraging violent reprisals against blacks, Watson also spewed hatred at the Roman Catholic Church and played a pivotal role in feeding the virulent anti-Semitism that led to the lynching of Atlanta factory superintendent Leo Frank in 1915. His frequently controversial views made their way throughout the South and beyond through his own weekly paper and monthly magazine, where his denunciations of U.S. involvement in World War I and opposition to the draft incurred the wrath of both the Justice Department and the U.S. Postal Service. Though his fortunes and allegiances in Georgia politics had been volatile and controversial to say the least, Watson managed to win one of Georgia's Senate seats in 1920, although he would serve less than two years before dying of a cerebral hemorrhage at age sixty-six in September 1922.

Though Woodward had not yet given up on "Seven for Demos" when he began writing in the summer of 1933, his decision to begin with Watson made it clear where his greatest interest and enthusiasm lay. Still, he found it slow going at first, lamenting to Rainey that he had reached "page ten and Tom is still in his angel infancy!" "I feel rather like I expect Bishop Sterne did when he got to page 578 and found that Trist[r]am [Shandy] was just a-borning."[35]

By September 1933, after seeking advice from friends in the publishing world, Woodward had concluded that "it has got to be a whole book on Tom." He had already done enough writing to see that a great deal more research would be required. The problem was that he had no real means of supporting himself while he gathered more information about Watson. Perhaps recalling his friend Ferguson's advice about how he might make the best use his scholarship to Columbia, Woodward concluded that his best prospect for completing the project lay in securing yet another fellowship. His ostensible purpose would be pursuing a PhD in history, but his primary objective was getting the income he needed to allow him to finish his book, which, almost incidentally, in Woodward's thinking at least, could also be submitted as his dissertation. In this case, the University of North Carolina was clearly best suited for his purposes because its library had recently acquired Tom Watson's private papers.[36]

Woodward had no direct acquaintance with anyone in the UNC history department, but once again the connections that he had established with Will Alexander (through his uncle Comer) stood him in good stead, for both men were well known to the famed sociologist Howard W. Odum, himself an Emory College graduate whose Institute for Research in Social Science with its influential journal, *Social Forces*, had put the University of North Carolina at the vanguard of research on southern issues. More so even than Alexander, Odum had the ear of the nation's foremost academics, publishers, New Deal bureaucrats, and, most important for Woodward, its philanthropic organizations. These included the General Education Board, created by John D. Rockefeller in 1902, which offered a program of assistance for promising young southerners seeking answers to their region's problems. In many cases, these awards had gone to recipients handpicked by Odum, and he thus became pivotal to Woodward's plan to secure enough financial support to see him through the completion of his book on Watson.

From the very beginning, the story of Woodward's fortuitous relationship with Howard Odum is both complicated and murky. In addition to having both an uncle in Comer and a mentor in Will Alexander to put in a good word for him, there was the sheer serendipity of Odum's family farm lying just down the road from where Woodward's parents lived in Oxford. Although Woodward recalled in his 1986 memoir that he had first met Odum and told him of his plans for the Watson biography in the summer of 1934, his correspondence indicates that their first meeting took place four years earlier, in late June 1930—well before Woodward had decided on the Watson project—when Odum was visiting his brother on the family farm. Although both Woodward and Rainey admired Odum's candid appraisal of the South's problems, they had recently heard him speak in Atlanta and had come away feeling something less than overwhelmed. When Woodward arrived at the Odum place, the famed sociologist was absorbed in weaning some prize calves. "I was expected to stand about admiringly while he went through the process," Woodward reported to Rainey, but "I'm afraid I did it none too gracefully. He appeared very much interested in my plans and talked a good while about them. . . . In spite of our unanimous opinion of his address the other night, I still cannot help being impressed by the largeness of the man in closer quarters. Whatever the quality of his work may be, the man is possessed of a remarkable energy and genuine disinterestedness."[37]

Woodward went on to describe the forthcoming final volume of Odum's "Black Ulysses" trilogy of folkloristic novels, tracing the black experience in the New South. As an admirer of H. L. Mencken, he was particularly impressed to learn that Odum "and H. L. are quite chummy, and see each other often. He believes that H. L. is still our greatest critic, and has done more for the South than any other of the literati."[38]

Despite its impact on the younger man, the meeting did not register as deeply with the perennially distracted and overcommitted Odum. In fact, in October 1933, when he received a letter identifying Woodward as one of the southern critics of the Commission on Interracial Cooperation's formal study of lynching in the South (with which Odum was affiliated), he demanded of Will Alexander, "What does this mean that Vann Woodward is questioning your organization?" Perhaps confusing Woodward with his uncle, he asked, "Is it the little Vann or the big Vann, and who is Professor Vann Woodward?"[39]

The kindly Alexander had by then forgiven his opinionated young protégé for his ill-considered remarks during the Angelo Herndon affair, and he hastened to assure Odum that Woodward's views on the lynching study had been misrepresented, explaining that "the Woodward referred to is Comer Woodward's nephew, a young man who graduated from Emory and who held one of our Southern fellowships [at Columbia]. He made a trip last year to Russia, came back and taught at Georgia Tech. He was let out with a number of professors as an economy measure and is now writing a life of Tom Watson. I've just spent considerable time reading his manuscript and from everything I can see he is very friendly to us." Before mailing the letter, Alexander discovered that Woodward was even then in "Chapel Hill working in your library," adding, "I have dropped him a note suggesting that he come in to see you."[40]

Already planning to "hit Odum for money later," after hearing from Alexander, Woodward hastily beat a path to the great man's office and quickly persuaded him that he had been misquoted about the lynching study. In fact, he dropped in twice to see Odum, who found him "very genuine and sincere" in his feeling that "some of the younger brethren can perhaps do something worthwhile." He had little difficulty persuading Odum of the potential importance of his study of Watson. "Odum says 'Important Hell! It ought to be worth two books,'" he reported to Rainey, although, he added, "he doesn't think I can do it, I could tell. Bit chagrined I thought. He was in a hurry, being brain truster and captain of (research) industry."[41]

In the meantime, though, he discovered that Odum's colleague Rupert Vance was doing something along the lines of his original idea of studying several southern demagogues, and in a foreshadowing of the close relationship they would form, Woodward found Vance very "pleasant and helpful." In much the same way that the proximity of his parents' home to the Odum family farm and his uncle Comer's connections with both Alexander and Odum had proven propitious, Woodward had previous ties to Vance, who, like Charles Pipkin, was also from Morrilton, where his father had once employed a teenaged Woodward at the swimming pool that he operated.[42]

Although Vance would go on to influence Woodward more than any historian, including his eventual dissertation adviser, Howard K. Beale, whom he would meet at Chapel Hill, Odum was unquestionably the key player in making Woodward's tenure at North Carolina possible. Not long after the two had visited in his office, Odum was making Woodward's case with the General Education Board's Jackson Davis, calling his attention to "Vann Woodward of Emory, who held one of the regional [Rosenwald] fellowships last year and went to Columbia, is writing on Tom Watson, and wants very much to stay here at the University of North Carolina after Christmas to continue his work on the subject. . . . Woodward is probably quite worthy of your consideration for a fellowship and for his development in the future. His father is principal of the Emory Junior Academy at Oxford, and his uncle is Professor of Sociology at Emory. Vann is an enthusiastic youth . . . and needs at this time guidance and development very much."[43]

Odum's efforts would bear rich fruit for Woodward, but it would take a while, and in the meantime, he was happy to have a job working on an unemployment survey for the Works Progress Administration. "The man[n]a still falls from on high," he exulted in 1934, "and I lie on my back in the grass with my mouth open and one eye on a restive Sinai. It [his WPA job] only takes the mornings now and I put in the afternoon contemplating the mechanism of the typewriter and occasionally hitting a key—gingerly, tentatively to see if they work." As May unfolded, he informed Rainey that while he had heard "nothing out of Rockefeller yet," fortunately "Roosevelt" remained "unflagging. . . . And apparently just as rich. One billionaire is as good as the next for me."[44]

For all his show of nonchalance, Woodward was clearly relieved when he informed Rainey at the end of May 1934 that he was "quitting On-Our-Way" Roosevelt's job. Odum had finally gotten word that his General Education Board stipend had come through and urged him to come up to Chapel Hill immediately so that he could "go ahead with his collection of material and studying" without delay. "Howard 'On-Our-Way' Odum informs me that John You-Can-Be-Had Rockefeller consents to make me a kept man," he explained, "and suggests I come over to Chapel Hill for nuptials before he (On-Our-Way) gets off to New York via California." Quickly making his way to Chapel Hill, Woodward reported a few days later that as "Odum got off with a huff and a puff," he had mentioned "while talking in a Dictaphone and conducting a telephone conversation that I had a fellowship of $90 per month for 12 months."[45]

Woodward's sarcastic references to the person who had just set him up handsomely in an era when such support was so very hard to come by might suggest the brashness and feelings of entitlement of a young man accustomed to having things go his way, but they likely reflected as well an already simmering disenchantment with Odum that he would sometimes be at pains to conceal in the years ahead. He was, however, all but ecstatic at this juncture about the prospect of life in Chapel Hill, and he confessed to Rainey that since his arrival he had "done practically nothing except drink deeply and well and talk to some of the best talkers anywhere. . . . I still don't know another place anywhere I'd rather be. When I consider that once I was such a goddam idiot as to go to Columbia University and listen to some Midwesterner Kipple Kipling. . . . Dear God. And people here of brains and accomplishment and charm. Do I slop over? Very well, I slop over. . . . I might be expected to. The beer is simply fine." As he drank deeply of Chapel Hill's best intellectual and alcoholic spirits, however, he also retained the single-minded sense of purpose that led him to see graduate study in history as merely the fastest route to completing his book on Watson, telling Rainey, "I think I convinced them I should not go to summer school at all, but devote my talents to research."[46]

On the research front, although Odum's assistance in securing the stipend from the Rockefeller Foundation was critical to Woodward's plans for finishing the Watson biography, there was another crucial figure who contributed heavily to making the biography as rich and powerful as it would become. Woodward had good reason to be particularly interested in the graduate program in history at the University of North Carolina because Tom Watson's papers had been deposited in UNC's recently established Southern Historical Collection. In the division of Watson's estate, these papers had gone to one of Watson's granddaughters, Georgia Lee Watson Brown, who had required some persuading before entrusting them to the new repository and did so only with the stipulation that the papers would be open for use solely by persons who had first secured her formal permission. Georgia Lee Brown was a jealous guardian of her grandfather's already contested reputation who had already rejected such requests from other scholars, and it seemed unlikely that Woodward, a young stranger without much in the way of credentials, stood much chance of getting the requisite approval. To make matters worse, although only twenty-seven, Brown was suffering from tuberculosis and in decidedly frail and declining health.

Surmising that, as a young outsider with dubious qualifications, he had little chance of winning her over, Woodward set out to persuade Watson's other granddaughter, Georgia Doremus Watson, to plead his case with her cousin. He pinned his hopes on this strategy because this Georgia Watson also held a master's degree in history from the University of Chicago, and she happened to be teaching at Salem Academy, a private school for girls, in Winston-Salem, North Carolina. Watson, an attractive young woman who would later marry her thesis director, historian Avery O. Craven, was surprised by her unannounced Sunday afternoon visitor, but he struck her as "dignified, polite, serious and interesting," and she found his passion for learning more about her grandfather both gratifying and intriguing. She agreed to intercede in his behalf with Georgia Watson Brown after going to dinner with him at the Robert E. Lee Hotel in Winston Salem and absorbing a heavy dose of Woodward charm in the course of an intense dialogue that went on for an astonishing eight hours. Two days later, Woodward followed up on his charm assault in a letter reminding Georgia of "how earnestly I hope you have succeeded in winning your cousin for me." He also assured her that he would stop by to visit with her on his way home, not simply because he had more questions, but because "even if they were all answered, I would want to see you." Woodward's mixture of flirtation and scholarly earnest apparently did the trick, because after an exchange of correspondence between the cousins, he became the first researcher to gain full access to the Watson papers.[47]

He was beside himself with excitement at the prospect of tearing into "five large packing boxes full of letters etc., and two full of scrapbooks—untouched except by rat's rage." He confessed to Rainey that knowing one of Watson's granddaughters was "an ally" left him "entirely relieved from the (unconsciously) depressing sense of betraying innocent and unsuspecting kinsmen . . . no matter what I write." Georgia had flatly rejected any notion of portraying Watson as "a man of meeker stuff. She sees the thing, intimately and analytically and dispassionately."[48]

At any rate, Woodward's sojourn to North Carolina had given him a great deal more material to work with, and even as he awaited official word on his fellowship from the General Education Board in the spring of 1934, he had plunged back into writing. Although he affected an altogether confident, sometimes even cocky air, his commentary on his early writing efforts suggested a certain lack of organization and direction, not to mention his difficulty with managing the information he had gathered and using it selectively in his text: "The trouble now, of course, is that I have too much stuff and that I clog up the works with it, *and* citations—ten to a page. Dear God! I am as thoroughly intimidated as any Ph.D. alive. . . . Then too I haven't the courage to burn up the first MSS, nor the strength to resist looking at it, nor the will to refrain from using old smooth sentences." Amazed at "how much stuff I've got and how much I'm packing in," Woodward fretted that he was providing too much detail and too little interpretation "without getting in enough between the lines."[49]

Such frustrations were hardly surprising, given Woodward's academic background. His strongest undergraduate concentration, and not a terribly serious one at that, had been in philosophy. Though he had managed a straightforward chronological narrative of Thomas Heflin's career in his MA thesis at Columbia, much of that study focused on events of the previous decade, and he had written it for political scientists rather than historians. His thesis had ultimately led to the decision to write a book on Tom Watson, but he had undertaken the book project with "no academic purpose in mind" and only "the faintest formal preparation in American history," acquired in an exceedingly dull course at Emory that had "been more than enough to discourage further curiosity." Thus, although for Woodward southern history was not so much a chosen field as one dictated by his choice of a biographical subject, he was forced nonetheless to accept the fact that "a Southern historian I must be—or somehow become."[50]

3

History, I Find, Is a Collection of Facts

Pursuing the "Cursed Degree" in Chapel Hill

With little idea of what to expect as he began his formal training in September 1934 for an academic career he had no intention of pursuing, Woodward willed himself to hope that "with a fresh if empty mind and exciting book of my own underway ... perhaps I would now see this unexplored field take on a new glamo[u]r and I would rise to the challenge." He also expected to find some semblance, at least, of the "surge of innovation and creativity" among contemporary southern novelists, poets, and playwrights whose search for new meaning in the South's past had them exploring the same terrain as the region's historians. To his utter dismay, however, instead of encouraging fresh, creative thinking about the South's past, he found most of the southern historians in Chapel Hill busily indoctrinating their charges in a peculiarly southern historical creed that had survived with but negligible alteration since their own mentors had passed it on to them.[1]

A proper sense of the intellectual stagnation and rigidity that a disappointed Woodward encountered among his professors at UNC entails a quick examination of how and why a distinctly purposeful historical mind-set that surfaced shortly after Appomattox could so quickly gain sway among historians and white southerners in general and maintain it virtually unchallenged some seventy years later. As historian E. Merton Coulter would soon observe, in the wake of the Civil War, for southern whites, their region's history served as "the last stronghold of the South, not for the defense of its nationality but for the protection of something more clear and sacred, its reputation." Jefferson Davis and other prominent former Confederates had just this end in mind when they formed the Southern Historical Society in 1869 as a means of amassing a formidable arsenal of historical documentation and/or propaganda "from which the defenders of our cause may draw any desired weapon." The defense of that Lost Cause soon took on the trappings of something more akin to a celebration, not only of the valiant champions of southern rights, but of the aristocratic and humane way of life they had supposedly fought to preserve.[2]

The militant, self-styled defenders of the Old South–Lost Cause legacy were so well organized and influential by the beginning of the twentieth century that William E. Dodd was quick to caution his fellow southern historians that the quickest route to an "enforced resignation" lay in questioning the legitimacy of secession or the wisdom of its advocates. University of Florida professor Enoch M. Banks met with precisely that fate in 1911, after foolishly presuming that, a half century after Fort Sumter, he could safely apply some "calm history" to the Civil War. He virtually sealed his own demise in an essay that identified slavery rather than "states' rights" as the true cause of secession and even dared to venture that, in the final assessment, "the North was relatively right, and the South was relatively wrong." The ensuing outcry from groups like the United Daughters of the Confederacy and a torrent of condemnations in the press, not to mention threatened cuts in university funding, ensured Banks's speedy departure from the Florida faculty.[3]

Beyond upholding the virtue of the South's cause and the actions of its leaders from 1861 to 1865, it was no less incumbent on southern historians to emphasize the innumerable wrongs visited on its white citizenry by Carpetbaggers, Scalawags, and their ignorant black pawns during Reconstruction. With that in mind, a number of young southerners had headed north, ironically enough, to study at Columbia under Professor William A. Dunning, who was known as a consistent critic of northern policies during Reconstruction. When Dunning's southern-born protégés dutifully published a number of state-level studies of Reconstruction in the South aimed at correcting what they believed was a prevailing northern bias in the written history of this period, they did so fully assured, as Peter Novick observed, that "any excesses or exaggerations" would serve only to "redress the balance."[4]

The Dunning School's account of the suffering inflicted on white southerners during Reconstruction seemed calculated to win the sympathy of other white Americans as well. Meanwhile, the Dunning narrative encouraged

History, I Find, Is a Collection of Facts

contemporary white southerners to celebrate the scions of the hallowed antebellum planter class and heroes of the Lost Cause as the heroic Redeemers who boldly overthrew the corrupt and vindictive Reconstruction governments in their respective states. This accomplished, the prevailing narrative had the Redeemers quickly ceding leadership to younger, more progressive men such as Atlanta editor and orator Henry W. Grady. Grady and his cohort then set out to drastically reduce the region's dependence on agriculture while fostering the urban, industrial, and commercial development once thwarted by slavery and the plantation system. Their efforts had borne fruit practically overnight, so the story went, in a prosperous and powerful New South, hailed by a Virginia-born historian in 1905 for overcoming "adversity such as no other section of North America has ever experienced . . . [to] become the pride of the union." It had been almost seventy years since Robert E. Lee's surrender when Woodward began his graduate classwork in Chapel Hill. Over that span, a succession of unwavering era narratives focusing on the Old South, the Civil War, Reconstruction, Redemption, and the rise of the New South had been almost seamlessly melded into what amounted to a single, broadly encompassing historical creed, which allowed of no piecemeal adoption but must be swallowed whole and undifferentiated, as if at a single gulp.[5]

While perhaps not all of the white historians of the South were still choosing to drink from that cup by the time Woodward arrived at UNC, the great majority of those comprising the region's historical establishment clearly were. This much was more than apparent during the early years of the Southern Historical Association, which was founded in Birmingham in November 1934, just a few weeks after Woodward began his classes at UNC. The SHA was formed ostensibly to encourage "the study of history in the South, with particular emphasis on the history of the South." From the outset, however, some of the organization's early leaders seemed less interested in objectively examining the region's history than in defending or even weaponizing it. E. Merton Coulter used the inaugural SHA presidential address to rebuke white southerners for their failure to do a better job of gathering and preserving the records necessary to defend the South from its northern critics. A few years later, Frank L. Owsley took to the SHA presidential pulpit to blame the Civil War on the "egocentric sectionalism" of the Yankees. Other early presidents blamed the contemporary South's multitude of problems on the damage wrought by Reconstruction or ongoing colonial exploitation by the North. In a summary of the first fifteen SHA presidential addresses, political scientist Herman Clarence Nixon would note that some of them were so stridently defensive and sectional in tone as to qualify as outright "polemics."[6]

As of the mid-1930s, the South's orthodox historical creed still imposed what amounted to a virtual gag order, enjoining its historians from writing anything straightforwardly critical of the actions and methods of its leaders in either the distant or the recent past, especially if it might reflect negatively on its present as well. This is not to imply that most historians at Wisconsin, Columbia, or any number of northern universities at that point were given to highly critical treatments of the South's past. The major difference, as Woodward discerned early on, was that the southern historians actively defending that past did so as a means of "vindicating, justifying, rationalizing, and often celebrating the present order." In this, these historians found themselves, by and large, not so much trailing as still bucking the curve set by not only the leading literary figures of the day but the sociologists who comprised the Chapel Hill Regionalists. Led by Howard Odum, this formidable cadre of researchers grounded their strikingly candid discussions of the problems dogging the South's present in their equally unflinching effort to identify the roots of these pathologies in its past. Although Woodward was already beginning to see Odum as too much of an establishment figure to suit him by the time he got to UNC in 1934, his benefactor had been less hesitant to make waves a decade earlier, when he declared in the journal *Social Forces* (which he had founded in 1922) that "the South needs criticism and severe criticism." No small part of that sort of criticism would appear either in *Social Forces* or in the many studies and special reports conducted under the aegis of the Institute for Research in Social Science, which he had launched in Chapel Hill in 1924 with generous funding from the Rockefeller family.[7]

As both Odum's colleague and protégé of sorts, his fellow sociologist Rupert B. Vance believed even more passionately than his mentor that "history, not geography" had "made the solid South." Known for his encyclopedic grasp of southern history (He even held informal history tutorials for graduate students), Vance earned such a reputation as a historian that the editors of Louisiana State University Press's History of the South series soon invited him to write the volume slated to cover the period 1913 to 1945.[8]

With ties to Woodward that stretched back to their Arkansas days, the generous and personable Vance would quickly become the closest thing to an intellectual soulmate Woodward was to find at UNC. His graduate school contemporaries readily concurred that Vance was probably the only faculty member who really influenced him at all during his time on campus, and later, in the preface to his Tom Watson book, he would acknowledge his profound indebtedness for "the many hours I have spent across a littered desk from Dr. Rupert B. Vance, plundering that storehouse of knowledge about the South."[9]

History, I Find, Is a Collection of Facts

In the years to come, Woodward's writing would repeatedly demonstrate the power of the past to clarify and reshape reactions to the present. Yet his formal instruction in history had hardly begun before he realized that the most historically minded critics of the contemporary South on the UNC campus were sociologists. Meanwhile, unlike Odum and Vance or the exciting young writers then rocking the southern literary scene, those held up to Woodward as role models in southern history were much less likely to draw on the past as a basis for challenging the present than to rely on it to forestall such challenges. This, of course, hardly inspired the brilliant—but sometimes brash—young man to approach his studies more seriously or, perhaps, less cynically.[10]

Some found it difficult to take one of America's most distinguished historians seriously when he insisted, as he did more than once in later years, that he had been, at best, a mediocre and dissatisfied graduate student at UNC, unmotivated by anything other than the prospect of completing his book. Yet this was not simply Woodward's trademark penchant for self-deprecation; he was being entirely candid. He may not have hated every minute of his PhD work, but he clearly hated a great many of them, particularly those when he was forced to spend time on coursework or exam preparation that he could have devoted to writing on Watson. From the beginning, his accounts of his days at UNC are shot through with signs of frustration, resentment, and sometimes even contempt.

Much to his dismay, the historians in Chapel Hill generally seemed bent on challenging, not his capacity for fresh, creative thinking, but his tolerance for wading through stacks of books whose authors seemed wholly bereft of any such capacity themselves. To his professors, it seemed, preparing graduate students in southern history came down primarily to catechizing them in the accumulated wisdom of their elders as found in musty old sets like the Yale *Chronicles of America* series, volumes written at least a generation earlier and left to languish wholly unrevised in the interim. Plodding through the likes of these, Woodward wondered if he had ever encountered "prose so pedestrian, pages so dull, chapters so void of ideas, whole volumes so wrongheaded or so lacking in point." Persuaded that becoming a professional historian meant little more than "a lifetime dedicated to inflicting such reading on innocent youth," not to mention himself, he recalled spending many a night during his first year pacing Chapel Hill's legendary Franklin Street, "debating whether I might fare better as a fruit-peddler, panhandler, or hack-writer."[11]

Scarcely settled into the spirit-crushing regimen of graduate study in the fall of 1934, Woodward observed to Glenn Rainey that, not unlike a Greek social order, initiation into the historical fraternity amounted to acquiring a load of trivial information "that no one else in the world knows but a Ph.D." By way of illustration, he reported that, after a lengthy presentation on state taxation systems before the ratification of the Constitution, his mind was "now a plum pudding of esoterica of the order."[12]

Beyond mucking up his mind, such distractions meant that his writing had "just about come to an impasse. Courses take up all my time." He was tempted simply to drop his classes for the next term with the aim of getting the book into the final stages, but "not complete—so I can get [my] grant renewed." His spirits improved but little as the term ground on. "I am in low state of mind generally and aching to unburden myself upon you unmercifully," he warned the long-suffering Rainey, who surely felt his friend had been doing that ever since his formal PhD studies began, and wondered what to expect when the two saw each other over the Christmas holidays. So habitual and unrelenting had Woodward become in his complaining that he found himself complaining about that: "I spend so much of my time rebelling against what I am doing that there is little time left in which to do it. Matter of being at war with myself. . . . It's actually embarrassing to be so out of sorts. What pains me chiefly is the fact that the stuff on Tom is getting colder all the while."[13]

Yet, if anything, Woodward's depression and self-pity seemed to consume even more of his time and energy after he returned to campus in January 1935. "For weeks," he confessed to Rainey, he had sunk "deeper and deeper in a muck of doldrums, till I was in up to the ears" and "the mere thought of myself wrung tears of compassion from my soul." The only slightly encouraging development Woodward could report was that, desperate for some sort of affirmation, he had asked history professor and director of the Southern Historical Collection, J. G. de Roulhac Hamilton, to read his manuscript. An established scholar, Hamilton had studied under William A. Dunning at Columbia, and to Woodward's surprise, he not only liked the manuscript but suggested "only a few changes to make it acceptable as a dissertation." Yet Woodward knew that Hamilton's archival duties would prevent him from directing his work, leaving him to admit, "Who will take it I do not know."[14]

Any relationship between the two would have been short-lived once Woodward got a taste of the dismissive racism and crass stereotyping Hamilton seemed to revel in during classroom lectures, but his concern about finding a dissertation director was not unfounded. He had been intrigued to learn that the history department had apparently looked into bringing Civil War era historian Avery O. Craven in from the University of Chicago.

History, I Find, Is a Collection of Facts

Woodward had met Craven while he was interviewing on campus, and the two had seemed to hit it off, but it was unclear at that point whether Craven would be coming to Chapel Hill or, if not, whether, according to Woodward at least, he might be joining Craven at Chicago. He had reported at the beginning of the 1934–35 academic year that the "history department here seems to be cracking up like the English Department did several years ago. People all on point of leaving. It's possible I might not stay after all." His suggestion that he might forfeit his handsome fellowship check by leaving UNC before finishing his book scarcely seems credible, and it is hard to see anything more than posturing in his explanation to Rainey, in April 1935, that he was staying put "since in all seriousness I can say that I have not gleaned a single scholarly idea from any professor here, I would be no more likely to fare any better with the professors who taught these professors."[15]

Although Woodward was well past his twenty-sixth birthday at this point, his flippant remarks could still be written off in some measure to the lingering cocksureness of youth. His extensive reading in philosophy may also have fostered a greater inclination to see his history professors as generally short of "ideas." Finally, his intense admiration for the thought-inspiring, creative imagination of writers like Thomas Wolfe may have left him impatient with the notion that the historian must master all the factual details of human events before addressing their larger meaning. Distressed that his instructors at Chapel Hill seemed concerned only with his command of the basic historical narrative, Woodward's tongue was probably not entirely in his cheek when he complained to Rainey, "History, I find, is a collection of facts. Should have looked into that before going so far. Nothing but contempt for facts. Opinion all that matters. Proper attitude."[16]

According to Woodward, his best friend in graduate school was J. Carlyle Sitterson, who admitted that his chum had little zeal for mastering "the bricks and mortar of historical information." Woodward was "never a nuts and bolts man" but a great "ideas person," observed Bennett H. Wall, another grad school colleague. In reality, Sitterson felt that there was simply an intellectual disconnect between the history faculty's emphasis on trying to "find out" precisely what happened in the past and Woodward's interest primarily in the meaning and consequences—as opposed to the details—of those developments. Sitterson felt that Woodward had come to Chapel Hill with "a definite point of view," and Wall found him "totally uninterested in history except for the post–Civil War South." Yet his classmates readily admitted in retrospect that they had never been that close to Woodward, who had been too much of a loner and not an especially communicative one, at that, to give them a fix on his thinking. Woodward's fellowship stipend gave him considerably more financial freedom than most of his peers. "We thought he was rich," Wall insisted, because he had generally lived in quarters beyond their means and socialized outside their immediate circle.[17]

With his first Rockefeller fellowship expired, Woodward was anxiously awaiting word of its renewal in April 1936 when he complained to Rainey that, in the meantime, he could count only on "the pittance" provided by a standard teaching fellowship to at least "soften the harder edges of slow starvation next year." Despite the economic and social distance between Woodward and his fellow graduate students, they all agreed that excelling in his courses or otherwise impressing his professors was of little concern to him compared to completing his book. With the loathsome prospect of his qualifying exams looming just ahead, he fumed to Rainey, "I still believe in the story strong, but, Hell, I can't call the choice of an adjective my own until I have that cursed degree behind me, and time for enough blasphemy to efface the memory of its every insolent recollection."[18]

Despite complaining that attending classes and meeting other program requirements had thrown his writing off schedule, Woodward refused to rein in his passion for literature. At this point, he was still not overly fond of William Faulkner, whose *Sound and the Fury* he did not finish. At the same time, both he and Rainey immediately devoured anything written by Thomas Wolfe, for whom Woodward later professed such "warmth of affection" that Wolfe's death in 1938 had caused him "personal grief." On the other hand, he harbored no such feelings toward Margaret Mitchell, whose story "about how a tart little bitch gets all the men in North Georgia in rut" triggered such a "violent muscular contraction in the esophagus" that he was forced to abandon it only 118 pages in. He saw no need to keep at it, he explained to Rainey, because "one doesn't have to drink all the sea to call it salt." As he suffered through his course assignments, complaining of having "7 6/7 volumes to go" in a dreary eight-volume history of England in the eighteenth century, he still found energy and time to tear through a two-volume set on English literature and a *Saturday Review* essay on Faulkner's *Sanctuary*.[19]

In addition to his literary indulgences, Woodward could seldom resist the distraction of a good real-world tussle with the forces of social injustice. Though discouraged from doing so by Howard Odum and others, almost immediately on arrival in Chapel Hill, he took to hanging out with local radicals and activists at Ab's Intimate Bookshop, whose proprietor, Milton Abernethy, was a self-professed communist. He later claimed that seeing his supposedly confidential comments about Dr. Will Alexander during the

Angelo Herndon affair pop up in the *Daily Worker* had taught him a powerful lesson "about collaboration with the communists." If so, that lesson was clearly slow to sink in. Amid the labor unrest across the Carolinas in the fall of 1934 and still in his first semester in Chapel Hill, he reconnected with Communist Party operative Don West. The two had met while working on Herndon's defense in Atlanta, and West enjoyed a reputation as a handsome, charming, resourceful, and utterly fearless organizer for the American Communist Party. In the middle of the 1934 textile strike in nearby Burlington, North Carolina, Woodward had ridden around with West as he tried to rally support for the strikers. He had clearly relished the vicarious notoriety of associating with someone with "warrants for his arrest in three southern states." He was also proud of his own role in helping West to "organize some protest of [the] terrorism, etc." unleashed on the workers.[20]

Rainey had expressed his enthusiasm for Socialist Party leader Norman Thomas, but Woodward thought Thomas's talk in Durham amounted to "pretty sissy tactics" compared to West's appearance in Chapel Hill with some of the workers bayoneted in the 1934 strike. He plunged directly into the fray himself when workers charged with bombing the Holt Mills plant in Burlington were summarily convicted on suspect evidence and sentenced to from two to ten years in prison. Woodward had no doubt that the men had been "framed," and he described their trial to Rainey as lacking even "a half-hearted regard for the formalities of legal decorum." Although he had been in Chapel Hill only a few months, he joined forces with several other local liberals to raise money for the men's defense and appeal. He had helped to arrange an on-campus meeting of their supporters, but much to his dismay, when the UNC campus newspaper, the *Daily Tar Heel*, carried a notice of the meeting, it also ran an editorial bemoaning the "feeble, misdirected, and ostentatious efforts that characterize such strivings toward social justice as this" and denouncing the meeting as "an imprudent move" that was likely to "jeopardize the interests of both strikers and University."[21]

Woodward immediately fired off a letter to the editor, pointing out that "the interests of the strikers are pretty much 'jeopardized' whether such meetings are held or not" and challenging the notion that such a gathering would be harmful to the interests of the university: "If you young gentlemen believe you are doing the university a good turn by writing such stuff as this for the consumption of timid legislators and mill owners, may I suggest that you take a look at the current Hearst [newspaper syndicate] editorials, and you will find your own president [Frank Porter] Graham and his predecessor in that office pilloried as Reds in about the same tone as you adopt toward this little meeting." He also reminded the editor that the paper had quoted approvingly from Graham's recent speech in which he cited liberalism and academic freedom as vital to "the common heritage of students and faculty" at UNC. Of all places, he thought, in Chapel Hill, which was known as the last "stronghold of the liberal tradition," that tradition "ought to be worth a better defense than it is getting." The editor stood by his comments, however, suggesting to Woodward and his fellow liberals that "social justice" might be achieved "without the sounding of brass and tinkling of symbols [sic] that are so dear to the hearts of those who see every mill owner as a swine and every breast-beater as a ministering angel."[22]

Sharing a clipping of the exchange with Rainey, Woodward explained rather dejectedly, "This gives you the prevailing undergraduate opinion. Strange situation here—or is it true elsewhere? The radical and advanced liberal opinion is mainly among the faculty (a very few, Two Socialists among them) and the graduate students in the English department. You know perfectly well that in our undergraduate days it was in the student body, if anywhere, that radical opinion lay. So soon are we superannuated?"[23]

Scarcely a year later, planters in northeast Arkansas responded to a share-cropper strike organized by the Southern Tenant Farmers' Union by unleashing a firestorm of violence against the strikers and those who organized and encouraged their actions. "The war in Arkansas has got me upset," Woodward announced to Rainey in early July 1936. "It looks like my planter uncles and cousins—with which Cross County is overrun—are out to barbecue all the nigger croppers along with the foreign devils [Southern Tenant Farmers' Union workers] from Memphis. I came pretty near going out there with a committee from Chapel Hill. I think you and I and the rest of us are not raising enough hell, and I think if we don't start it pretty soon we're going to suffer a severe deflation in self-esteem."[24]

In the meantime, regardless of how little "self-esteem" Woodward had riding on faculty evaluations of his academic performance at UNC, the terms of his fellowship required that he show satisfactory progress toward his degree. With the end of the spring 1936 semester approaching, if he hoped to retain the support he needed to finish the Watson book, he could no longer postpone submitting himself to the requisite exams over his coursework and reading in his selected fields. As all of his graduate student companions acknowledged, up to that point, his obsession with finishing the Watson manuscript had led him to "cut classes with abandon" and, as Wall observed, "crib notes from classmates, and put off course assignments until the last minute."[25]

History, I Find, Is a Collection of Facts

Regardless of how his fellow graduate students felt about such behavior, he knew it had not escaped the notice of the faculty, either, and with his formal PhD orals in the offing, he was forced to get beyond his generally low estimates of most of his instructors at least long enough to gain their approval to remain in the program and proceed with his dissertation. By all accounts, Woodward's response to this crisis was to frantically beg and wheedle notes from his fellow students, particularly his onetime roommate, Joseph R. "Spec" Caldwell, with whose invaluable assistance he flung himself into a paroxysm of intense, utterly panicked cramming. In later years, Caldwell would confirm that "Vann just borrowed people's notes so he'd learn enough to pass those examinations."[26]

He did pass, but "just barely" would be an exaggeration of how well he apparently performed. It would become a virtual commonplace of departmental lore in the years to come that the history program's most famous and influential graduate had come as close as was humanly possible to failing his PhD oral exams. Queried about this perception more than forty years after the fact, UNC history professor George Tindall admitted that he had heard that the orals had not gone well because, before the exam, Woodward had focused largely on what was of interest to him and then dismissed questions on other topics by saying something like "I don't know. I never was much interested in that." For his part, Tindall doubted that Woodward's responses were quite so flippant as that, but the legend of his almost ostentatious indifference toward his orals and coursework made him something of a heroic, antiestablishment figure among succeeding generations of graduate students at UNC.[27]

These feelings surfaced in a flyer titled "Food for Thought," which later made the rounds purporting to describe Woodward's experience with his orals: "He flopped the first question, on the European field, as he did the second question, on the American field." At the end "all but one member of the committee wished to fail him." If true, the lone holdout was surely Howard K. Beale, a recently arrived Harvard PhD, who, in the course of an agonizingly protracted debate, somehow managed to persuade his new colleagues that the young man whose dissertation he had just agreed to direct should be allowed to proceed with it unimpeded by further coursework.[28]

Though certain embellishments have doubtless been attached in the retelling over the years, this general version of events is not terribly at odds with Woodward's own comments about his orals. From his perspective, he reported to Rainey, the exam had proven "rather formidable, as expected. I performed adequately, of course, but not brilliantly. There is simply nothing in the idea of examinations that challenges my temperament. I seldom rise to them more than sufficiently. A new man in the Department, Beale, whom I count a friend, and under whose direction I will do the thesis, was generously enthusiastic." In any case, he seemed not the least bit humbled by his experience when he claimed the day after the exam to be "indulging myself the dubious pleasure of some extravagant forgetting. No niggardly date here and a dictator there, but whole dynasties at a time—Poof there go the Hapsburgs, poof the Hohenzollerns. (I made the mistake of forgetting Hanoverians before the orals.) A continent or two, an ocean of diplomacy, and a library of books—alcohol proves an excellent solvent for the unused impedimenta of information after examinations."[29]

If Woodward's subsequent performance on his written examination for Beale was any indication, he may well have followed through on his commitment after his orals to "extravagant forgetting," at least when it came to some significant dates and details. Beale, who may not have shared in full measure the "facts first" orientation of his fellow faculty examiners in history, awarded Woodward an "A" on his overall performance, even though some of his responses were a bit short on specifics. Answering a question about the changing fortunes of the Fourteenth Amendment in the courts over time, he named only the *Slaughterhouse Cases* (1873), *Munn v. Illinois* (1877), and *Berea College v. Kentucky* (1908), attempting to date only the first as "about 1872," and, ironically enough in light of his later writings, he made no specific mention of either the *Civil Rights Cases* (1883) or even *Plessy v. Ferguson* (1896), both obviously major Fourteenth Amendment cases. Elsewhere, although the major Grant-era scandals were spread over a seven-year period, Woodward provided no chronology whatsoever in his fairly jumbled allusion to them, and when explaining the rise of pro-tariff sentiment in the late nineteenth century, he mentioned specifically only "the war tariff of 1862." Woodward's performance clearly satisfied Beale, who was by then well aware of his student's considerable talents and potential. Yet his frequent failures to support his broad generalizations with specific examples or to supply useful chronology would have confirmed the suspicions of other UNC history faculty that Beale's new charge, as Woodward's friend Sitterson put it, "simply did not know many facts of history."[30]

Even with exams and coursework behind him, Woodward continued to complain. He was "rusty of ideas and words have to be dragged out," he reported to Rainey, "but God, what would I expect after two years of lectures and examinations? It's a wonder I have an idea left in my head." Woodward would never deny his good fortune in finding a benefactor in Howard Odum and such a propitious setting for completing his book as Chapel Hill. Yet well read and widely traveled, with a master's degree from Columbia and two years of college teaching already under his belt when he arrived in 1934, he seemed from the outset to feel less grateful than put-upon. However legitimate and even prescient his critique of how southern history was being written and taught may have been, he made it more than apparent to his fellow students that he saw meeting the same standards of preparation imposed on them as little more than a waste of his valuable time. He was, to be sure, neither the first nor last graduate student to harbor such sentiments, but his manifest indifference to concealing them was nonetheless striking in an era when acquiescing to an ordained hierarchical standard remained a central fixture of academic life. Certainly, the famously self-effacing public persona of his later years was little in evidence during his years at Chapel Hill. Still, even if few faculty might have given him an "A" for his attitude, in early May 1937, less than three years after he arrived on campus with a manuscript already well underway, C. Vann Woodward successfully defended his dissertation, "The Political and Literary Career of Thomas E. Watson."[31]

It is difficult to gauge how much influence Howard Beale was able to exert over a manuscript that was largely drafted before he agreed to become Woodward's dissertation adviser. In the preface to his book, Woodward chose his words carefully in thanking Beale for "advising me in the latter stages of the work," and he acknowledged privately that "because Beale was the director of the work I was allowed much more latitude than otherwise." A friend and disciple of the enormously influential historian Charles A. Beard, Beale came to the University of North Carolina as an ardent proponent of the Beardian perspective—also identified with other historians of the so-called Progressive school—in which history is essentially the story of conflict between competing economic interests. Five years before he arrived in Chapel Hill, Beale had applied Beard's model to Reconstruction in *The Critical Year: A Study of Andrew Johnson and Reconstruction*, where he presented the Radical Republicans largely as the agents of an aggressively capitalist northeastern business and industrial order determined to gain and maintain economic and political dominion over the rural, agricultural South and West. Woodward had read Beard before he got to Chapel Hill, and it is fair to assume that some of Beale's enthusiasm for his work may have also rubbed off on his student, whose dissertation and later work showed a strong Beardian presence.[32]

Howard Odum's intellectual influence on Woodward may have paled beside that of Beale or Rupert Vance, yet in the end, it was Odum who not only secured the funding Woodward needed to complete his manuscript but provided crucial assistance in getting it into print. The dissertation topped out at a hefty 556 pages of manuscript. University of North Carolina Press director William T. Couch, whom Woodward initially considered his "best bet" for publication, had advised that some 150 to 200 of those pages would have to go before he could even hope to see it in print. Although Odum had not yet read the manuscript, both he and Vance encouraged Woodward to send it to a publisher, if only to get a read on what cuts and revisions might be necessary. At that point, Woodward felt his unrevised manuscript was "in pretty poor shape as it stands . . . for anything except a dissertation," but in July 1937, roughly two months after it had been approved by his doctoral committee, he sent it, still essentially unaltered, to Macmillan, where editors had agreed to review it at Odum's request. Convinced that such a high-profile press would never really consider publishing it without big cuts and perhaps a heavy subsidy, Woodward professed to hope for no more than some helpful suggestions out of Macmillan.[33]

Meanwhile, as he awaited those suggestions, July was slipping away without any real prospect of employment. "I might not get one this summer," Woodward allowed to Rainey, but if he was worried, he gave no indication of it as he jokingly boasted of having "done a damn good job of dodging scummy jobs—and that's no little accomplishment. For example: one military school, one debutante's, one A&M in darkest Arkansas, and a third 'University' in the dismal swamp, to say nothing of a brace of prep schools and an earth-departing 'experimental' school. One develops skill at it. To one prospective employer of the blue-stocking persuasion who inquired about my denominational preferences I gravely responded 'vegetarian.'" Woodward was likely exaggerating a bit for Rainey's benefit, but he might still have seemed a trifle selective for someone whose future means of support was not the least bit visible, especially when the sort of jobs for which he was apparently saving himself were not exactly plentiful.[34]

Yet, as it had so often been since he left Arkansas, fortune smiled on him once again, and he was soon on his way to the University of Florida, where he would be an assistant professor, not in the history department, but in the new General College, teaching interdisciplinary social science courses to freshmen and sophomores. Within the space of another two months, in early September, just as he was settling rather uncertainly into his teaching duties at Florida, he received a letter from Macmillan offering to publish his dissertation. Woodward was almost too giddy for speech after picking up the letter on his way to a meeting with his dean. Though he could not entirely suppress a muted "Zoweee!," he complained to Rainey, the circumstances had otherwise obliged him to stifle his feelings and spend "an hour and a half pretending that I was listening to what the ass was saying about this course 'Man and the Other World' or something." When he got a chance to read the letter more carefully, he was stunned to discover that editors at Macmillan had offered no advice on how to improve the manuscript but instead assured him that they were "very much pleased" with it as it was and "shall be glad if we may publish it for you." Instead of suggesting cuts, they counseled against them unless he thought they were absolutely necessary because "we like the book about as it stands, and we hope you do not change it too much." Woodward's elation at the news would not have been surprising even for a senior scholar, much less for a newly minted PhD receiving what amounted to an author's "dream" letter from so prominent a publisher. "On the strength of this news," he reported to Rainey, "I rented a five-room apartment just so I could walk up and down in it and think what a fine fellow am I."[35]

This turn of events was especially gratifying to Woodward, who claimed he "had given up hope" some two weeks earlier after finally receiving Odum's belated comments on the manuscript. Odum had advised that, at "its present length," it was "utterly impracticable as a publishing venture" and even suggested that Woodward might as well ask Macmillan to return the copy he had sent so that he could either "send it on to Prentice-Hall" or, more realistically, "start cutting it down for Couch." It was perhaps understandable that the almost gushy letter he received from Macmillan spurred him, in the headiness of the moment, to mock Odum's solemnly definitive pronouncement. On the other hand, although he would continue for some time to take the liberty of dropping Odum's name from his fellowship and grant applications, Woodward's attitude toward the person who had thus far done the most to help him achieve his aims seemed strikingly disrespectful and ungrateful, suggesting an already prickly relationship that would become more apparent in years to come. In a stark contrast to the warm appreciation he expressed to Vance in his book's preface, Woodward would offer only a terse thanks for Odum's "consistent encouragement and support," and he even had to be prompted to "by all means send an autographed copy to Dr. Odum" by Vance, who reminded him that "it's just the little touch that does the most."[36]

Woodward would later credit Howard Beale's hard-nosed editing and criticism for minimizing the time "between dissertation and published book." In reality, Beale was clearly taken aback by Macmillan's speedy and unqualified acceptance and would have preferred to see the process slowed down to allow Woodward to rework the entire manuscript "into a little better style for publication" before it was submitted. As Woodward readied his text for copyediting, Beale spluttered in October 1937 that he "did not dream you would have to rush the manuscript off as you seem to be doing" and urged him to insert a chapter discussing "the extent to which Watson did or did not keep up his old interests while pursuing his various phobias after 1900."[37]

When Woodward resisted this call to approach his subject more analytically, he revealed a critical difference between his and Beale's ideas of what he should be trying to accomplish in the book. He had consistently shown more interest in developments on the literary than historical front throughout his largely indifferent pursuit of a PhD in history. This preference for literature over history came through repeatedly during his work on the dissertation, as he typically referred, not to the history or biography he was writing, but to "the story" he was telling, and he complained that his struggle to do justice to Watson's saga simply affirmed for him "the sheer inadequacy of biography vs. fiction." While Woodward was clearly writing the former, in many respects, he approached the task as if he were writing the latter.[38]

When he worried that the minimally revised work he was preparing to send back to Macmillan was "not up to my true standard," he was referring not to a historical standard but to a literary one. He feared that too much of it had been written with "the attitude that after all, this is 'just a dissertation and what the hell.'" Though he knew it would have taken him much longer to write, he felt "the book would have been better . . . if I had been prey to all the pangs of a literary conscience—instead of sometimes mearly [sic] the Ph.D. conscience, which is something else." Yet both stylistically and structurally, the influence of Woodward's "literary conscience" was much in evidence throughout, while his perhaps still emerging "historical conscience" was more apparent at some points than at others.

Shortly after hearing from Macmillan, Woodward had vowed "not to let them rush me on this business," because he felt "some cutting would help and a lot of polishing." Yet with his editors urging him to "make only such changes as seem to you entirely wise" and asking him to return the manuscript within "a month or so" in order that it might be put into production in November, roughly seven weeks after he learned of its acceptance, he had shipped it back to Macmillan. In the end, he reckoned that in the whole process of revising the text, rather than cutting, he had wound up inserting "something like 15 pages . . . in all I guess, mostly dealing with [Watson's] personal life and feelings."[39]

The final stages of turning Woodward's dissertation into a book coincided with the final stages of his courtship of Glenn Boyd Macleod of Greensboro,

History, I Find, Is a Collection of Facts

North Carolina, whom he had begun seeing in 1936, while still in Chapel Hill. After graduating from the North Carolina College for Women, Glenn had headed north to Columbia University, where she earned a master's degree in 1932 after, coincidentally enough, taking some classes with her future husband. It was not until she had returned to Chapel Hill to work at UNC, however, that she and the handsome, quietly imposing, perhaps a tad aloof PhD student two years her senior began to establish a relationship.

Woodward had been slow to develop ties with women in Chapel Hill, in no small part because he persisted in comparing them to his beloved "Nina," Antonina Jones Hansell, a divorcee and aspiring writer with whom he began a torrid affair in 1933 while both were still living in Atlanta. Their correspondence brimmed with powerfully emotive allusions to love and lovemaking, interspersed with references to the writings of William James, William Faulkner, and Stephen Vincent Benet, and Woodward's ardor not simply for the physical charms but for the worldliness and intellectual sophistication of a woman ten years his senior knew no bounds. Shortly before he left to begin his formal graduate study in Chapel Hill in 1934, he assured her that although he had once "wondered vaguely whether we would drift away from each other, lose interest, [or] find other attachments," he "could see now that this will not happen." He knew he would "always want to see you when I can and will go a long way to do so." Even if he became interested in another woman, Woodward insisted he would "still have the same affection and interest for you" regardless of "this current predilection with monogamy, which precludes 'all but one.'" When the matter of her potential suitors came up, he simply declared that it would "be utterly ridiculous for me to go about respecting any of your hypothetical marriage vows."[40]

When Nina decided to move to New York, the two agreed that their current arrangement could not continue, but they kept up a lively and sometimes intense correspondence. It was difficult to tell whether he was trying to convince Nina or himself when he allowed that he was "pretty sure I am not romantically in love with you." Still, he had discovered that it was "easier by far to find one with whom one can sleep, than it is to find one with whom one can laugh. . . . You might prove the last as well as the first I find." Seemingly fearful that she might have been truly exceptional in her affectionate but irreverent reaction to him, Woodward made it clear that he was searching for a woman of independent spirit and emotion like Nina, not one who simply looked on him in "Christ-like patience and mute martyrdom."[41]

Though he did not claim to have found such a partner, he confessed to Nina in August 1936 that his recent encounter with "an agreeable young lady of charm and parts" marked "the first time I have been unfaithful to you since we met [some three years earlier]." The next thing he knew, the two were planning to go camping in the mountains for a few days. And why not? "She is nearly my age," he explained, "rather pretty, matured, traveled, taste, intelligence—we had a class together at Columbia, but didn't know it—experienced, never married, never in love. She does not love me and does not expect me to love her."[42]

The relationship had grown closer and more complicated by May 1937, when, still referring to Glenn as "She," Woodward acknowledged that she "loves me a great deal, I am sure." Yet he worried that his warm feelings for her arose largely out of gratitude for her unselfish devotion to him and guilt over his own "irresponsibility, selfishness, pride, [and] stiff-necked independence." He was quite certain that he would be "doing her as well as myself a great injustice by marrying her for reasons such as that."[43]

Although he professed some six months later that his enduring devotion to Nina still left him "transfixed with a pang of guilt when I catch the hungry, eager eye of some freshman pinned upon me," he was still sorting out his feelings about "the girl." He was more persuaded than ever that "her genuine love for me has done more than anything to deepen my feeling for her." Still uncertain about asking her to marry him, he noted airily that, for the time being, he felt "inclined to leave it up to impulse." At that point, he may have still held out hope that, given a little more time, the woman whose love and companionship he clearly still craved above all others might yet discover that she could not live without him after all. When six weeks passed with no sign of such an epiphany on the horizon, however, he and "the girl in Chapel Hill" were wed, just four days before Christmas in 1937. According to Woodward's account, he had insisted on a civil ceremony, but after Glenn refused to be married by a justice of the peace in a hardware store, the couple were eventually pronounced man and wife on December 21, 1937, by a minister, with local bookstore owner and fabled Chapel Hill communist Milton "Ab" Abernethy as their witnesses.[44]

When, as luck would have it, the galleys for his book showed up right before their honeymoon, nothing would do for his unselfish new bride but that he bring them along. After he finished checking them against the manuscript, he had left them on the floor of their Miami hotel room, only to return from the beach a little later to find them gone. There ensued "a long & frantic search," he reported to Rainey, before they were "finally unearthed . . . at the bottom of the hotel ash can along with sundry cigarette butts, beer bottles, etc. The maid explained it looked like trash to her. . . . I started to remonstrate but Glenn reminded me that one does not descend to cavil[l]ing with one's critics. "Despite this little scare, in early March 1938, scarcely six months after he first heard from Macmillan, Woodward was holding a copy of his book. *Tom Watson: Agrarian Rebel* would go on to win acclaim as a historical monograph, even though its author had indicated from the outset that this was not exactly what he had in mind in writing a book that not only bore the mark of a literary as well as historical imagination but suggested, in some aspects at least, that the literary might be the more powerful presence of the two.[45]

4

A Better Read Than
Huxley's New Novel

Telling the Tom Watson Story

In company with Ernest Hartsock and Glenn Rainey, Woodward had regularly heaped scorn on the Old South–Lost Cause romanticism that had dominated southern fiction since the Civil War. Yet as he pounded out his first few pages about Watson in July 1933, struggle as he might to remain "hardboiled," he found it surprisingly difficult to avoid slipping into that genre himself. Sitting at his typewriter in his parents' antebellum-era house in Oxford while gazing out through the magnolias at a local farmer in his field, he claimed to be suffering from "a severe attack of the Faulknerian galloping-hooves." "The poor, poor Old South," he complained, "I write and snatch a blotter to save the MSS from the briny ruin of a heart wrung sob. . . . Nobody should write anything about the South right here in the middle of it all. . . . Goddammit, I say, how can you *help* sounding like Thomas Nelson Page and Al Jolson?"[1]

Though Woodward had clearly been exaggerating for effect, his ultimate portrayal of Tom Watson's origins and boyhood revealed a stronger attachment to certain aspects of the Old South legend than he cared to acknowledge. He suggested as much by relying on Watson's own partly autobiographical novel to frame the account of his boyhood. *Bethany: A Story of the Old South* was Watson's intensely romantic and frequently maudlin tale of the scion of a fine old family whose wealth and standing, much like those of his own, had been decimated by the Civil War. Looking to convey the traumatic impact of this experience on the young Watson, Woodward drew on the childhood recollections of the novel's protagonist, who was haunted by the strains of "Lorena" and other melodies of tragedy and sorrow that Tom might have heard frequently during the final months of the war as the certainty of defeat sank in for thousands of white southerners.[2]

Eight-year-old Tom was devastated when his beloved grandfather was felled by a stroke toward the end of the war and died shortly after Appomattox. Despite Watson's later claims that his grandfather had never risen out of the middle class, Thomas Miles Watson's forty-seven slaves and 1,372 acres of land comprised an estate valued at $55,000 in 1860, meaning that the loss of his human property alone might have cost him well over 80 percent of his wealth, not to mention the labor needed to work all that land. When young Tom's father, John Smith Watson, returned from the conflict, he pridefully turned a blind eye to his family's dramatically diminished circumstances and began to build what would have passed for the grandest of antebellum mansions. The place went to his creditors soon enough, and John ultimately fell prey to despondency, drunkenness, and a serious gambling habit.[3]

This abrupt reversal of family fortunes and status, Woodward observed, had "jolted" the nine-year-old Tom Watson out of "his warm nest" into a childhood and adolescence defined chiefly by "insecurity and poverty." Woodward also let his subject speak through the narrator in *Bethany* who, in middle age, still clings to his boyhood image of his grandfather, walking slowly over his fields, orchards, and woods, "with the calm, dignified air of a master who expects to find everything going as it should." Looking back across two intervening generations of upheaval and tumult, it seemed to the grandson that, under its master's watchful eye, life on the farm had proceeded in perfect human and natural balance. So it must have been for Watson, too, Woodward ventured, for he would remain fiercely loyal to the values of the old agrarian aristocrats like his grandfather for the remainder of his life. In fact, many of those days would find him doing battle with the agents of industry and commerce who seemed eager to trample on those values while heralding the meteoric ascent of a triumphant New South.[4]

Until well into the nineteenth century, scientists and physicians conceived of nostalgia not as a relatively harmless form of romantic escapism but as a dangerous "psychopathological condition," bordering on, or at least conducive to, mental illness. Woodward seemed to echo this perception in suggesting that "an irrational core of nostalgia for a lost paradise of childhood" lay concealed beneath the adult Watson's exaggerated sense of personal pride and hypersensitivity to slight, not to mention a marked propensity for compensatory blustering and aggressive self-assertion.[5]

These tendencies were apparent even in his teen years, when his family's severely strained finances allowed for only two years of study at Mercer College in Macon, Georgia, and dictated a lifestyle and wardrobe that fairly screamed of his near destitution. Still, Woodward quoted a classmate of Watson's who declared that he had never seen "a purer piece of grit" than the ill-clad fifteen-year-old savoring the wide swath he cut as he "swaggered" about the campus, often "with one or two worshipful henchmen in his wake." This affected swagger and bravado struck Woodward as a classic indication of an inferiority complex that Watson would never outgrow, as witnessed by his lifelong propensity for emotional overreaction and flights of cruel and vengeful behavior. As a struggling lawyer barely into his twenties, he would slap an opposing lawyer in the courtroom and assault a landlord who had struck and cursed his sharecropper brother. A few years later, he faced charges of attempted murder after shooting a legal and political rival in the course of a fight that Watson himself had provoked.[6]

Despite bragging about such behavior at times, Watson understood early on that he had a problem, though he blamed others for it. "The better part of me is poisoned," he complained at age twenty-six to his wife, because as a frail and sensitive child, he had been mocked and belittled by the parents who should have nurtured him, leaving him now to see "enemies where there were none" and lash out at "indignities" that were purely of his own conjuring. Beset at every turn by "a presence that poisons every joy," he could not escape "a shadow that follows like a hungry wolf." (Bertram Wyatt-Brown and others have noted the similarity of the "wolf" reference to Winston Churchill's description of his depression as "the Black Dog.") Watson's propensities for exaggeration and self-pity cast doubt on his attempt to blame his self-destructive tendencies on his upbringing. Yet there was no avoiding that, even as a young man, Watson gave solid evidence of the emotional pathologies that appeared to turn the later stages of his life into little more than a constant swirl of what Woodward saw as delusions—"of persecution, of grandeur, delusions of many kinds."[7]

His tendencies toward dysfunctional behavior did not obscure the younger Tom Watson's consistently superior and quite lucrative courtroom skills. He would soon restore the family fortunes and more, eventually becoming landlord to more tenants than his grandfather had slaves. Yet, even as his own landholdings and tenant rolls continued to swell apace, with his political fortunes also on the rise, Watson steadfastly refused to acknowledge any divergence in interests despite the growing economic divide between Georgia's large landholding farmers and the tenants who worked successively smaller plots of their acreage. Woodward seemed reluctant to make this distinction himself in tracing Tom Watson's agrarianism back to Robert Toombs and Charles Colcock Jones, two postbellum advocates of the antebellum planter elite's ostensibly anti-capitalist worldview. In this, he seemed very much attuned to the thinking of Charles Beard, who, historian Staughton Lynd insisted, simply assumed that all "Jeffersonians—slaveholders or no—were defending economic democracy."[8]

Writing in the shadow of Beard eight years earlier, Howard Beale had blamed the Radical Republicans for holding the South's recovery in check long enough to ensure that, by the end of Reconstruction, a new, predominantly northern, economic and financial order reigned supreme and impervious to attack. Woodward largely echoed his adviser when, setting the stage for the agrarian political insurgency, he presented Reconstruction as merely "a Yankee euphemism for capitalist expansion." Caught up in that capitalist expansion, some in the old planting class had become bankers, merchants, businessmen, and, for the most part, sworn enemies of the Populists. Yet, even as one of the state's largest landholders, Watson readily embraced the role of spokesman for Georgia's increasingly impoverished rural masses. Looking to explain this apparent irony, Woodward also invoked Beard's Jeffersonian era model of a planter aristocracy presiding over "a democracy of small farmers," who had rallied behind the segment of the "agrarian class" they felt best equipped to provide "dominant direction" in the struggle against the rising might of capitalism.[9]

No Georgian before or after the war was ever more confident of his capacity for "dominant direction" than Watson's boyhood idol, the brilliant orator Robert Toombs. Watson freely admitted that he had "*gloried* in Bob Toombs," who had been one of Georgia's foremost proponents of secession and an unapologetic champion of the antebellum planter class. After the war, Toombs stridently opposed efforts by journalist Henry W. Grady and other prominent Atlantans who promised to lead Georgia to unparalleled prosperity as the capital of New South industry and commerce.[10]

Woodward believed that Watson's earliest expression of agrarianism had also come in response to the "aggressive capitalism" propounded by Grady, and in this, he found Watson's views nearly identical to those of Old South planters turned New South critics like Toombs or Charles Colcock Jones, who floridly deplored "the creation in our midst of giant corporations intent on self-aggrandizement" at the expense of the agrarian values that marked southerners as a distinctive people. Woodward saw men like Jones and Toombs providing a transitional link between antebellum agrarianism and the less rhetorically adorned, but ultimately more practical postbellum version first espoused in Georgia by the reform-minded political Independents of the 1870s and 1880s. As precursors to the Populists, Independents like William H. Felton spoke more directly to and for the masses of "farmers . . . mechanics and [other] wealth-creators" of the countryside who were being pushed aside or simply rolled over by the greedy, exploitive agents of a new postbellum capitalist regime.[11]

Historian Charles Crowe observed that, by essentially making agrarians of any farmer, irrespective of wealth or social pedigree, who appeared to resist the incursions of modern industrial and commercial capitalism, Woodward had created a model of agrarianism broad enough to accommodate either a "Peruvian feudal landlord or [a] Russian collective farmer." Woodward saw Watson endorsing "relentless class conflict with the enemy classes," meaning industrial, financial, and commercial capitalists both outside and within the South whose aims were self-evidently at odds with those of any and all farmers, be they planters, yeomen, or tenants. Whatever resentments they might also harbor against greedy or dishonest landlords, for Woodward, the rank-and-file Populists represented more than anything a "vanguard against the advancing capitalist plutocracy" and their eventual defeat virtually assured the South's "capitulation to capitalism."[12]

In many respects, Watson the Populist seemed not only to personify Beard's badly outmanned agrarian South gamely battling the emerging northern industrial colossus but to exude Woodward's personal distaste for the wealthy and powerful capitalists, either of Watson's era or of his own. In *Tom Watson* and elsewhere in his formal writing and private correspondence, he also revealed a pronounced personal aversion to self-styled capitalists of any sort. In his younger days he and Glenn Rainey had regularly appended "capitalist" to the names of those they meant to mock or ridicule, as when Rainey described rising from the audience at a YMCA banquet to rebuke the speaker, "Samuel Candler Dobbs, Capitalist," for boasting about getting an instructor at a small Methodist college "fired off the campus the same day" for daring to suggest that there might be certain imperfections in the U.S. Constitution. (Ironically, four years later Dobbs, a cousin of Coca-Cola founder Asa Griggs Candler, would make an unrestricted gift of $1 million to Emory University, Woodward's and Rainey's alma mater.) Woodward eagerly assured Rainey that he "gloried in your baiting Capitalist Daniel Snobbs [*sic*]" and "enjoyed some vicarious comfort from the reflection that there was a time when I was fit for such noble sport."[13]

In 1931, Woodward observed to his former English teacher at Henderson College, Boulware Martin, that the downside of the "skinny [Rosenwald] scholarship" that was funding his year at Columbia was that it was restricted to study in the social sciences. He had been forced to "say farewell to my classics," he reported, because "damn the capitalists, they will not pay you to study classics." Though he would benefit more than once in his career from philanthropic funds made available by the likes of the Rosenwalds and the Rockefellers, his attitude toward even the most philanthropic of the uber-capitalists fairly dripped with condescension and disdain, especially for those of the homegrown variety such as Emory's principal benefactors, the Candlers, who had amassed huge fortunes under the mercenary New South order.[14]

Arriving for a one-year teaching stint at the University of Virginia in 1939, he encountered a "primness and formality and smug tradition" that he found "pretty hard to stomach," but whenever Virginia's "stuffiness" began to re-mind him of Emory, he had only to "lift up mine eyes to Monticello and re-flect that these colonnades were not constructed on the profits of Coca-Cola stock." (Apparently, he did not reflect on the likelihood that those vaunted colonnades had instead been constructed on the backs of enslaved laborers.) Likewise, he declared it "a case of loathe at first sight" for Duke Univer-sity, which had invested some of its windfall from tobacco magnate James B. Duke in garish "concrete gargoyles," fake chimneys, and other pretentious and incongruent architectural imitations. Overall, the campus gave him the impression of "middle Gothic in cellophane." Certainly, neither Emory nor Duke came close in his estimate to Chapel Hill, which was both "lovely" and "unraped by Coca-Cola or Chesterfield."[15]

It did not seem quite so bold to bemoan the postbellum South's surrender to capitalism in a book published in the Depression-wracked 1930s when critics of the system were by no means scarce as it would later in *Origins of the New South*, which appeared with McCarthyism on the ascent in 1951. Wood-ward invited controversy nonetheless when he declared that "Tom Watson was perhaps the first native white southern leader of importance to treat the Negro's aspirations with the seriousness that human strivings deserve," after inserting the qualifying "perhaps" only at the urging of Howard Beale.[16]

Having said of the Watson of the 1880s and 1890s what could scarcely be said of any but a very few white southerners of the 1930s, Woodward cited Watson's appearances before racially mixed audiences, his endorsement of a black appointee to the Populist Party's state executive committee, and his often-dramatic calls to white Populists to defend their black counterparts from angry white Democrats. In the main, however, he rested his case for Watson as a revolutionary champion of racial tolerance and cooperation on his boldly unrepentant language in calling on his fellow Populists to make "lynch law odious to the people" and declaring that "the accident of color can make no difference in the interests of farmers, croppers, and laborers," who were "kept apart [so] that you may be separately fleeced of your earnings." Woodward conceded that Watson stopped well short of embracing social equality between the races but insisted that he had never flinched in his support of "political equality," as embodied in his pledge "to wipe out the color line, and put every man on his citizenship, regardless of color."[17]

Woodward may have been safe in observing that, as of the mid-1930s, at least, blacks and whites in the South had never come "so close together as they did during the Populist struggles." He ventured well out on what proved to be a highly suspect limb, however, in insisting that, "under Watson's tutelage," the South's rural white masses were coming to see blacks as true political allies, "bound to them by economic ties and a common destiny." Woodward's claim that Watson's vision of interracial cooperation had made significant headway among the Populist rank and file rested almost entirely on a single incident involving a young black minister, H. S. "Seb" Doyle, who, despite repeated threats on his life, gave numerous speeches in Watson's behalf during his 1892 reelection campaign for Congress against Democrat J. C. C. Black. On Sunday, October 23, 1892, Doyle got word that a mob of white Democrats in Watson's hometown of Thomson planned to lynch him, and he sought refuge at Watson's place. Watson agreed to shelter Doyle, and as a small local posse was assembled for protection, he and his friends dispatched several riders to recruit enough supporters from the surrounding area to repulse any mob that might show up at his home.[18]

Over the next two days, Woodward reported, "fully two thousand" men answered the call, assembling at Watson's home and escorting him and Doyle into Thomson, where Doyle spoke briefly before Watson delivered a lengthy address. After that, Doyle later declared, "Mr. Watson was held almost as a savior by the Negroes." Meanwhile, Woodward observed, "the spectacle of white farmers riding all night to save a Negro from lynchers was rather rare in Georgia." This would have been an understatement of truly epic proportions had it accurately depicted what transpired.[19]

Whatever else may be said of it, the Doyle affair spoke to the anxieties and animosities that, by the close of the high-stakes contest, had risen to the point that Georgia's Democratic governor W. J. Northen was heard to say that Watson should be killed, and both the threat and reality of violence were sufficient to send some of the Thomson area's outnumbered Democrats into hiding as election day drew near. These feelings dissipated but little in the aftermath of Watson's highly suspect defeat amid widespread charges of blatant fraud, including, but not necessarily confined to, what Woodward identified as "wholesale repeating, bribery, ballot-box stuffing, voting of minors and intimidation." He found abundant indications of all these abuses and more in an official congressional investigative report on the thoroughly tainted election. At the same time, however, the report also offered ample evidence that, had he chosen to share it, would have revealed his portrayal of the Doyle incident as highly questionable, if not deliberately misleading. Regardless of their feelings about Watson, the white witnesses called to testify in the investigation uniformly agreed that the throng of white men who assembled at his house in October 1892 had come solely out of concern for Watson rather than Doyle. Though Doyle himself was inconsistent on whether the initial, smaller local posse had been gathered "to defend Mr. Watson" or "to protect Mr. Watson and myself," even he conceded that the much larger group of men from surrounding counties had come in response to a report that "Mr. Watson was probably in danger of being hurt because Doyle was at his house."[20]

This much was confirmed by the local sheriff, a Populist, who testified that the group had simply gathered "to protect Mr. Watson" and might even "have come because they heard Mr. Watson was killed." Although Woodward noted the sheriff's presence at Watson's home that day and his footnotes indicated that he had read the testimony of both Doyle and the sheriff, he made no mention of their comments contradicting his version of events in the book itself. In fact, although Woodward also declined to share it, Watson himself had confirmed the sheriff's speculation, saying that the "crowd" from Lincoln County "came over here greatly excited because news had reached Lincolnton that I had been killed."[21]

After reviewing the testimony given to congressional investigators, historian Barton Shaw doubted that many of the white men who came were even aware that Doyle was involved in the incident before they reached Thomson. While the large group of men who hurried to his defense in October 1892 spoke volumes about Watson's remarkable personal sway over his white supporters, it said little or nothing about his white supporters' interest in showing solidarity with his black followers. On the contrary, although Woodward offered several examples of Democrats intimidating black voters in 1892, he seemed to overlook evidence that Populists sometimes did much the same, essentially treating blacks whose votes they could not control in much the same menacing and abusive fashion as did the Democrats, down to nightriding in Klan-like regalia and killing or whipping blacks who might be inclined to vote Democratic.[22]

In his later work, Woodward would cite the biracial southern Populist insurgency as one of the "forgotten alternatives" of southern history. In this book, however, his primary aim was not to chronicle the insurgency itself but to tell the story of a man whose meteoric rise and tragic demise mirrored that of the movement he had so fervently championed. How compelling that story proved to be depended on how sharp a contrast Woodward managed to draw between the earlier Watson and the later. Before the humiliating Populist defeat in 1896, the Watson who leapt from Woodward's pages could be mercurial, irrational, and even self-destructive to be sure. Yet, in his political discourse of that era, he generally came across as articulate, keenly insightful, and focused on real rather than illusory concerns of substantive import to his followers.

In Woodward's account, though, after returning from less than a decade of relative political exile following the 1896 debacle, Watson appeared largely to lose his way and wander into a swamp of bigotry, irrationality, and paranoia from which he seldom emerged throughout the rest of his life. The remainder of the story Woodward told came down to one man's seemingly abrupt, irreversible descent into what appeared to be mental illness. It played out chapter by agonizing chapter in socially destructive and self-degrading campaigns of rhetorical terror against enemies and conspiracies whose existence was confined largely to his imagination.[23]

Regardless of how real or consistent the later Watson's perceived madness may have been, there was no denying that the same man who, in the 1890s, had openly mocked whites who stoked fears that "the Negroes will 'dominate us,'" had reemerged a decade later sounding his own, near hysterical warnings of "the 'HIDEOUS, OMINOUS, NATIONAL MENACE' of Negro domination." If anything, Watson appeared not simply to join those whom he had once taunted yet could not beat but to move well beyond them in his bitter and lurid racial invective. Rather than dismissing "the accident of color," he now ranted about its monumental importance, condemning the savagery of a race scarcely removed from the jungles where, not so long ago, they practiced cannibalism and exhibited the most animalistic sexual urges imaginable. "Civilization" owed them "nothing! . . . Nothing!! NOTHING!!" The only thing to be done, he claimed, was to consign them to the status of

A Better Read Than Huxley's New Novel

a permanent "peasantry" laboring always under the strict control of their white superiors.[24]

To that end, reversing a position he had taken in the 1890s, Watson promised in 1904 that he and his fellow Populists would rally behind any Democratic candidate who would pledge himself to "perpetuat[ing] white supremacy in Georgia" by taking the vote away from blacks. In another racial about-face, where in 1893 he was urging the Populist Party to dedicate itself to making "lynch law odious to the people," two decades later he was insisting that "*lynch law is a good sign: it shows a sense of justice yet lives among the people.*"[25]

Watson let fly with similarly egregious racial invective as he touted the pro-disfranchisement gubernatorial candidacy of Hoke Smith in 1906 in a campaign that culminated in four days of bloody, antiblack violence in Atlanta. Beyond that, his powerful, artfully orchestrated diatribes may have been responsible for numerous other outrages against the people whose votes he once courted. In certain respects, this obsessive spewer of racist vitriol bore but the scantest resemblance to the earlier champion of white-black cooperation depicted by Woodward. Yet Woodward was still awaiting his first copy of the book when Glenn Rainey challenged the sincerity of Watson's earlier interracial appeals. Researching his own dissertation on late nineteenth-century Georgia politics in 1938, Rainey did not conceal his misgivings about his friend's take on Watson as "a real white hope" for blacks. Based on what Rainey had seen of Democratic politics in the 1880s, which featured its own "frantic" bidding for black votes, he could conclude only that appeals such as Watson's "were absolutely standard and almost universally insincere." In Rainey's view, Watson had pursued black votes only so long as he felt the need, and when he no longer did, he promptly reverted to the standard political practice of race-baiting, to which he simply brought "new expressions of violence and hatred." Absent evidence of Watson's continuing loyalty to blacks thereafter, Rainey told Woodward rather pointedly, "I doubt that you can prove anything other than he said what he thought he must say to get the Negro votes without losing too many whites doing it."[26]

This would not be the last time that Rainey's criticism of Woodward's work in manuscript would foreshadow what was later said of it in print. Woodward responded at this point that Rainey was "probably right that I paint too glowing a picture of Tom's position on the Negro, but I don't think I am as far wrong as you say." The critical question, of course, was how "far wrong" he could be before his carefully constructed wall separating the younger and older Tom Watson began to crumble? Certainly, there was no lack of evidence more favorable to Rainey's position than his own.[27]

Historians would later cite instances in the 1890s when, despite Watson's continuing appeals for black votes, as editor of the *People's Party Paper* he had readily resorted to racially inflammatory and derogatory language in hopes of persuading white voters that it was not the Populists but their Democratic antagonists who could not be trusted to safeguard their racial supremacy. His targets included President Grover Cleveland, "who was elected by southern Democrats," but nonetheless welcomed Frederick Douglass and his white wife into the White House and Virginia's Democratic governor Charles O'Ferrall for hosting a black guest from Massachusetts who, after dining with socially prominent whites, had "wiped his distinguished lips with O'Far-rell's napkins just as if he had been at it all his life." These and other episodes suggested that Watson's racial tactics and language in the mid-1890s generally bore more resemblance to what he would be doing and saying a decade later than Woodward had given readers reason to believe. When Rainey chalked Watson's appeal for black votes up to pure political expediency, he was fore-shadowing what would become a scholarly consensus, later summarized by Charles Postel, that the Populists never really "questioned core beliefs in white supremacy and the master race ideology" and that their "commitment to biracial cooperation" was always "more rhetorical than substantive."[28]

If both Watson's initial pursuit of black voters and his later push to elim-inate them as a factor in Georgia politics altogether were both mere matters of strategy, the apparent changes in Watson's racial attitudes more likely re-flected changes in his perception of the political realities confronting him and his fellow Populists. Although Woodward professed puzzlement at how Watson could have gone from espousing "his radical democratic doctrine" to endorsing the idea of disfranchising "a million citizens of his state," Wat-son himself had explained his reversal rather straightforwardly. So long as blacks were voting and their votes could be used effectively against them, it behooved the Populists to capture as many of those votes as they could. By the end of the 1890s, however, it was abundantly clear that "the white people dare not revolt so long as they can be intimidated by fear of the Negro vote," and, as Watson himself later explained, eliminating this "bugaboo" now be-came a more urgent political necessity for him and his followers. Woodward introduced an element of drama by suggesting that, in endorsing disfran-chisement, Watson "abandoned his old dream of uniting the two races against the enemy." Yet he also acknowledged that, with blacks no longer voting, Watson and his followers now represented the "balance of power" between

A Better Read Than Huxley's New Novel

the two warring factions in the Democratic Party, much as blacks had once done with the Populists and Democrats.[29]

In truth, it would have been more accurate to say that the balance of power belonged to Tom Watson himself, a reality he was never loath to demonstrate thereafter, typically in flamboyant and often vindictive fashion. Though he would go on to capture a U.S. Senate seat in 1920, the sizable political impact he registered in Georgia during this period came primarily in advancing and thwarting the ambitions of other aspirants for office, sometimes even doing both for the same aspirant over the course of several elections. Watson supported would-be reformer Hoke Smith's successful pro-disfranchisement gubernatorial bid in 1906. The new governor could hardly have been more solicitous of his benefactor, and despite powerful opposition from legislators and lobbyists, in Woodward's view, Smith "accomplished wonders," not the least of them being more stringent regulation of the railroads. This achievement alone should rightly have warmed Watson's Populist heart, but it seemed to count for little after Smith declined to commute the death sentence of an obviously guilty murderer who had been a longtime Watson supporter.[30]

Abruptly turning on the man he had so recently anointed but now renounced as a "selfish and cold-blooded politician," he dared to ask the unthinkable of many former Populists by urging them to abandon Smith in 1908 in favor of Watson's anointed challenger, Joseph M. Brown. As a railroad executive and the son of the Redeemer era governor and senator, Brown's procorporate, antilabor, antireform credentials were well known. Still, out of loyalty to their longtime champion, enough of his "boys" apparently managed to swallow their principles to put Brown in the governor's mansion. As he claimed credit for ousting the man he had just helped put in office two years earlier, Watson assured his supporters that they need only "sit steadily in the boat and trust me. And if God spares my life, we will dominate the state during the next decade."[31]

There were setbacks; Watson's opposition failed to keep Smith from reclaiming the governorship in 1910 or to foil the reelection bid of his onetime lieutenant, Congressman Thomas Hardwick, whom he now spurned for refusing to break with Smith or to offer a minor appointment to a Watson crony. From that point on, however, as Woodward noted, Watson simply redoubled his efforts to regain his grip on Georgia, and the fruits of those efforts were soon apparent. With the Democrats of the state deeply divided and Watson in apparent command of some 17,000 fanatically loyal Populist diehards, representatives of rival Democratic factions "kept a beaten path to Hickory Hill [Watson's home], and news of Watson's favor or disfavor made or unmade many a candidate." From 1906 until his death in 1922, to some degree at least, every Georgia governor owed at least one of his terms to Watson's backing. By the same token, "some of the men he elected he [just] as surely defeated," for Watson clearly demanded a "high degree of subservience" from those whose power he seemed to feel was merely an extension of his own.[32]

In certain respects, Watson's efforts to turn what remained of Georgia Populism into what Barton Shaw called a "personality cult" were no doubt a reflection of his long-standing emotional volatility. On the other hand, like many of his actions in this period, they were likely more calculated than Woodward chose to indicate. Watson's readiness to shift his loyalties in the batting of an eye struck Bertram Wyatt-Brown as the mark of someone so obsessed with demonstrating his own importance "that he took pleasure in the potency of betrayal." As emotionally gratifying as demonstrating that potency to his rivals might have been to Watson personally, however, it was hardly less so for his fanatical following. As a constituency painfully sensitive to their own powerlessness, they fairly reveled in their hero's ability to force "big men," such as senators and governors and others aspiring to those offices, to do his bidding and to hold them strictly accountable if they displeased him, which, in Watson's case, seemed all but a foregone conclusion at some point. He prided himself on understanding his "peepul," and he knew full well that the spectacle of the high and mighty scraping and bowing to their champion, the old "Sage of Hickory Hill," would never grow old or unsatisfying for them. Likewise, while it would have been better for either Democratic faction that won his favor at any point to maintain it over time, it did not suit Watson's purposes to see one faction gain the upper hand and hold it. It was the fervent competition between the two groups, after all, that sustained his emotionally intoxicating and politically intimidating position as kingmaker from election to election.[33]

There was also more method in the apparent madness of Watson's rabid assaults first on blacks and later on Catholics and Jews than Woodward chose to affirm. In fact, his wild-eyed hatemongering proved quite conducive to his simultaneous efforts to expand both his influence and his wealth via his writings and publishing interests. Watson's redoubled effort to regain his sway over Georgia politics after his anointed candidates lost to Thomas Hardwick and Hoke Smith in 1910 came as he was in the final stages of consolidating his numerous publications under his own control. In the interim between the rout of the Populists in 1896 and his return to active involvement in politics less than a decade later, Watson had written not only his novel, *Bethany*, but biographies of Napoleon and Thomas Jefferson, as well as a two-volume history of France, which sold an astonishing 50,000 copies for Macmillan, before Watson purchased the rights to it and his other books in 1910–11.[34]

He had gained a substantial national and regional following as the editor of the *People's Party Paper* from 1891 to 1898 and enjoyed early success with *Tom Watson's Magazine*, which was launched, improbably enough, in New York in 1905, and quickly gained a place among the popular reform and muckraking journals of the day. A dispute with his business partner soon led Watson to sever his connection with this offering, in favor of *Watson's Jeffersonian Magazine* (rechristened in 1912 as *Watson's Magazine*), which was published in Atlanta along with its new weekly counterpart, the *Weekly Jeffersonian*. By 1910, however, both were on the move again, this time to Watson's estate near Thomson, where he bragged of erecting "one of the best equipped printing plants in the South," at a reported expense of $100,000. Though his wealth had continued to swell, this sum amounted to almost 40 percent of Watson's self-estimated worth as of two years earlier. Woodward pointed out that, with this huge new investment on the line, both the appearance and the perceived tone of his publications began to change, as "italics and capitals and bold-faced type came to sprinkle virtually every paragraph," and headlines were soon leaping off the page in red ink. Meanwhile, his assaults on politicians and other prominent figures elevated slander to "a fine art." Not only was Woodrow "Professor Woodpile" Wilson an "arrant liar," but the hated Hoke Smith, now a U.S. senator, was "the vilest of rascals," whose alleged crimes included, but were not limited to, "seduction, kidnapping, adultery, . . . [and] rape." It was soon clear, as Woodward did admit, that Watson felt that holding on to "his renovated power" came down to recruiting hordes of new subscribers, drawn to his publications by the wild-eyed vendettas he conducted therein.[35]

These crusades were markedly different from his older, more substantive, and penetrating David versus Goliath critiques of the capitalist plutocracy and the corporate state. Ground down by precisely those entities, small farmers and the urban masses now welcomed the chance to do some bullying of their own by lashing out against what Woodward called more "vulnerable antagonists: against anything strange, and therefore evil." In this hunger for at least some measure of psychic satisfaction, "a frustrated man and a frustrated class found their desires and needs were complementary." Thus it was that, by 1910, Roman Catholicism and its adherents had joined blacks as another convenient and virtually defenseless target for Watson's demonizing invective. Over the next seven years, he would offer readers of his weekly newspaper and monthly magazine a steady diet of almost wholly fabricated, luridly sensational articles and outlandish charges aimed at exposing the Roman Catholic Church as "The Deadliest Menace to Our Liberties and Our Civilization." As Woodward noted, any pretense of the fairness and accuracy that Watson had once professed to hold dear was gone, along with any but the scantest regard for human decency, much less dignity. He delighted in publishing photos of Roman Catholic dignitaries and reaching all manner of denigrating conclusions based on their facial features: "Look at that nose! . . . Such a proboscis *always* marks the sensual man. It is thick, and I shouldn't wonder if it is red." In Watson's writing, convents were invariably overflowing with women held against their will as sex slaves for the priests who routinely murdered their illegitimate babies. Such excesses in print led ultimately to his prosecution for sending obscene literature through the mails, proof positive to Watson that, in addition to conspiring to kill or imprison him, the Roman Catholic "Hierarchy" had infiltrated the government and made the White House "little more than a Vatican annex."[36]

Although Woodward acknowledged that Watson's vicious anti-Catholic campaign was "deliberately planned," he also maintained that even "the personal motivation of a Martin Luther" would not be sufficient to explain it. Perhaps not, but readers might have found it relevant that Watson was by no means fulminating solo on this issue, for the sentiments he expressed were generally in sync with a substantial segment of popular opinion at the time. Noting the breadth and virulence of America's hostility to "Popery" at that point, Justin Nordstrom has pointed to a profusion of anti-Catholic publications enjoying "huge financial success" easily rivaling that of the more established print outlets of the day. Woodward did not note that two months after his anti-Catholic campaign began in earnest, Watson, who had complained a year earlier that his publishing enterprise was "in the hole $20,000," was exulting in a letter to a friend that his serial attacks on the "Hierarchy" had proven to be a financial "ten-strike." Watson admitted that the cartoons used to illustrate his articles were "too crude to appeal to the scholarly taste, but . . . seem to be effective with many of our readers," but Woodward avoided any suggestion that he was consciously orchestrating the series to maximize the sales and subscription revenue it generated.[37]

Watson could not resist bragging openly in the *Jeffersonian* that his revelations about the scourge of Catholicism had "gained him thousands of new readers." For once, he was not exaggerating. As figures gathered by Nordstrom revealed, so voracious was the public appetite for his anti-Catholic tirades that the circulation of *Watson's Magazine* exploded from 16,000 in 1911 to an astonishing 80,000 just two years later, when it claimed, for a time at least, 10,000 more readers than *Harper's Magazine* and fully 50,000 more than the *Atlantic Monthly*. Meanwhile, his assaults on the Vatican boosted not only his financial standing but his political clout. He had "forced the popery issue into Georgia politics," he crowed to a friend in 1914, "where it is now cutting a wide swathe to the consternation of the old-line politicians." These included, of course, his preferred whipping boy, Hoke Smith, whom he condemned as "a truckler" to Rome.[38]

Woodward observed that Watson would soon be nearly as well known for his ravings on the Roman menace as for his jeremiads against Wall Street. Yet he would owe even more of his ultimate notoriety as a hatemonger to actions that proved even more vicious and tragic, while further boosting his publishing income. Public interest had run fever high during the lurid trial of Leo Frank, the Jewish superintendent of an Atlanta pencil factory who was convicted and sentenced to death in 1913 for the murder of one of his employees, thirteen-year-old Mary Phagan. The evidence against Frank had been thin at best, and as demands for a new trial poured in, many originating in the northern press, and even the *Atlanta Journal* briefly took up Frank's cause in March 1914. Watson had remained uncharacteristically quiet about the affair up to that point, but the *Journal* was the unofficial political organ of its former publisher, his archenemy Hoke Smith, and he leapt full into the fray.[39]

Although a precipitous drop in the *Atlanta Journal*'s circulation quickly led its editors to rethink their position, Watson warned that outgoing governor John M. Slaton might yet be pressured into commuting Frank's sentence to life imprisonment, and quickly launched into a sustained barrage of anti-Semitic, not to mention stridently sectional, class-polarizing, and sexually charged sensationalism. Stressing Frank's many "wealthy connections in the North," Watson insisted that these "rich Jews" meant to assure that "no aristocrat of their race should die for the death of a working-class Gentile." Sexual innuendo and gossip had swirled around the case, and Watson eagerly condemned Frank as "the typical young libertine Jew," whose lust had been stoked in this instance "by the racial novelty of the girl of the uncircumcised." As he had done in his anti-Catholic onslaught, from the picture of Frank he ran in his *Jeffersonian*, Watson thought anyone might tell that the young man was "a lascivious pervert," simply by observing "those bulging, satyr eyes. . . . The protruding fearfully sensual lips; and also the animal jaw."[40]

When, in response to pleas from 10,000 Georgians and many others from across the nation and world, Slaton did in fact commute Frank's sentence, the man who had been elected governor by a landslide with Watson's support was quickly beset by a howling mob of 5,000 assembled outside his official residence. Not surprisingly, Watson's outrage knew no bounds. Crying that "our grand old Empire State HAS BEEN RAPED," he vowed that "THE NEXT JEW WHO DOES WHAT FRANK DID, IS GOING TO GET EXACTLY THE SAME THING THAT WE GIVE TO NEGRO RAPISTS." Even before the sentence had been commuted, Watson had demanded to know "*how much longer is the innocent blood of Little Mary Phagan to cry in vain to heaven for vengeance?*" Finally, on the evening of August 16, 1915, he got his answer, and apparent wish, when a group of armed men forcibly entered the state prison at Milledgeville, removed Leo Frank, took him back to Mary Phagan's hometown of Marietta, and hanged him from a tree. Watson, who knew of the plan in advance, was notified of its success around two o'clock the following morning.[41]

With condemnations raining down on Georgia from above the Mason-Dixon Line, Watson defiantly praised the lynchers and warned that "the North may rail itself hoarse" but Georgians had "already stood as much vilification and abuse as we intend to put up with." To those who would persist in meddling in the state's affairs, he hinted that "another Ku Klux Klan may be organized to restore HOME RULE." Sure enough, a few months later, in November 1915, the Klan was formally resurrected atop Georgia's Stone Mountain. Woodward was surely correct in observing that "if any mortal man may be credited (as no one man may rightly be) with releasing the forces of human malice and ignorance and prejudice, which the Klan merely mobilized, that man was Thomas E. Watson."[42]

Once again, like his anti-Catholic smear campaign, as monstrous as Watson's behavior in the Frank affair may have been, it was not exactly bad for business. Where Hoke Smith's paper had hemorrhaged subscribers after briefly adopting a moderate stance on the Frank case, every escalation of Watson's bloodthirsty rhetoric fueled more interest in his *Weekly Jeffersonian*, as copies melted away "like snowflakes" on the streets of larger cities and people in the towns lined up to meet incoming trains carrying their "'Jeff's." Woodward cited "a convincing itemized statement," compiled by longtime Watson antagonist Thomas W. Loyless of the *Augusta Chronicle*, showing that, from the beginning of his verbal pogrom in April 1914 to early September 1915 (shortly after Frank was lynched), the *Jeffersonian*'s circulation leapt from 25,000 to 87,000. Over this time, Loyless added, Watson had also effectively doubled the price that he charged dealers for the paper. At its peak circulation in this period, Loyless estimated, the magazine turned a weekly profit of $1,123.75 (the rough equivalent of $30,500 in 2021).[43]

A Better Read Than Huxley's New Novel

Woodward simply reported these numbers matter-of-factly, apparently to illustrate passionate public interest in the Frank affair, again without commenting directly on the possibility that, as he almost certainly had done in his anti-Catholic rampage, Watson might have consciously exploited the hatred that he whipped up in the Frank case for personal gain as well. Loyless showed no such hesitation, although Woodward failed to pass along his allegation that Watson had jumped on the Frank case "like a duck on a June bug" and proceeded "to capitalize it and commercialize it to his own account."[44]

Loyless was clearly something less than an objective observer where Watson was concerned. Still, Watson himself not only gave ample indication that he was aware his diatribes against both Catholics and Jews were enhancing both his wealth and his influence but that he delighted in pointing it out to others. This revelation was not incompatible with the idea that Watson's behavior grew progressively more psychotic in the years after 1896. Yet it did suggest that, regardless of how severe his psychosis may have been, his vicious campaigns against blacks, Catholics, and Jews were also the work of a man still keenly attuned to his own economic and political interests. Still, Woodward resisted any suggestion that the profit motive may have factored into Watson's hate-filled diatribes, noting only that that "the same pathological state of mind" he revealed in his anti-Catholic harangues also lay behind "many of his wild utterances on the Frank case." He did point out, however, that, with Watson still stirring the pot post hoc on the Frank case throughout the 1916 campaign season in Georgia, his anointed candidates were "victorious all along the line."[45]

Whatever buoyancy of spirit Watson may have gained from yet another demonstration of his prowess as a kingmaker in Georgia politics would dissipate thoroughly over the next eighteen months. His incessant attacks on Woodrow Wilson's preparedness program, American involvement in World War I, and especially his calls for resistance to military conscription, led the postmaster general to deny him the use of the mails for his publications in August 1917. His daughter died a few days later, and his son and final surviving child died the following April. Seeking some diversion from his crippling melancholy, he ran for Congress in 1918, and though his patriotism was under continuous assault, he showed surprising strength even in defeat.

Two years later, with postwar disenchantment now surging and a new print organ, his *Columbia Sentinel*, to disseminate his invective, he managed, in what surely was one of his sweetest personal victories, to oust the hated Hoke Smith and take his place in the U.S. Senate. Watson had managed this unexpected triumph by reprising his time-tested warnings about the Roman Catholic hierarchy, citing it as a far greater "menace" to individual liberties than the Bolshevism of which he found himself accused by the "100 percent idiots" of the "100 percent Americanism" crowd. In doing so, Woodward observed, Watson had, however improbably, mobilized the Ku Klux Klan against the American Legion.[46]

Watson's eighteen-month stint in the Senate seemed like little more than an extension of the last twenty years of his life, complete with a succession of belligerent and outlandish accusations against his colleagues and other members of the Washington establishment, punctuated by what Woodward called "spells of black melancholy and morbid drinking." As he saw it, Watson's death from a cerebral hemorrhage on September 26, 1922, marked the end of a "recapitulation—an ironic epilogue," tacked on merely to "assure an ending on the true theme" of his life and career.[47]

Woodward had certainly pulled no punches in depicting the later Watson's vicious, vengeful behavior or its frightful consequences. Even so, in suggesting ways the manuscript might be revised for publication, Howard Beale confessed to a certain uneasiness that "your handling of Watson left me with a very friendly and sympathetic feeling" toward a man whose "chief lasting influence" might well have been "the conversion of thousands of present-day Georgians to bigotry and intolerance." Though Beale surely hoped that his comment might lead Woodward to put a darker tint on his depiction of Watson, it did precisely the opposite. Beale's uncertainty about what to make of Watson was precisely the effect Woodward wanted to achieve with his readers, and he set out to reinforce it as he followed up on his adviser's suggestion to provide more "personal" details that would "keep Tom Watson the man before your reader."[48]

A comparison of dissertation and completed book reveals that, wherever Woodward seemed to heed this advice, the material he added appeared to run directly counter to Beale's concern that he had made Watson seem too sympathetic a figure. When he inserted material about Watson's personal life at Hickory Hill in the decade after 1896, he presented a man who, though quick to lash out at anyone who violated his tyrannical and quirky sense of privacy and propriety, might also be found in the evening, fiddle in hand, patiently showing his granddaughters how to waltz. While the people for whom he cared the most were drawn to these displays of "tenderness," they dared not get too close to him, because they knew that his other, utterly repellent traits might surface at any instant. "The psychological tragedy of his life was just this misfortune," Woodward observed.[49]

Woodward also expanded his treatment of Watson's personality and temperament with a discussion of the "genuine devotion" revealed in his letters to his wife. When he wrote Georgia Durham Watson in 1908 to affirm this devotion, promising that he would spend more time with her and "we will be . . . perfectly happy," Tom revealed that he had been moved to make such a pledge by a painful recollection of his "ugly fit of temper" that had spoiled an occasion for her some twenty-eight years earlier. Watson lament's that "no man has ever been more cruelly punished by his passions" might strike some as deflecting blame with pleas of victimhood, but Woodward saw such letters revealing a "pathetic struggle to express a tenderness that his perverse nature was eternally thwarting." Finally, hinting further that Watson's seemingly most despicable behavior might have been linked to an emotional disorder beyond his control, Woodward added a passage showing that, in the middle of his hatemongering spree during the Frank affair, Watson had complained to a physician friend about "a baffling nervous trouble" that recurred almost monthly and "for several days I am so despondent & distressed, *about nothing,* that it is difficult to live." Unflinching as Woodward's portrayal of Watson at his worst may have been, in other respects it was not unlike Watson's portrayal of himself—as an ill-fated victim of forces beyond his capacity to control.[50]

When Watson died, a *New York Times* writer surmised that he had been plagued by "a certain mental instability" throughout his career. Woodward had given his readers ample reason to suspect as much, but he was content to leave it at that, venturing only that Watson's life and career were simply "a paradox . . . especially when the two parts of his career, divided by an interval of eight years that began in 1896 are considered."[51]

Journalists may get away with simply writing off what they cannot explain as a paradox and leave their readers to sort it out, but historians typically enjoy no such dispensation. Yet this particular paradox was the central compelling element of the intensely personal story that Woodward had set out to tell, and he chose to leave it unresolved. Like most of what he added to the text at the last minute, the book's preface did nothing to mitigate his adviser's concern about the book leaving him too charitably disposed toward Watson. Instead, Woodward seemed to hint at his own sympathy for him when he took serious issue with a writer for the *Nation* for charging him with fomenting "the sinister forces of intolerance, superstition, prejudice, religious jingoism, and mobbism." Watson "did not produce those forces," Woodward countered, "he was produced by them. They thwarted at every turn his courageous struggle in the face of them during his early Populists battles and . . . led him into the futility and degeneration of his later career."[52]

Privately, Woodward gave fuller vent to his personal feelings about Watson and his mental state during his final years in his withering reply to F. M. Reeves, an irate Georgian who charged that he had "heaped calumny and falsehood" upon the memory of a heroic defender of "the honor and fame" of Georgia and the South. Turning the tables on his detractor, Woodward insisted, "It was not I . . . who heaped 'calumny and falsehood' upon the Georgia hero. . . . It was the 'respectable' leaders of Georgia, the Gov.'s, Senators, bishops and bankers, who, as Watson himself said, 'outlawed and vilified and persecuted and misrepresented, howled down and mobbed and threatened until I was well-nigh mad.' . . . No, Mr. Reeves, I have sought to defend this Georgian from 'the calumny and falsehood' that his fellow Georgians heaped upon him, and whom Watson himself blamed for driving him 'well-nigh mad.' . . . Frankly, having read the record, I do not understand why he was not driven completely mad." More than anything, Woodward contended, it was, "the persecution of his own state" that prevented him from keeping "his balance" toward the end of his career. He wished that Watson had not been so "abused," Woodward added, "and . . . that he had kept his balance. The fact that he was abused and, as he said, driven 'well-nigh mad' is the tragedy that I have attempted to relate."[53]

For all the seemingly genuine sympathy he expressed after the fact, however, at the end of the book itself Woodward had simply inserted two sentences into the original dissertation text, quoting a popular ballad that hailed Watson as "a mighty man of power" who "fought and struggled," before adding his own postscript: "and in the end, failed." His decision to bring his book to such an inconclusive conclusion was in keeping with his response to *Journal of Southern History* editor Wendell Holmes Stephenson's comments on "Tom Watson and the Negro in Agrarian Politics," an article lifted directly from his dissertation. Though Stephenson advised the young author that it would be a "distinct improvement" if he could "clarify" his explanation of how Watson arrived at the "liberal views" he espoused in 1892 only to abandon them several years later, Woodward demurred, going no farther than to observe vaguely at the end of the article that "Watson's changing attitude toward the Negro was symptomatic of the changing racial views and policies of agrarian politics in the South."[54]

Woodward claimed years later that he had consciously "avoided explicit analysis of his [Watson's] change" because, at the time, it had seemed sufficient simply "to describe the incredible career," punctuating the narrative with occasional "interpretative suggestions." Rather than an "evasion of the biographer's duty" he preferred to see his strategy as "deferential sidestepping." Such restraint might seem befitting for an author who undertakes such a book still several months shy of his twenty-fifth birthday. Yet the young man who wrote so boldly and heretically about the genuine racial and class insurgency inspired by Watson and the Populists was, to say the least, hardly given to deference. Once again, his literary inclinations may have been the real culprit here. In their first meeting, Georgia Watson had told him that she envisioned writing "a novel of her family," and he readily agreed that "[it] would make as powerful stuff' as Wolfe's *Look Homeward, Angel*—"drunken, raw, and full of passion." After their eight-hour "chat," about her grandfather, he confessed to a sensation "such as I feel after being swept off my feet by a highly improbable novel." He had also promised that his rendition of Watson's story book would be "a better read than Huxley's new novel [presumably *Eyeless in Gaza*]." In his mind, realizing that ambition may have dictated greater emphasis on dramatizing Watson's personal "story" than expounding on its broader historical significance, much as a novelist might artfully arrange the elements of a compelling tale and then leave readers to do some of the piecing together before making of it what they will.[55]

Such a minimalist approach to interpretation also came through in Woodward's ideas about the book's illustrations. He had enlisted Glenn Rainey to scour the state of Georgia for portrait photos showing "striking contrasts" in Watson's appearance at various stages in his life. After rejecting two of the shots Rainey turned up "for the entirely unworthy reason that they did not corroborate my theories," he settled on seven that showed Watson from age twelve to sixty-five. He pushed his editors to place them in chronological sequence but uncaptioned, leaving readers to draw their own inferences from the "distinct change in Watson's face" as the bitterly intense personal and political conflicts and his tragic descent into the hatred and delusion of his later years progressively took their visible toll. His editors agreed to the sequencing but balked at withholding the captions, arguing that "the reader and the students like to have dates and descriptions which indicate definitely for reference and other purposes the exact nature of the picture in question." At least one astute reviewer grasped Woodward's intention, however, observing that "the several photographs of Watson that are reproduced tell . . . the same story that is told by the book."[56]

Woodward's preference for letting readers draw their own inferences from Watson's photographs presaged his later confession to Rainey that he had yielded "only when I had to" when Beale prodded him to provide "more help to the gentle reader—transitions, summaries, etc." When Woodward contended that "the reader should do some of the work, appreciates the flattery, and in the end, enjoys more what is not spoonfed," or revealed that he some-times felt "there is virtue in lack of clarity," he was once more espousing an approach more commonly associated with the novelist than the historian.[57]

Given his resistance to offering a central, straightforward thesis for his book, it is not surprising that reviewers read *Tom Watson* in a variety of ways. Journalist Gerald W. Johnson saw its "true importance . . . as a case history of a Southern liberal" and made no mention of Populism whatsoever. Mean-while, fellow southern historian Alex M. Arnett, who had also written a book on Georgia Populism, focused almost entirely on recounting Woodward's narration of what seemed to be Watson's strikingly dichotomous career. Only John D. Hicks, whose recent study, *The Populist Revolt*, had greatly influenced Woodward, seemed to appreciate some of the historiographical potential of this "understanding portrayal of a man, a movement, and a section," adding for good measure that "if the Pulitzer Prize judges for 1938 overlook this extraordinary biography, they will have committed a rather larger blunder than usual."[58]

First books by fledgling historians rarely receive as much favorable notice as Woodward's, which was reviewed in a number of high-profile print outlets. None garnered more attention, surely, than the one on the first page of the *New York Times Book Review* by Allan Nevins, who was arguably the most influential U.S. historian of his day. He could claim no admirer, however, in Woodward, who resented Nevins's generally disdainful treatment of south-ern Populists in his biography of Grover Cleveland, particularly his terse dismissal of Tom Watson as "a voluble hothead who made political demagogy and the editorship of a Populist weekly pay well." While his book was still in press, Woodward had explained to Rainey that "if there was any one con-temporary biographer that I had in mind as in a measure 'answering,' it was Nevins." Although he had taken issue with Nevins directly only in a footnote suggesting that he had been "mistaken in asserting that Watson's [*People's Party Paper*] was a source of riches," he professed surprise upon learning not only that Nevins had served as a reviewer for his manuscript but that his enthusiastic endorsement had apparently "sold the book to Macmillan." Though he was happy with this outcome, of course, he confessed to Rainey that he was feeling "a little dashed at being taken into [Nevins's] school and just a little resentful." In a rare concession on this front, he added, "Maybe I wasn't forceful enough." Perhaps not, for in what amounted to a stunning mischaracterization of the book's implications, Nevins declared in his review that its greatest contribution lay in revealing that "popular ignorance and

A Better Read Than Huxley's New Novel

the race question" had given the "Populist movement in the South . . . a bitterness, violence and crudity that never stamped the Northern movement."[59]

Seizing on Woodward's apparent decision to leave it to readers to determine the book's meaning, Nevins had leapt into the interpretive void to impose his own highly improbable thesis. In much the same fashion, noting that the author had made little effort to "explain the direction" of Watson's racial and religious "phobias," reviewer Frank L. Owsley decided to take a crack at it himself. Although he relied overwhelmingly on evidence presented within the book, his assessment of Watson's career departed dramatically from what his biographer had in mind. Principally, Owsley believed that, rather than a sharp break with his past, "Watson's [later] racial and religious bigotry were logically and psychologically identified with his populism." Watson's overriding objective had always been advancing the Populist agenda, rather than promoting biracialism. When the latter proved to be an impediment to achieving his primary aim, he readily abandoned it for what he saw as a better strategy. Owsley made a similar case for continuity in arguing that Watson's incendiary rants during the Leo Frank affair derived in no small part from his sense that Frank's backers represented the same "great money power" that he had assailed constantly throughout his career. Anticipating the conclusions of later historians, Owsley found sufficient evidence in Woodward's book to persuade him that "Watson was basically consistent and he died as he had lived an unregenerate populist and agrarian rebel."[60]

Some half century after the fact, Woodward explained in *Thinking Back* that he had chosen to write about Watson because "not only was it a fascinating story in itself, but it plunged the historian into all the dark, neglected, and forbidden corners of Southern life shunned by the New South school," and thus enabled a fledgling scholar to mount an "oblique" rather than "head-on" attack on "the ramparts of the establishment in Southern historiography" in the 1930s. In reality, as he admitted himself, he had settled on his subject and completed most of the writing with no such broader aim in mind, and the book itself offered little or no historiographical engagement with what was an admittedly limited body of relevant work. Still, even if somewhat inadvertently, he had presented a compelling case that it was time to rescue the marginalized Populists from the lunatic fringe and reconsider their cogent critique of the New South order. In later years, Woodward was quick to admit that *Tom Watson: Agrarian Rebel* was "certainly not the book I would've written later," but regardless of his intent at the time he undertook it, he had registered a remarkable achievement in what was, at most, a minimally revised dissertation. He was scarcely three years out of Emory and effectively untutored even in studying history, much less writing it, when he began the project, and he had completed much of it without direction or input. Yet he had produced a beautifully written, compelling, and informative narrative about one of the most fascinating but least understood figures in southern politics since the Civil War.[61]

Even if some of the critical meaning and importance of what he had done became fully apparent to him only in hindsight, he was no less correct in looking back on it as "a book *for* the 1930s and *of* the 1930s . . . a book for the Okies and the Arkies who were the rednecks and lintheads and the Samboes [of the 1890s] further down the road but no nearer salvation" and finally, "a book of, as well as for, the provincial at odds with the metropolis, . . . the colonies against the colonizer, [and] the exploited against the exploiters."[62]

Woodward's 1986 retrospective on his book reflected not only the meaning and significance *Tom Watson* had taken on over nearly half a century in print but the changes in his own perspective over the same span. His comments at seventy-seven hardly call to mind the brash twenty-nine-year-old who, a few days after Allan Nevins's mangled interpretation of his book appeared, declared that he was neither surprised nor concerned "that it is not understood. I did not expect it to be." While a certain obscurantism may sometimes be employed to good effect by poets and novelists, it is an indulgence not granted to the scholar committed to elucidating the past. Woodward was not yet such a scholar, however, or even indicating much interest in becoming one. This would change over the next few years, however, as the promise he had shown in his first book brought him enough notice and new opportunities that he was forced to admit, however grudgingly, that the profession he had so firmly and consistently resisted was the one for which he was ultimately best suited.[63]

5

A Chance to Have My
Say about the Period

The Origins of *Origins*

Although his day of reckoning with the reality of his future would not be long in coming, Woodward continued to see himself as a biographer rather than a full-blown narrative historian for some time after his Watson book appeared. For the balance of 1938, he devoted the time his teaching assignments at Florida left him to searching for a suitable new subject whose story he could tell. Despite warnings from Beale that it would take him "a long time to get oriented" in a new historical period, he flirted with books on both John Randolph of Roanoke and John C. Calhoun before returning, as Beale advised, to more familiar terrain on "this later field where you are already at home." Even there, however, Woodward struggled to find an appropriate subject. The family of the late senator Oscar Underwood of Alabama had offered Woodward access to his papers, but Beale wondered if Woodward would "do as good a job" writing on Underwood as he had done with Tom Watson when he was not so much "in sympathy" with his subject.[1]

Glenn Rainey also weighed in to urge his friend to take a break from demagogues and choose a genuinely upstanding figure like UNC president Frank Porter Graham or crusading liberal Texas congressman Maury Maverick. Doing so, Rainey explained would "put wind into the sails of the folk who deserve it" like Maverick, who had just been defeated by anti–New Deal forces in his race for a third term and stood in peril of becoming "a has-been." After all, the ever-insightful Rainey reminded his friend, "in the South, it takes more guts and imagination and largeness of spirit to stand for the elementary decencies than it does to make a revolution anywhere else." Woodward was intrigued by Maverick and even contemplated coauthoring a book with him, but with Beale urging him to settle on a subject or topic likely to solidify his reputation as a scholar, he eventually gravitated toward doing a biography of Socialist leader Eugene V. Debs.[2]

In the meantime, Woodward had scarcely begun his second semester at Florida when he declared to Rainey that "serious research and writing is virtually impossible while teaching." He had even toyed with the notion of seeking a Rosenwald grant for the following year until it dawned on him that asking "for a year's leave of absence after only one year" at Florida might just be frowned upon. A year later, however, he put aside such qualms and sought support from both the Rosenwald Fund and the Social Science Research Council to pursue his book on Debs. In the end, however, despite his considerable investment of time and effort, Woodward was forced to shelve plans for the Debs biography after learning that the family no longer held most of his papers, while other sources that once seemed promising proved to be of "paltry significance."[3]

He would have little time to brood, however, for in a matter of days he would be offered an opportunity that forced him to make a realistic assessment of his career options and accept, however reluctantly, that the best of them was becoming the academic historian that he had repeatedly vowed he would never be. Ironically, this new opportunity arose out of the same New South insistence on historical orthodoxy that had steeled Woodward's determination to avoid becoming a practicing historian at all costs. In 1913 the History Committee of the John Bell Hood Chapter of the United Confederate Veterans raised a howl of protest over the University of Texas's use of "[Harvard historian Edward] Channing's *Student's History* 'so called' *of the United States*," which they condemned for its "narrow, contracted, bigoted New England Stand Point." Writing to Major George W. Littlefield, a Confederate veteran and wealthy and influential banker, the History Committee of the Hood Chapter reminded him that "the insidious effort to prejudice the minds of the rising generation in our Southland against the action of their parents in the great war of the '60s has been going on for years." The UCV representatives thought it better to teach no history at all than to subject students to the "untruth and sophistry of a book like Channing's *History* or others of its ilk."[4]

A Chance to Have My Say about the Period

Clearly sympathetic to the UCV's concerns, Littlefield, a member of the University of Texas's Board of Regents, led a behind-the-scenes effort to force its history department to stop assigning two texts that Littlefield and his cohorts deemed too critical of the South. Turning a pressure campaign into an opportunity, the enterprising department head, Eugene C. Barker, managed to persuade Littlefield that the best way to address this problem was for the University of Texas, presumably with generous support from the major himself, to establish an archival collection to support research by southern scholars looking to write books more sympathetic to the white southerner's point of view. Littlefield donated an initial $25,000 to fund such an effort in 1914, and his will provided for another $100,000 contribution (which became available when he died in 1920) with the expectation that the archive would eventually support the publication of a "history of the United States with the plain facts concerning the South and her acts since the foundation of the Government, especially since 1860, fairly stated." The primary objective of this new history was assuring that "the children of the South may be truthfully taught and persons matured since 1860 may be given opportunity to inform themselves correctly."[5]

Over the next fifteen years or so, the University of Texas built up a more than respectable archival collection in southern history, but it was not until the end of 1937 that a group headed by Civil War historian Charles W. Ramsdell began to move forward with plans for writing the history of the South that Littlefield had anticipated. The initial plan called for a four-volume series spanning the years from 1783 through 1900, apparently with the possibility of an additional volume on the colonial period, with Ramsdell serving as the general editor. As Ramsdell began approaching potential contributors to the series, he was contacted by fellow historian Wendell Holmes Stephenson of Louisiana State University, who invited him to write one of the ten volumes in a very similar series he and his colleagues had been planning for at least a year. Ramsdell and Stephenson quickly agreed that offering "competing" series in southern history made no sense and decided to merge the two projects into a single, ten-volume series to be published by Louisiana State University Press, with Ramsdell and Stephenson sharing the general editorship duties.[6]

An impulse to push back against the New South's orthodox historical creed could be detected here and there at this point, yet there was still no shortage of self-styled watchdogs eager to pounce on anything that smacked of an unsympathetic treatment of the region's past. One of these was Mrs. William A. Coleman, "Historian of the Virginia Division, United Daughters of the Confederacy." The "chief objective" of her division, Coleman explained to Stephenson, was "fair and impartial history," and they had already made great strides "in eliminating objectional [*sic*] text books from our schools and having others revised." Ever vigilant on this front, Coleman cautioned that, "before getting too excited about this proposed history," she had decided to run the information about the project and contributors by her ally and confidant, Dr. Matthew Page Andrews, who was essentially her counterpart for the Sons of Confederate Veterans in Maryland. Thinking it nothing less than her duty, she had forwarded Andrews's estimate of their undertaking to Stephenson and Ramsdell. Although Andrews professed satisfaction with most of the contributors the editors had selected, he questioned their choice of Wesley Frank Craven of New York University to write the proposed volume on "The Southern Colonies in the Seventeenth Century." Andrews objected because Craven's earlier book, *The Dissolution of the Virginia Company*, with its emphasis on the failure of this venture, was "an amazing historical distortion" and quite at odds with the far more positive, even prideful treatment Andrews had offered in his own book, *Virginia, the Old Dominion*. Craven's misguided view of the early history of Virginia, which was absolutely vital after all, to understanding the origins of the entire nation, left Andrews deeply concerned that his volume in the series might well "misrepresent the beginnings of the Republic."[7]

Stephenson politely thanked Coleman for her letter and her interest in the project, but neither he nor Ramsdell appeared to take heed of her "note of warning" about Andrews's objections to Craven. This is not to say, however, that they had not been extremely cautious in their own right when deciding whom to invite as contributors. Both had been mentored by traditionalists of the first order, Ramsdell by William A. Dunning at Columbia and Stephenson by U. B. Phillips at Michigan. Neither was as conservative in outlook as his respective mentor, but as the two sought out prospective authors for the series, they showed a clear preference for older scholars less inclined to controversial revisionist interpretations. Shortly before he was invited to write volume 4, dealing with the period 1789 through 1819, Thomas P. Abernethy demanded to know of kindred spirit Frank Owsley, "Why has the South so long taken the interference and sneers of the Yankee lying down?" It puzzled and frustrated Abernethy that "northerners have . . . rarely been able to see . . . the superior merits of southern society," and he could conclude only that "they simply don't want to understand it."[8]

E. Merton Coulter of the University of Georgia had devoted his inaugural presidential address for the Southern Historical Association to rallying white southerners to preserve the manuscript materials needed to defend

A Chance to Have My Say about the Period

their heritage. A diehard Dunningite even after the blatant racism inherent in the Dunning perspective had begun to elicit winces from many of his peers, Coulter was chosen to write the volume on Reconstruction. (When Ramsdell died in an automobile accident in 1942, Coulter not only succeeded him as coeditor but agreed to write what was to have been Ramsdell's volume on the Confederacy.) The editors tapped Duke University historian Charles S. Sydnor to write volume 5, encompassing the years from 1819 to 1849, and Avery O. Craven of the University of Chicago agreed to do the next install-ment, which would follow the South through to the Civil War. Both were less defensive of southern whites than Abernethy or Coulter, but it is fair to say that few names on the original list of contributors would have troubled adherents to the traditional orthodoxy that Woodward meant to challenge. Rather than a springboard for any sort of youth movement in southern his-tory, Ramsdell and Stephenson seemed to see their series as anything but. Stephenson had prefaced his suggestion of Wesley F. Craven for the volume on the southern colonies in the seventeenth century with "if we must resort to a younger scholar." He went on to describe Craven and Philip Davidson of Vanderbilt, who was in the running to write the succeeding volume on the eighteenth century, as "two youngsters," as he urged Ramsdell to let him know if he could come up with "some mature scholar who seems better qualified."[9]

Ramsdell and Stephenson ultimately settled on both Craven and David-son as the best options available for their respective assignments, though until he learned about Craven's North Carolina background, Ramsdell was a bit concerned about him, explaining that while he did not feel "southern origin is a *sine qua non*" for writing one of the volumes, he thought "it should be worth something in the way of familiarity with the southern scene." A similar concern arose when Harvard's Paul H. Buck, whose *Road to Reunion* had recently won the Pulitzer Prize, came up as one of the possibilities for the final, post-Reconstruction volume in the series. Despite his sympathetic take on the New South, Buck had never lived, taught, or been taught in the region and therefore lacked the firsthand acquaintance with the South that the coeditors considered "absolutely essential."[10]

Instead of Buck, the initial nod for this volume went to Benjamin B. Kendrick of the Women's College of North Carolina, but with the contract on his desk and awaiting his signature in January 1939, Kendrick abruptly withdrew from the project, citing both the scarcity of the relevant second-ary sources he would need to write a purely synthetic account of the period between 1880 and 1910 and teaching obligations and other commitments that precluded the archival research he would need to fill in the gaps. As he apologized vigorously for withdrawing from the series, however, he did offer "the gratuitous suggestion" that Ramsdell and Stephenson should "consider Professor Vann Woodward of the University of Florida" as his successor. Ramsdell's first response was to try to get Kendrick to reconsider by offering him more time to complete the project. When that effort failed, the editors first considered Francis Butler Simkins. However, Simkins's boldly revisionist writings on Reconstruction included a recent paper urging fellow southern historians to rethink their assumptions about "the innate inferiority of the blacks" and to reject the fatalistic notion that southern blacks must continue to play their "present inferior role." While he conceded Simkins's familiarity with the field, Stephenson feared that his penchant for "sensationalism" might preclude "a judicious handling of certain important questions, especially the race issue."[11]

Ramsdell and Stephenson had reason, then, to take Kendrick's suggestion of Woodward more seriously than they might have otherwise, although it was clear that both editors were still mindful of the language of a draft of the "Editors' Preface" describing the series as "a logical culmination of the pioneering efforts of historians whose labors began in the closing years of the nineteenth century." (By and large, of course, these were the same historians whose work struck Woodward as dedicated to rationalizing the current order in the South.) So it was that as Ramsdell and Stephenson went about selecting authors for the various volumes, both persisted in their preference for the "more mature scholar" over "youngsters" like Woodward, who had just turned thirty.[12]

Ramsdell professed to have "a very good opinion of Woodward," although he had not yet read his Watson biography and thought he recalled Stephenson saying that he felt John Hicks's review of it had been a little on the generous side. He also wondered whether "so young a man can have the maturity of judgment and acquaintance with the broad field" necessary to produce a volume suitable for the series. For his part, the "only serious fault" that Stephenson could find with Woodward's book on Watson was that he "was not as careful as a scholar should be" in accurately documenting the material he quoted. The time he had spent verifying sources while editing Woodward's 1937 article in the *Journal of Southern History* "demonstrated the need for greater care in future studies," but Stephenson nonetheless foresaw him producing "a very readable volume" requiring only "a modicum of editorial supervision."[13]

The two decided to press Kendrick to elaborate on his recommendation of Woodward and to assess his viability compared to a much older scholar,

A Chance to Have My Say about the Period

Holland Thompson of the City College of New York, whose *The New South: A Chronicle of Social and Industrial Revolution* had appeared in 1919. Kendrick alluded primarily to Thompson's recent health problems and described him as "on the way out," while Woodward was "on the way in." Kendrick did allow that Woodward "likes his liquor quite a little better than he should, and I am somewhat afraid that he may let it get him down," although he added that so far as he knew, Woodward "indulges over much only when he is on some sort of excursion." If, however, Woodward managed to reach his full promise, Kendrick felt "quite safe in predicting that in five or ten years from now, he will be recognized as being superior to anything Thompson has ever been." UNC history department chairman Albert R. Newsome seconded this appraisal, pointing out that Woodward "had youth, ambition, promise, a brilliant style, an analytical and comprehending mind and an eagerness to seize upon some definite work project." Given the choice between Woodward and Thompson, Newsome preferred "the young man who still has his spurs to win." Similar praise was also forthcoming from Woodward's loyal mentor and friend Rupert Vance, who would soon be on board as the author of volume 10, the final contribution to the series, then slated to cover the period 1913–40.[14]

Still, the two editors hesitated. Hoping to find an author who could be "genuinely objective" without becoming "too much of an advocate," Ramsdell remained leery of the "evidently brilliant" but indisputably young Woodward. Owing perhaps to his minimally interpretive approach in the Watson biography, neither Ramsdell nor Stephenson nor anyone else who participated in the discussion seemed to pick up on a revisionist impulse in the book. On the other hand, Thompson, who had published an admiring history of the New South some twenty years earlier, struck Coulter as clearly the "best man" for the assignment, because "he certainly has the background and mellowed knowledge about the period which is not given to many." When Stephenson sought his appraisal of the "youngster," a wary Coulter responded that Woodward "could do it, but he is still quite young and has some distance to go yet."[15]

Judging from Thompson's earlier work, had his declining health not factored heavily in the final decision, Volume IX of the History of the South series might now be offering its fourth generation of readers some decidedly un-Woodwardian pronouncements about the unparalleled "economy and fidelity" of the Redeemer governments, which were all but free of "scandal" and "dishonesty." In the end, though, Ramsdell decided that he was less "worried" about Kendrick's reference to Woodward's drinking than about the age and health of Thompson, who would, in fact, be dead inside two years. Even so, after almost two months of agonizing, he admitted that there was "still a small measure of doubt in my mind" when he finally contacted Woodward about replacing Kendrick in early March 1939.[16]

There was not the slightest doubt, however, in the mind of Comer Vann Woodward, who had been doing a bit of soul-searching in the wake of his setback on the Debs biography project. He eagerly accepted Ramsdell's invitation, thanking him profusely for the "unusual honor" bestowed on him. Woodward was then in his second year at Florida, where he taught only interdisciplinary freshman-sophomore courses on the Western heritage. Like it or not, he recognized that securing a lighter teaching load and the chance to teach upper-level courses in southern and United States history (at Florida or elsewhere) meant demonstrating his expertise in a traditional academic field that he had entered only as a means of becoming a biographer. Despite all the media notice it commanded, his Watson biography had sold only 559 copies in its first year in print, and the most encouraging words H. S. Latham at Macmillan could offer were his hopes that "it will continue to sell in a small way." Forced to acknowledge that "it is from my teaching and not my writing that I am going to have to make my living," he knew that his next step must be strengthening his credentials as an academic historian. This, he explained to Glenn Rainey, was why the History of the South volume was "more important professionally than anything I could write just now." Perhaps mindful of the interpretive loose ends he had left dangling in the Watson book, he leapt at the chance to have "my say on the period . . . to lay down the main lines of interpretation and to do something fairly definitive."[17]

He had already seized the opportunity to clarify some of the ambiguities of his treatment of Watson and the Populists when he was selected to deliver the University of Florida's inaugural Phi Beta Kappa Address in December 1938. As the 1930s drew to close, Woodward meant to leave no confusion about the legitimate heirs to the Watsonian-Populist tradition. The decade had begun with the publication of *I'll Take My Stand*, a collection of essays by twelve so-called Nashville Agrarians affiliated in most cases with Vanderbilt University. In the main, the collection combined searing critiques of modern industrialism, long touted by others as a panacea for all the South's ills, with largely uncritical celebrations of life on the land as the vital bedrock of southern cultural identity. Not surprisingly, the latter efforts rang hollow at a time when southern agriculture was all but suffocating under the weight of the Great Depression.

Woodward's respectful, almost deferential tone in his correspondence with Agrarian Donald Davidson suggested a certain spiritual empathy with

A Chance to Have My Say about the Period

the group, and he conceded years later that their "ideologies and strategies" had shaped his take on Watson. He was not about to admit that publicly in 1938, though. The distinct empathy for Watson Frank Owsley revealed in his review of Woodward's biography had given him serious pause. In stressing Tom Watson's lifelong fixation on the despoiled agrarian paradise of his early childhood, had he somehow implied that this "agrarian rebel" of the 1890s was the spiritual ancestor of the cloistered academic dissidents who took their "stand" in the 1930s? Watson clearly believed that agricultural pursuits were morally and spiritually superior to industrial or commercial ones, but he was too keenly attuned to the severe hardships facing most southern farmers at the end of the nineteenth century to indulge romantic fantasies of farm life. In Woodward's view, like Watson, the entire Populist movement exhibited a "tough-minded realism, a fact-encrusted hardness that was modern." Accordingly, he was now attempting to distance Watson and his fellow Populists from Nashville and situate them closer to Chapel Hill, where Howard Odum, Rupert Vance, and their Regionalist cohort were rejecting both the Agrarians' "never-never land of the past" and the boosterist New South school's "never-never land of the future." Instead, by candidly acknowledging southern problems and mounting a serious, scientific effort to gather the information needed to address them, the Regionalists sought to lead the South "down the hard, narrow path of realism."[18]

As he set out down this path himself, Woodward quickly encountered a somewhat unlikely fellow traveler in former Nashville-Agrarian-turned-regional-critic Herman Clarence Nixon. In a 1938 review, he praised the "Hillbilly Realism" of Nixon's new book, *Forty Acres and Steel Mules*, in which he spurned both the "pessimistic romanticism" of the Agrarians and the "optimistic romanticism of the New South school." Nixon blamed the New South's reckless, single-minded courtship of northern industrial carpetbaggers for binding the region ever more tightly to a colonial economy. In this, Nixon sharpened the critique of the Redeemer–New South regimes that Woodward had offered, more often implicitly than explicitly, in *Tom Watson* and foreshadowed the more direct attack that he would unleash in the book he had just undertaken.[19]

Woodward's progression from biographer to narrative historian was not entirely linear. Despite his genuine enthusiasm for the new book project, he found his old predilections hard to shake. He was soon yearning "for a return to the beautiful simplicity of the biographer's job." Convinced that biography was "much better suited as a vehicle of expression *for me* than the straight history that I am now struggling on," some two years after receiving his contract for *Origins of the New South*, he signed another one with Little, Brown for a (never delivered) volume of biographical essays focused on "Henry Grady and the Makers of the New South."[20]

In the main, however, he had little time for such distractions. The contract for volume 9 of the *History of the South* called for a completed manuscript in three years, and the scarcity of published research on the New South era in 1939 meant that Woodward's book would require "more pick-and-shovel work" than volumes devoted to earlier periods. He realized immediately that the University of Florida's anemic library holdings could not support even the secondary reading, much less the substantial archival research, that he felt would be needed for the book he—though not necessarily his editors—envisioned. With this in mind, he took what was supposed to be a one-year leave from Florida and accepted a temporary part-time teaching appointment at the University of Virginia. The move brought not only access to a vastly superior library but the opportunity to teach just one course and earn almost the same amount he was paid "for three times the work" at Florida.[21]

Perhaps still harboring some misgivings about his choice, Ramsdell pressed Woodward for an outline of his plans for the book by August 1, 1939. The outline arrived a little later than requested, and understandably perhaps, both sketchier in detail and less comprehensive in scope than Ramsdell hoped. Tersely descriptive rather than interpretive or thematic, it largely amounted to a sparse listing of the details and personalities to be covered in each chapter. For example, presenting his proposed chapter "The Industrial Revolution," he offered:

> D. Textiles and the Piedmont
> E. Coal and Iron
> 1. The rise of Birmingham
> 2. The rise of Chattanooga
> F. Tobacco.
> 1. The rise of Durham and Winston.

Meanwhile his chapter, "The Redeemers and the Redeemed," promised:

> C. The configuration of the Redemption regimes.
> 1. Railroads.
> 2. Convict leases.
> 3. Bonds and treasury scandals.
> 4. Compared with antebellum and Reconstruction governments.[22]

Although he found no "soul mates" on the faculty, his time in Charlottesville proved fruitful nonetheless. The library's expansive holdings left him so awash in reading material that he confessed to Rainey to feeling at times that he had been tricked into trying to "[bail] out the ocean with a sieve." True to character once again, however, despite the demands of his work at Virginia, Woodward found time to take a stand against social injustice. In April 1940, just thirty-one years old and not quite three years out of graduate school, he testified before the U.S. House of Representatives Committee on the Judiciary in support of abolishing the poll tax, which, he charged, was instituted largely at the behest of "commercial and industrial interests in the South" in order to "emasculate" the political potential of "the agrarian masses who have not a sufficient voice in their own state governments, much less in their representatives in Congress."[23]

Though he was supposed to return to Gainesville in the fall of 1940, Woodward had grown dissatisfied with a position where his only possibility for teaching southern history came in the summer and he was otherwise restricted to general education social science courses. A few weeks short of the end of his second semester at Florida, he had complained to Beale that his despair "of the future of this place, not to speak of its present low condition, grows the longer I stay here. Academic standards are shockingly low." Beale had passed along Henry Steele Commager's observation that Woodward was "too good a man to be down in Florida," and he agreed that it might be a good time to move on "to a better place." After calling on all his connections to make sure that the Tom Watson book got strong notice in the New York papers and elsewhere, Beale launched an all-out blitz to find a more suitable situation for his protégé, touting him for jobs at a variety of schools, from Vassar to Virginia to the history department headship at Georgia State College for Women at Milledgeville. Accepting the final position would mean dealing with the quite "formidable" former department head, but Beale felt entirely confident that Woodward could "exercise good sense and tact sufficient to get along with this very difficult woman." Apparently, Woodward was not so sure, for he reported to Rainey that the prospect of a higher salary notwithstanding, he had turned down this job because he "couldn't fit myself into that picture even at twice my present pay."[24]

As he literally sang Woodward's praises from coast to coast, Beale had mentioned him in November 1938 to Ernest Jaqua, president of Scripps College, a small, recently established women's school in Claremont, California, some thirty-five miles from Los Angeles. Well aware of Woodward's substantial expectations, Beale warned him not to "be snooty about it. Scripps is one of the Pomona group close to LA." The well-regarded Huntington Library was also nearby, and Beale added, "Claremont is, I am told, a heaven on earth." Woodward would later describe Scripps rather disparagingly as "a sort of Hollywood Garden of Eden," but his reaction to it mattered little at the time, for he would not hear from Jaqua until April 1940, when he was nearing the end of his stay at Virginia.[25]

When he contacted Woodward, Jaqua asked whether he preferred a one-year temporary position or a permanent appointment. Flung squarely on the horns of a dilemma, Woodward earnestly sought Beale's advice. "I would rather have had the decision to make at almost any other time than just now," he complained. He had applied for funding from the Guggenheim Foundation but as of yet had heard nothing from them, and there would be no news on a similar application with the Rosenwald Fund until May. If either came through with sufficient funding to allow him to devote a full year solely to research, Woodward allowed that he would "be tempted to turn almost anything down for this chance. I am completely absorbed in the New South book, much steamed up over it, and want to finish it more than I want to do anything else. Furthermore, I'm going to do it whatever else I do." From Beale he wanted to know what a move to Scripps would mean, in terms of both time and materials for research on this book. Looking forward, he also wondered about the consequences for "my contacts, career, and future, which so far have been completely wrapped up in the South. . . . I don't believe I know a single individual in California." Would the Huntington collection have enough material relevant to his interests "to compensate for the thousands of miles between me and the Library of Congress?" Despite such misgivings, Woodward acknowledged that the job at Scripps offered not only a more appealing locale but a more substantial boost in his career fortunes "than I can hope for in the South for years to come, or in the East either."[26]

Woodward's remarkable propensity for hitting pay dirt with funding agencies would soon complicate matters further, for the Rosenwald Fund responded to his request for $1,875 with an actual award of $2,400. His first inclination was to reject the Scripps position on the spot, but he eventually negotiated an agreement with President Jaqua that would allow him a semester off during the upcoming academic year in order to take advantage of the Rosenwald grant. At that point, he accepted Jaqua's offer of a three-year appointment as associate professor of history at a salary of $3,500 with $500 in traveling expenses, along with a reduced teaching load to give him extra time for writing. This arrangement would afford him a total of nearly eight months to work at the Library of Congress and conduct research at manuscript repositories in the South and elsewhere between June 1940 and September 1941.[27]

In addition to Beale, Woodward had continued to seek the counsel and support of Rupert Vance and Howard Odum, whom he had listed as a reference for several fellowship applications. When Woodward sought Odum's opinion on whether to take the Scripps offer, Odum warned him that the school was simply not big enough to hold "major scholars," and his professional profile might suffer if he was there very long. Therefore, he advised, "if you get sufficient fellowships, take them and complete your writings. The South needs you, and there will be no doubt about a good place waiting you when you have completed these works." When Woodward wrote to explain the arrangement he had worked out with Jaqua, he assured Odum that "one thing I would like for you and perhaps a few others to know is . . . that I shall want to come back to [the South] before so very long."[28]

Woodward's fears that the Scripps position would distance him both from the sources he needed for his book and the scholarly cohort where he had already made a name for himself were soon borne out. He found his students at Scripps far superior to those at Florida and seemed to enjoy teaching undergraduates there a great deal more than anywhere he taught throughout his career. Yet after scarcely two months on campus, he was already "fighting a haunting feeling that I have disastrously lengthened my supply lines in pushing this campaign to the West Coast." Not only was he disappointed with the holdings of the Huntington Library, but he complained of finding "few congenial spirits" on the faculty, which, as a group, struck him as fairly mediocre. Woodward's instinctive reserve in the company of new acquaintances did not serve him well in the tight social milieu that was all but imposed on the Scripps faculty, leading him to admit to Beale that he had never "fully appreciated the anonymity and impersonality that offers one shelter in a large university." The conscious integration of the social and academic environments at Scripps meant that "social life among the faculty is less escapable," and to his even greater distress, "there is a deliberate encouragement of student-faculty social relations."[29]

Having already warned Woodward about his vaguely condescending attitude toward Scripps, Beale was clearly put out to find his protégé proving every bit as quick to find fault there as he had been at Florida, nor was he happy to find himself delivering a lecture on mature behavior that might otherwise be reserved for a college undergraduate to a thirty-two-year-old man three years out of graduate school. . He was not surprised at his reaction to Scripps, he told Woodward, but "I should merely like to feel that in such physically pleasant surroundings with good students to teach you could be somewhat happier than you sound." Beale had taught at both Bowdoin and Grinnell and knew something about the expectations of "being pleasant socially and giving a lot of time to people you do not particular care about" that Woodward had encountered at Scripps. He seemed to be pleading more than lecturing when he counseled Woodward that "you must for your own sake, if not theirs, be pleasant and agreeable to such people and make them like you. That's part of what is known as success in teaching in any small college, and I hope you do not let them guess, as I fear you may, the feeling about them that you express in your letters to me."[30]

Woodward's frustration with the social expectations at Scripps would soon give way to larger concerns. Although he had found much to like about the brisk and direct Ernest Jaqua in his early dealings with him, the first and only president of Scripps, who had held that office even before its official opening in 1926, had been embroiled in controversy long before Woodward arrived. In May 1938 a student group had sent a letter to trustees, administrators, and influential alumnae, detailing their concerns about what they saw as the instability of both the faculty and the academic programs at Scripps, as well as undue administrative interference in student affairs. Faculty relations with the president had improved but little by February 1941, and though he was still in his first year at Scripps, Woodward let Beale know he wanted to move on. His name would be bandied about in connection with positions at the University of Wisconsin, the University of Delaware, Connecticut College, and Brooklyn College, where Beale had offered to recommend him because "in spite of the Red Hunt, there is great security of tenure in the New York colleges for anyone not actually a communist." With the situation at Scripps steadily deteriorating, Woodward's tone grew more urgent as he stressed to Beale that "it is pretty important that I get away from here soon—preferably to the East," and when he learned that Jaqua might be trying to recruit Joe Russell, an old Chapel Hill colleague, to Scripps, he insisted that Beale tell Russell to contact him before making any commitment to Jaqua.[31]

Although Woodward confessed that he was "really having a lot of fun" in his classes, where he had stopped lecturing and "thrown out the textbooks," the enthusiasm and capability of his students did not brighten his outlook on either the future of Scripps or the course of world affairs. By 1940, the growing likelihood of American intervention in the war in Europe sorely upset Woodward, Beale, and Rainey, all of whom openly and earnestly opposed it. In doing so they found themselves in the company of one Charles A. Beard, who had suggested in the mid-1930s that American leaders might seize on going to war as the best means of pulling the United States out of the Great Depression. In good Beardian fashion, Woodward also saw the New Deal's failure to spark thoroughgoing recovery leaving the U.S. economy dependent on Britain's wartime spending to stay afloat. With hopes for America's economic future pinned to "the hopeless dream of saving not only Britain but a vanished world economy of free trade." He predicted that "we will be driven to fight for that lost world and I believe, like you, that the fight is lost before it is done." Woodward had supported Franklin Roosevelt in 1940 solely because of his domestic initiatives but now found himself "sickened" by the president's increasingly militant rhetoric. Though he feared all was already lost, he continued to deliver anti-interventionist speeches and worked to get Beale's own attack on the "Fallacies of the Interventionist View" in print and widely circulated.[32]

On the day before events at Pearl Harbor would render this question effectively moot, Woodward reported in detail on a speech at Scripps by the distinguished European historian Bernadotte Schmitt, in which, to Woodward's horror, Schmitt called not only for a merciless military onslaught that would "make the Germans feel what war is" but an indefinite period of deliberately punitive occupation, along with forced reparations and complete removal of the nation's railroad network "rail by rail and tie by tie." Schmitt readily acknowledged that these measures "would cause great suffering" and, in the end, substantially reduce the population, but after all, at 80 million strong, there were now "too many Germans" in comparison to 45 million British and 40 million French. Aghast at the prolonged applause for Schmitt, Woodward reported that he had risen "to ask where was I? In Berlin? What was the Godly community of Claremont thinking about? Was this our slogan—to out-Hitler Hitler?"[33]

If he was shaken by the enthusiastic local response to Schmitt's remarks, Woodward was stunned to see how abruptly and dramatically the climate of suspicion and fear had intensified within hours after the Pearl Harbor attack on December 7, 1941. On the very next day, he was in a faculty committee meeting in President Jaqua's office "when the door suddenly opened and four men, one a policeman, entered with the remark 'We'll have to break up this little party.' They took my colleague [Arnold] Bergstraesser, sitting next to me, without permitting him to see or speak to his family, or without telling his wife where he was being taken or for how long." More than two weeks later Bergstraesser was "still locked up, along with another German from Scripps. . . . It was a week before we learned where he was, and two weeks before he was permitted to write anyone. His house was ransacked the night he was taken and any of his private papers and those of his wife seized—a thing that never happened to them in all their scraps with the Gestapo, so his wife tells me."[34]

Bergstraesser had been a stridently nationalistic German conservative during the Weimar era, and his run-ins with the Gestapo may have had less to do with his perceived political beliefs than with a family tree boasting a Jewish grandmother, which might also account for his expulsion from Nazi Germany on "racial" grounds. The FBI had been observing him for nearly two years before his detention, not only because of the positions he had taken before deportation, but because he remained every bit the staunch German nationalist even after immigrating to the United States, so much so that some fellow refugees shared authorities' suspicions that he was a Nazi sympathizer. After his colleague was seized by the FBI, however, Woodward swore under oath that Bergstraesser had given no evidence of being a Nazi collaborator but, on the contrary, had "repeatedly expressed to me in conversation his abhorrence of the principles, practices, and leaders of the present German government."[35]

It was roughly four months before Bergstraesser was released and able to resume his duties at Scripps, where his return and that of fellow German detainee Fritz Caspari created an even greater uproar than their detention by the FBI in 1941. From the moment they reached campus, Woodward reported, the two were subjected to "constant suspicion, investigation and petty persecution." Upon learning that Bergstraesser and Caspari were back on campus, the local American Legion chapter sent a letter to all parents of Scripps students, declaring that retaining the "enemy aliens" on the faculty was "dangerously unwise."[36]

In keeping with his already stout record of defending civil liberties, Woodward showed no hesitation in jumping squarely into the middle of this uproar, in which faculty-community divisions had broken along roughly the same lines as the dispute over Jaqua's leadership at Scripps. Meanwhile, he reported to Rainey, students had taken to "rending the air with petitions and serving as intermediaries between professors who did not speak to each other. Parents protesting and counter protesting mass meetings, demonstrations, breast beatings, resignations, faculty meetings at the top of one's voice, spying, counter-spying. You would never believe how much hell can be packed into such a small place."[37]

In Woodward's view, the effort to save his German colleagues and fend off the American Legion had ramped up the tensions generated by the battle with Jaqua and brought the crisis to a head. By the time Jaqua resigned in early June 1942, faculty had practically taken control of university administration,

A Chance to Have My Say about the Period

and Woodward regretted that the affair had led to such a "sharp break" between him and the president. According to Woodward, at one point, Jaqua accused him of falling in with a "small clique of people who were working against the best interests of the college." Jaqua claimed that he felt compelled to convey his disappointment with Woodward to him directly "for my own good since he would probably have considerable to do with my present situation and perhaps my future as well." This veiled threat was enough to give Woodward pause. "He will be quite dangerous to me in the future. That is perfectly clear," he told Beale. As it turned out, though, he would have little to fear from Jaqua, who held a couple of obscure bureaucratic positions during World War II and could manage no better thereafter than an even more obscure two-year stint as president of a tiny college in Oregon.[38]

In the short run, however, the whole affair had taken a personal toll on Woodward. He confessed to Rainey in October 1942 that the conflict and upheaval of the previous academic year had left him at "low ebb for me—an all-time low, I believe, though I have gone through such fits of depression before. Never so protracted nor so low as that one, however. . . . A few obvious factors—the war, the treatment of my German friend, the policy toward the Japs, and worst of all—our own teapot tempest, the revolution that overthrew the college president. The combination just about finished me off." Yet after an entire summer spent "dreading facing a class, hating teaching, and everything about it," suddenly with the start of the fall semester, "the whole stupid fog lifted overnight, magically and for no reason I have been able to discern. Teaching from the start became the true delight it can be on rare occasion—and kept on being." Despite taking on additional classroom responsibilities, he had managed thus far to write as much since he began teaching in the fall term as he had back in the summer when he had nothing to do but write, and to his mind, it was "better writing, at that." Woodward was also clearly pleased to reveal that he and Glenn were "in a family way," though he tried to conceal it with his professed qualms that "in all probability the creature will be expected to live here in this house, with me!"[39]

Woodward's newfound optimism also came through when he reported in October 1942 to Wendell Stephenson that he had completed two of approximately fifteen anticipated chapters. If things continued as they were until May and he had the anticipated benefit of an extended summer break afforded by a compressed wartime instructional schedule, he might be able to complete the first draft of the book by the end of the following summer. If so, allowing time for revisions, fact-checking, and compiling a bibliography, Stephenson should have his completed manuscript by Christmas 1943.[40]

Woodward knew that these were likely little more than "fond hopes," however, as the first anniversary of Pearl Harbor approached and the prospect of military service loomed ever larger and more likely. He had already sought Rainey's appraisal of his options, admitting, "like everyone in III-A," that he had wondered whether he should pursue a commission in the army or navy or continue to wait. For the time being, he had chosen to wait. He knew of no one with legitimate dependents who had been drafted in California, though some friends in Florida or North Carolina had not been so fortunate. In any case, he reckoned that "if 4.5 million more are inducted this year as planned," his and Rainey's age cohort were bound to be hit hard within the next six months or so. Woodward remained indecisive, although he sought Beale's assistance in securing a noncombatant post as a writer or an instructor, such as several of his academic acquaintances had managed. Though Beale had filed for conscientious objector status himself, he tried unsuccessfully to get Woodward a wartime teaching position at West Point because "it would let Glenn be with you and it would be better than being drafted." He also suggested in February 1943 that if Woodward were drafted, he might at least be able to take leave from UNC and "take your place and hold it for you" for the duration of the war.[41]

With his father's military future still much in doubt, the arrival of Peter Vincent Woodward on February 17, 1943, provided another, more welcome distraction. Six weeks later, with his typical resort to humor as a mask for his real feelings, Woodward was feigning distress that his "only begotten son, . . . in whom I am not at all hours of the night well pleased," had proven thus far to be "a serious, humorless, and uncompromising savage as ever interrupted the meditations of civilized man and made him yearn for the comparative privacy of the sailor's fo'c'sle. In spite of daily and nightly lung exertions that would have debilitated the veriest demagogue, this Peter Vincent continues to increase in wisdom and stature and in disfavor with God and man at the rate of an ounce and a quarter a day until he now weighs nine pounds five ounces and tears any passion to tatters at no provocation whatsoever. In all these afflictions I beg no sympathy—only understanding."[42]

By that point, Woodward had finally submitted his application for a commission in the navy, and while awaiting the response, he was "stalling off the local [draft] boards with deferments requested by the local college presidents," as he taught American history to 200 army meteorological trainees. "Unfortunately," he confessed to Rainey in early April, "the local draft board, my eloquent demonstrations to the contrary notwithstanding, has of late not always been able to appreciate the true worth of American history in this matter of meteors. So obtuse have these gentlemen proved, in fact, that they propose to classify me as I-A next week." This unwelcome development left him doubting that he could "devise to continue my instruction of the board and the meteorologists until my commission comes through." As it turned out, his good fortune held. His commission arrived some three weeks later, and he warned Rainey that "you will doubtless hear of me next as Lieutenant. j.g. Woodward, (Ph.D., A-V(s), Squadron Leader of Falstaff's Falcons, vigilantly patrolling the coast line of Bolivia."[43]

In fact, Woodward was destined for considerably less adventurous duty, though not immediately. Uncle Sam's navy moved far less expeditiously than he had anticipated, and thanks to his folder being lost for a time, he had been able to "knock off three more chapters," he told Rainey in July 1943. Although he knew that his friend had sought a deferment, Woodward warned him that the "38+ [age] class is to be invaded momentarily." Instructors in "ballistics and botany" might be spared the draft, he surmised, but it "looks bad for the comma engineers." Since they were "still handing out Navy commissions with both hands to anyone who can take nourishment and has a B.A.," he advised Rainey to apply for one, "otherwise, they will plump you in an Army Officer Training Camp and sweat living hell out of you." Finally, after spending the summer, "lost," as he put it, "in inactive service," he was summoned for training as a combat naval air intelligence officer at Quonset Point, Rhode Island. At some point, though, he explained later, "I was discovered to have written a book and ordered to report to the office of Naval Intelligence in Washington."[44]

Apart from struggling to find suitable housing for his family and living for a time with the uncertainty over whether he would be stationed permanently in D.C., Woodward found few grounds for complaint. "The job," he wrote Rainey in early May 1944, "has turned out to be pretty interesting. . . . My commanding officer is a reasonable and quite intelligent and well-informed man. My associate officers are for the most part a congenial lot, some of them excellent company. As a point of vantage for keeping up with current military goings on it could scarcely be improved upon." His duties in the Naval Intelligence Office fell well within his comfort zone as a historian, for his division was responsible for providing "brief classified accounts of battles" as quickly as possible. While in service, Woodward had written three such accounts, two of which were stamped "Confidential" and made available only to certain qualified naval personnel. The third, Woodward's expanded treatment of the

Battle of Leyte Gulf, off the coast of the Philippines in October 1944, would be published in 1947 by Macmillan.[45]

Although his official assignments kept him occupied during duty hours, he eventually decided to have his research notes and other materials for his book on the New South shipped to him in Washington. By the time a forwarded letter from E. Merton Coulter reached him a few days before Christmas in 1944, he could report that he had managed to "put in a few licks . . . during my evenings and Sundays" drafting an additional chapter, bringing him up to nine of the planned fifteen.[46]

Woodward went on to inform Wendell Stephenson in late January 1945 that, depending on how long it took him to complete his final assignment for the navy, he might even be able to get him a manuscript by September 1, but by the end of the year he was forced to admit that he had made "no progress . . . since my last report." Realistically, there was little reason to expect any until Woodward returned to civilian life, but not long after he did, he was advising Stephenson that his timeline for completing the manuscript had been too ambitious. Near the end of November 1946 he explained that his "optimism of last spring . . . was unwarranted. . . . It turns out that notes taken four and five years ago, some of them six and seven years ago, are not nearly as usable as I had imagined." As a consequence, in addition to the expected "revision and rewriting," there would be several wholly unforeseen visits to archives, primarily to examine new sources only recently made available to researchers. Moreover, what he uncovered on these forays might require even further revision or reorganization of the manuscript.[47]

This would become an all too familiar refrain for Stephenson. Hoping to speed up his progress, he advised Woodward in June 1947 that the publishers and editors were "most anxious" to wrap up the entire series by the end of 1950. Though Woodward promised to "make every effort to hurry my manuscript along," he followed up with a steadily lengthening list of "unforeseen things that have slowed me up." He had recently accepted a position at Johns Hopkins after securing a Guggenheim Fellowship that allowed him take the first year off before assuming his teaching duties. He had found Hopkins attractive not only because of its proximity to the Library of Congress but because of its "rather special" policy of granting reduced teaching loads to new faculty actively engaged in research projects. Even so, there was no chance that he would be delivering the manuscript by March 1948, as he had most recently promised.[48]

As it turned out, the entirety of 1948 and half of 1949 would pass before Stephenson received that manuscript, and even then, it was not a complete

A Chance to Have My Say about the Period

draft. Woodward was still working on chapter 2, "The Forked Road to Re-union," which concentrated on the maneuvering for sectional advantage that led to the "Compromise of 1877" and thus the de facto end of Reconstruction. If he offered no real apology for the tardy and still incomplete manuscript, neither did he seek mercy from his editor, asking instead that Stephenson pull no punches in critiquing either the style or the substance of what he had written. He was "not a sensitive writer," Woodward assured him, and he urged Stephenson not to shrink from challenging him on any questionable point. Having "crawled out on several limbs in this book, challenged accepted beliefs, etc.," he was all the more determined to eliminate errors and shore up its defenses against "the criticism it is likely to get."[49]

Woodward's words had the crackle of "let us then be up and doing" about them, suggesting an author eager to clear the final hurdles and get his much-awaited book in print. If, however, the long-suffering Stephenson thought that the maddeningly elusive end of this project might at last be in sight, he would soon learn otherwise. Scarcely two weeks had elapsed before Wood-ward was back in contact, seeking his reaction to a "problem" that had arisen in the course of trying to complete the "Forked Road to Reunion" chapter. Since dispatching the rest of the manuscript to Stephenson, his efforts to rewrite this chapter had led him to the inescapable conclusion that the ex-traordinary length and detail required "to tell the story I have unearthed" in a single chapter would mean "distorting the book out of all proportions." Rather than risk doing that, he thought it preferable to "publish the complete story elsewhere first" before summarizing it in the New South volume. He was putting forth "an entirely new story" of the Compromise of 1877 and its implications, and his findings stood to require significant revisions to what southern historians and others had written about this episode and to the way it had been presented in U.S. history textbooks. He wanted Stephenson to know that he had no thought of devoting so much attention to the Compro-mise until he had the good fortune to stumble on some critical documents that led him to follow a trail of clues. Over the span of nearly a decade, that trail wound through a variety of archival collections, major and obscure, requiring him to search out "smaller bits and pieces of the jigsaw puzzle," the last of which he had uncovered that very summer while teaching at the University of Chicago.[50]

At the same time, he assured Stephenson that he did not want to delay the publication of his New South volume further. After some back and forth, Ste-phenson agreed to Woodward publishing his treatment of the Compromise of 1877 first, so long as the New South book "at least include[d] the cream of your researches" on the affair. The bottom line for Stephenson, though, was that "we should make every effort to publish your 'Beginnings of the New South' in 1950."[51]

In reply, Woodward agreed in August 1949 that "it would not do" to post-pone publication of his volume in the series until the spring of 1951 (though, as it worked out, the book would not appear until several months later.) There was a bit more jockeying about with Stephenson, but for the most part, the advantage at this juncture lay with Woodward. Although more than a de-cade had passed since he signed the contract to write volume 9 of the History of the South series, he sensed that Stephenson and Coulter were not likely to turn their backs on a much-anticipated book that was, at long last, virtually completed. Although he professed otherwise, Woodward had clearly been pondering this move longer than he let on. He had already consulted W. T. Couch, now at the University of Chicago Press, who had persuaded him that he could easily find a publisher for such a concise and intriguing book. Heartened by Couch's comments, Woodward assured Stephenson that he did not "believe much delay should be necessary."[52]

Stephenson could surely be forgiven for putting little stock in yet another such assurance. Yet the manuscript, or at least the book it represented, would prove well worth the wait, for it would become easily the most widely read and influential volume in the History of the South series. It would also serve as a powerful interpretive beacon for well over a generation of historians who followed Woodward's lead in exploring the racial, political, and economic forces that came together on the heels of Reconstruction to shape the foun-dation of a new southern order.

6

Juleps for the Few and Pellagra for the Crew

Reckoning with the Redeemer–New South Legacy

In persuading his editors to allow him to publish a monograph spun off his research for a volume in their series before that volume itself appeared, Woodward had insisted that this could be done expeditiously enough to minimize the added delay in completing a book already nearly twelve years in the making. He had no time to waste if he meant to avoid disappointing those editors yet again. After sending Stephenson the full manuscript, including chapter 2, in April 1950, he turned quickly to Stanley Salmen at Little, Brown to let him know he had finally finished the book "that has held me up so long" and was well along with another project. This book would be more national in scope, though its regional implications were also substantial.[1]

In barest outline, his proposed book would revisit the critical factors in resolving the volatile partisan standoff over the disputed outcome of the 1876 presidential election. With the initial tally awarding Samuel J. Tilden 184 of the 185 electoral votes required, while his Republican opponent Rutherford B. Hayes had amassed only 165, the Democrats seemed virtually assured of returning to the White House for the first time in twenty years. There had been no decision, however, about assigning the 20 remaining electoral votes, 19 of which belonged to South Carolina, Louisiana, and Florida, the only southern states then still under Republican governments. To add to the uncertainty, each of these states had submitted two sets of returns, one awarding its electoral votes to Tilden, the other to Hayes. With tempers flaring on both sides, Congress moved to defuse the dispute by creating a fifteen-member Electoral Commission, drawn in equal numbers from the Republican Senate, the Democratic House of Representatives, and the Supreme Court, with Justice David Davis, a political independent, expected to serve on the body in order to ensure a partisan balance. Yet Davis's sudden resignation from the Court in order to assume a seat in the U.S. Senate ultimately led to an eight-to-seven Republican advantage on the commission, a partisan breakdown reflected precisely in a series of eight-to-seven tallies in favor of awarding all the disputed electoral votes, and thereby the presidency, to Hayes. Outraged congressional Democrats reacted with a fury sufficient to raise genuine concerns that, either by political or, if necessary, by physical means, they meant to prevent Hayes's inauguration, leaving the country effectively without a president, as of March 5, 1877.

According to the prevailing account, this impending crisis was narrowly averted only by some intense backroom political horse-trading culminating in a meeting at Washington's Wormley Hotel, where southern Democrats agreed to desert their own party's filibuster against certifying Hayes's election, supposedly in exchange for Hayes's pledge that, as president, he would immediately remove the remaining federal troops from the region. This, in turn, would assure the collapse of the Republican governments still clinging to authority in South Carolina, Louisiana, and Florida and pave the way for restoring the racial and political home rule that white southerners had so earnestly sought since the beginning of Radical Reconstruction a decade earlier.

Not the least of Woodward's corrections to this narrative was that the withdrawal of the troops had been virtually guaranteed several days before the meeting in question, when House Democrats managed to block the appropriations necessary to keep those troops in place. In Woodward's considerably more complicated and expansive version of events, the real bargain that put Hayes in the White House had not grown out of a partisan struggle over the presidency or even the final removal of troops from the South. The actual precipitant had been a competition between two powerful railroad magnates, Tom Scott of the Pennsylvania Railroad and Collis P. Huntington of the Southern Pacific, to secure federal subsidies for completing a southern transcontinental line from New Orleans to California. Scott also owned the

Texas and Pacific Railroad, which he hoped would be subsidized to construct the portion of the line within the South, and a number of prominent southern leaders, including John B. Gordon in Georgia and L. Q. C. Lamar in Mississippi, showed great interest in his venture. A proposal from the Hayes camp that would provide subsidies for Scott, as well as Huntington, brought the men together long enough to lobby southern Democrats and others elsewhere to accept Hayes rather than Tilden as the duly elected president. The Republicans further sweetened the pot for the southern contingent with promises of additional appropriations for levee construction and repair and other internal improvements, as well as the appointment of a southern Democrat to Hayes's cabinet as a means of restoring the flow of federal patronage into a region where scarcely a trickle had been seen since 1865.[2]

From Woodward's perspective, the agreement that defused a potentially violent clash over presidential succession in 1877 took on even greater significance when understood as the product of an active alliance between a new wave of ardently probusiness southern leaders, many of them former Whigs, and such titans of industry and finance as Scott, Huntington, Jay Gould, and others. This was what he meant when he promised his prospective editor "a refreshingly new picture of Reconstruction, the overthrow of the carpetbaggers, and the nature of the New South and its leadership. It also gives the first full story of one of the great sectional compromises of our history."[3]

Woodward's brief sales pitch clearly hit its mark at Little, Brown, for by July 4, 1950, he was expressing pleasure with the advance and royalties offered him, and promising editor Angus Cameron a final manuscript within a month. The project must be fast-tracked, he stressed, because the Little, Brown book must be published in advance of the New South volume, where it would be summarized. As he hoped, Little, Brown did manage to get his *Reunion and Reaction: The Compromise of 1877 and the End of Reconstruction* out in April 1951, well ahead of *Origins of the New South, 1877–1913*, which would not appear until November.[4]

Of the two, *Origins of the New South* would not only make a much bigger splash initially but demonstrate a great deal more staying power. *Reunion and Reaction* was nonetheless a revealing book, owing not simply to the provocative new interpretation it offered but also to what it revealed about the mindset of its author at that point in his career. Woodward had followed Charles Beard's historical model in framing his sympathetic treatment of Tom Watson's continuous struggle to prevent agrarian interests from being crushed by the relentless advance of a northern industrial and commercial juggernaut. Beard's influence would be more obvious still in both *Reunion and Reaction* and *Origins of the New South.* In the former, Woodward seized on Charles and Mary Beard's treatment of the Civil War and Reconstruction as the "Second American Revolution," which, like the first one in their view, had been more the product of conflicting economic objectives than actual differences over political structures or governing systems. Likewise, where Beard saw the U.S. Constitution effectively embodying an antidemocratic backlash against the liberal, egalitarian principles set forth in the Declaration of Independence, Woodward cast the Compromise of 1877 in much the same mold.[5]

Howard Beale fairly idolized Beard, and Woodward took great pride in a letter from Beard praising his Watson biography and singling out its author as "a flash of light in the fog of academic mediocrity," as well as the positive notice the Beards later accorded his book in *America in Midpassage.* As a younger scholar, however, he had resisted Beale's prodding to pay a visit to the man who both inspired and lauded his work. Beard had died in 1948, and Woodward's effusive tribute to him in the acknowledgments to *Reunion and Reaction* likely reflected his regret at failing to properly pay his respects while Beard was still alive. In any case, Woodward's praise came at a time when kind words about Beard were exceedingly rare. Not only had his perceived economic determinism fallen out of fashion by the 1950s, but he had already damaged his public and professional standing seemingly beyond repair through his strenuous, high-profile opposition to American involvement in World War II, including his accusation that President Franklin Roosevelt had orchestrated the events leading to the attack on Pearl Harbor. For this, Beard had been openly jeered at meetings of both the American Historical Association and the American Political Science Association, and a number of his former disciples hastened to distance themselves from him. Without calling names or citing examples, Woodward took pains at the outset of *Reunion and Reaction* "to express the hope that American historians will never permit honest differences of opinion over foreign policy to withhold from the late dean of the craft the honor that is justly due him."[6]

Just as Beard's work had inspired Woodward to challenge, implicitly at least, the New South historical consensus that prevailed in the 1930s, both his praise for Beard in the book's preface and the thoroughly Beardian interpretation of the Compromise of 1877 that followed amounted to an aggressive challenge to another line of historical thought that had gained sway by the 1950s. Members of the so-called Consensus School of American history held that the defining reality of the nation's past was not class or regional conflict but an overarching sense of common purpose and allegiance to its core institutions. Woodward acknowledged years later that his personal feelings for the late, but still "much-denigrated," historian may have spurred him to wax a bit too assertively Beardian in *Reunion and Reaction* purely as a means of answering Beard's critics in the Consensus School.[7]

Woodward's take on the Compromise of 1877 had been edgy and provocative from the outset. The "Thermidorian reaction" referred originally to the overthrow of radical rule in the aftermath of the French Revolution. Woodward simply adopted it to analogize the Compromise of 1877 with the Constitutional Convention of 1787, which historians Samuel Eliot Morison and Henry Steele Commager had already cast "as the Thermidor of the first American Revolution." Woodward posited to Glenn Rainey that the political machinations that effectively brought down the curtain on Reconstruction were also typical of conservative reactions to other examples of revolutionary extremism such as "Cromwell, Stalin, etc." Conceding that further research was needed to truly sustain this comparison and admitting he had always been something of "a drunken metaphorist," he nonetheless thought he had come up with "one of those suggestive analogies that one could afford to send up as a flare in the darkness, but should not attempt to employ as a searchlight."[8]

As he had with Woodward's work on Tom Watson, Rainey seemed to anticipate some of the criticism the book might encounter in trying to persuade his friend to show more restraint on several fronts. Where Woodward saw the Compromise of 1877 defining the fundamental modus operandi of the American political system for the next twenty years, for Rainey the agreement simply came down to the Republicans cutting a "hard-boiled" and thoroughly opportunistic deal. Long aware that their continued support for black rights had become a political liability, they had leaped at the chance not only to withdraw from "a battle already lost" but to extend their four-term grip on the presidency in the bargain.[9]

Woodward was in no mood to be constrained, however, as he demonstrated in the book by presenting the Compromise of 1877 as "the most enduring" of the four great sectional compromises of the nineteenth century (in addition to those of 1820, 1833, and 1880). Beyond assuring the final overthrow of Reconstruction, he believed the compromise had been much more influential than the constitutional amendments of the era in shaping "the future of four million freedmen and their progeny for generations to come." If the agreement registered the triumph of political and economic pragmatism over the idealism once espoused by northern Republicans, Woodward also saw it as the harbinger of a regime change, reflecting the rising influence among southern Democrats of a newly ascendant political class drawn from the ranks of the old business-friendly antebellum Whigs.[10]

If Woodward made little effort to conceal his distaste for this southern contingent, he also reserved no small amount of loathing for the Radical Republicans, whom he condemned for reducing the Constitution to tatters as they made voters of more than 700,000 former slaves while whittling the white electorate down to about 627,000, displacing six governors, purging three legislatures of conservatives, suppressing or ignoring the civil courts, and denying freedom of speech. Like Howard Beale, he believed that all these abuses and many more were committed at the behest of dominant northern economic interests who feared that allowing the Democrats to regain control in the South could lead to a coalition with "discontented elements" in other agricultural areas. This interregional coalition of have-nots (such as the Populists would attempt to forge a generation later) might then dismantle "the elaborate structure of capitalist legislation," including the tariffs, currency restrictions, banking acts, and government subsidies that provided the institutional foundations of eastern economic might.[11]

While this view of the Radical Republicans was fully consistent with the Beardian perspective, it was also in keeping with what would become a consistent pattern in Woodward's reaction to self-righteous northern critics of the South, be they historical or contemporary. Though he was anything but a southern apologist, he nonetheless felt an enduring affinity for his native region that led him to bristle, almost instinctively, at what he saw as unfair and hypocritical criticism emanating from north of the Mason-Dixon Line. There was more than a whiff of this sentiment in his angry reaction to Allan Nevins's disparaging treatment of southern Populism, but it was also apparent in his exchange with Little, Brown editor Angus Cameron about his frequent and clearly pejorative use of the term "carpetbagger" in *Reunion and Reaction*. Woodward grudgingly conceded that some of the northerners who involved themselves in southern politics or business after the war might have been motivated primarily by altruism. Even so, he maintained, "I have yet to find one who was not used—consciously or unconsciously—to further the pragmatic and economic gains of the revolution. However zealous they proved in defending Negro rights and equality in the South (and they rarely had any political plums to spare the Negroes), the men they sent to Washington voted right down the line with [James G.] Blaine & [Roscoe] Conkling ... and the rest of the new [northern] economic order."[12]

In the end, however, the most striking aspect of Woodward's perspective on the Compromise of 1877 was not how "southern" it was but how Beardian. Historian Michael Les Benedict would later characterize *Reunion and Reaction* as "one of the last, most important, and most sophisticated works of the

Progressive school." Writing at the midpoint of the twentieth century, Woodward may have also seen reflections of the historic intersectional alliance that had finished off Reconstruction in the contemporary affiliation of southern Democrats and right-wing northern Republicans bent on neutralizing the advantages secured by blacks and organized labor during the New Deal. He had recently observed this latter convergence of interests at work in the 1948 election, as the insurgent Dixiecrat Party's efforts to roll back advances, not only by black Americans in the South, but by organized labor throughout the country, won them notable support among representatives of northern manufacturing.[13]

Although Woodward expressed doubt that *Reunion and Reaction* would get much attention, it was both widely reviewed and, for the most part, favorably, especially in the popular press, where even scholarly commenters were inclined to accept Woodward's new version of events in 1877 with little apparent hesitation. In the *New York Times*, historian Dumas Malone praised the book as "illuminating and exciting" and its author as "a southern historian who is as fearless and frank as he is competent." Although he was hardly a Woodward soul mate, even E. Merton Coulter lauded him in the *Saturday Review* for showing "a detective skill" in producing "a superb bit of historical craftsmanship."[14]

While the response in academic journals was generally positive as well, here and there, a reviewer raised questions that would resurface full-blown only after a generation had passed. Wallace E. Davies found Woodward's account of the more "sensational" economic aspects of the bargain fairly "dubious," given that he offered "no explicit evidence that a real economic bargain was ever made or fulfilled." Also foreshadowing future criticism of the book, Dan M. Robison of Vanderbilt noted the scarcity of evidence supporting Woodward's bold claim that southern Democrats in Congress consistently broke ranks with their northern counterparts in their determination to see the terms of the compromise fulfilled. Had he paid proper attention to roll call votes, Robison charged, Woodward would have found a number of instances when differences in the voting patterns of northern and southern Democrats were negligible at best.[15]

Later analyses of several relevant roll call votes would bear out this claim, and closer attention to the only one Woodward discussed would have raised even greater concern. Having once again advanced an argument much too weighty for the body of evidence he had gathered to support it, Woodward had misrepresented some of the scant evidence he had collected in much the same disingenuous fashion that he had employed in his Watson book. To document his claim of a probusiness alliance between southern Democrats and northern Republicans, he had relied on a single House roll call vote, taken in December 1875, on a resolution designed to prevent Congress from granting further subsidies to corporations (such as Tom Scott's railroad), which passed by a final tally of 223 to 33. In order to support Woodward's argument, the breakdown of the vote needed to show southern Democrats aligned with pro-business northern Republicans against the resolution, and he presented the measure as passing "over Southern opposition," noting that "of the 33 votes against the resolution, all but 7 were cast by Southerners." Yet he failed to disclose that more than a quarter of the southerners opposing the ban on subsidies were Republicans rather than Democrats, nor did he mention that only 19 of the 54 southern Democrats who participated in the vote had in fact opposed it, while 35, or 65 percent, had backed it.[16]

Later critics would take note of additional roll call votes that cast doubt on Woodward's argument, but as with his other research monographs, it would be some time before *Reunion and Reaction* met with a detailed, in-depth challenge. In the interim, textbook authors eagerly incorporated his explanation of how the Compromise of 1877 came about into their accounts of the period, as what began as a decidedly revisionist appraisal quickly emerged as the established treatment of the affair. Irwin Unger's *These United States* dutifully described key southern leaders, "many of them former Whigs," striking a bargain with northern Republicans to accept Hayes as president "in return for a promise to remove the troops, give some political rewards to Southerners and support a Texas and Pacific land grant." For good measure, Unger's book even offered an artist's rendition of one of the "secret sessions" in which the attendant "wheeling and dealing" was accomplished. Woodward's take on the compromise would, of course, also take center stage in the account of the abandonment of Reconstruction he offered in *The National Experience*, one of the most popular and influential U.S. history textbooks published in the latter half of the twentieth century.[17]

Reunion and Reaction had been in print for roughly a generation by the time other historians began to take serious issue with both the substance and the framing of Woodward's account of the Compromise of 1877. Allan Peskin even questioned whether there had been any such formal agreement, given that so many of the major commitments it was said to entail (such as the promised subsidies to the Texas and Pacific Railroad) were never fulfilled. "A deal whose major terms are never carried out," reasoned Peskin, "appears suspiciously like no deal at all." In his view, Hayes became president in 1877 instead of Tilden simply because of the formidable advantages enjoyed by the Republicans, who controlled the White House, the Senate—where the presidential votes were to be tallied—and the Supreme Court. Keith Ian Polakoff soon echoed some aspects of Peskin's argument while pointing to more recent research indicating that Woodward had greatly overestimated the capacity of Democratic and Republican leaders to control the actions of others within their respective ranks. This led Polakoff to suspect the two parties of simply "blundering" their way into a solution to the electoral crisis.[18]

There would be further challenging commentary from other historians, whose arguments, in combination with those of Peskin and Polakoff, ultimately left Woodward squarely on the defensive on these and other parts of his argument. He had long since become a towering presence in the profession by this point, but though these critics adopted a low-key, even deferential posture toward him, they nonetheless exposed his exaggerations on several fronts, including the involvement of business-friendly former Whigs in facilitating the compromise itself. Woodward had been so adamant in this latter contention that he even proposed initially to title the book "A Whiggish Affinity," relenting only after Howard Beale insisted that "it still means absolutely nothing to me after reading the manuscript," and feedback from friends and colleagues ranged from "very precious and therefore faintly ridiculous" to "pretentious and deliberately clever and obscure." Woodward had paid less heed, however, to his former Florida colleague Manning Dauer, who had warned him after reading the manuscript that he claimed far too much for the involvement of old Whigs, and a little more digging on his part would have revealed practically all of the major southern players in the affair as reliably staunch Democrats. In a footnote, Polakoff respectfully suggested that Woodward was "apparently unaware that he was . . . confusing a political party (the Whigs) with an economic doctrine ('Whiggery') and both of these with the political factionalism characteristic of the Democrats and Republicans alike in the nineteenth century."[19]

Woodward had made it clear in *Reunion and Reaction* that he saw the Compromise of 1877 marking the historic instant when—and the means whereby—what remained of the humanitarian ideals of the Civil War and Reconstruction were effectively sacrificed to the racism of southern whites and the rapacity of an ascendant capitalist order. In reaching this assessment, however, he had posited a more cohesive and systematically functional relationship between—and among—southern Democrats and northern Republicans than had ever existed in fact.[20]

Woodward could and should have paid more attention to congressional voting records at the very beginning of his research, but by the time he seized on the idea of *Reunion and Reaction* as a separate monograph, the urgency of getting it in print before the LSU volume left no time for further digging. Meanwhile, the critics who trained their sights on his book roughly a quarter of a century after it was published enjoyed access to a lot more documents and correspondence, as well as relevant secondary sources, than had been available to him.

In any case, Woodward apparently foresaw none of the later objections to the arguments he offered in *Reunion and Reaction* when he squeezed them into a single chapter in *Origins of the New South*. He wanted to show at the outset that the implications of the Compromise of 1877 went well beyond the removal of the remaining contingents of federal troops that presaged the collapse of the three surviving Republican state governments in the South. His most passionate concern in *Origins* was demonstrating that, contrary to both popular and academic wisdom, the conservative politicians who redeemed their respective states from Republican rule were not the selfless and heroic scions of the old antebellum planter aristocracy. Rather, he insisted, the region's fate lay primarily in the hands of unscrupulous, self-serving men "of middle-class, industrial, capitalistic outlook, with *little but* a *nominal* connection with the old planter regime." In fact, stripping the Redeemers of their cachet as the esteemed descendants of the still-hallowed antebellum defenders of the agrarian tradition was central to Woodward's revisionist agenda in *Origins*. Perhaps aware that he had struck the New South historical orthodoxy little more than a glancing blow in *Tom Watson*, he clearly meant to leave no room for ambiguity this time around by offering up what he later described as "a sort of historiographical black mass in the eyes of true believers."[21]

After questioning the Redeemers' bloodlines, Woodward set his sights on their morals, showing that their state governments were neither more honest nor more fiscally responsible than their oft-maligned predecessors in the Reconstruction era. Shamelessly complicit in the ruthless exploitation of the South's laboring classes and its natural resources, in their relentless pursuit of northern capital, the Redeemers had willingly, even eagerly, shackled the region with a colonial economy. Meanwhile, the rural masses of both races found themselves caught up in the seemingly endless and hopeless cycle of tenancy, dependency, and debt that was the sharecropping and crop-lien system.

Nearly three-quarters of a century later, with latter-day southern politicians vowing to save their white constituents from a return to the racial horrors of the First Reconstruction and proclaiming themselves worthy heirs to the Redeemer legacy, Woodward understood the contemporary relevance of discrediting that legacy and the men behind it. This was reason enough to dispute the Redeemers' reputed ties to an antebellum planter aristocracy, but his relentless assault on their character and values also reflected his own personal disgust at seeing such men lumped in with others he found more deserving of such lofty status. Woodward had already shown in *Tom Watson* that he shared Watson's admiration of the wisdom and integrity of men like Charles Colcock Jones, Robert Toombs, and Alexander Stephens, critics of New South materialism who represented Georgia's old planter order. In *Origins*, he allowed Jones and his Virginia counterpart Robert L. Dabney to give full vent to anti–New South feelings that were strikingly similar to his own.

These men were associated with the Lost Cause, but in rejecting the mercenary New South ethos, Woodward saw them espousing doctrines that were "closer to Thomas Jefferson than Jefferson Davis." He quoted liberally from a discourse in which Dabney, Stonewall Jackson's biographer and former chief of staff, exhorted southerners to spurn the shallow materialism of those who would make Gods of "factories, and mines, and banks, and stock boards, and horse-powers of steam, and patent machines."[22]

It would seem that any enemy of New South capitalism was effectively a friend of Woodward's by default, but his appreciation of these men was rooted in what he believed they had stood for—and against—before as well as after the Civil War. In fact, curiously enough, his critique of the South's leadership after Reconstruction may offer the best window we have into his feelings about their Old South predecessors and what he saw as their distinctly precapitalist mind-set. More than one observer has picked up on what Woodward's former Florida colleague Bill Carleton called his sense that there was "a genuine aristocracy in the South" whose traits he found admirable in many respects. Carleton recalled that, later in his career when Woodward was working in the Mary Boykin Chesnut Papers, he shared his pleasure at encountering what he called the "real aristocrats" who moved in Chesnut's antebellum circle. (Carleton also suggested that this sentiment accounted for Woodward's obvious distaste for W. J. Cash and Louis Hartz, both of whom lampooned notions of aristocracy and enlightenment among southern whites in the antebellum era.) Southern literary specialist Louis D. Rubin Jr. echoed Carleton's appraisal, noting that although "Woodward has written comparatively little about the Old South as such . . . what he has [written] puts him more or less in the school of Ulrich B. Phillips or, in our own time, Eugene Genovese." That is, he, too, believed that the Old South had given rise to "a distinctive landed gentry with a set of values and attitudes qualitatively different from the finance-capital-dominated plutocracy of the Northeast."[23]

Woodward might have flinched just a bit at the association with Phillips, whose sympathy and regard for the planters clearly did not extend to their bondsmen. Still, with its impersonal, almost clinical focus on conflicting economic interests as the catalyst for the Civil War, the Beardian model favored by Woodward did not directly engage the moral dilemma posed by slavery. At the same time, this perspective was also conducive to a certain empathy with hopelessly outmatched antebellum southern planters foredoomed to fail in their struggle against the industrial and financial behemoths of the North. Woodward went well beyond empathetic, however, in a later essay describing the Old South as "a great slave society. . . . [that] had grown up and miraculously flourished in the heart of a thoroughly bourgeois and partly puritanical republic." Nor did he shrink from casting its leaders as men of "skill, ingenuity and strength, who, unlike those of other slave societies, invested their honor and their lives, and not merely part of their capital, in that society." When the crisis came, they, unlike the others, chose to go down fighting in what amounted to "the death struggle of a society that went down in ruins."[24]

Woodward's esteem for members of the Old South's ruling elite was neither universal nor unqualified, but he made it inescapably clear nonetheless that he found the Redeemers to be wholly unworthy as claimants to their legacy. In *Tom Watson*, he had made no secret of his disdain for the Bourbon Triumvirate of Governor Joseph E. Brown, General A. H. Colquitt, and General John B. Gordon, who dominated the Georgia political scene for nearly a generation after Reconstruction. Yet he felt that the term "Bourbon"— implying adherence to the aims and values of a bygone order—was not really an apt descriptor for such men, who portrayed themselves as faithful defenders of a vanquished Old South but gave little evidence of embracing what he saw as its true ideals. Instead, they spoke fervently of a "New Departure" in which they would lead the region away from its agrarian traditions toward a more prosperous industrial and commercial future. Rather than credit them for their realism in embracing economic change, Woodward largely saw them as traitors to the old order, which, by implication, was both less capitalistic and more admirable. Gordon's aims, he wrote, "were not those of the planter aristocrat his manner proclaimed, but rather the acquisitive zeal of the rising capitalists and industrialists whom he served." One of these, railroad magnate Collis P. Huntington, a key player in Woodward's version of the Compromise of 1877, had recognized Gordon as "pretty clearly . . . one of our men." Thanks to the influence of men like Gordon, Woodward noted in *Reunion and Reaction*, state governments that were once the "bailiwick of planter statesmen" became the instruments of the industrial and financial classes.[25]

Woodward seemed even more openly contemptuous of the rise of capitalism in the post-Reconstruction South in *Origins* than he had in *Tom Watson*, noting Mark Twain's reference to the fast-talking up-and-comers of the New South whose God was "the dollar" and "how to get it their religion." As Woodward saw it, for the thoroughly bourgeois New Man of the South, the niceties of manners and personal or family pride that marked the dealings of the old planter-statesmen were now but a hindrance to his "pursuit of the main chance."[26]

Woodward was also repulsed by the eagerness of the same men who heartily proclaimed, for local consumption, their undying fealty to the failed crusade against Yankee domination to sell out the region's laboring masses in order to win the favor of ruthless northern industrialists. He found it strikingly ironic, he told Carleton, that the men who engineered this capitulation to northern colonizers managed to conceal their true ambitions by adopting the rhetoric, symbols, rituals, and other signifiers of continuing devotion to the antebellum ideals of "regional patriotism and independence." Recounting the efforts of New South entrepreneurs to enshroud their projects in the trappings of the old Confederacy, he noted how eagerly subsidiaries of northern corporations pounced on an "some impoverished brigadier general to lend his name to a letterhead." Carleton believed that his friend despised the Redeemer–New South leaders primarily for "betraying the Lost Cause," but Woodward's anger stemmed less from any Lost Cause affinities of his own than from seeing its emotional appeal appropriated and exploited as a means of achieving that betrayal.[27]

Woodward himself had nothing good to say about sappy literary indulgences in Old South–Lost Cause nostalgia, and neither, for that matter, did most of his peers among southern intellectuals who came of age in the years after World War I. Still, he clearly felt that something worthy had been lost, not simply in the South's defeat, but in the changes in leadership and dominant values that came in its wake. He was not alone in this view. William Faulkner, Thomas Wolfe, and other key contributors to the Southern Literary Renaissance also seemed to envision postbellum southern history as a sort of grand declension narrative. A morally elevated and intellectually refined planter aristocracy had given way to a postbellum parvenu order driven by materialism and greed and short on both breeding and respect for ideas or principles or anything else from which financial gain could not be wrung. Woodward and his peers had been affirmed in this perception by the Baltimore critic, satirist, and New South–baiter extraordinaire Henry Louis Mencken. While he was thoroughly despised by the southern boosters whose ballyhoo about progress he delighted in puncturing, as we have seen, Mencken enjoyed near-iconic status among intellectually rebellious young southerners like Woodward and his friends at Emory in the 1920s.[28]

Mencken had lampooned the cultural and intellectual barrenness of the boastful, pretentious New South but good in the "Sahara of the Bozart," yet as he did so, he was also lamenting its shortcomings in relation to the Old South, which, to his mind, had been "a civilization of manifold excellences— perhaps the best that the Western Hemisphere had ever seen." It had thrived under the leadership of extraordinary men, urbane, lettered, and thoroughly aristocratic in both manner and lineage. Tragically, these superior men of the Old South had been swept away by what Mencken called the "Calamity of Appomattox," which, to him, marked the transfer of power and influence from the "gentleman" to the shallow, thoroughly mercenary "Babbits" and other such hustlers bent on enslaving the South to the "Chamber of Commerce metaphysic." Though Woodward's racial sensibilities would not have allowed him to describe the outcome of the Civil War as a "calamity," Mencken could hardly have anticipated his take on the Redeemer legacy more accurately. Later, Woodward would draw on Faulkner's fictional account of the demise of the aristocratic Compson family at the hands of the grasping, ill-bred ar- rivistes of the Snopes clan to explain that the triumph of the New South mind-set effectively meant "the Compsons going to work for the Snopeses."[29]

Though it bore the distinct imprint of Woodward's distaste for capitalism and its practitioners, his indictment of the Redeemers and their New South successors did not lack for substantive particulars, including scandals aplenty, ranging from embezzlement, kickbacks, and forgeries to outright thievery and numerous absconscondings with public funds. Although the Redeemers claimed that their draconian retrenchment efforts were a necessary corrective to the fiscal excesses of the governments they overthrew, Woodward charged them with establishing "cheapness, even niggardliness . . . as the criterion of good government." Deep tax cuts allowed the recovery of millions of acres forfeited for taxes during Reconstruction, but the levies they left in place were aggressively regressive. Meanwhile, with expenditures for public edu- cation slashed to the bone, illiteracy soared. Indifferent to the ravages their policies had visited upon already woefully underfunded schools and other public services, the governing classes had abandoned any pretense of social responsibility while exalting the vaunted principle of laissez-faire to the point that it "almost became a test of Southern patriotism."[30]

These principles proved quite pliable when a railroad or manufacturing executive sought a subsidy or tax exemption, but for farmers staggering under tax burdens wholly disproportionate to the value of their property, much less their capacity to pay, the rule of laissez-faire was iron-handed and impassive. The life of such a farmer, Woodward eloquently summarized, consisted of "the annual defeat of the crop market and the tax collector, the weekly defeat of the town market and mounting debt, and the small, gnawing, daily defeats of crumbling barn and fence, encroaching sagebrush and erosion, and one's children growing up in illiteracy."[31]

The great majority of such farmers soon found themselves hopelessly entangled in the "crop-lien system," a horrendously inefficient and disheartening arrangement reflecting the desperate scarcity of capital and, for that matter, of financial institutions themselves, in the postbellum South. With such lenders as there were unwilling to accept worn-out, tax-encumbered land as collateral, the landowner's only hope of obtaining the financing he needed to produce his crop lay in agreeing to a lien against that crop before planting it. With the ultimate value of the crop and the cost of producing it so dependent on the vagaries of both the weather and the marketplace, the interest rates set by the lender were almost prohibitively steep. At the same time, all the inherent disadvantages and perils of the crop-lien system were merely compounded by the reliance of severely cash-strapped landowners on some form of sharecropping, where, in lieu of wages, tenant laborers worked parcels of their land in exchange for a share of the crops they produced.[32]

"Judged objectively, by its economic results alone," Woodward declared, "the 'new evil' [of the crop-lien system] may have worked more permanent injury to the South than the ancient evil [of slavery]." He did not exaggerate the defects of the new arrangement, but in hindsight, instead of measuring its ill effects against those of slavery, he might have done better to conjoin them. Subsequent research on the economics of slavery demonstrated that the capital starvation that led to the crop-lien system was in large part a legacy and consequence of the massive concentration of antebellum southern investment in slaves whose monetary value had been destroyed by a single stroke of Abraham Lincoln's pen. In this case, it seems, an "ancient evil" had not so much given way to a "new evil" as given birth to it.[33]

When Bill Carleton tweaked his friend about his general antipathy to capitalism shortly after *Origins* appeared, Woodward readily admitted "an unconcealed animus toward certain kinds of the article, particularly of the colonial type," that had been imposed on the postbellum South. This "neomercantilism" was so objectionable to him because it sacrificed the vital interests of the region itself to those of the external investors who were really calling the shots. Worse yet, instead of resisting this criminally disadvantageous system, the politicians who rose to power in the wake of Reconstruction vowing to restore the South's fortunes and standing had not only accepted but aided and abetted it.[34]

This argument was hardly original to Woodward, of course. Liberal or conservative, few southerners of that era could resist linking the South's economic and institutional backwardness relative to the rest of the nation to northern colonial control. Benjamin Kendrick anticipated Woodward's arguments in both *Origins* and *Reunion and Reaction* by roughly a decade in his 1941 presidential address to the Southern Historical Association, especially in noting that after the Compromise of 1877, "the native southern elite would guarantee the protection of northern imperialist interests in the region."[35]

Fairly echoing Kendrick, Woodward contended that, as in many Latin American republics, with the absentee owners of southern manufacturing operations channeling their profits into more attractive investments elsewhere, the South had become little more than "a tributary" of distant "industrial powers." He may have even gone Kendrick one better in insisting that northeastern capitalists exercised greater control over the New South's economy than British tobacco merchants had enjoyed back in their colonial heyday. The enduring effects of the South's stunted neocolonial economy were glaringly apparent in any comparison of regional economic well-being. Its total bank deposits accounted for but 9 percent of the nation's total in 1914, and its per capita income was roughly 46 percent below the national average in 1919.[36]

Subsequent research has suggested that, in presenting these deficiencies as by and large the bitter fruits of the Redeemers' misguided and self-serving policies, Woodward took too little account of the decidedly unfavorable circumstances they inherited. Again, not the least of these was the scarcity of indigenous capital or collateral in the wake of emancipation, which not only spawned the crop-lien and sharecropping system but also imposed severe restrictions on the nature and scope of postbellum industrial development. The Redeemer–New South regimes would have been hard-pressed to overcome these deficiencies regardless of the governing approach they adopted.

Beyond that, as Gavin Wright and other economic historians have shown, not only was the consciously self-colonializing strategy itself not so economically ill-advised as many believed, but it may have been the most productive option available. In fact, Wright argued, increasing the pace of southern industrial development in the wake of Reconstruction would have meant

Juleps for the Few and Pellagra for the Crew

attracting far higher levels of external investment and thus expanding the "very 'colonial' relationship that Woodward and many contemporaries decried." As it was, capital investment in the southern states was less likely to have come from outside the region than in faster-growing rural states in the Midwest, where 50 percent of Iowa's total nonagricultural wealth and 47 percent of Nebraska's was held by outsiders in 1900, compared to only 17 percent in Virginia and 19 percent in Georgia.[37]

In sum, rather than its overreliance on outside capital, the New South's sustained economic woes more likely reflected its failure to attract a great deal more of it, which, in turn, left it all the more dependent on the painfully scarce indigenous variety. With such local capital as might be scraped together typically coming in exceedingly modest amounts from people who could ill afford to lose even a penny of it, concentrating on relatively safe investments in small, labor-intensive, low-value-added operations was less a matter of choice than necessity. Likewise, maximizing the region's primary advantage, its abundance of cheap but unskilled labor, meant encouraging industries such as textiles, lumber, and mining that frequently involved little more than extraction or early-stage processing of agricultural products or raw materials. At the same time, the prospects of such operations spinning off large numbers of new jobs or more lucrative investment opportunities were simply too remote to entice entrepreneurs, inventors, or engineers to the region. Greater and more consistent support for public education beginning in the Redeemer era might have yielded more opportunities over time, but in light of the late-arriving South's historically disadvantaged position within the industrial investment marketplace, what Woodward later bemoaned as its "fatal attraction" for such industries was in truth more like a mutual need.

For the most part, what Woodward called his "savage exposures" of the Redeemers' misdeeds and motives seemed to assume that the power and reach of "the people who ran things," as he put it, was so extensive that they bore primary responsibility for the suffering and misfortunes of "the people who were run, who were managed and maneuvered and pushed around." In the first place, as historian Edward L. Ayers observed later, southerners of all sorts in that era "had their own struggles with poverty, injustice and prejudice that had nothing to do with the Redeemers." Beyond that, before he fashioned his indictment of the Redeemers for stunting the economic and social development of the South after Reconstruction, Woodward might have harkened back nearly a century to the words of Karl Marx, who observed in 1852 that while "men make their own history . . . they do not make it as they please . . . but under circumstances existing already, given and transmitted from the past." For the Redeemers, those historically transmitted circumstances obviously included the deterrents to entrepreneurialism and to investments in education, diversification, and resource development posed by slavery. This burdensome legacy seriously restricted the options of Redeemer–New South representatives who were competing for investment capital with the more dynamic and advanced industrial economies of the northern states. All told, the economic system the region's leaders appeared to impose on the laboring masses of their states had also been imposed on them to a greater extent than Woodward seemed to recognize.[38]

This is not to say that much of Woodward's criticism of the Redeemer regimes was not thoroughly warranted or that the people of the post-Reconstruction South might not have benefited substantially from more honest, humane, and enlightened leadership. Still, he likely overestimated what might have been accomplished even then. If, as he suggested, the demise of the Populists at the hands of the Redeemer–New South Democrats and their powerful northern allies destroyed the last hope for economic, political, or racial justice in the region, it did not necessarily follow that this hope had been very realistic in the first place. Certainly, there were many later scholars, who, drawing on both their own research and the broader perspective afforded them by several decades of research by others, found good reason to doubt that conditions in the New South would have improved significantly had the Populists prevailed. Economist William N. Parker had taken much the same line, arguing that "the remedy for Southern poverty—the alternative growth path that might have been followed after 1866—lay outside the reach of decision by farmers, tenants, and planters, acting either individually or as a group." Rather, Parker believed, in the first seventy-five years after the Civil War, southern regional development could hardly have gone much differently without redistributing both labor and capital on a national scale, a process that would ultimately be triggered only by the conjoined systemic shocks delivered by the New Deal and World War II.[39]

Woodward's indictment of the Redeemers and their New South successors was not confined solely to their economic policies, of course, and when he charged in *Origins* that they had also "laid the lasting foundations in matters of race, politics, . . . and law for the modern South," he hinted at the contemporary racial and political objectives of his attack on their legacy. If the politicians currently vowing to quash any attempt to launch a second Reconstruction were eager to liken themselves to the Redeemers, then, not only their judgment but their motives and moral values should immediately be suspect. In essence, he meant to discredit the kingpins of the

Juleps for the Few and Pellagra for the Crew

contemporary southern political order by revealing the ethical bankruptcy of the men from whom they claimed spiritual descent. Historian Bell Irvin Wiley picked up on this message. In his review of *Origins*, he alluded to a contemporary political operative's reference to his candidate as "the greatest statesman produced by our Commonwealth since the days of Gen. John B. Gordon." If the speaker ever had occasion to read Woodward's book, Wiley ventured, "he will probably discard, and permanently," any such comparison to Gordon or, for that matter, to Henry Grady or a great many others in the Redeemer–New South ranks.[40]

Reviewers of *Tom Watson* had failed to pick up on what Woodward himself thought in retrospect were obvious connections between the plight and prospects of the marginalized rural southerners of the 1890s and "the Okies and the Arkies" of the 1930s. Vowing not to be found guilty of "intentional obscurity" a second time, when he sent manuscript chapters of *Origins* asking for Beale's and Rainey's feedback, he urged both of them to "give me hell for it" whenever they caught him at it in *Origins*. Both were happy to oblige. Rainey did not hesitate to point out spots where he felt Woodward's thinking was tangled or circuitous, and called for "clear summaries of intent and accomplishments" at the beginning and end of paragraphs, along with "plain unadorned transitions within the chapters!" Meanwhile, as he had done before in reading his former student's work, Beale chided him for repeatedly assuming "too much intelligence and imagination" on the reader's part, pointing to specific passages where he thought Woodward could state his argument "much more explicitly than you do without spoiling the artistic effect of it as it is."[41]

Woodward's greater receptivity to such advice this time around paid off handsomely. Notably more straightforward than *Tom Watson*, *Origins* made it harder to miss the connection between the contemporary South's manifold deficiencies and the racial, political, and economic transgressions of the Redeemers, whose self-styled political heirs continued to thwart the region's material and human development as the second half of the twentieth century began. In his review of *Origins*, David Donald observed that "today's southern problem is a result of the historical processes which Professor Woodward so admirably analyzes."[42]

Donald was not the only fellow historian who seemed to pick up on the contemporary relevance of Woodward's message, but there were still some who clearly did not. Woodward had been frustrated since his collegiate days with well-intentioned liberal scholars and journalists who continued to embrace the New South School's whitewashed version of history and its greatly exaggerated claims of progress and hollow promises of imminent prosperity. It was the maddeningly tenacious grip of the myth of New South progress on the minds of white southerners that fueled his determination to reduce it to rubble. Thinking he had surely managed that in *Origins*, he found it particularly galling that, ten years later, noted University of Texas historian Walter Prescott Webb was urging his fellow white southerners to turn away from some recent critical historical writing—including Woodward's, perhaps— where "the story is so unpleasant" and fix their gaze instead on what he saw as "a future so bright as to be unbelievable to some." With his frustration finally boiling over, Woodward forcefully reiterated what he had hoped readers would take away from *Origins* ten years earlier, that the contemporary South remained so backward and troubled in so many ways precisely because it was still "continuous in its economic, political and racial institutions with the order established in 1877."[43]

In an uncharacteristically biting and sarcastic address in Little Rock that later appeared in the *Washington Post*, Woodward bemoaned the "misguided sense of identity" that led latter-day southern liberals to see themselves carrying on the good work of the "New South movement" under the naive and uninformed assumption that "this associates them with industry and progress and dissociates them from slavery and the old regime." On the contrary, Woodward insisted, it attached them to a thoroughly regressive social and economic mind-set almost certain to hold the region back rather than move it forward. Instead of a bright and progressive future, those who were still clinging to "the New South credo bag and baggage" nearly a century after Appomattox should expect nothing more than the same old "caste and segregation and paternalism" and glaring economic disparities that still translated into "juleps for the few and pellagra for the crew."[44]

Back in his graduate school days, Woodward had pontificated that " besides teaching people what to hate and what [to] cherish," education "should equip them with proper heroes and proper villains." The ill-fated Populists were about as heroic as the characters came in *Origins*, and Woodward aimed to demonstrate forcefully that in venerating the Redeemer–New South regimes while scorning or simply dismissing their Populist challengers, white southerners had been hissing the heroes and applauding the villains. Noting that hardly a Redeemer or New South proponent of any consequence managed to escape Woodward's wrath, historian James Tice Moore observed wryly that, judging from *Origins*, among Democratic leaders of this era, "men of character, integrity, and foresight" were about as common as "godly inhabitants of Sodom." Moore also chided Woodward for minimizing Redeemer efforts to address such problems as tight money, overreliance on property taxes, and other ills besetting the farmers while exaggerating the coziness of Redeemer relationships with railroad and manufacturing interests.[45]

Woodward had heard all this before. Critiquing the *Origins* manuscript in 1949, Rupert Vance had worried that his esteemed protégé held "such high ideals that nobody ever reaches them" and that his study conveyed "the impression that no progress was made throughout the period." Vance's associate Harriet L. Herring praised Woodward's revelation that the Redeemers were not "the saviors and the haloed saints which political speakers in my youth would have led us to think," but she also felt that his treatment of retrenchment in the Redeemer era was "pretty hard on those old boys," given that there was "not too much to tax" nor "too much to pay taxes with." Vance's and Herring's cautions went largely unheeded, for Woodward's principal concern in *Origins* was not balance or complexity but producing what reviewer Avery O. Craven called a book that "wrecks most of the old notions that have grown up about southern life after the Civil War."[46]

Urgently needed as it so often is, notion-wrecking can be a risky business, nonetheless. As historian Daniel J. Singal has pointed out, in their zeal to correct the excesses of their predecessors, revisionist historians are often driven to certain excesses of their own. Conceding that he might have gone a bit overboard in his scorched-earth campaign against the heroic Redeemer–New South legend, Woodward explained years later that "the familiar line of Southern historiography was the one I was trying to overthrow, so I had to speak out rather forcibly to be heard. In such circumstances it's perhaps natural to overemphasize some points, and I think I did that." Not surprisingly, the excesses Woodward committed in his determination to discredit the Redeemers' ties to the old planter classes and reveal their regimes as no less corrupt and self-serving than those of the Republican governments they overthrew would eventually prove the most inviting and vulnerable targets for those bent on revising his own interpretations.[47]

On the twentieth anniversary of the publication of *Origins of the New South* in 1971, Woodward protégé Sheldon Hackney marveled that there had been so little fundamental challenge to the narrative crafted by his mentor. Hackney was certainly correct in noting the extraordinary length of the book's exemption from criticism, but that exemption was about to expire. The next fifteen years or so would see vigorous reexamination and debate on some of the fundamental tenets of Woodward's argument. His insistence on the wholesale demise of the old planter class at the hands of upstart businessmen and industrialists seem to draw the most sustained fire. The most controversial challenge came from Jonathan M. Wiener and Dwight B. Billings Jr. In their respective studies of postbellum Alabama and North Carolina, both argued for the persistence of the planter class, which they likened to the nineteenth-century Prussian Junkers, a landed agrarian elite that remained powerful enough to restrict the efforts of a shaky new business middle class to promote the expansion of commerce and industry.[48]

In the end, other scholars who reexamined the political economy of the late nineteenth-century South found very little that smacked of Prussia or the Junkers, including Michael O'Brien, who allowed that "as Prussians, Alabamans cut a sorry figure." What they found instead was many different arrangements prevailing across a variety of geographic and economic contexts, some favoring planters and others the commercial and industrial classes. What Woodward presented as a revolutionary seizure of power by an upstart new business class, then, might just as readily be seen as an incomplete and inconsistent restoration of the old planter class. Nor was it by any means clear that the two groups were nearly so polarized in their aims and values as either Woodward or the proponents of planter persistence would have their readers believe, perhaps because they shared a compelling common interest in keeping wages and taxes low and governments small and fiscally austere.[49]

As valid as some of the retrospective criticisms of *Origins* may have been, it is important to remember that, writing in 1951, Woodward had no access to the mass of relevant data or historical or economic analysis that would be gathered and processed over the next four decades. Much of the later work on the South in this period emphasized not just the regional but the national and global scope of the forces impinging on its development at the close of the nineteenth century. Yet few if any books written about the South by the middle of the twentieth century (or, for that matter, well into the twenty-first) could rival *Origins of the New South,* either in the breadth and force of its unflinching analysis or in the formidable array of sources on which it drew. Likewise, as with Woodward's other books, the number of challenges to *Origins* that began to pop up in its third decade in print begs the question of how many historical works retain such seminal importance long enough to invite serious revisionist challenges so many years after they were published. Simply put, Woodward had written a truly remarkable synthesis of a complex and tumultuous period with no more than a scattering of relevant published sources at his disposal. *Origins* represented not only a crowning personal research achievement but a masterful marshaling and fusion of specific evidence into a powerful and persuasive metanarrative of an era then still largely unexamined by others. Avery O. Craven was wholly justified in touting the book for a Pulitzer, but the Frederic Bancroft Prize (awarded annually by Columbia University for a distinguished book in American history) was perhaps a sounder testament to how deeply *Origins* had impressed Woodward's professional peers.[50]

An estimated sales of 7,000 copies during its first six years in print was quite respectable by publishing standards of the day, especially for a university press book, but *Origins of the New South* would gain much broader exposure after 1966, when it became the first volume in the *History of the South* series to appear in paperback. In reality, it had already gained sufficient international notice to spur an Italian publisher to bring out a translated edition in 1963. This recognition might have seemed gratifying enough in its own right to turn some heads at LSU Press, but as in all his dealings with publishers, Woodward's gaze remained firmly fixed on his financial bottom line. He did not shrink from confronting LSU Press director Richard Wentworth about why he had still received no compensation from the Italian publisher after the translation had been in print for five years, which should have been more than enough time, he reckoned, to "jar loose a suitable remission by these lousy wops."[51]

Not everyone was thrilled with the widespread notice accorded the book or its author. Dismayed by its revisionist bent, disgruntled series coeditor E. Merton Coulter agreed with a friend that *Origins* had been written primarily "to please Gunnar Myrdal, the Civil Rights Advocates and All the Northern Left-Wingers." He would have "objected to the MS," Coulter explained, "if there had been any way to bring it more into line with the facts; but the point of view permeated the whole. And so we could not afford to reject the MS." The upshot, Coulter noted resentfully, but not altogether inaccurately, was a book that "put C. Vann on the pinnacle in Yankeeland."[52]

Still, whatever their private quibbles, Woodward's contemporaries largely agreed that he had written a truly extraordinary and lasting book, which historian-turned–editor and publisher Roger W. Shugg believed was destined to become "one of the masterpieces of our historical literature." Dumas Malone not only saw *Origins* superseding "all previous accounts of the New South" but warned that, because of it, significant revisions in "the general history of the United States between reconstruction and Woodrow Wilson" were now in order. The almost awestruck reaction to *Origins* from such a stellar cast of reviewers suggested that, in having what he called "my say about the period," at age forty-three, Woodward had also secured his legacy as a truly transformative figure whose work lent new meaning and direction to a field of historical inquiry where both had long been sorely lacking.[53]

7

Cordially Invited to Be Absent

_____

Integrating the Southern Historical Association

Even the stringent demands on his time and attention posed by the frenetic final push to ready *Origins of the New South* for its long-delayed publication had not dulled Woodward's sensitivity to social injustice. His fervor for protecting free speech and civil liberties had shone through in his stout defense of his German colleagues at Scripps, but his time in uniform had allowed little leeway for social activism. Soon after his discharge from the navy, however, he began to make up for lost time. He spent the first months of his tenure at Johns Hopkins on leave, but shortly after arriving on campus in 1947, he lodged a protest with the board of governors of the Johns Hopkins Club after a black graduate student at Hopkins was denied membership, a ruling Woodward thought inconsistent with the school's "liberal tradition."[1]

He was also intent on challenging the Southern Historical Association's continuing acquiescence to Jim Crow practices at its meetings, as well as what he saw as the sterile traditionalism that was stifling innovation and fruitful discourse in its program sessions. His opportunity to pursue both of these ends materialized in 1948, when Lester J. Cappon, the incoming president of the organization, asked him to chair the program committee for the 1949 meeting in Williamsburg, Virginia. Though Woodward made a show of his reluctance to take on the assignment, Cappon was insistent, pointing to Woodward's well-known "criticism of previous meetings." As Cappon indicated, Woodward had long made little secret of his dissatisfaction with the provincial and defensive tone that still marked far too much of southern historical scholarship, and his letter revealing his ideas about the program to fellow members of his committee fairly brimmed with subversionary intent. First, he proposed that "the sessions be (1) *shorter* and (2) *better*. . . . Never more than two papers per session, even one for some if it's good enough. . . . That flat rule ought to take some of the torture and boredom out of the meeting—as well as some load off our shoulders. As for quality, I can't see why we should not shoot for top-flight stuff." By this, he meant no more "dreary dishes of spade-work, but interpretive essays, synthesis, revisionist challenge[s] if any. Something to keep them awake. A fight if possible." Next, in order to "break up the tradition of parochialism," he proposed to "import a few live Yankees who are unabashed by their ignoble origins," one of them being Arthur Schlesinger Jr. Woodward hoped to match Schlesinger up on a session on the South in the New Deal with his own Johns Hopkins colleague in political science V. O. Key, whose massive study of southern politics would be in print the following year.[2]

Looking to use the program to shake up the entire organization, Woodward also enlisted his old Emory classmate David Potter, then teaching at Yale, to offer a paper appraising the articles that had appeared in the first fifteen volumes of the *Journal of Southern History*. Potter's exploration revealed that just 28 percent of all contributors were responsible for 58 percent of the articles published, with twenty-six of those articles coming from just six authors. Although Woodward might have seen this breakdown confirming his concerns about the rather narrow and dated scholarship that had appeared in the journal to date, Potter preferred to see it simply as evidence that its contributors included practically all the distinguished scholars in the field. Potter also appeared less concerned than Woodward surely hoped about the racial blind spot in southern historical writing, suggesting only that "there is reason for more attention to the Negro in the South." Potter did seem to foreshadow Woodward's own future effort to fill that void, however, when he noted that, so far, the journal had offered no treatments of segregation in southern schools, churches, hospitals, and other institutions.[3]

Woodward's efforts to stir things up at the 1949 meeting yielded more provocative fruit when he asked his friend and kindred spirit Vanderbilt political scientist Herman Clarence Nixon to prepare what he already knew would be a pointed critique of the addresses delivered by the group's first fifteen presidents. After all, Woodward reasoned, though Nixon was not a historian himself, he knew enough about how the game was played "to stand behind the pitchers and call the strikes for us" without being terribly bothered by any howls of protests his assessments might elicit. Nixon's assignment "really ought to be some fun" if, rather than reading each of the addresses line by line, he simply scanned them for "some judiciously chosen quotations that would raise provocative questions about where this outfit is bound and what century it is living in." Nixon was quick to accept, provided he could count on the support of Woodward in what he gleefully dubbed this "decidedly iconoclastic undertaking."[4]

Eager to oblige Woodward, Nixon composed a paper that clearly showed little deference to icons of any sort, human or institutional. He lampooned the strident sectionalism of many of the orations, many of which were either "pretty well spiked with the hard liquor of polemics" or simply polemics from beginning to end. Overall, Nixon also found too much emphasis on sectionalism and too little inclination to criticize the South for anything beyond failing to collect and preserve the records and other materials needed to rebut the criticisms of outsiders. The addresses were also notably lacking in the thoughtful or broadly philosophical fare frequently served up in presidential addresses of the American Historical Association. On the other hand, the SHA presidents showed a gift for romanticizing the Lost Cause and antebellum planter order that put Sir Walter Scott to shame while glossing over the harsh realities of the region's racial history. Southern historians might not be responsible for solving the South's problems, but at the very least, Nixon ventured, they should avoid compounding them by shoring up "a regional iron curtain against the interchange of ideas" or providing "fuel for the Nordic [KKK] signal fire which sometimes burns on Stone Mountain."[5]

Sarcastic and satiric, Nixon's paper, which appeared in the February 1950 issue of the *Journal of Southern History*, showed little effort to spare the feelings of his principal targets, including his former agrarian colleague Frank L. Owsley and others whose identity was made unmistakably clear. A delighted Woodward declared Nixon's paper "a real Mickey Finn" and assured him that those whom he called out or satirized "would have to laugh or be laughed at."[6]

Nixon's paper may have caused agitation in certain quarters, but its potential impact was much less explosive than the real bombshell Woodward planned to drop on the Southern Historical Association in 1949. When the group was formed in 1934, the founders had not even discussed the possibility of black participation, and there was nothing in its constitution or bylaws to suggest that this was or might become a reality, much less a problem. Four years after its founding, Owsley had extolled the group to Robert Penn

Warren as "the white hope of the South." In 1941 SHA president Benjamin Kendrick had to admit that he had no idea the organization might actually have black members until he received an inquiry from a historian at historically black Atlanta University concerning the extent to which he and his colleagues would be allowed to participate in the group's upcoming meeting at Atlanta's Biltmore Hotel. Caught off guard, Kendrick had responded that black members enjoyed "all the rights and privileges of any other member, subject only to local city ordinances, state laws, or practices of the hotel in which the meeting is held."[7]

Kendrick's ad hoc imposition of Jim Crow contingencies on the "rights and privileges" of black members struck his fellow SHA leaders as just the ticket for avoiding conflict with the Biltmore and other southern hotels down the road, not to mention segregationist whites within the organization itself. Leaving the Biltmore's policies unchallenged, the executive council affirmed Kendrick's position, voting to dump oversight of this prickly matter on local arrangements committees for upcoming meetings but offering no assurance of support should a future committee opt at any point to challenge southern racial mores.

The council's reluctance to adopt a more progressive stance cost the group one of its most prominent members of either race in W. E. B. Du Bois, who was also teaching at Atlanta University and contended that the Biltmore might well have relaxed its prohibition against integrated dining in the hotel had the SHA leadership pressed the matter. Seeing their failure to do so as a "revelation of your attitude toward colored members," he tendered his resignation shortly after the meeting. Elsewhere, Du Bois observed wryly that the association's official stance effectively meant that black members were "cordially invited to be absent." Those who chose to attend the annual meeting paid their money and took their chances. Some of their white colleagues welcomed them while others avoided even eye contact, much less physical proximity. Jim Crow's constraints were a bit looser in some cities than others, but generally, black members were well advised to expect treatment little better than that accorded the black employees of the host hotel. This meant entering the building by the back door, seating themselves as inconspicuously as possible at the rear of the meeting rooms, and relieving themselves only in the toilets designated for the black custodial and kitchen workers. They could sit with white members for none of the luncheons or dinners that were a part of the annual meeting, although they might be allowed to eat in the kitchen and then enter the main dining area in order to hear a speaker once the white members had finished their meals.[8]

For the most part, even the more liberal white members of the SHA who found this tradition of internal apartheid embarrassing and degrading both to them and to their black colleagues went along with it, each waiting on someone else to summon the temerity to challenge the practice openly. However quiet or even shy Woodward might seem in certain social settings, when issues of true concern to him were involved, his temerity was not to be doubted, and now, as program chair, he intended to literally push his friends to take a stand that was long overdue.

John Hope Franklin had received his PhD from Harvard in 1941 and had already published a book on free blacks in North Carolina when his *From Slavery to Freedom: A History of American Negroes* appeared in 1947 and quickly became the standard textbook in black history. In the same year, Franklin had also joined the faculty at Howard University in Washington, D.C. The two men were already acquainted, but Franklin's newfound proximity to Woodward in Baltimore proved conducive to a closer personal and professional relationship. Woodward congratulated Franklin on his new book and invited him up to talk to his seminar students at Hopkins. Franklin later recalled in his memoir that in the fall of 1948 (about the time that Woodward was contacted by Cappon about chairing the SHA Program Committee for the 1949 meeting), Woodward had asked him "if he became chair of the Program Committee . . . and if the next annual meeting was not held in one of the more racist towns, would I be willing to read a paper at the meeting?"[9]

Woodward had informed his fellow committee members at the outset that he wanted to invite a black scholar to present a paper at the 1949 meeting, and at least two of the four singled out Franklin as a likely candidate, though he had just published a scathing critique of diehard Dunningite E. Merton Coulter's *Reconstruction* volume in the History of the South series and taken it upon himself to distribute off-prints to around 200 people. Given Woodward's desire for controversial sessions, University of Wisconsin historian William B. Hesseltine asked, "Why not a Negro speaker on the race issue?" and allowed that he would like to see "J. Hope Franklin and E. Merton Coulter tangle." From Millsaps College, Vernon L. Wharton also volunteered that Franklin would be his first choice to break the color barrier. Gerald M. Capers of Tulane assured Woodward that he too had long favored having a black scholar on the program, though he thought it best not to make the occasion even more stressful by asking him to focus his presentation directly on race. Capers need not have been concerned on this count, for Woodward expected all along that Franklin would read a paper drawn from the research on the martial tradition in the South that would later be incorporated into his book *The Militant South*.[10]

Meanwhile, back in Williamsburg, Cappon was just beginning to realize what a whirlwind he had unleashed in his choice of program chair. He had been supportive when Woodward broached the subject of Franklin's involvement, but after discussing the matter with his colleague Carl Bridenbaugh, both agreed that they should not attempt to shatter both on-campus and systemwide public higher education precedent in Virginia without the blessing of William and Mary president John E. Pomfret. After meeting with the president, Cappon wrote immediately to inform Woodward that, although "Mr. Pomfret agrees with us in principle that a Negro scholar should not be excluded from our programs, . . . he doubts very seriously the advisability of the proposal from the standpoint of the College as a public institution of Virginia and the present status of public opinion in the state on racial discrimination in education." The situation had grown particularly tense in some Tidewater counties, Cappon explained, and Pomfret was "inclined to feel that a stand on principle, without due regard for attending circumstances and prevailing social attitudes, will lose more than it gains for both the College and the Negro." Pomfret had promised to take it up with the chair of William and Mary's board of visitors, but Cappon anticipated, "with a high degree of certainty," that this would come to naught. Despite the almost palpable sense of relief his note conveyed, Cappon was doubtless sincere in declaring, "I regret the situation very much," but at least, so he presumed, Woodward had "not approached Franklin as yet." After all, there was nothing to prevent him from attending the meeting, and, confident that Franklin understood the ways of Virginia with respect to meals and lodging, Cappon offered to arrange a room for him with "a colored family."[11]

Cappon may have thought the matter settled and done with, but Woodward did not. As soon as Cappon's letter arrived, he fired off a wickedly disingenuous telegram: "Assuming your earlier letter on tentative program was a green light I spoke to Franklin/Retraction embarrassing to Association should think [stop] Would not Association instead of college have responsibility and blame"? In reality, although Woodward had quietly sounded Franklin out several months earlier about his willingness to be on the program, he had not yet issued a formal invitation. Instead of letting the convention hosts at William and Mary off the hook, however, he seized on this ploy, hoping to bluff them into living up to their earlier, at least tacit agreement.[12]

Woodward could hardly have resisted a chuckle or two upon learning how readily his sleight-of-hand had done the trick when a letter quickly arrived from Cappon, reporting that his telegram had shown up just as he was preparing to write with the good news that President Pomfret had had a change of heart over the previous weekend and now "thinks we can go ahead and include Franklin on the program," reasoning that the chances of any untoward incident were slight and that, even if one arose, he could simply say that it happened at "a private meeting of a learned society." Pomfret had asked whether any SHA member might object to Franklin's participation, and although Cappon suggested to Woodward that they should be alert to this possibility, he had assured Pomfret that Franklin was "not the sort who courts publicity," and he saw no reason to worry that "any group of Negroes or race agitators" might show up on the campus.[13]

Not the least bit remorseful over hoodwinking Cappon, Woodward now lost no time in formally inviting Franklin to make history as the first black scholar to read a paper before the Southern Historical Association. Though the invitation was official, its tone was casual rather than formal, giving Franklin, who surely knew better, no indication that the decision to ask him to participate had caused any sort of stir or was likely to, or that his experience in delivering a paper might be even the least bit stressful: "Our plans for the Williamsburg meeting next November are taking shape, and I want to know if you will be able to read us a paper on the Martial Spirit of the Old South. I particularly hope you will agree to do this for it is important to the shape and character of the program planned. The invitation is not, be assured, something I put over on my own. I was determined to press the matter, but it did not prove necessary. Two other members of the committee suggested your name independently and the others fell in quite heartily. There was no disagreement within the committee. The invitation is therefore unanimous and cordial." There would be no "discussion leader." The session chair would simply invite comment from the floor. There would be a second paper, though Woodward professed to be "at a loss for a man to pair with you," and asked Franklin to suggest someone, preferably a white southerner, in order "to balance a good many Yanks on the program."[14]

Franklin must have found Woodward's last comment as deliciously ironic as Woodward surely intended it to be, especially since some of the old line southern-born members of the SHA had in fact been complaining for some time about what they saw as a "Yankee" takeover of the group. Franklin assured Woodward that he was deeply grateful to him and his committee and sought Woodward's guidance on whether his paper should concentrate on a single facet of the growth of the military tradition or offer a broader summation of his findings and interpretations. In seeking Woodward's input, he also made it clear that he would be likely to follow his advice.[15]

Woodward had thought it better not to involve Franklin in any session dealing with race, but neither did he want him to appear tentative or intimidated in any presentation he made. His response also revealed his own preference for ideas over heavy emphasis on factual detail or documentation in historical writing. He urged Franklin to be as bold and sweeping in his observations as he dared. Neither he nor any other speaker at this meeting would have to worry about getting any flak from a "discusser," Woodward explained, "because I think they inhibit speakers and obstruct intelligent exchange of ideas and good conversation—and if these affairs don't result in that, then what good are they? That means you won't have to submit a formal paper to anybody. . . . Nobody will be running down your citations and picking you up on some silly 'point.'" Because Franklin's remarks would be essentially off the record, he would be "free to make such sensible observations as are tedious or sometimes impossible to 'document' and therefore often get omitted from 'scholarly' productions."[16]

In the meantime, there was much scurrying about and fretting in Williamsburg about how best to assure that Franklin's participation went off without incident or embarrassment to him or the SHA or the College of William and Mary. Cappon and Bridenbaugh mentioned that Franklin might drive down from Washington and find overnight lodging at historically black Hampton Institute, about thirty miles from Williamsburg, although that would not address the matter of where and with whom he would eat during the day. Cappon thought it would "be simpler for him to get a room with a colored family and I think we could work something out in advance, although the room he could get would not compare very favorably with what our white members will get at the hotels and tourist houses. We shall have to give some further thought to the problem of meals. One of us could take care of him at home, but we shall be pretty much involved in the meetings at the same time."[17]

Amused by their obsessive concern with what he saw as the essentially trivial details of Franklin's appearance, Woodward proceeded to toy with both Cappon and Bridenbaugh, at one point promising to "ask Franklin about the car and see if he can bring a pup tent and k-rations" before airily assuring the nervous SHA president, "We can work it out some way. He doesn't want trouble, I'm sure." To Franklin, he gleefully reported, "Our good Yankee friends [Cappon was from Wisconsin and Bridenbaugh from Pennsylvania] down the coast are in a buzz-buzz over the intricacies of Southern race ritual. If I didn't think you had a sense of humor, I would never have let you in for this. Our friends amuse me no end, and I am giving them no help. Just watching with detached irony."[18]

Franklin responded that he had "just howled at what you had to say about our Yankee friends. I rather regret that my impending appearance is causing them so much anxiety and discomfort. Frankly, it is not regret; it is pity. As you can imagine, I am much too preoccupied with other things at the present to worry about where I shall sleep and eat, or indeed, if I shall sleep and eat at all. . . . You are at your very best in helping them to squirm! Let me know of developments as they transpire."[19]

Woodward remained evasive as Cappon pressed him repeatedly during the spring and summer of 1949 for "specific directions about what I should do to take care of John Hope Franklin." After getting no direct response to his repeated offers to find lodging for Franklin with a "good colored family," Cappon decided to be more specific. He knew of a particularly "fine colored family here by the name of Baker" who were said to take in tourists, although they did not provide meals.[20]

Still in the dark about Franklin's plans at the end of September, with the meeting now scarcely six weeks away, Bridenbaugh all but begged Woodward to ask him unequivocally "whether he plans to stay at Hampton Institute or whether he would be happy staying with Mrs. Baker . . . who has a nice house not far from Lester's house. . . . Also when he plans to arrive so that we can make arrangements for his meals. We will want to invite him at least once at our house." His inquiry, Bridenbaugh explained, merely reflected his "desire to make everything as easy as possible and as comfortable as I can."[21]

When Franklin's program containing registration materials for the convention arrived in September, Woodward encouraged him to request a room at the Williamsburg Lodge, the host hotel, just as any white number attending the meeting would have. Knowing nothing of this, Bridenbaugh informed Woodward that he had "asked the Lodge not to reply to his request because they would have to turn him down," appending to his note the by now wholly predictable reference to a "nice colored family." On the matter of what Franklin would or would not be allowed to do at the meeting itself, Bridenbaugh went into excruciating detail: "Dr. Pomfret says that from the point of view of the College, the whole problem is to be handled by the Association; this means that Franklin can eat with us there and use the toilet facilities. The Williamsburg Inn says that he can attend all dinners which are exclusively for the Association." Regrettably, however, the manager of the inn indicated that he would "have to refuse the use of the public toilet facilities," though

Cordially Invited to Be Absent

"he says that he very much dislikes having to ask Mr. Franklin to use those of the help." Bridenbaugh lived nearby, and to avoid this embarrassment, he proposed simply taking Franklin to his house "at such times" when he needed to relieve himself. Regardless of whether Franklin would have found this arrangement any less of an indignity than using the Jim Crow toilets at the inn, Bridenbaugh was clearly sensitive enough to his feelings to suggest that he and Woodward should see to it that he did not lack for dining companions "in order that he be made to feel at home."[22]

Woodward passed along this elaborate explication of protocol in what Franklin called a *"priceless"* letter so "explicit in detail" that "there is no possible way for me to go wrong after so much time and thought have gone into the planning. If I were in the field of Chinese History," he added, "I think I would change to Southern history. There is nothing anywhere more fascinating than 'Southrons' and their history!" Even when Franklin informed him he would be staying with Douglas Adair, a friend on the faculty at William and Mary, Woodward waited another week to let Bridenbaugh finally know, now scarcely three weeks before the meeting, that "Franklin feels that he can make satisfactory arrangements for himself." Though clearly relieved, Bridenbaugh continued to fret about Franklin's access to a proper toilet, offering yet again to "give him a key to my house where he will be welcome at all times."[23]

Bridenbaugh's fixation on the logistics of addressing Franklin's toilet requirements may have struck Woodward as truly laughable, but the absurdity of Jim Crow rituals and taboos did not make the practical obstacles they posed any less real. Woodward's rather cavalier disregard for the challenges facing those charged with the practical implementation of his plan was that of someone who would be leaving Williamsburg immediately after the meeting, regardless of how his bold experiment played out. Meanwhile, Bridenbaugh and Cappon knew full well that, however transformative Franklin's appearance on the program might be for the Southern Historical Association, the codes of conduct governing routine activities in the rigidly segregated environment in which they lived and worked would neither be suspended for the meeting nor fundamentally altered thereafter by what transpired in the course of it. Yet it had fallen to them to see it that Woodward's plan came off without an ugly incident that might, among other things, discourage further efforts to free the SHA from the unjust and burdensome constraints of Jim Crow. Also genuinely concerned about any untoward episode that might embarrass Franklin personally, not to mention cast the institution where they taught in a very bad light nationally, they had good reason to fret about where he ate or used the toilet or other practical concerns as well.

Already on edge because he could get no helpful response from Woodward, an agitated Bridenbaugh had informed him in mid-June that a member of the group, "presumably at Chapel Hill where the word is known," had written "to high powers at h. q. to try and cut our Negro out of the program." Although the mysterious troublemaker had been "turned down flat," Bridenbaugh thought it important for Woodward "to know that some diehards are not dead." This hardly came as news to Woodward, of course, but foreseeing potential future flareups as the meeting drew nigh, Bridenbaugh urged him to "marshal all your arguments in case we need them" and promised that he would "handle the Richmond newspapers when the time comes." Two weeks later, fearing the worst, Bridenbaugh let Woodward know that the defiantly unreconstructed E. Merton Coulter had contacted Cappon to find out who was chairing the program committee. "I guess you know why," he explained, "so I want you forewarned. . . . Apparently some word has gotten out around." As an afterthought, he speculated that Coulter's inquiry might indicate that "he read J. F. H.'s review of his book." As it turned out, Woodward soon discovered that Coulter was simply interested in letting Woodward know that he was available to read a paper.[24]

Ironically, the single greatest thorn in Woodward's side during the whole affair turned out to be one of the most enthusiastic supporters of what he was trying to do. His former adviser Howard Beale had become a vigorous crusader against racial discrimination within professional historical organizations across the board. (He would campaign ferociously a few years later to integrate the Mississippi Valley Historical Association, which was the forerunner of the Organization of American Historians.) Beale had impulsively volunteered to secure a hotel room in Williamsburg under his name and then share it with Franklin, only to have Woodward forcefully veto this deliberately provocative arrangement, which Franklin would almost certainly have declined in any event. This "won't work according to local ritual," he patiently explained to his fire-breathing mentor, who had surely known that well enough all the while, adding that both he and Franklin were content for now to let "my good Yankee friends down that way stew in that one."[25]

As it happened, Woodward's laid-back approach to the whole affair was no more satisfactory to the volatile Beale than it was to Bridenbaugh and Cappon, whom he took it on himself to confront about certain "rumors" concerning Franklin's participation in the upcoming meeting, one of them being "that the hotel is not going to house him." Beale had also gotten wind of Coulter's inquiry about the program chairman, and presuming both that he meant to lobby against Franklin's appearance and that he might well succeed, he raised the thinly veiled threat of a concerted effort to inform the membership that William and Mary was "reluctant to have Franklin." After receiving panicked notes from both Cappon and Bridenbaugh, Woodward was furious with Beale, not simply because "they probably suspect me of egging you on and want me to call you off the crusade," but because he recognized that Beale's actions had thrust him into the unfamiliar and uncomfortable role of "councilor of moderation" in a situation where "it would be more fun to raise hell." He was tempted, so he told Beale, to amuse himself by simply sitting back and watching "you Yanks . . . fight it out," and he would, he insisted, "were it not a fight between my friends in which a third friend [Franklin] is likely to get hurt."[26]

After assuring him that Coulter's inquiry had nothing to do with Franklin, he demanded to know "what earthly good would it do to circularize the members with a report that William and Mary was 'reluctant to have Franklin'?" Whether this was true or not, Franklin had been invited with the knowledge of its administration, and at that point, apart from simply trying to make trouble, he saw little reason for Beale to "question whether W&M's hospitality . . . was genuine and heartfelt, etc." On the matter of the hotel refusing Franklin a room, Woodward really got his dander up, asking "in all candor, Howard, do you think this is the time and place for a campaign against race discrimination in American hotels?" If so, "why not pick the Pennsylvania Hotel in New York two years ago at the AHA meeting? Or the Mayflower in Washington last year? Or the Parker House in Boston next Christmas? It's the same story as in Williamsburg, and you don't have to rely on 'rumor' for its authenticity! Ask John Franklin, or the clerk at the Stevens Hotel in Chicago. Any time you want to organize a picket line of the above hostelries, let me know, and I will fall in line. But I can't launch the crusade in Williamsburg—and keep my sense of humor." Finally, knowing that Beale was very proud of supposedly shielding Franklin from certain indignities at other meetings, Woodward asked, "Have you considered the effect of [your] crusade on John's reception?"[27]

After this blast from his protégé, Beale appeared to calm down for a spell, but even as Woodward tried to reassure Bridenbaugh in mid-October that his former mentor would not be a problem, Beale's simmering outrage exploded once more, and he favored Cappon and Bridenbaugh with a hide-peeling six-page, single-spaced excoriation of the kind for which he was rightly— though seldom affectionately—known. For starters, he lit into Bridenbaugh for failing, as local arrangements chairman, simply to invite Franklin to stay at his home. Likewise, before launching into a lengthy recitation of Franklin's achievements, liberally sprinkled with references of his own acts of kindness toward him, Beale demanded that Cappon consider how many white members of the organization would be satisfied with "the arrangements you describe for John"?[28]

Beale raised valid points, but in this instance, as in many others, his self-righteous presumption and eagerness to condemn the moral shortcomings of others marked him as more of an overzealous agitator than a constructive critic. This was precisely why Bridenbaugh had already let Woodward know that President Pomfret at William and Mary had stipulated that "every effort must be made to keep Beale away from Franklin, since he always seems to be more concerned with stirring up things than with solving vital but delicate problems." Beale had other ideas, however, and he insisted on driving Franklin down from Washington for the meeting.[29]

Beyond the matters of Franklin's living arrangements and whether he would be allowed to attend banquets or luncheons, there was great interest in the makeup of the session itself. Still in his early forties, with three well-received books already in print, Emory University Civil War specialist Bell I. Wiley was clearly an accomplished scholar, and he eagerly agreed to pair his paper on "Southern Reaction to Northern Invasion" with Franklin's discussion of "The Martial Spirit of the Old South" in a session titled "The South at Arms." When the distinguished Columbia University historian Henry Steele Commager got wind of Franklin's appearance on the program, he volunteered to chair the session. Some white SHA members may have known little or nothing about John Hope Franklin's scholarship or even the color of his skin until they showed up in Williamsburg. Wiley and Commager lent major "star power" to the proceedings, however, and that, plus the drama of Franklin's unprecedented appearance on the program, seemed to promise a large turnout, although, just in case, program organizers had deliberately scheduled his session opposite a likely less attractive one on U.S. relations with Latin America.[30]

It was soon clear that no such contingency measure had been necessary, when at 3:00 P.M. on Thursday, November 10, 1949, a crowd well in excess of what the room on the ground floor of William and Mary's Phi Beta Kappa Hall could accommodate had gathered to see southern historians making history while talking about it. "You couldn't get in that place," Franklin recalled, noting that a number of curious William and Mary faculty as well as townspeople had gathered outside the first-floor room to peer in the windows. Others in attendance offered much the same account and confirmed Franklin's impression that his paper "got a good reception." The only potentially

Cordially Invited to Be Absent

awkward moment, Franklin remembered years later, came during the discussion from the floor when a white woman who looked to be in her sixties demanded to know, "How we can sit here and hear him use the term, 'Civil War,' when he should call it the War Between the States?" To Franklin's relief—and perhaps surprise, the audience immediately "broke into laughter." The incident seemed more noteworthy when Franklin learned that his questioner was the widow of Lyon G. Tyler, son of President John Tyler (born in 1853 when his father was sixty-three) and a historian who had been a dedicated defender of the Old South, not to mention president of William and Mary from 1888 to 1919. Both Franklin and his listeners that day might have seen even greater import in the audience's less than deferential reaction to her comment had they realized that Susan Ruffin Tyler was herself the great-granddaughter of the fatally irreconcilable Virginia secessionist Edmund Ruffin.[31]

Franklin had also broken new ground by joining with some friends to dine at the annual banquet held in conjunction with the presidential address. Meanwhile, reporting matter-of-factly on the historic session, the *Richmond Times-Dispatch* made no mention of Franklin's race, indicating only that he taught at Howard University. All told, it seemed, the SHA had come a long way since the previous year's meeting in Jackson, Mississippi, where black members had to enter the hotel via the back door and confine themselves to the rear of the room when attending sessions. In the association, as in the South and the nation at large, though, progress on the racial front soon proved anything but linear.[32]

There was still good reason in the wake of the Williamsburg meeting to think that more changes were coming, however. When he was dressing down Lester Cappon in advance of that gathering, Howard Beale had assured him that there were now "countless younger men" within the SHA and the field of southern history in general whose thinking was no longer distorted by the racism that seemed to come as second nature to so many of their elders in the profession. Though the excitable Beale was given to rather sweeping generalizations, something of a youth movement was definitely afoot in both the field and the association in the wake of World War II. As historian Bethany Johnson notes, during its first decade of publication (1935–45), half of the academic authors whose articles appeared in the *Journal of Southern History* held the rank of full professor. Over the next decade, that proportion fell to just over a third. Meanwhile, Thomas D. Clark was forty-three years old when he served as president of the association in 1947 and not coincidentally, perhaps, when Clark took over the editorship of the journal in 1949, it featured a review of Rollin G. Osterweiss's *Romanticism and Nationalism in the Old*

South by John Hope Franklin, marking its first publication of a black scholar's review of a white scholar's book. Clark also went on in 1951 to remove the familiar image of a plantation house that had long graced the journal's cover. Meanwhile, J. Carlyle Sitterson of the University of North Carolina was but thirty-eight when he became the organization's secretary-treasurer in 1949. Two years later, he was succeeded in that post by Bennett H. Wall, age thirty-five, of the University of Kentucky. Both Sitterson and Wall were graduate school contemporaries of Woodward's at Chapel Hill.[33]

When cajoling Clarence Nixon into delivering his provocative paper on past SHA presidential addresses, Woodward had argued that both he and Nixon enjoyed a greater freedom because they were among the very few who apparently did not aspire to be a future "president of the Sanhedrin." Yet scarcely a year after engineering the most provocative and subversive program in the association's fifteen-year history and just a few days past his forty-second birthday, Woodward was writing his friend Lyle Sitterson to accept the nomination to serve as the group's president in 1952, professing his amazement at "what a committee will do in a moment of irresponsibility and absentmindedness."[34]

At that point, it was still difficult to see John Hope Franklin's participation in the 1949 program and banquet as much of a breakthrough. After members of the local arrangements committee for the 1951 SHA meeting in Montgomery warned that "it would be extremely difficult for a Negro to appear on the program without creating many problems and much embarrassment," the pall of Jim Crow once again descended on the proceedings. In late November 1951, a few weeks after the Montgomery meeting, incoming president Woodward's choice as program chair for 1952, Thomas P. Govan of Sewanee, wrote to ask whether "the Negro situation in Knoxville" (where the next meeting would be held) would make it "possible and practicable . . . to have one or perhaps two papers on Negro leaders by Negroes." This would be in keeping with Govan's idea of organizing the program around the theme "This Too, Is the South" and would emphasize, through the appearance of black scholars on the program, that "these too are Southerners." Perhaps with this end in mine, Govan's suggestions for fellow committee members had included Bell Wiley, who had been an eager accomplice in setting up the session with John Hope Franklin at Williamsburg, as well as Bennett Wall, Woodward's friend and former grad school classmate. He also hoped to have Robert Penn Warren as the principal speaker at one of the key sessions and "make him wrestle with the problem of the Negro which he has so successfully dodged until now." Overall, his goal was to organize the regular sessions by pairing

Cordially Invited to Be Absent

someone who was challenging some aspect of the received wisdom about southern history against someone of a more traditionalist bent. In short, he meant to make the program lively and attractive enough to ensure that the meeting became something more than simply an opportunity for members to socialize.[35]

Replying to Govan's query about the racial climate in Knoxville, Woodward advised him that he had requested that, insofar as possible, local arrangements committee chair J. Wesley Hoffman of the University of Tennessee make dining and other arrangements that would allow black members to participate without incident or embarrassment. Hoffman had taken the request "without blinking," he reported, and "I assume, but do not know for sure, that the arrangements will be made accordingly." Woodward encouraged Govan to make the most of this apparent dispensation, but he was also concerned that the beachhead established at Williamsburg could be eroded if subsequent black speakers gave less than stellar performances. Accordingly, he cautioned Govan that "colored talent is scarce and we would not want to make a choice purely on the basis of colored." Govan's proposed theme for the program seemed to lend itself to black participation, but Woodward urged him to take care, lest, in pursuing that objective, "the theme could be strained to the point of appearing forced." As "not only an admirer but an envyer [sic] of Warren's historical talent," Woodward urged Govan to "do everything you can to enlist his interest. Of course, we would take anything he suggested, but if you can get him on the theme of the bane of Southern history, which he has in mind in all his novels and his projected novel, it would be wonderful. I would consider a paper by him as the triumph of the occasion."[36]

There is no record in Woodward's correspondence of any exchange with Hoffman specifically addressing the issue of black members attending the meeting, although he might have talked with him a few weeks earlier at the SHA meeting in Montgomery. At any rate, regardless of whether Woodward truly saw no reason to worry about things going awry on that front in Knoxville at that point, he had recently removed another racial barrier within the group by appointing John Hope Franklin to the membership committee, and he advised Franklin, in January 1952, that "the Knoxville situation seems promising, so far as the inter-racial situation is concerned." Govan remained skeptical, however, and as he and Wiley prepared to invite several black scholars to participate in the program, he thought it best that Woodward seek reassurance from Hoffman that this could be done without fear of any untoward incident. Woodward followed up with Hoffman in early February, letting him know that Govan planned to place one or two black scholars on the program and was seeking assurance that this could be done without awkwardness or embarrassment. "I told him that I thought it could," he added, but "I am writing you for confirmation."[37]

Several weeks later, still with no confirmation from Hoffman in hand, Govan again prodded Woodward, telling him that he was heading down to Atlanta shortly to meet with Wiley, "so if you can give me any information in regard to our colored brethren it would be helpful." After conferring with Wiley, Govan sent Woodward a tentative copy of the program, which included a paper by Elsie Lewis, who, he explained, was "colored" and a student of Avery Craven at the University of Chicago, and "well thought of by him." Woodward responded that "the tentative program sounds swell to me, with a lot of variety, color, and interest." His only suggestion was that Govan might want to contact "Rayford Logan, the Negro historian," who, he added, "has something of a chip on his shoulder, but might be mollified by an invitation." In the meantime, as February drew to a close without a response from Hoffman, Woodward had again let him know of the committee's interest in having one or two black speakers on the program, adding, "I trust that is all right." It was almost mid-March before he finally heard from Hoffman, who wrote then only to resign from his local arrangements post, ostensibly because he planned to go on leave in order to teach in the University of Maryland's extension program in Europe. Hoffman informed Woodward that his junior colleague LeRoy Graf would succeed him as committee chair, but he still made no mention of how black members might be received in Knoxville hotels, and curiously, neither did Woodward when he wrote Graf to thank him for assuming Hoffman's duties.[38]

From that juncture forward, Woodward appeared to proceed, much as he had three years earlier in Williamsburg, on the blithe assumption that this further effort to push the racial envelope would likewise come off without incident. Yet barely a week before the members were to assemble, he registered sheer panic as he informed Govan that "Knoxville hotels have struck against Negro diners and things are in a mess at the moment. I had been positively assured that this had been taken care of." There is no record of his receiving any such assurance from anyone in Knoxville, although the management of the Farragut Hotel had apparently agreed to allow integrated dining during official SHA functions only to back out at the last moment. Bennett Wall was still finding his way as secretary-treasurer of the SHA, but he knew quite well that, for all his former classmate's prowess as a scholar, "Vann couldn't organize anything!" Knowing Woodward would neither stand for a segregated presidential banquet nor be of any help in devising the means whereby this could be avoided, Wall realized that it would fall to him and Graf to somehow resolve this crisis. To Graf's dismay, the University of Tennessee's faculty club also flatly refused to host an integrated banquet. After faring no better with other dining establishments within the city, he seized upon the idea of contacting the management at Whittle Springs, a small resort just north of Knoxville that catered to summer tourists. When a deal was struck, he informed the appropriate people at the Farragut Hotel that he was taking the banquet and an estimated 270 diners elsewhere, dismissing their threat to sue the SHA by pointing out that he had negotiated with them as an individual rather than as an official representative of the organization. In the interim, he had persuaded university officials that they should at least provide buses to take some of the historians out to Whittle Springs, and other members agreed to form carpools to ensure that no one missed the banquet. It was a memorable evening, to be sure, but, coupled with Woodward's customary halting and mumbled delivery, the drama and distracting circumstances of the occasion largely blunted the immediate impact of his presidential address. Only in print would the brilliance and timeliness of "The Irony of Southern History" begin to shine through.[39]

Although a group of younger, more liberal white members showed both pluck and commitment in refusing to abide by the Jim Crow allegiances of a host hotel in 1952, the SHA was still a long way from being able to guarantee black members' full participation in a given meeting, much less from one year to the next. This became painfully apparent the following year when the headquarters hotel for the 1953 meeting in Jacksonville refused to allow an integrated banquet before the presidential address. At this, SHA president Kathryn A. Hanna called on the association's executive council to develop a formal policy on the treatment of all members, black or white, in convention hotels. In the ensuing deliberations, Woodward introduced a resolution requiring that future meeting sites be chosen only "with the understanding that it is the policy of the Association that every reasonable effort be made to accommodate all members at all formal sessions of the convention." Although this proposal failed to specify that black members could not be barred from eating or sleeping at convention hotels, there was enough opposition to deadlock the council and force ex-officio member Secretary-Treasurer Ben Wall to break the tie by voting in the affirmative. If approval of this resolution, even by the thinnest of margins, suggested that a new generation of movers and shakers were eager to see the Southern Historical Association shake free of the region's racial encumbrances, the very thinness of that margin indicated that certain members of the preceding generation were not. One of these was the incoming SHA president for 1954, Francis Butler Simkins, who went on to use his presidential address to lecture his fellow southern historians about tolerating the South's past, including its racial traditions.[40]

In 1955, Simkins's presidential successor, Bell Wiley, pressured the Peabody Hotel in Memphis into hosting a banquet session featuring speeches by not only William Faulkner but prominent black educator Benjamin E. Mays. Yet the barrier to securing rooms at convention hotels for black members held fast. John Hope Franklin illustrated the difficulties imposed on him by this practice when he agreed to serve on the program committee for the Memphis meeting only so long as he did not actually have to attend. He refused, as he explained to Howard Beale, to "subject myself to the inconvenience and risk of humiliation involved" because Memphis was "a terrible town with the most rigid patterns of segregation." He would be left effectively stranded at a hotel where he could not stay, Franklin explained, because white cabbies would not pick up black passengers, while black cabbies disliked venturing into "'the white part of town' since return fares are impossible."[41]

It was not so surprising to encounter such a stance at the Peabody, the storied watering hole of the Mississippi Delta's planter elite, but in fact, the National Association for the Advancement of Colored People failed to find a single hotel in the South in the mid-1950s that would accommodate black lodgers under any circumstances. By the end of the decade, hotels of suitable convention size in three Florida cities, plus Kansas City, Saint Louis, Oklahoma City, and Williamsburg had abandoned their proscriptions against renting rooms to blacks. Yet, despite several aggressive attempts to move beyond it, the so-called Woodward resolution would define the SHA's position on the treatment of its black members at its annual meeting until 1961, when it was amended to stipulate that blacks must be allowed "to attend all official functions . . . including those at which meals are served." This move still fell short of requiring convention hotels to accept black members as overnight guests, but, despite the absence of such a formal policy, beginning with the 1962 meeting in Miami, Secretary-Treasurer Wall and members of the executive council appeared simply to take it on themselves to ensure that black members attending the meetings would enjoy the same access to lodging and all the privileges accorded white guests at the host hotel. Only at that point could it be said that the old Jim Crow taboos that had tainted the spirit and undermined the purpose of SHA meetings for nearly three decades were finally yielding to the forces of change that Woodward had brought to bear on the Williamsburg proceedings in 1949.[42]

Cordially Invited to Be Absent

Meanwhile, after playing his own key role in the breakthrough achieved on that occasion, John Hope Franklin was soon trying to build on it through his work with Thurgood Marshall and the NAACP Legal Defense Fund. He first did this in a case that led to the admission of a young black teacher, Lyman Johnson, to the graduate program in history at the University of Kentucky in 1949. By August 1952 Marshall's team was preparing to make their initial arguments before the Supreme Court in the massive *Brown v. Board of Education* suit against de jure segregation in public schools, although, pleading prior commitments, Franklin managed initially to sidestep a request to prepare briefs for the suit.[43]

He would soon find Marshall's calls for help harder to resist. After hearing the case in December 1952, the justices opted in June 1953 to place it back on the docket for argument during the Court's fall session. At the same time, they also asked both parties to the case to consider, among other things, whether the framers and supporters of the Fourteenth Amendment in Congress and later in the ratifying states believed "it would abolish segregation in the public schools." If the answer here was that they did not, the Court wanted to know whether framers of the amendment felt that certain of its provisions might either empower members of later Congresses to take such action or allow the Supreme Court, in consideration of future circumstances, "to construe the amendment as abolishing segregation of its own force." At that point, Marshall did not so much ask as summarily decree that Franklin would be spending much of his time over the next several months working with him in the Legal Defense Fund's New York offices.[44]

While Franklin was spending his weekends digging out every possible example of southern whites' efforts to circumvent the Fourteenth Amendment, John A. Davis, who headed the LDF's research task force, took the Court's questions to mean that its "background knowledge of the historical period" was incomplete at best. Looking to remedy this, he turned to Woodward in July 1953, asking if he would provide a report outlining "the main political and economic factors at work with regard to the South from 1865 to 1913." Though he anticipated that part of the report might amount simply to a summation of the two books Woodward had recently published on the period, it needed to be sufficiently detailed and documented. Woodward was teaching at the University of Tokyo that summer and would not be back in the United States until August 21, at which point, he explained, he would be tied up for at least ten days, leaving him little more than two weeks before he must resume teaching at Johns Hopkins. Despite the prospect of drawing primarily on his work in *Origins* and *Reunion and Reaction*, Woodward was concerned about the limited time he might have to complete the assignment and wondered if he could do full justice to Davis's request. Beyond that, he cautioned Davis that "in preparing such a document, I shall feel constrained by the limitations of my craft," meaning that he did not "want to get out of my role as historian" and become an advocate instead. Finally, he wanted to know if his paper would be "subject to alteration by counsel" and "whether any compensation might be expected." If he could be reassured on all these concerns, Woodward agreed "to make the attempt."[45]

Davis responded that there would indeed be an honorarium (which proved to be $400), but the best news was that the reargument had been postponed until December 7, meaning that Woodward would now have considerably more time to prepare his report. Addressing Woodward's concerns about maintaining his scholarly integrity and independence, Davis assured him that "your conclusions are your own" and explained that "if they do not help our side of the case, in all probability, the lawyers will not use them." In any event, Davis felt that Woodward's contributions would be most helpful to the lawyers charged with "answering some of the arguments of the opposition." Davis also confirmed that he wanted Woodward to trace postbellum race relations to their "political and economic base." To Davis, this meant first examining the intent of the framers of the Thirteenth and Fourteenth Amendments and the Civil Rights Acts of the Reconstruction era and the way they were understood by opponents as well as members of the state legislatures and conventions that ratified them. Then Woodward could proceed to show how economic and political forces worked to thwart or otherwise alter their original intent, with the eventual concurrence of the President, Congress, and Supreme Court. Ideally, Davis thought, Woodward's report would demonstrate that the Reconstruction era crusade for full and immediate equality for the freedmen "was caught up in a complex economic, historical and political situation." The constitutional basis for these earlier efforts was still there, however, and Davis believed that the current national and global racial, economic, and political climate not only favored such action but demanded it. Still, lest he appear to be dictating what Woodward would write, he asked him to "note that I say the resultant impact of what you have to say will be this; you do not have to say it."[46]

As it turned out, Woodward did not say it or come any closer even to suggesting it than he had in *Reunion and Reaction*. Nor did he go beyond general references to the "equalitarian purposes and idealistic aims" of the Radical Republicans to examine the specific intent of the framers of the Civil Rights Acts and the Fourteenth Amendment or the way these were understood

Cordially Invited to Be Absent

by those who supported or opposed them. Instead, perhaps taking Davis a bit more literally than he had hoped, he submitted a twenty-seven-page, double-spaced typescript on "The Background of the Abandonment of Reconstruction" that was essentially lifted, often verbatim, from *Reunion and Reaction*.[47]

Although Woodward had granted a degree of sincerity to the Radicals' idealism in that book, he found it no match for the overpowering greed and determination of northern industrial and commercial interests. Hence, his report began with a cautionary reminder. Not only were "the equalitarian purposes and idealistic aims" of the Radical Republicans pursued with less ardor and firmness as Reconstruction progressed, but they were forced to coexist from the outset with other, largely pragmatic and material objectives, consisting primarily of advancing the tightly conjoined interests of the Republican Party and those of "a [northern] sectional economy." Moreover, any conflict between the more idealistic objectives and those more nakedly partisan and regional in nature was almost always resolved in favor of the latter.[48]

In fact, Woodward noted, the short-lived heyday of Radical Republicanism was largely confined to the years 1866–68. From that point on, despite the lip service still accorded the righteous outrage of Thaddeus Stevens and Charles Sumner, the party's true priorities shifted rather abruptly to representing northern business interests through policies geared to establishing and maintaining social and political order and promoting sectional reconciliation at the expense of further agitation for racial equality or black rights. In fact, this overriding Republican emphasis on acquiring and protecting private wealth and property left the hard-won rights of the freedmen to be steadily chipped away through a process of "compromise and concession." Woodward offered this observation on page 2 of his report and made no further mention of the fate of the former slaves until page 25, where he simply quoted an editorial from a once staunchly Radical Washington newspaper touting the wisdom of allowing old white ruling orders of the South to reassert their dominion over "the native menial classes."[49]

Relying almost exclusively on *Reunion and Reaction* throughout, he devoted much of his report to the behind-the-scenes political and economic maneuvering and machinations leading to the Compromise of 1877. Instead of directly addressing the NAACP legal team's central question about the intent of the framers and supporters of the Fourteenth Amendment, Woodward came closer to dismissing it as largely academic when he concluded that "the future of four million freedmen and their progeny for generations to come" had turned not on the "constitutional amendments and wordy statutes" that marked the beginnings of Reconstruction but "on the bargain that sealed its demise."[50]

NAACP lawyer Jack Greenberg recalled a half century later that part of Woodward's argument had ultimately been incorporated into a section of the team's brief concerning early interpretations emphasizing the egalitarian focus of the Fourteenth Amendment. Greenberg also believed that Woodward's views had been encapsulated in a few sentences in their "Summary Argument," which held that the intent of the amendment as framed was to effect "a revolutionary change in our state-federal relationship by denying to the states the power to distinguish by race." Woodward himself, however, had made direct mention of the Fourteenth Amendment only once, in the first paragraph of his report, and he came no closer to addressing its specific intent than listing it as one of several manifestations of the initial "idealistic and humanitarian aims of Reconstruction [that] were concerned with the liberation and protection of the Negro freedman." Another LDF historical consultant, Rayford W. Logan, did not criticize Woodward directly for his heavy emphasis on economic forces. Yet, fearing that his report might be construed as simply saying that the Compromise of 1877 "had nothing to do with the Negro, Reconstruction or the Fourteenth Amendment," Logan warned Thurgood Marshall that "economics must not be overstressed" at the expense of "the political aspects of the Compromise . . . that necessarily had overtones of the growing concept of the inferiority of the Negro."[51]

Whatever the overall importance of Woodward's commissioned report to the NAACP's argument, not a great deal of its actual content or argument surfaced in the final brief. His suggestion that the "pragmatic and material ends" of Reconstruction ultimately prevailed at the expense of its earlier, more idealistic aims made its appearance, as did his observation that the Compromise of 1877 did more than the Fourteenth and Fifteenth Amendments and various other civil rights measures to shape "the future of four million freedmen and their progeny." On the other hand, his attempt to explain the economic forces behind the compromise got no more than a brief mention in a footnote referring readers to *Reunion and Reaction* for "an elaborate and detailed explanation of the argument."[52]

On the other hand, seeking an academically credible interpretative summary of the emergence of the Jim Crow South that was compatible with their argument, the lawyers seized on two sentences from *Origins*, where Woodward had written: "Whether by state law or local law, or by the more pervasive coercion of sovereign white opinion, 'the Negro's place' was gradually defined—in the courts, schools, and libraries, in parks, theaters, hotels and residential districts, in hospitals, insane asylums—everywhere, including on sidewalks and in cemeteries. When complete, the new codes of white supremacy were vastly more complex than the antebellum slave codes or the Black Codes of 1865–66, and if anything, they were stronger and more rigidly enforced."[53]

By these means, the authors of NAACP brief explained, "the Negro was effectively restored to an inferior position through laws and through practices, now dignified as 'custom and tradition.'" When the Supreme Court upheld the doctrine of "separate but equal" accommodations and facilities for blacks in the precedent-setting *Plessy v. Ferguson* ruling in 1896, it affirmed the "reasonableness" of Louisiana's railroad segregation statute because it reflected "the established usages, customs and traditions of the people." The NAACP lawyers in the *Brown* case countered that surely no "Constitutional sanction" should be accorded "customs, traditions and usages" that once buttressed the institution of slavery and now thwarted the intentions of the framers of the Thirteenth, Fourteenth, and Fifteenth Amendments to ensure a "complete break" with the era of slavery. Therefore, drawing on Woodward's analysis in *Origins*, the LDF team contended that the separate but equal doctrine advanced in *Plessy* must be seen as "part of an overriding purpose to defeat the aims of the Thirteenth, Fourteenth and Fifteenth Amendments." The current Court now had the opportunity at long last to overturn this egregious ruling and move to remediate the injustices it had perpetuated, and the first and most vital step in the process lay in fully and finally repudiating the concept of "separate but equal."[54]

Woodward had participated in conference discussions of the NAACP legal team's arguments and joint critiques of early drafts of the reports filed by his fellow advisers, and he alerted Thurgood Marshall to some troubling evidence that ran counter to his team's arguments. Yet neither he nor any of the other scholars working with the LDF attorneys put in the hours logged by John Hope Franklin, who spent several months commuting each weekend from Washington to New York, working at the frenetic pace set by the indefatigable Marshall. Neither was Woodward as directly involved in the strategizing as other research consultants including constitutional experts Alfred H. Kelly and Howard J. Graham.[55]

Along with the noncommittal and dispassionate tenor of his report, Woodward's restrained role in other efforts to bolster the NAACP's case may have reflected his genuine concerns about becoming less an objective historian than an active advocate. In voicing these concerns, which had not appeared to trouble him terribly in the past and would seem even less of a deterrent in the future, he may have also been trying to avoid revealing another reservation that he was reluctant to share. Although he obviously supported the NAACP lawyers' aims, he was deeply skeptical from the beginning of their contention that the framers of the Fourteenth Amendment truly intended to outlaw or preclude racial segregation in the schools. In fact, some four years after the original *Brown* decree, he would admit to "numerous doubts . . . about the depth and extent of the original Republican commitment to racial equality." In the years to come, he would expand on some of these doubts, especially concerning the motivation behind both the Fourteenth Amendment and its immediate predecessor, the Civil Rights Act of 1866.[56]

In the meantime, Woodward's rather narrowly focused report for the NAACP lawyers had left it up to others to respond to the Court's request for evidence that the framers and supporters of the Fourteenth Amendment believed that it either would or potentially could prohibit school segregation. If the Justices were already leaning toward overturning the *Plessy* decision when they issued this request, they may have hoped to ground such a momentous and almost certainly controversial ruling in a determination of the "original intent" of the parties sponsoring and supporting the Fourteenth Amendment. In keeping with Woodward's suspicions, however, the NAACP team uncovered scarcely any direct evidence that many, let alone most, of the amendment's backers saw it prohibiting segregation at that point or even offering a judicial basis for doing so in the future. There was also the rather disquieting fact that the very same Congress that submitted the amendment to the states had provided for segregated schools in the District of Columbia, while most of the states ratifying the amendment had either continued to maintain segregated schools or established them thereafter.

Appearing neither surprised nor concerned, however, Thurgood Marshall had explained to his empty-handed researchers that, even though they lacked adequate proof to win the historical argument outright, with the Court apparently leaning their way, he felt that simply fighting the other side to a draw "means we win." Thus, he exhorted his staff to go back to their notes and tease out at least enough substance for their argument to "get by those boys down there.'" One adviser took this to mean putting sufficient "gloss" on certain "fateful events" to persuade the Justices that they at least had "something of a historical case" for their expansive take on the Fourteenth Amendment. Ironically enough, the historians who cooperated in this effort ultimately registered perhaps their greatest contribution when the Court declared the

Cordially Invited to Be Absent

evidence offered in the case "inconclusive" and shifted its focus to the injurious effect of segregation on blacks.[57]

As Woodward seemed to anticipate, Marshall's strategy obviously put the other scholars on his research team in a tough spot by forcing them to choose between what Alfred Kelly called "my professional integrity as a historian" and his personal "wishes and hopes" about how the Court would rule. Although they had not stooped to the point of submitting outright fabrications, Kelly admitted that he and some of his colleagues had nonetheless "manipulated history" by "carefully marshaling every possible scrap of evidence in favor of the desired interpretation and just as carefully doctoring all the evidence to the contrary, either by suppressing it when that seemed plausible, or by distorting it when suppression was not possible." John Hope Franklin later acknowledged that, working under Marshall's direction, he, too, had "deliberately transformed the objective data provided by historical research into an urgent plea for justice." This was essentially what Woodward had expressed his unwillingness to do upon his first contact with the NAACP's John A. Davis, and there was nothing in the final report he submitted to indicate that his position had changed. In pushing for racial integration to date, he had largely spoken through his actions as an individual rather than through his words as a historian. A few months after the *Brown* decree, however, he would prove more amenable to straddling the line between scholarship and advocacy in the interest of furthering what would stand as the worthiest American cause of the twentieth century.[58]

8

A Fundamental Attack upon the Prevailing View

Launching *The Strange Career of Jim Crow*

Woodward had largely stuck to his vow to exercise scholarly restraint in his role as adviser to the NAACP legal team in the *Brown* case, resisting the impulse to join some of his colleagues in manipulating the meaning of what little evidence they could find to suggest that the framers of the Fourteenth Amendment saw it precluding racially segregated public schools. In the end, he may have thought it just as well that the Justices had grounded their opinion, not in the findings of historians, but in what he called "sociological evidence" of the damaging social and emotional impact of school segregation on black pupils. Reflecting on the experience some thirty years later, though, he could see that, although his involvement with the NAACP legal team was hardly crucial to the outcome of the case, it had left him deeply and openly "committed" to doing what he could to encourage public support for the decree. In any case, once the ruling came down, he clearly proved less squeamish about breaching the line between scholarship and advocacy than he had indicated in his early communications with the NAACP lawyers.[1]

In May 1953, nearly a year to the day before the *Brown* decision was announced, Professor S. V. McCasland of the University of Virginia had invited

Woodward to deliver the university's James W. Richard Lectures in the fall of 1954. The Richard Lectures ranked as one of the school's most prestigious lecture series. Recent lecturers included the distinguished historian of ideas Crane Brinton and noted philosopher and theologian Paul Tillich, and the university provided an honorarium of $1,000, quite a hefty sum by the standards of the day. The lectures also carried the assurance of publication, although, as McCasland explained, the University of Virginia would retain the rights to the book itself and hence receive all the royalties it generated. After some exchanges over scheduling the lectures so as to allow Woodward to meet his commitments as the next Harmsworth Professor at Oxford University, which required him to be in residence before the end of the year, the lectures were set for September 28–30, 1954.[2]

John Hope Franklin recalled spending a whole day brainstorming with Woodward in 1953 over his plan to use the lectures at Virginia to counter "the segregationists and their Jim Crow," but as of late June 1954, with scarcely three months remaining before he was to deliver the lectures, Woodward had yet to settle on a topic. As he often did in such circumstances, he turned to Rupert Vance for advice. At that point, he was toying with the idea of using the lectures to mark the end of a discrete period in southern history that might be called "The New South" or "The Era of the Compromise." The proposed lectures, he explained, would argue that the racial, political, and economic arrangements secured by the Compromise of 1877 had "crumbled in the last five, ten, twelve (How many would you say?) years." Seeking Vance's help in choosing a development or event that best signaled the end of the era defined by these arrangements, he floated FDR's more reform-oriented "Second New Deal," World War II, and finally "The Segregated Schools Decision of May 17?" Though this was his only direct reference to the recent *Brown* ruling, he clearly saw its potential to upend the entire southern racial system and thus open the curtain on a distinctly new stage in the region's history. Even so, Woodward hastened to assure Vance that he was by no means wedded to this theme for the lectures, and he might still decide to go in another direction in "the next week or so."[3]

And so he did, although it is not precisely clear when he reached his decision. Not until late August, with the lectures now barely a month away, did Woodward write Edward Younger, his fellow southern historian at Virginia, to assure him that, after devoting what he called a "hard summer" to the task he was about to finish a full draft of all the lectures, although he still wanted to "juggle a bit with the titles" of the three presentations. The tentative title for the set of lectures, however, was "The Strange Career of Jim Crow." The topic might not be appealing to some, he conceded, but the lectures were at least "fairly timely."[4]

Scarcely three months had passed since the *Brown* decree rendered the South's racial future uncertain, but Younger did not seem concerned that Woodward's lectures might further aggravate already sensitive feelings about the ruling. Rather, he saw Woodward's topic offering "a great opportunity to do some immediate good here in this state." Younger assured Woodward that UVA president Colgate Darden seemed "as enthusiastic about it as I am" and reported that, provided Woodward's message was "temperate," Darden even wanted "to get a copy of the book into the hands of each member of the legislature. . . . I think he is sincere."[5]

"I hope I won't let President Darden down," Woodward replied, but he surely had reason to wonder what Darden, a former governor once tied to the forthrightly segregationist Virginia senator Harry F. Byrd, might have meant by "temperate." At that point, Darden was still contending that segregation could be preserved in undergraduate as well as secondary and primary education. On the other hand, he was also savvy enough to understand that racially separate, indisputably unequal programs of graduate and professional education had no hope of surviving judicial scrutiny. As Woodward doubtless knew, the University of Virginia had already admitted several black graduate and professional applicants, although another year would elapse before the first black underclassmen arrived on campus. What Woodward probably did not know as he prepared what he called a "fundamental attack upon the prevailing view . . . used to justify and defend the system of segregation" was that, back on May 18, the day after the *Brown* decision was announced, the "prevailing view" that he meant to assail had found its classic expression and affirmation in UVA's *Cavalier Daily*. Ignoring the feelings of black southerners altogether, the editor of the campus paper had flatly declared that "the people of the South are justified in their bitterness concerning this decision," which ran "contrary to a way of life" and "violates the way in which they have thought since 1619."[6]

In the space of a couple of sentences, the editorial substantiated Woodward's observation that when the *Brown* ruling came down, most southern whites and many northern ones as well still believed that segregation had emerged almost simultaneously with slavery, meaning that the two shared a common history stretching back for centuries. This notion of segregation's "antiquity" as "an institution sanctioned by long usage and hoary with age" was vital to its defense, he noted, "because it fit in with popular sociological theories of the time . . . [which] held that reform could not alter ancient custom." Woodward meant to shatter this perception of segregation's longevity, which, by buffering it against would-be assailants, also helped to preserve the white privilege it sustained.[7]

Woodward's thinking here largely anticipated that of sociologist Barrington Moore Jr., who later argued that seeing the mere persistence of such inequities as an indication of their legitimacy—or at least inevitability—amounted to assuming "that societal and cultural continuity are simply the natural state of things and do not require explanation." This inherently laissez-faire notion, Moore added, ignored the reality that, in order "to maintain and transmit a value system" over time, "human beings . . . [have been] punched, bullied, sent to jail, thrown into concentration camps," and, in some cases, even "stood up against a wall and shot." Therefore, accepting the status quo (and whatever fundamental continuities it might represent) as merely a reflection of the naturally recurring order of things sometimes meant accepting at face value the rationales that ruling elites frequently offered for some of their most brutally repressive actions.[8]

Hoping to counteract just this kind of passive and uninformed acceptance of the justifications offered for leaving racial segregation be in the South, Woodward explained that he had chosen this lecture topic because the current "national discussion . . . of how deeply rooted . . . ineradicable, and . . . unamenable to change the segregation practices really are" was proceeding on the basis of insufficient and often incorrect historical information. Likewise, some of the most influential sociological theories underscoring the difficulty of eliminating segregation were also "based on erroneous history." The theories in question could be traced to sociologists Herbert Spencer, William Graham Summer, and Franklin Giddings, who had argued in the late nineteenth and early twentieth centuries that doctrines or decrees fashioned in the distant chambers of government ("stateways") were simply no match for "ancient custom" ("folkways") formed in the actual crucible of human experience and affirmed by their persistence over many generations. As Giddings put it, whenever the two came into conflict, "Every time, the folkways will defeat the stateways." This assumption also seemed to shape the thinking of Supreme Court justice Henry Billings Brown, who had declared in the 1896 *Plessy v. Ferguson* opinion, upholding separate accommodations for blacks and whites on the railroads, that "legislation is powerless to eradicate racial instincts, or to abolish distinctions based on physical differences, and the attempt to do so can only result in accentuating the difficulties of the present situation." Woodward had also seen this thinking up close in the more contemporary writing of his benefactor Howard Odum, who had studied under Giddings at Columbia and often emphasized the potency of the South's "concentrated folkways of racial purity and dominance." Years later, Woodward would confess that although he had set up Sumner as his principal "target" in *Strange Career*, he was actually "shooting at Odum."[9]

A deeply ingrained sense of segregation as an ancient folkway and of folkways as the unassailable determinants of societal behavior lay behind the *Cavalier Daily's* defense of segregation as a "way of life" as well as the *Macon Telegraph's* warning that the federal government could not "forcefully change customs overnight." The pervasiveness of this notion posed a significant concern for those hoping for Jim Crow's speedy demise. For example, deplore racial discrimination as he might, in declining to testify for the NAACP team in the *Brown* case, Odum had warned of the "disastrous" consequences of forcing immediate integration of public schools in the South and elsewhere. Likewise, in his response to the ruling, *New York Times* columnist James Reston worried that in reaching an essentially "sociological decision," the Court had ignored the historical and cultural background to segregation. Meanwhile, on its editorial page, the *Times* hailed the *Brown* decision as good news for "All God's Chillun" but cautioned nonetheless that "the folkways in Southern communities will have to be adapted to new conditions" if black and white teachers and students were to truly enjoy "not only equal facilities but the same facilities in the same schools."[10]

Some two years after the original *Brown* decree, Democratic presidential candidate Adlai Stevenson was warning black audiences that, in implementing school desegregation, "we must proceed gradually, not upsetting habits or traditions that are older than the Republic." While he was perhaps less liberal on race than on some other issues, Stevenson practically bubbled with enthusiasm for enforcing *Brown* compared to his incumbent Republican opponent, Dwight D. Eisenhower, who simply declared, "You cannot change people's hearts merely by law."[11]

Here again, the conviction among liberals and conservatives alike that segregation was virtually impregnable to legal assault rested primarily on their impression of its longevity, because they saw its survival over so many generations as proof that no better means could be devised to assure peaceful coexistence between the races in the South. Seeing this line of thought at once bolstering Jim Crow's defenders and discouraging his would-be assailants, Woodward set out first to show that, rather than being a socially ingrained habit dating back to the early seventeenth century, segregation of the races had emerged as a rigid and pervasive practice in the South only near the end of the nineteenth, and then only because it had been mandated by law. In this he not only challenged the traditional chronology of segregation but transformed segregation itself from a supposedly invulnerable folkway into a stateway subject to removal by the same means as it was imposed.

Because segregation had largely been taken for granted as simply a fact of southern life rather than a discrete social and historical phenomenon in need of serious examination, its nature and origins had attracted little attention from American historians prior to World War II. (Even the term "segregation" had been employed only sparingly in reference to the region's racial practices before the 1920s, although its usage would spike in the 1940s.) Meanwhile, the widespread popular and even scholarly impression of its longevity struck Woodward as particularly ironic, given that middle-aged or older southerners and other Americans of the 1950s had actually grown up in the period when the system itself was still maturing. Yet, unable to remember a time without segregation, as adults, they had simply assumed that "things have always been that way."[12]

Realizing that this common assumption stood to undermine the cause of racial integration, Woodward set out in his lectures to dispel it forthwith. Though hard evidence was sorely lacking, one way or the other, he simply reasoned that segregation had not emerged in tandem with slavery because there would have been little need for it so long as slavery could be counted on to control black mobility and proximity to whites. Proceeding from one assumption to another, he reasoned further that emancipation had suddenly left southern blacks and whites with neither laws nor traditional codes of behavior to govern their interactions in such new and unfamiliar circumstances. Contrary to what southern historical and political apologists alike had long insisted, then, the ensuing civil rights legislation and constitutional amendments of the Reconstruction era could not have been foolhardy attempts to use the law to change long-established customs because no such customs existed in the first place. By the same token, the collapse of Reconstruction could not have signaled a return to so-called normal race relations, because there was no general sense of what that meant in 1877, nor would there be for quite some time. Woodward conceded that racial separation had already become the norm in certain aspects of southern life by the end of Reconstruction. Yet, he insisted, rather than marking an immediate return to a stringently restrictive, uniformly enforced code of racial conduct, the collapse of the Republican regimes ushered in a period of general inconsistency and flux marked by fewer and less rigid constraints on racial interaction than would later be imposed and defined by law, primarily in the 1890s. Coming roughly two decades after Reconstruction ended, these latter, harsher, legally mandated practices like segregation and disenfranchisement had been in place for scarcely half a century in 1954, hardly long enough to qualify as "immutable 'folkways' . . . impervious alike to legislative reform and armed intervention." Indeed, Woodward would soon venture elsewhere that "many of those who are currently defending the Jim Crow laws as ancient and immemorial folkways are older than the laws they are defending."[13]

Attacking a perception that lent aid and comfort to the defenders of segregation only four tense and uncertain months after the *Brown* ruling was announced hardly promised to win him many new white friends in Charlottesville, other than among the UVA faculty, perhaps. Still, the *Cavalier Daily* reported dispassionately on each lecture, even when Woodward pronounced it "unthinkable" that a final day of reckoning with the *Brown* decree could be staved off "indefinitely." He seemed not merely relieved but genuinely elated when he reported to Howard Beale immediately after his final lecture that his talks had "been received with an enthusiasm that quite surprised me" by large audiences, including several black students on each occasion. Reflecting on this reception a few weeks later, he chalked it up to "a powerful concern over the subject, a genuine eagerness of troubled people to know what to think and feel and say about a deeply disturbing problem." At a time fraught with tension and uncertainty about what lay ahead, he had found "tremendous interest in the South on this subject," and he assured Beale (who was by then at the University of Wisconsin) that if he were to return to the region, he, too, might be "surprised and perhaps unprepared for [the] changes in attitudes."[14]

Woodward quickly realized that this "tremendous interest" in the origins and nature of segregation was hardly confined to the South. He later professed both amazement and a certain bewilderment that what began "as a modest communication to a Southern academic audience" would ultimately reach "a national and quite mixed audience of vast numbers." Although he must have held out some hope that his published lectures would somehow reach readers outside the scholarly realm, he could hardly have anticipated how quickly this would come to pass. He had announced his topic in late August, barely a month in advance of the lectures, and there were but three weeks to go when, seeking feedback, he sent copies of the 132-page manuscript to John Hope Franklin, Howard Beale, Rupert Vance, and his former colleague at Florida Manning Dauer. Franklin recalled spending "about a half day" going over a draft of the lectures with Woodward before urging him to deliver them just as they were written. Among the other readers, only Beale, who critiqued the lectures after they were given, recommended a significant number of changes, most of them stylistic rather than substantive. For his

A Fundamental Attack upon the Prevailing View

part, Vance declared himself perfectly happy to see them published "as is," and Dauer seemed to speak for all the readers when he declared the manuscript "so timely that I think it is a shame to delay. It should come out now."[15]

Getting Woodward's take on segregation into the hands of general readers as quickly as possible left little time for considering how a book so hastily conceived and written might fare under close examination by his scholarly peers. Still, he had given no indication that he planned any major revisions before publication in any case, and this suited the editors at Oxford University Press just fine. He had left for England to assume his Harmsworth duties on the day after the final lecture, but sensing the dearth of historically informed commentary on a matter of such urgent contemporary concern, they pounced on him for a copy of the manuscript almost immediately. On October 19, 1954, less than three weeks after receiving the typescript of the lectures, they asked to publish them essentially without changes other than any he felt were absolutely necessary. And the fewer of these the better, counseled Oxford's Lee Grove, who stressed the press's desire to get the book in print by early the next spring at the latest. Because Woodward was still settling into his routine as Harmsworth Professor and had already indicated that his revisions would be limited, Grove even suggested that he might provide Oxford with only the individual pages where he had made changes, which could then simply be inserted in the larger manuscript. Three weeks later, after doing as Grove advised, Woodward noted in his personal journal that he was "rather pleased, but not wholly satisfied with the results."[16]

The galleys for the book arrived in late January with an urgent request for a fast turnaround. Woodward quickly discerned that they had not been "carefully read" by the editors. (Actually, in keeping with Oxford's standard practice, they had not read them at all, although they later relented in this case.) He was even more disturbed to find that his own rereading of the manuscript had not "produced that glow of confidence" that should come with having a new book in press, leaving him to muse that "it could have been a better book, but there wasn't enough time." Although he had concurred wholeheartedly from the start with Oxford's extraordinarily tight schedule, not long after the book appeared, he responded to critical comments by his friend Bill Carleton by lamenting once again the "haste from which the whole book suffered" because he had "to get the thing done in less than three months."[17]

Still, for better or worse, barely six months after he had delivered them, the lectures were in print as *The Strange Career of Jim Crow*, and what readers found in the book was very nearly to the word what listeners had heard the author say in Charlottesville. Although Woodward insisted that he had tailored his lectures to an academic audience, he had readily assented to rushing them into print, essentially unrevised and scarcely even reflected upon. Like his editors, he also felt that time was of the essence if he hoped that his views on the origins and development of segregation might encourage a more positive public response to the *Brown* decree. In any case, whatever qualitative compromises the accelerated publication schedule might have entailed seemed of little consequence at the time to Oxford's Lee Grove, who let Woodward know that the early reaction to his book after scarcely two months in print had already given him and his colleagues good reason to feel proud, an assurance borne out in Oxford's decision to nominate it for a Pulitzer Prize. The mad rush to get the book in print surely made such a positive first impression all the more gratifying.[18]

Some historians have assumed that the argument that Woodward was making so passionately in *Strange Career* was an outgrowth of his collaboration with the NAACP legal team in the *Brown* case. As we have seen, though, in lifting his report for them practically verbatim from *Reunion and Reaction* and scrupulously maintaining his scholarly detachment, he had effectively sidestepped some of the key contemporary concerns he would soon address more directly in the Richard Lectures. Here again, his seemingly abrupt shift to a more socially engaged posture was in keeping with his sense that, in working with the NAACP lawyers, he had incurred a certain moral obligation to do his part to ensure that the full promise of the historic ruling would be realized. To that end, he set out in the lectures to persuade pessimists and skeptics alike that the obstacles to swift and consistent enforcement of the *Brown* decree were not so formidable as many seemed to think. In doing so, he would appear more than once to allow the sense of a higher social purpose he brought to the task to take precedence over some of the professional historian's customary constraints on the use of evidence.

Although Woodward maintained that parts of his argument in *Strange Career* could be traced to some of his earlier work, the progression was not always as clear or as linear as he indicated. The NAACP lawyers in the *Brown* case had found his formal report far less useful than *Origins of the New South* in supporting their argument that, after 1877, much of the advance toward black equality registered during Reconstruction had been quickly reversed "through laws and practices, now dignified as 'custom and tradition.'" Although the language employed here belonged to the lawyers, it seemed in retrospect to offer a remarkably precise blueprint for the primary thesis Woodward would advance in *Strange Career*. Certainly, Woodward relied upon anecdotal examples lifted from *Origins* in suggesting that, before the

A Fundamental Attack upon the Prevailing View

Jim Crow laws were in place, blacks and whites sometimes drank at the same bar in Mississippi saloons and ate in the same rooms at restaurants, while blacks and whites rode together without incident in railroad cars in both South Carolina and Virginia. Such scenes would become progressively rare, however, as, over a five-year span, with Florida leading the way in 1887, eight southern states enacted statutes requiring racial separation on railways operating within their boundaries. Thereafter, Woodward had noted in *Origins*, "'the Negro's place' was gradually defined" in a multitude of settings, ranging from courts, schools, and hospitals to theaters, hotels, and public parks, and even to sidewalks and cemeteries. When finalized, he explained, not only did these "new codes of White Supremacy" prove much more detailed and complex than either the old slave codes or the Black Codes, but "if anything, they were stronger and more rigidly enforced."[19]

Yet Woodward had also pointed out in *Origins* that many of these new laws simply codified established practices, reflecting the more "pervasive" and coercive influence of dominant white opinion. If he meant in *Strange Career* to challenge the widespread perception of segregation as an indomitable, historically and culturally ordained folkway, his earlier take in *Origins* must be modified to place substantially greater and more singular emphasis on the impact of the Jim Crow laws and a great deal less on the force of established white racial attitudes and practices. Otherwise, he would be hard-pressed to make a persuasive case that, before the imposition of these statutes near the end of the nineteenth century, the South enjoyed what he later described as a period of greater racial flexibility in which "segregation was not the invariable rule."[20]

Strictly speaking, of course, a single exception would show that segregation was not "the invariable rule." The principal question was how many exceptions—and of precisely what sort—would be required to make his suggestion of an era of relative inconsistency in black-white interactions seem at least plausible. This judgment seemed especially critical because the aspect of southern life and history that Woodward's thesis addressed directly was relatively limited from the beginning and narrowed further after the lectures appeared in print in successive editions. He admitted from the outset that his argument did not apply to a number of critical institutions where segregation had gained a foothold during Reconstruction, including churches, public and private hospitals and asylums, and, most notably, the public schools. Ironically, although his lectures clearly sought to lend historical perspective to the crisis over school integration, when he argued that rigid racial segregation was a relatively recent practice imposed by law, his focus was largely confined to public transportation and public accommodations such as theaters and restaurants.[21]

Even with his thesis restricted to these categories, the body of evidence he had frantically scraped together to support it was far from imposing. One of Woodward's most admiring but incisive critics, his friend David Potter, later identified only seven discrete primary sources (although by my count, there were actually eight) for his contention that blacks and whites often commingled on trains and in restaurants, bars, and other public spaces before the Jim Crow laws appeared on the books. He had already used five of these sources in *Origins*: two first-person accounts by white southerners, two southern newspaper editorials, and one narrative of a British traveler. He supplemented these with the additional reports of two northern visitors, another southern newspaper editorial, and the perceptions of a southern black expatriate returning to visit his native South Carolina in 1885 after several years' absence, the latter two borrowed from George B. Tindall's *South Carolina Negroes, 1877–1900*, published in 1952.[22]

Had Potter examined these sources and how Woodward approached them more closely, he could have added that much of the material quoted in *Strange Career* had been lifted with strikingly selectivity from reports and accounts that, read in their entirety, might have served just as well to counter the book's thesis as to bolster it. Yet other than Potter, few readers appeared to take notice of the paucity of Woodward's evidence or to how he presented it, perhaps because *Strange Career* provided no formal footnotes directing the reader to the specific location of any of the material he quoted. The matter of formal documentation had not come up in Woodward's preliminary discussions with his editors at Oxford University Press, although at least one of his friends who read a draft of the lectures clearly anticipated that there would be "some footnotes at the back," and Alfred Knopf, who sought the rights to publish the book in paperback, advised Woodward that he wished he had provided the sources for "the extremely interesting quotations" featured in the text. While the rush to get the book in print might help to explain the absence of documentation, the sources he quoted were too few and generally too familiar and accessible to him to suggest that inserting notes would have consumed more than a few hours of his time. Although he gave no hint that he deliberately avoided footnotes in *Strange Career* in order to discourage anyone from consulting his sources, the lack of them did precisely that. He identified the specific issue of only one of the magazines and two of the newspapers he quoted. A reader interested in considering his other sources in their original context would have to be sufficiently curious to put in the extra legwork required to track down some combination of author, title, and volume number before thumbing through the publication in search of the relevant pages.[23]

Propping up so substantial a claim with so spindly an array of sources meant making every shred of the testimony he offered seem as consistent with his thesis as possible, and Woodward revealed a distinct aptitude for surgery in excising precisely the quoted material he wanted to share with his readers from what was often a mass of otherwise contradictory testimony. His selective approach accorded well with his heavy reliance on the often scattered observations of travelers such as Sir George Campbell, MP, whose published account of his sojourn through much of the South in 1878 appeared the following year. Although he did not share the title of the volume, Woodward reported that Campbell had been "impressed with the freedom of association between whites and blacks," quoting his observation that, on street cars or local trains in the South, "the humblest black rides with the proudest white on terms of perfect equality and without the smallest symptoms of malice or dislike on either side. I was, I confess, surprised to see how completely this is the case; even an English Radical is a little taken aback at first."[24]

Woodward failed, however, to share Campbell's lament, at the beginning of the same paragraph, about the increasingly "pronounced" separation of Americans "into two castes." Instead of the more relaxed racial posture afforded them by slavery, whites now aggressively asserted their dominance through "social exclusion" of blacks, who responded by seeking, insofar as possible, to avoid the settings where the two races had once regularly encountered each other. Musing over his experience serving the Crown in India, Campbell likened white and black southerners at the end of the 1870s to "separate Hindoo castes" and saw little evidence of "any abatement of [this] caste feeling."[25]

Despite the more troubling reflections that he chose not to pass on to readers, Woodward indicated that Campbell's observations about the equitable treatment of black passengers on the railroads were "corroborated" by a white South Carolinian, identified earlier in *Origins* as Belton O. Townshend, whose account appeared in the *Atlantic Monthly* in June 1877, scarcely two months after the official withdrawal of federal troops from his state. Here again, although Townshend reported that "the Negroes . . . are permitted to and frequently do ride in first-class railway and street railway cars," Woodward neglected to share succeeding sentences in the same paragraph, in which Townshend qualified his remarks by noting that while white employers might ride on the same seats with their black nurses and servants, "they would die before doing the same if the latter were traveling as equals."

Meanwhile, although white riders reacting to a black passenger entering their car might not object verbally, they were almost certain to make no secret of their "aversion" to the "intruders" and do their best to keep their distance. Overall, however, such awkward incidents were relatively infrequent, simply because, as Townshend explained, other than "politicians," few blacks could afford to ride in the first-class cars favored by whites. From the same page, Woodward lifted the writer's observation that blacks were "freely admitted" to theaters and "other exhibitions, lectures, etc." in Columbia, though whites gave them a wide berth "if the hall be not crowded." He skipped the next sentence, however, which would have informed his readers that blacks were forbidden to enter such venues "in Charleston and the country towns."[26]

For testimony on the Old Dominion, Woodward turned to a rare southern white critic of racial practices in the region. George Washington Cable had insisted in *The Silent South*, his 1885 treatise on southern race relations, that "in Virginia [blacks] may ride exactly as white people do and in the same cars." Woodward noted, off-handedly and without elaboration, that Cable's remarks about Virginia came as he "protested vigorously against discrimination elsewhere." Calculated or not, this was an understatement of substantial importance, for surely none but a handful of the readers of *Strange Career* could have any idea that he was actually referring to Cable's searing six-page indictment of racial practices on railroads in other southern states, which altogether dwarfed his brief allusions to more favorable conditions in Virginia and South Carolina. Unbeknown to the great majority of Woodward's readers, Cable had declared that as of 1885, there was not a railroad refreshment stand between Washington, D.C., and Texas where even well-groomed, fastidious blacks, regardless of their fine manners or lighter complexion, might dine in the company of whites. Woodward seized on Cable's Virginia and South Carolina references as evidence of fluidity in black-white relations before the Jim Crow laws without sharing Cable's explanation that he had not presented them as hopeful indications of racial progress in the region. Rather, as the sole variations from the harsh and rigid practices he found prevalent elsewhere, they were meant to demonstrate that black people traveling by rail were likely to find their rights trampled upon with "an ever-varying and therefore more utterly indefensible and intolerable capriciousness." Notably, all the troubling events and reports that Cable rolled into his highly critical assessment of black-white relations in the South as of 1885 had come more than two years before Florida enacted the first state law since the Black Codes requiring separate accommodations on southern railroads.[27]

Woodward also tailored the evidence to fit his argument when he turned to the Lower South, where he maintained that, although slavery had reputedly been more severe and Jim Crow laws had been enacted earlier, "segregation and ostracism were not nearly so harsh and rigid" early on as they would later become. To support his contention, he drew on passages plucked strategically from Vernon Lane Wharton's *The Negro in Mississippi, 1865–1890*, published in 1947 and one of the few relevant scholarly publications available in 1954. There, as elsewhere, when he found evidence to support his thesis, it was often nestled tightly against evidence that did not. By way of suggesting that sentiment for racial segregation was slow to coalesce among white southerners after the collapse of Reconstruction in 1877, Woodward had observed matter-of-factly that it would be "more than a decade" before the first Jim Crow law was enacted in a southern state. In this, he took no apparent note of what Wharton called the "first 'Jim Crow' law in the South," making it illegal in Mississippi to allow persons of color to ride in first-class cars designated for white passengers. The measure had been signed into law in November 1865 as part of the state's Black Codes, and similar prohibitions appeared in the contemporary Black Codes of Texas and Florida, although even at that point in Mississippi, Wharton observed, they had simply lent legal authority to an already common practice.[28]

Wharton also noted that when black legislators managed in 1870 to push through a countermanding measure prohibiting infringement on the rights of black passengers on the state's railroads, steamboats, or stagecoaches, the new law had minimal effect. No hint of this information made it into the first edition of *Strange Career*, however, even though Woodward quoted Wharton's observation, only one paragraph removed, that "most of the saloons served whites and Negroes at the same bar" in the first years after the war. He also passed along Wharton's references to a certain park and a dance hall in Jackson used on separate occasions by both races before the 1890s. He did not acknowledge, though, that Wharton had prefaced this information with a reminder that the insistence of "a large mass" of whites on imposing "a code of racial distinctions" on any place or occasion where the two races might come in contact left no doubt that "the matter [of segregation] was not entirely a problem of law."[29]

To bolster his contention that racial interaction was more relaxed and fluid in the Deep South before the passage of the Jim Crow laws, Woodward quoted Massachusetts-born essayist and journalist Charles Dudley Warner's report that during the 1885 International Exposition in New Orleans "white and colored people mingled freely, talking and looking at what was of common interest." He made no mention, though, of Warner's next paragraph, in which he alluded to the wholesale "exclusion" of blacks from hotels in the South and cited instances where, despite purchasing the appropriate tickets, "perfectly respectable and nearly white women" were denied access to certain cars while "dirty and disagreeable white people" met with no discrimination whatsoever.[30]

While Woodward's professional contemporaries in southern history either failed to pick up on his use of sources in *Strange Career* or opted not to challenge him on it, a PhD candidate at the University of Virginia showed no such restraint. Charles E. Wynes was working under Woodward's friend Edward Younger in 1956 when Woodward agreed to critique Wynes's MA thesis, later expanded into his dissertation and subsequent book, *Race Relations in Virginia, 1870–1902*, which appeared in 1961. At Woodward's invitation, Wynes reciprocated with his own evaluation of *Strange Career*, which was strikingly skeptical, especially coming from such a fledgling scholar. Pulling no punches, Wynes observed rather bluntly that, in making his case for more relaxed racial interactions before the Jim Crow laws, Woodward had "selected instances that tended to prove your thesis—as we, of course, all do when we have something to prove." Even so, Wynes added, he was "convinced that there are just as many instances of the other kind," and he had "tried to recall both sides" in his thesis.[31]

In addition to quoting the evidence provided by certain individuals quite selectively, Woodward also drew on the testimony of others, who, as subsequent research suggested, might not have been the most reliable or objective sources for a book like *Strange Career*. These included an 1878 travel account provided by Col. Thomas Wentworth Higginson, a one-time militant abolitionist who had conspired with John Brown before the Harper's Ferry raid and later commanded a regiment of black troops during the Civil War. Higginson claimed to have come south as a "tolerably suspicious abolitionist" who wondered immediately if the apparently peaceful coexistence of freedmen and whites he observed were merely a facade to conceal "some covert plan for crushing or re-enslaving the colored race." If so, he reasoned, he was bound to observe cases of whites abusing blacks and trampling on their rights and privileges. Yet his stays in Virginia, South Carolina, and Florida had yielded not a single such incident, leading him to conclude that, based on what he had observed in his three-state sojourn, southern whites seemed about as tolerant and accepting of blacks as whites in his own state and region. What more could be expected, after all, of states so recently "in rebellion" than to be already "abreast of New England in granting rights and privileges to the colored race." Higginson seemed even more bedazzled by what he had seen in a passage Woodward did not share, where he summarily declared that "the bulk of thinking [white] men see the old southern society is as annihilated as the feudal system and that there is no other form of society possible except such as prevails at the North and West."[32]

Such observations seemed strikingly credulous, especially from a former confidant of John Brown and a Union officer to boot. Yet, as other historians have shown, Higginson had grown skeptical of what direct federal intervention could achieve in the South even before the end of Reconstruction. In fact, shortly after the official redeployment of the remaining federal troops in the South in 1877, he had endorsed the move "heartily, cordially, and unreservedly." If Woodward knew of Higginson's change of heart at the time, he gave no indication of it in the original version of *Strange Career*, noting only that six years later, as he revisited the racial situation in the South, the former abolitionist had stuck to his earlier appraisal. Although Woodward would concede in a later edition that Higginson had "lost some of his zeal" for restructuring southern race relations by the time he made his 1878 excursion, he had reason to suspect this from the beginning. Based on the sources he had consulted for *Origins*, he knew that, by 1884, Higginson had left the Republican Party he had helped to found. Woodward had even noted in *Origins* that Higginson had "dissolved in tears" in the 1890s while reading Old South apologist Thomas Nelson Page's "Marse Chan," featuring an old black man who recalls his years in bondage as "good ole times, marster—de bes' Sam ever see." As historian Scott Poole later revealed, by 1904 Higginson was telling a Harvard audience that the principal issue behind the Civil War was differences, not over slavery, but over "states' rights and the sovereignty of the nation."[33]

Of the various testimonies he offered in the original version of *Strange Career*, Woodward initially felt that the most "pertinent and persuasive" came from "the Negro himself," who spoke in this case through black lawyer, minister, and journalist T. McCants Stewart. A native of Charleston returning to South Carolina in 1885 after roughly an eight-year absence, Stewart explained that as he embarked on his homecoming tour, he had "put a chip on my shoulder and inwardly dared any man to knock it off," only to return with the chip still securely in place. He had occupied seats in railroad cars so crowded with white passengers that some of them were compelled to sit on their luggage. Apparently drawing on the reports of others, Stewart declared that in the old slave states along the Atlantic Seaboard "a first-class ticket is good in a first-class coach; and Mr. [Henry W.] Grady would be compelled to ride with a Negro or walk."[34]

Upon arriving in his native state, Stewart was particularly surprised and pleased to find that he felt "about as safe" in Columbia as in Providence, to the point that he could expect to enter a soda shop "and be more politely waited upon than in some parts of New England." Not only did he witness blacks and whites dining together in Columbia, but he saw a black policeman arrest a white man without incident in the same city. With what seemed entirely genuine pride, Stewart likened the South Carolina he observed to a guiding star leading the entire South "on and on into the way of liberty, justice, equality, truth, and light."[35]

If anything, Stewart seemed more enthused about what he had seen in the South than any of the white observers whose testimonies Woodward shared. The question of whether his impressions of southern racial conditions at that juncture were by any means in tune with the perceptions of other blacks was another matter, however, for Stewart himself was anything but a representative figure. Perhaps attempting to bolster the significance of Stewart's reports, Woodward noted that they came shortly after the inauguration of Grover Cleveland as the first Democratic president in more than a generation and speculated that Stewart might have secretly come south looking to substantiate Republican warnings that a Democratic victory in 1884 would be a disaster for blacks.[36]

As with Higginson, however, there was still much to be discovered about Stewart when he popped up in *Strange Career*. One such discovery was that he was certainly no blind Republican loyalist in 1885. Indeed, like his friend *New York Globe* editor T. Thomas Fortune, whose paper had come close to endorsing Cleveland the previous fall, Stewart had already challenged the idea that blacks had no choice but to cast their lot with the Republicans. Not long after his sojourn in the South, he joined a group of prominent northern blacks who even bolted to the Democrats for a time, and in 1888 he would campaign actively for Cleveland, whose history of dealing fairly with blacks made him eminently preferable to his GOP opponent, Benjamin Harrison. Woodward may also have been unaware at that point of the close personal friendship and strong philosophical bond with perceived racial accommodationist Booker T. Washington that led Stewart, who had a framed photograph of Washington in his home, to place his two sons under Washington's stern tutelage at Tuskegee. Woodward did not quote from Stewart's 1890 account of a subsequent visit to Charleston in which he seemed to see Washington's gospel of patience and positive thinking paying off in a city "full of public schools for colored children" and alive with black lawyers and physicians.[37]

Stewart's buoyant outlook of 1890 would dissipate rapidly, however. By 1898, he had become so disillusioned with the prospects for further black advancement in the United States that he renounced his citizenship, eventually becoming a citizen of Liberia. Writing from there in 1907, he declared that crusading for black equality in America was but "a hopeless struggle." Perhaps by 1966 Woodward had learned enough about Stewart's mercurial, perhaps even manic, temperament and erratic behavior to conclude that he was less than the ideal witness, for in the second revised edition of *Strange Career*, he downgraded his initial description of Stewart's account as "more pertinent and persuasive" to "more pertinent, whether typical or not." This strategic tweak amounted to a tacit admission of the risks he had taken in offering the testimonies of individuals whose backgrounds and biases had been so little examined at the time.[38]

The paucity of Woodward's sources in *Strange Career* lent greater importance to questions about how representative their observations might be. Of the personal accounts he used, only two came from individuals likely to be familiar with the recent history of day-to-day racial practices and attitudes in the vicinity. Woodward had not passed along T. McCants Stewart's glowing appraisal of the racial climate in Charleston in 1890, but at that point, he had spent scarcely a week in South Carolina over the last thirteen years. He gave no indication in 1890 that he knew the South Carolina legislature had recently repealed the state's antidiscrimination statute. Meanwhile, his extravagant optimism about the prospects for further racial progress seemed remarkably out of sync with reality just three months later, when the race-baiting, self-styled champion of the white masses Benjamin R. Tillman took office as governor. Less than five years after Stewart's sunny assessment of the future, in a darkly ironic twist (not to mention a cautionary tale for those inclined to attach great significance to racially integrated railroad cars), Tillman sat on a train beside a black reporter candidly detailing his plans for disfranchising the state's black voters, which he soon brought to fruition in the redrawn state constitution of 1895.[39]

Brazen as Tillman's actions might seem, as the process of stripping blacks of the vote unfolded in 1895, he felt compelled nonetheless to urge the disfranchisement-minded framers of the new constitution to be circumspect enough to at least "give the [northern] people the idea that we are going to have fairness," lest "a Republican President and Senate and House come here and turn your Constitution down." If Tillman was still fretting about this prospect some eighteen years after occupying federal troops were removed from the state, it was surely of greater concern to whites in the first eighteen months after the actual withdrawal in 1877, when three of the reports from South Carolina that figured quite prominently in Woodward's text had been filed. He acknowledged northern suspicions that, once the troops were gone, white southerners would attempt to resubjugate the freedmen as quickly and as firmly as they could. Yet he apparently failed to consider the possibility that, fully aware of those suspicions, whites in the recently occupied southern states might be wary of any overt move against blacks that might provoke calls for returning federal troops to their midst. In 1878 a white South Carolina Republican assured Thomas Wentworth Higginson that northern party leaders who come down to rally their black followers need not worry that their meetings would be disrupted by white Democrats because "it would ruin them with the nation."[40]

Moreover, although the Civil Rights Act of 1875's sweeping prohibitions against racial discrimination in public accommodations would prove difficult, if not impossible, to enforce, that hardly could have been as obvious in 1877–78 as it would later become. Early on at least, the act's provision for up to $500 in federally adjudicated damage awards for victims of discrimination, plus fines of up to $1,000 and even imprisonment, could not have escaped notice, especially among railroad officials. A later study revealed that the U.S. attorney general's office reported 158 cases still pending for prosecution under the act in 1880. Beginning in the second revised edition of *Strange Career* (1966), Woodward himself noted that, emboldened by the new law, blacks in North Carolina "successfully tested their rights in railroads, steamboats, hotels, theaters, and other public accommodations."[41]

Although the Supreme Court struck down the Civil Rights Act of 1875 in 1883, on occasion the courts would still force the railroads to pay substantial sums in a number of private civil suits arising out of the same issue. The amounts varied considerably, but in a widely publicized Texas case, the U.S. circuit court eventually granted $2,500 in compensation to Lola Houck, a light-skinned, pregnant black woman whose brutal physical ejection from the first-class car led to a miscarriage in 1886. Damage awards were typically smaller, but they still invited enough litigation to spur a Tennessee judge to instruct a jury in 1885 to be wary of plaintiffs who appeared to have entered the first-class car solely to get themselves ejected "for the purpose of bringing a suit." In his study of race relations in Virginia during this era, Charles Wynes suggested that the propensity of federal courts to award damages to black

A Fundamental Attack upon the Prevailing View

litigants who filed charges of discrimination might help to explain some of the racial intermingling reported by passengers before a 1900 law mandating racial separation on the state's railroads. Although George Washington Cable had made reference to such a suit, Woodward seemed unaware, either in *Origins* or in *Strange Career*, of this potentially mitigating influence on the way black passengers were treated on southern railroads or streetcars during this period.[42]

Concerns about interventions by the courts or federal authorities may also help to explain why it was not until 1887 that the first of such laws requiring separate accommodations for blacks and whites traveling by rail begin to appear on the statute books, with Florida leading the way, followed quickly by Mississippi (1888) and Texas (1889). Not until the U.S. Supreme Court upheld the validity of the Mississippi statute in 1890, however, did Louisiana legislators write these separate-but-equal mandates into state law, with the remainder of southern states following suit in the years 1890–1900. Historian Roger A. Fischer later attributed much of the hesitation in Louisiana to lingering "constitutional uncertainty" rather than any reluctance on the part of its Democratic establishment to institutionalize Jim Crow in their state.[43]

Woodward, on the other hand, largely ascribed the delay in imposing statutory Jim Crow to the resistance of the surviving remnants of the South's old racially paternalist planter class, who sought to protect blacks from the depredations of poor whites quick to see any hint of black advancement as an incursion on their own status and prospects. He had already observed in *Origins* that South Carolina's Wade Hampton, Mississippi's L. Q. C. Lamar, and other political representatives of the old planter class were notable for their casual, easy manner toward blacks and that, so long as their influence prevailed, the "racial code" was much less severe than it became later. From the outset, though, postbellum planter-paternalists had been forced to make concessions to the "developing phobias of the hillbillies in the white counties," which intensified in the face of growing competition with black labor, not only in the cotton fields but in the mining and industrial towns of the southern uplands. Woodward had also noted in *Origins* that "it took a lot of ritual and Jim Crow to bolster the creed of white supremacy in the bosom of a white man working for a black man's wages." It was easy enough, then, to see the clamor for legislation guaranteeing white supremacy arising, not from what a black editor in North Carolina called "the best people," but rather from "the lower instincts of the worst class of whites." It was no mere coincidence, Woodward had concluded in 1951, that "the barriers of racial discrimination mounted in direct ratio with the tide of political democracy among whites."[44]

He bore down even harder on these class-differentiated racial attitudes in *Strange Career*. He pointed to an 1879 South Carolina editorial that might have "put the case too strongly" but seemed logical enough in reasoning that, with no cause to regard blacks as a threat to their socioeconomic status, the former slaveholders were naturally more sympathetic to educating them and furthering their overall development as a race. On the other hand, Woodward also cited a Florida railroad official who explained that his company's racial policies "had to be shaped to suit the crackers, as the road ran through a good bit of territory settled by that class."[45]

The first bill requiring racially separate railroad cars in South Carolina was introduced in 1889, although years of debate and bickering lay ahead before such a measure became law in 1898. In crediting the more racially moderate white upper crust for resisting such a measure, Woodward drew heavily on the perspective of the *Charleston News and Courier*, which was known to reflect the views of the Low Country elites. He quoted the paper's 1897 editorial denouncing the separate-car law as "a needless affront to our respectable and well behaved colored people" but failed to share the editor's additional concern that the requirement also stood to increase "the burdens and troubles of the already over-burdened railroads without due cause." He had already revealed in *Origins* that racial paternalists such as Wade Hampton and other like-minded South Carolina patricians had aligned themselves with the business classes of the state's major cities, but he gave no such indication in *Strange Career*. Moreover, although Woodward lifted the *News and Courier* quotation from George B. Tindall's recent study of blacks in South Carolina after Reconstruction, he took no apparent note of Tindall's conclusion that the objections of railroad executives lay behind the efforts of "conservative Low Country senators" to delay passage of a separate-car bill.[46]

Regardless of the economic motives of what he called the "Conservatives" who resisted separate coach laws for the railroads, Woodward presented their more moderate racial stance as one of a trio of alternatives to the Jim Crow solution that ultimately gained sway among southern Democrats. The others were the "radical" Populist formula of unifying and mobilizing struggling black and white farmers politically along lines of common economic interests and, finally, a liberal doctrine of equal rights and equal protections regardless of race. In terms of viability, however, it is hard to fathom why Woodward attempted to present the latter position as even remotely viable in the real world of the late nineteenth century South. George Washington Cable, whose not exactly voluntary self-exile to Massachusetts in the mid-1880s he had mentioned in *Origins* but not in *Strange Career*, was the only noteworthy proponent of this point of view that he could cite, after all (at least until the 1966 edition, in which he added Virginia's Lewis Harvie Blair to that category). Therefore, it effectively came down to only two alternatives to the hard-bitten racism of the Jim Crow era: the paternalistic approach of the Conservatives and the ostensibly colorblind model of interracial cooperation advanced by the Populists.[47]

As Woodward saw it, the Populist challenge to the Conservatives' economic and political agenda forced many of them to accede, however reluctantly, to incendiary race-baiting by their own forces in order to win over enough poor white voters to ensure that establishment Democrats could turn back the Populist insurgency. This defeat, in turn, led frustrated and bitter Populists such as Tom Watson to abruptly turn the blacks whose goodwill they deemed essential to their victory into convenient scapegoats for their defeat. This had come to pass not simply because of a sudden spike in racial extremism among lower-class whites, Woodward thought. It also reflected the slackened resolve of the white upper crust to hold such forces in check.[48]

Meanwhile, as the nineteenth century wound down, the Supreme Court was readily signing off on efforts to disable or circumvent most of the civil rights protections established during Reconstruction. As powerful economic interests beat the drums for sectional reconciliation, white northerners seeking to curb the influence of a new wave of racially ambiguous immigrants from southern and eastern Europe grew more sympathetic to the complaints of white southerners. At the same time, an expanded American presence abroad further emphasized the frustrations of riding herd on nonwhite peoples elsewhere in the world. The upshot, as Woodward noted wryly, was that "just as the Negro gained his emancipation and new rights through a falling out between white men, he now stood to lose his rights through the reconciliation of white men." Frederick Douglass had foreseen this prospect as far back as 1875, when he asked in a famous July 4 oration, "If war among the whites brought peace and liberty to the blacks, what will peace among the whites bring?" Later, in *Black Reconstruction* (1935), W. E. B. Du Bois lamented the compromise between northern capitalists and southern capitalists who "accepted race hate and black disfranchisement as a permanent program of exploitation." Still, even if the insight was not original to Woodward, he had put the sharp decline in the fortunes of southern blacks at the end of the nineteenth century into the broader national and even global context in which historians continue to explore it today. He seemed equally prescient, foreshadowing later work by George Fredrickson and John Cell, in suggesting that southern whites and South African whites of the World War I era seemed to be following similar, potentially disastrous paths in dealing with the black masses among them. Fortunately, as Woodward saw it, those paths had seemed to diverge because, however grudgingly, whites in the American South had generally adapted to the racial changes they had witnessed over the three-decade span between the end of World I and the end of World War II. How they would react to the changes wrought by the *Brown* decision remained to be seen, but at least they need not fear "the madness of self-destruction" now haunting their contemporaries in South Africa.[49]

Hindsight confirms the prescience of many of Woodward's observations in *Strange Career*. Yet it also points to his single-minded emphasis on the paramount importance of the law in imposing and maintaining racial segregation as the most tenuous aspect of his thesis, and the one most responsible for its ultimate historiographical demise. This would hardly come as a surprise to Howard Beale and Rupert Vance, both of whom cautioned him before the book went to press about leaning too heavily on laws as either reflections or determinants of social attitudes and practices. Sending a draft of the lectures for Vance's perusal some two weeks before they were to be delivered, Woodward admitted that he was "in places being a shallow optimist (an unaccustomed role for me)." After reading the draft, Vance declared himself "cheered by your optimism," but as a sociologist, he felt compelled to add, "it's an open question whether quotations from a few politicians represent the attitudes of a people, whether changes in attitudes can be dated by changes in laws."[50]

Less than a year later, with *Strange Career* still awaiting the formal appraisal of his scholarly peers, Woodward rather uneasily echoed Vance's concerns himself in reacting to an assessment of the relationship between slavery and the law written by Stanley Elkins and Eric McKittrick. Conceding that his own "recent venture on the subject of segregation invites showers of stones which I will no doubt receive," he felt compelled nonetheless to "throw a few pebbles . . . about the use of law as historical evidence." Despite the convenience of relying on legal statutes, he worried that "they are rather poor evidence for dating a practice, that they lag behind actual practice sometimes and anticipate it at others, and that they are not a very reliable indicator of what practice was actually followed."[51]

This was a rather startling admission for someone whose brand-new book described the Jim Crow statutes as "the most elaborate and formal expression of sovereign white [racial] opinion" and credited them with introducing "racial ostracism" into practically every aspect of southern life. He did allow that "custom" might have helped to make that ostracism a fixture in all modes of public transportation, not to mention a host of other venues, ranging from hospitals to funeral homes. He also cautioned that "there is more Jim Crowism practiced in the South than there are Jim Crow laws on the books" and warned that, in and of themselves, "laws are not an adequate index to the extent and prevalence of segregation and discriminatory practices in the South." (He went on to italicize the latter reminder in the revised editions of 1966 and 1974.) Yet none of these disclaimers prevented his observations from being, as he later complained, "misread," both by those who questioned his thesis and those who not only embraced it but read a great deal more into what he was saying than he had intended.[52]

For all his protests, however, it is hard to see how Woodward could have genuinely expected to be read much differently. However seriously he meant the careful hedgings and cautionary asides sprinkled throughout the book to be taken, their tone might easily be perceived as more obligatory than earnest. Neither in succeeding editions of *Strange Career* nor in his subsequent efforts to defend its thesis elsewhere would he give reason to think that he was backing off his contention that racial segregation was not fully in effect in the South until the statute books declared it so. He had mined George Tindall's 1952 study of blacks in South Carolina from 1877 to 1900 for bits of evidence that appeared to support his thesis in *Strange Career* but paid no apparent heed to Tindall's observation that the two races had rarely interacted on equal terms in South Carolina even when there was "no basis in law for segregation," which was enforced "then, as now," overwhelmingly by custom. In this, of course, Tindall largely echoed Vernon Wharton, whose earlier study of blacks in postbellum Mississippi Woodward had also quoted without referring to his conclusions. Despite such findings clearly at odds with his argument from the beginning (which would only accumulate as the years passed), Woodward was convinced in 1954 that his best hope of persuading his readers that segregation might be destroyed by legal action lay in persuading them that it had been created by the same means. Hence, rather than the mere force of old habit, the Jim Crow system must, in overwhelming measure, owe its origins and implementation to the "force of law."[53]

To support his position, Woodward turned to the testimonies of a number of black southerners who had been around when the Jim Crow laws were enacted, which, upon examination, had already led Gunnar Myrdal to conclude in his *American Dilemma* that these statutes were critical in "tightening and freezing—in many cases instigating—segregation and discrimination." As Woodward noted, the Jim Crow laws applied to all blacks rather than singling out the most unruly or ignorant among them. In this, they enhanced the authority of conductors and railroad officials while simultaneously stripping them of the discretion they might once have exercised in deciding whether reserved, well-dressed, middle-class black travelers were likely to provoke disruptive behavior by white passengers in the first-class cars. Although he did not raise the possibility, some of the racially mixed seating in first-class coaches observed by some of Woodward's travelers before the passage of the Jim Crow laws may have reflected little more than a single conductor's willingness to give the benefit of the doubt to black passengers of obviously substantial means and status.[54]

Woodward's claim that the Jim Crow laws further emboldened "the hoodlum of the public parks and playgrounds" and "accorded the majesty of law to mass aggressions [against blacks]" was certainly plausible enough on its face. The same did not apply to his conjecture that, absent these statutes, such outrages and abuses "might otherwise have been curbed, blunted, or deflected," which came with no hint of how this might have been accomplished, given the rising white racial animosities in the South and the growing white indifference to the plight of black southerners nationwide that he saw setting the stage for these laws in the first place.[55]

Bolstering an argument about the significance of a historical event with an essentially counterfactual hypothesis about what *might* have happened if what *actually* happened had not hardly squared with what his professional peers would have deemed "best practices." Still, if he hoped to persuade general readers that the force of the Jim Crow laws was both necessary and sufficient, in and of itself, to impose and sustain rigid racial separation in the South, then suggesting that their pernicious reach extended well beyond the routine interactions of individual blacks and whites surely could not hurt. Woodward made it clear enough, both in the book and elsewhere thereafter, that he had not set out to offer a full-blown scholarly chronicle of Jim Crow's past so much as to correct certain widespread misconceptions about his origins that might hinder contemporary efforts to effect his demise. His paramount objective in *Strange Career* was countering the assertions of segregation's defenders—too commonly accepted at face value by others hesitant to challenge them—that separation of the races was too historically embedded as a fixture in southern life to be removed solely by judicial decrees. As he later explained, he had set out to show that the Jim Crow system originated, not in ancient habit or custom, but in a legal framework dating back scarcely half a century, thinking that "reformers might take hope that segregation was not all that invulnerable." His intentions were clear enough to the president of historically black Atlanta University Rufus E. Clement, who hailed the timely arrival of *Strange Career* at the very moment when it could make the greatest contribution to "the embattled forces of law and order."[56]

Despite his claim that the Richard Lectures had originated as nothing more than "a modest communication to a Southern academic audience," if Woodward truly meant to influence would-be civil rights activists, he had surely envisioned his remarks attracting a much broader readership from the outset. *Strange Career* had been out in hardback scarcely a year when he inquired in May 1956 if Oxford University Press might be amenable to an arrangement allowing Alfred A. Knopf to publish it in paperback. Although Oxford's Lee Grove passed on that proposal, a few weeks later, he and Woodward were discussing plans to bring out an updated version of his book in Oxford's own Galaxy Paperback series. By the time the paperback appeared in 1957, demand for the book seemed be accelerating in tandem with the quickening pace of developments on the civil rights front. It was soon selling fast enough that Oxford ran out of copies entirely at one point in 1959, leaving its editors to order a reprinting every six months or so.

If Woodward hoped that the message he meant to convey in *Strange Career* would reach as many readers as possible, he had good reason to feel a certain fulfillment in seeing the book so quickly become "a mass paperback publication for a national and quite mixed audience of vast numbers." Yet he would never cease in the years to come to complain that too many in the massive audience that *Strange Career* attracted had failed to read it carefully enough. "Searching for the cheering and hopeful message," he lamented, his "truly naïve" popular readers had simply ignored his cautions and qualifiers as they searched for "quotable passages to confirm views, advance an argument, [or] make a point." In this, they "often discovered what they sought and used it as they wished." Woodward's reaction seemed doubly ironic. Not only had he admitted that a "hopeful message" was precisely what he set out to send, but his depiction of the way many had gone about reading his book also amounted to a reasonable approximation of what appeared to be his own approach to writing it.[57]

His complaints about nonacademic readers who found too much cause for optimism in his text might have carried more weight had he not begun to take his own relatively encouraging slant on the prospects for a timely takedown of Jim Crow into the popular arena shortly after *Strange Career* appeared in print. By 1956, he was pointing out to readers of the *Nation* that many who defended the segregation laws as "ancient and immemorial folkways" had actually been around when they were enacted. Over the latter half of the 1950s, he would publish other articles that generally accentuated the positive, even in the face of burgeoning white opposition and the ugliness in Little Rock in 1957. Despite strident, ongoing calls for last-ditch resistance, Woodward drew on both the language and optimism of *Strange Career* to assure a larger reading audience that southern racial attitudes and practices should not be regarded as "unchangeable folkways," especially when the re-actions of white southerners to the *Brown* decree had thus far revealed "a considerable degree of diversity as well as some fluidity."[58]

Succeeding editions of *Strange Career* would also attach more cautions and clarifications to Woodward's original arguments about the integral role of the law in establishing the Jim Crow system. Yet, regardless of how skimpy and sometimes shaky his evidence continued to be, from the first version of the book to the last, the text declared unequivocally that before the enact-ment of the first Jim Crow laws blacks "could and did do many things" that they were forbidden to do thereafter. Where black passengers riding "upon equal terms" with whites was once seen as "normal, acceptable, and unobjec-tionable" in some states, the supposed "folkways" on the "railways" had soon proved no match for the new "stateways" embodied in the segregation laws, which quickly made separation of passengers by race the universal practice. Determined to establish both the immediate and the enduring impact of the new railroad laws, Woodward also saw them as the critical first step in extending Jim Crow practices into practically every corner of southern life. Just as the new segregated arrangements on the railroads soon seemed as "normal, unchangeable and inevitable as the old ones," so would it shortly be with "the soda fountains, eating places, bars, waiting rooms, streetcars, and circuses. And so it probably was with the parks in Atlanta, and with cemeteries in Mississippi."[59]

Here again, if the law had been so swift and brutally efficient in imposing rigid, thoroughgoing racial segregation on the South, there was surely rea-son to believe it might be equally effective in removing it. In light of where things stood in 1955, other aspects of Woodward's take on the origins of the Jim Crow system seemed to cast doubt on its future. In coming years, histo-rians would challenge Woodward's depiction of ignorant, bigoted, rural poor whites as the real driving force behind the move to make segregation a matter of law. Yet in the mid-1950s the South was very much caught up in what he would soon characterize as "the Bulldozer Revolution," an unprecedented wave of economic expansion triggered by World War II. The region was also just beginning to feel the effects of a serious, long-overdue campaign for ed-ucational improvement. It followed, then, that, if the white South's poverty

A Fundamental Attack upon the Prevailing View

and educational deficiencies were critical to Jim Crow's survival, his days might truly be numbered.

Though Woodward stressed that the process of bringing incomes and educational opportunities for both races in line with national standards had scarcely begun at that point, he ended the original version of *Strange Career* on a largely promising note. He devoted much of the final chapter to a narrative of largely encouraging developments, ranging from President Harry Truman's integration of the armed forces in 1948 to voluntary desegregation of a number of private schools, as well as public libraries and parks. There was also, the *Brown* decision itself, and what he saw as the "surprisingly mild" reaction to it in the southern press. (Woodward had written this in mid-September 1954, of course, meaning his observation applied only to the four months since the ruling was announced.) Some stalling tactics might be expected, he cautioned, but it was, after all, a "unanimous decision" with "all the moral and legal authority of the Supreme Court behind it," and therefore it was "unthinkable that it can indefinitely be evaded."[60]

Woodward was writing squarely in the shadow of that landmark ruling in September 1954 and before the forces of white resistance had time to coalesce. At that point, he largely envisioned the cause of racial justice advancing inexorably, if gradually, via an effectively cut-and-dried, top-down legal process, mandated and sustained by the power and authority of the Supreme Court and the Justice Department. While this approach was bound to trigger legal skirmishes, he found reason to hope in 1955 that it would prove less conducive to conflict outside the courtroom. In this, he had not reckoned with the prospect that many southern blacks were poised to adopt a more directly confrontational extrajudicial strategy rather than continue to wait until the cumbersome legal process ran its course. *The Strange Career of Jim Crow* had been in print for nearly nine months when a sizable contingent of the black citizens of Montgomery stepped outside the judicial process on December 5, 1955, by launching an organized boycott of its segregated bus system. In acting so forthrightly, they immediately incurred the wrath of most local whites by putting the lie to their claims that the city's blacks were satisfied with the status quo. With her entire family under attack because her husband, attorney Clifford Durr, had been active in defending boycott participants, Woodward's friend Virginia Durr warned him that his "'Jim Crow' book" now seemed "a little optimistic from the point of view of Montgomery, Alabama." He gently conceded that if he had written *Strange Career* after witnessing more than a year's worth of increasingly hostile public reaction to the *Brown* ruling, not to mention the boycott, he "would not be as hopeful as I was then." Scarcely a month later, segregationist forces across the South began to rally to the call for "massive resistance," paving the way for a violent outburst over the integration of Central High School in Little Rock in September 1957. (Though the new paperback edition of *Strange Career* went to press before the upheaval in Little Rock, the new chapter Woodward added to bring it up to date subtly tempered the optimism that he had encouraged at the close of the original text.)[61]

Woodward might well have lumped Virginia Durr with the mass of non-academic readers, who, he claimed, had ignored his numerous scholarly cautions in taking his thesis about the origins of segregation to mean that dismantling it should be a relatively easy matter. The same could hardly be said, though, of some of the leading black scholars of the day who seemed to read him much the same way. Reviewing *Strange Career*, historian Rayford W. Logan suggested that some recently observed cracks in Jim Crow's armor might be attributable to "the relative recency of many of the segregation laws" and that "additional breakdowns of the barriers may be easier for the same reason." Black sociologist E. Franklin Frazier thought that Woodward had demonstrated that "the race problem was *made* and that men can *unmake* it, as they are attempting it today." That Frazier and Logan especially, both of whom surely had tangled with Jim Crow enough to know what a tough old bird he was, could come away from the book exuding such optimism begs the question of how Woodward could possibly have believed his eloquent, skillfully crafted attack on the historical and cultural legitimacy of segregation would be interpreted otherwise by a readership less discerning than his professional peers.[62]

By the same token, *The Strange Career of Jim Crow* would almost certainly have created less of a stir among the reformers whom he hoped it would encourage had they actually taken his qualifiers as seriously as he professed to hope they would. Contrary to what became a mainstay of Woodwardian legend, the Reverend Martin Luther King Jr. did not describe the book as "the historical Bible of the Civil Rights Movement" when he spoke in Montgomery on March 23, 1965, at the end of a three-day march from the recently bloodied voting rights battleground of Selma. Still, Woodward and several other prominent historians who had come to show their support that day did hear King invoke "the noted historian, C. Vann Woodward [and] his book, *The Strange Career of Jim Crow*," as his authority in declaring that "racial segregation as a way of life did not come about as a natural result of hatred between the races immediately after the Civil War. There were no laws segregating the races then." As Woodward had clearly shown, King maintained, racial segregation was merely "a political stratagem employed by the emerging Bourbon interests in the South to keep the southern masses divided and southern labor the cheapest in the land." When leaders of the Populist movement set out to unite the sorely exploited masses of both races in order to overthrow Bourbon rule, "to meet this threat, the southern aristocracy began immediately to engineer this development of a segregated society." In reality, Woodward had made no mention of the "Bourbons" in *Strange Career*, and he portrayed "the southern aristocracy" as reluctant capitulators to de jure segregation rather than its eager architects. Still, despite mangling certain details of his argument and failing to invoke the biblical metaphor, in drawing on his book to challenge the legitimacy of segregation and suggest its vulnerability in 1965, King was using it just as Woodward had hoped it might be ten years earlier.[63]

9

Wrong in All Its Major Parts

Strange Career Returns to Earth

More than one commentator has alluded to the "strange career" of the *Strange Career of Jim Crow* itself, but in reality, "strange careers" might be more appropriate for a book that, however inadvertently, enjoyed at least three of them. The original book had launched the first of these careers—as a treatise aimed at encouraging readers to embrace the *Brown* decision as a viable means of eradicating racial segregation—and it had entered its final phase by the time Dr. King invoked *Strange Career* in Montgomery in March 1965. After a decade in print, though, *Strange Career* was still gathering steam in its second career, extended by the new chapter added to the 1957 paperback, as a brief, up-to-date history of segregation attracting an increasingly broad audience of students and lay readers. Finally, the book's third and thus far relatively high-flying career as a pathbreaking contribution to historical scholarship on segregation, also derived from the 1955 version, was about to encounter heavy turbulence.

The 1957 Galaxy paperback version of *Strange Career* had left the text of the original book virtually intact, save for a sentence or two revised to prevent it from appearing dated in light of developments since the original went to press. "Deliberate Speed vs. Majestic Instancy," the title of the new chapter Woodward added to the paperback edition, played simultaneously on the Supreme Court's reference in the second *Brown* decree in 1955 to school integration proceeding with "all deliberate speed" and the haunting refrain, "Deliberate Speed, Majestic Instancy," from Francis Thompson's 1893 poem "Hound of Heaven." Thompson's sense of the greater virtue of "deliberate speed" foreshadowed the message Woodward meant to convey in a chapter where he sought to justify his rather encouraging take in the original version of *Strange Career* and yet tamp down the expectations of Jim Crow's speedy demise that his earlier optimism may have encouraged.[1]

There were numerous instances in Woodward's career where his real-time assessment of events foreshadowed conclusions reached by a later generation of historians only in hindsight. One of these came when he suggested that, by declining to set a firm deadline for school integration in the second *Brown* ruling (1955) and simply directing local officials to bring their districts into compliance with "all deliberate speed," the Justices may have unwittingly given southern politicians reason to believe that their persistent foot-dragging might yet result in an "indefinite postponement of school desegregation." Scattered acts of mob resistance in a few communities where desegregation attempts moved forward in 1956 merely gave further reason, Woodward conceded, "to speculate whether the New Reconstruction, in spite of its promising start, is not doomed to repeat the frustration and failure of the First Reconstruction."[2]

Despite offering a list of reasons to fret that this "Second Reconstruction" might also be derailed, Woodward devoted the concluding pages of the new chapter to tempering such concerns, noting, for example, that unlike the first federal effort to secure and protect black rights, the second one currently enjoyed significant backing from both political parties. Also, in contrast to the penniless and illiterate freedmen, contemporary black activists had already demonstrated an impressive capacity for organization and leadership. At the same time, the resolve to defend segregation seemed to be crumbling, not only among whites in the old Border States, but among younger white southerners throughout the region. The air might still be thick with vows of last-ditch defiance, but the "preponderant evidence," Woodward insisted, "points to the eventual doom of segregation in American life and the triumph of the second Reconstruction—*in the long run*." As his choice of words implied, however, he meant to caution both the supporters and the foot soldiers of the civil rights crusade that, like it or not, "gradualism" would be the means by which the "New Reconstruction" achieved its ends. Accordingly, he advised anyone who had lost patience with the "deliberate" pace of current desegregation efforts "to ponder the unhappy history of 'majestic instancy' in the First Reconstruction." However frustrating, even maddening, its seemingly glacial progression might be at times, he added, "the Second Reconstruction would seem to promise more enduring results'"[3]

The new chapter featured in the 1957 paperback of *Strange Career* almost certainly reflected Woodward's concern that faith in the ultimate effectiveness of the *Brown* decision had begun to flag. Developments since the original appeared had failed to bear out its hopeful implications, a pattern that would only grow more pronounced over the next few years. Although the courts continued to demand compliance and blacks served notice of their determination to force the issue in sit-in campaigns and the Freedom Rides, the generally hostile reactions of whites to these nonviolent protests gave clear indication that they were by no means ready to part company with Jim Crow just yet. With white resistance apparently on the rise, the relentless Virginia Durr did not hesitate to chide Woodward yet again, admonishing him in early 1963 to "be humble, you did prophesy wrong in the Jim Crow book and all hell has broken loose since then." The brutal assault on black marchers at Selma just a few days before King's remarks in Montgomery in 1965 did little to dispel the growing sense that, in his eagerness to energize Jim Crow's would-be attackers, Woodward had almost certainly underestimated the enduring resolve of his defenders.[4]

His successive efforts to update the narratives of previous editions of *Strange Career* show his guarded optimism steadily receding in the face of his mounting disappointment and frustration with the direction and prospects, not simply of the civil rights movement, but of race relations in America in general. While the new chapter added to the 1957 edition counseled greater patience in the face of stiffened white resistance, the 1966 version indicated that Woodward's own patience was nearing exhaustion, despite the apparent breakthroughs embodied in the Civil Rights Act of 1964 and the Voting Rights Act of 1965.

The new final chapter of the 1966 edition retained much of the material from its predecessor in the 1957 edition, supplemented with a powerful critique of President Eisenhower's refusal to provide vigorous support for implementing the *Brown* decree and the failure of the Democrats to push him on this. Woodward's take on these and other events leading up to 1960 revealed his continued expectation that federal action would be the primary vehicle for advancing the civil rights agenda. Still, he had already noted a growing assertiveness among black leaders in the 1957 edition, and in the 1966 revision he pointed to a critical shift toward more aggressive public activism among civil rights leaders. Despite the Montgomery Bus Boycott of 1955–56, Woodward ventured that, before 1960, most white southerners remained sufficiently persuaded that black southerners were genuinely content with their lot to simply dismiss the push for racial integration as the work of "outside agitators." This illusion clearly took a beating after 1960, which proved to be "the year of massive awakening for the Negroes of the South—indeed Negro Americans generally."[5]

Meanwhile, with de jure segregation steadily retreating under fire in southern public schools, de facto segregation in northern schools had also attracted judicial scrutiny. Protests against segregation north of the Mason-Dixon Line had grown increasingly common by 1964 and on a much larger and less disciplined scale than anything yet seen in the South. More ominously still, Woodward observed, even as Congress debated the Civil Rights Act in 1964, black anger had exploded in bloody and destructive riots in several major northern cities, including New York, Chicago, and Philadelphia. With a nationwide "white backlash" already building, five days after President Lyndon Johnson signed the Voting Rights Act into law in August 1965, Watts, a black enclave in Los Angeles, erupted in a firestorm of deadly and destructive violence that raged for several days.[6]

With the old state laws that he had seen largely creating and sustaining the South's rigid racial practices now countermanded by new federal statutes, Woodward affirmed that, "as a legal entity, Jim Crow could at last be pronounced virtually a thing of the past." Yet the violence in Watts stood as "a harsh reminder that civil rights laws were not enough." Most of the gains in income, education, and status accruing from the civil rights movement had gone to a relatively small urban black middle class. Much of the remainder of the black population still faced joblessness, decaying neighborhoods and disintegrating families, and de facto segregation in housing and school attendance. The newly enacted civil rights laws could not mitigate these deplorable circumstances; all of them demanded "broader and more drastic remedies." If de jure Jim Crow was truly dead at long last, Woodward observed, "his ghost still haunted a troubled people and the heritage he left behind would remain with them for a long time to come."[7]

As the 1960s unfolded, Woodward had become progressively more involved in writing for a public audience. The growing distress over the direction and future of the civil rights movement that he signaled in the final chapter of the 1966 edition of *Strange Career* was a pervasive theme in his increasingly frequent essays and opinion pieces in mass market publications. In these, he was sometimes scarcely able to contain, much less conceal, his mounting anger and bewilderment at seeing the long and courageous crusade for racial integration unraveling right before his eyes. By the time the

1966 edition of *Strange Career* appeared, black agitation had taken on a noticeably more radical and uncompromising cast, and for that matter, so had white resistance to it. "Looks like the Second Reconstruction is about over, 1954–1966," he observed privately to Robert Penn Warren in August 1966. "The reaction is on us and strong, northern liberals in full retreat and nothing in sight to turn them back. Colored ranks in confusion or knifing each other. . . . Congress wiping its hands of the whole cause, LBJ backtracking, backlash lashing, Kluxers kluxing, G. Wallace booming. All the classic [18]'77 signals are up. . . . It had to come sometime, and it looks like the twelve-year cycle is par for the course as in [18]'65–'77. Same thing only different."[8]

Woodward would soon make much the same point for a public audience in "What Happened to the Civil Rights Movement?," a widely read and discussed *Harper's Magazine* piece that appeared in January 1967. Harkening back to the Compromise of 1877 that ended the First Reconstruction, he envisioned a book on "The Triumph of Tokenism," in which some future historian might tell of the "Compromise of 1966" that effectively brought down the curtain on the Second Reconstruction. Alluding to inner-city racial violence, the rise of militant black separatists, and a swelling tide of angry white reaction, he foresaw the hypothetical historian first explaining "how the people wearied of the annual August ghetto riots and the inevitable call for troops, of the farcical war on poverty, and . . . the rise of racist demagogues, black and white, and their shameless antics in New York, Baltimore, Atlanta, and Los Angeles." From that point, the historian need only describe how white conservatives in both parties cooperated to bring a halt to all this while black leaders became increasingly divided, leading their former white allies to withdraw "in . . . confusion and timidity." Meanwhile, some of these whites and some blacks as well had "tacitly acquiesced in the consensus of tokenism," as a few of them even "took high office and endorsed it." Woodward's concise and adroit projection of a later historian's possible take on the untimely demise of the civil rights movement would have been impressive enough had it derived from several decades of reflection. As an on-the-scene, technically premortem postmortem that still holds up well more than half a century later, it was nothing less than brilliant.[9]

Despite his disappointment, Woodward still held out at least a sliver of hope in 1967 that the energy and drive of some of the younger civil rights advocates might yet fuel a "Third Reconstruction" that would address the shortcomings of its predecessor. The *Harper's* piece resurfaced a year later in the second edition of Woodward's *Burden of Southern History*. The book had gone to press shortly after Dr. King's assassination in April 1968, and his essay now bore a hastily appended caveat, cautioning that King's death "necessarily modifies even the cautious words of optimism with which the above essay was concluded in 1966."[10]

As Woodward had noted in that essay, rather than staying true to the integrationist aims espoused by King, in a designedly dramatic and conspicuous about-face, some black leaders now embraced a racially exclusionary doctrine of their own and rallied to the cry of "Black Power!" Elaborating on their views, Woodward had cited a Student Nonviolent Coordinating Committee position paper declaring that "true liberation" meant that "we must cut ourselves off from white people . . . form our own institutions . . . and write our own histories." With Dr. King gone, he was dismayed to find other established black leaders refusing to take a firm stand against not only the separatists but the cynical and damaging behavior of others within their ranks. On this point, publisher Alfred A. Knopf found Woodward's *Harper's* piece "too calm, cool and collected." In particular, Knopf was incensed to see highly respected black figures supporting Adam Clayton Powell Jr., the flamboyant, freewheeling congressman from Harlem whose forthright stand for black equality attracted less notice than numerous allegations of egregious ethical abuses, such as keeping a former wife on his payroll long after she ceased to be either his wife or his employee.[11]

Knopf was preaching to the choir on this issue with Woodward, who conceded that he had added more "targets of indignation" to his list since he wrote the *Harper's* article, particularly such established black leaders as A. Phillip Randolph, who had rallied to Powell's defense when some of his House colleagues called for his ouster. "I think they are driving nails in their coffin," he added. He had been especially "dumbfounded" to hear his friend John Hope Franklin apologizing privately for the black establishment's support of Powell while admitting that "he would not go on public record" with his apology. Woodward could only conclude that "we whites have lost contact with the Negro mood. I now think I was too optimistic in my article— another way of admitting I was too calm, cool, and collected." A few days later, a letter from Woodward in the *New York Times* warned against allowing Powell to become "the symbol of Negro rights and grievances." Sensing yet another opportunity to invoke a lesson from the past, Woodward pointed out that whites looking to derail the first Reconstruction managed to "discredit the Negroes and their cause" by linking both to a handful of corrupt politicians. "It would be doubly ironic," he ventured, if those bent on thwarting the Second Reconstruction also profited from the equally misguided actions of otherwise reputable black leaders.[12]

Woodward's perspective grew even darker in his subsequent appraisals of the direction of black-white relations, including the third (and final) edition of *Strange Career*, which appeared in 1974. He did concede, however, that the turn for the worse on the racial front in the mid-1960s might have been less upsetting to him and other white liberals had they not been so quick to assume at the outset that segregation had been almost wholly to blame for all the problems besetting its victims. He also chided himself and other white liberals for failing to recognize that, rather than diving headlong into the proverbial melting pot, black Americans had hoped all along "to preserve a sense of cultural identity and racial pride and unity." Seen in this light, with victory over legally enforced segregation seemingly at hand by the mid-1960s, it was less surprising to see this "suppressed yearning" finally break free "with startling force."[13]

Despite professing to understand this reaction, Woodward gave little indication that he regarded it with anything other than resentment and dismay. He made no effort in *Strange Career* or elsewhere to conceal his utter contempt for the likes of former Student Nonviolent Coordinating Committee activists Stokely Carmichael and H. Rap Brown, whom he blamed for perverting black Americans' understandable craving for a distinct and prideworthy racial identity into an angry, full-throated call for black separatism. In addition to belittling the hard-won advances in racial integration achieved by Dr. King, they had mocked his doctrine of nonviolence, even urging rioters in Washington, D.C., in 1968 to "do more shooting than looting." The cries of "Burn Baby, Burn!" had largely faded away by 1974. Yet Woodward had not forgotten, much less forgiven, those he blamed for not only condoning but inciting the 150 major riots that left television screens awash in scenes of violence and destruction between 1965 and 1968. Heedless of the practical political consequences of their incendiary bombast and indiscriminate threats, a few provocateurs speaking for a small minority of their people had cost black Americans the continuing support and goodwill of many liberal-minded and moderate whites. He thought the radical authors of *Black Rage* had, however unwittingly, revealed the utter futility and moral bankruptcy of their tactics in 1968 when they flatly declared, "No more patience, no more thought, no more reason. Only . . . a tidal wave of fury and rage." He reserved his bitterest resentment for Carmichael, who undertook a purge of whites from SNCC and vowed that the Black Power movement "will smash everything Western civilization has created."[14]

Several days after Carmichael vowed in his historic July 28, 1966, "Black Power" speech to "build a movement in this country based on the color of our skins that is going to free us from our oppressors," Woodward had bluntly rebuffed a SNCC request to sponsor a drive to solicit contributions from university faculty members. Doing so, he declared, would amount not just to "sponsoring a split in the civil rights movement" but to choosing Carmichael's way over that of "A. Philip Randolph and Martin King." Participants in the First and Second Reconstructions, Woodward later observed, had passed through similar stages, progressing from idealism and an early sense of great achievement to "self-doubt, disenchantment, and withdrawal" before "signs of the final phase, reaction, had set in." In the case of the Second Reconstruction, the protracted firestorm of inner-city violence had lent powerful ammunition to white opponents bent on reducing concern about "law and order" to a simple matter of race.[15]

This reaction had prompted race-based appeals to southern whites by Barry Goldwater in 1964 and by both George Wallace and Richard Nixon in 1968. Wallace's strong showings in each of his northern presidential primary campaigns gave proof that the backlash against the Second Reconstruction was no more confined to white southerners than it had been with the First. However grudgingly, Woodward seemed to make prophets of many diehard southern segregationists of the massive resistance era by pointing out that so long as segregated schools could be construed as a purely southern problem, "the heat was on," and brought surprising advances across the region. On the other hand, as soon as the courts showed an inclination to challenge de facto segregation in their schools, white northerners' enthusiasm for integration all but evaporated. Even northern white liberals, whose hypocrisy he seemed to delight in mocking throughout his career, took to recycling the arguments of southern segregationists who condemned integration efforts as a catalyst for unrest and a threat to neighborhood schools as well the neighborhoods themselves.[16]

A few months after Woodward lamented this betrayal of the integrationist cause by many of his liberal northern allies, the Supreme Court effectively blocked further efforts to alleviate de facto school segregation in northern cities by striking down court-ordered busing across school district lines. Woodward's earlier examination of northern Republicans' rather hasty retreat from the First Reconstruction left him persuaded that he was now witnessing a similarly fateful and climactic turn of events for the Second. Yet he studiously avoided any identification with the sorely disenchanted liberals whose references to the Second Reconstruction as a total failure played squarely into the hands of the conservatives who had opposed their efforts from the beginning. These naysayers had surely been "perverse and shortsighted," he complained, to ignore the substantial advances in income, education, career opportunities, and even social status that blacks had registered in the 1960s.[17]

Woodward offered this cautionary perspective because he understood full well how white Americans' sense of the First Reconstruction as a failure had impeded the launch of the Second, and he feared a similar focus on the shortcomings of the latter might well dash any prospect for a Third. Meanwhile, he saw an emergent mutuality of interests, every bit as toxic as ironic, between white diehards and black separatists, both of whom seemed intent on halting the civil rights movement dead in its tracks. Till the end of his days, he would never cease venting his bitterness and frustration at seeing crusaders for racial integration delivered into the hands of their enemies by an irresponsible, self-serving black minority pursuing an agenda wholly inimical to the goals and principles of a great cause in which he and many others had invested so much.

By the time Woodward was forced to admit that his optimism in the original version of *Strange Career* had been more wishful than historically justified, his book's historiographical honeymoon had also run its course. In addition to bringing the original text up to date by inserting a new chapter at the end of the 1957 edition, he had hoped to mitigate some of the scholarly criticism that he knew was certain to come by making revisions or corrections elsewhere in the book, based on suggestions he solicited from historians more familiar with the field. His Oxford editor Lee Grove had readily agreed to adding the new chapter, but in order to avoid the expense of resetting the type for the entire book, he asked Woodward to do his best to squeeze any other corrections or clarifications into the foreword of the new edition.[18]

Mindful of Grove's strictures about keeping the original text intact, Woodward managed in the foreword to incorporate, in passing at least, some comments on the proofs of the first edition that he had sought from George Tindall, whose findings in his book on blacks in South Carolina from 1877 to 1900 largely ran counter to Woodward's thesis about the origins of segregation. Tindall responded with a prediction that the book would "have a happier career than Jim Crow." Yet where Woodward argued that segregation had not emerged in the immediate aftermath of emancipation, Tindall saw the "almost monolithic unity" in white racial thought reflected in the old proslavery doctrine, not simply surviving the war fundamentally intact but making rigid racial segregation essentially a foregone conclusion in the postbellum South. Segregation itself might have been new as a practice in certain respects, but even so, Tindall maintained, it merely represented a "new application of a

Wrong in All Its Major Parts

very old idea or set of ideas." Citing antebellum restrictions on free blacks as well the Jim Crow practices mandated in the short-lived Black Codes enacted in 1865–66, he also questioned whether postbellum white sentiments for formal de jure segregation were as slow to coalesce as Woodward suggested.[19]

With Tindall's comments clearly in mind, Woodward affirmed succinctly in the foreword to the 1957 edition that "segregation is, after all, only the latest phase in the long history of the white man's ways of fixing the Negro's status" and noted that its underlying racial assumptions were "based on the old pro-slavery argument." He also conceded that some restrictions on free blacks in the antebellum era could be seen as precursors to segregation and that many "railroads, steamboats, and other carriers" had been quick to deny first-class accommodations to newly freed blacks. Finally, he acknowledged that the Black Codes enacted in 1865–66 gave "the force of law" to racially separate accommodations on the railroads in Mississippi, Florida, and Texas. When Tindall saw that Woodward had addressed at least some of his concerns in the foreword to the forthcoming paperback, he allowed that "this may serve to guard you against some possible criticism." Perhaps it did, though only for a time.[20]

Though sales of the 1957 paperback remained brisk, with the civil rights movement poised to enter a new phase, Oxford editor Sheldon Meyer approached Woodward in April 1960 about the possibility of bringing *Strange Career* up to date yet again. Not inclined to undertake another revision so close on the heels of the previous one, Woodward asked if such a move was necessary to keep the book from going out of print. Meyer hastened to assure him that whether he revised it or not, the 1957 edition was selling too well for Oxford to allow that to happen.[21]

Thus assured, Woodward resisted further revisions until February 1965, when, just a few weeks before Bloody Sunday in Selma, he informed Oxford editor Byron Hollinshead that he felt it was now time for a new edition, offering a more current perspective on the events of the past eight years and addressing recent challenges to his Jim Crow thesis by fellow historians. After more than a decade in print, the book's career as a version of the past dedicated to reshaping Americans' attitudes toward the present had a last reached what would be a fateful intersection with its hitherto uneventful career as a historical monograph subject to the judgments of Woodward's professional peers.

In considering the latter career, it bears noting that Woodward was not the only historian of his generation who published a book in this period that stood to alter its readers' perspectives on the *Brown* decision and the civil rights cause. Kenneth M. Stampp's *The Peculiar Institution*, which appeared in 1956, put the lie to earlier treatments in textbooks and elsewhere that portrayed slaveholders as generally benign masters trapped in an unprofitable system and generally passed rather lightly over the pain and damage inflicted on their human property. Pulling no punches about the horrors suffered by enslaved blacks, Stampp also sought to make their suffering more relatable to whites, by insisting that "innately, Negroes are after all, only white men with black skins." Substantial scientific evidence showing no significant physical or mental differences between the races had been around for a while, but by putting such a fine point on the fundamental sameness of blacks and whites, Stampp made sure that, like *Strange Career*, *The Peculiar Institution* lent a greater sense of moral urgency to efforts to redress the historic injustices done to black Americans. The major difference between the books was that, while the appearance of Stampp's was also timely, unlike Woodward's, it reflected a massive research effort. Some of the more conservative reviewers of the day criticized it as not so much a detached study of slavery as an outright polemic against it, but there was no disputing the strength of the evidence behind its argument.[22]

By way of further comparison, we should also remind ourselves that, despite later references to himself, perhaps with tongue in cheek, as "the Jim Crow historian," in the absence of any comprehensive scholarly treatment of the topic, Woodward's slender volume was by default not just *a* history—but for some time to come, actually, *the* history—of segregation. (Perhaps anticipating its career as such, the book's editors decided to add the subtitle, "A Brief Account of Segregation," to the 1957 paperback, although it was absent from subsequent editions.) *Strange Career* offered little evidence that could not be found elsewhere, and it by no means did justice to the overall complexity of the process it described. Still, as the only free-standing scholarly overview of the history of racial segregation in the South available, it provided both a de facto introduction to the subject and an inviting historiographical target for others looking to establish themselves in the still scarcely explored but potentially most relevant topical field in southern history.

Woodward had explained in the original version of *Strange Career* that he thought the uncertainty and skepticism engendered by the *Brown* decision demanded some attempt to shed light on the origins and development of segregation in the South. Still, he admitted that his lectures represented a "somewhat premature effort" in light of the wholly inadequate body of pertinent secondary sources available to him in 1954. He conceded that errors were all but inevitable under these circumstances and professed to "expect and hope to be corrected." Still, even giving him full benefit of the doubt, is unlikely that Woodward truly anticipated, much less welcomed, the protracted, multifront onslaught of critical attention his book would attract. *Strange Career* presented such an inviting target for aspiring revisionists because, by insisting that widespread racial segregation had emerged only after the Jim Crow laws were enacted, Woodward effectively dated its arrival back only to the final decade of the nineteenth century. By presenting the Jim Crow system as relatively new, he hoped to persuade would-be racial reformers that segregation was not so impregnable a fortress as it might seem, though he would later add that "usefulness to reformers or embarrassment to conservatives should, of course, never be regarded as an admissible test of the validity of any historical thesis."[23]

Therein lay the rub, however. In tracing the timeline of consistent and widespread segregation of the races back only to the 1890s, he essentially opened a vast chronological expanse to exploration by other historians eager to test the validity of what was known almost immediately as the "Woodward thesis." Vernon Wharton's findings in Mississippi and George Tindall's in South Carolina were effectively at odds with that timeline well before Woodward had proposed it. One of the first appraisals of his Jim Crow thesis to appear in print was the work of Charles E. Wynes, who, while still a graduate student at the University of Virginia in 1956, had shown the temerity to tweak Woodward about the way he chose his sources for the original version of *Strange Career*.

By the time his own book on race relations in late nineteenth-century Virginia surfaced in 1961, however, with Woodward's prominence now risen to even greater heights and his own professional savvy perhaps kicking in just a bit, Wynes's reaction to *Strange Career* was more affirmative, though not quite so much as Woodward later implied. Wynes did grant that Woodward's argument was essentially sound for Virginia railroads before a 1900 law requiring separate accommodations. The same did not hold, though, for bars, theaters, or other such public accommodations, where black Virginians typically had little chance of gaining entry, or of remaining inside for long if they did. The Woodward thesis should not be taken at "complete face value," Wynes counseled, because it was possible "to deduce or conclude too much, as Professor Woodward sometimes does, from relatively few and isolated occurrences."[24]

Four years later, Joel Williamson's research on South Carolina blacks from the beginning of the Civil War to the end of Reconstruction led him to echo George Tindall's skepticism about Woodward's vision of somewhat flexible race relations before the relatively belated appearance of the state's separate car law in 1897. Segregation had been a fixed practice in South Carolina long before the last federal troops were withdrawn in 1877, Williamson maintained. In fact, contrary to Woodward's claim, the state's first segregation law had been slow in coming not because postbellum white racial attitudes took a while to harden or coalesce but for precisely the opposite reason. These attitudes had already hardened thoroughly well before the Civil War and survived Reconstruction so fully intact that whites had seen little need for a statute to create in principle what "already existed in fact," especially when it might have offended "influential elements in the North." Overall, Williamson was less concerned with the timing of segregation or the means by which it had been accomplished than the reality that "the real color line" had held sway in the minds of white and black South Carolinians for many generations before it was written into law.[25]

Elsewhere, Richard C. Wade's 1964 study of slavery in southern cities offered evidence of the long-standing pattern of physical separation that Williamson had seen dating back to the antebellum era. Like Williamson's, Wade's findings were problematic for Woodward because he had simply taken it for granted that slavery would have made segregation both unnecessary and impractical.[26]

With these and other related studies to answer, the 1966 edition of *Strange Career* featured the most significant revisions to the original text that Woodward would undertake. The most notable of them appeared in a new first chapter in which he attempted to counter some of the recent studies whose conclusions seemed to be squarely at odds with his own. In doing so, he offered a first glimpse of what was to be his standard tactical response to criticism of *Strange Career*, which consisted of seizing on some aspect of his critics' findings that might somehow be construed as compatible with his own. Accordingly, he found affirmation in Wynes's suggestions of "a considerable range of tolerance" in race relations in Virginia between 1870 and 1900. He faced a bigger challenge in Wade's research on slavery in antebellum southern cities, which ran directly counter to his own emphasis on Jim Crow's relatively recent arrival in the South. Without disputing that a crude form of segregation might have existed in some southern cities in the antebellum era, Woodward was nonetheless quick to note that it was neither "uniform" or "complete," nor was it always backed by "the force of the law," which, for him, at least, remained the sine qua non of thorough and effective racial segregation.[27]

Likewise, despite acknowledging the legal mandates for racial separation on the railroads that appeared in the Black Codes enacted in Mississippi,

Florida, and Texas in 1865–66 in the foreword to the 1957 edition, he now discounted them, citing both their brief stay on the law books and their limited scope. Giving the impression that he was suddenly elevating the standard of proof, he pointed out that none of the Black Codes had required separate cars for blacks while simultaneously prohibiting racial mixing on second-class cars. Not until "much later," Woodward insisted, would laws both requiring segregation in second-class accommodations and making it "universal" in first-class cars mark "the arrival of the full Jim Crow system."[28]

Woodward found it more difficult to dismiss Joel Williamson's contention that segregation had "crystallized into a comprehensive pattern" many years before South Carolina's first separate coach law appeared on the books. Williamson's argument was based on exhaustive research, and although South Carolina had supplied more than half of *Strange Career*'s relatively few examples suggesting racial fluidity in the post-Reconstruction South, Woodward could only allow that perhaps the state's experience during Reconstruction itself "may have been exceptional in some respects." Even so, he contended that the period had been marked by too much uncertainty, contradiction, and "violent reactions" to say that black-white relations had been "crystallized or stabilized [or] . . . become what they later became."[29]

Woodward would make no further attempt to respond to his critics eight years later in the third and final edition of *Strange Career*. In the interim, however, he had kept his eyes peeled for additional studies that seemed to support his thesis, even as he continued to insist that he welcomed any and all would-be correctives. By 1971, he was sufficiently weary of sparring with other historians over his book to admit that the prospect of a continued proliferation of "monographs, pro and con," might "well be viewed with dismay." In all likelihood, he lamented, the controversy would not be put to rest even if "the preponderance of new studies continued to sustain the disputed thesis, as in the past."[30]

This was an artfully inserted dig at his critics but hardly an objective assessment of how well his Jim Crow thesis had fared at the hands of his fellow historians. Two years earlier, his close friend David Potter had observed that, taken alone, the evidence Woodward presented would "lead a reader to minimize the importance of segregation in the South in the 1870s, 1880s, and 1890s, far more than the general bulk of other evidence would do." In keeping with Woodward's proclivity for detecting fine points of agreement with his critics where others did not, two of the books on which Potter based his judgment about the relative weight of the evidence running contrary to his friend's thesis, Charles Wynes's study of Virginia and Frenise Logan's study of North Carolina, had been cited by Woodward himself as supporting his argument.[31]

By 1969, of course, the "general bulk" of evidence on this topic had grown much bulkier compared to 1954, when scarcely a handful of southern historians had done significant research on the origins of segregation and Woodward's last-minute decision to make it the focus of his lectures precluded further digging on his own. Historian Forrest McDonald later cited *Strange Career* as "an example of a historian's letting what his heart told him influence what his research told him." In reality, Woodward had done too little research of his own on this topic to tell him much of anything in 1954. Still, rather than heed the cautionary findings of George Tindall and Vernon Wharton, he was indeed more receptive to what his heart had to say. As a consequence, he had attacked the received wisdom about the history of segregation as it stood in the mid-1950s armed with nothing more than a slender, highly selective collection of scattered incidents and observations that seemed at first blush to run counter to the prevailing consensus. Here and elsewhere in his work, rather than establish the generalities of the past, Woodward chose to emphasize the exceptions that might, in turn, justify his vision of an alternative historical path leading to an alternative present. Though he insisted that he had "always tried to point out that they were exceptions and not the rule," he conceded privately in 1977 that "in emphasizing them I may have given the impression of neglecting the rule for the exceptions." In this and other instances, Potter saw Woodward caught up in an "inner struggle" pitting his professional commitment to "historical realism" against "his liberal urge to find constructive meanings in the past for the affairs of the present." When Potter posited an ongoing career dialectic in which his friend's liberal instincts "constantly impelled him to emphasize viewpoints which his realism constantly impelled him to qualify and dilute," he could surely have rested his case on *Strange Career* alone.[32]

Woodward claimed in all sincerity that Potter possessed "a remarkable gift for telling me what I think" or at least "what I would have written if I had understood what I thought when I was writing it," and Potter likely knew and understood his friend, both intellectually and temperamentally, as well as anyone. As we have seen, Woodward did not flinch in admitting that his primary purpose in the lectures came down to persuading readers, and would-be racial reformers in particular, that Jim Crow was not so formidable an opponent as he might seem at that point. In pursuing this objective, Potter suspected, Woodward's animus toward segregation in the present may have encouraged him to minimize its prevalence in the past, just as his desire to show that meaningful cooperation between the races had been a genuine possibility as recently the 1890s may have also led him to exaggerate the significance of Populist appeals to black voters in that era.[33]

In offering what remains the most incisive and probing assessment of the mind-set reflected in *Strange Career*, Potter maintained the same respectful— at times almost deferential—tone favored by almost all of the book's critics to date. The first notable exception was David Hackett Fischer, who came out swinging in his provocative 1970 book, *Historian's Fallacies*. As Fischer saw it, facing a steady barrage of contradictory findings from other historians, over the course of the 1957 and 1966 revisions of *Strange Career* and in his efforts to defend his thesis elsewhere, Woodward had taken cover behind the "fallacy of the overwhelming exception." Lest anyone miss his point, Fischer mocked Woodward for successively narrowing the scope of his original argument in the two revised editions until "it [now] applies to all southern institutions *except* churches, schools, militia, hotels, restaurants, public buildings, jails, hospitals, and asylums, gardens, railroads in several states, and the New Orleans Opera house." Fischer likewise bemoaned Woodward's stubbornness in continuing to defend what remained of the original thesis with what he described as "a tenacity worthy of a better cause." To his mind, studies by Williamson, Wade, and others in the 1960s had exposed Woodward's thesis as "wrong in all its major parts." In a classic example of the "telescopic fallacy," Fischer added, Woodward had essentially "falsified" the "very long story" of racism and race relations in Anglo-America by trying to "reduce an extended trend into a momentary transformation." Fischer's rather summary dismissal of *Strange Career* might have seemed overly harsh, but despite his markedly more abrasive and heavy-handed approach, in some key respects he had simply put a sharper point on Potter's critique of the year before.[34]

There would be other challenges to Woodward's take on the origins of segregation and other, increasingly strained attempts on his part to defend it. Despite a substantial, if largely tacit, consensus that continuing to debate the book's primary historical argument amounted to the historiographical equivalent of bludgeoning a dead horse, he went on in his 1986 career retrospective, *Thinking Back*, to refer to the "continuing debate" over his Jim Crow thesis. He likewise persisted in his by then thoroughly predictable strategy of replying to his revisionist challengers on all fronts by making small strategic concessions while playing up even the tiniest and vaguest points of agreement between their disparate arguments. John Cell had concluded four years earlier that Woodward's argument did not square in the least with the actual experiences "of most Southerners" of the post–Civil War generation.

Yet Woodward insisted in *Thinking Back* that Cell found it "hard to choose between [the Woodward thesis] and the revisionists." Likewise, Joel Williamson described the findings of his massive 1984 study of race relations in the South since emancipation as "essentially and vitally different" from Woodward's. Undeterred, Woodward pounced on Williamson's acknowledgment that "there are congruences between the Woodward interpretation and the one advanced here," taking the liberty to exaggerate just a bit in reporting that Williamson actually found "many congruences" between their points of view.[35]

Woodward was reduced to such semantic sleight of hand because his desire to make the past speak to the present at a critical moment had led him to advance an argument that, however carefully hedged and qualified, still went well beyond what the evidence available to him in 1954 could possibly justify. If he truly did not expect that his provocative, hastily assembled four-lecture foray in Charlottesville would quickly achieve the status normally reserved for a seminal research monograph, then he certainly did not anticipate spending the rest of his life defending its central argument.

Strictly speaking, though, it was not simply the steadily accreting mass of research disputing his primary thesis that helped to push *Strange Career* out of the spotlight and into the historiographical shadows. As an enduring version of the past tailored to address the specific concerns of a particular moment in the present, it was destined to bear the imprint of that moment long after the moment had passed. Eager to stress the urgency of ending racial segregation once and for all in the immediate aftermath of the *Brown* decision, Woodward had left the distinct impression that it was the most harmful and degrading condition that might have been imposed on southern blacks at the end of the nineteenth. In the short run, the crude, incendiary rabble-rousing of contemporary defenders of segregation such as Orval Faubus or Ross Barnett seemed to confirm Woodward's premise in *Strange Career*, that the practice had originated primarily as a means of pacifying the incorrigible and vindictive racists who occupied the lowest rung of the white social order.

The crusading urgency of the civil rights era had passed by the 1970s, however, opening the way for the more detached observations of historians such as Howard Rabinowitz, who argued that historians might now be better served by shifting their attention from "when segregation appeared [to] what it replaced." By this, he meant the wholesale exclusion of blacks from public institutions, organizations, and accommodations that he found dating back to the antebellum era and remaining a common practice up to the onset of congressional Reconstruction in 1867. Blacks had protested their exclusion, and insofar as possible, they had also responded to it by forming organizations and institutions of their own, but in the end, surely, they preferred separate, even if inferior, spaces, and facilities to having none at all.[36]

In the face of Rabinowitz's findings, Woodward admitted that his preoccupation with destroying segregation in 1954 had blinded him to the possibility that blacks might have actually seen it improving their circumstances at one point. This oversight, he conceded, simply underscored the "dangers of allowing present-day issues to shape or define historical investigation." He had sculpted the message he teased from the past with an eye to influencing the way Americans outside the academy reacted to specific "present-day issues," but without regard for how useful that message might be in helping them to cope with the questions and concerns that might arise in the days to come. Woodward had encouraged optimism in the wake of the *Brown* decree. Such optimism seemed sorely outdated scarcely a decade after *Strange Career* appeared, when 98 percent of the South's black children were still attending segregated schools, and efforts to end other forms of racial discrimination were meeting with violent white resistance. At that point, Woodward's readers might have been better equipped to make sense of what they were witnessing had they consulted Joel Williamson's thoroughly researched monograph showing that black South Carolinians had consistently faced not only segregation but other forms of white repression from the very moment of their emancipation.[37]

The persistence of segregation seemed all the more plausible several years later when John Cell cast it not as a capitulation to the racial extremism of the South's ignorant, impoverished rural whites but as a sophisticated and evolved system that represented "the highest stage of white supremacy." His comparative analysis of the origins of segregation in South Africa and the American South offered a bold new synthesis indicating that, contrary to Woodward's argument, "Jim Crow" was not "born and bred among rednecks in the country. First and foremost, he was a city slicker." In fact, as Cell saw it, segregation had grown more widespread and fixed in virtual lockstep with urbanization and industrialization in the South, to the point where it, too, might qualify as one of the "indexes of modernization."[38]

In practical terms, the growth of cities, the expansion of manufacturing, and especially the creation of an extensive, consolidated transportation network meant that whites and black were regularly thrust into the same relatively confined spaces. By restricting their potentially volatile interactions, legally mandated racial separation might serve as a vital lubricant for the machine of southern economic progress. It was no coincidence, then, that, as a matter of law, Jim Crow first arrived in the South by train and riding first class. In the years ahead, historians such as Edward L. Ayers and Barbara Young Welke would affirm Cell's impression that, as Ayers put it, segregation on southern railroads was no "throwback to old-fashioned racism [but] a badge of sophisticated, modern, managed race relations." Welke concurred, placing laws mandating segregation on southern trains in an emerging Progressive Era pattern of regulatory measures signaling the arrival of "the modern American state."[39]

As Williamson and others would point out, some of the strongest proponents of segregation were not necessarily hate-mongering advocates of racial persecution like Mississippi's James K. Vardaman and South Carolina's Ben Tillman. Rather they were racial paternalists like Episcopal clergyman Edgar Gardner Murphy, for whom the best hope of mitigating the brutal agenda of Vardaman and his ilk lay in trying, insofar as possible, to keep the races apart. By 1971, Woodward was willing to admit that, to some extent, the onset of legal segregation might be seen as an "extension" rather than "an end of the paternalistic order," though he remained steadfast in his contention that the Jim Crow laws themselves were put on the books primarily "to please the crackers."[40]

Finally, after more than thirty years in print, *Strange Career*'s narrow emphasis on the overriding importance of laws imposed on blacks by whites did not appeal to many in a new generation of scholars inclined to favor history written from the bottom up, which in this case meant showing blacks as something other than mere helpless victims of white racism. Rabinowitz, Cell, and others, for example, had pointed both to efforts by blacks to form their own racially separate institutions and organizations and to the role of prominent black leaders in negotiating at least some of the terms on which segregation would be observed and enforced in local communities.

Woodward had observed in *Strange Career* that "as a rule . . . Negroes were not aggressive in pursuing their rights," even when Reconstruction era amendments and statutes appeared to afford them a measure of protection. He made no mention of black boycotts pushing back against Jim Crow practices on the streetcars in any edition of the book. When he did acknowledge them elsewhere, he was quick to note that a 1968 study showed them failing in every instance. Later research, however, would show that because local streetcar companies were so heavily dependent on a black clientele, in several cities, the simple fear of such boycotts was sufficient to delay enforcement of state Jim Crow laws on the trolleys for periods ranging from seven to fifteen years.[41]

On the other hand, the whites who comprised a substantial majority of the passengers on major railroads might well see the mere presence of any black traveler with the wherewithal to ride first class and actually look the part as a distinct threat to their feelings of superiority. From the bottom-up perspective, then, the genesis of the Jim Crow statutes lay not simply in the desire of whites to preserve their dominance but in their sense that blacks were not only in a position to challenge it but disposed to do so when the opportunity afforded itself. As early as 1965, Williamson had noted that even as the fundamental resolve to maintain white supremacy continued to hold sway, the contours of racial interaction in South Carolina had always shifted when confronted with what he called "vigorous assaults by one side or the other." Nearly four decades later, Steven Hahn's sweeping examination of black politics in the rural South from slavery to the Great Migration affirmed that Jim Crow was not so much "an imposition . . . as a product of struggle"[42]

In a real if deeply ironic sense, the true importance of a historian's contribution is measured not simply in how effusively others in the field praise it at the outset but in how long they deem it relevant enough to warrant their continued criticism. For *Strange Career*, this period encompassed at least three decades. Such a span would have been remarkable enough for a patiently crafted monograph based on several years of scrupulous research, let alone a hastily conceived and composed set of lectures advancing a more sweeping and provocative argument than the evidence provided could possibly justify. Woodward's book was a daring attempt to make the past say precisely what he thought Americans in general needed to hear at a specific moment. As such, it was all but certain to draw fire from historians concerned with what it had to say about the past rather than the present. That so predictable a development would play out is hardly surprising, then, and its cumulative implications by no means offer the full measure of all that Woodward accomplished in a little book that David Donald hailed as "a landmark in the history of American race relations."[43]

Surely no historian did more fundamental damage to the Woodward thesis itself over that thirty-year span than Joel Williamson. Yet none was quicker to acknowledge the profound importance of *Strange Career* in establishing the history of race relations in America, theretofore largely the province of black scholars, as a rich and vitally important field of inquiry for whites as well. Moreover, by challenging the presumption that rigid racial separation had been a fixed and pervasive practice in the South long before the end of Reconstruction, Woodward had taken segregation out of the backdrop, moved it center stage, and assigned its origins and development a critical role in a historical drama that he saw still playing out in the mid-1950s. As Howard Rabinowitz added, the scholarly curiosity piqued by Woodward's provocative assault on the traditional wisdom soon led to a host of "new findings that transcended the narrower issue of the origin and extent of segregation."[44]

Regardless of what *The Strange Career of Jim Crow*'s standing among historians after more than sixty-five years in print may tell us, it is hardly a register of the book's importance outside the scholarly arena, where it reached a vast audience of readers over more than two generations. In a progression of updates over a twenty-year stretch, Woodward had succeeded, not only in historicizing recent events on the fly, but in weaving them into a brief, readable, and reliable narrative, not necessarily of Jim Crow's beginnings, but certainly of his rise, dominion, and demise. These attributes were not lost on a great number of instructors looking for just such a text to assign to their undergraduates, and more than thirty years after *Strange Career* made its debut, Rabinowitz deemed it still the "best available brief account of American race relations," noting that Woodward's treatment of events in the twentieth century had gone virtually unchallenged.[45]

The magnitude of Woodward's achievement in this respect may have escaped the notice of some academic critics, but it did not go unrewarded by any means, as evidenced in the steady stream of substantial royalty checks destined to flow his way over *Stranger Career*'s extended career as a concise account of the long struggle for racial justice in America. Although the $1,000 (roughly equivalent to $10,000 today) honorarium he received for the Richard Lectures was generous by the standards of the day, the terms of his assignment stipulated that all royalties from sales of the initial published version of the lectures were to go to the University of Virginia. Pointing to the additional time and effort required of him to come up with a revised paperback edition in 1957, he and his editors managed to strike a bargain with university officials whereby he would collect 2.5 percent of the list price of the new edition. As he undertook the second (1966) revision of the book, Woodward balked at Virginia continuing to share in the royalties at all. University administrators again proved amenable to some renegotiation but declined to forego all of the royalty proceeds, and understandably so, given that from December 1964 to April 1965 alone, sales of the now seven-year-old paperback edition of *Strange Career* had totaled nearly 19,000 copies.[46]

At slightly over 31,000 copies, Oxford's initial print run of the 1966 paperback edition had seemed a bit optimistic at first, but with roughly 18,000 of those already sold well before the official publication date, by late January, a second printing was already in the works. Though not given to bragging and gloating publicly, Woodward was not above aiming a subtle private barb or two at those he felt had sold him or his work short. Shortly before the original Richard Lectures were delivered, he had contacted Little, Brown trade books editor Arthur Thornhill to see if he might have any interest in publishing them. When Thornhill quickly responded that the project was "too short and specialized" for Little, Brown's list, Woodward persisted, suggesting to Little, Brown's editor-in-chief Ned Bradford that the press might be "overlooking a bet." He apparently backed off, though, after Bradford agreed in rather half-hearted and almost patronizing fashion to take a look at the manuscript, just on the "odd chance" that Woodward might be correct. Later, as *Strange Career*'s sales continued to soar, the vindicated author could not resist reminding Thornhill and Bradford of the opportunity they had fumbled, reporting to Thornhill that the newly revised *Strange Career* registered sales in excess of 50,000 in 1966 and making sure Bradford knew that, even after thirteen years in print, the book had sold 81,000 copies in fiscal 1968 alone.[47]

In 1974, with what would be the final edition in the works, Woodward would once again lobby Oxford University Press to ask the University of Virginia to forego further royalties. The university's president Edgar F. Shannon agreed to a new arrangement more favorable to Woodward, but only after a polite reminder that, in inviting Woodward to deliver the Richard Lectures some twenty years earlier, the university had effectively subsidized a book that had not only "profited [him] financially" but "also served to enhance Mr. Woodward's distinguished and well-deserved reputation in the scholarly world." When Oxford's Sheldon Meyer proposed a new royalty plan offering him 6.5 percent on the paperback sales, Woodward assured Meyer that he hated "to be a pig" but asked whether Oxford might be willing to boost that rate to 10 percent, noting that he had "heard of other contracts that call for a royalty of that amount after sales on the book have got above one-quarter of a million," a figure that *Strange Career* had surely surpassed by that point.[48]

Meyer agreed to look into the possibility but explained that increasing the royalty would make it difficult to maintain the current price of $1.95, and Oxford's sales representatives had already warned that raising the price above $2.00 could mean losing a goodly portion of course adoptions, not only at the college level, but in high schools, where pricing was even more critical. Although the earning potential for Woodward under this royalty and pricing arrangement might seem relatively modest, assuming new paperback sales of 50,000 copies yearly, his annual royalty payments would have totaled $6,337. He collected another $19,000 in royalties in 1974 as one of the contributors to the popular U.S. history textbook *The National Experience*. The proceeds from these two books amounted to a hefty 64 percent supplement to his $39,000 salary in 1974, pushing his income from these three streams alone to more than $64,000, the rough equivalent of $361,000 in 2022.[49]

Meanwhile, cumulative new-copy sales of *Strange Career* would go on to top 800,000 by the time of Woodward's death, indicating that, with used and library copies taken into account, the book had long since reached well over a million readers. To all appearances, at least, when its career as something of a historical call to arms finally collided with its career as a free-standing scholarly monograph, the latter clearly got the worst of it. Yet as David Potter mused in 1969, what proved to be Woodward's "least substantial book" by traditional academic standards, was the one that would make "his public, as distinguished from . . . [his] professional, reputation." In fact, however, even though Woodward's Jim Crow thesis had been tested and found wanting in several specific cases by the end of the 1960s, most of his fellow historians had seemed oblivious to its weaknesses up to that point. In the interim, *Strange Career* had also helped to fuel its author's meteoric rise to the pinnacle of his profession while showcasing his talent for writing for a broad general audience as well. The combination stood only to enhance his appeal as both an accomplished scholar and a highly readable commentator on public affairs.[50]

10

A Basis for Criticizing the American Legend

Southern History as Both Asset and Burden

The Strange Career of Jim Crow had showcased Woodward's rare gift for deftly and concisely interpreting the past and persuading a contemporary popular audience of its relevance. This peculiar talent was also on display in a number of essays he had published in the 1950s, and by the end of the decade, a number of high-profile publishers, such as Little, Brown and Alfred A. Knopf, were clamoring to add a collection of these pieces to their catalogs.

He had delivered the Walter Lynwood Fleming Lectures in Southern History at Louisiana State University in 1951, focusing on exiled southern dissenters, including Kentucky abolitionist James G. Birney and abolitionists and women's rights activists Angelina Grimké Weld and her sister Emily Grimké. It was standard contractual procedure for these lectures to be published in timely fashion by LSU Press. Yet Woodward's many commitments, which included serving as president of the Southern Historical Association, holding a visiting professorship at the University of Tokyo, preparing the Richard Lectures at the University of Virginia, and discharging his duties as Harmsworth Professor at Oxford, had left him little time to put together a publishable book manuscript based on the Fleming Lectures. As he hastily pieced together his lectures for Charlottesville in September 1954, he could do no more than assure LSU editor Donald Ellegood that he meant to get the Fleming Lectures ready for publication as soon as he returned from England the following year.[1]

Finally, in 1958, three years after Woodward's return, still with no manuscript in hand or any apparent prospect of receiving one, Ellegood suggested that, in lieu of publishing the lectures, he would be interested in putting together a collection of Woodward's previously published essays. Woodward seemed open to pursuing this venture as the best means of fulfilling his contractual obligation to LSU Press. Yet that obligation notwithstanding, with other publishers also eager to bring out such a collection, he did not shrink from pressuring Ellegood into extricating him from another dilemma "that rather stumps me." His thoughtful and provocative essay, "The Search for Southern Identity," had been published a few months earlier in the *Virginia Quarterly Review*. This piece, Woodward thought, should rightly "embody the theme" of any collection of his work, but alas, it was already committed to what he called an "ill-starred" effort to publish a volume of essays organized around the theme of "The Southerner as an American." Woodward knew that Ellegood was all too familiar with the project because LSU Press had long been slated to publish it, and the editor had already suffered through numerous delays and missed submission deadlines. He had long since lost any enthusiasm for the volume, whose contributions were "uneven to start with," and given reports of several similar collections in the works, he felt "the whole thing should be reconsidered or abandoned." Certainly, Ellegood had "already exceeded any reasonable limits of patience," and he should not feel guilty in the least about letting the project editor, Charles G. Sellers of the University of California, know that LSU Press was no longer interested in publishing the collection. If the project were scrapped, he explained to Ellegood, he would then be "free to incorporate this key essay in my own collection." Five days later, he had a copy of Ellegood's letter advising Sellers that it was "highly unlikely that we can now undertake publication" of the volume in question.[2]

Pleased (but obviously not surprised) to learn that Ellegood had "put the quietus" on the Sellers project, Woodward immediately pronounced himself ready to proceed with assembling his own collection, complete with the crucial "Search for Southern Identity" essay. Assuming that "The Southerner as an American" venture was effectively dead in the water, Woodward did not inform Sellers and other contributors that he had committed his piece elsewhere until more than two months later, at which point the proposed volume, with Woodward's essay still prominently featured, was already under

A Basis for Criticizing the American Legend

consideration by the University of North Carolina Press. Upon learning that Woodward had withdrawn his offering, George Tindall, another long-suffering contributor to the volume, implored him to reconsider. Woodward's essay was a vital summation of the themes pursued by the other writers. "Without you, we are probably dead," he pleaded.[3]

Woodward responded that, while Tindall's letter "distressed me a good deal," he felt that "my obligation to LSU is more than simply a matter of a wish to get a book out of my own, for I do owe them a book in lieu of the Fleming Lectures." Although he could not go back on his arrangement with LSU Press, he managed to sing a more upbeat tune about the troubled project for Tindall's benefit than he had for Ellegood. Even without his own contribution, he assured Tindall, the essays still represented "an unusually good collection as it stands," and he even offered to encourage UNC Press director Lambert Davis to publish it. As it turned out, not only did the University of North Carolina Press publish *The Southerner as American* but later, as Woodward fretted about the early sales of his own volume, he could not resist prodding his editors at LSU Press for a better publicity effort by pointing out that "Chapel Hill is making quite a plug for 'The Southerner as An American.'"[4]

As is often the case with such projects, after assembling the essays he planned to use in his book, Woodward worried about how well they would hold together as a book. Ellegood did not share his concern, though, pointing to the collection as "one of the most generic and provocative statements to historians, or, for that matter, any history-minded reader, to come along in a long time." He was confident that the book would appeal to professional historians, but Ellegood thought it even more important to get the book in the hands of "the general history-minded reader and better still that mythical 'intelligent layman' who likes ironies, social problems, and even historiography if made palatable—the reader of *Harper's*, *Atlantic*, *The Reporter*, and so on." In keeping with what had become Woodward's preferred practice in recent years, only one of the previously published essays had been footnoted, and Ellegood thought it was better to forego notes altogether rather than risk putting off nonacademic readers, who stood to embrace the book "if it is appealingly entitled, popularly reviewed, . . . forcefully promoted and not priced too high." There was also an excellent prospect of reaching even more readers through a subsequent paperback edition. In any event, Woodward should know that, for the press, "the main thing is that your book be read," and he and his colleagues were prepared to "do anything reasonable" to accomplish this.[5]

The initial collection offered eight essays, seven previously published, all in the 1950s, and five within the past four years. Their subjects ranged from the essence and regional and national import of southern identity to the peculiarly historical inclinations of southern writers and the limitations of the northern commitment to racial equality before, during, and after Reconstruction.

The expert readers asked to comment on Woodward's bundle of essays in manuscript were some of the best-known contributors to humanities scholarship in America in their own right, and they were uniformly unstinting in their praise. David Potter believed that "there is nothing in print which interprets the intrinsic significance of the Southern factor in American life with as searching and subtle a probe." Southern literary expert Louis D. Rubin was equally enthusiastic, predicting that most readers would be drawn to the essays, not simply because of what they said, but "because it is Vann who is saying it." Rubin had identified Woodward as "that rarest of birds," a "southern ironist" who "interprets everything from that standpoint," and his fellow reader Daniel Boorstin suggested "The Irony of Southern History" as the title for the collection that would best "sum up the unifying theme of the essays for me." Sensing that this title might imply a closer connection to Reinhold Niebuhr's *Irony of American History* than Woodward might prefer, he added a fateful "P.S." to his report to Ellegood: "Another possible title: 'The Burden of Southern History.'"[6]

After sifting through a list of options including "On Being a Southerner," "Southern Experience and National Myth," and "The South in Search of Identity," Woodward would eventually go with Boorstin's second, almost offhand suggestion, although he professed some unease, not so much with the "ambiguity in the word 'burden,'" "but with the possibility that he might "be accused of a pretentious title." He dedicated the book to Robert Penn Warren, with whom he already enjoyed a fast and mutually admiring friendship. A quarter century later, in a draft of his memoir, *Thinking Back*, Woodward explained that the title was not conceived originally as a reference to Jack Burden's warning in Warren's *All the Kings Men* that "if you could not accept the past and its burden there was no future." By the time the revised draft of his memoir was in print, however, Woodward appeared to have forgotten entirely that the title had been proposed initially by Boorstin, telling readers that it was, in fact, "suggested" by the line that Warren had put in Burden's mouth, and he did essentially the same in the preface to the third edition of *Burden*, published in 1993.[7]

Woodward had not only rejected Boorstin's preferred title, "The Irony of Southern History," but objected to proposed jacket copy referring to the "ironic perspective" of his essays, arguing that, in common parlance, "irony" was too often "confused with mockery or sarcasm" and seen, however erroneously, to suggest an air of "flippancy or unfriendliness." Beyond that, he added, "I simply feel that irony is hardly a quality one can afford to advertise, even if it is present." In this instance, irony surely needed no advertisement. It was an inescapable presence in practically all his essays, not to mention implicit in the title he had chosen for a book whose contents suggested that in some respects the troubled historical experience of southerners could actually prove to be more of an asset than a burden.[8]

The two pieces in the collection that proved most broadly engaging and thought-provoking were closely related, and taken together, they offered the foundation for an alternative perspective on southern identity and, in almost equal measure, on American identity as well. "The Irony of Southern History" had been Woodward's presidential address to the Southern Historical Association in November 1952. Delivered in his trademark mumble, his insights proved no match for the dramatic distraction posed by relocating the presidential banquet so that black members of the association could attend. After registering little immediate impact, the address had gained wider though still not exceptional notice when it appeared in the February 1953 edition of the *Journal of Southern History*. Thanks to global and national developments in the interim, however, Woodward's message had taken on much greater relevance by the time it resurfaced seven years later in *The Burden of Southern History*.[9]

Woodward readily acknowledged that his essay drew heavily on Reinhold Niebuhr's *The Irony of American History*, with its focus on the illusion of a peculiarly American "innocence and virtue." As early as 1783, this illusion had led Yale president Ezra Stiles to cast the new nation as "God's American Israel," untainted by the wickedness of the Old World and ordained by Providence to "create a new humanity and restore man's lost innocence." As the United States grew and prospered, its growing military formidability and mounting achievements had quickly given rise to a national "legend of success and victory," which, in turn, simply reinforced Americans' faith in their nation's exceptional virtue and an invincibility born of acting in perfect accord with the designs of the Almighty.[10]

Woodward saw the effects of this historically emboldening elixir kicking in with a vengeance as the United States stepped forward after World War

II to claim the mantle of free-world leadership, committing itself to global containment of communism with little regard for the possible consequences, at home or abroad, of playing both policeman and evangelist to the rest of the world. America's intoxicating myths, coupled with its once unthinkable power at the dawning of the atomic age, had actually made it more vulnerable than ever before to what Niebuhr called the same "ironic perils . . . of over-weening power and overweening virtue" that had taken their toll on ancient societies like Israel and Babylon. By 1952, Woodward noted, Americans had grown "exasperated by the ironic incongruities of our position." Despite their nation's unprecedented power, with the Soviet Union now also armed with nuclear weapons, they actually felt less secure than before. Meanwhile, efforts to strengthen America's position in the world by extending the presumed blessings of its way of life to less fortunate nations had yielded little more than frustration as "the liberated prove[d] ungrateful for their liberation, [and] the reconstructed for their reconstruction." Although Woodward did not refer to it directly, talk of employing nuclear weapons in the still ongoing conflict in Korea in 1952 may have spurred him at the time to cite the danger "that America may be tempted to exert all the terrible power she possesses to compel history to conform to her own illusions," even if it meant striking the first blow in a "so-called preventive war."[11]

Ironically, America had become such a danger to itself and the rest of the world largely because its record of prevailing in every major crisis that had come its way thus far had fostered oversized faith in the nation's continued progress, prosperity, and military invincibility. Such "unique good fortune," Woodward warned, "has isolated America . . . rather dangerously" from the rest of the world's peoples, who, "without exception, have known the bitter taste of defeat and humiliation."[12]

The critical implications of America's isolation from global historical real-ity notwithstanding, Woodward did not want readers to overlook the irony of the nation's peculiar experience according it a peculiar standing in respect to the rest of the world, not unlike the exceptional position of the South within America itself. As he clearly understood, the perception of the South's dis-tinctiveness relative to the rest of the nation really derived from its differences with the northern states, which constituted the idealized embodiment of the national success story. Compared to other nations of the world, it was not the South, with its troubled and uninspiring history of military defeat, occupa-tion, and ensuing impoverishment, but rather the North, with its record of uninterrupted success and progress and reputation for unimpeachable virtue, that actually stood out, for that record was "not shared by any other people of the civilized world." Here, then, lay the ultimate "Irony of Southern History": The same heritage of frustration, failure, and loss that set southerners apart as the only Americans for whom "history" was not just "something unpleasant that happens to other people" actually put them on common ground "with nearly all the peoples of Europe and Asia."[13]

Woodward had effectively suggested a new perspective on southern identity, grounded not in defending its distinctive racial system but in a defining historical experience dramatically different from that of the North. Rather than flesh out this argument in "Irony," however, with the *Brown* decision still two years away, he seemed more interested in drawing on the South's past to offer potentially vital lessons for Americans confronted with the challenges and fears of the Cold War. The fervent defense of slavery prompted by the abolitionist stirrings of the 1830s had quickly become the sum and extent of the South's "whole cause, its way of life," and thus its primary, if sometimes unspoken, concern in all its major disagreements with the North, leading ultimately to the disastrous consequences of secession and civil war. Here, in their own past, lay a cautionary precedent for contemporary white southerners to consider before allowing an all-out defense of segregation to become what amounted to a regional raison d'être. Yet he also drew on the same analogy with the proslavery crusade in questioning America's haste amid the resurgent prosperity of the 1940s to make defending and extending modern capitalism "our whole cause" as a nation after the jarring uncertainties of the Great Depression had rendered it suspect even in its own backyard. As relations with the Soviet Union and China grew more confrontational, dedication to capitalism had quickly hardened into a rigid orthodoxy that equated even the mildest internal criticism of this system with a desire to undermine the nation's efforts to combat the global advance of communism. Meanwhile, embracing American-style capitalist doctrine became the litmus test of loyalty for our allies abroad and the endgame of our misguided efforts to win the allegiance of "uncommitted peoples" by forcing our own values and practices on them with no regard for their actual relevance to the "real needs and circumstances" of these peoples.[14]

As it had with northerners and southerners in the late antebellum era, Woodward suggested, such an unyielding insistence on the universal superiority of their own institutions and values had now left both sides in the Cold War with so little prospect for compromise that it might well foster notions of yet another "irrepressible conflict." If so, the use of force would become not only acceptable but, at some point, inevitable. This prospect was especially disquieting to America's European allies, who foresaw potentially catastrophic consequences arising from the impetuosity and naïveté rooted in its obliviousness to the prospect of failure and defeat that had loomed so large in the experiences of other nations. In reality, Woodward suggested, it was not so much that the nation's history was truly lacking in such "tragic and ironic implications" but that these implications had been "obscured by the national legend of success and victory and by the perpetuation of infant illusions of innocence and virtue."[15]

Woodward had ventured at the outset that, for all its peculiarity in national context, the region's globally relevant experience might actually be more of an advantage than a "handicap" for southern historians looking to deepen their understanding of American history and clarify it for others throughout the world. With its fate and perhaps that of the entire world hanging in the balance, America needed more desperately than ever to brush myth and illusion aside and face up to the reality of its history. The key to this lay in "criticism from historians of her own who can penetrate the legend without destroying the ideal," and Woodward could think of none better suited for this assignment than southerners who studied the South, for whom, unlike their northern counterparts, it was "common knowledge that history has happened to their people in their part of the world." Who, he implied, could better document "the futility of erecting intellectual barricades against unpopular ideas [and] employing censorship and repression against social criticism"? In doing so, southern historians would offer a vital lesson about the contemporary dangers of McCarthyite witch-hunting and other attempts to make rigid, reflexive anticommunism the ultimate proof of national loyalty. With American messianism and megalomania surging in the early 1950s, southern historians might also find a critical cautionary tale in the thwarted northern idealism of the Reconstruction era. This, in turn, would leave them better equipped to school presumptuous would-be nation builders in the perils and unintended consequences of imposing their ideas on other peoples vanquished with military force. The same would apply to setting out to overthrow repressive regimes and indoctrinate supposedly liberated peoples around the world in the superiority of the American ideas and institutions. Surely southern historians should enjoy unrivaled credibility in warning America's Cold War zealots that "an overwhelming conviction in the righteousness of a cause is no guarantee of its ultimate triumph."[16]

Heedless of the fate of their counterparts a century earlier, southern politicians were still demanding wholesale resistance to the Supreme Court's 1954 school desegregation in 1958 when Woodward offered a variation on the argument he made six years earlier in "The Irony of Southern History."

A Basis for Criticizing the American Legend

His primary aim in "The Search for Southern Identity," however, was not prodding Americans outside the South to consider the peculiarity of their nation's defining historical narrative or the lessons offered by a starkly contrasting but more globally resonant southern experience. This time, he urged contemporary white southerners to embrace the true roots of their region's identity in its distinctly "un-American" past, rather than continuing to defend segregation as the cornerstone of the "Southern way of life" in much the same tragic fashion as their ancestors had done with slavery a century before.

Woodward's argument that white southerners were bound to each other by a distinct "collective experience" shared by no other Americans took no account of the historic divisions and conflicts among them based on class and economic interests, some of which he had chronicled himself. Moreover, if southerners were distinguished as a people by their peculiar history of "frustration and failure and defeat" and their consequent immunity to any delusion of invincibility, then, by all rights, blacks not only qualified as southerners but arguably even more so than whites. Yet in the 1950s, for both liberal and conservative whites North and South, "southerners" was a term interpreted almost universally as a generic reference to whites, and save for a single sentence, the essays published in the original version of *Burden* did not depart from this usage. What Woodward saw as the South's most "cherished myths"—such as the planter class's alleged ancestral connection to the old English Cavaliers, the Old South legend of planters' gentility, grace, and refinement, and the "hallowed memory of the Redeemers who did in the Carpetbaggers"—were legends embraced almost exclusively by whites. Finally, though southern blacks were surely no strangers to "frustration" and "failure," the enduringly painful, character-defining "defeat" suffered by white southerners in the Civil War was, for them, a victory to be savored and celebrated.[17]

Woodward did acknowledge at a single point, however, that blacks were "also Southerners" who simply had yet to "achieve articulate expression of their uniquely un-American experience." Key figures in the Harlem Renaissance such as Sterling Brown, Jean Toomer, and Langston Hughes, as well as Ralph Ellison, who was later to become a close friend of Woodward's, might have taken issue with him on this point. In all likelihood, however, Woodward's assessment of the work of southern black writers would have drawn little, if any, disagreement from his white contemporaries studying southern literature except, perhaps, for his prescient suggestion that "the Negro" might one day acknowledge "that he is also a southerner as well as an American."[18]

When that day came, black southerners would, in fact, ground their identity as southerners in their own distinctive historical experience, but at this point, Woodward was essentially writing for and about whites. Just as he had sought in *Strange Career* to encourage white Americans at large to support vigorous enforcement of the *Brown* decision, so he was now trying to give white southerners reason to rethink their resistance to it, despite a raging horde of demagogues likening any move against segregation to an attack on the very foundation of southern identity. Yet if, as Woodward had maintained, rigid racial separation was not so historically rooted in southern tradition as many believed, it followed that southern whites who ceased to defend Jim Crow would not also be abandoning their identification with their region in the bargain. Woodward's argument ran counter not only to majority opinion among white southerners but to a prevailing perception among historians, southern and otherwise, that a consistent and pervasive dedication to maintaining white supremacy actually qualified as "the central theme of southern history." Such had been the precise contention thirty years earlier of Ulrich Bonnell Phillips, who was seen at his death in 1934 as the nation's foremost authority on southern history, a standing that arguably belonged to Woodward by the time he penned his rejoinder to Phillips. Although he nodded respectfully to Phillips's stature, Woodward took vigorous issue with his declaration that subscribing to "a common resolve, indomitably maintained," that the South "shall be and remain a white man's country," was, in fact, "the cardinal test of a southerner."[19]

With the South of the late 1950s in the middle of a rapid economic and social transformation that had already "leveled many of the monuments of regional distinctiveness," Woodward understood why some white southerners who felt threatened by this seismic upheaval might cling to Phillips's maxim as a potential "bulwark" against further changes in their lives. Much as he had suggested earlier in "Irony," Woodward observed that the South once again had "a morally discredited Peculiar Institution" on its hands, and he foresaw dire consequences if white southerners at the end of the 1950s should emulate their forebears at the end of the 1850s by once again making the identity of their region synonymous with its most vulnerable institution. Updating the portrait of racial progress he had recently drawn in the final chapter of the most recent edition (1957) of *Strange Career*, he pointed to the many pillars of white supremacy that had already fallen. At that point, a number of southerners, white and black, might have seen little more than wishful thinking behind Woodward's vision of Jim Crow's imminent demise. Still, he warned that if defending segregation to the bitter end were allowed to become virtually synonymous with "Southernism," the younger generation

A Basis for Criticizing the American Legend

might even start distancing itself from any regional identification whatsoever, including even the term "southern" itself.[20]

Woodward later explained that he did not set out in this essay to deny the enduring reality of racism, or racial subordination, which he deemed an indisputable truth requiring no further proof. On the other hand, what he felt "*did* need proof and demonstration" was that there were ever any exceptions to the prevailing wisdom "that things have always been the same" and, therefore, as Phillips had put it, "'shall be and remain' the same." After all, Woodward reasoned, "if there had been no exceptions, no breaks, and things had always been the same, there was little hope of change."[21]

Confronted with this rationale, David Potter simply asked, "What has the historian to do with hope?" Though he and Woodward remained the best of friends, they kept up a running debate about the risks and rewards of historians examining the past with a view to addressing the concerns of the present. Doing otherwise, Woodward contended, was akin, as Tolstoy had put it in *War and Peace*, to "a deaf man answering questions nobody had put to him." This, Potter countered, was precisely why the deaf man would "be worth listening to," because he was reporting on what he had found without regard for what his contemporaries wanted to hear.

For Potter, the historian's primary obligation was to offer a thoroughly detached and straightforward assessment of "what the past was 'really' like," based solely on the evidence available and with no punches pulled. Yet Woodward seemed to suggest in this essay, and in *Strange Career* as well, that, in gauging how fervently southern whites had once identified with slavery, segregation, and white supremacy, a historian should consider how that assessment might affect the readiness of contemporary white southerners to identify themselves with more affirmative aspects of their regional identity. As Potter saw it, Woodward's desire to use history to sanction "meritorious values" sometimes seemed to take precedence over using it to accurately portray "the evils of the past."[22]

Apparently, this was a choice Woodward was ready to make if it stood to counter what he saw at the end of the 1950s as the greatest threat to the South's future well-being. Although the Agrarianism of *I'll Take My Stand* had long since proven to be yet another "lost cause," he feared that, standing helpless as the modernizing "Bulldozer Revolution" began to "plow under cherished old values of individualism, localism, family, clan, and rural folk culture," white southerners might stake all their hopes for maintaining a distinctive regional identity on yet another self-destructive last stand, this time in defense of racial segregation. (A few years later, disgusted by virulent white opposition to school integration, novelist Walker Percy quipped that, in New Orleans, "the 'Southern Way of Life'" came down to nothing more than "Let's keep McDonough No. 6 segregated.")[23]

"The Search for Southern Identity" may be read profitably in a variety of ways, but building on the premise he lay down in *Strange Career*, Woodward's primary objective in the most widely read essay in *The Burden of Southern History* was to persuade white southerners that rallying to the defense of a manifestly unjust racial order already on the brink of destruction was neither a valid nor a viable means of sustaining their claims to a distinct cultural identity. The operating premise behind this essay was wholly in keeping with Woodward's earlier suggestions in *Strange Career* that Jim Crow was all but done for, and by 1958, surely, it was beyond foolish for southern whites to squander further energy in trying to rationalize or defend the indefensible.

Although he obviously welcomed the day when dedication to white supremacy would no longer be the "cardinal test" of regional loyalty, he by no means relished the prospect of seeing any real sense of a peculiarly southern identity swept away by the steadily intensifying currents of change sweeping across the South. He pointed to newly arrived immigrant groups "with traditions far more ancient and distinctive than those of the South" who showed no apparent reluctance to jettison their cultural identities in their haste "to conform as quickly as possible." It pained Woodward to think that, suddenly stripped of some vital elements of his own cultural heritage, "the Southerner" might also come to "regret or forget his regional identification" as well. He could only hope that, instead of abandoning that attachment, his fellow southerners might look to their distinctive historical experience, where they should find many lessons conducive to a much-needed realism that, as he had suggested in "Irony," would ultimately "balance and complement the rest of the nation."[24]

It is easy to understand why Woodward was so determined to include "The Search for Southern Identity" in his collection because, when paired with "The Irony of Southern History," the two essays delivered a critical and timely historical message to both a region and a nation in dire need of guidance. How, and even whether, that message would be received was another matter. Woodward's fellow southerner and southern historian David Donald saw little prospect of contemporary white southerners setting aside their stubborn identification with white supremacy to seize on other broadly defining aspects of their past. As a native Mississippian, Donald felt he knew

A Basis for Criticizing the American Legend

a thing or two about white southerners' day-to-day priorities and predilections, and he doubted that many of them were even aware of the additional historical factors that Woodward saw contributing to their region's distinctive identity. Casting niceties aside, he allowed that, while Woodward's solutions might appeal to an "intellectual," they "overlook[ed] the ignorance and indifference of the average southerner."[25]

There is certainly no means of determining how many white southerners ultimately read these two essays in *The Burden of Southern History*, much less came away from them eager to embrace their distinctly "un-American past" as both the foundation of a new regional self-awareness and a powerful corrective to Cold War presumptions of American virtue and invincibility. If the enduring appetite for massive resistance and militarism among so many southern whites of this era hardly suggests that Woodward's message in these essays won a lot of converts, it was not solely for want of exposure. Comprehensive long-term sales figures for *The Burden of Southern History* are hard to come by, but LSU Press's original 1960 hardback run of 5,000 (compared to 3,000 for *Origins* in 1951) sold briskly enough to quickly attract the attention of several commercial presses, including Random House, whose original paperback printing of *Burden* was estimated at a minimum of 24,000. By 1969 the original hardback had sold out, and there were actually three paperback versions on the market simultaneously, one of them a revised edition, which appeared in 1968. At that point, the Random House edition was selling nearly 7,500 copies per year, and LSU Press had signed a paperback contract with the New American Library with a likely first printing of 75,000 copies. Even without a regional breakdown of sales figures, the book's early and consistent availability in paperback would suggest that a goodly number of southern college students might have encountered it as an assigned text.[26]

In any case, readers who focused too narrowly on the two lead essays in the collection missed out on several others that affirmed Woodward's talent for integrating national and regional perspectives on the past and revealed how his southern roots factored into both. The importance of literary influences in shaping his perception of how historians should approach their work came through in "The Historical Dimension," which had appeared in the *Virginia Quarterly Review* in 1956. Although he now valued the contributions of southern historians a great deal more than he had as a graduate student, he still believed that some of the most powerful lessons to be drawn from the South's past were to be found, not in the writings of its historians, but in those of its novelists, poets, and playwrights.

He had been drawn to several of these even as an undergraduate at Emory and was so in awe of Thomas Wolfe that he could not bring himself to approach him when he caught sight of him in Chapel Hill in 1937. William Faulkner, on the other hand, had been an acquired taste for him, but by 1942 he was praising his work for its "high sense of tragedy and humor as rich as W. Shakespeare and more so than Mark Twain's." By the end of World War II, he was reading Faulkner with both reverence and understanding. There was a distinct sense of déjà vu in his account of discovering that the "small man just in front of me" as he waited to check out of the Algonquin Hotel in New York in 1954 was William Faulkner. A bit overwhelmed as he headed off to assume his Harmsworth duties at Oxford, he confessed to feeling much in need of Faulkner's blessing. "But no," he sheepishly admitted later to David Donald, once again, "my nerve failed me, and I never met another of my heroes." He would go on to hang Faulkner's portrait in his office and concede to an interviewer that "he was always a powerful influence on me, even though I didn't always realize it."[27]

He had also formed a deep and admiring friendship with Robert Penn Warren by the time he wrote "The Historical Dimension," which saluted the peculiarly powerful historical consciousness of these southern writers whose works had "given history meaning and value and significance as events never do merely because they happen." Southern historians should commit themselves, not only to achieving the same effects, but to approaching the challenge with the "same fortitude and honesty."[28]

Woodward saw the best southern writers of this era subtly affirming his own argument that, for all the potentially transformative changes now coming to their region, southerners could still claim a distinctive common identity and mindset born of a shared and no less peculiar historical experience. Where New England novelists generally approached their central characters as "an individual alone with his conscience or his God," their southern counterparts more typically made their protagonists "an inextricable part of a living history and community," constantly beset by the consequences, not only of their own actions, but of the actions of others in both the present and the past.[29]

Here again, the title of *The Burden of Southern History* was as deeply ironic as the theme of any essay in the collection, for, as Woodward presented it, rather than a complete and enduring encumbrance, the South's past also stood to be an asset, particularly in endowing southerners with a more realistic and detached perspective from which to critique both their nation's history and its current condition. In fact, he had set out in several selections in the book to do precisely that. After sharing a copy of his SHA presidential address with fellow historian Henry F. May, he had explained that, in reality, "The Irony of Southern History" reflected his own search for "a base from which to criticize the American legend." A quarter century after *Burden* appeared in print, Woodward reaffirmed that "it was current national policies, obsessions, moods, myths, fallacies, and blunders that mainly inspired the themes of this book." Upon reflection, he realized that he had likely written a number of the essays with the North as much in mind as the South and that "when Southern history is brought in, it is to illustrate or compare with or admonish some current national or northern tendency I deplored."[30]

This inclination to rely on a southern perspective in criticizing American myths was not peculiar to Woodward or his fellow southerners. In "A Southern Critique for the Gilded Age," he pointed to leading late nineteenth-century New England writers such as Henry Adams, Henry James, and Herman Melville, each of whom offered sympathetic treatments of a fictional Confederate veteran who expresses or symbolizes their own concerns about "the mediocrity, the crassness and the venality" that so permeated northern society in that era. In Adams's anonymously published novel *Democracy* (1880), John Carrington, a Virginian and former Confederate, rescues a widow from the clutches of a corrupt and hypocritical Yankee politician. By revealing her suitor's acceptance of a huge bribe from a shipping lobby, Carrington exposes her would-be husband as a man who "talked about virtue and vice as a man who is color-blind talks about red and green." Amid the hollow, self-congratulatory rhetoric enveloping America in and around its centennial year, Carrington and his counterparts in the works of Melville and James were playing the role of deflater and skeptic that Woodward envisioned for southerners in both "Irony" and "The Central Theme."[31]

Some readers might have been surprised to find so much direct or implied criticism of northern attitudes and scruples in a book whose title suggested a focus on southern shortcomings. Woodward would surely have ranked near the top on any list of the leading southern liberals of his day. Still, as several of the essays in *Burden* readily attest, his liberalism made him no less a southerner, nor any less likely to take exception to what he saw as self-exculpatory, holier-than-thou attacks on his fellow white southerners by critics of northern extraction, regardless of the era. From the outset of his career, he had made no secret of his distaste for the Radical Republicans, whose ill-concealed ardor for tearing down the old planter ruling class struck him as perhaps exceeding their enthusiasm for lifting up the freedmen. This impulse to punish southern whites had revealed what Woodward saw as a callous disregard among the

Radicals for the social and economic consequences of such an abrupt regime change, not to mention the legal and constitutional constraints they were also trampling under foot. Neither was he a great admirer of the Radicals' fiery abolitionist predecessors, whose uncompromising views and pretensions to moral superiority made them, in his eyes at least, almost as culpable in assuring the Union's dissolution and triggering the ensuing bloodbath as the South's proslavery, secessionist hotheads.

Woodward gave vent to these feelings in his *Burden* essay "John Brown's Private War," which had begun as his contribution to a lecture series at Bennington College and was subsequently published in a collection that appeared in 1952. In Woodward's appraisal, John Brown was not only a study in human dysfunction but a serial liar and consistent defaulter on his financial obligations throughout what was his ultimately failed business career. He found it especially troubling that, spread across Brown's fifty-five years, such a record of personal instability, corruption, and failure had seemed to raise no red flags with a cohort of affluent northern abolitionists who helped to subsidize his second career as a violent and incendiary antislavery agitator and guerrilla.[32]

These well-heeled patrons apparently chose not simply to overlook, but to tacitly condone, both Brown's marauding, murdering, and mutilating guerrilla campaign against proslavery residents of Bleeding Kansas in 1856 and his occasional forays into horse rustling during the same period. Among those working behind the scenes in Brown's behalf, he singled out a group of six of the most prominent representatives of wealth and social preeminence that the northeastern states had to offer. "The Secret Six" included, among others, Thomas Wentworth Higginson, whose testimony on postbellum southern conditions Woodward presented in *Strange Career*, as well as the eminent theologian Theodore Parker and the wealthy philanthropist and former congressman Gerritt Smith of New York. By secretly diverting funds and arms to Brown that had actually been contributed to support antislavery forces in Kansas, this group had helped to underwrite Brown's notorious, insurrectionary assault on the federal arsenal at Harpers Ferry, Virginia, in 1859. Only later, Woodward wrote, would "thousands of innocent contributors" to the antislavery cause in Kansas learn "that they had furnished arms for a treasonous attack on a federal arsenal."[33]

Brown had denied any treasonous intent or actions at his trial, but Woodward could not fathom how anyone who set out to "seize a federal arsenal, shoot down United States marines and overthrow a government" would not be guilty of treason. (This perspective begs the question of whether

Woodward also considered such ex-Confederates as Charles Colcock Jones and Robert Toombs, whom he treated so sympathetically in his own writing, to be traitors as well.) After suggesting that Brown's well-heeled collaborators had also been party to treason, Woodward got in a few licks at New England's "cultural and moral aristocracy," including the likes of Ralph Waldo Emerson, Henry David Thoreau, and Theodore Parker, whose fervent defense of Brown after his raid soon became a crusade to declare him a martyr and eventually even anoint him a "SAINT." The real tragedy here, Woodward thought, was that the affair bolstered extremism on both sides, as fire-breathing southern secessionists immediately made every Republican a John Brown, much as their abolitionist foes made every southern planter into Simon Legree. The result was a rapidly expanding whirlwind of paranoia and demonization that would culminate, of course, in disunion and war. More than thirty years after his essay on Brown's raid and the reaction to it had first appeared in print, Woodward remained convinced that "few events illustrate so well the consequences of unbridled self-righteousness."[34]

Though Woodward never flatly equated the extremism of those who fought to destroy slavery to that of those determined to preserve it, he seemed to come close enough to it to draw some criticism. He was not by any means alone among his southern contemporaries in his low estimate of John Brown and his supporters, however. His friend Robert Penn Warren, who had published a book on Brown's martyrdom in 1929, praised Woodward's essay as "the best thing I know on the old homicidal maniac and his pals." At that very point, Warren was reading Mississippian David Donald's scathing treatment of Radical Republican senator Charles Sumner of Massachusetts, whom Warren pronounced "a rotten tomato if there ever was one." Certainly, neither Donald nor Warren would have gotten any argument on that point from Woodward, who had already confessed that Sumner "nauseates me."[35]

Some twenty years after he heard the Reverend Martin Luther King Jr. invoke *The Strange Career of Jim Crow* in "support for his crusade," in his March 1965 speech in Montgomery, Woodward admitted to "mixed feelings" at the time "because I knew perfectly well what those Montgomery white people who silently lined the streets were thinking and saying about a certain Yale professor of southern origins being quoted by Martin King in those circumstances." In reality, apart from the historians with whom he had made the trek to Montgomery, it was unlikely that more than a few others in the crowd that day knew anything of Woodward or his origins, but the setting and occasion made him all the more acutely aware of them himself. Though wholly persuaded of the rightness of the cause he was there to uphold, he could not escape a certain feeling that publishing a high-profile book geared to undermining support for segregation amounted to something of a breach of faith with his fellow white southerners.[36]

In a sense, his own role in focusing critical attention on the South's racial past and its historical myths in particular may have left Woodward feeling all the more obliged to refute any attempt to reduce the struggle for racial equality to a simple, straightforward conflict between a morally enlightened North and a morally delinquent South. He offered a counterbalancing perspective in two essays that were published soon after *Strange Career*, and then included in *Burden*, both geared to situating more of the moral responsibility for America's enduring racial inequities north of the Mason-Dixon Line. With the Civil War Centennial rapidly approaching in 1958, Woodward had set out in "Equality: The Deferred Commitment" to caution historians who were struggling to get their appraisals of the conflict in print in timely fashion not to "flatter the self-righteousness of either side," meaning that just as the South should not be presented as "fighting for the eternal verities," so the North should not be portrayed as "burning for equality since 1863 with a hard, gem-like flame."[37]

The North's first objective, after all, was restoring the Union. Whatever Lincoln's personal feelings about slavery, abolishing it became the second war aim principally by the force of unforeseen complications, including widespread uncertainty among Yankee commandants about the status of the thousands of slaves pouring into Union encampments. Even then, it had been a haphazard progression; the division of northern opinion on emancipation meant that it had to be sold as a "war necessity" rather than a moral imperative, and even Lincoln would have preferred a more gradual process.[38]

Rather than quieting the abolitionist clamor, Woodward saw the Emancipation Proclamation provoking calls to move beyond emancipation and make "equality" a third war aim. The "radicals" who pushed the issue had found it a tough sell, however, especially to a number of white Union troops who had been slow to embrace even the more limited aim of emancipation. Sentiments expressed by northern whites in the wake of Appomattox persuaded him that the radical minority had essentially stampeded other whites in the North into a greater commitment to racial equality than general popular sentiment could justify, much less sustain. The Union had "fought the war on borrowed moral capital" to begin with, only to see the radicals compound that debt to the point where it was "beyond the country's capacity to pay." As a consequence, the U.S. had effectively defaulted on the huge outstanding balance on its moral indebtedness in the Compromise of 1877, leaving what was a truly "national" obligation in arrears for more than three-quarters of a century until the Supreme Court finally called in the note in 1954. At this point, Woodward observed, the burden of finally fulfilling this national commitment fell disproportionately on the South, marking the second time, he added, that it been "called on . . . to bear the brunt of a guilty national conscience." Although Woodward's argument was not without some validity, he seemed almost to imply that, in failing to push harder for black equality on all fronts in the wake of emancipation, white northerners were as morally culpable as white southerners who swore to do everything in their power to thwart any such effort.[39]

In fairness to Woodward, there was far less documentation of the ferocity and extent of that southern white resistance at that point than has come our way since. He had at least conceded in "The Political Legacy of Reconstruction," which first appeared in 1957, that the violence accompanying white efforts to overthrow the first Reconstruction meant that "the North and its selfish interests" could not be held solely responsible for its ultimate collapse. In the end, though, he saw the key to the eventual undoing of Reconstruction in the same wariness of black equality that prevented most northern blacks from voting even after "freedman's suffrage had been imposed upon the South." As a consequence, blacks in the northern states in that era had managed not even a fraction of the modest political advancement registered by their southern counterparts. Even if what Woodward saw as "the North's loss of faith in its own cause" had indeed hastened the end of Reconstruction, subsequent research would definitively assign the central role in its early demise to the unyielding resolve of white southerners to restore white supremacy and political self-determination in their region by whatever means required.[40]

The distaste for the presumption of northern moral superiority so much in evidence in the foregoing pieces came across as something closer to unbridled hostility in a piece published shortly after *Burden*, which was later included in another collection of Woodward's essays. In a devastating 1962 review of Dwight Dumond's *Antislavery*, Woodward lit into Dumond for acknowledging "no complexities or ambiguities beyond the fixed categories of right and wrong" on the slavery issue. Save for William Lloyd Garrison, the abolitionists enjoyed Dumond's "unqualified admiration," while the accomplishments of the likes of Patrick Henry, George Washington, and Thomas Jefferson counted for little or nothing simply because they were slaveholders. Woodward also bemoaned what he saw as Dumond's apparent delusion that, from Congress to the White House to the battlefield itself, the entire northern war effort was, from the first, a closely coordinated crusade "to abolish slavery at the earliest possible moment."[41]

Woodward was, if anything, angered even more by seeing Dumond's one-sided, emotionally overwrought evocation of "the antislavery myth" win consistent, "unqualified praise" from some of the nation's most prominent historians, including, among others, the likes of Oscar Handlin, Richard B. Morris, and Allan Nevins. Struggling to understand why these learned historians had so uncritically embraced what he saw as such a seriously biased and genuinely flawed book, he observed, that in their comments, several of them linked the heritage of slavery to the ongoing struggle against Jim Crow. Yet surely, he argued, taking the appropriate stance on "clear-cut contemporary moral problems" should not entail "compromising the standards of historical criticism."[42]

In the end, he suspected that Dumond's "ponderous, fierce, and humorless" book had been accorded such gentle treatment primarily because it harkened back to "one of the great American myths," even though, in Woodward's view, "serious history is the critique of myths . . . not the embodiment of them." To him, Dumond's book and the almost knee-jerk acclaim it received demonstrated that "the Yankee remains to be fully emancipated from his own legends of emancipation. Confront him with a given set of symbols and he will set his sense of humor aside, snap to attention, and come to a full salute." Woodward was surely justified in criticizing Dumond's overly moralistic approach, but Woodward's "tendency to take pot shots at white northerners" did not escape the notice of historian Brooks Simpson, who found it emblematic of the "'you, too' approach to history that seems to capture the imagination of some white southerners (regardless of their position on the political spectrum)." Southern white liberals' resentment of Yankee condescension was certainly understandable, but as Simpson noted, in their compulsion to call attention to "northern shortcomings and hypocrisy, sometimes to excess, they tended to let their fellow white southerners off the hook."[43]

This inclination by no means marked the majority of Woodward's writing about the South or America in general, and it may be no coincidence that he seemed more susceptible to it during the later 1950s and early 1960s, when many northern liberals seemed eager to blame all white southerners for racial transgressions committed by any one of their number. Woodward himself would almost certainly have been a welcome presence at any point in a gathering of the best and brightest liberal thinkers that New York or New England might offer. Yet he never lost his sense that his southern roots, which

A Basis for Criticizing the American Legend

he never sought to obscure, much less deny, kept him just the least bit out of step in northern intellectual circles. In this case, however, feeling out of step did not necessarily mean feeling a step behind. After all, the reasoning he employed in "Irony" and "The Search for Southern Identity" indicated that his own roots as a southerner gave him a different and frequently more detached and realistic perspective on the American experience, historical or contemporary, than he sometimes found among his northern colleagues.

He also thought this true of other southern-born historians, especially his dear friend and former Emory classmate David Potter. Potter had earned his PhD at Yale under his fellow Georgian U. B. Phillips, and when he succeeded Phillips at Yale in 1942, Potter was the only southerner on the history faculty. (The same was true for Woodward when he replaced Potter at Yale twenty years later as the only member of Yale's history department who was not only southern-born but, in his case, southern-trained. The latter distinction, it seems safe to assume, would likely have held true across history faculties throughout the Ivy League at that point.)

Woodward had nothing but praise for Potter's 1962 essay on "The Historian's Use of Nationalism and Vice Versa." Potter had pointedly exposed the fallacy of dismissing the efforts of antebellum southerners to defend their particular regional interests as mere "sectionalism," while the North's rapidly expanding influence in Washington allowed its representatives to pursue their regional interests as if they were one and the same with national interests. Woodward admitted to Potter that he found it "impossible to imagine this contribution originating along Boston-Detroit latitudes." "The ironical thing," he thought, "is that those latitudes will agree and consider it another reason for resisting your thesis." In her recently released biography of Radical Republican Thaddeus Stevens of Pennsylvania, Fawn M. Brodie had praised Woodward for pointing out that if Reconstruction had ever "set the bottom rail on top, it was not for long," and "[demonstrating] brilliantly that it was not Reconstruction but the 'Redeemers' who truly laid the modern foundations for race relations in the South." Apparently noting that Brodie's recent critique in the *New York Times Book Review* of southern historians who still seemed inclined to downplay the importance or brutality of slavery had left both of them unscathed, Woodward confessed that he had gotten "a wry grin out of Mrs. Brodie's efforts to make decent citizens out of both of us."[44]

Woodward did venture, though, that neither he nor Potter "would have made the list [presumably of more objective southern historians]" had Brodie seen Potter's essay or Woodward's "strictures on Dumond." In the end, he warned jokingly, "the curse of our origins will out. There is no cure." He was also curious, he confessed, about whether there would be "a regional pattern" in the responses "provoked" by Potter's piece. The reception of his critical appraisal of Dumond's book, he reported, "was strictly according to the M&D [Mason-Dixon] Line: pro below, con above. NO exceptions."[45]

If Woodward's southern roots had been a professional "burden" in any real sense, it was certainly not apparent in the rapidly intensifying competition for his services in the decade or so after the publication of *Origins* in 1951. In the same year, in fact, the distinguished U.S. historian Richard Morris followed up a job offer to Woodward at Columbia with the assurance that "there isn't a soul in the entire profession whose coming is wanted or welcomed with such entire and hearty unanimity here, or anything approaching it. . . . Just to speak for myself . . . your decision to come would be the most heartwarming event in ages." Woodward had already turned down an offer several years earlier from the University of Wisconsin (before helping to secure the position for his mentor Howard Beale), and Morris's entreaties proved to be no more persuasive. Johns Hopkins received a flurry of unsolicited applicants for Woodward's position in 1954 after word leaked that he had been approached by the University of Chicago. Even though his department chair, Sidney Painter, warned him that Hopkins was in no financial condition to enter into a bidding war with such an exceedingly well-heeled competitor, Woodward opted yet again to stay put, and when the University of California, Berkeley, came calling the following year, the result was the same.[46]

He did seem to seriously consider a position at Princeton in 1959, at least to the point of securing promises from his prospective new employer of two years' leave over the next six. Already assured by Johns Hopkins that he could be free from teaching obligations for a semester in order to concentrate on researching a proposed book on Reconstruction, he also approached the school's president for additional leave time, a request rendered considerably more problematic, he conceded, by the fact that his department currently boasted only eight permanent faculty. Princeton history department head Joseph Strayer laid out a stratagem that would afford him three terms off within the following six years. He also promised support for Woodward's pursuit of outside funding for yet another year off and suggested ways that his teaching obligations might be further reduced. In response, Hopkins administrators granted Woodward not only paid leave for the spring term in 1960 but unpaid leave for the academic years 1961–62 and 1963–64, meaning that he could be free from teaching responsibilities for five of the next ten semesters. Once Woodward determined that "the leave problem . . . can be solved here also," he politely declined Princeton's offer, expressing his hope that no one there felt he had "abused your patience and good will."[47]

Woodward may have given the impression at that point that he was settled in at Hopkins for the duration of his career, but although he was loath to admit it even to himself, he did not feel totally fulfilled. When he discussed the prospect of a move to Berkeley in 1955, he had found Carl Bridenbaugh's assurance that his salary would "be more than ample" a bit beside the point, because his decision would not hinge on the size of his paycheck. He liked Johns Hopkins's "emphasis on graduate training, small classes, and small lecture obligations," but for him, the choice came down to "whether I want to remain out of the mainstream you are in the middle of, or whether to jump in." He called on the same imagery five years later when he admitted that, although he had told himself that moving to Princeton was "an opportunity I could not afford to pass up," for all his "heaving at my bootstraps, I have been unable to get myself off the ground." It would be a mere matter of months, however, before he was confronted with another opportunity to jump squarely into "the mainstream," perhaps precisely the opportunity he had been awaiting all along, but in any case, one that, in the end, he could not bring himself to refuse.[48]

11

Tortured for Months

The Agony of Moving to Yale

George W. Pierson was a direct descendent of Yale's first president. He had taken all of his degrees there and would never teach anywhere else. He joined the faculty immediately on receipt of his BA in 1926, earned his PhD in 1933, and took over as head of the history department in 1956. Yale could claim no fiercer loyalist, but even Pierson's deeply partisan squint told him that its standing in the field of history had fallen off badly in recent years. . . He managed to build on the recent appointment of Harvard-trained colonialist Edmund Morgan by hiring another Harvard PhD, political historian John Morton Blum, away from MIT in 1957. When David Potter decided to leave Yale for Stanford in 1960, Blum and Morgan descended on Pierson immediately, insisting that "there was only one way to replace David," and that was by bringing in C. Vann Woodward, who, in Blum's view, was "already the premier historian of the American South." Although the acutely pedigree-conscious Pierson might have been expected to raise an eyebrow at Woodward's North Carolina PhD, he reportedly took only "a minute" to concur, and proceeded on the spot, apparently, without further consultation with anyone, to call Woodward and offer him a Sterling Professorship, "the most prestigious and remunerative chair available at Yale," on the spot.[1]

Pierson's alacrity and boldness in offering Woodward such a position over the phone may have seemed aggressive, even in a bygone era when restraints on the academic hiring process were few, but in his mind, the sense of urgency his actions conveyed was entirely justified. Despite his concerted efforts to energize the department by bringing in outstanding historians trained at elite institutions other than Yale, when Pierson called Woodward, six of thirteen full professors and six of ten associate professors on the history faculty had one or more Yale degrees and four of the "Yale men" had been teaching there since the 1920s. In addition, half of all the associate professors had come to Yale before World War II and had yet to win promotion to full professor. Not surprisingly, even with the recent appointments of Morgan and Blum, the general intellectual climate in the department hardly crackled with energy or enthusiasm. It was also fair to say that Yale's PhD program in history looked all more anemic in comparison to its rival program at Harvard, which, along with Radcliffe, granted 20 PhDs in 1959, compared to Yale's 10; across the preceding decade, Harvard's total stood at 280 compared to Yale's 94.[2]

As reflected in the academic pecking order, however, contemporary realities are often slow to undermine an institution's historic reputation or cachet. British historian J. H. Hexter considered Washington University in Saint Louis "one of the most endearing of all American universities," but he admitted that by the time he had the opportunity to move to Yale in 1963, he had long since grown weary of explaining that the institution where he taught was in neither the state of Washington nor the District of Columbia. After accepting the offer, Hexter was never sure how much he had been swayed by the certainty that "when you tell someone that you are at Yale, he does not ask 'In Lost Nation, Iowa?' or 'In Painted Post, New York?' or 'In Cambridge, Mass.?'" Likewise, Edmund Morgan recalled that when he was being recruited by Yale in the mid-1950s, his department chair at Brown had readily advised, "Brown is Brown, but Yale is Yale. . . . You should go."[3]

Pierson had actually extended preliminary feelers to Woodward the year before, and he assured him in July 1960 that he believed "an overall agreement will not be hard to reach." Still, from that point, the official courtship and back and forth on details stretched out over more than four months. The formal campus visit and interview for Woodward and his wife, Glenn, came in mid-October 1960, complete with the familiar regimen of lunches, dinners, receptions, and meetings with administrators, who, in Woodward's case, included Yale president A. Whitney Griswold. After the fashion of the era, Glenn Woodward was placed under the care of a coterie of faculty wives when her husband was involved in formal meetings and discussions. The requisite reciprocal thanks and compliments were exchanged in the wake of the visit, but the courtship was far from over, for Woodward's professional and personal concerns were both complicated and very real. It would be another three weeks before Pierson even tendered an official offer in a letter running to seven single-spaced, typed pages. His letter began with an urgent emotional appeal uncharacteristic either of the genre or of Pierson himself: "We want you here with us. Very much indeed. Do come. You won't regret it." He assured Woodward that his invitation came with the unqualified and wholly enthusiastic approval of everyone at Yale, from the president down to "the lower ranks" of the history department, not to mention others outside the department. Woodward was to be one of only twenty-five Sterling Professors at Yale, whose positions currently carried a maximum salary of $20,000, with excellent prospects for future increases, of course, along with an additional $500 for basic secretarial support.[4]

When Pierson had contacted him in May 1959 about visiting for a term at Yale, Woodward had responded that he "would like to visit Yale sometime, but for the next five years it seems improbable that I could work it in. . . . I expect to have considerable leave in that time but want to devote it to research." Mindful that Woodward had recently been granted a one-year fellowship from the Lilly Endowment and promised leave for two of the next three years at Hopkins, Pierson proposed that his tenure at Yale begin officially on July 1, 1961, though Woodward was to be on unpaid leave for the 1961–62 academic year with additional leave time to be determined "on a fair and friendly basis when you and we know better what will make sense to all concerned." Woodward's typical teaching load at Yale was to be but two courses a year. That would include sharing responsibility for History 180, the foundational course for graduate training in American history, as well as offering a graduate seminar on a topic in keeping with Woodward's interests and expertise. Aware perhaps of Woodward's concern that devoting too much time and energy to teaching might impede his research and writing, Pierson suggested rather tentatively that in alternative years or terms, he might consider offering an advanced undergraduate seminar, "with enrollment strictly limited." All of his teaching duties could, of course, be "adjusted in later discussion," and so they would be, as Woodward steadily distanced himself from undergraduate teaching over the next few years.[5]

In addition to the retirement program in which Yale would contribute 10 percent of Woodward's salary and Woodward 5 percent per annum, Woodward's son, Peter, who was already enrolled at Yale, would receive the $650 supplement to defray tuition and other costs that was standard for the children of Yale faculty. Yale also offered moving expenses, which Pierson promised to get jacked up beyond the usual $1,000 allotment in Woodward's case.

Finally, Yale also subsidized home mortgages for faculty at a standard rate of 4.5 percent over thirteen years.[6]

In the end, however, Pierson knew that the financial terms he offered were not more appealing in and of themselves than what Woodward enjoyed at Hopkins, including the $20,000 salary. Sensing that he must also be sold on the monumental importance of his coming to Yale at that precise moment, Pierson could hardly have laid it on any thicker. Beyond the practical necessity of finding a successor for the departing David Potter, it was nothing less than a matter of "national obligation or duty" for Yale "to stay at the front of American universities." This meant not only greater attention to the sciences but "all the more urgently . . . a continued insistence on the liberal arts and on pre-eminence in at least some of the humanities and social sciences." It was vitally important, then, for "one of the most distinguished American historians of our day" to join a cohort of "able American historians" already in place and needing only the addition of "a man of your calibre and quality to stand close to the top, or at the top itself." Woodward's presence would also be critical to efforts to rejuvenate Yale's graduate program in history, and doubtless aware of Woodward's decided preference for graduate teaching, Pierson promised that he would find like-minded colleagues ready to push for greater emphasis on graduate training. Beyond that, however, he begged Woodward's indulgence as he, "a Yale man and a Yale historian," argued that the institution's "accumulated power and resources . . . and [its] variety of distinguished scholarship" would allow Woodward to achieve a great deal more than if he stayed at Hopkins. Woodward was about to turn fifty-two, and Yale's mandatory retirement age was sixty-eight. Pierson did not hesitate to assure him that, "in the next sixteen years, you can do more here than you could in any place in the country."[7]

Woodward responded to Pierson's effusive offer with appropriately elaborate thanks: "What a letter. What an invitation. What a temptation. Before I read it, I did not see how I could accept. After reading it I do not see how I could refuse. My impulse is to say 'yes' and be done with it." Woodward knew that was not going to happen, of course, even if Pierson had secretly fancied that it might. Such a spur-of-the-moment decision, Woodward explained, "would be too easy and too unfair and I cannot do it that way," without listening "to the other side," meaning the administrators and his longtime friends and colleagues at Johns Hopkins. "I only wish there was one real son of a bitch among them," he complained. "Someone I hated and could blame. Unfortunately, I can't think of one." There was also the matter of whether Hopkins would extend a counteroffer, which could not be resolved quickly because, at the moment, the school's president was confined to bed with a slipped disk and awaiting surgery. "Being flat on his back," Woodward explained, "he has the greater claim on my fairness." Still, he assured Pierson that he would not draw the matter out any longer than necessary and promised a decision within three weeks, at the outside. In the end, the process would take more than a month, and a busy, at times almost frenetic interim it would be.[8]

Ironically, it was Pierson, who so desperately wanted him to come to Yale, whose manner and observations about the history and character of his alma mater seemed to give Woodward the greatest pause. It's fair to say that George Pierson wasted little energy pretending to be a man of the people. A few years earlier, he had complained to Yale's president Griswold about the modest family circumstances of many graduate applicants in his department. As Pierson saw it, the English major still drew to some degree "from the cultivated, professional, and well-to-do classes," but "history tends to appeal on the whole to a lower social stratum." Rather than "sons of professional men, far too many [history majors] list their parent's occupation as a janitor, watchman, salesman, grocer, pocketbook cutter, bookkeeper, railroad clerk, pharmacist, cable tester, mechanic, general clerk, butter-and-egg jobber and the like. One may be glad to see the sons of the lower occupations working upward. . . . It may be flattering to be regarded as an elevator. But even the strongest elevator will break down if asked to lift too much weight."[9]

In addition to such unabashed elitism, Woodward was concerned that Pierson, in his 1952 history of Yale College, had seemed to find something almost endearing about a campus culture in the 1890s that "preferred discipline to free thinking, organization to originality, athlete to scholar [and] customs to books." In the main, Woodward's own preferences ran in precisely the opposite order, he confided to David Potter, allowing that, by now, that might be true of "George's and modern Yale's" preferences as well." Yet he could not shake his unease about other passages in which Pierson emphasized that the patriotism and conformity of the Yale of that era were "qualities that were so marked and would prove so enduring. . . . The joiner and the man of faith was perfectly at home." Were these traits still "enduring," some seventy years later, Woodward wondered. He was not "unpatriotic" or "a beatnik," but as Potter doubtless knew well, neither was he "a joiner or a man of faith or a conformist."[10]

The most obvious person to consult about Pierson's comments would have been Pierson himself, but for all his professed desire to diversify his department academically or intellectually, his personal loyalty and devotion to Yale were so much the stuff of institutional legend that Woodward feared he might bristle at questions that smacked even in the least of negative impressions of the place he loved so fiercely. (Pierson took an interest not only in the academic "breeding" of the Yale faculty but also in the proportion of "Yale blood" in a still all-male Yale College student body, where, he later reported, more than one in four were "sons of Yale" in 1962.) It seemed safer to sound out Potter and have him quietly share his reservations about Yale with Edmund Morgan and John Blum, who, like Potter, were not products of Yale College.[11]

Potter would be leaving for Stanford in a few months. Though he reportedly felt "underappreciated" after eighteen years at Yale, he was understandably hesitant to say anything that might sway such a critical decision for his close friend one way or the other. He conceded that there might have been a small contingent of faculty and administrators who once placed "the making of Yale men" above developing the potential of individual students, but this stereotypical notion was by now at least a generation out of date. In sum, Potter felt that if there was any lingering inclination toward conformity at Yale, its presence was "inappreciable" and should not factor into his decision.[12]

Blum and Morgan more or less echoed Potter's response. Morgan insisted that he had never felt the least bit of pressure to conform, though he allowed that he was not particularly fond of New Haven, which he found "provincial and too much in the shadow of New York." Woodward heard much the same thing about New Haven even from Pierson, who insisted that the town boasted a "cosmopolitan society of unusual diversity and vivacity and charm" but admitted with his trademark condescension that "the quality and quantity of cultivation in the town element still leaves something to be desired."[13]

In its day-to-day functioning, Morgan also found a great deal more emphasis on faculty rank than he liked, meaning that "the full professors have the last word, and often the only word, on most matters." Despite this, Morgan sensed a pervasive commitment to seeing the university excel. The days of faculty inbreeding were fading fast, and the best of Yale's graduate and undergraduate students were "very good indeed." He went on to assure Woodward that if the passages from Pierson's book that he had quoted were descriptive of what he had found at Yale, "I would not only reject it but would clear out." He added that "you know we want you, and the fact that we do want you is another sign that the things you hear about us are not so."[14]

Blum offered up much the same message: conceding that Yale might yet harbor some students, and maybe even a few professors, who preferred to "live in an Edwardian fantasy," but reporting that, overall, he had found his faculty colleagues not only intelligent but open-minded and energetically outspoken on all matters of import, including academic freedom. New, more academically demanding undergraduate admissions criteria promised to cut into the advantages once enjoyed by "sons of Yale" or other prep-school graduates. Lest Woodward think Yale was just "a big Princeton," however, Blum emphasized that "all of the best historians here devote more than half their time to graduate work." Like Morgan, Blum assured Woodward that if Yale's intellectual and cultural climate was by any means as constraining as he seemed to fear, "I honestly couldn't tolerate it." He also went on to describe his own three-and-a-half-year tenure at Yale "as close to ideal as I expect any could be," to the point even that he could "imagine myself nowhere but here."[15]

Woodward held Potter, Morgan, and Blum in high regard as his professional peers, but he also sought the perspective of Robin Winks, a Johns Hopkins PhD who was then still an assistant professor of history at Yale. Winks had quietly expressed some reservations about Yale during Woodward's campus visit, but in keeping with Yale's (and certainly Pierson's) seniority-conscious approach, the prospective new Sterling Professor had talked primarily to senior faculty who, if they had reservations, failed to pass them on. Making little effort to conceal his lack of enthusiasm for undergraduate teaching, Woodward observed to Winks that Yale appeared to devote the "great bulk of teaching energy" to the undergraduate program, "perhaps not so much as at Princeton, but a great deal." He could only hope that the bump in graduate enrollment over the past two years meant that Yale's administration truly meant to put more emphasis on graduate education. Yet he was still torn, and he entreated Winks to offer any more thoughts he might be inclined to share.[16]

In what was clearly a carefully considered response, Winks ventured some comparisons between what he had seen at Hopkins and now saw at Yale. Although he felt certain that the majority of Yale's faculty were not wealthy, he conceded that a noticeably greater share of them appeared to have additional sources of income than he had detected at Johns Hopkins. In any case, he felt scholarly achievement was far more important to faculty standing at Yale than personal wealth. Because Woodward's teaching would be largely confined to graduate students, he would rarely encounter "the easy arrogance of wealth" that was most pronounced in the undergraduate ranks, and Winks went out of his way to assure him that Yale was wholly committed to putting more emphasis on graduate training. "Sterling Professors here are looked at with incredible awe," he added, a factor that could serve as an additional buffer against unwanted interactions. At the same time, Winks anticipated that Woodward would benefit from his common interests with Morgan and Blum, suggesting that Johns Hopkins "induces a kind of scholarly isolation which Yale overcomes without intrusion." He also admitted to worrying that Woodward might choose to stay at Hopkins "largely out of loyalty to the institution rather than to yourself," when Yale offered a much better platform for him "to articulate the things which I know that you feel strongly about."[17]

Winks had provided information about the productivity of Yale's junior faculty, as well as the PhD program, detailing recent job placements and comparing recently completed and/or published dissertations with those produced at Hopkins. Woodward saw little qualitative difference; the greater distinctions seemed to lie in size and approach. Yale's history program was larger and more diverse, while Hopkins offered greater simplicity and intimacy. Though he realized that he must make a decision soon or "call the game on account of darkness," with his mind still caught up in a "tug of war," he admitted that he was still seeking "a surge of assurance that will sweep me off dead center."[18]

Surely no one other than Woodward, and perhaps not even he, wished so devoutly for that "surge of assurance" to materialize than George Pierson. Yet though Woodward professed to have been swept away by Pierson's letter offering him the job, he quickly came up with a good number of logistical questions and potential sticking points wholly apart from his personal reservations about Yale's intellectual ambience. Because he had been assured that he could be on leave and not in residence during 1961–62, his first year of official employment at Yale, he concurred with Pierson that his original plan at Hopkins to go on leave again in 1963–64 would have to be revised because it would not do for him to be on leave for two of his initial three years at Yale. Accordingly, he had agreed to at least push his second year of leave back to 1964–65, which still meant that he would actually be teaching during only two of his first four years at Yale.

This did not deter him, however, from seeking to further minimize his time in the classroom when he was not on leave. Yale's History 180 was a team-taught graduate course on American historiography. It typically consisted of a single weekly two-hour lecture and a pair of two-hour discussion sessions, each session covering the same material and involving roughly half of the students, allowing them to report on and criticize the work of various authors. Woodward had asked whether the discussion sessions might be combined into a single meeting, but Pierson made it clear that the smaller sections were meant to create an environment more conducive to student participation. Beyond that, he noted, because four professors were assigned to the course, each would be actively engaged with it for approximately seven weeks, amounting to a total of only forty-two classroom hours per year.[19]

Woodward had readily agreed to a starting salary of $20,000, which his fellowship from the Lilly Endowment would cover while he was on leave for 1961–62. Yet a devil still lurked in other financial details, particularly his retirement benefits. He pushed Pierson on the question of whether, like Hopkins, Yale would guarantee faculty who retired "at the regular time" an income equal to at least half their annual salary at the point of their retirement and wondered if Yale did the same. Pierson had shown uncharacteristic patience in responding to his prospective new colleague's inquiries about what he likely saw as trivial financial details, but in this instance, he responded bluntly that "the answer is that it never has, and does not, and sees no prospect of doing so."[20]

Eager as Pierson was to bring in outstanding scholars, like many of the Yale-bred senior faculty on campus, the man known, affectionately or otherwise, as "Father Yale" felt that the inherent privilege of teaching there justified expecting new faculty to "suffer for Yale," even if he, as a man of independent means, would not be suffering alongside them. Alvin Kernan had been forced to teach additional courses elsewhere to make ends meet as an assistant professor of English at Yale in the late 1950s. He later mused that the sense of at least genteel poverty as the natural condition of junior faculty was so pronounced that even those with additional means "were oddly appealing in their desperate need to seem poor like the rest of us." Even when dealing with established scholars, Pierson took it for granted that Yale's cachet obviated any need to offer them higher salaries than they were receiving in their current positions. Not only was the thirty-six-year-old John Blum asked initially to come to Yale for less than he made at MIT, but after being courted by Pierson, he was stunned on his campus interview to have the imperious and often unsubtly anti-Semitic department chair demand to know, "What business have you, at your age, looking at a Yale professorship?"[21]

When Pierson grew impatient with Woodward's dogged focus on such mundane details as salary and benefits, he allowed that his prospective new colleague's reasons for accepting his offer should "lie near the heart of the university and its faculty, rather than its fringes." Woodward had been genuinely apologetic about pressing Pierson on financial particulars, but his response this time was different. "My concern over retirement annuities," he replied rather pointedly, "is that of a man who expects to live largely on his salary and has no expectation of a legacy to help out later." He went on to admit that he had "felt from the start that a move to Yale would be good for me" and "would probably get more out of the old frame than staying put would." Yet he had also known that he could not be happy about the move if it came "at substantial sacrifice," and he assured Pierson that he was simply "trying hard to make a case that will justify the terrific effort and loss that pulling up stakes will cost."[22]

Woodward clearly recognized the enhanced influence, more powerful connections, and greater institutional support that he would enjoy at Yale. Still, he refused to allow the professional benefits of the move to undermine his resolve to keep his personal and family interests foremost throughout the negotiations. He had recently opened himself to serious courtship by Princeton, despite its heavy emphasis on undergraduate education, which he clearly did not find attractive in the least. Yet his vigorous pursuit of guaranteed future leave in his communications with Princeton had helped to secure the appropriate assurances from Hopkins on that score. These, in turn, would ultimately strengthen his bargaining position with Yale as well. Despite his humble, retiring posture, like his aggressive efforts to secure better royalties and advances on his books, his exchanges with George Pierson showed a deft and determined negotiator rather than the hapless, improvident academic he had seen in his father. Details of what transpired in the immediate aftermath of his attempt to exact further assurances from Pierson are scant, but there is good reason to suspect that further concessions were forthcoming before Woodward finally telegrammed his acceptance to him on December 12, 1960.[23]

Woodward's friend Robert Penn Warren, who had been affiliated with Yale for roughly a decade, had played a key role in his decision to join him. Warren had given a party for him and Glenn where he had encountered enough southern expatriates, such as writer William Styron and southern literary scholar Cleanth Brooks, to persuade him that he would not "feel too lonely in Yankeedom." When he wrote to tell Warren that "after a powerful lot of backing and filling and pulling and hauling, I finally said I would come to Yale," he allowed that knowing Warren "found the place congenial" encouraged him to believe "I cannot have gone terribly wrong." Yet even so, Woodward realized that "it will be some time before I know, and longer still before I know for sure."[24]

Although Woodward felt that going to Yale stood to be of substantial benefit professionally, he made no effort to conceal the pangs of personal loss that the move inflicted. "I don't think I ever had a decision that gave me such difficulty," he confided to Edmund Morgan. "The main thing was the ties here. . . . Breaking them proved almost an act of violence against myself as well as others." The wounds would surely heal in time, "but there is no use pretending they are not sore now." He offered much the same appraisal of his and Glenn's emotional state to his close friend and confidant Bill Carleton, after being "tortured for months" by a decision whose wisdom only time could validate.[25]

On the other hand, his future colleagues showed no ambivalence whatsoever in their reactions to his decision. "You should have seen the faces of our Professors of History," Pierson reported, when he read them the telegram. John Blum called it "the best news since V.J. Day." A newcomer to Yale himself, Arthur Wright, a distinguished historian of China, declared that he felt "rather like my small children must have felt when they sang 'Happy Birthday to Me.'"[26]

Woodward would eventually get beyond second guessing the move, but its emotional toll was still evident even in 1963, some eighteen months after he and Glenn had actually taken up residence in New Haven. He confessed to Glenn Rainey that at first it had seemed "all strange and confusing and obsessed and suddenly everybody seemed younger than I was. . . . This year it's better and I rather like it and besides, I would have regretted it if I hadn't [moved] just like I knew I would if I did. . . . It is an exciting place and powerful and marvelous human beings all about, young and old but terribly demanding, and I obviously won't live as long as I would had I stayed put, but what the hell."[27]

George Pierson hoped to build on Woodward's appointment to strengthen his department further, and Woodward was more than willing to serve as his chief talent scout. At his new colleague's urging, Pierson contacted the eminent cultural and literary scholar Henry Nash Smith of the University of California, Berkeley. Smith was seen as one of the principal creators of the discipline of American studies, and Woodward's suggestion drew an enthusiastic response from faculty of that program, as well as the departments of history and English at Yale. Yale's courtship of Smith ultimately went unrequited, leaving Woodward to ask suggestively whether "Dan Boorstin will be next in line for consideration." The reasons why Woodward's trial balloon for Boorstin gained little altitude among his future colleagues are not clear, although Boorstin's "consensus" perspective on U.S. history, which stressed the unity and continuity of the national experience, had begun to fall out of favor and would soon come under fierce attack from a younger, left-leaning scholarly cohort bent on emphasizing conflict and upheaval in American history.[28]

Although Woodward's suggestion of Boorstin did not pan out, he remained a valued adviser and consultant on faculty recruitment. Pierson even sought his input on bolstering Yale's ranks in Russian history, where he was scouting for a scholar "of the first magnitude." When he pondered additions to the department, Pierson clearly did not think small. His targets included the renowned Cold War and foreign affairs expert George F. Kennan and the eminent economic historian David Landes, both of whom turned him down, as did the University of London's Russian specialist Leonard Schapiro.[29]

In essence, Pierson was intent on bulking up his department at and from the top, and despite the departure of four promising young American historians for jobs "too good to turn down," Woodward knew full well that Yale's history department was on a recruitment roll in the early 1960s. The enthusiasm generated by his appointment and Pierson's commitment to bolstering the department even further had proven downright contagious. Yale provost and later president Kingman Brewster was so warmly disposed toward the history department, Woodward joked, that "if Kingman overheard you saying you liked [a historian's work], he'd hire 'em the next day."[30]

Headhunting for superstar professors was the order of the day in the early 1960s, as increased public and private support for higher education sparked an ultracompetitive scramble among universities looking for a quick means of making up the distance between themselves and the nation's truly elite institutions. The same was true for universities concerned with maintaining their exalted status, of course, with Yale's pursuit of Woodward as a case in point. He would be rudely reminded of this when widespread "faculty raiding" finally captured the attention of major news outlets and a certain recently hired Sterling Professor of History at Yale became "Exhibit A." *Time* magazine led the way with its January 1962 exposé of "The Faculty Raiders." Woodward had been stingy with the specific details of his arrangement at Yale, and he was not the least bit pleased to find some of those details, including "a blue-ribbon chair and a year's leave with pay before he ever reaches New Haven," highlighted in the clincher sentence of the *Time* report. Without mentioning that his leave was funded by the Lilly Endowment rather than Yale itself, the reporter cast Woodward as part of a wheeler-dealering cohort of pampered high-profile academics bent on maximizing their salaries while minimizing their teaching. Nor were they above demanding library acquisitions or laboratory accommodations tailored strictly to their particular research interests.[31]

After complaining to the editors at *Time* that his arrangement with Yale had been portrayed inaccurately, Woodward managed to exact a private apology but no promise of a public correction. More than two months later, at the end of March, he admitted that he was "still sore about this," only to find himself sorer still two months later, when he was blindsided yet again by a similar, though more expansive *New York Times* front-page exposé of the increasingly competitive and high-stakes game of "faculty raiding" by universities looking to poach "'Name' Professors" away from their academic rivals. Here again, the *Times* education writer Fred Hechinger described substantial salaries (Woodward's $20,000 seemed to be just about the "going offer" for "the most desirable schools") and dramatically reduced teaching loads, apparently down in some cases to one course every other semester. With these, Hechinger reported, came other perks such as tuition subsidies for the professors' children and subsidized mortgage assistance, both of which, of course, Woodward had received from Yale as standard benefits for all tenure-track faculty.[32]

Although, publicly at least, Woodward directed the bulk of his anger toward the reporter who wrote the piece, he could not have been terribly pleased to see an unnamed Yale administrator quoted as calling the competition for distinguished scholars "strictly a dog-eat-dog business" and sounding every bit the alpha dog himself as he "point[ed] with pride" to "the acquisition of Professor Woodward." Hechinger also noted that Woodward's first year at Yale would be spent on leave and claimed that his standard teaching load was to be one seminar, so that he could otherwise "devote himself to writing." Regardless of whether this information was accurate (or how much Woodward may have secretly wished it so), he was anything but gratified to find the issue of his teaching load in print yet again for millions of readers, including his new colleagues, to see.[33]

The administrator who appeared to have provided the reporter with some details of his arrangement with Yale and seemed to liken him to a prize won in a fierce dogfight had not been identified. Yet Woodward seemed more than a little miffed to find Provost Kingman Brewster speaking on the record as he waxed breezily philosophical in likening intensely competitive faculty recruitment efforts to a fishing expedition, explaining that "you've got to enjoy fishing without catching all the fish." When Woodward made sure Brewster and Pierson knew of his displeasure, both tried to redirect his anger solely toward the *Times* reporter who, according to Pierson, had simply displayed his "wonderful capacity for putting his foot in it," despite the efforts of "King Brewster . . . to educate him gently." If Woodward was mollified by Brewster's assurance that he "would be worried about you if you were not 'sore as a boil'" about the whole business, he gave no evidence of it in his reply. He was indeed "burned up and boiling mad," he fumed, because it was "hard enough to change universities anyway. But to arrive plastered by the press as a sharp bargainer and a shirker makes it harder."[34]

Though embarrassed by having his light teaching load and generous leave allocation exposed, not once, but twice, in the national press, Woodward did not shrink thereafter from jealously guarding his time for research and writing. Scarcely two years after the *New York Times* affair, his new department chair, Edmund Morgan, asked faculty members for an update on their activities and concerns. Woodward responded that, while he was uncertain about how much research time it was reasonable to expect, under the current arrangement, at least, he "found it difficult to maintain the continuity of work that is essential for productive scholarship." Momentum gained during the summer or periodic semesters on leave was difficult to maintain "between September and June." He acknowledged that his "share of the burden of teaching and committee work" was modest relative to that of some of his colleagues. Yet he claimed that he had already done more "committee work and teaching (four courses the second term)" in his first two years on campus "than . . . in twenty years in other institutions." He knew that his colleagues with greater teaching and committee obligations must surely feel even greater frustration, leaving him to worry all the more about "the overall impact on faculty morale and productivity."[35]

To remedy this situation, Woodard suggested that two courses should be the normal teaching load, and with the expanding enrollment in the graduate program, he felt it was unavoidable that "some members of the department" must confine their teaching almost exclusively to graduate courses. (It's highly unlikely Morgan felt the need to ask if he had anyone specific in mind for such an assignment.) Beyond that, Woodward also proposed that the lecture requirements for undergraduate courses be reduced from three hours to two, so as to "enable a man to set aside consecutive time each week for research and writing." As to the excess of committee work, he thought more decision-making authority should simply be delegated to the department chair, while most of the duties now assigned to the directors of both graduate and undergraduate studies might at some point be "taken over by high-grade secretaries." This response may not have immediately secured Woodward's exclusive involvement with graduate students, but Morgan and John Blum did go on to persuade Kingman Brewster, who was by then president of Yale, to allow productive faculty a semester off every three years.[36]

Woodward would later recall having been asked initially only to offer a graduate seminar every year and deliver a lecture or two here or there in undergraduate courses taught by others at Yale. In any case, the editor of the student newspaper thought it was front-page news when the history department announced in April 1963 that he would finally teach his first undergraduate course, a small, highly selective seminar for seniors and juniors, the following year. Details of the specific teaching responsibilities of distinguished senior historians at Yale are generally too murky to allow for much in the way of comparisons. J. H. Hexter, also worked largely with graduate students, and Morgan, a highly regarded U.S. colonial historian, typically spent no more than five hours a week in the classroom. Regardless of whether Woodward's actual teaching load differed significantly from those of his high-profile senior colleagues, his greatest contributions to the graduate program were not to be registered while he was in formal classroom mode.[37]

Even the most devoted of Woodward's charges were forced to concede that he was far from the most effective classroom instructor they had encountered. Yet whether they studied with him at Johns Hopkins or Yale, many of them looked back appreciatively at what Louis Harlan called "the unique blend of direction and non-direction" he offered in his graduate seminars, where he gave students considerable latitude, both in choosing their topics and in how they approached them in their research and writing. Making his students "carbon copies of the master" was never Woodward's aim, Harlan thought. "Rather than tell us what it is and how to do it, he helped us frame the problem and sent us off to solve it. We learned by doing. . . . This approach further developed us into independent thinkers, scholars, and writers." Woodward's Yale PhD student Mills Thornton thought he was at his best in a "one-to-one conversation in his office, talking about how you could develop projects or the meaning of things." Thornton echoed Harlan in explaining that Woodward "never wanted disciples. . . . He wanted you to find your own way." Rather than "toe the party line or embroider positions that he had already laid out . . . he expected me to go out and figure out all of the stuff on my own. Now he was prepared to comment about it. But he did not demand that I agree with him, just [that I] take account of criticisms or holes in the argument that were apparent to him, for my own welfare."[38]

Recalling his tutelage under Woodward at Johns Hopkins, James McPherson agreed that he did his best teaching in private discussions with individual students. He was "not a particularly good lecturer," McPherson admitted, but he was much "more effective as an example, his books, his ideas. He was also a very good critic of what his students wrote. A sympathetic, but constructive and tough critic." One of Woodward's later students at Yale, Lawrence Powell, agreed that when a student gave him something to read, "nine times out of ten, you would get back incisive commentary, poetically expressed." When Woodward retired in 1977, responsibility for directing Steven Hahn's dissertation passed to Howard Lamar. When that dissertation appeared in print as

The Roots of Southern Populism, however, Hahn was quick to acknowledge his debt to Woodward, who "asked hard questions, steered me away from unpromising scholarly paths, and held out an example of learning and historical imagination to which I, like all of his students aspired."[39]

Regardless of how highly they valued his guidance, Woodward's PhD students did not seem to relish the prospect of going to his office to seek it. Arriving at Johns Hopkins in 1957, Bertram Wyatt-Brown quickly realized that, despite his quiet manner, his adviser-to-be did not exactly put graduate students at ease in one-on-one conversations about their work. Anyone reporting that "I must go see God this morning" need not elaborate to win the commiserations of his or her peers. After all, Wyatt-Brown soon realized, "'A good word from Vann Woodward,' as the old Hopkins saying went, . . . would reanimate a sorely depleted graduate student ego," while "a note of criticism, usually deftly, courteously stated, or still worse, a silence, could be temporarily devastating." Lawrence Powell agreed that "the thing you dreaded most were the silences." He spoke for many of his fellow Woodward students when he described a visit to the darkened, deathly quiet office in Yale's Hall of Graduate Studies, its atmosphere rendered all the more intimidating by the steely presence of William Faulkner, who gazed down from the portrait behind his mentor's desk. It was "unfailingly a terrifying experience," Powell recalled, for flustered student visitors who "often stumbled through the meeting, which was punctuated by enigmatic nods from the great man himself. Rehearse your lines as you might, you always left with the sinking feeling that this was probably the last casting call you would ever get." Although Woodward could be relaxed and affable in other settings, few of his students seemed to feel any impulse to prolong their office visits or to sense any encouragement to do so on his part.[40]

Only nine PhD students had completed their dissertations under his supervision during his fourteen years (1947–60) in residence at Johns Hopkins, although as his fame grew, he had begun to attract more disciples, six of whom had dissertations in progress when he decided to leave in 1960. By way of comparison, over roughly the same time span (from his actual arrival on campus at Yale in 1962 until his formal retirement in 1977), Woodward would direct an additional twenty-four dissertations to completion, with two more to come by 1979. Twenty-three of the twenty-six done at Yale dealt with topics in or closely related to southern history. Of these, nineteen would eventually be published.

For a number of Woodward's students, getting a dissertation in print was merely the first milestone in what would become a distinguished and influential career. One of his Yale PhDs, William S. McFeely, went on to win a Pulitzer Prize for his biography of U. S. Grant (*Grant: A Biography*), while Johns Hopkins advisees James McPherson (*Battle Cry of Freedom: The Civil War Era*) and Louis Harlan (*Booker T. Washington: The Wizard of Tuskegee, 1901–1915*) also received Pulitzers. Several of his students from both institutions joined him as winners of the coveted Bancroft Prize given by Columbia University for an outstanding book in American history. Although it is impossible to say that each of the forty-one students whose dissertations he directed received the precisely same degree of his attention, there is no indication that he was in the habit of giving any of them less than he thought they required, even if the numerous other demands on his time meant it sometimes took a while.[41]

From his earliest days at Johns Hopkins until his retirement from Yale and beyond, Woodward frequently showed remarkable patience and diplomacy in dealing with his dissertation students. The demands of his role changed over the years, but it could be particularly challenging before the mid-1960s, when jobs were so plentiful that some of his students were able to win spots at leading universities even before they completed their dissertations. A few weeks before James McPherson began teaching at Princeton in the fall term of 1961, he submitted fifteen dissertation chapters devoted to the abolitionists during the Civil War and gave his mentor notice that five more, apparently devoted to the Reconstruction era, were soon to follow. Woodward's task was further complicated by the presence on McPherson's dissertation committee of distinguished Civil War and Reconstruction historian David Donald, who also happened to be his senior colleague at Princeton. This rather unorthodox arrangement became downright awkward after September 5, 1962, when Donald dashed off a letter to Woodward complaining that "your Mr. McP. has just deposited on my desk his formidably large manuscript with the request that I have it read so that he can make all the corrections and have the entire book typed up in final form by October 1." Woodward certainly agreed with Donald that honoring this request was "simply out of the question," and anticipating this reaction to the uncommon length of the manuscript, Woodward had just written Donald, conceding that, perhaps because of McPherson's "prodigious research," he "tends to over prove/over document points" and thereby "risked writing himself out of the limits of practicability of publication and straining the patience of his readers." Still, he allowed, "the boy's efforts obviously deserve serious attention from us both."[42]

After further communication with Donald, Woodward let McPherson know that there was not even the remotest possibility of meeting his October

1 deadline. Though he had no precise sense of how Donald felt about the quality of McPherson's work, Woodward added that the two of them were of one mind in recommending McPherson amend his title to indicate that he was covering only the Civil War era and include only the fifteen chapters dealing with that period. This would leave a manuscript that was still "longer than the average dissertation" and "save you money and time in the typing and editing and put less of a strain on the patience of your examining committee."[43]

Rather than cut whole chapters, McPherson ventured that by drawing on the comments of Woodward, Donald, and his own former graduate school colleague Willie Lee Rose, he could reduce the overall length of the manuscript without weakening his argument simply by culling out superfluous paragraphs, sentences, and quotations. To McPherson's relief and perhaps Donald's dismay, Woodward not only relented in his call to cut the last five chapters but, setting aside his customary practice of withholding his recommended changes until he saw a full manuscript, he also agreed to provide comments on the parts he had seen that could be incorporated into revisions before it was passed on to Donald.[44]

Though Donald had just begun to read the dissertation as January 1963 drew to a close, Woodward worried less about his ultimate appraisal of it than his view of his brand-new and thus untenured colleague. Hence, Woodward conveyed to McPherson his sense that while Donald seemed to have little doubt about the "acceptability of the work," he did, however, "entertain some doubts about your native endowment in the matter of tact, deference, etc." Without passing judgment on the validity of Donald's impressions, Woodward could "only urge that you muster whatever resources you may have in the exercise of these qualities." With that bit of lecturing accomplished, however, he reassured McPherson there was "no reason to doubt we will come through with the degree in the required time." Not only would this come to pass, but almost eight months later to the day, McPherson was signing a contract with Princeton University Press, which would publish his dissertation the following year.[45]

With McPherson, as with so many other of his students, Woodward moved quickly from advising him about his dissertation to advising him about his career. It might seem that McPherson's book contract should have left him sitting pretty at Princeton. Yet the arrival in 1962 of fellow American historian Martin Duberman, who already had a Bancroft Prize–winning book to his credit, understandably left him a bit uneasy about his role in the department going forward, especially in light of apparent suggestions that he might consider changing his focus to the history of education. Woodward counseled McPherson not to apply for positions elsewhere until his book came out the following year, but he did not encourage him to stay at Princeton if it meant that he would be "diverted from your true line of interest." On the contrary, he thought that if Duberman stayed there, McPherson should probably count on leaving because "it would not be healthy either for your own career or your relations with him to sit around and watch another man do the things you want to do yourself." As to where McPherson might go, Woodward saw little reason for concern. Once his book came out, he should be "in a very strong position to move to a good job" and enjoy "a wider range of choice and opportunity." He had already called Michigan's attention to his newly minted PhD and promised that he would recommend him "for anything I think would be really desirable."[46]

Cocksure as it might seem in light of today's anemic job market for historians, Woodward's confidence about McPherson's job prospects was not unfounded. Not only were McPherson's talent and potential plain to see but, in a time well before requirements that positions must be advertised or hiring decisions held accountable, the status and connections of one's adviser stood to be of pivotal importance. As McPherson himself recalled, "My own path to Ivy League employment . . . was ridiculously easy. One day in 1962 the chairman of the History Department at Princeton phoned my Hopkins adviser, C. Vann Woodward, and asked him if he had a 'young man' to recommend for an instructorship (then the first rung on the tenure-track ladder). Woodward recommended me—I don't know if he even had to put it in writing—and Princeton offered me the job, without a real interview and without having seen any dissertation chapters."[47]

Sheldon Hackney was also hired at Princeton before completing his PhD under Woodward's supervision at Yale. Woodward already knew Hackney as the son-in-law of his friends Clifford and Virginia Durr before he began his studies at Yale in 1961. By the time Hackney began teaching at Princeton in 1965, Woodward had read an entire draft of his study of "Populism and Progressivism in Alabama." He would read another revised draft and significant parts of the manuscript beyond that, as Hackney struggled to get it in shape while staying abreast of his teaching and expanding administrative duties at Princeton. Hackney's case was fairly indicative of Woodward's general approach to directing dissertations. His initial perusal of chapters and manuscript segments was dedicated largely to seeing that his protégé was on track or suggesting the appropriate course corrections. Once this was accomplished, he tended to take a more detached approach unless the student sought his further guidance on specific issues. Though not at all hesitant to convey skepticism or to express disappointment about a chapter that seemed "a little thin," Woodward typically remained positive and optimistic, though guardedly so. Only when he saw the final product was he likely to offer a definitively affirmative, though still seldom effusive, assessment. Hackney's submitted dissertation had drawn a "quite favorable" response from his reading committee, Woodward reported, but the strongest formal commendation he offered was that it had given him "a new appreciation of the work you have done."[48]

Knowing full well that his mentor was not given to gratuitous praise, Lawrence Powell had good reason to savor Woodward's observation that one of the chapters in his dissertation on northern planters in the South during the Civil War and Reconstruction "measure[d] up, for the most part, to the high standard set by Willie Rose" (in her acclaimed study of wartime northern occupation of the Sea Islands off the coast of South Carolina). True to form, however, Woodward followed up on his gratifying appraisal with several gentle suggestions about how the chapter might be further fleshed out and enriched.[49]

If the situation required, Woodward was not averse to a more straightforwardly critical approach to getting a dissertation in shape. He praised the "great stuff" in his Yale PhD student John Blassingame's statistics-laden third and fourth dissertation chapters on blacks in New Orleans but thought considerable revision would still be necessary and asked to see them before Blassingame submitted the full manuscript to his reading committee. He also tried to rein in what struck him as Blassingame's uncritical exuberance about the accomplishments of New Orleans's black bourgeoisie: "I am sure they were black and beautiful, but I think you go too far with your details about some of the petty entrepreneurs." He also questioned Blassingame's emphasis on "the deep sense of *noblesse oblige* and racial commitment professed by free negroes, since there was very little evidence that they did anything for their starving brothers." On the other hand, he lauded the potentially "revolutionary significance" of Blassingame's data on the stability of the black family despite his concerns about the trickiness of identifying male heads of households and compiling reliable figures on illegitimate births.[50]

Though he seemed more critical of Blassingame's early efforts than those of some other students, Woodward's "tough love" approach should not obscure his genuine admiration for a young black man who grew up with few advantages in Social Circle, Georgia, some twelve miles from Oxford, where Woodward and his family had lived for several years. This much was evident in his praise for Blassingame's book *The Slave Community*, which appeared in 1972, a year before his dissertation was published. Drawing primarily on published slave narratives, the book was one of the first major efforts to present slave life from the perspectives of the slaves themselves, and Blassingame used their testimony to challenge the arguments of Stanley Elkins and other historians and sociologists that enslavement had essentially stripped African Americans of their cultural identity and sense of dignity and worth. Although Woodward had urged him to get his dissertation in print first, he had read *The Slave Community* with "pleasure and profit—and I should say vicarious pride," he reported to Blassingame in September 1972, declaring it "a fine piece of work" that "sets a high mark for others in the field." The book "smashes many old and many new stereotypes," he added, "but the one that I take most satisfaction and pride in your shattering will not be found in the index, nor is it mentioned in the text. It didn't have to be. We all know what it is."[51]

Although Blassingame's career prospects seemed bright, there was still a hurdle to be cleared. He had accepted a position as an instructor at Yale in 1970 and moved into an assistant professor slot after his dissertation was approved the following year. Now on what was assuredly a "fast track," he was up for tenure and promotion to associate professor in 1972, awkwardly enough, with his mentor chairing his promotion and tenure committee. As propitious as this arrangement might have seemed for Blassingame, there was reason for concern. His dissertation had been accepted for publication at that point, but as Woodward had feared, it would not be out until the following year, meaning that external reviewers of Blassingame's published work to date would have to focus most of their attention on *The Slave Community*. Moreover, in light of his personal and professional ties to Blassingame, Woodward was acutely conscious of avoiding any impression that his student was being held to less exacting standards than any other promotion and tenure candidate in his department. Hence, among the scholars whose appraisals of Blassingame's work he sought were Winthrop Jordan and Kenneth Stampp, two of the most highly respected historians of race and slavery of their generation, and the latter one of the historians who had come in for some significant criticism in Blassingame's book.[52]

For his part, Stampp informed Woodward in mid-November 1972 that he couldn't provide much in the way of an assessment of Blassingame's work because he had read only a couple of his articles and had not yet been able find a copy of *The Slave Community* in any bookstore in Berkeley. Though he had ordered it directly from Oxford University Press back in January, he still had no idea when he might get his copy. With the time fast approaching for his committee to make its recommendations in Blassingame's case, however, Woodward pressed Stampp to "write me about it as soon as you can. Surely your copy of it will turn up in the next few weeks, and I hope you will have the time to write me a reaction. The reason for my insistence is that Blassingame's case for tenure is unusual in view of his age [40] and experience, yet I feel the case must be made."[53]

Though he had still heard nothing more from Stampp, in late December, Woodward finally got a response from Jordan, who explained that he had been delayed by the illness and subsequent death of his father but hoped that his note would not be "too late to be of use" "in what he saw as "a difficult decision." He praised Blassingame for trying to correct certain "deficiencies" by taking "black" sources seriously and noted that "just being sensible on the subject . . . is a considerable achievement in itself." Yet for all that, Jordan felt that *The Slave Community* "does not have much analytical power, nor does it seem to me particularly perceptive or imaginative in dealing with the thoughts and feelings of slaves," though he conceded that he knew of no other book on slavery that was any more successful in this respect. In the end, Jordan concluded that if he "were voting on the matter here," he would "with some misgivings, vote for promotion," although he was of the opinion "that whatever decision you make will be a controversial one in the profession."[54]

However gently and tactfully it was delivered, Jordan's endorsement was, at best, a few degrees warmer than tepid. At that, however, it was practically glowing in comparison to the response Woodward eventually received from Stampp, who had gotten a copy of the book only at the end of January 1973 and clearly did not seem to think it worth the wait. Though he was uncertain whether Woodward still wanted his evaluation, he could at least tell him that "I do not think the book is very good." Published slave narratives or autobiographies were suspect as sources in the eyes of many scholars because it was likely that they had been edited by white abolitionists looking to sharpen their condemnations of slavery. Stampp felt that Blassingame had approached these volumes "most uncritically" while making little or no use of other potentially important sources. Though he also found "much evidence of carelessness" in the misspelled names of key characters and elsewhere, Stampp's major criticism echoed Jordan's in terms of the "lack of originality" in a book that struck him as largely a "synthesis of recent scholarship." Blassingame's discussion of rebellious and runaway slaves, he noted, was "derived almost entirely from secondary sources, with [Marxist historian Herbert] Aptheker appearing in his footnotes far too often."[55]

With its focus on slave agency, *The Slave Community* presented something of a counter to Stampp's heavy emphasis in *The Peculiar Institution* on the thoroughly debilitating impact of slavery on its well-nigh helpless victims. Where Blassingame saw interactions among the slaves within their own semiautonomous "community" bolstering their sense of worth and insulating them from some of the worst effects of their condition, Stampp had seen their relationships with their owners as the dominant factor in their lives. Though it was hardly surprising that Stampp found so much to dislike about the book, Woodward informed him nonetheless that, had his letter not arrived two weeks after the committee made its recommendation, "it would have stopped the promotion." This was obviously not Stampp's fault, he added, "and neither of us is to blame for the delay." Why Woodward felt the need for such disclaimer is not exactly clear. On the one hand, if he had any intention of trying to protect Blassingame, he surely would never have asked Stampp to assess his work in the first place, much less persisted in begging for his appraisal despite Stampp's difficulties in getting his hands on the book. On the other hand, if he was truly intent on having Stampp's input before the committee's deliberations began, as the author of one of Oxford University Press's best-selling books of the twentieth century and the editor of the Oxford History of the United States, he surely could have seen to it that Stampp got a copy of *The Slave Community* in plenty of time to meet his committee's deadline. Be that as it may, Woodward assured Stampp that he was "disturbed at the shortcomings you find," adding that he had "repeatedly cautioned [Blassingame] that he was going too fast with it, and the mistakes are in large part due to haste." His justification for recommending the promotion was his high opinion of Blassingame's dissertation, which was to be published in a few months. Sensing that this rationale might cut little ice with Stampp, he appealed to his liberal sensibilities by reminding him that Blassingame "is a young man in a great hurry, who has come up from far down. One has to take chances, and I hope his future record will justify this one."[56]

Woodward's hopes for Blassingame would soon be more than fulfilled, but in the meantime, he felt that Stampp's comments left him all but obligated to rain on his protégé's parade. He assured his former student and current colleague that he surely could have found no fault with the list of external reviewers contacted for their appraisal of his work. The majority of their letters had favored his promotion. A few, however, had suggested that the book bore signs of having been done in haste. Though the names of the referees were to be kept strictly confidential, Woodward explained that there was one letter that he must call to his attention "because of specific errors it cites and the possibility of your correcting them in the future." Much as he had told Stampp, he advised Blassingame that, in his view, had this letter arrived in time for the committee's consideration, "I'm afraid it would have blocked our efforts." Envisioning a message that was more sobering than devastating, he maintained that he still thought "our decision was justified," but in a classic mentor's "I-told-you-so," he also implied that if Blassingame had followed his advice and made the dissertation a priority, the referees would have then "been able to base their opinions on your dissertation instead of exclusively on the book published."[57]

In a reaction many a mentor of graduate students would recognize all too readily, Blassingame seemed less chastened than irritated, perhaps more so with Woodward than with his unknown critic. "Quite frankly," he told Woodward, "I find nothing exceptional in the commentary." Misspellings could be corrected in future editions, and "the reliability of certain kinds of evidence" would always be subject to debate. As for the reader's questions about the originality of his contribution, Blassingame professed to have been "wracking my brain to come up with the title of any general study of slavery which has a chapter on the family, culture, or the African background treated in the same fashion as in *The Slave Community*." On this point, Blassingame came close to echoing the studiously upbeat and affirming appraisal of the book that Woodward had offered in his earlier letter congratulating him on how well it had turned out. This may well explain why Blassingame added rather pointedly, "Your reaction is somewhat surprising." Woodward apparently pursued the matter no further, but the striking forbearance he demonstrated in deftly tightroping his way through Blassingame's potentially tricky promotion and tenure review often came through in his efforts to help others of his students weather career crises of their own.[58]

Although Woodward's contributions to the graduate program were critical to Yale's rapid emergence as the most desirable place to study southern history in the entire country, his labors with graduate students at Johns Hopkins had yet to bear much of their ultimately bountiful fruit when Yale began courting him in 1960. His appeal as David Potter's successor had rested in large measure on his impressive record of publishing original and influential scholarly monographs. Yet in an ironic twist truly befitting the career of such a master of irony in his own right, it would turn out that, by the time he arrived in New Haven, Woodward's own days of writing the kind of books that had established his reputation (and that his students would soon be contributing in such profusion) had effectively been over for more than a decade.

12

Therapist of the Public Mind

The Strange Career of C. Vann Woodward

There had been substantial buzz well before Woodward left Johns Hopkins about his rumored plans to undertake a "serious" book on Reconstruction, preparatory, perhaps, to a larger book on the entire century between Emancipation and the civil rights movement. When word of this broke in publishing circles, he quickly found himself beset by ardent suitors such as Oxford University Press, where he was assured that "we are interested in anything you do," and Random House, where he was promised that "any manuscript you submit here will be read with the greatest pro-Woodward bias."[1]

In late September 1958, Woodward finally made his own direct pitch to Little, Brown, which technically held the option on his next two books by virtue of the contract he signed when they published *Reunion and Reaction*. He had done some work on the Reconstruction book in fits and starts, but he told Little, Brown's Arthur Thornhill that in order to finally get himself going on it, he needed a formal contract. The book he had in mind, Woodward explained, might be seen as something of a companion to *Origins*, though free of the constraints often imposed on books written for a series. The new book stood to attract more attention, he reasoned, owing to its "thundering relevance" to the rapidly escalating civil rights struggle of the late 1950s, which Woodward had already dubbed "the Second Reconstruction." This second crusade for black rights "will be with us for some time to come," he predicted, and would surely rekindle interest in the "First Reconstruction." Where Americans had generally accepted the changes that marked the Progressive Era and the New Deal, the concerns and challenges raised earlier by Reconstruction remained uniquely "unresolved and live." Given the raucous chants of defiance and resistance to school desegregation currently blaring from the old Confederacy, he ventured, "we will probably celebrate the centennial of the first Reconstruction before its principles and aims are achieved by the Second."[2]

Noting the sales of the "more academic" *Origins*, which amounted to about 7,000 copies, Woodward foresaw better prospects for his Reconstruction book and suggested a $2,500 advance. Thornhill readily agreed and proposed a royalty rate of 10 percent on the first 7,500 copies sold, rising to 15 percent after 10,000. Thinking the matter settled, Thornhill was startled a few months later to learn from Woodward that George P. Brockway of W. W. Norton had telegrammed to ask if an advance of $10,000 might "persuade" him to write a book on Reconstruction for his company. According to Woodward, when apprised of his contract with Little Brown, Brockway was undeterred and simply encouraged him to seek a release from that agreement. "In view of these special circumstances," Woodward explained to Thornhill, he had decided to do precisely that, hoping, of course, that this request would not spoil his relationship with a publisher he held in such "high regard."[3]

Stunned by Woodward's letter, as well as word of a fellow editor engaging in behavior he considered not only a gross violation of professional standards but downright "barbaric," Thornhill contacted Brockway, who professed to agree with Thornhill that it made no sense "for publishers to go around asking authors to tear up contracts and sign with competitors." Though he was still puzzled about what had transpired, rather than push Woodward for more clarification, Thornhill simply reminded him of the losses Little, Brown had incurred in publishing *Reunion and Reaction* and sermonized a bit about the risks inherent in reckless proffers of large advances before explaining, "In other words, Vann, I honestly don't think you should ask us to cancel the contract for your book on Reconstruction."[4]

If Thornhill expected contrition, Woodward failed to deliver, insisting that he had given Brockway "the full story," and "he left no doubt in my mind that in his opinion a request for a release from the contract would involve no breach of accepted publisher-author ethics." In any case, he maintained, "I still consider his position above board and beyond reproach." Thornhill had pointed out that the original $2,500 advance was the figure Woodward had requested. Woodward conceded as much but added, "You are not right in assuming that I needed no more than I asked for. I have two sick parents in Florida and a son who starts college in the fall of 1960. I cannot do that on an academic salary, even a good one." In light of these obligations, he asked Thornhill to "look at it from my point of view. Here comes another good publisher offering me an advance four times the advance I requested of you, ... before he met me, and with obvious confidence that he was not going to lose money... in spite of the large advance." Advancing rather than retreating, he urged Thornhill to "reconsider the venture in light of these developments and see if you cannot improve the terms of advance and do so in the entire consistency with a realistic appraisal of the book's possibilities." Thornhill did not buy into Woodward's contention that Brockway's tactics were either "above-board or beyond reproach," but in April 1959 he reported that, after some recalculations, he had persuaded his colleagues "that we should go all out to support you," and was prepared to raise the advance to $7,500. Though still short of the Norton offer, this was three times the figure agreed on initially, and it proved sufficient to satisfy Woodward, who had once again proven himself a hard-nosed steward of his financial interests.[5]

At that point Woodward knew he would be on paid leave from Johns Hopkins in the spring semester of 1960, and he had plans to seek outside funding that he believed, however unrealistically, would allow him enough free time over the next four years to complete his manuscript by October 1964. In addition to the contemporary relevance of his proposed book, he noted in a funding proposal for the Lilly Endowment that, despite a recent flurry of activity in the field, the standard studies of Reconstruction largely dated back more than fifty years and, whatever their merits, rested on racial views and historical assumptions that were "no longer tenable." With the exception of W. E. B. Du Bois, the authors of these studies were whites who generally assumed that blacks were simply not up to the challenges "of self-government and full participation in democratic government." Astutely connecting some critical dots, he observed that because of the intensely negative impressions of the First Reconstruction conveyed by these racist authors, subsequent federal efforts to help blacks had struck whites as a recipe for "disaster." E. Merton Coulter's 1947 book on Reconstruction in the *History of the South* series illustrated Woodward's point perfectly. Coulter was both an unabashed segregationist and a diehard proponent of the Dunning view of Reconstruction as an unwarranted and ill-considered intrusion into southern affairs. His book simply underscored Woodward's contention that such treatments of Reconstruction had provided "a bulwark" for Jim Crow's defenders and proven to be a significant hindrance to "a 'Second Reconstruction,' now underway."[6]

Beyond its potential implications for the ongoing crusade for racial justice, Woodward saw his book as a dramatic departure from the simplistic "century-old debate" about "whether Reconstruction was benevolent or malevolent, philanthropic or vindictive." Rather, he planned to approach Reconstruction more from the feelings and experiences of those directly affected by it, focusing on "what was it like to be emancipated, conquered, disfranchised, redeemed, segregated?"[7]

The ground-level focus he described would have represented a decided shift in perspective for a historian whose previous monographs were largely dedicated to major players in the broader political, economic, and racial struggles that shaped the South in the wake of Reconstruction. In fact, the focus of Woodward's early research on the new book hardly suggested a departure from his old approach, as he concentrated primarily on the correspondence of such prominent Radical Republicans as Charles Sumner, Thaddeus Stevens, and Lyman Trumbull, for whom he continued to show an undisguised distaste. In his jotted research notes, he deplored the Radicals' concerns with patronage while allowing that "the very nature" of Andrew Johnson's position required him to bargain for support in exchange for political appointments. Woodward's notes also affirmed his longtime suspicion that a great many white northerners calling for black suffrage in the South did so largely in hope of pursuing their own political and economic interests in the region without interference from white southerners. On this point, returning to yet another of his pet peeves, he also gathered information that seemed to indicate that the number of white southerners disfranchised during Radical Reconstruction was far more substantial than had been acknowledged thus far.[8]

Although he cited the fresh research on Reconstruction recently conducted by his PhD students at Johns Hopkins, in funding requests to the Lilly Endowment and Guggenheim Foundation, he made it abundantly clear that he was not preparing a "mere synthesis of new monographs done by my students and others" but going "back to the archives" to "do original research myself." He had already done that in a string of manuscript repositories stretching from Boston to Detroit when he launched his southern research initiative with visits to major archives in both the Carolinas in the spring of 1960.[9]

After some work in Knoxville the previous fall, in January 1962 he and Glenn began a three-month southwestern sojourn that would take them down through Alabama and Mississippi and ultimately out to Austin, where he would find the archives "so rich and abundant" that he quickly resigned himself to a return visit. While notes from Woodward's earlier northern research on Reconstruction are largely concentrated in seven folders in two regular archival boxes, his notes from research in southern newspapers and archives account for the majority of the contents of but two twelve-by-five-by-eight-inch file card boxes. These notes are also generally less detailed, with quoted material less likely to be annotated than those from his earlier work in northern archives.[10]

Although Woodward continued to work on the Reconstruction book as he was settling in at Yale and even drafted a bit of text here and there, as the next few years unfolded, his momentum and engagement with the project began to slip away. He had planned to rely on certain parallels between the First Reconstruction and the Second as the book's interpretive foundation. Michael O'Brien has suggested that Woodward may have lost interest in the project as he saw those parallels beginning to break down in the mid-1960s, when the Black Power movement sapped the energy and widened divisions within the civil rights crusade. In reality, however, Woodward's enthusiasm seemed to fade even before this scenario had played out.[11]

When he first contacted Arthur Thornhill about the project in September 1958, he foresaw October 1962 as the earliest possible date for completing the manuscript. This deadline was wildly unrealistic from the beginning and obviously out of the question after he decided to go to Yale. Woodward explained to Thornhill in February 1961 that his change of employment necessitated a new timetable because being on leave for his first official year at Yale (1961–62) made it prudent to defer his second leave to 1964–65, when he hoped to have his research well enough along to devote the year to writing. Yet even before he embarked on his big southern research excursion in 1962, he was already confessing to Bill Carleton that completing the book was "going to be a struggle." By the end of 1964, when he was supposed to have been finishing up the manuscript, he was fending off queries from Carleton and others about his progress on the book, pleading to his friend that he "must wait until there is an opportunity to talk with you about it at length." Some two months passed before he finally confided to Carleton that he was "not about to come out with the book on Reconstruction."[12]

One of the reasons that Woodward's confidence in the project and his drive to complete it had faltered over the previous few years may have simply been that, as the civil rights movement began to expand and escalate at the end of the 1950s, he was not alone in sensing both the historiographical importance and the contemporary relevance of a fresh perspective on Reconstruction. In November 1959, six months after Woodward and Arthur Thornhill had reached a renegotiated publishing agreement, the *Journal of Southern History* published Bernard A. Weisberger's remarkably perceptive and penetrating assessment of "The Dark and Bloody Ground of Reconstruction Historiography." Arguing that the need for a new "general history of Reconstruction" was all the more critical amid an ongoing "New Reconstruction of the South," Weisberger sounded what amounted to a historiographical call to arms because it was now more vital than ever to gain a better understanding of "the issues raised in the 'old' Reconstruction of 1865 to 1877."[13]

Two years later, with Woodward's southern research scarcely under way, John Hope Franklin, who also agreed that "the need was urgent," finally sent his oft-delayed *Reconstruction after the Civil War* to his publisher. In this concise revisionist treatment, he vigorously attacked the old Dunning view, arguing that Reconstruction era governments in the South were neither dominated by ignorant, easily duped black politicians nor any more egregiously corrupt than many northern state governments of the era. In 1965, Kenneth Stampp's *Era of Reconstruction* launched a more concentrated frontal attack on what he called "the tragic legend of Reconstruction," denying that the Radical Republicans were either as malicious or as self-serving as the Dunning School had maintained. Like Franklin, instead of dwelling on Reconstruction's supposed failures, Stampp emphasized historically undervalued achievements such as the Fourteenth and Fifteenth Amendments and the advances registered in public education. In reality, neither book offered the broad scope or in-depth research Woodward envisioned, but both authors had to some extent beaten him to the punch by challenging the historical foundation of claims by opponents of the "Second Reconstruction" that the first one had been misguided from the beginning and could only be judged a failure in the end.[14]

Stampp's and Franklin's books stood out but were hardly alone amid what amounted to a revisionist groundswell in the 1960s. David Donald's revised edition of what had long been the standard textbook on Reconstruction, James G. Randall's *Civil War and Reconstruction* (1937), appeared in 1961, and a few years later came Donald's own *Politics of Reconstruction* (1965). In the meantime, Eric McKittrick and John and Lawanda Cox had weighed in with fresh interpretations that reinforced Stampp's suggestion that the Radical Republicans were something other than mere vengeful and mean-spirited opportunists. Although Woodward warned in 1966 that Rembert Patrick's manuscript for a book on Reconstruction was lacking in "new insights or interpretations" and therefore unlikely to "make a very exciting or original book," the editors at Oxford University Press, who were doubtless thinking in terms of timely textbook adoptions, had it in print scarcely a year later.[15]

Woodward gave no hint that he felt his planned book had been pre-eclipsed by any one of these other works, and he was openly skeptical of some of the conclusions they offered. Yet the sudden profusion of works on Reconstruction as the 1960s unfolded, along with reports of still others on the way, surely raised concerns about the appeal of yet another book on this subject, not only in his own mind, but in the mind of his editor. In May 1965, with Stampp's book on Reconstruction out and capturing strong reviews, Arthur Thornhill assured Woodward that he and his colleagues at Little, Brown remained confident that "our project is more comprehensive and will become the definitive work in the years ahead." Still, perhaps wondering just how many "years ahead" lay ahead before he saw Woodward's manuscript, he began to press for a meeting to discuss "your thoughts about completing your Reconstruction book." Woodward was clearly in no great hurry to have this discussion. He had already put off a request from Little, Brown's editorial representative in the New York area, A. L. Hart Jr., for an appointment to talk about the project before Thornhill discovered that he would be in New Haven himself at the end of June and suggested a meeting. "What a pity," Woodward replied, because although he had "hoped very much to talk with you," he had promised "to take my wife on a trip beginning the 24th and will not be back until July 1." Not to be denied, Thornhill urged him to contact Hart upon his return and proposed yet another meeting with him on July 7.[16]

At this point, if Woodward's editors at Little, Brown were beginning to sense that something was amiss, his former student, now close friend and frequent confidant, Willie Lee Rose, could have confirmed their fears. Having pressed Woodward several times about his progress on the book, Rose was distressed to learn from him in September 1965 that his intentions for it had been "revised." Was there actually "some overwhelming reason that makes it seem impossible to approach the presentation as you had originally planned?" she wondered. David Donald's reworking of the old James G. Randall volume struck her as "not a whole lot better . . . than it was." Unfortunately, it seemed, "there just is no really good single book," and, she added, "I had hoped yours would be the BOOK."[17]

Precisely when Woodward next met with Arthur Thornhill is not clear, but rather than concentrating on the Reconstruction book, their conversations going forward focused primarily on his ideas about a collection of his essays dealing with race and slavery that promised to put the current

Therapist of the Public Mind

racial crisis in historical perspective. By October 1965, Woodward was also pushing for a Little, Brown reprint of *Reunion and Reaction*, and he decided to hold back temporarily on the book of essays while getting this new edition ready for publication. In July 1966 he informed Thornhill that he was also working with Basic Books on yet another volume of essays addressing the "Comparability of American History," drawn from lectures prepared by "a brilliant group of historians" he had recruited for the Voice of America's "Forum Lectures." Nearly three years would pass before Woodward's request to meet with Little, Brown's editor-in-chief Larned G. Bradford to discuss "several problems on my mind" led to a formal agreement in February 1969, canceling the contract for the Reconstruction book in favor of a new contract for not one but two books of his collected essays. Meanwhile, the fruits of the research Woodward had done solely for the Reconstruction book would be little in evidence in his academic writing for the remainder of his career. Neither the Messenger Lectures at Cornell in 1964, which he devoted to the Reconstruction period, or his "Seeds of Failure in Radical Race Policy," published in the *Proceedings of the American Philosophical Society* in 1966, appeared to draw on his primary research for his ill-fated book.[18]

Whatever may be said of Woodward's decision to abandon his Reconstruction book, it amounted to more than a simple strategic withdrawal from a suddenly crowded field. It reflected other considerations, including his standing in the academic world at that juncture and the demands and expectations his stature conveyed. There is also good reason to see the abandoned project as an indication of Woodward's desire to change the focus and direction of his career going forward. By 1969 it had been almost two decades since he had published a traditional research monograph. Yet however thinly documented and conjectural, *The Strange Career of Jim Crow* was still a timely must-read on the history of segregation. His thoughtful and accessible essays on the nature of southern identity and its relation to national identity in *The Burden of Southern History* solidified his preeminence in his field and lofty stature among American historians in general. As a consequence, he found himself far busier and more sought after when he reached age sixty in 1968 than he could have imagined ten years earlier.

Though his classroom obligations were surely not onerous in and of themselves, the time and energy he devoted to directing PhD dissertations was not insignificant. From April 1959, when the terms of the contract for his Reconstruction book were settled, until the contract was canceled almost ten years later, he directed twelve dissertations to completion, six at Yale and the six holdovers from Johns Hopkins. Woodward's involvements as a manuscript reader and critic also extended well beyond the dissertations he supervised. As his reputation grew, friends and colleagues eagerly sought his evaluation of their work, meaning that he wound up reading drafts of a number of the books destined to become major works in American history, poring over them with the same care he typically devoted to one of his students' dissertations. It was not uncommon for publishers to solicit his appraisal of a promising book manuscript that he had already read and critiqued privately at the author's behest. This was true for Stanley Elkins's dissertation, an appraisal of the impact of bondage on the slave, written under the supervision of Richard Hofstadter at Columbia, but with copious input from Woodward, who was serving on Elkins's reading committee. After reading and commenting on the manuscript previously, Woodward expressed his disappointment to Elkins in January 1958 "that you are able to make no more concessions to my criticisms than you evidently do." He also chided Elkins for his high-handed and dismissive treatment of other historians' appraisals of slavery, especially Kenneth Stampp's recently published book, *The Peculiar Institution*, and urged him to be more cautious in drawing analogies between the experiences of slaves and those of inmates of a Nazi concentration camp. Despite these and several other reservations he offered in a roughly 1,300-word critique, perhaps mindful of Elkins's obstinance on certain issues, he conceded that he was "prepared to go along with you, provided you can make reasonable concessions to my criticisms." Later published as *Slavery: A Problem in American Institutional and Intellectual Life*, the dissertation was destined to become a highly controversial book, so controversial in fact, that Woodward's endorsement was necessary to counter the harsh criticisms of others who read it in manuscript for the University of Chicago Press.[19]

Instead of plowing ahead with his Reconstruction book in May 1962, Woodward was reading the manuscript of Richard Hofstadter's *Anti-Intellectualism in American Life*, where he found "some of the most masterful and penetrating pages of intellectual history in our historical literature." Yet, though the two were fast friends, Woodward was never comfortable with Hofstadter's generally unsympathetic treatments of the Populists and the white masses in general. In this case, he took him to task for his sweeping indictment of religious fundamentalists, past and present, as the driving force behind American anti-intellectualism. Woodward took particular exception to Hofstadter's facile assumption that contemporary fundamentalists were simply promulgating the same "ancient and thoroughly indigenous refrain" offered up by their predecessors for centuries. Showing an uncharacteristic impatience, Woodward insisted, "Dick, you just can't do this. . . . If you mean by fundamentalists those addicted to 'literal scanning of the scripture' you take in a hell of the proportion of the population from the seventeenth down through the nineteenth centuries—including a hell of a lot of intellectuals.... Being a fundamentalist before the 20th century was, I should guess, 'normal' for the vast majority of Catholics and Jews as well as Protestants. If a lot of them turned out to have some poisonous prejudices, I doubt it was because they were fundamentalists."[20]

A few months later, in the middle of a major research sojourn for the Reconstruction book, he was immersed, not in his own notes, but in reading John Hope Franklin's outline for an ultimately ill-starred book detailing the history of civil rights in America, written for the United States Commission on Civil Rights. Soon he would be reading Franklin's entire manuscript. Woodward had cautioned him that the "ethnocentrism" of his very nearly exclusive focus on blacks might offend other minorities such as Japanese Americans, Jews, and Native Americans who had serious civil rights grievances of their own. Franklin persisted, however, in making the unrequited struggles of black Americans the dominant theme in a book that, after all, was supposed to appear in conjunction with the centennial of the Emancipation Proclamation. To his dismay, however, the Civil Rights Commission ultimately rejected the manuscript as submitted, apparently seeking a more positive portrayal of what had been accomplished in the pursuit of racial equality by 1963. For his part, Woodward would likely have winced at Franklin's recollection years later that his friend had "seemed completely satisfied" with the manuscript that had been rejected.[21]

Woodward was surely no less frustrated after devoting considerable time to a close reading of the manuscript of Ole Miss historian James W. Silver's explosive exposé, *Mississippi: The Closed Society*, which he had received from Silver in late September 1963, scarcely a week before it was due at the publisher. He praised Silver's courage in offering such a "terrible and impressive indictment" of the mind-set of white Mississippians, but he fairly pleaded with him "not to publish this draft without extensive revision, reorganization and re-writing. I do not think it will do as it stands." The crux of Woodward's concerns lay in the fiery and impetuous Silver's lack of restraint, embodied in such gratuitously antagonistic assertions as "Statistically, Mississippi has contributed nothing since World War II to the defense or even the running expenses of the national government." This statement, Woodward thought, seemed almost "consciously calculated to bring down on your head every Korean Gold Star mother and every indignant taxpayer in Mississippi," and he warned that such excesses undermined "the dignity and seriousness of your assaults." "The state legislature may be 'a snarling pack of jackals,'" he added, "but is this the place for that?" When the book appeared, Woodward doubtless noted that while some of the specific examples he cited had been addressed, taken as a whole, the book was still more akin to a catalog of outrages than a carefully, subtly crafted piece of scholarship.[22]

If Woodward rarely seemed to stint on the time and energy he invested in evaluating manuscripts, the same was surely no less true of the some 250 or more books he reviewed over the span of more than six decades. He was scarcely into his twenties when he began contributing brief reviews to the Atlanta newspapers in 1930, and by the end of the ensuing decade, he was regularly reviewing books for the *New Republic*, as well as several scholarly journals. He remained committed to this practice, and even though he entered military service late in 1943, he still managed to churn out five reviews during 1944–45. Upon returning to civilian life, he plunged headlong back into the reviewing whirl, publishing ten reviews between 1947 and 1950, while scrambling to complete what turned out to be two books in *Origins* and *Reunion and Reaction* and assuming a new position at Johns Hopkins after enjoying a year's leave in 1946. Despite wrapping up final revisions of the two books, composing his presidential address to the Southern Historical Association, writing the lectures that became *The Strange Career of Jim Crow*, and spending a year at Oxford as Harmsworth Professor, between 1950 and 1960, Woodward published no fewer than fifty book reviews, not including thirty-two thumbnail synopses of books that he prepared for the *Key Reporter* between 1957 and 1960. Though his review total slipped to thirty-three in the 1960s, nineteen of these appeared in the first half of the decade, when he was still generally presumed to be working in earnest on his Reconstruction book.[23]

Along with reviewing books at an astonishing clip and wading through an unrelenting torrent of manuscripts written by students, colleagues, and students of colleagues, all eager for his appraisal—and, hopefully, his endorsement—of their work, Woodward had signed on with Richard Hofstadter in 1961 to coedit the new Oxford History of the United States. This quickly proved to be a frustrating and voraciously time-consuming responsibility, involving voluminous correspondence and incessant scrambling to replace a steady stream of authors who failed to deliver on their commitments to write volumes for the series.

Woodward was also awash in organizational commitments and other extraordinary demands on his time. In addition to the committee and leadership assignments he took on enroute to the presidency of both the American Historical Association and the Organization of American Historians in 1969, there were his activities within other groups such as the American Academy of Arts and Sciences and the American Philosophical Society. Beyond these were all manner of editorial boards and prize committees (including, not infrequently, the Pulitzer). Informed in May 1963 that he had been nominated for the Council of the American Association of University Professors, he was moved to take stock of his organizational commitments. A bit shocked by his findings, he explained to AAUP general secretary William P. Fidler that he was already obligated to "twenty-one out-of-town meetings of committees, councils or boards during the academic year—all of them professional in one way or the other, and this after recently resigning from a couple so as to join the board of the ACLS [American Council of Learned Societies], which meets five times a year!" "How," he asked almost prophetically, "is a man to get on with his book?"[24]

In mid-May of 1960, Woodward offered a rare accounting of the day-to-day demands on his time when he explained to Glenn, who was then visiting Woodward's family in Florida, that, instead of working on his Reconstruction book, he was completing revisions on "The Age of Reinterpretation," an article for the *American Historical Review*, while still caught up in pulling together his essays for *The Burden of Southern History*, which was slated for publication later that year. At the behest of his former lover, Antonina Looker (formerly Hansell), he had just labored through a draft of her husband's novel—"bad enough to read it, but far worse to write him about it and not hurt Nina." In the midst of fending off recruiting advances from Brandeis and the University of Pittsburgh, his pressing "chores" included a lunch meeting the next day in New York with an American Council of Learned Societies committee, followed two days later by lunch in Philadelphia with "the meeting committee of the American Philosophical Society." While in New York, he also needed to talk with the editors at Harcourt, Brace, who were "breathing down my neck about the text book revision." As if his report on recent activities and upcoming obligations was not wholly sufficient to answer the question, he added, "And where, you might legitimately ask, has my leave for research gone to[?]"[25]

For all of Woodward's complaints about such individual and organizational demands on his time, the very prominence and widespread respect that lay behind those demands also put him in a position to say "No" a lot more often than he did. Yet even after making such a forceful case to William Fidler against pursuing a seat on the AAUP council, in the end, Woodward had told him, "If you should tell me that in spite of all this I should agree to run . . . I guess I will do it." Likewise, much of whatever compulsion he felt to review so many books seemed to come from within, for it was often Woodward himself who was seeking the assignment from the editor rather than the other way around. His proclivity for organizational involvement and nonstop book reviewing may have arisen in part from an inner sense that, as a southerner, the improbability of his lofty standing among the American intelligentsia left him constantly obliged to prove himself deserving of it. It may also have been simply his means of extending and sustaining his professional influence. Although it seems that completing his much-anticipated, potential blockbuster of a book on Reconstruction would also have served this aim, the priorities he appeared to set for himself seemed almost calculated to prevent him from doing that.[26]

In trying to understand Woodward's apparent reluctance to devote more of his time and energy to finishing the research for his Reconstruction book, we might also recall that he had never been by nature an avid hunter and gatherer of primary historical information. From the outset of his indifferent pursuit of a PhD in history, he had made it abundantly clear that, as his classmates readily confirmed, he was more interested in crafting and massaging ideas than in simply acquiring more facts. One of the greatest of his many complaints about graduate school, after all, had centered on both books and professors spouting facts but "void of ideas." Several years later, while teaching at the University of Virginia, he commiserated with a young Englishman who had studied at Virginia and perceived, to his dismay, that "in America as in England . . . ideas are about the last thing professors of history care for." Woodward heartily agreed, citing old-guard Virginia historian Thomas P. Abernethy as "an extreme example of the research for research's sake school" and observing that "some of the young American scholars are going to have to stage a deliberate revolt from this academic Philistinism or our scholarship will lapse into an untimely dotage." Though he winced at some of his friend Richard Hofstadter's prodigious interpretative leaps of faith, he maintained that "an original and brilliant failure is of a higher order than a pedestrian success," thinking in the latter case of the work of colonial historian Carl Bridenbaugh, a "collector of instances, illustrations [and] information" who made but little "contribution . . . to interpretation and understanding."[27]

This is not to say, of course, that Woodward disputed the need for new, innovative research that promised to challenge previous historians' long-fixed and little-examined notions about the past. He had done this in *Tom Watson*, but complain as he might about the distraction of classes and exams while in Chapel Hill, he could hardly have asked for better fortune than to have the research mother lode for his dissertation, the Watson Papers, within walking distance and at his disposal at least five days a week. Two years after graduate school, Woodward's second plunge into historical revisionism essentially forced him to undertake a much more demanding and prolonged multiarchival research effort that would eventually produce both *Origins of the New South* and *Reunion and Reaction*. As conceived, the History of the South series envisioned contributors focusing primarily on synthesizing the accumulated writings of senior scholars, which, at that point, consistently reaffirmed the New South school's historical orthodoxy and, by implication, the region's racial and political status quo. Relatively few relevant secondary works had been available when Woodward signed up for the project in 1939, and he was familiar enough with those to realize that if he truly meant to turn "the orthodox credo . . . upside down" in *Origins*, it was to the archives he must go.[28]

And this he had done, repeatedly, both before his military service and for some time thereafter, when, more than once, the appearance of a new and undeniably relevant manuscript collection prolonged his search for closure on certain aspects of the book. In essence, save for his three years in uniform, the period from 1939 to 1951 had been a grueling, protracted stretch of traveling, researching, writing, and rewriting for Woodward. At some point, all of this would likely have come to be less a labor of love than of wearisome necessity for any scholar. This was true especially for one never temperamentally reconciled to the extended slog through a swamp of often extraneous and mundane information required to produce thoroughly researched and meticulously documented historical monographs. This may explain why, before he began work on the Reconstruction book in earnest, Woodward had sought some practicable means of avoiding "the almost endless task of thorough research of eleven state histories."[29]

He had done scarcely any additional research in advising the NAACP legal team or in crafting the essays that became *The Strange Career of Jim Crow*, and when David Donald got wind of Woodward's plans for a monograph on Reconstruction, he saluted him "for tackling a big job and for sticking at research, even when it would be easier to sit down and turn out 'syntheses' by the hour." By the end of 1958, with contract negotiations for the book still ongoing, he declared that "after a three-year-energy-and-confidence slump (to which I have been susceptible before)," he was "once more teeming with plans and notions." Still, if he had somehow forgotten how much "dreary . . . spade-work," as he had once put it, was required to make realities of a historian's "plans and notions," he got a quick refresher course during his research in northern repositories at the end of the 1950s. Once he began his time- and energy-consuming research trips to southern archives, there was no escaping the reality that he had committed himself to what promised to be yet another arduous and protracted grind of tedium and trekking. Hence, it was not so surprising perhaps that, even in December 1961 as he prepared to embark on a three-month research trip in the South, he was admitting to Bill Carleton that he was just then coming to terms with the enormity of the task he had set for himself.[30]

Beyond how he actually felt about the nuts and bolts of historical research, Woodward's misgivings about having taken on the Reconstruction book may have also reflected an inner struggle so personal that he was reluctant to discuss it, even with Carleton, who, with Glenn Rainey now a more distant presence, now ranked as his closest confidant. Always candid, sometimes almost brutally so, Carleton felt comfortable in pointedly criticizing Woodward's thoughts and writings in a way that few others did. Both Vann and Glenn Woodward delighted in his company, and they worried about the health and at times even the safety of the pugnacious Carleton, who had never married. With McCarthy-era anticommunist paranoia and homophobia still very much alive in the Sunshine State in the late 1950s, he and other outspoken faculty colleagues had come under intense and intrusive scrutiny by members of the state legislature. After seventeen years as chair of the Department of Social Sciences at the University of Florida, he had finally stepped aside in 1957 and was looking to retire altogether in a few more years.

In December 1958, Woodward advised his friend, who, unlike him, was a powerful, self-confident speaker, that the "lecture circuit" would be the "easiest, most remunerative" way of "earning your bread" and "far preferable to teaching." Given his flair for writing for nonacademic audiences, Carleton could also sign with a literary agent, as well as tap into one of the foundations, such as the Guggenheim, "which should be a soft touch." Either way, Woodward foresaw little difficulty for Carleton in making "a better living" outside the academy, adding for emphasis, "*I couldn't but you can* and should!"[31]

This was no exercise in false modesty on Woodward's part, for it was certainly true that, absent his cachet as a scholar, his speaking skills would not have carried him far. Still, he gave reason to suspect that certain aspects of the plan he urged on Carleton actually intrigued and appealed to him as well. In December 1961, with Carleton's full retirement from Florida about to become official and with still quite a long way to go on his Reconstruction book, Woodward observed that while his friend's "crisis" was "over and resolved," his own "personal career problems" were anything but. There was still much uncertainty about the then pending physical relocation to Yale, but the "heavier crisis" lay in "the conjunction of two major challenges" presented by "the new job *and* the new book," and he found it frankly "hard to say which is more severe." Carleton had offered his reassurances about Woodward's "fear of the new book," but he had been less soothing in delivering what Woodward called a "homily on the slavery of careerism and its dangers, the treacherous water treading of prestige, [and] the toadying to the establishment (especially one that really isn't there.)." Notably, Woodward admitted to having his own "sessions of self-accusation and doubt on this score" even before Carleton's "timely sermon" had left him wondering if he was "already, as you half-imply, half-enslaved and don't know it."[32]

In keeping with this admission, Woodward reciprocated with a telling little sermonette of his own. Carleton should see his own planned book on the history of political parties in the United States "as the fruit of a lifetime of reading" and approach it deliberately, rather than with any sense of urgency, lest he deny himself the "satisfactions" of his accustomed routine of writing essays and articles. Inwardly, at least, he may have been fancying such a course for himself as much as for Carleton. Certainly, the direction and focus of Woodward's energies in the years that followed suggest that he was not thinking solely of his friend when he observed that "of the several persons we might have been, we simply come by a certain age to accept the one or few we can be and try to realize some degree of contentment with that." For all his air of detachment, Woodward's philosophizing was that of someone much absorbed in his own process of self-reappraisal. Having achieved a great many things in the course of being "several persons" at once, he was now looking to devote more time and energy to being the one that offered him the most satisfaction, or "contentment," as he put it.[33]

He had given a hint about the person he aspired to be well before he had reached the pinnacle of his profession or was even sure about what that profession would be. From his involvement in the Alonzo Herndon case while teaching at Georgia Tech to his testimony before Congress against the poll tax as a barely dry-behind-the-ears PhD, he had made it abundantly clear that he was not content to sequester himself securely inside the academic cloister while real-world injustices cried out for remedy. Despite his professed concerns about maintaining a certain scholarly detachment, he had emerged from his work with the NAACP Legal Defense Fund in the *Brown* case feeling an obligation to advance their cause. He had acted on this feeling a few months later in the Richard Lectures at Charlottesville. The response, as he gauged it, at least, encouraged him to think that he might wield more influence on popular reactions to contemporary social crises and concerns as a historian writing for a broad public audience rather than as an individual activist who also happened to be a historian.

Genuinely heartened by the interest and responsiveness of his listeners at UVA, he had explained to Howard Beale shortly thereafter that "in this situation I felt the historian would play a legitimate role as therapist of the public mind, could probe the public memory and bring to light the repressed, if unpleasant truth." The powerful positive response to the published Richard Lectures in *Strange Career* had only reinforced this perception. As so many of his writings going forward reveal, Woodward did not envision himself as a traditional therapist who simply hangs out a shingle and waits for the troubled and confused to beat a path to his couch. His approach would be more proactive, and he would not only do his counseling in public but offer it, by and large, to a mass clientele.[34]

Woodward understood, of course, that writing primarily for the benefit of other academic specialists was not the best means of reaching such a clientele. Save for a handful of contributions to the *New Republic*, his book reviews in the 1940s had appeared in academic journals. This would change dramatically in the 1950s, however, as his appraisals of new books began to reach a much broader audience in more widely distributed publications, such as the *Saturday Review*, the *New York Herald Tribune*, *Commentary*, the *Nation*, the *New York Times Book Review*, and shortly after it began operation in 1963, the *New York Review of Books*. Because the *NYRB*'s distinctive review-essay format afforded contributors both the length and latitude to incorporate their own perspectives on the topics treated by the book under review, it quickly became Woodward's platform of choice. Between 1964 and 1995, he would contribute fifty essay reviews to the *New York Review of Books*, compared to twenty-one for the *New York Times Book Review*. Of some eighty-three reviews or essay reviews he published in the 1950s and 1960s, only roughly a third appeared in academic journals, and he wrote scarcely a dozen reviews for scholarly publications over the remainder of his life.[35]

Meanwhile, Woodward moved even more decidedly toward popular outlets for his own original articles and essays. Roughly half of the pieces Woodward published between 1950 and 1970 appeared in one of the aforementioned high-profile publications. Beyond that, even among journals catering to academic audiences, Woodward showed a decided preference for those favoring the essay format over the formally documented research article. By the end of the 1950s, his work was much more likely to appear in the *American Scholar* or the *Virginia Quarterly Review* than any of the more traditional scholarly journals. In fact, between 1950 and his official retirement from Yale in 1977, apart from his presidential addresses to the three organizations that respectively published the *Journal of Southern History*, the *Journal of American History*, and the *American Historical Review*, he contributed only two additional articles to the "big three" journals, both in the *American Historical Review*. Moreover, not only did his SHA presidential address, "The Irony of Southern History," appear in the *Journal of Southern History* without footnotes, but except for the other two presidential addresses, only five of Woodward's eighteen articles in academic journals of any sort during that period came with formal documentation.[36]

Only five of the ninety-eight boxes currently comprising the C. Vann Woodward Papers are specifically designated as containing "Research" items, although this material can also be found in scattered folders dealing with specific writing projects. All told, however, the great bulk of the contents of those boxes and folders representing the fruits of Woodward's personal research in archival sources points to work completed by 1951 or earlier. Likewise, neither the *Strange Career of Jim Crow* nor his subsequent books—consisting largely of previously published and typically undocumented essays—and only one of his eleven articles in traditional historical or social science journals over the next forty-odd years gives direct evidence of archival research undertaken after the publication of *Origins of the New South*. Ironically enough, by the time Woodward's arrival made Yale the mecca for studying southern history in academic circles, he was spending ever more of his own time and energy as a writer and analyst operating outside those relatively tight circles, where he would emerge as one of the nation's most significant and prolific public intellectuals during the latter half of the twentieth century.

This is not to say that, in largely steering clear of the archives going forward, he became any less the dedicated historical analyst he had always been, as he consistently demonstrated in the well over 100 essays and opinion pieces he went on to write for readers outside the academy. He had begun to make himself heard in the public realm well before he came to Yale, but from his arrival there practically until his death almost forty years later, Woodward was rarely silent on any crisis or issue of critical national import. Shortly after the assassination of John F. Kennedy in November 1963, in one of the first of many pieces for the *New York Review of Books*, Woodward pondered the "fate of the Union" moving forward under the leadership of President Lyndon B. Johnson. Kennedy, he noted, had been cut down before his efforts to promote national renewal could bear much fruit. In a critical time of trauma and conflict, rife with conspiracy theories and racial and regional antagonism, the "metropolis" now found itself facing a simmering rebellion in the "provinces" that had spilled over into the halls of Congress. Johnson was a man both of the provinces and of the Congress but was part of the rebellion in neither and thus brought certain potentially significant advantages to the office of the presidency, Woodward thought. He had risen to his nation's highest office despite "the practically insuperable obstacle of being a Southerner," but once in the White House his southern roots left him better positioned "than President Kennedy ever was, to tell his fellow Southerners what needs to be done." Johnson's widely acknowledged experience and skill in shepherding controversial legislation through the Congress also promised to be a major asset. His subsequent leadership on civil rights seemed to justify this guarded optimism, but his militant interventionism in Southeast Asia would soon mark him in Woodward's eyes as yet another southerner who failed to learn the lessons of his region's tragic past.[37]

Woodward was truly angered and dismayed by disruptive and destructive behavior that marked many of the campus protests against the Vietnam War, and in 1965 he saw the future of the civil rights movement seriously jeopardized by the distracting and increasingly divisive escalation of America's involvement in that conflict. He was surely one of the most prominent of the 462 Yale faculty members who signed a public letter to President Johnson protesting the bombing in North Vietnam in 1967. Then, less than a week after the May 4, 1970, killings of Kent State University students protesting U. S. military incursions into Cambodia, he was one of eight distinguished historians, including Richard Hofstadter and William E. Leuchtenburg, who cosigned a letter to the New York Times condemning President Richard Nixon's "disastrous and indefensible re-escalation of the war." Appealing to "all like-minded citizens everywhere" to express their opposition to Nixon's policies, they cautioned that "the hour is late and the country's danger great."[38]

Four years later, Woodward blamed Nixon for putting the country in even greater peril through his attempts to cover up the Watergate affair. In May 1974, John Doar, chief counsel for the Congressional Impeachment Inquiry Staff Investigating Charges against Richard M. Nixon, directed his assistant Hillary Rodham to commission a study of abuse of power allegations against previous presidential administrations. Rodham, a recent Yale Law School graduate, asked Woodward to assemble a team of historians and gave them only a few weeks to file their report. Woodward's cohort of twelve established scholars, including William E. Leuchtenburg and Merrill D. Petersen, swung into action immediately and managed to meet what had seemed an impossible July 1 deadline. Beginning with George Washington and concluding with Lyndon Johnson, their report offered a remarkably thorough accounting of every previous president's experience with charges of corruption and abuse of power within his administration. Yet, for all the emphasis on meeting the July 1 deadline, when Nixon officially resigned the presidency on August 8, the entire report was still tightly under wraps, so much so that members of the congressional investigating committee themselves reportedly knew nothing of its existence until it later appeared in a commercial paperback edition bearing an introduction written by Woodward.[39]

Woodward had no way of knowing this would be the outcome, of course, as August dawned with the articles of impeachment submitted by the House Judiciary Committee still awaiting a vote by the full body. At that point, he worried that the sordid story of President Andrew Johnson's impeachment more than a century earlier had left such a bitter aftertaste that Americans' reaction to the prospect of a second impeachment effort, however justified, might simply come down to "Never again!" Fearful that such an aversion to another attempt to oust a sitting president might somehow spare Nixon the punishment he so richly deserved, he fired off an essay to the *New York Times* that was meant to establish a clear distinction between "That Other Impeachment" and the one confronting Nixon.

For all the trumped-up charges against Andrew Johnson in 1868, Woodward noted, he "had broken no law" nor violated the Constitution. Unlike Nixon, Johnson had not compiled a long list of offenses such as defying court orders and congressional subpoenas, evading income taxes, or using "government agencies to discredit or defame opposing candidates and political critics." Most pertinently, perhaps, Johnson had not ordered or condoned spying on political opponents or paying "hush money" to prevent testimony against him.[40]

Despite their disgust at the illegal and reckless manner in which the Republican Radicals pursued their vendetta against Johnson, Woodward hoped Americans would understand that "the abuse of a constitutionally granted power is no argument for its abandonment—especially on the basis of one precedent." In addition to undermining governmental institutions in general, foregoing impeachment in this case could leave "the great sword the Framers forged for the defense of constitutional liberty . . . [to] rust unused and never again be drawn." Persuasive as it may have been, Woodward's argument became moot when Nixon resigned two days before the piece appeared in the *Times*.[41]

It would seem that Nixon's coerced departure in August 1974 might have restored some of the flagging faith in his country that Woodward revealed the previous November in declining an invitation to write a volume in a series of books celebrating the American Bicentennial, explaining, "Your letter catches me in a non-celebratory mood. I am, in fact, beginning to wonder what there is to celebrate and whether the U. S. was a mistake." Yet he seemed no more optimistic about the nation's prospects when he again took to the pages of *New York Times* in the dwindling days of its bicentennial year to reflect on the meaning of the orgy of celebrations and commemorations that had consumed the previous twelve months. Behind all the hoopla, Woodward saw a familiar, though now perhaps increasingly desperate, desire to reaffirm what he had repeatedly described as America's defining myths of innocence and invincibility. Both had taken quite a pounding in losing a war in Vietnam and then enduring the national shame of Watergate. The ultimately failed military adventure in Vietnam had shattered the illusion of American triumphalism, and before the nation could fully extricate itself from this swamp of failure and futility, the deeply embedded faith in America's innate virtue had absorbed a telling blow of its own in the Watergate scandal. Even so, to Woodward's dismay, instead of acknowledging the sobering lessons of its more recent past, the bicentennial observances gave little indication of a nation chastened by the disillusioning failures of the 1970s. Rather, Americans seemed intent on recapturing the supposed moral purity of the 1770s by immersing themselves not only in the military campaigns but in the rhetoric, garb, and manners of the Revolutionary era. This impression led him to label America "the eternal Peter Pan of nations, still seeking comfort and refuge in the illusory innocence of its youth.⁴²

In the wake of the 1976 election, Woodward had been at least modestly encouraged by America's willingness to look to the South for leadership. Four years later, however, his hope that Jimmy Carter's southern background might better enable him to dispel long-held presumptions of national innocence and entitlement was crushed in the overwhelming embrace of a challenger bent on doing just the opposite. In Ronald Reagan, Woodward quickly recognized a champion and master manipulator of the old mythology of America's peculiar virtue and national stature, and he foresaw "a return to fatuous complacency and self-righteousness" with him in the Oval Office. Woodward was even less kind after eight years with Reagan at the helm. On top of Reagan's reckless nationalism, Woodward argued that no previous president "nor all of them taken together, left the country such staggering burdens of national debt, interest payments, budget deficits, and trade imbalances, or left American industry, its banking system, and education in such a crippled and uncompetitive plight." Woodward also thought Reagan's legacy all the more damnable for his strong endorsement of "such a shallow-minded and unprincipled successor as George Bush—and such a vice-president [Dan Quayle] as the latter deliberately chose."[43]

Woodward had also seen in Reagan's election in 1980 a resurgence of Republican efforts to roll back the hard-won advances of the civil rights era. Testifying in June 1981 before a House of Representatives subcommittee considering legislation to revise or extend the Voting Rights Act of 1965, he warned that narrowing the purview of the act would open the door to widespread efforts "to abridge, diminish, and dilute, if not emasculate, the power of the black vote in southern states." This was precisely what had happened, he explained, when the removal of federal supervision at the end of Reconstruction created a "vacuum of permissiveness," in which "extremists . . . set out to destroy black rights utterly at the cost of popular government and democratic principles." Asked to expound on whether these historical developments had any bearing on what might transpire a century later, he responded, "My history teaches me that if it can happen once, it can happen again." His warning surely proved nothing less than prophetic. Yet here and elsewhere, Woodward drew on history, not so much to foretell the future, per se, but to encourage his fellow Americans to ponder carefully the meaning and potentially far-reaching implications of what was being done in the here and now. It is impossible to know how many took the lessons he offered to heart, but we can be certain that, across the second half of the twentieth century, no historian, academic or otherwise, was more dedicated to making the past speak effectively to urgent popular concerns about the present than C. Vann Woodward. His decision to abandon his Reconstruction book may well be recorded in red ink in the scholarly side of the ledger, but the ensuing redirection of his intellectual energies toward writing for a broader audience left the public side decidedly in the black.[44]

13

I Mean to Do All I Can

The Mentor Flexes His Muscles

Though Woodward himself grew steadily less involved in traditional scholarship after he moved to Yale, his professional stature did not suffer for it in the least. Even as his presence continued to lure top-flight graduate students to New Haven, he drew, subtly but skillfully, on his reputation and the deference accorded him to boost the careers of those who had studied with him in the past, as well as many others whom he knew as friends and colleagues.

The generally high quality of the work done by Woodward's former PhD students as a group speaks for itself. Taking note of the support offered by their mentor should not imply in the least that the professional recognition so many of them received was anything other than wholly merited. James McPherson went on to become the foremost Civil War historian of his generation and beyond. Yet even in McPherson's case, it did him no harm early on to open the *New York Times Book Review* in January 1965 and see a highly favorable review of his recently published revised dissertation written by the distinguished director of said dissertation. McPherson alluded to "eyebrow-raisers who might question the ethics of your reviewing a book by a former student," only to have Woodward respond, tongue firmly in cheek, that he hoped the review "will cause you no embarrassment. . . . Even if it does, I think you will be able to take it."[1]

It also seems safe to assume that Bertram Wyatt-Brown was not the least bit displeased when, with his book on the fabled Percy family of Mississippi just out in 1994, Woodward passed along the "cheering news" that when Bob Silvers of the *New York Review of Books* sought his opinion on the *House of Percy*, he had not only told him it was "an absolute MUST" but agreed to review it himself. "You know what I think of the book," he added, "and I mean to do all I can." That turned out to include more than writing a powerfully positive review of both this book and a related collection of Wyatt-Brown's essays. He had intervened several years earlier to dissuade Walker Percy from withdrawing his cooperation with the project by reassuring him that Wyatt-Brown did not plan to include what he called "the sensational gossip" he had heard from another Percy family member concerning the supposed homosexual escapades of Walker's cousin and adoptive father, William Alexander Percy. After reading Woodward's review of the book, the source of that "gossip," Boston University historian William Armstrong Percy III, wrote a letter to the *NYRB* criticizing Woodward for failing to emphasize the homosexuality that was "rampant in virtually every generation" of his family and describing William Alexander Percy as a member of the "international homosexual elite." Knowing that publishing the letter would not only embarrass Wyatt-Brown but infuriate Walker Percy, Woodward again stepped in to persuade Bob Silvers not to run it. There had been no such backstage machinations when Woodward reviewed Wyatt-Brown's earlier book, *Southern Honor*. All told, Woodward wrote reviews of at least thirteen books written or edited by former students, all of which appeared in the *New York Times*, the *New York Review of Books*, or the *New Republic*.[2]

Woodward's habit of reviewing his students' books was perhaps more common in the tighter, more personalized and patriarchal academic sphere of the 1940s and 1950s in which he rose to prominence. Yet he persisted in this habit throughout his career, long after his senior peers had abandoned the practice. Not until 1987 did Stephen J. Whitfield become one of the few historians who took him to task publicly on persisting in a "dubious reviewing practice which, if it can be justified at all, ought to require that an interest be declared (which Woodward has not done either)."[3]

Given the opportunity, some of Woodward's students showed little hesitation in reviewing his books as well, but perhaps the most striking act of reciprocity came from Sheldon Hackney when he delivered a paper in a session at the 1971 meeting of the Organization of American Historians devoted to the twentieth anniversary of the publication of *Origins of the New South*. Woodward confessed to Joel Williamson that he wondered about "the propriety of having one of my students on the panel," but he added, "I do think that Sheldon Hackney is one of the most thoughtful and independent-minded minds now engaged in this field." Yet when Hackney sent him a draft of his paper asking for his comments, Woodward obliged him, despite feeling "a bit conspiratorial . . . in participating in a critique of my own work." In response, Hackney pronounced himself ready to "concede that conspiracies exist if you will admit that they can be beneficial," adding, "in any case, I'm glad you agreed to conspire on our paper." In fact, Woodward offered only a few suggestions, dealing mainly with evidence and scholarship supporting his view of the Compromise of 1877 and of the prominence of former Whigs among the Redeemers. The session itself had the earmarks of what might today be called a sweetheart arrangement. The only panelists were Hackney and Robert H. Brisbane, a member of the political science department at Morehouse College, whose principal publication to date was a book on the origins of black civil rights activism, published by a small press in Valley Forge, Pennsylvania, and seemingly geared to general rather than scholarly readers. The session chair was Paul M. Gaston, then of the Southern Regional Council and a Woodward admirer of the first order. What Hackney called "our" paper appeared the following year in the *Journal of Southern History*. In it, he declared, "the pyramid still stands," meaning that *Origins* had been in print for twenty years without attracting significant criticism, perhaps, Hackney ventured, because "Woodward is right about his period." Ironically, as we have seen, it would be a mere matter of months until *Origins* was under critical fire from several angles. Woodward would later observe somewhat sheepishly that Hackney had written his tribute during his "more impressionable years." Hackney had been thirty-nine at the time.[4]

Efforts by Woodward in his students' behalf were more common, of course, including not simply endorsing their published work but helping to ensure that it was not only published, but by the right publisher or in the right journal. Scarcely a month after his glowing review of James McPherson's first book appeared, Woodward recommended his article on the Civil Rights Act of 1875 for publication in the *Journal of American History*. He would go much further when he was asked by the editor of the *American Historical Review* to appraise Sheldon Hackney's article on "Southern Violence." In this case, although Woodward praised the "courage and imagination" of the piece, he reminded editor Henry R. Winkler of what he had doubtless known before sending him the manuscript, that Hackney was a former student whom he did not want "either to profit or to suffer from my association with him." Hackney's piece relied on data and theory drawn from several disciplines in the social sciences, and Winkler had sent the manuscript to specialists in some of those fields who had apparently criticized it solely according to their own disciplinary standards. Woodward allowed that such input should be used to strengthen Hackney's work, rather than to tear it down. Accordingly, he urged Winkler to take an active role in mediating "between the author and the specialists." Woodward also recommended that Winkler send the manuscript to someone with command of the various social science disciplines involved, perhaps someone like famed psychologist Erik Erikson. After dutifully complying with Woodward's suggestion only to be turned down by Erikson, Winkler contacted a "distinguished and very broad-gauged sociologist." Although this reader was just the sort recommended by Woodward, when he submitted an evaluation that Winkler thought "fairly critical both from a methodological and analytical point of view," rather than let that be the end of it, he turned to Woodward yet again. Breaking with precedent, he even shared a copy of the problematic report with him. Of the seventeen critical points raised by the sociologist, Woodward found only three that he agreed were truly significant enough to demand a thorough response. He also allowed that he found some of the criticisms "a bit tendentious," and "unlike the sociologist," he believed that Hackney "has a grasp on the line of analysis that will prove fruitful if he persists."[5]

In the end, Winkler went with Woodward's suggestion to stick it out with Hackney a bit longer, and the result was a provocative and influential article that seemed in every respect to bear out Woodward's recommendation. Still, for all that Hackney accomplished in the essay, the story of how it made its way into the *American Historical Review* surely says every bit as much about Woodward's standing in the profession. In fact, it virtually compels the question of how many scholars of any era acquire the cachet necessary to have the editor of the most significant journal in their field ask them to evaluate an article submitted by one of their own students in the first place, let alone seek their advice on how to counter or circumvent the objections to the piece raised by other readers?[6]

Woodward's touch with editors was not always golden. He made a strong pitch to Oxford University Press for Willie Lee Rose's roughly 560-page manuscript for *Rehearsal for Reconstruction*, which began as a dissertation written under his direction, concluding breezily with "Shall I have the author send it on up?" Despite his endorsement, the press board was concerned about its length and salability and ultimately passed on publishing it. Informed of this decision by editor Sheldon Meyer, in a terse note tinged with a hint of irony, Woodward professed to be heartened to learn that it had been "a close decision," which made him "feel better about suggesting that you consider it." Woodward and Rose no doubt found considerable satisfaction in seeing the book, later published by Bobbs-Merrill, go on to win several major prizes.[7]

Beyond using his influence to help his students get their work published, he drew on his professional savvy to counsel them on how best to advance their careers themselves. This sometimes called for a bit tougher version of the tough-love approach he had employed when they were still writing their dissertations. Woodward was especially fond of J. Morgan Kousser and felt he deserved more recognition than he had thus far received. He waxed almost effusive in 1988 as he praised the manuscript of Kousser's original and "inspired" essay on the respective fates of prointegration legislation in Louisiana before the 1896 *Plessy* ruling and in Kansas before the 1954 *Brown* decree. He was not pleased, though, to see that the piece was to appear in a collection of essays coedited by two "unknowns" that was certain to "virtually escape notice." As he had learned from personal experience, there was little career benefit in "giv[ing] away such gems to passersby" as opposed to publishing them in a book of his own essays. "Please don't do this again," he admonished.[8]

Decisions on promotion and tenure for Woodward's former charges frequently rested on the strength of published dissertations that he had supervised, but deans and department heads regularly solicited his input just the same. Though Bruce Palmer's book on the Populist vision of American capitalism began as a dissertation directed by Woodward, Palmer's department chair at the University of Houston–Clear Lake nonetheless sought his appraisal of the work. He responded that, despite the pitfalls of wading into the contentious historiography of Populism, Palmer had persevered and written a "fine book" destined to "earn a prominent and important place in the literature of the subject." Woodward's recommendations of his students were clearly positive and supportive, but he was rarely extravagant in his praise, a tendency that possibly lent even greater weight to his more forthrightly emphatic endorsements such as the one he offered when the University of Michigan asked for his appraisal of his former student J. Mills Thornton III, who was up for promotion to associate professor with tenure. "I doubt," Woodward responded, "that among the several generations of graduate students I have taught, I have encountered a keener or more versatile mind or one better adapted to the study of history."[9]

Woodward also seemed to ratchet his enthusiasm up a notch when recommending William McFeely. He was not only "one of my best graduate students at Yale," his mentor observed, but "one of the outstanding American historians of his generation." The same was true of Louis Harlan. While his letters for his other students were unmistakably positive and supportive, there was a qualitative difference between Woodward's "I encourage you to fund this proposal," and his declaration, in Harlan's case, that "I am for this project strong."[10]

When asked to evaluate more than one student at a time, Woodward typically responded with scrupulously balanced appraisals, and he was especially careful about assessing the potential of those still in the early stages of their development. Queried in 1968 by James McPherson about the relative merits of two of his black PhD students, Robert Engs and John Blassingame, he suggested that while Engs might potentially be more "promising," Blassingame seemed "the more productive and determined." Both were still writing their dissertations, and while Woodward expected "something original and significant" to come out of Blassingame's research on blacks in New Orleans during Reconstruction, he also thought that Engs's study of "the Negro personality in emancipation . . . just might be really important." He hoped to keep them working on their dissertations until they had degrees in hand, but both Engs and Blassingame were already attracting keen interest from prospective employers. The "weekly inquiries" he received about black historians, he joked, had led him to endorse "the burnt cork solution. They are simply not available."[11]

When Woodward informed his PhD students that he would be retiring in June 1977, he made it clear that he would "continue my interest in your work and help you any way I can. . . . That includes writing recommendations and helping you get jobs, promotions, grants, fellowships, National Book Awards and Nobel Prizes." Though he was trying to introduce a little humor into what might be unsettling news, in light of the future achievements of so many of his charges, references to such exalted possibilities seem a bit less hyperbolic in retrospect than they might have at the time.[12]

This is not to say that Woodward saw all his students as likely contenders for such awards or represented them as such to others. Contacted in 1951 about one of his students who was close to finishing his dissertation at Johns Hopkins, he responded that, while the student merited serious consideration, "If you have applicants with imagination and distinction *plus* training, competence, and dependability, then ——— is out of the running. But if you have to be content with the latter qualities—but those in satisfactory quantity—then I feel safe in putting him in the race." (We should note here that in 1951 the pool of history PhD students was neither as large nor as rich as it would be even a decade later, and it was understood that some schools would have little option but to appoint candidates who might not be their ideal choices.) Elsewhere, even his appreciation of the "keen, alert, and critical mind" and "clear, brisk prose" of one of his former charges did not deter Woodward from cautioning a prospective employer about this candidate's reluctance "to call something finished and submit it" to a publisher. On the other hand, he might spare no effort to illuminate the strengths of former students such as Lawrence Powell, who struck him as the "type of writer too often overlooked by Guggenheim award committees . . . a scholar's scholar." To Woodward's mind, Powell had shown "all the skills, talents, techniques and all the qualities of thoroughness and patience" that, with the assistance of a Guggenheim fellowship, virtually guaranteed that he would produce "a distinguished book."[13]

If Woodward's students were fortunate to have so influential an adviser, his friends were not lacking for benefits, either, for not only was he generous in reading their manuscripts, but he did not let his involvement with a book before it was published stand in the way of reviewing it when appeared in print. He did such double duty with Robert Fogel's and Stanley Engerman's venturesome and provocative econometric assessment of the slave system, *Time on the Cross*, and with Eugene Genovese's monumental *Roll, Jordan, Roll*. Well before praising Genovese's confident presentation of his certain-to-be-controversial case for the reciprocity of the master-slave relationship—"Gene, you are the only one who could get away with this. Who else would dare?"—he had contacted editor Bob Silvers about reviewing both this book and Fogel's and Engerman's in the *New York Review of Books*. Woodward had also asked to review James Silver's *Mississippi: The Closed Society* after reading it in manuscript.[14]

Woodward did not limit his active support to close friends or those who agreed with him. Although Joel Williamson's dissenting take on the origins of segregation led some to cast him as Woodward's historiographical nemesis, Woodward wrote several strong letters of recommendation for him. When Williamson turned his attention away from race relations to undertake a study of William Faulkner, Woodward backed the project to the hilt. He urged the applicant screening committee at the National Humanities Center to offer Williamson a fellowship, assuring them that although he and Williamson had differed in some of their interpretations, he had the highest regard for Williamson's abilities and thought Faulkner a "quite natural and logical subject for him to undertake at this point." Woodward also seemed generously supportive of another critic of his Jim Crow thesis, Howard Rabinowitz, writing letters of recommendation in his behalf and penning the introduction to a paperback version of Rabinowitz's book, in which Woodward was respectfully taken to task for failing to note the practice of simply excluding blacks from public accommodations that preceded the onset of de jure segregation.[15]

Though he seemed to strive for fairness, Woodward was not always so positive when asked to evaluate grant or fellowship proposals submitted by scholars whose interpretations ran explicitly counter to his own, especially if he questioned the soundness of their methods or approach. He had already referred privately to Jonathan Wiener as "this Harvard chap who is afflicted with econometric dysentery" before Wiener challenged his conclusions in *Origins* by arguing for the persistence of the planter elite in postbellum Alabama. In a review of Wiener's Guggenheim fellowship proposal for a study of the historiography produced by American historians in the 1960s and 1970s, he invoked the "spirit of open-mindedness and tolerance that I try to maintain toward bright young scholars with whom I do not agree." He could not "pretend enthusiasm for the project here represented," in part because of the author's "identification . . . with one side of a two-sided argument." Still, he allowed that "Mr. Wiener is well-informed about the historiography of that period," and "he may well contribute something of significance" on the topic. "This," he concluded, "is about as far as I can go in my estimate of the project and the applicant's qualifications for carrying it through."[16]

When he felt the situation warranted it, Woodward revealed a well-nigh unrivaled mastery of the fine art of damnation by faint praise. Contacted by a representative of the MacArthur Foundation about an up-and-coming fellowship nominee, Woodward described him as worthy of "serious consideration" because even though he could "think of some who are better, he measures up to some in the discipline of history who have received fellowships." When the MacArthur Foundation sought his appraisal of the distinguished historian Gordon Wood as a prospective fellowship recipient in 1988, Woodward indicated that his "esteem for Professor Wood's ability" had led him to ask Wood to write a volume in the Oxford History of the United States. That said, however, although Wood had signed a contract for the Oxford volume several years earlier, with the understanding that he had another book that must be completed first, Woodward was "disappointed that [Wood] has not been able to make more progress on the new book." He took heart in Wood's recent assurance that he meant to "fulfill the contract." Yet perusing a listing of Wood's priorities for 1986–87, he found "completion of several books," but neither of the two mentioned specifically was "the big book for the Oxford History." This led Woodward to confess "some puzzlement over the omission," adding that he could "only hope that it represents no change of intentions."[17]

Wood had likely done himself no favors with Woodward with his decidedly critical 1982 review of Robert Middlekauff's book *The Glorious Cause*, the first volume of the Oxford series to appear in print. Though he had recently signed up for the series himself, he saw Middlekauff's volume illustrating the many weaknesses of the "narrative history" format that Woodward and his coeditor, Richard Hofstadter, had made the cornerstone of the entire undertaking. At any rate, for whatever reason, Wood did not receive a MacArthur Fellowship in 1988, although one of his books he listed as then in progress won a Pulitzer Prize in 1993.[18]

Historian Bernard Bailyn had kept Woodward and Hofstadter waiting for more than six months before declining their invitation to write a volume for the Oxford series, but when he approached Woodward in 1963 about submitting his name as a referee for Bailyn's application for fellowships to support his research sabbatical, Woodward readily agreed. Except for the ACLS, where his position as a director prevented him from writing in support of an applicant, Woodward urged Bailyn to "list me for anything else up to the Nobel Prize." When he was called on to write in Bailyn's behalf, he praised his work as editor of the John Harvard Library pamphlet series and predicted great things for his proposed book on the origins of American politics. Bailyn might have winced just a bit, however, at Woodward's assessment that while "what he has produced has been of the first rank," he had "not been as productive in his field as others of his age." Lest Woodward's assessment seem unduly harsh, at that juncture, in the ten years after receiving his PhD, Bailyn's major publications included a book based on his dissertation, another coauthored with his wife, and a slender volume comprising two lectures on the history of education in early America. Though he had gone on by 1991 to publish eight more books and win two Pulitzers, a National Book Award, and a Bancroft Prize, Bailyn still fell short of winning Woodward's unqualified endorsement. Consulted by representatives of the University of Chicago about Bailyn's merits as a potential recipient of an honorary degree, Woodward conceded that Bailyn had made "genuinely significant contributions to his special field" but allowed that he had not always "been the most original in his ideas" or "the most productive" in his writing. "Both those distinctions," he added, "could be more readily assigned to [Woodward's friend and Yale colleague] Edmund Morgan," though, he conceded, "to few of any others in this field."[19]

When asked where a particular scholar might stand relative to the leading figures in southern history, Woodward usually managed to throw a few of his favorites into the mix even if he had not been queried directly about them. Asked in the course of a search at Brandeis in 1985 to rank Drew Faust among historians in her field, he allowed that this would mean considering her in relation to Carole Bleser, Michael O'Brien, Daniel J. Singal, James L. Roark, and, "at a more advanced level," Eugene Genovese and Bertram Wyatt-Brown. Though he commented favorably, if briefly, on Faust and the others he placed in her cohort, he put Genovese "in a class by himself," while "Bert Wyatt-Brown, in my opinion, deserves much more than he has received from the profession and he has much more to come."[20]

When Princeton sought a similar ranking of senior scholars in southern history the following year, he again mentioned Genovese, but noting that Princeton's previous discussions with him had ended with Genovese declining their offer, he devoted the balance of his response to expansive praise of Wyatt-Brown and his recent book on southern honor, which he deemed "social history at a high level." He did offer a brief nod to the productivity of Michael O'Brien and the "quality" of his work. Joel Williamson might be a possibility because of his interest in postbellum race relations, although Williamson's current work on Faulkner's use of history struck him as a project better suited for Wyatt-Brown. Finally, his former student Morgan Kousser, who pursued a wider range of interests, was working on a book in judicial history, and putting his own skepticism about quantification at least temporarily aside, he praised Kousser's "awesome command of quantifying techniques." Woodward could hardly be faulted for pushing his former students in these rankings, especially those as well qualified as the ones he most frequently recommended, and the same might be said of the friends he also suggested. In the end, if his appraisals of the historians he recommended gave little reason to question his judgment, the sheer frequency with which his appraisals were sought gave even less reason to question his influence.[21]

Some within Woodward's circle of former students, friends, and colleagues seemed to see it as an egregious oversight if not an outright injustice if the *New York Times Book Review* or the *New York Review of Books* failed to run a proper review of their clearly very important new book, and when this happened, some looked almost instinctively to Woodward for redress. George Fredrickson complained to Woodward that his 1971 book, *The Black Image in the White Mind*, had gotten only a thumbnail synopsis review in the *New York Times Book Review*. He had already invoked Woodward's high regard for the book in his own letter of protest to the *Times* book review editor, but he asked Woodward to weigh in as well, reasoning that, coming from him, such a letter would "make the editor think twice before he consigns another book of importance to the dustbin of *et al* rather than sending it to a competent reviewer." Apparently, Woodward never wrote the letter, but he came through for his friend in a big way a few weeks later in a review in the *New York Review of Books*. That review, Fredrickson assured him, "more than made up for what the *Times* did to me," adding that "it's wonderfully gratifying to be understood and interpreted in such a profound and sympathetic way." The frequency of pleas such as Fredrickson's was at once a testament both to Woodward's lofty professional standing and to his reputation for personal generosity. He was still fielding such requests at age ninety, when he was contacted about sending a note to editor Robert Silvers at the *New York Review of Books* by a former student who felt that his new book was important enough to merit a review.[22]

Woodward had been friends with writer William Styron for some time by 1967, when he took the manuscript for Styron's novel *The Confessions of Nat Turner* with him as he vacationed in Grenada. It had induced "absolute skin-prickling horror" even as he sat reading it on the beach, he reported. Styron's success in getting behind the "black mask" in his portrayal of Nat Turner struck him as a singular achievement, which "stands alone. . . . And I think very high."[23]

Woodward went on to review the book in the *New Republic*, calling it "the most profound fictional treatment of slavery in our literature" and marveling at Styron's "native instinct for the subtleties and ambivalences of race in the South." As he sometimes did for friends and students alike, Woodward attempted to use his connection and clout with *New York Times Book Review* editor Raymond Walters to see that Styron's novel was placed in the hands of a receptive reviewer. When Walters told him that the book was already assigned to Wilfred Sheed, book review editor of *Commonweal*, Woodward subtly conveyed his doubts, and perhaps his displeasure, at not being consulted in the choice, by expressing his hope that "this man, Sheed, really knows something about slavery and appreciates the remarkable merits of Styron's book. In my opinion, not all will, but all should." As Woodward feared, although Sheed praised Styron's achievement in conveying "the physical condition of slavery," his general reaction was that attempting to write historical fiction was simply a waste of Styron's time and talents.[24]

Woodward did not always use his influence to pair authors with sympathetic reviewers. He had written several letters in support of Lee Benson and seemed to reveal a certain grudging personal fondness in describing him as "the most amiable madman of my acquaintance." Still, having made no secret of his skepticism about what he called the "quantification fad" that seemed

I Mean to Do All I Can

to be taking the profession by storm in the late 1960s, he recoiled from what he saw as Benson's uncritical enthusiasm for using quantitative methods to reach clear-cut, definitive conclusions about no less weighty and complex issues than the causes of the Civil War. In an aside to a letter to Bob Silvers, Woodward suggested that "if Lee Benson ever comes out with the proposed book on the [Civil War as an] 'Irrepressible Revolution' . . . Barrington Moore would be just the man to repress Lee Benson."[25]

To his credit, beyond a subtle dig or two in a letter of recommendation for someone who had crossed or disappointed him, Woodward seldom used the influence he enjoyed to settle scores. He made a striking exception, however, in the case of a writer who had been dead for nearly thirty years. He had written a brief but favorable review of W. J. Cash's *Mind of the South* when it appeared in 1941. As Woodward's thinking on the South evolved, however, Cash's relentless insistence that white southerners' distinctly warped mindset remained impervious to change regardless of the challenges and upheaval they faced ran directly counter to his own emphasis on fundamental discontinuities in the southern experience. The appearance of Joseph L. Morrison's sympathetic biography of Cash, which Woodward reviewed rather critically in 1967, spurred him to take another closer and more analytical look at *Mind of the South*. This he did in a long, uncharacteristically sarcastic and petulant paper presented at the 1969 meeting of the Southern Historical Association, which was then quickly published by his friend Bob Silvers in the *New York Review of Books*.[26]

It was certainly fair for Woodward to point to the limited geographic, cultural, racial, and chronological scope of Cash's treatment, and he did so quite effectively. He was also justified in taking Cash to task for refusing to acknowledge anything approaching a southern intellectual tradition and passing too lightly over the likes of Thomas Jefferson and James Madison as "exceptions that prove the rule." Yet for all the considerable merit of Woodward's professional objections to what he saw as a genuinely flawed book, in his comments on the paper at the SHA session, David Donald noted a "curious tone of personal hostility" to Cash in some of Woodward's criticisms. In truth, the same might be said of Donald's critique of Woodward's critique of Cash, where he found "misrepresentations and misconceptions in almost every line." Still, there was, in fact, more than a trace of resentment in Woodward's comments about the enduring regard and even reverence accorded to what, noting Cash's Piedmont roots and perspective, he mocked as "an unbiased history of the South from the hillbilly point of view." As a "non-academic," he complained, Cash had enjoyed a "charmed immunity" from criticism by scholars who in fact quoted him "un-jealously and flatteringly with a freedom they normally begrudge their fellow academicians." Journalists and popular writers had also been party to this orgy of "unstinted praise" to the point that "no other book on southern history rivals Cash's in influence among laymen and few among professional historians."[27]

Woodward may have been more right than wrong in the substance of his critique, but the response to it indicated that, in this rare instance, he had come up wide of the mark in his manner and tone. Beyond David Donald's strikingly emotional rebuke at the SHA session itself, even Woodward's former student Sheldon Hackney was "surprised by the vigor of your attack" in what he called "the bluntest bit of criticism you have done." Perhaps, he suggested, the fact that Cash is "somehow sacred" is why "you were relatively harsh." In any event, Hackney claimed to be perplexed by the negative reaction to the essay, which marked it as "your least enthusiastically received work."[28]

Few objected to the piece more fervently than Cash's biographer, Joseph Morrison, whose rebuttal letter to the *NYRB* expressed high regard for Woodward as one of his former professors but declared him "100 percent wrong" on Cash. Morrison's letter did not impress editor Bob Silvers, who saw it as more of a personal defense of Cash himself than a direct response to Woodward's arguments about Cash's book. Still, after sending him Morrison's comments, he assured Woodward that he would be happy to run them if they included anything "you might want to have published so you can reply to it." (This was hardly the only example of Silvers's long-standing protective regard for Woodward. In April 1990 he sent him an advance copy of an exceedingly favorable review of his latest book, *The Future of the Past*, by Woodward's friend and Yale colleague David Brion Davis, "just in case you should feel some reply is needed."[29]

Though Woodward declined this offer to set up Morrison for additional pummeling, his resort to ridicule and show of petulance in his re-review of Cash's book was out of keeping with his typically respectful and restrained professional demeanor. It is impossible to say definitively that his personal trials were affecting his temperament at this point, but the end of the 1960s marked the beginning of a prolonged period of deep personal anguish and loss. He had delivered his SHA paper on Cash scarcely two months after the death of his only child.

Woodward had lost both his parents several years earlier. For her part, Bess Woodward was much given to motherly doting and fretting. She had journeyed to New York to visit her son before he sailed for Europe in 1932 and inquired frequently about the well-being of her son, daughter-in-law,

I Mean to Do All I Can

and grandson while they were off in England during Woodward's stint as Harmsworth Professor at Oxford in 1955. She cautioned his parents against leaving Peter alone for any extended period because "so many things might happen" and worried especially about Vann's continued involvement in defending his Johns Hopkins colleague Owen Lattimore against accusations of communist sympathies. Even though "you feel sure he has no red leanings," she counseled, "just stay out of his fight." Bess likely realized that her admonition would go unheeded, but her readiness to offer it nonetheless bespoke a more relaxed and reciprocally affectionate relationship with her son than her husband ever enjoyed, as witnessed, perhaps by his determination after securing his job at Georgia Tech in 1930 to see that "the Mater" made it to every Grand Opera performance in Atlanta.[30]

On the other hand, Jack Woodward would be dead well before Vann acknowledged that his harsh youthful assessment of his father's reticence on social justice issues had been more than a little unfair. After leaving his post at Emory Junior College in 1934, Jack rendered dutiful, though not terribly remunerative, service as an instructor at both Georgia Tech, where he regularly taught six classes per quarter, and Oglethorpe College (later University). By 1952, though, at age seventy-six and in declining health, he was, to say the least, struggling as a sales agent for the Lincoln National Life Insurance Company. "If I were younger it might be possible for me to succeed in the insurance business," he ventured to Vann, but while "the young fellows who can work night and day six or seven days each week succeed fairly well ... as it is, I'm making very little out of it." The palpable sense of defeat conveyed here by a father whose career had reached its brief and relatively modest peak some twenty years earlier must have been especially poignant for a son whose future by then promised one great achievement after another. Yet there was also a familiar strain of instinctive hesitation and aversion to change that had marked Jack Woodward's outlook and demeanor throughout his adult life and continued to underscore the differences in personality and outlook between him and not only his brother, Comer, but his son as well. Knowing that Vann and Glenn were thinking of building a house, he allowed that his advice on that project "would not be worth very much" but added with characteristic caution that "some of my friends have run into many difficulties and most of them seem to regret starting." Though clearly wary of the undertaking, he could only hope "for Glenn's sake especially ... that you may find it possible to proceed successfully with your plans."[31]

Jack and Bess Woodward would soon relocate to Florida, where they would live near their daughter, Ida, but with some of their financial support coming from Vann and Glenn, who also looked in on them frequently. Though Bess was younger and had seemed healthier, she would die first, in 1962, followed by Jack two years later. Meanwhile, Woodward's kindly and affectionate uncle Comer had also died in 1960.

Although Vann would never quite succeed in sorting out his feelings about his father, he and Glenn were deeply saddened by the deaths of both his parents and uncle. Still, each of them had lived well into their eighties. Surely, nothing could have prepared the couple for the untimely, soul-crushing loss of their beloved only child, Peter Vincent Woodward, who was only twenty-six, recently married, and seemingly poised for a brilliant academic career of his own only to see his life cut brutally short by cancer in September 1969. Handsome, hardy, athletic, and an enthusiastic outdoorsman, Peter spent several summers out in the wilds as a teen, hiking and canoeing. Though he was more outgoing than his famous father, the two enjoyed a powerful bond, not only of affection, but of mutual pride and respect. Peter had shown himself an intellectual prodigy at every stage of his education. He attended the academically demanding Gilman School in Baltimore before moving on to Yale, where he had graduated in 1964, then moving on to study politics, philosophy, and economics at Oxford. In February 1966 while at Oxford, Peter confided to his father that he was deeply distressed about his girlfriend back home, who seemed to be suffering from separation anxiety to the point of being "in a distraught state right now—emotionally unbalanced and very depressed." Fearing that she was struggling in her studies, apparently at Yale, he advised his father that he might soon ask him "to see her, to talk with her, to give her any advice you can." For the time being, he asked his dad not to tell his mother of this, preferring that "you, alone would know about this for right now." Regardless of whether it ever fell his father's lot to lend his counsel to the young woman, it said a great deal about his son's feelings about him that Peter not only seemed comfortable asking for his help in such a potentially awkward matter but felt confident that his father could make the situation better.[32]

After entering graduate school at Princeton, Peter met and married Susan Lampland, a fellow student in political science, a union ardently embraced by his parents, who assured him, "We could not have hoped for better for you or for ourselves." Secure in the love and approval of his parents and his new wife, Peter appeared to have the world at his feet as he pursued his studies at Princeton, only to be cruelly blindsided by a diagnosis of advanced stage melanoma, which necessitated massive and aggressive surgery on his lymph nodes and upper body in September 1968. Still, despite a less than sunny prognosis from his physicians, he and Susan moved to Montreal so that he could continue research for his dissertation on Canadian federalism.[33]

Though clearly fearful that the cancer would recur, Woodward supported his son's determination to proceed with his studies. Writing in late September 1968, he could not resist a fatherly remonstrance about Peter's reliance on a variety of credit cards, warning that the "credit card neurosis is one symptom of American Jonesmanship syndrome, and I do hope you will not get hooked on that." Yet he also clearly took great pleasure in serious intellectual exchanges with his son, with whom he shared bits of writing in U.S. history such as Lee Benson's call for a more "scientific" approach to Civil War causation, which impressed the son no more than it had the father. Shortly before the 1968 presidential election, Peter had raised a question about the supposed "populism" of George Wallace, and his father explained why he rejected this label for Wallace as "a distortion of history and a disservice to a valid tradition of protest." The original Populists had "rational" economic grievances and sought redress in a politically rational manner, whereas Wallace, like Joe McCarthy before him, had simply manipulated the anxieties and prejudices of his followers. He did not share Peter's hopes for "a Kennedy takeover of a demolished Democratic party" or his sense that a decisive Nixon victory might at least offer greater social and political stability. "I fear the influence of your unstable [Princeton] mentor in this," he teased. His letter was not totally dedicated to keeping Peter's mind off his illness, for his daughter-in-law was about to take her doctoral exams at Princeton, and he wanted "Sue" to know of his "distinct premonition that she will wow them."[34]

When doctors discovered the resurgence of Peter's cancer in June 1969, he and Susan returned to New Haven for further treatment and moved in with his parents, who would share with Susan the agony of watching his courageous but futile battle against the cancer that was ravaging his body. When Peter, racked by pain, was unable to stay outside on his family's annual beach sojourn, his father refused to leave his side even briefly to go swimming, explaining to a visiting friend, "I just want to stay here with him." Though Peter struggled valiantly, he lasted scarcely three months after the recurrence was diagnosed, succumbing on September 20, 1969. "The ordeal," his devastated father mused, had been "mercifully short, but all the more poignant and bitter. The most haunting and unbearable part was watching those two living up their last two months together in knowledge that it was the last of it all."[35]

Coping with such a devastating loss would have been hard enough in the least demanding of circumstances, and Woodward's were far from that. After achieving the great distinction in 1969 of serving as president of both the

Organization of American Historians and the American Historical Association, he had dispatched his obligations as the former a few months earlier. When Peter died, however, his bereaved father had but three months left, not only to prepare his AHA presidential address, but to ready himself for the enormously taxing obligation of presiding over what proved to be the most confrontational and protracted business meeting in the organization's history to date. He had known for several months that a "Radical Caucus" of leftist historians planned to propose a new "counter-constitution" for the AHA. In addition, the radicals intended to challenge the traditional practice of choosing the group's president from a slate of candidates drawn up by an official nominating committee by submitting a petition nominating one of their own to oppose the "establishment" candidate, Robert Palmer of Princeton. The radicals' choice was Staughton Lynd, who had been denied tenure at Yale a few years earlier and claimed thereafter that the decision had been based on his leftist politics. Beyond that, the group planned to enliven the typical, matter-of-factly sedate atmosphere of the business meeting even further by, among other things, introducing a resolution stating that the AHA condemned U.S. involvement in Vietnam. Indeed, some in the Radical Caucus proposed that they actually shanghai their own regular program session on the state of leftist history by turning it into what amounted to a pep rally designed to get the combative juices flowing in preparation for the business meeting that was to begin immediately afterward. As Radical Caucus leader Jesse Lemisch envisioned it, the session program would "document our indictment of the profession on every front possible," including an attack on Woodward for his recent "preposterous" OAH presidential address in which he had criticized certain aspects of current black history programs.[36]

Lemisch's plan was spread around quite a bit by the radicals themselves and publicized even more widely by those who stood to be their opponents at the December meeting. Woodward and AHA executive secretary Paul Ward had also sent the entire membership copies of the organization's recently amended constitution, which they felt responded to many of the concerns about centralization and undemocratic policy-making procedures raised by the Radical Caucus. In essence, AHA officials were publicizing the radicals' agenda in the hope of rallying opposition to it. In addition to preparing to deal with Lynd, Lemisch, and others, Woodward also had to worry about his volatile friend Eugene Genovese, who, despite coming from the left himself, had been quite vocal in expressing his personal as well as professional distaste for these particular leftists and their tactics.

I Mean to Do All I Can

Lemisch's widely circulated letter outlining a proposed radical strategy for the meeting and mocking Genovese's "servility to Woodward" was sufficient to elicit what he called one of Genovese's trademark "faux Brooklyn-tough death threats," although he admitted to taking it "a little seriously" when he read, "It will be to the knife." Scarcely a fortnight after Peter's death, Woodward would learn from a concerned Paul Ward that he had just fielded a call from Genovese, who complained that the AHA was giving "too much of a platform" to "a small unrepresentative clique" of radicals bent simply on disrupting the business meeting. Genovese foresaw the radicals bringing in many nonmembers and "volunteered his own services if we wished to set up security procedures." In the end, however, neither Genovese's worst fears about the meeting nor Ward's worst fears about Genovese were confirmed. Thanks to Ward's tireless work over the Christmas holiday in preparing for multiple contingencies and Woodward's uncharacteristically meticulous attention to logistics and detail, not to mention considerable strategizing and politicking on his part, the business meeting saw every Radical Caucus initiative turned back without anyone coming to blows, let alone "to the knife."[37]

The radicals had held a preparatory meeting of their own before the convention began and, as Woodward suspected they might, succeeded only in embarrassing themselves by failing to agree on their proposed counter-constitution. Woodward also knew in advance that 27 of the 207 names on the petition nominating Lynd were "phoney." Rather than go public with the information, however, he decided to use it for leverage, summoning Lynd, Arthur Waskow, and the radical icon Howard Zinn to tell them that he could prevent the executive council from disqualifying their nomination petition, provided the radicals were willing to "be a bit cooperative." Though jeers erupted when Lynd read this pledge to the Radical Caucus, he felt that Woodward had been largely honest and forthright in his dealings with him when he was denied tenure at Yale a few years earlier, and he vouched for his former colleague as a man of his word.[38]

The AHA had brought in additional security personnel and secured a professional parliamentarian (whom Woodward found more hindrance than help), and the atmosphere was both tense and potentially volatile as, by his estimate, some 2,200 jammed the room. This was ten times larger than any known previous turnout for a business meeting. The radicals, Woodward later reported to Susan, "screamed [and] ranted a good bit but observed most of [the] amenities," with the "only breach of decorum" coming when "[Art] Waskow called George Pierson a liar," for which he quickly apologized. Apparently, Woodward did not consider decorum breached when, by his own account, Genovese delivered "a searing indictment of Lynd & Co. as totalitarian barbarians" and, by the accounts of others, warned the audience that "we must put them down, put them down hard, once and for all."[39]

There was also the matter of Howard Zinn grabbing the microphone to propose postponing further discussion until the following evening so that the radicals' antiwar resolution could be voted on before the meeting was officially adjourned, only to have the mike wrested from him physically by the previous AHA president, John K. Fairbank of Harvard. Despite the interruption, Zinn's proposal for postponement eventually carried the evening, and the meeting was adjourned at twenty minutes past midnight, nearly four hours after it had begun. By that time, Robert Palmer had easily bested radical presidential nominee Staughton Lynd, despite Lynd receiving a surprising 400 votes, and it was clear that the proposed new constitution for the AHA was also dead in the water. The suspension of the proceedings also offered time for the hotter heads to cool. For Woodward, however, it meant that, instead of delivering his presidential address the following evening and abandoning the podium to be feted at a huge congratulatory reception, he would be taking up the gavel yet again and trying to keep the lid on as the radicals continued to press their antiwar agenda.[40]

The next evening's proceedings had seemed to be off to a shaky start even before the business meeting reconvened when, as Woodward reported to Susan, just as he was about to be introduced for his presidential address, "four dashikied blacks suddenly swarmed [the] podium to grab the mike," whereupon he, gavel tightly in his grasp, "asked [the] leading dashiki what the hell he wanted." Shown a two-sentence announcement of a meeting, Woodward agreed to let the man read it, after which he and his contingent had "retired, marching to hidden tom-toms." After he had delivered his "immortal words of wisdom" and seen them received "in surprising respect and gratifying acclaim," at 10:00 P.M. it was back to the contentious business of the business meeting. The principal item on the agenda was the radicals' call for an official AHA endorsement of a sweeping resolution, not only demanding withdrawal of the troops from Vietnam, but casting the war itself as a brutal attempt to "extend our modern American empire." For good measure, it also condemned the government's alleged political assassination of the Black Panthers and called for the release of various radical activists currently held as "political prisoners." Authored by Howard Zinn, the statement provoked discussion of the critical issue of "politicizing" the organization, but most of the remaining time was consumed by parliamentary wrangling until what Woodward called "Zinn's resolution against Sin & Running Dog Capital Establishment

I Mean to Do All I Can

pigs" was finally defeated by a vote of 822 to 493. Only then could President Woodward bring his gavel down for the final time, declaring the meeting adjourned at around 1:00 A.M. The longest business meeting in AHA history had stretched over nearly seven exceedingly stressful hours, and this after several days of intense discussion and negotiation, not to mention preparation for his presidential address, all of which had doubtless taken its toll on Woodward, who, though still fit, was no longer a young man at sixty-one.[41]

Still, even a day or so after "the whirling had stopped," he confessed to his widowed daughter-in-law that he was still feeling "some giddiness, but with it a good deal of quiet satisfaction and—I might as well admit it—some elation and secret twinges of euphoria about the academic politics." By mutual agreement, Susan and the Woodwards had spent Christmas apart, she in Oslo and they down in Barbados, where they were joined by Richard Hofstadter and his wife, Beatrice, and their Yale friends, Alex and Joanne Bickel, both the other couples with lively youngsters in tow. With all the noise and activity, Woodward mused, "it was as many light years as it was possible for us to put between this and Christmas last. And, it was just as well. Just as well, too, that we were not together this time. Next Christmas, maybe. I simply couldn't have taken it at home. Even so, there were paroxysms of blinding anguish. I hope Oslo served you better. And maybe we had both best wait and hope for time to do what no amount of space seems capable of doing."[42]

In the meantime, Woodward's season of anguish and loss would continue. Within the next four years he would also lose three of his dearest friends to cancer. Richard Hofstadter died in 1970, David Potter the year after, and then, in 1974, his Yale colleague, legal scholar Alexander Bickel. Woodward had his philosophical and interpretive differences with all three. He and Potter had known each other since their undergraduate days at Emory, though Potter, who studied under U. B. Phillips at Yale, favored a more straightforward, socially neutral approach to writing history, in contrast to Woodward's more activist and presentist orientation. Woodward had become friends with Hofstadter while teaching summer classes at Columbia when he was still trying to finish the research for *Origins*, and the two had coedited the Oxford History of the United States until Hofstadter's death. They remained close despite Hofstadter's much more critical and skeptical appraisal of the Populists, whose rationality of purpose and thwarted promise Woodward had trumpeted.

Bickel had secured his place in Woodward's heart forever by his intense devotion to Peter in the immensely difficult final days, and he was reportedly at Peter's bedside when he died. He was the newest friend of the three and perhaps the least likely, given that he was highly critical of the Earl Warren Supreme Court and especially the *Brown* decision, a ruling that Woodward had provided his assistance in helping to secure. As Woodward's former student William McFeely put it, the two men "did not exactly meet on the March to Selma." Yet their spirited intellectual jousting led to a warm personal friendship. "Alex," Woodward observed after Bickel's death, "gave me trouble for the thirteen years I knew him" on matters ranging from "integration" to "populism" to broader considerations of "liberalism and conservatism" and "free speech and revolution. Troubles, troubles—about virtually every bent and bias that clung to my hair. . . . Sometimes I thought I would have hated him had I not loved him."[43]

The Woodwards, Hofstadters, and Bickels had vacationed together, shared their joys and their sorrows, and comforted and consoled one another before and after the great losses they suffered. Potter was far away at Stanford, but he had kept close tabs on Peter's illness, and Woodward was one of the first people he informed when his own wife died by suicide in 1969. In short, Potter, Hofstadter, and Bickel were some of the closest friends of a man who did not have that many truly close friends, and coming so closely on the heels of Peter's, their deaths pained him all the more. One of his closest surviving friends, Bill Carleton, recalled that with the pain over Peter's death compounded by losing his friends in such rapid succession, a shaken Woodward confessed that he sometimes felt "I have contaminated everybody I am with" and even feared that his emotional suffering might be "what I have to pay for all this fame and success."[44]

Although most thought the passage of time eased Vann's pain more than Glenn's, his Yale colleague John Blum believed that appearances might be deceiving in this case because his friend simply refused to grieve and thus kept the pain of the personal losses he suffered tightly bottled up inside. Blum reported seeing these feelings unloosed only once, when Woodward, upon learning that Blum's wife was also being treated for cancer, "pounded on a table with his big hands" and declared, "Cancer is my enemy!" Such a rare emotional outburst persuaded Blum that despite Woodward's outward calm and reserve, he was struggling desperately to keep the fury and frustration seething within him in check. When this inner cauldron boiled over, Blum ventured, Woodward's unchecked anger sometimes led him to take it out "on some people in some quixotic campaigns."[45]

As he struggled with a succession of painful personal losses that began with Peter's death, Woodward also found his early, paradigm-shifting contributions to scholarship under sustained critical fire for the first time. Despite his repeated insistences for public consumption that he not only expected criticism of his work but welcomed it, his private responses to this development suggested otherwise. Four months before Allan Peskin's 1973 article challenging his take on the Compromise of 1877 ran in the *Journal of American History*, editor Martin Ridge sent a copy to Woodward, advising him of a new editorial policy giving authors whose work was the primary focus of a critical article appearing in the journal the opportunity to respond in the same issue. Woodward took him up on the offer, but he let Ridge know that he was expecting his comments to appear "immediately following [the critique] and that this will be the end of the matter in so far as the two of us are concerned. I do not want to become involved in rebuttals of rebuttals." He was sorely displeased to learn from Ridge that, as a matter of editorial policy, his rejoinder could not be placed in the text immediately after Peskin's article but would appear instead in the *Journal*'s "Communications" section as a letter to the editor. At this, Woodward protested vigorously. Not only did the letter-to-the-editor format "impl[y] the right of the critic to reply," but having long counseled his students against complaining about critical reviews in letters to the editor, he would now seem to be doing just that himself. "Worse," he added, he would "appear to be overreacting with an unprecedentedly long letter in response to criticism which (though I refrain from saying so) does not command my respect. Can you see what an embarrassing position I am caught in? ('Man, that cat must have insecurity problems!')." Though he continued to press Ridge to "take my article out of the communication section and place it immediately following Peskin's article," the editor did not relent. Several years later, as the flow of books and articles critical of his writings continued, an exasperated Woodward wondered aloud to *American Historical Review* editor Otto Pflanze whether there were "any limits to the profession's interests in criticisms of my work." Meanwhile, as we have seen, he was increasingly hard put to maintain the charade of finding affirmation of his Jim Crow thesis in the challenges posed by historians such as Joel Williamson and John Cell. Accumulating personal pain and professional frustration may have contributed to some of the more contrarian stances Woodward adopted over the final decades of his life. On the other hand, while the positions he took may have both surprised and dismayed some of his admirers, many of them were nonetheless grounded in the aims and values he had embraced in the past.[46]

14

An Ever More Conservative Old Liberal

Moving to the Right or Standing Fast?

Despite C. Vann Woodward's seemingly lifelong association with liberal causes, a number of writers have commented on what they saw as a distinct rightward tilt in his thinking that began in the late 1960s, which, according to his former student William McFeely, marked the beginnings of his mentor's "Tory period." Historian David Moltke-Hansen likewise observed later that, as he aged, Woodward was seen "not as a radical any longer, but as an ever more conservative old liberal and scion of progressivism."[1]

In partisan terms, certainly, an aging Woodward remained very much the liberal Democrat he had been since putting aside his youthful flirtations with more radical platforms. It was in the sociocultural and academic realm where he appeared to track to a distinctly more conservative arc as he grew older. As Sheldon Hackney suggested, however, in many cases Woodward was not changing his stance so much as simply standing fast on values and principles he had long held dear but now found increasingly under attack. Instead of championing cherished causes like racial integration and freedom of speech in the face of opposition and encroachments from the right, he now saw himself defending them from the onslaughts of the left. It is fair to say, though, that while his fundamental personal values may have changed but little over the course of his adult life, he defended them in a more overtly confrontational, even vengeful manner as his years dwindled down. So it was with his reaction to the rise of militant black separatism, which, as we have seen from his writing, he condemned for repudiating and undermining the aims of the civil rights movement and exacerbating the white backlash that threatened to stop it dead in its tracks in the last half of the 1960s.

Not surprisingly, Woodward was hardly less distressed to see the doctrine of black separatism sweep across college campuses, where calls for speeding up the racial integration of the student body were suddenly drowned out by demands for separate dorms, campus gathering places, and even discrete programs of study for black students. With some black students demanding a separate black student center at Yale in 1969, Woodward advised president Kingman Brewster that he thought that the impulse sprang primarily from the fundamental "insecurity" of younger black students who were now being admitted in much greater numbers under Brewster and found themselves thrust into academic competition with white students for the first time in their lives. Hoping that the "separatist impulse" would soon "fade out as confidence grows," he urged Brewster to make any concession a temporary one, warning that a formally established black student center would "be very hard to get rid of" and likely "become the source of endless trouble." A few weeks later, when Yale's black Divinity students issued their own set of de-mands, Woodward advised Brewster, "with unfaltering piety and mounting anxiety," that in response to "the threat of the Black Seminarians to resort to 'any means' . . . to get their way," he should propose "that if the divinity students promise to refrain from invoking the intervention of Divine Power, you would refrain from invoking the police power."[2]

Woodward's exasperation with this turn of events led him to assure vet-eran southern liberal journalist Gerald W. Johnson that "in order to appreci-ate fully how intolerable the boredom over Negro rights can get, you really have to be a card-carrying member of the academic community. I know it looks bad enough from the outside, but inside it's much worse. Twenty-four hours a day—gabble, gabble, yak-yak. Integration, separation, autonomy, black history, black studies, black math, black magic, black deans, black co-eds. Back in the Good Old Days the firing line was in the Black Belt where it belonged, the latitude of Selma and Montgomery. Now the firing line is along the Cambridge-Berkeley axis, and the targets are not the Bull Connors and the Jim Crows, but the Kingman Brewsters and the Clark Kerrs."[3]

Yale's Brewster would soon come under fire from Woodward himself for what he and some other faculty members saw as his unduly conciliatory response in April 1970 when militant blacks threatened a campus takeover in connection with a massive May Day rally in support of Black Panther Bobby Seale, who was then on trial for murder in New Haven. At one point, the militants even prodded students to arm themselves and break Seale out of jail or "at least," burn down the Beinecke Library. Instead of condemning their efforts to intimidate him and the entire campus community, however, Brewster seemed to make an awkward attempt to ingratiate himself with them by offering his unsolicited opinion that no "black revolutionary" was likely to receive a "fair trial anywhere in the United States." At this, Woodward had immediately joined Alexander Bickel and other faculty colleagues in taking Brewster to task, declaring forthrightly that they knew of "no evidence that the responsible legal and judicial officers of the state of Connecticut are unable or unwilling to see to it that the defendants get a fair trial."[4]

There had been only three black students enrolled at Yale in 1960, but under Brewster's leadership, a much more aggressive effort to recruit blacks boosted the size of the black freshman class from 14 in 1964 to 100 in 1969. Meanwhile, despite their almost nominal presence, the 14 black freshmen who arrived on campus in the fall of 1964 would have a decidedly significant impact on black student life that would be felt long after their time in New Haven had passed. This group was instrumental in forming BSA, the Black Student Alliance, which, in turn, began to push Brewster on a variety of issues, including, at the beginning of 1968, the need for a designated black studies curriculum leading to a major in black studies. When Woodward got word of this in February 1968, he reminded Brewster that students had long been taught that "race was the least useful of explanatory variables in account-ing for human worth, variety, and behavior and for distinctions based on the concept." Indeed, until recently, the consensus in academic circles had been that "race was a dangerous generalization of demagogues and an obsession of white supremacy fanatics." Now it seemed, race was suddenly worthy of serving as "the vital organizing principle of a curriculum," and it was "integra-tion" that had become the "bad word," because the new ascendant wisdom held that "to be equal, we must be separate."[5]

Woodward found his skepticism about freestanding black studies pro-grams reinforced by a letter from his black PhD student, Robert Engs, whose work with black studies programs in the state of New Jersey led him to report that, sadly enough, many of the faculty and administrators of these programs had seized on them as "the best hustle goin'," with many faculty more than willing to "manipulate historical fact so as to give completely distorted inter-pretations of the past," while "any scholar whose bag is genuine intellectual inquiry is likely to be chased off the campus." Woodward pronounced himself "fascinated and appalled without being surprised" by Engs's account, adding that he had shared it with John Blassingame, who also confirmed some "incidents of fraud and farce and frustration."[6]

Woodward would also find himself at odds with zealous proponents of black studies who were incensed by his friend William Styron's 1967 novel *The Confessions of Nat Turner*. Sales had been brisk, early reviews, including Woodward's, had been largely positive, and the novel would bring Styron the Pulitzer Prize in 1968. Still, an angry chorus of black intellectuals howled in outrage at a southern-born white man's attempt to probe the psyche of an enslaved black man, and not just any black man at that but one long-cherished by black Americans as "our hero" and a "Prophet."[7]

The Nat Turner of black legend was in every respect a virile, courageous, fiercely committed warrior who, oblivious to the consequences, had executed a bold, carefully conceived plan for a slave uprising with ruthless efficiency. Yet a white writer had dared to imagine a different Nat Turner outside the heroic mold—intellectually gifted but emotionally weak, unstable, and full of racial self-loathing. In Styron's telling, Nat's only real sexual fulfillment comes in a homosexual encounter, although his lust for a white woman dominates his fantasies and ultimately drives his urge to lead a rebellion that quickly deteriorates into a blind, drunken, bloody, and ultimately futile rampage. In the eyes of many incensed black intellectuals, by presenting Turner as irresolute and ill-suited for leadership, not to mention obsessed with a white woman, Styron had come close to serving up the same racial stereotype that white racial demagogues had long invoked and one that Styron's black critics were out to destroy once and for all.[8]

Styron quickly found himself under attack in both interviews and editorials. By 1968 his appearances on college campuses amounted to venturing into a veritable lion's den of angry black students and faculty seemingly bent on taking issue, not only with what he had written in the novel, but with anything he might say by way of explanation or defense. Then, at the end of the summer came a somewhat redundant mix of protest, accusation, and implacable anger packed into a slender volume offering the irate responses of ten black scholars to Styron's novel. This slender collection offered little that had not already been written or said or much of anything beyond repetitive assaults on Styron as a white racist unable to "transcend his southern peckerwood background" and eager to defame the memory of "a slave who led a heroic rebellion against the dehumanization of chattel slavery."[9]

From the outset, Woodward made no secret of his contempt for "the racist campaign against Bill Styron's novel" or of his opinion that some of "our black Nationalists . . . are taking a decidedly Fascistic, racist, and anti-intellectual line." When Styron sent him a copy of what Woodward called "the Black Mafia's book on William the Infamous," he confessed that he had "only dipped into it and quickly withdrawn with the dry heaves." Still, he knew that he "must drain the dregs in order to discover the depth of the madness." Woodward may have been instrumental in setting up what he called Eugene Genovese's "masterful dismemberment" of the black scholars' critique soon to run in the *New York Review of Books*, and he promised Styron that if he got the chance on an upcoming NBC television appearance, he would "take a crack at this" as well. Yet if he imagined that the assault on Styron had been by any means repulsed, he would soon learn otherwise in a setting of his own making that provided his first truly up-close-and-personal exposure to the unquenchable ferocity and unswerving absolutism that marked some black nationalists at that time.[10]

Perhaps looking to affirm his high regard for his embattled friend's talents as a writer, Woodward invited Styron to join him, Robert Penn Warren, and Ralph Ellison for a session on "The Uses of History in Fiction" at the November 1968 meeting of the Southern Historical Association in New Orleans. The writers' presentations and panel discussion went well enough and yielded some rich general insights into the novelist's approach and obligations to the past, but the ensuing questioning from the audience proved another matter entirely. It consisted largely of one ad hominem verbal assault on Styron after another, including one from a questioner who announced proudly that he had already called him "a liar" earlier in the year at Harvard and now was in New Orleans to do precisely the same thing. And so it went, until, finally despairing of any prospect of browbeating concessions or apologies from Styron, the last assailant from the floor settled for declaring that "the book must not be valid if all the black intellectuals put it down."[11]

The association's secretary-treasurer Bennett Wall declared the uproarious session "the highlight of the program," and for public consumption at least, Woodward insisted that he, too, was pleased with the outcome. Styron, however, was not at all happy about yet another volatile confrontation over his novel and seemed to come away fully persuaded that further such public discussions of his book would prove equally frustrating and fruitless. Robert Penn Warren also offered a grim take on the experience, reporting that "Black Power people turned [up] to give Bill the once-over, with a few sideswipes for Ralph, who [because of his refusal to embrace black separatism] has now been declassed to Uncle Tomism." Pointing to a recent shooting at a Black Power rally at UCLA, he fretted that Ellison himself might "get it someday."[12]

For all his professed satisfaction, the New Orleans session likely strengthened Woodward's conviction that "a bit of rough and tough ridicule is in order." He seemed bent on administering such a dosage at several points in his presidential address to the Organization of American Historians in April 1969. Later published in the *Journal of American History* as "Clio with Soul," his talk was an unflinching, go-against-the-flow commentary on an emotionally volatile issue of the sort rarely encountered in the academy, so much so that it is hard to imagine it coming from any of Woodward's white contemporaries, save perhaps the pugnacious Eugene Genovese. Though it was destined to anger and offend some black scholars and intellectuals especially, Woodward's address began by acknowledging that white scholars had failed to integrate black history sufficiently, into either their courses or their research and writing in American history. Even those who had made the attempt, Woodward noted, had largely presented blacks as a "passive element" to whom much was done by whites, while they seemed to have done little more than react to what whites were doing—or trying to do—to them. In this, white historians had done a great disservice not only to black Americans but to all Americans regardless of race. By way of making amends, he called for "an infusion of 'soul'" as "an essential corrective in line with the tradition of countervailing forces in American historiography."[13]

Woodward's message to those calling for more attention to black history seemed supportive and conciliatory up to that point, but his remarks soon took on a sharply critical and seemingly almost consciously confrontational tone. Despite admitting that he saw the task of making black history a more dynamic and interactive presence in the broad narrative of the nation's past as largely the responsibility of "the Negro historian," he made it clear that this should not lead to "the exclusive preemption of a subject by reason of racial qualification." Though he knew full well that such a preemption had already been granted on many campuses, he was particularly aggressive on this point. He was having none of the argument that the field should rightly be ceded to black scholars because they were said to be uniquely capable of supplying the "black perspective." If the black experience was critical to a fuller understanding of the American experience, then "Negro history [was] too important to be left entirely to Negro historians." Beyond that, trying to exclude whites from writing about black history solely because of their race came down, ironically enough, to catering to "an extreme brand of racism" and practicing precisely the kind of racial discrimination that blacks and their white allies, including Woodward himself, had labored so long and so diligently to discredit.[14]

The upshot of this exclusionary stance, Woodward feared, would be a "fantastically abstract" presentation of black history, tailored largely to furthering the aims of the contemporary black nationalist movement and thus long on celebrations of black heroes and black culture but short on documentation or critical reflection. In this, Woodward saw certain parallels with the "overwrought nationalism" of newly independent African states where, in their zeal, "some black patriots" had even declared that "Moses and Buddha were Egyptian negroes." Woodward knew full well he was poking a hornet's nest here, but he proceeded to rile its volatile inhabitants further by pointing out that Liberia, "named for liberty" and "ruled by former slaves from the United States," had itself "established a flourishing slave trade," while Haiti, born out of a slave rebellion, had subsequently embraced an "oppressive system of forced labor remarkably similar to state slavery." Aghast at the rise of what he saw as a historically and culturally fraudulent Afrocentrism throughout American academe, he did not mince words in declaring flatly that "Afro-Americans . . . are far more alien in Africa than they are at home" or in insisting that "many old black families of Philadelphia and Boston are less African in culture than many whites of the South."[15]

Turning to well-meaning white historians concerned with seeing "full justice done at long last to Negro achievements and contributions," Woodward cautioned against a "misguided form of white philanthropy and paternalism that would attempt to compensate by exaggerating or by celebrating ever more obscure and deservedly neglected figures of the past." The accompanying impulse to deprecate European civilization and reduce its legacy to a chorus of "*mea culpas*" struck him as a reminder that "the demagoguery . . . and the charlatanry of historians in service of a fashionable cause can at times rival that of politicians."[16]

This was strong stuff indeed at a time when it seemed that many thoroughly intimidated white administrators were virtually falling over themselves to comply with demands for freestanding black studies programs and separate dorms and cultural centers for black students on campus. As heard by his OAH audience and read later in the *Journal of American History*, his original remarks would have been sufficient to cause a stir in their own right even had Woodward not arranged in advance to have a slightly modified but no less confrontational version appear in the *New York Times Magazine* just three days after his address was delivered.[17]

Among the number of critical reactions to Woodward's *Times Maga-zine* piece, none were more openly contemptuous—or bizarre—than that of black poet LeRoi Jones (aka Amiri Baraka), who assailed Woodward as "somebody's idea of a historian," though only among "the self-hypnotized and their trainees." Jones could only marvel at Woodward's "ignorance" in lampooning Afrocentrists' claims that Buddha and Moses were black: "Yes, man, Buddha [and] Moses, were BLACK. Can you dig it?" So, among oth-ers, were "Christ and Krishna." Having settled the matter to his satisfaction by simply declaring Woodward clueless, Jones bade him "return to yr. lit-tle scramble of American White Nationalismus, wretched little man. And [to] the rest of your tribe, you ignoramuses, you small-minded, fearful little fakes."[18]

Woodward's presidential address later drew a more objective and temper-ate critique in an essay by African American historian Sterling Stuckey, who found him much more open to the importance of black history than his white peers but nonetheless felt that his remarks represented much that "is wrong with the way in which the past is viewed by white historians." Beyond dis-playing what Stuckey thought was an appalling ignorance of African history, Woodward's greatest offense was failing to recognize contributions of black scholars in writing "the history of Afro-Americans and . . . in helping their people preserve their sanity in an America mad with racism."[19]

When Woodward sent Stuckey his reactions to the essay, the two began a respectful dialogue in which he made some concessions to Stuckey's criti-cisms and Stuckey politely took him to task for conflating the work of black historians with the rhetoric of "certain militants." Given the horrendous crimes perpetrated against black Americans, Stuckey felt that black scholars had actually been "not a little measured in their attitudes toward the larger society." Woodward conceded that he "tended sometimes to confuse the rhetoric of black militants" with the actual arguments and findings of black historians, though he thought Stuckey might also "admit on further reflection that the two sometimes overlapped." He did not press the matter further with Stuckey, but he would never have much use for the black intellectuals of that era who "loudly demand[ed] black withdrawal, separation, nationalism, exclusion of all whites, and pre-emption of all teaching and monopoly of all writing of black history by blacks." Such behavior was simply unconsciona-ble to someone who, as his former student J. Mills Thornton observed, had consistently worked toward "a society in which race was recognized as an identity imposed by others, rather than something innate."[20]

If the blowback from his "Clio with Soul" address and articles was more substantial than Woodward anticipated, he gave no sign of being the least bit chastened in the third and final edition of *The Strange Career of Jim Crow* in 1974, where he charged that what were supposed to have been formal, legitimate courses on the Afro-American experience had been coopted by separatists bent on turning them into platforms for "dramatiz[ing] their causes and act[ing] out their fantasies." Campus environments had not only been corrupted intellectually but even rendered physically unsafe, Woodward noted, citing the case of Cornell, where administrators "found themselves solemnly signing concessions surrounded by gun-bearing students and members of the press."[21]

Woodward also saw the hostility to anything other than to a rigidly uniform (and in his view, grossly distorted) narrative of black history that emanated from black studies programs as a threat to academic freedom and the free expression of ideas within his profession. In the past, such threats had come primarily from zealous anticommunists bent on rooting out or silencing professors whose loyalty they deemed suspect. His friend Clarence Nixon and some of his colleagues had come under fire on these grounds at Tulane in the late 1930s. Woodward was directly involved in the higher-profile case of his beleaguered Johns Hopkins colleague the international affairs expert Owen Lattimore, whom red-baiting senator Joseph R. McCarthy targeted as "the top Soviet espionage agent in the United States." Lattimore's criticism of hardline anti-Soviet attitudes and his seemingly tolerant attitude toward controversial Soviet moves in Asia led McCarthy and other Cold War era powerbrokers to demand his ouster. Although some Hopkins faculty actually found Lattimore difficult to work with and doubted whether, as one put it, he truly "belonged in the academic profession," he had been granted tenure, and the principle of academic freedom itself seemed to be under direct attack in this case. Much to his mother's dismay, that had been enough to draw Woodward into the front ranks of a campus cohort who managed to persuade the university's higher-ups to retain Lattimore, despite his indictment for perjury in 1952.[22]

Woodward continued to stand behind Lattimore until he was finally cleared of all charges in 1955, despite indications that some of his own previous actions and affiliations had raised suspicions that he might be harboring some communist sympathies as well. In 1951, with Senator McCarthy running amok against the backdrop of a Cold War now gone hot in Korea, prominent naval historian Samuel Eliot Morison recommended Woodward for a post as historical adviser to the Joint Chiefs of Staff, only to see the requisite security

An Ever More Conservative Old Liberal

check derail the appointment. An earlier background check pursuant to his appointment in naval intelligence during the war had failed to find anything more noteworthy than his defense of his German colleagues at Scripps. This time, however, investigators delved into his involvement in Angelo Herndon's defense "under the auspices of communist influence." To that end, they had sought out John H. Hudson, the rabid, red-baiting prosecutor in the Herndon case. Hudson promptly revealed that, although he had never heard the twenty-three-year-old Woodward say he was a member of the Communist Party, he did hear him identify himself as a "socialist." Hudson also recalled Woodward declaring that every American had "the right to revolt" and repeatedly condemning the "tyranny of capitalism."[23]

Harmful as these allegations might seem, what was likely the most damning and influential testimony about Woodward came from one of his biggest benefactors. Howard Odum had warned the youthful Woodward about mixing with the "wrong crowd" of leftists and radicals who made Ab's Intimate Bookshop their headquarters in Chapel Hill, and he surely took an equally dim view of his protégé's gadding about with the likes of Don West in the early weeks of his first semester on campus. Despite Odum's role in getting the funding Woodward needed to finish his Tom Watson manuscript and in persuading Macmillan to look at it for publication, he almost surely picked up on Woodward's greater personal affinity for Rupert Vance and for Frank Graham, whose emergence as another prominent spokesman for reform in the South may also have sparked jealousy on Odum's part.[24]

When naval intelligence investigators came to Chapel Hill in the summer of 1951, Vance assured them that Woodward's youthful indiscretions were behind him now and that he considered his "character, discretion, and loyalty beyond question." They got quite a different take, however, from Odum, who reported that Woodward had traveled to Europe in 1932 because he "questioned the democratic form of government in the U.S." The young man might have returned the wiser for his experience, Odum allowed, but he believed nonetheless that Woodward's "restlessness and inclination toward liberalism" during that period "would not have allowed him to trust [the] subject," who did not always seem to be "stable intellectually or emotionally." Though he felt Woodward was now "OK," according to the investigator, Odum still "didn't know that he could recommend him."[25]

When Woodward learned in January 1952 that his security clearance had not been approved, he found the news "naturally disturbing" and pressed the officer who informed him to share whatever details he could about the reasons his clearance had been withheld, although this request was apparently declined. More than a decade later, he could only ascribe the denial of his security clearance to his own seemingly evasive response to an investigator's query about belonging to the Southern Conference for Human Welfare, which was allegedly a communist front organization. When he replied that "he may or may not have been considered a member," a security officer had quickly confronted him with documentation that he had even held a minor office in the group in 1938. He had done so, he then recalled, solely at the behest of SCHW co-founder Frank Graham, for whom he "would have done anything [he] asked me to do." It was this memory lapse and the contradictory evidence uncovered, Woodward eventually persuaded himself, that had surely derailed his security clearance.[26]

Woodward had still been processing the implications of this episode in 1954 when he found himself embroiled in yet another dispute over academic freedom, this one stemming from the strikingly politicized process of selecting the Harmsworth Professor at Oxford each year. The U.S. ambassador to England was an ex-officio member of the selection committee, and reports had surfaced from years past that the appointment of Arthur Schlesinger Jr. had twice been vetoed by ambassadors who found Schlesinger's politics too far to the left for their tastes. There were further rumblings in 1954 that U.S. Ambassador Winthrop W. Aldrich had objected to the selection of Pulitzer Prize–winning historian Merle Curti for the 1954–55 Harmsworth slot because Curti was an avowed pacifist, which amounted to prima facie evidence of disloyalty among the hard-core Cold Warriors of that day. That appointment then went to Woodward, giving what was, for him at least, the discomfiting impression that he had been chosen because he was safer and "less controversial" than Curti. He raised this concern with Lord Halifax, the chancellor of Oxford University, noting that if these reports were true, it would undermine his relationship with his Oxford colleagues and jeopardize "the prestige of the chair itself."[27]

After much back and forth, including a rather testy meeting between Woodward and Ambassador Aldrich, the ambassador decreed that he and his office would henceforth have no direct role in screening candidates in advance of the selection committee deliberating. The former selection process, which seemed to give influential American historian Samuel Eliot Morison almost sole discretion in submitting nominees for the ambassador's approval before they were sent on to officials at Oxford, would be scrapped. Going forward, a formal committee of the American Historical Association would send their suggestions directly to the secretary of electors for the Harmsworth Professorship. Though Woodward later shrugged off a chorus of kudos for his handling of the affair, the praise was wholly in order. Thrust into a tense, awk-ward, and extremely delicate situation, he had quickly sized it up and resolved it through firmness and careful diplomacy, with some assistance from both sides of the Atlantic. Woodward was not only smitten with the Oxford setting but charmed by his faculty colleagues in Queen's College, who, he declared, "could not have been more hospitable." He also delighted in the "leisure and freedom" he enjoyed courtesy of the minimal lecturing and student contact hours required of the Harmsworth Professor. Still, though he had sought throughout to limit adverse publicity concerning the incident, he had left no doubt that he was determined to defend the principles of academic free-dom and free speech against political encroachment, even if it might mean resigning from a post he truly relished.[28]

Woodward's involvement in free speech controversies had thus far fit into a general pattern stretching back to the early days of the Republic, in which individuals or groups who challenged the prevailing verities or the practices of the reigning political majority often met with determined, aggressive efforts to silence them, either through the resources of government or by other coercive means. By the 1960s he had begun to see a striking reversal of the traditional polarity in free-speech debates and conflicts, especially on college campuses, as, increasingly, efforts to silence dissenting voices came from the left instead of the right. As a champion of free speech, Woodward bristled at the grim irony of seeing self-styled champions of dissent, such as militant black stu-dents or anti–Vietnam War activists, move to silence or shout down anyone who took issue with their viewpoints or tactics. Such a turn of events was anathema to someone who thought periodic conflicts, even potentially vola-tile ones, sparked by the expression of controversial or unpopular views were vital to maintaining a vibrant, energized campus intellectual environment.

Woodward was more than a little dismayed, then, in September 1963, when then provost and acting president Kingman Brewster persuaded a stu-dent organization to rescind its invitation to segregationist Alabama governor George Wallace to speak at Yale. Brewster would later be named president in his own right, but he was clearly chastened by the backlash against his use of his office to restrict free speech in a setting where it was supposed to have been a thoroughly hallowed tradition. Though Woodward had actually been on campus at Yale barely a year at that point, he had not hesitated to let Brewster know of his own disapproval. Nearly a decade later, he would be, if anything, even more upset when student protestors were allowed to physically prevent Gen. William Westmoreland, former U.S. commanding officer in Vietnam, from taking the podium in 1972.[29]

In a letter to the *Yale Daily News* in January 1974, Woodward pointed out that "Harvard recently disgraced itself and the academic community" by canceling a debate featuring renowned physicist and infamous proponent of the genetic inferiority of blacks William A. Shockley and Roy Innis, director of the Congress of Racial Equality. He hoped, Woodward added, that "Yale students will prove more sophisticated and less imitative." Alas, however, they did not, as Yale followed suit by canceling a similar event involving Shockley. Shockley was later shouted down at Yale by screaming protesters at what was supposed to be a debate pitting him against *National Review* editor William Rusher. In the wake of the Shockley debacle, Brewster asked Woodward to chair a committee to draft a policy that would "ensure freedom of expression at Yale."[30]

The committee consisted of five faculty members, including Woodward as chair and the eminent political scientist Robert Dahl. They were joined by five students, two administrators, and an alumnus, who just happened to be powerful Washington attorney Lloyd Cutler, a close friend of Brewster. The committee spent the fall 1974 semester drafting a report addressing the principle of free speech, recounting its history at Yale, and recommending a comprehensive policy to guarantee that it would be upheld on campus. Woodward was responsible for overseeing the composition of the historical component of the report, though a student was heavily involved in writing the first draft, which was forthrightly critical of Brewster's handling of free speech issues dating back to his time as provost. A later report had Cutler warning Woodward, "You can't write this. If you write this, Kingman Brewster will have to resign," and then "bull[ying]" him into damping down the criticism of Brewster. In reality, the moderated tone of that revised section of the final report more likely reflected Woodward's role in simply bringing the overzealous efforts of a student writer in line with the careful, measured language that was a hallmark of his own writing. Anyone familiar with that language needed only to read that the Yale president's past statements on free speech priorities had sometimes appeared to assign "equal if not higher value to law and order, to town-gown relations, to proper motives, to the sensitivity of those who feel threatened or offended, and to majority attitudes" to understand that Kingman Brewster was not getting off scot-free.[31]

In the end, however, it was not the language of the historical summary of free speech issues at Yale that ensured that what was soon known as the "Woodward Report" would become that rarest of academic documents—a committee report with both immediate and lasting impact, even beyond the campus where it originated. The document owed the near canonical status it achieved in some quarters to its eloquent and compelling opening statement on "values and priorities," which was apparently more the responsibility of Dahl than of Woodward. The statement straightforwardly established free speech as the absolute and inviolable principle by which all universities worthy of the name must abide: "The history of intellectual growth and discovery clearly demonstrates the need for unfettered freedom, the right to think the unthinkable, discuss the unmentionable, and challenge the unchallengeable. . . . We value freedom of expression precisely because it provides a forum for the new, the provocative, the disturbing, and the unorthodox." It followed, then, that even though a university might also be seen as "a special kind of small society," it could not "make its primary and dominant value the fostering of friendship, solidarity, harmony, civility, or mutual respect" and remain true to "its central purpose." By way of driving this point home, the framers had added for good measure, that "it may sometimes be necessary in a university for civility and mutual respect to be superseded by the need to guarantee free expression." Even if these words were not precisely Woodward's, the values and priorities they conveyed certainly were, and the report bearing his name seemed to bolster his bona fides as what journalist Nat Hentoff called Yale's "most renowned paladin of free speech."[32]

Had the Woodward Report surfaced a generation earlier amid the intense efforts to silence campus dissidents during the McCarthy era, it would surely have been hailed as a courageous, forthright assertion of the most cherished principles of American liberalism. Yet, for all the instant acclaim it won in the administrative ranks of American higher education, its sweeping guarantees of free speech, no matter how offensive or divisive, struck some on the Yale campus as having as much potential to sanction harassment and persecution of minorities as to safeguard their freedom of expression. This was no isolated or ephemeral sentiment. It would gain astonishing traction and soon become nearer the norm than the exception at many universities, where left-leaning faculty and students now demanded limits on speech that might offend racial and cultural minorities. In this new environment, Woodward observed, he and other traditional liberals found themselves either "voiceless or pushed into conservative identification," to the point that having his name affixed to Yale's protections of free speech soon branded him as a "reactionary." Much the same had happened, of course, as the unwavering advocacy of racial integration that had marked him as a liberal in the 1950s had become a badge of conservativism in the eyes of some twenty years later.[33]

If this perception of a liberal to conservative metamorphosis bothered him, his behavior going forward offered no hint of it. In fact, the fabled

Woodward Report had scarcely been bound and distributed when he took a position that some saw contradicting its central premise and leaving little doubt that he was steadily gravitating to the right. It all began quietly enough when students in Yale's Davenport College submitted a proposal in October 1975 for an undergraduate seminar devoted to W. E. B. Du Bois. These seminars typically met once a week, lasted one semester, and were not even accepted for credit in some undergraduate majors. Though they required formal sponsorship by an appropriate academic department or professional school, they were sometimes taught by nonacademics in a variety of fields, including famed sportscaster Howard Cosell, who would be offering one during the upcoming spring 1976 semester. Up to this point, approval of the seminars had been all but a foregone conclusion. At the outset, there seemed no reason to suspect otherwise in this instance. The proposed instructor, Herbert W. Aptheker, held a PhD in history from Columbia, he had published several books on African American topics, including an edited volume of Du Bois's correspondence, he was the literary executor of Du Bois's estate, and he had been a close associate of Du Bois from 1946 until his death in 1963. Surely, it seemed, he was eminently qualified to offer a single undergraduate course focused on someone whose work he knew so well. The only possible hitch seemed to be that Herbert Aptheker had also been visibly committed throughout his adult life to furthering the aims and interests of the American Communist Party. Woodward had included Aptheker's published dissertation, *American Negro Slave Revolts*, on his early assigned reading lists when reliable historical treatments of slavery were still hard to come by. Still, like many white scholars of the era, he looked askance at Aptheker's claim to have discovered as many as 250 documented cases of slave revolts and conspiracies. Woodward was not alone in seeing this number as a gross exaggeration driven by communist dogma and calculated to convey the impression of an enslaved black proletariat bent on seizing the first opportunity "to overthrow the master class by force."[34]

Questionable as many of Aptheker's historical arguments might have been to some, they nonetheless appealed to scholars on the left bent on affirming an enduring radical tradition in American life. He had been invited to more college campuses than any American communist of his day, and seeing an "extreme threat" in Aptheker's appeal among "the intellectual segment of the academic community," FBI director J. Edgar Hoover had once branded him "the most dangerous communist in America."[35]

Aptheker's busy speaking schedule and voluminous writings dedicated to boosting the Communist Party's image and cause left him little time for serious scholarly research and cast further doubt on the validity of his earlier, more academically oriented work. Arthur Schlesinger Jr., who had tangled with him in a spirited debate in 1949, had come to regard him as a mere "communist hitman," and Aptheker seemed to play the part to the hilt, nowhere more so than in his disingenuous defense of the Soviet Union's brutal suppression of the Hungarian uprising in 1956.[36]

When the Yale history department was asked to sponsor Aptheker's proposed seminar on Du Bois, a special ad hoc committee, chaired by Woodward and including John Blum and John Blassingame, recommended unanimously that the department decline the request. There were hearty assurances all around, that Aptheker's "politics," that is, his communism, had no bearing on the committee's decision, which, Woodward explained, came down to their collective sense that Aptheker did not rise to "the standard of scholarship we try to maintain for Yale teachers." After all, "none of his work may be said to have achieved distinction, and for the most part, it is second rate." He also shared that both he and Blassingame were disappointed with Aptheker's approach to editing the first volume of Du Bois's correspondence, which had been published two years earlier. Without elaborating on specifics, Woodward allowed only that the committee felt that "if we could not trust him to edit Du Bois's papers—a matter of public record—we were even less able to feel confident of his teaching, of which there would be no public record."[37]

Woodward's subsequent attempts to explain his opposition to allowing Aptheker to offer the seminar rarely went much beyond this terse and not terribly forthcoming rationale, fueling whispers in some quarters that his stance had less to do with Aptheker's record as a historian than with his long-standing role as, by David Horwitz's estimate, "the Communist Party's most prominent Cold War intellectual." Although Woodward and his supporters repeatedly dismissed this suspicion out of hand, it was not entirely unwarranted, in his case especially. Woodward was hardly the only young American intellectual of his generation who had developed a fascination with communism in the 1930s and indulged in a bit of flirtatious fellow traveling with its adherents. Four decades later, however, as with many others, his youthful captivation had long since given way, not simply to a resolute hostility to the doctrine, but, if anything, to an even deeper antipathy toward its avowed disciples.[38]

Woodward admitted at the time that he was "greatly concerned" about the decision to deny his security clearance in 1952, and he would continue to turn the meaning of the affair over in his mind in the years to come. There was no escaping the implication that regardless of how lightly he had once taken his youthful associations with alleged communists and communist front organizations, others took them seriously enough to question his own feelings about communism. This revelation did not deter him from continuing to support his embattled Johns Hopkins colleague Owen Lattimore, who was accused of being a communist agent. It did give him sufficient pause, however, that he made it a point to clarify that he was not defending Lattimore's actual views per se but rather his "academic freedom." Going forward, his responses to queries about his early reactions to what he had seen during his initial visit to the Soviet Union would be distinctly measured. Interviewed some fifty years later, Woodward conceded that, with "the Western system" apparently crumbling in the early 1930s, it had seemed "an exciting time to go there." By his later recollection, however, 1932 had actually been "a bad year for Russia," marked by famine, violence, and repression. All told, he now recalled his visit as "a sobering experience" and certainly not one to incline him to embrace the Soviet system. He was even more circumspect about his earlier interactions with known or suspected communists. He did not seem so eager to be associated with Don West as he had been in 1934, after West listed him as a reference in a grant proposal submitted to the Rabinowitz Foundation in 1961. Foundation trustee and Woodward's former Little, Brown editor Angus Cameron readily perceived that Woodward's comments on the proposal effectively amounted to "damning it with faint praise," an interpretation that Woodward subsequently confirmed.[39]

Woodward made no effort to conceal his disdain for communists and communism in general when he warned historian and Student Nonviolent Coordinating Committee activist Staughton Lynd in 1965 that, while current allegations in the press of communists infiltrating the group may have been overblown, he was fully persuaded that they were an active presence within the organization. This was an issue that could "destroy the movement," and he feared that SNCC's leaders were taking it too lightly. He understood why there was impatience with the "lessons" that older generations sought to pass down, but he added, "My generation had more experience with the Communists than the present generation. We learned the hard way. I hope the present generation will not have to learn it all over again." SNCC's very name, he reminded Lynd, bespoke a commitment to nonviolence, which he felt was neither "consistent [n]or compatible with Communism," and he could not but doubt "the sincerity of any Communist who professes non-violence."[40]

Despite his distaste for communists, Woodward might not have opposed Aptheker's proposed seminar so vehemently had it not been focused on someone he held in almost worshipful esteem. Woodward's only personal contact with W. E. B. Du Bois had come while he was still casting about for a thesis topic in 1931. When he met with him at the New York editorial office of the NAACP's magazine *The Crisis* to discuss doing a thesis on "his ideas," he got no encouragement from Du Bois, who, Woodward thought, might have been put off by "that Deep South accent of mine." Determined to give it another try, Woodward sent him a reprint of his 1938 article in the *Journal of Southern History*, which encapsulated Woodward's favorable depiction of Tom Watson's racial attitudes before 1896. At this point, Du Bois was teaching at Atlanta University, and Woodward, making no mention of their previous encounter, included a note with the reprint assuring him that the article had been written "in a spirit that I hope you will approve, whether you can agree with my conclusions or not." He added that he had long followed Du Bois's work with "interest and profit" and expressed particular appreciation for the insights offered in his "admirable book, *Black Reconstruction*." Finally, perhaps hoping for a more satisfying personal encounter the second time around, he allowed that when he was in Atlanta again, he would "like sometimes to talk with you over a plan of research I have in mind, if I may come out to see you." Woodward may have been angling for an endorsement of his take on Watson, but Du Bois merely thanked him for the reprint and his "kind words." Though Du Bois added that "anytime you are in Atlanta, I should be very glad to see you," starstruck as he was, Woodward knew a pro forma invitation when he got one, and their less than satisfactory first meeting would also be their last.[41]

Some forty years later, Woodward conceded that he had been "a much over-awed and nervous young man" when he paid his personal call on Du Bois back in 1931, but even as he matured, he continued to hold this hero of his youth in extremely high regard. In addition to praising Du Bois's pioneering contributions to the history of Reconstruction, he hailed his prescience in grasping "the true nature of the New South rulers, northern colonization and the essential discontinuities of Southern history." Du Bois's *Souls of Black Folk* had been one of his first "literary loves," he wrote to Bernard Bailyn in 1967, and he was still struck by its "lyrical beauty, its melancholy passion, its keen insights, its prophetic passages."[42]

In the end, though, Woodward reserved his greatest admiration for Du Bois's profoundly analytical and dispassionate approach not only to history but to questions of political economy. This, in turn, made it difficult for him to understand, much less accept, Du Bois's decision to join the Communist Party near the end of his very long life. He had professed skepticism of communism as a strategy for improving the lot of black Americans for the better part of that life, citing the obstinate refusal of its spokesmen to acknowledge that "the split between white workers and black workers was greater than that between white workers and capitalists."[43]

Yet, as the Cold War unfolded, Du Bois's increasing coziness with communist regimes around the world led many of his former patrons to distance themselves much from him and federal authorities to place him under constant scrutiny. In Woodward's mind, it was the push-pull effect of isolation and harassment in the United States and the warm words of praise and welcome offered by communist leaders throughout the world that finally led Du Bois to announce his official affiliation with the Communist Party in November 1961, on the eve of his departure for Ghana, where he would spend the rest of his days.[44]

Woodward acknowledged that, in the decade leading up to that decision, Du Bois had praised Joseph Stalin as a "great man" wholly deserving of the "worship of his people" while placing President Harry S. Truman alongside Adolf Hitler as "one of the greatest killers of our day." Yet Woodward could still write, "Given what we know of this man, I simply find it hard to believe he could have become that much of a true believer." Du Bois, he noted, consistently emphasized his willingness "to change my mind when I see reason to do so." Though Du Bois had lived for ninety-three years before he formally embraced communism, Woodward chose to believe that "had his search for truth been extended long enough," the communist-inspired bloodshed ravaging much of "his beloved Africa" alone would have quickly led Du Bois to yet another "drastic change of heart." Woodward's wishful conjecture bespoke an almost unshakable faith in his own vision of Du Bois as simply too intelligent to swallow the corrupt, false-fronted doctrine of communism whole and too deeply principled to tolerate the duplicity, corruption, and ruthlessness of those committed to propagating it. Anyone who denied the possibility of his recanting his commitment to communism, Woodward insisted, must surely be ignoring Du Bois's well-deserved reputation for "intelligence and integrity."[45]

The strength of Woodward's conviction on this point had left him profoundly disturbed that Du Bois's papers had fallen under the control of Aptheker, who struck him as little more than a propagandist in historian's pose. Critics of Aptheker's earlier work on Du Bois had already accused him of "casting Du Bois in the writer's own image" by exaggerating his inclinations toward communism and socialism over the entire course of his long career. Woodward himself fumed that, instead of doing justice to the profound complexity of a man of such vast experience and intellectual depth, Aptheker's primary aim in editing Du Bois's papers for publication was conveying the false impression that, despite joining the Communist Party scarcely two years before his death, he had actually been a communist at heart for most of his career.[46]

When the first volume of Du Bois's correspondence appeared in 1973, it appeared that Woodward's sense of what Aptheker was up to might not be far off the mark. The correspondence in the book spanned roughly fifty-eight years, from 1877 to 1934, a period well before Du Bois announced his formal association with the Communist Party, but one encompassing the fifteen years between 1905 and 1920, when he emerged as a high-profile advocate for black rights. Yet correspondence from these years accounted for less than a third of the text, while slightly more than half was allotted to the remaining fourteen years down to 1934, when Aptheker saw Du Bois gaining a greater appreciation of the "relevancy of Marxist dogma." (Notably, the second volume would be devoted entirely to a single decade, 1934–44, when Aptheker presumably saw this process accelerating.)[47]

Meanwhile, although Aptheker claimed that Du Bois had actually been a socialist "for the better part of his life," most of the references in the volume to Du Bois's purported socialism or communism came from someone else, several of them from Aptheker himself. (By Clarence Contee's calculation, some 54 percent of the letters in the volume were written by someone other than Du Bois.) When he included examples of correspondents asking Du Bois to clarify his views on socialism and communism, Aptheker rarely supplied his response, and when he did, Du Bois came across as almost deliberately vague on this point. All told, despite what he claimed or implied in editorial asides and annotations, Aptheker provided almost nothing of substance in Du Bois's own words to suggest a consistent, ongoing gravitation toward communism over the entire course of his career.[48]

When Du Bois finally made his application for Communist Party membership official in 1961, few had been more exuberant than Aptheker, who wrote to him hailing "the news of the Doctor's choosing to join the Party," and exulting in its "prominent treatment in yesterday's TIMES." Woodward and Aptheker were surely two of the greatest Du Bois admirers among whites of their generation, and both found his relationship with communism frustrating, the former because he had formed any relationship at all and the latter because it took him so long to do so.[49]

Here in a nutshell lay the fundamental explanation for Woodward's determination to keep Herbert Aptheker from coming on the Yale campus to promulgate a consciously distorted vision of Du Bois as a communist at heart for the majority of his long life and career. Despite his general antipathy to the Communist Party and its adherents at this point, he had befriended and grown to respect a number of Marxist historians, including some of his students, as well as others, like Eugene Genovese, who was a former communist. In Aptheker, however, Woodward saw not simply a historian who also happened to believe in communism but one so blindly committed to it that he had repeatedly sacrificed scholarly objectivity at the altar of ideological expedience. Though he would probably have passed on the opportunity to hear him, he would have raised no formal objection to Aptheker coming on campus to deliver a lengthy oration about the manifold evils of capitalism and laud Karl Marx to his heart's content. He was not challenging Aptheker's right to say what he pleased in a public forum. On the other hand, in Woodward's mind, the principle of academic freedom applied to the expression of ideas grounded in thorough, objective research and contemplation. It did not extend to the dissemination of mere dogma and propaganda of the sort he saw Herbert Aptheker trying to pan off as the fruits of legitimate scholarship.

Woodward seemed to feel fully justified in his efforts to prevent this from happening at Yale. Yet he could scarcely have imagined that they would spark a divisive, and at times heated, dispute on campus that would also involve the nation's two largest historical organizations before an official resolution would be reached nearly three years later. Although broader interest was destined to fade as the matter dragged on, this was one tempest in a teapot that mattered a great deal to those directly caught up in it. Not only would Woodward's role in instigating the controversy fuel the errant notion that his devotion to the liberal principles was faltering as he aged, but his uncharacteristic display of hubris and vindictiveness throughout the affair would do him no credit. In the end, the unexpected resistance and unmuted criticism his actions provoked along the way would leave him more shaken than he cared to admit as his official tenure at Yale drew to a close.

15

I Do Not See How I Could Have Been Misunderstood

___

Sorting Out the Aptheker Debacle

Woodward's deep admiration for W. E. B. Du Bois and protective concern with how his life and legacy would be represented virtually guaranteed that, at some point, he would find himself at cross purposes with the stalwart communist who served as the executor of Du Bois's literary estate and zealous guardian of his papers. Unfortunately for Woodward, regardless of how he felt about Aptheker's designs on Du Bois's papers, Du Bois himself clearly had no such misgivings about a man whom he first invited to share his office in 1946 and asked to edit his correspondence just a few months later. When a white doctoral student sought permission to continue working in his papers in July 1950, Du Bois responded that he was "sorry indeed" to turn him down but explained that he had given custody of the papers "to Miss [Shirley] Graham [later Du Bois] and Mr. Aptheker and am honor bound to take their advice."[1]

Aptheker's personal devotion to Du Bois was beyond question, but his extraordinarily tight-fisted control of access to the papers gave reason to suspect that his interest in Du Bois's legacy was not simply protective but proprietary as well. Woodward definitely got this impression in 1964 when he contacted Aptheker in behalf of one of his graduate students, Eugene Levy, who was seeking access to Du Bois's correspondence with James Weldon Johnson, only to have Aptheker reply that he was bound by "specific instructions limiting physical access to the papers." Seven months later, he informed Woodward that he had found thirty to forty letters between Du Bois and Johnson, though "the terms of my trust forbid that these papers leave me," and the items could not be quoted.[2]

While polite on the face of it, their correspondence reflected a mutual wariness that would never recede. Aptheker, who professed great regard for Woodward's scholarship, commended his critical reappraisal of W. J. Cash's *Mind of the South* in 1969, noting that his own review of the book in *New Masses* had offered a similar perspective. Woodward professed pleasure at finding "so many points of agreement" with Aptheker, though after chairing a session at a Marxist scholars conference in 1966 featuring papers by Aptheker and his fellow Marxist Eugene Genovese, he reported gleefully to Robert Penn Warren that "Comrade Aptheker was apoplectic and Genovese had the better of the battle." He painted much the same picture for *Richmond Times-Dispatch* editor Virginius Dabney, allowing that Aptheker's "explosion of outraged indignation" at Genovese's "devastating" critique of his book had been "a lot of fun."[3]

The two maintained their polite, if thoroughly stilted exchanges, however, as Woodward continued to press Aptheker to make the Du Bois Papers available to "qualified research students in some good and accessible library." For his part, Aptheker maintained a stolid, stiff-lipped resolve in the face of Woodward's hectoring. Their relationship became increasingly strained, however, after Aptheker revealed in a January 1971 letter that the forthcoming first volume of Du Bois's correspondence covered the entire period between 1877 and 1934. Woodward immediately voiced his concern that, with only four published volumes of the papers projected, the first would come all the way down to 1934. He simply could not believe, he explained, that this arrangement could possibly give adequate coverage of all of Du Bois's activities before that point. Both the Booker T. Washington Papers, edited by Woodward's former student Louis Harlan, and a proposed new edition of the Frederick Douglass Papers, to be compiled by his current student, John Blassingame, were projected to run to at least ten volumes. "Is there any chance of expanding the project," he asked, noting that "such a limited publication" might not meet the needs of many interested scholars.[4]

Aptheker responded that there was nothing to prevent the publication of a more comprehensive collection of the Du Bois correspondence at some later point. Noting that, in accordance with "the late Doctor's direction and

I Do Not See How I Could Have Been Misunderstood

decision," he had the "greater proportion" (an estimated "85 or 90%") in his own "custody," he even floated the idea of Yale University Press taking on this project. Regardless of whether Aptheker truly expected Woodward to even pass along this feeler, he had already been rebuffed by enough prominent university presses to know better than to expect any expression of interest from Yale University Press if he did. What he probably did not know at that point was that Woodward was one of six reviewers for a grant proposal that he had recently submitted to the National Endowment for the Humanities. The review panel also included Woodward's colleague John Blum, who objected to Aptheker's "particularly doctrinaire" approach to history, and African American writer and literary critic Blyden Jackson, who also feared that he would approach Du Bois "solely from the Marxist angle." Jackson's fellow literary specialist Louis D. Rubin flatly declared that Aptheker's "Marxist bias would wreak havoc with the meaning of Du Bois's life," because it precluded "[any] kind of disinterested, subtle, psychologically acute inquiry." Save for the African American historian Benjamin Quarles, who gave the proposal a "5" on a scale of 5, Woodward's was actually the most affirmative of the other reviews. The project, which he rated a "4," was of "first-rate importance," he felt, and curiously enough in light of subsequent events, he even allowed that the "PI's competence from [his] published work" was "persuasive."[5]

Despite Woodward's fairly positive appraisal of the proposal, he was deeply concerned that such a treasure trove of historical material should be entrusted to the control of any single individual, let alone stored in that individual's private residence, and he continued to press Aptheker to make all the papers accessible to scholars, even suggesting the Library of Congress as a possible repository. Surely, he ventured, "you must regret having to reject legitimate use by others." In reality, of course, he had long sensed just the opposite—that Aptheker thoroughly relished his control over the papers and the opportunity it gave him to lord it over other historians, many of whom, he knew, held him in low professional regard. Finally grown weary of Woodward's prodding, Aptheker promised tersely in March 1971 to pass his suggestions on to Du Bois's widow, Shirley Graham Du Bois, who actually owned the papers and held the final word on their "disposition."[6]

And there things had stood until August 1973, when despite recently consenting to serve on the Du Bois Papers project's advisory board, Woodward agreed once again to review Aptheker's application for a National Endowment for the Humanities grant to support his work on the project. Possibly at Woodward's urging, NEH research grant director William Emerson had queried Aptheker directly about whether, with respect to future volumes, he meant the term "papers" to include Du Bois's correspondence. Aptheker replied that he did not, but referred instead to a great variety of unpublished essays and manuscripts, including papers Du Bois had written as a student. When Emerson sent Woodward a copy of Aptheker's letter, he responded that he had agreed to serve on the project advisory board under the impression that the reference to Du Bois's papers surely included his correspondence and that, after learning otherwise, he could not support the grant application. Recommending that the NEH committee defer action on the proposal, he promised to urge Aptheker to reconsider his plans but added that "until he does, my attitude toward his application is quite negative."[7]

True to his word, Woodward wrote Aptheker immediately, advising him that if he did not intend to include correspondence in the forthcoming volumes, he "could not in good conscience remain on your board in support of your present plan." Aptheker slyly professed puzzlement about how Woodward had gotten word of his plans for the next volumes, knowing that it could only mean that he was in on the deliberations on his application for NEH support. He promised that, henceforth, the advisory board would be allowed more input on the content of the volumes.[8]

Unmoved by this assurance, Woodward officially cut his ties with the project at the end of January 1974 in a terse, two-sentence note to Leone Stein, informing her of his withdrawal from the advisory board, principally because he disagreed with the editor's approach to selecting and editing Du Bois's correspondence. Woodward had also been in contact with Louis Harlan, whose letter of resignation from the board arrived almost simultaneously with his own and also read much like it, even though Harlan had actually reviewed and endorsed the prepublication galleys of the first volume of Du Bois's papers. There would be a little more back and forth between Aptheker and Woodward, revisiting Woodward's objections to the first volume and his concern with how thoroughly Aptheker had searched for Du Bois's letters in other collections.[9]

Although Woodward professed his willingness to "be of further help," he clearly had no intention of supporting the Du Bois Papers project further so long as Aptheker remained the editor. Indeed, his intention was quite the opposite. Some two years later, in February 1976, he moved once again to discourage NEH funding for the enterprise, citing the project's "inferior standards of editing" and the "great disappointment" of his fellow historians with the first published volume of the Du Bois correspondence.[10]

Had Woodward's participation in this review been public knowledge, it might have raised some eyebrows because, by this point, word of his negative comments about Aptheker's work had spread well beyond the Yale campus. Though he may have fancied the matter settled in October 1975 after the history department formally accepted his ad hoc committee's recommendation, he was soon meeting with Davenport College students and faculty to explain his committee's objections to allowing Aptheker to offer the seminar. In the face of an unanticipated barrage of pointed questions, as his history department colleague Ramsay MacMullen sized it up, he had been "unable to spell out in intelligible (Blunt) terms just what the problem was." Meanwhile, when the history department declined to sponsor the seminar, its proponents, including both students and faculty, had quickly formed a special "Committee to Support the Du Bois Seminar," which joined with the Black Student Alliance in spreading word of what they saw as a blatant effort to "suppress Aptheker's point of view."[11]

The controversy seemed to have been defused when, a week after the history department had appeared to torpedo the proposed course for good, the political science faculty voted unanimously to resurrect it under their sponsorship. From that point, the proposal had only to pass through several levels of what was normally a progression of little more than perfunctory faculty and administrative reviews. The final stage of the process entailed the traditionally pro forma approval of temporary faculty appointments for those slated to offer the seminars the following semester. This responsibility belonged to Yale College's Joint Board of Permanent Officers, composed of the tenured full professors in each arts and sciences discipline. With the political science department's action, a student journalist declared, "the curtain fell on what might have been this year's cause célèbre." There should be no further difficulty in getting the course approved, and the matter would be "quickly forgotten," he predicted. The historical basis for this prophesy may have been sound, but the prophesy itself proved anything but.[12]

Though the political scientists' actions promised to end the matter and still leave Woodward with the satisfaction of having at least kept Herbert Aptheker off his own disciplinary turf, he was anything but happy with this turn of events. Irked that the political scientists would presume to second guess him and his history colleagues on a decision so squarely within their area of expertise, he had made his displeasure known to Yale College dean Horace Taft. Taft also chaired the committee on junior appointments, which would soon pass judgment on the seminar. In that capacity, Taft had asked Woodward to prepare a formal statement for that committee explaining his ad hoc committee's opposition to the Aptheker appointment. Although Woodward pushed Taft to solicit the input of both Kenneth Stampp and

Eugene Genovese, whose assessments he assumed would be distinctly critical of Aptheker's scholarship, Taft thought it preferable to collect published reviews and other scholarly commentary on Aptheker's work instead. Discussions of the dispute and the material submitted, Taft promised, would be "kept in strictest confidence," and he assured Woodward that he "greatly regret[ted] the trouble and anguish which this affair has caused all of us."[13]

Little did Taft imagine at that point that the "trouble and anguish" had scarcely begun. Woodward's report to the junior appointments committee expanded but little on his by now familiar list of criticisms. Few took Aptheker's writing seriously "by any standards of scholarship." His biases as a historian were readily apparent in the first published volume of Du Bois's correspondence, where his tendency to skirt questions on which of Du Bois's views differed from his own had left "the scholarly integrity of the work" in doubt. In support of his appraisal, Woodward included with the report a review of the volume by Clarence Contee of Howard University, who also noted Aptheker's neglect of issues where Du Bois's stance was not in keeping with his own ideological agenda and charged that the editor's "continued use of selections on socialism overemphasizes this aspect of [Du Bois's] thought." Contee's objections to what he saw as Aptheker's attempt to exaggerate Du Bois's identification with socialism seemed very much in line with a student journalist's impression that Woodward's opposition to even a temporary appointment for Aptheker stemmed from his perception that "Aptheker, a Marxist, overemphasizes Du Bois's years as a Communist in editing the latter's correspondence."[14]

Whether Woodward was overreacting in this case or not, one of Yale's most influential faculty members had not only spoken but done so with uncharacteristic force. Yet much to Dean Taft's chagrin and to Woodward's shocked indignation, the committee on junior appointments did not see things his way and voted unanimously to approve the Aptheker seminar under the sponsorship of the political science department. Taft informed Woodward of this not "entirely pleasing" development on December 2, 1975. By that point, only two days remained before Aptheker's appointment to teach the proposed seminar would be submitted for the final approval of the joint board of permanent officers. All such appointments were typically rubber-stamped by acclamation as a single package attached to a committee recommendation, but Taft assured Woodward that, as chair of the proceedings, he would honor any request for "a ballot" on any individual seminar proposal. Though he hoped that "no major confrontation" would ensue, Taft was effectively telling Woodward that he and his colleagues still had a shot at blocking Aptheker's appointment, and to the surprise and dismay of many, they managed to do precisely that.[15]

With most of Yale's political scientists simply assuming that approval of Aptheker's appointment was a foregone conclusion at that point, Woodward had crisply and quietly marshaled his weapons and rallied some of his colleagues for a surprise last-minute counteroffensive that struck some as more like an outright ambush. Fellow ad hoc committee member John Blum could not attend the meeting but encouraged Woodward to make his own opposition to the seminar known. Woodward, Blassingame, and eight of their colleagues were there, however, so that the history department accounted for ten of the roughly forty faculty who bothered to show up for the historically uneventful meeting. The majority in attendance were clearly taken aback when Woodward and Blassingame shattered the accustomed matter-of-factness of the proceedings by rising to speak aggressively and at some length against Aptheker's appointment.[16]

Ramsay MacMullen sensed that if his history colleagues succeeded in carrying the day, they would be called upon immediately to clarify the reasons behind Aptheker's denial, with the likely upshot being an "unpleasant and public war of words." Under the circumstances, it seemed better to him to simply let the seminar proceed. Though not alone in this view, MacMullen was decidedly in the minority. When the ballots were tallied, the "nays" had it by a vote of twenty-five to seven, leaving all the remaining appointments to be approved immediately by acclamation with a single voice vote.[17]

Though he had gotten what he wanted at that juncture, Woodward was still clearly displeased that the faculty in another discipline with no "claim of authority" in the field could undermine the recommendation of his ad hoc committee of distinguished historians and its subsequent approval by the history department. Responding to Dean Taft's suggestion that his report to the junior appointments committee "failed to convey fully our objection," Woodward protested that, though he was "not given to strong words," he had surely questioned Aptheker's work vigorously enough to make his position clear, and "I do not see how I could have been misunderstood." The problem was not so much the intensity of his opposition, Taft responded, but the scarcity of detailed specifics offered to justify it. The review he submitted and others collected by the committee, including one by Eugene Genovese, had actually cast Aptheker's scholarship in a much more favorable light than Woodward had indicated was generally the case.[18]

While Taft's explanation seemed plausible enough, had he read between the lines just a bit, he would have understood that Woodward was so upset primarily because his own appraisal of Aptheker's work was not sufficient in itself to close the book on the matter then and there. Though he did not make a habit of openly wielding his clout on campus, from the president on down, administrators regularly sought his input before implementing a new policy or amending an old one, and his endorsement of either move sometimes became a big selling point in securing its acceptance on campus.[19]

He did not always get his way, of course, as his futile opposition to creating separate dorms and cultural centers for black students at Yale made clear. Still, to his mind at least, his reputation and expertise should surely have earned him the benefit of the doubt in this case. Yet sixty-two Yale faculty went on to sign a document challenging the way the seminar approval process was conducted and pointing to the "vague, conflicting and unsubstantiated charges" against Aptheker as "a blot on the record of this university." Even worse, from Woodward's perspective, nine of those signatures belonged to fellow historians, meaning that only the mathematics and economics departments, with ten each, showed a stronger objection to the decision and the procedures leading up to it than his own. Political science department chair Joseph LaPalombara also took to the pages of the campus newspaper to charge not only that Aptheker's qualifications had faced "a degree of scrutiny . . . manifestly unprecedented" for temporary appointments of seminar instructors but that Woodward and his allies had collaborated in "the utmost secrecy" to ambush the appointment at the virtual eleventh hour.[20]

Woodward could not resist a bit of needling a few weeks later when he wrote LaPalombara offering to share his "information and views" the next time the political science department received a "college seminar proposal from Davenport College." He also assured LaPalombara that he had "no secrets at all in this matter" and truly regretted "that we did not consult freely last fall. Give me a ring anytime." In fact, he added, "in these and all other collegial matters, please be assured, dear Joe, that if mine eye doth offend my brother, I will forthwith pluck it out," signing his letter, "Cordially and collegially, One-eyed Vann."[21]

If LaPalombara found Woodward's facetiousness the least bit disarming, it was not to last. Just a few days later, the *Yale Daily News* ran a lengthy protest piece by Aptheker himself, who scoffed at history department chair John Hall's attempt to justify withholding the specifics of his colleagues' objections to the appointment as "a protection for the individual." For his part, Aptheker declared, he needed "no protection from anyone at Yale and want[ed] none." What he did want and, in fact, absolutely demanded, was

I Do Not See How I Could Have Been Misunderstood

"that this evidence be made public so that I have the opportunity of refuting it." There was, he added, "no other way I could think of for settling this matter."[22]

Some 2,200 undergraduates, amounting to more than half the enrollment of Yale College, signed a petition insisting that Aptheker be allowed to teach his seminar in the fall term of 1976, and students and faculty organized a two-day campus visit by Aptheker in February 1976, capped off by an impassioned lecture that reportedly drew a lengthy standing ovation from some 250 people in attendance. Woodward would have been well advised at this point to keep silent and hope that the emotional furor over the affair would soon die down. Instead, he leapt back into the fray, ostensibly to correct "a misapprehension" voiced more than once, most recently by Aptheker, that the history department's decision to deny his appointment "was based on secret evidence that has been withheld from him and from the public." Not so, Woodward insisted in the Yale Daily News, for the evidence, consisting of the "published works of the applicant," was not only "public" but available for all to see in the Yale Library. Those works, he and his colleagues had concluded, simply did not "measure up to the standard of scholarship desired for teachers at Yale, in appointments where scholarly standards can be applied."[23]

For all his initial reservations about the place, Woodward had soon become a bona fide Yalie. He felt compelled to add that Yale's reputation for exacting standards and highly selective hiring made it a place where "hundreds of people apply to teach . . . and only a handful are appointed" each year. As a result, there was "neither the time nor the taste for debates with candidates about their credentials such as Mr. Aptheker proposes." Seemingly unmindful of how his studied air of condescension might play both on and beyond the Yale campus, he pressed on, offering a gratuitous personal jab at Aptheker: "Most disappointed applicants go about their business with the perfectly plausible consolation that teaching or studying at Yale is not the only possible way to pursue an honorable and rewarding career and that there are other good colleges available, even some good community colleges [such as Hostos College in the Bronx, where Aptheker was then teaching]. A healthy response of this sort is encouraged."[24]

In its acute tone-deafness, Woodward's letter conveyed a smugness and mean-spiritedness that seemed very much at odds with his public persona. It is hard to imagine him doing anything at this point more likely to present himself in an unfavorable light while making Aptheker seem a more vulnerable and sympathetic figure. This single act seems to bear out his former student William McFeely's assessment that his mentor had simply "lost all perspective on this thing." John Blum was not so straightforward, but despite his own sense that Aptheker was a "second-rate intellectual" whose editing work on the Du Bois Papers "stinks," he, like McFeely, thought that the seminar was of too little consequence on campus to justify the enormous fuss Woodward was making. Jesse Lemisch would later observe that one of the dangers that came with all the "power and deference" that Woodward enjoyed was that "no one will tell you when you have done something really awful." Sure enough, cringe and commiserate with each other as they might, there is no indication that even his closest colleagues urged him to soften his stance or back away from a controversy almost wholly of his own making that ultimately embroiled their department in what became, for a time at least, a cause célèbre within their profession.[25]

Events began moving in that direction when Aptheker lodged a formal complaint against Yale with the American Historical Association in February 1976, declaring that because of Woodward's airy dismissal of his scholarship, "the damage to my work is manifest and cries out for remedy." Almost simultaneously, John H. Bracey Jr., who chaired the Afro-American studies department at the University of Massachusetts and worked closely with Aptheker on the Du Bois project, opened fire on another front. Knowing of John Blassingame's supporting role in blocking Aptheker's appointment at Yale, Bracey pressed him for any information in his possession that cast doubt on Aptheker's qualifications. His inquiry, he explained, arose from discussions with the University of Massachusetts's attorneys about possible legal action to quiet rumors that might hurt the Du Bois project in terms of its publication and sales as well as ongoing efforts to secure grant support.[26]

Although Bracey's lawsuit never materialized, there was actually little reason for him to worry that Yale's rejection of Aptheker might undermine the project's future grant prospects, for those prospects were next to nil in any case so long as Woodward was around. Even as Bracey was composing his letter to Blassingame in February 1976, Woodward was firing off one of his own to NEH, deploring Aptheker's approach to editing the first published volume of the Du Bois Papers and warning that "it would be a mistake to subsidize this project."[27]

A month later, the Aptheker controversy was once again headline news on campus after the "Committee to Support the Aptheker Seminar" called for adding the course to the schedule for the fall semester in 1976. Woodward had already ruffled feathers in his department by what some saw as his rather high-handed and secretive attempt the previous December to present his views and those of his fellow ad hoc committee members as those of the entire history faculty. Their displeasure only mounted in the spring of 1976, when a second request for their department to sponsor Aptheker's seminar was dispatched in what appeared be similarly undemocratic fashion.[28]

According to Ramsay MacMullen's account, the history faculty had agreed that, should a second request to sponsor the seminar be forthcoming, the chair would convene the tenured faculty to decide the matter. Instead, when the Davenport College seminar committee resubmitted the Aptheker seminar proposal to the department, chairman John Hall had apparently consulted with only a small contingent of his senior colleagues before announcing that the seminar proposal had been rejected yet again and the matter settled "once and for all," through his exercise of "the chairman's prerogative." Several tenured as well as junior faculty were genuinely upset by this action, none more so than MacMullen, who charged that no department chair at Yale enjoyed "any prerogative at all in recommending a teaching appointment."[29]

Predictably enough, the proposal wound up back in the lap of the political science department, which once more agreed to sponsor it, albeit with the stipulation that the approval was based, not on Aptheker's scholarship, but on his close personal relationship with Du Bois and his storehouse of knowledge about Du Bois's life and career. When Aptheker returned to campus to address a March 1976 rally in support of his seminar, students had also pressed for an appearance by Yale president Kingman Brewster, who declined their request, explaining that he would not "be forced into addressing rallies" because "that's not the way to discuss University business."[30]

The atmosphere remained tense and potentially confrontational three weeks later as the joint board of permanent officers again met to vote on new appointments for the upcoming fall term. Upward of ninety full professors showed up for this meeting, more than twice the previous year's attendance, while pro-Aptheker picketers and demonstrators milled about outside. The verdict on Aptheker's appointment was different this time around, although more than 40 percent of those present voted against it. Still, though it would be rolled out some nine months later than first envisioned, "W. E. B. Du Bois: His Life and Thought" was coming to Yale. Woodward had feared that this might happen, but he claimed to hope that "for his pride and that of other Marxist historians," Aptheker might decline the appointment this time. He surely knew better than to expect this, for the spotlight was rarely too bright or too hot for Aptheker. He would soon demonstrate as much by announcing that he was running for the U.S. Senate from New York on the Communist Party ticket. Woodward had also misjudged the shifting trajectory of a controversy whose political overtones had now been detected well beyond Yale and its environs. From this point forward, the brunt of the embarrassment and discomfort would fall, not on Aptheker, but squarely on Woodward and his colleagues.[31]

Shortly before the Aptheker seminar was finally approved in March 1976, the executive secretary of the Organization of American Historians, Richard Kirkendall, had informed Woodward that a member of the organization had requested that the OAH "look into the matter on Dr. Aptheker's behalf." Professing complete ignorance of the case, Kirkendall asked Woodward to fill him in and let him know whether the matter should be taken up by the "Joint Committee [of the OAH and the AHA] on the Defense of the Rights of Historians under the First Amendment." Seizing on what struck him as an opportunity to make short work of the matter, Woodward responded rather breezily that he had "looked into the matter thoroughly" and could assure Kirkendall that "due process . . . was scrupulously observed" throughout the deliberations on the appointment. There had been absolutely "no opposition on political grounds" and no significant disagreement on the "limitations" of Aptheker's scholarship. He also wanted Kirkendall to know that, while he was all for the OAH defending historians when there was compelling evidence that they had faced discrimination purely because of their political views, he did not think it should undertake to "investigate all rejected applications. There would be thousands of them."[32]

Woodward hoped to forestall any investigation by reducing the affair came to little more than a case of hurt feelings over missing out on an academic appointment, but although he clearly had prestige and influence going for him, the deck was not stacked quite as decidedly in his favor as he and some others at Yale may have assumed. The principal champion of Aptheker's cause within the OAH was Jesse Lemisch of the State University of New York at Buffalo. He had been instrumental in mounting the Radical Caucus challenge at the AHA meeting in 1969, and though he had earned both his BA and PhD at Yale, he was also one of its most persistent critics. With the cooperation of Marvin Gettleman, who had taken classes with Woodward at Johns Hopkins and currently taught at the Polytechnic Institute of New York, Lemisch had drawn up and circulated a petition requesting a poll of the membership on whether the OAH should investigate the Yale history department's actions in the Aptheker case.

For his part, Gettleman had already taken it upon himself to alert Woodward back in February of an effort to "mobilize" the "widespread" concern about the matter. Before he committed himself to this undertaking, Gettleman explained, he wanted to know if Aptheker's critics at Yale had prepared

I Do Not See How I Could Have Been Misunderstood

any formal statement justifying their position. Thus began a protracted series of exchanges in which Woodward seemed to enjoy toying with the unfailingly earnest Gettleman. "Do you really think our friend Herbert is that good?" he asked. Surely Gettleman was not referring to Aptheker's book on slave revolts, much less "the slighter things on Nat Turner or labor in the antebellum South. . . . Have I missed something of importance?" As their exchanges continued, Woodward's apparent equanimity in the face of Gettleman's warnings about the potentially "far-reaching repercussions" of the matter left Gettleman so frustrated that he finally served notice that his fondness for his former teacher would not keep him from fighting "for what, I believe, is right in this matter." Along with this somber declaration, Gettleman sent him a pro-Aptheker pamphlet, which would surely be of interest to Woodward, because it would be distributed at the upcoming OAH meeting in Saint Louis and circulated in New Haven as well.[33]

Despite his calculated show of indifference to Gettleman's missives, Woodward shared the gist of them with Eugene Genovese, complaining that he was being "misrepresented, misquoted, and lied about daily, here and elsewhere," only to have the fiery Genovese matter-of-factly counsel a general attitude of "Fuck 'em!" toward his detractors. However disinterested he sought to appear, though, Woodward was sufficiently concerned about public perception of the affair to quietly reach out to Alden Whitman, the reporter who would be covering the upcoming OAH meeting for the *New York Times*, alerting him to the plan to introduce a "resolution censuring Yale" for its handling of the Aptheker matter and including a copy of his earlier letter to Kirkendall. In the end, however, Whitman's decidedly bland accounts of the meeting gave no hint that Woodward's lobbying had any effect.[34]

An examination of the petition calling for an investigation of the Aptheker affair that was introduced at the April 9 OAH business meeting revealed more than the 100 signatures required by the by-laws for it to be submitted to a vote of the entire membership by mail ballot. At that point, a near-ecstatic Lemisch and Gettlemen reported to Aptheker from the meeting that "'the establishment' is freaked out—and we're having a swell time—wish you were here." Meanwhile, when word reached New Haven, Woodward abruptly abandoned his previous air of detachment and immediately took command of efforts to formulate Yale's response. After the OAH's Kirkendall requested that the history department respond to a handbill of allegations drawn up by Lemisch and his associates, Woodward sent his department chairman, John Hall, "a draft of a telegram from you to Richard S. Kirkendall" indicating that "if our critics have charges against us they believe would justify an investigation of Yale for violations of academic freedom, they must place such charges before us before we can reply to them. We are aware of no such violations. To expect us to reply to a handbill that is not a matter of public record, not recorded in the OAH minutes, and that few of the 12,000 members have seen or heard of would be preposterous. We expect resolute support from officers of the OAH for our demand to be confronted with charges we are required to answer." In addition to this strong language, which went out almost verbatim in Hall's letter to Kirkendall the following day, Woodward also advised his colleagues that "we must put pressure on Secretary Kirkendall and [OAH] President [Richard] Leopold. Perhaps John Blum should call the latter and I the former after the telegram is sent."[35]

Kirkendall responded to Hall's letter by suggesting that, instead of the handbill, the Yale historians respond to Lemisch's essay, "If Howard Cosell Can Teach at Yale, Why Can't Herbert Aptheker?" (Though he likely posed it purely for dramatic effect, the answer to Lemisch's question might have been that, like other nonacademics invited to offer a Yale seminar, Cosell stood indisputably at the top of his profession, which could scarcely be said of Aptheker.) Otherwise, although Lemisch's piece was short on substantive evidence of Woodward's alleged misdeeds, he nonetheless accused him of "genteel McCarthyism" and charged the history department with taking "unprecedented steps" to block Aptheker's appointment.[36]

Submitting a response in behalf of the Yale history department, John Hall insisted that the only thing that struck him as truly "unprecedented" about this case was an individual academic department being asked to explain to a professional organization why it had failed to make a particular appointment, especially one such as this that it would never have considered making of its own volition. Following Woodward's lead in questioning the OAH's "right to know what arguments were made in discussion of the appointment," Hall's statement invoked the principle of academic confidentiality, which, though not always upheld in practice, was nonetheless an official policy at Yale. If the final vote did result in an investigation, he promised the history department's cooperation, but not to the point of violating the university's rules regarding confidentiality.[37]

Both Lemisch's essay and Hall's response appeared in the July 1976 OAH *Newsletter*, along with a note from Kirkendall indicating that a favorable vote for conducting an investigation meant that the matter would be referred to the Joint Committee on the Defense of the Rights of Historians under the First Amendment, which had been created some ten years earlier in cooperation with the American Historical Association. OAH members had until the end of September to send in their ballots, and when the official count was announced in early October, it was clear that the general membership was not nearly so caught up in the controversy as those in Aptheker's camp may have hoped. The 1,663 ballots that were marked and returned represented the opinions of less than 20 percent of active members. Of these, while 833 voted to proceed with the investigation, 818 opposed it, and there were 12 abstentions, meaning that the resolution had actually garnered but a 3-vote plurality, representing less than 0.2 percent of all the ballots cast.[38]

Still, the membership having spoken, however faintly, Kirkendall then moved in cooperation with the AHA leadership to convene the joint committee, consisting of the presidents, executive secretaries, and a single historian from each group. In this case, the AHA was represented by President Charles Gibson, who had received his BA and PhD from Yale, its executive secretary, Mack Thompson, and member Paul Conkin. The OAH representatives included its current president, Kenneth M. Stampp, Executive Secretary Kirkendall, and member Paul L. Murphy.

Lemisch, Aptheker, and others pressed the joint committee to visit Yale and personally interview the principals in the dispute there and elsewhere, but the committee's legal advisers counseled against such an unprecedently aggressive, not to mention expensive, approach. In the end, the investigators relied on written questions addressed to Woodward, Hall, Blassingame, Taft, and others at Yale and to Aptheker, who volunteered to share additional pertinent documents in his possession but was not taken up on the offer. Thus, there ensued between December 1976 and October 1977, a massive outpouring and exchange of paper bearing words chosen with excruciating care, some with an eye to clarifying certain issues and details and at least as many others to achieving just the opposite effect. In either case, the torrent of correspondence and reports ultimately yielded surprisingly little of substance not already known about what had transpired at Yale and why.[39]

Woodward worked painstakingly through several drafts of his answers to the questions posed to him, and the result was a truly artful piece of wordsmithing in which his precision frequently served better to safeguard specific information than to convey it. Despite offering a lengthy rehash of his history with the Du Bois Papers project, he demurred at a request to explain how that experience factored into his own opposition to the Aptheker appointment because, as his questioners surely knew better than most, "the causes of things . . . are often complex," and, in case they had not noticed, "human memory is fallible." He was more tight-lipped still about details of the events leading up to the denial of Aptheker's appointment. He had spoken out after his meeting with the Davenport seminar committee only to correct what he described as a "garbled" account of his comments that had somehow been leaked to the press. On the other hand, he knew of no leaks from the junior appointments committee and joint boards meetings that were in need of correction, and in keeping with Yale's confidentiality policy, he would provide no further comment.[40]

Here, in essence was the core strategy for all the Yale respondents. Knowing that some information about proceedings in the Aptheker case had already been leaked in direct violation of university policy made it all the more imperative that Yale's representatives strictly adhere to that policy going forward, by withholding further details about what was said when and by whom during the debate on Aptheker's appointment. In this, Woodward insisted, Yale's stated policies differed little from those at "Michigan, Wisconsin, Berkeley, and Indiana," whose faculty included, respectively, joint committee members Gibson, Conkin, Stampp, and Kirkendall.[41]

By holding fast to this position, Woodward and his colleagues effectively hamstrung the investigation. Critics charged that the committee should have adopted a more aggressively adversarial posture by demanding to interview the parties involved in person and even contacting students and faculty not directly targeted by the investigation. Yet such an approach might have been fraught with not only professional but legal implications. In point of fact, the joint committee's official title and charge limited it to the "Defense of the Rights of Historians under the First Amendment." Yale was a private institution, after all, and its legal counsel, José Cabranes, allowed that he could not see how the First Amendment's "protections against actions by the state . . . are brought into play in this context." Even the presidents of both the organizations involved had conceded that the issues involved might not "relate to First Amendment rights." Absent such a connection, the committee had arguably exceeded the limits of its foundational charge simply by launching its investigation, making its authority in this case all the more suspect and, as the AHA's official summary of the investigation noted, leaving its members with no "means of prying secret information from Yale."[42]

Had it been feasible, a more aggressive approach might have turned up more information, but at the price of lending further plausibility to Woodward's ominous specter of professional organizations running amok on university campuses, second-guessing decisions on faculty appointments and challenging established policies and procedures. Hammering away at this point, he allowed that the committee had no business asking him to explain his own vote on an appointment because "in my judgment, the AHA and the

I Do Not See How I Could Have Been Misunderstood

OAH have no right to make such inquiries of their members and will do great harm to the profession by suggesting the existence of such a right." Giving the distinct impression that he was switching from defense to offense, he allowed that the committee's report on this case stood to be "of great importance," if it managed simply to "reassert the right of confidentiality in appointment procedures and . . . discountenance resort to massive organized pressure to force appointments." By way of underscoring his message, he shared with each recipient of his responses a copy of a piece he had published in *Daedalus* bemoaning "the erosion of academic privileges and immunities."[43]

In any case, so long as Yale's representatives invoked its rules of confidentiality, there was little hope of proving that Aptheker's opponents acted out of ideological bias. Nor had any of the evidence uncovered suggested any departures from Yale's standard procedures or that these procedures infringed on Aptheker's academic freedom. Hence, the six historians on the joint committee felt that they could only conclude: "The evidence available to us suggests that the Yale History Department simply decided that a candidate for a position did not meet its standards." The committee did acknowledge in its report, however, that the procedural issues in the case "skirt a most critical charge against the Yale History Department," because proof that ideological or political bias had not factored into the opposition to Aptheker's appointment might still lie "either in unconfessed motives or voiced considerations hidden in confidential records."[44]

On November 8, 1977, one month shy of two years after Yale's joint board of permanent officers initially rejected the Aptheker appointment, the *Yale Daily News* offered a front-page story announcing that the official investigation into the affair was complete. There was no indication of the specifics of the committee's findings, but former history department chair John Hall offered assurances that, even if the report officially censured his department, its "high national standing" would not be diminished. The story also quoted OAH president Kenneth Stampp as saying that the report itself would not be released until "the OAH and AHA have gone through the formality of having the decision approved by their board members."[45]

Where his own organization was concerned, at least, Stampp's presumption that the remainder of the process would be purely procedural proved to be well off the mark. The AHA's executive council did, in fact, quietly sign off on the full report at the end of December, but the OAH executive board would not even take up the matter again until the following April, and when it did, what transpired was anything but a formality. Executive board members Stanley Katz and Robert Wiebe were willing to go along with a resolution to accept the report's conclusions, so long as it stipulated that they were reached purely "on the basis of the evidence available," but they also wanted the board's statement to reflect their sense that "special but unstated criteria" had been used to block Aptheker's appointment and damage his reputation in the process.[46]

Brushing aside these concerns, Kenneth Stampp offered a tersely worded resolution simply affirming the board's acceptance of the joint committee's conclusion that "on the basis of the available evidence, neither Yale University's Department of History, nor individual members of the department violated Herbert Aptheker's academic freedom or his rights under the First Amendment." Katz later indicated in an interview that he and Wiebe had been pressured outside the meeting by Stampp and Frank Freidel (Katz's dissertation adviser) to accept the report as it was, essentially on the basis of Woodward's stellar record as a proponent of liberal causes. Stampp himself recalled saying, "This is an attempt to censure C. Vann Woodward, [who] has been a staunch supporter of academic freedom and civil rights, and he had reasons why he did this. You all don't know what his motives are. You are, in effect, going to say that this man is an enemy of academic freedom." Katz observed that although Stampp and Freidel conceded privately "that Vann might have erred," their primary concern seemed to be protecting someone "they loved and admired." Stampp was, of course, a friend of Woodward's as well as one of his coauthors on the U.S. history textbook *The National Experience*, and he had asked Woodward to provide a reference letter for a fellowship application just as the investigation was gearing up. Freidel was also a friend and had confided to Woodward before the original petition for an investigation was taken up at the 1976 OAH business meeting that he hoped enough "non-radical historians" would show up "so that a motion of censure will not pass there." Despite the lobbying by their respective mentors, Katz and Wiebe "politely demurred," as Katz put it, explaining that "we believed Vann had behaved badly, and that it was important for the OAH to stand up for the rights of scholars and teachers, and not to give in to elite institutions and academic elites when they behaved inappropriately."[47]

Katz and Wiebe were not alone in expressing reservations about the report and the procedure that generated it, but after lengthy debate the executive board voted eleven to four to accept the joint committee's findings as "reasonable," though solely with respect to the information it had managed to accumulate. Two days later, when the executive board's resolution came up for a vote up at the OAH business meeting, Stampp, who had by then relinquished the presidential gavel to his successor, Eugene Genovese,

I Do Not See How I Could Have Been Misunderstood

moved to circumvent yet another a protracted discussion by offering a substitute motion simply declaring that those at the business meeting accepted the executive board's action on the joint committee report. Opponents saw this as nothing but a straight power play, and the ubiquitous Marvin Gettleman immediately offered an amendment to Stampp's resolution, aimed at strengthening the committee's authority to intervene in cases such as this but offering no particulars as to how this might be done. In the end, Gettleman's proposal came to naught after newly installed President Genovese reported that the executive board had already agreed to "review the procedures and composition" of the committee going forward. By the time the final tally was taken, the once sizable crowd at the meeting had dwindled to 100, and the Stampp resolution to accept the committee's report was approved by a vote of 59 to 41. With but two exceptions, Gettleman reported, "every male over 50 voted against us. We had the women and youth, but ... not enough of them stayed to 6:15 when the votes were taken."[48]

Disappointing as this loss of resolve may have been, there remained at least a flicker of hope for Aptheker and his supporters because, in accordance with procedural guidelines, the official end to this excruciatingly drawn-out process awaited the outcome of yet another balloting of the membership by mail, which would not be known until October. In the meantime, Aptheker protested—as usual, to no avail whatsoever—that by acquiescing to terms virtually guaranteeing that little or no new information damaging to Yale would come to light, the committee had effectively ensured that it would have no basis for any finding other than an academic department had simply decided "that a candidate for a position did not meet its standards." In doing this, Aptheker charged, the committee gave the appearance of exonerating Woodward and his colleagues outright. He underscored his point by citing a *New York Times* piece captioned, "Panel of Historians Backs Yale Denial of Job to Aptheker" (January 15, 1978), and the *Yale Daily News*'s announcement that "OAH Clears Yale Historians in Aptheker Seminar Dispute" (January 17, 1978). Despite the valid questions he raised about the ethics and professionalism of Woodward and his colleagues, Aptheker's statement was at heart a deeply personal plea for respect and what he saw as justice. "Confidentiality" might well be "precious," but for him, so was "the good name of a scholar. . . . Even if he or she is a Communist."[49]

There was little doubt in Aptheker's mind that he had been done in by the historical establishment once again, but however legitimate his call for redress may have been, too many people who had once been agitated by his plight had long since grown fatigued of hearing about it, thanks, in some measure at least, to the glacial pace of the OAH's extraordinarily cumbersome bureaucratic process. The original balloting on whether to conduct an investigation in the first place hardly suggested widespread interest even at that point, but by the time the vote on whether to accept the joint committee report finally came around, the indifference was almost staggering. When the ballots were finally counted, the resolution had been approved by a tally of 272–220, which reflected a response rate of less than 6 percent of the 8,281 ballots mailed out.[50]

If Woodward considered this underwhelming outcome a victory in any sense, it was surely a Pyrrhic one at best. Not only, as Arthur Schlesinger Jr. noted prophetically, had he managed to assure Herbert Aptheker's "tenure forever in the pantheon of the Left," but even though the protracted controversy eventually overtaxed the attention span of most OAH members, it had left a lingering suspicion of duplicity hovering over Yale's history department. Finally, Woodward had clearly done himself no favors by triggering a heated dispute over a matter of so little apparent consequence, where the biggest thing actually at stake seemed to be his ego. He had done little to discourage this impression with his less than forthcoming, sometimes overtly condescending and cavalier responses to questions about his actions, along with his occasional failures to conceal his displeasure at having them questioned at all.[51]

University of Massachusetts Press director Leone Stein and Du Bois Papers project collaborator John Bracey wrote to NEH in July 1976 to protest yet another rejection of an Aptheker grant proposal after what they correctly presumed was another thumbs-down from Woodward. It was "generally agreed," they claimed, that Woodward's unrelenting attacks on Aptheker had "exceeded all the bounds of propriety, academic honesty, and human decency." "Generally agreed" may have been a stretch, but Bracey and Stein were clearly not alone in questioning Woodward's behavior or the motives behind it. His longtime friend Eugene Genovese, who would turn against him with striking ferocity a few years after the Aptheker affair, told an interviewer in 2001 that after assuring him otherwise at the outset of the controversy, Woodward later told him without hesitation that "of course his opposition [to the appointment] was political." If Genovese's claim was indeed factual, it amounted less to a revelation than an affirmation of what there was already reason to suspect.[52]

Taken aback by the unaccustomed criticism he had drawn, both within his profession at large and on his own campus, Woodward admitted privately to Boston University historian Aileen Kraditor in December 1976 that he

I Do Not See How I Could Have Been Misunderstood

had let "the petition against me [which, in this case, was actually directed against the History Department for refusing to sponsor the seminar] signed by 2,200 Yale undergraduates get under my skin more than I pretended to myself. Not to mention those 833 OAH members [who had initially voted in favor of the joint investigation]." As he later recalled, he not only had to face the disapproval of his own left-leaning faculty colleagues, who had arrived "in waves in the 1960s," but his "correspondence was drenched with outraged criticism," and some of his former students were "outraged" as well. Although he failed to mention it, some of those still under his tutelage at the time had also raised questions about his actions. John Blassingame, John Blum, and Edmund Morgan had backed his play against Aptheker, perhaps in part out of personal loyalty, but again, nine of his junior colleagues in history had come forward publicly to sign a petition protesting Woodward's and Blassingame's actions at the joint board of permanent officers meeting in 1975.[53]

Rather than subsiding quickly after Aptheker had finally offered his seminar in the fall semester of 1976, the dispute took on an even more vituperative and unseemly cast. With the spring term scarcely under way in January 1977, a series of heated, sometimes bitter exchanges over Aptheker's effectiveness in the classroom raged cross the pages of the campus paper. Fourteen of the fifteen students in his seminar came together to rebut disparaging comments about Aptheker's teaching, and a former member of the Committee to Support the Aptheker Seminar saw the "wounded pride" of Woodward and his colleagues fueling what he saw as an "ex-post facto smear campaign" against Aptheker.[54]

Charges of a "smear campaign" resurfaced several months later, when on November 8, 1977, the front page of the Yale Daily News offered what proved to be an inaccurate report on the settlement of a lawsuit allegedly charging Aptheker with "plagiarism" and "fraud" in which he had chosen not to contest the allegations. The suit had been filed by freelance bibliographer Paul Partington, who charged that his work or something closely approximating it was included in Aptheker's published bibliography on Du Bois without his permission. Woodward had been in contact with Partington for well over a year at that point and was fully aware of the suit. The story quoted Partington extensively but offered not a word from Aptheker or his publisher and indicated that word of the settlement "came to light" only when Partington placed certain materials in Yale's Beinecke Library. In fact, however, Partington had contacted the paper directly about the settlement at the urging of Woodward, who explained that he preferred "not to take any initiative myself" but suggested that "you might do so yourself without mentioning me." A few days after the story ran, Woodward sent Partington a copy, congratulating him on getting his story out there but allowing that he felt it "deserved a wider audience," perhaps meaning wide enough to include members of the joint committee, which had not concluded its deliberations at point. Several months later, Woodward would contact Kenneth Stampp about whether they were aware of the suit before reaching their decision, only to learn that they were not.[55]

Word of the story brought an outraged demand for an immediate retraction from Aptheker, whose publisher explained that the suit centered not on plagiarism but on common law copyright infringement and that the settlement entailed no admission of "culpability" on Aptheker's part. From the publisher's perspective, with the judge pressuring for an expedited resolution, the $1,000 required to settle the suit with Partington, who made his living as a grocery clerk, seemed too modest an outlay to justify the expense of mounting a full-blown defense. Despite the protests from the Aptheker camp, however, it was not until January 19, 1978, more than two months after the initial story appeared, that the Yale Daily News issued a near-microscopic "correction" in a small block at the bottom of page 2, advising that it had erred in reporting that Aptheker had been "sued on the grounds of 'plagiarism' and 'fraud.'" This should not have surprised Woodward because, shortly after he filed the suit in April 1976, Partington had sent him a copy of his legal complaint clearly alleging a common law copyright violation rather than plagiarism. Even so, shortly after the campus paper published its mini-correction, history department chair Henry Turner was quoted in the Yale Alumni Magazine as saying that the favorable findings of "six distinguished historians" on the joint committee, "along with the outcome of a recent plagiarism suit against Aptheker," should put an end to insinuations that efforts by Woodward and his colleagues to block the seminar had been politically motivated. Aptheker's publisher contacted Turner to provide clarification, but in this case, as in so many others, correcting erroneous information after the fact hardly dispelled the false impression that information conveyed.[56]

There is no indication that anyone else at Yale knew of Woodward's role in generating what proved to be an inaccurate and perhaps even defamatory account of the lawsuit. Yet based on what was known about his actions throughout the affair, it is hard to imagine finding more than a very few on campus—faculty, students, or otherwise—who would have argued that the way he had conducted himself had left either his department or the university any better for it.

This is not to say that he no longer enjoyed genuinely high regard among his colleagues. Even so, however, with his formal retirement scarcely two months away, he surely found little affirmation in an April 1977 *Yale Daily News* report suggesting that, while his fellow historians certainly saw his departure as a "most conspicuous" loss, some of them felt no great sense of urgency about naming his successor. There were several members of the faculty whose fields overlapped with Woodward's, after all, including David Brion Davis, who, at that juncture, also appeared to have supplanted him as the department's most sought after dissertation adviser. A more immediate concern for the history department was the retirement of the versatile Robert Palmer, who was well versed and widely published, not only in French history, but in European and world history as well. As one historian put it, "The department must replace Palmer," and as quickly as possible.[57]

Woodward would retain his office in Yale's Hall of Graduate Studies and continue to be a significant presence at Yale for nearly twenty-five years. Yet his actions in the Aptheker controversy had left the campus rife with discord in June 1977. It was probably just as well that, having reached Yale's mandatory retirement age of sixty-eight, he ceased to be an official member of the faculty at that point, more than a year before the final curtain finally came down on the whole sad, embarrassing, and exhaustingly prolonged affair.

16

The Masterpiece That Became a Hoax (and Won a Pulitzer)

Rewriting Mary Chesnut's Diary

Although the circumstances surrounding Woodward's official retirement from Yale were, to say the least, not entirely to his liking, the extra time it afforded did allow him to devote more attention to a project he had taken up with great enthusiasm several years earlier. He had long been intrigued by antebellum diarist Mary Boykin Chesnut, whose incisive, often penetrating social commentary he felt had been given short shrift in previously published editions of her journal. The daughter of South Carolina congressman and senator Stephen Decatur Miller, Mary had married James Chesnut, a scion of one of the state's largest landowning families, who was a United States senator before South Carolina seceded and went on to serve the Confederacy as a brigadier general and a personal aide to President Jefferson Davis. In early 1861, she began a diary destined to become the most celebrated personal account of life among the Confederate elite during the Civil War.[1]

Woodward would later note in his edition of the Chesnut diary that, as the wife of a Confederate officer and bureaucrat, Mary managed consistently to "stumble in on the real show" regardless of which direction the tides of southern fortune might be taking. Possessed of a brilliant and stinging wit, she could be an audacious flirt, exulting in her "power to make myself loved" wherever she went and clearly reveling in high-society partying to the point that her husband rebuked her for showing "too much levity" in such a time of crisis. In Woodward's view, however, Chesnut's private scribblings revealed her true persona as a strikingly detached and critical observer who "repeatedly declared her hatred for slavery . . . called herself an abolitionist . . . and rejoiced at the collapse of slavery at the end of the war." She was also guilty of the "heresy of militant feminism and defense of oppressed womanhood," and he claimed that her hostility to the Old South's dominant patriarchal order was, "if anything, more vehement" than her dislike of slavery.[2]

Chesnut would achieve posthumous renown only after the first publication in 1905 of her diary as it was purportedly written during the Civil War, though it had actually been drawn from several drafts of the original journal as revised and expanded by Chesnut in 1870s and 1880s, in hopes of getting it published herself. She had already toned down her earlier criticism of slavery and southern society in her revised drafts, but as edited by Isabella D. Martin and Myrta L. Avary, the first print version was all but purged of such naysaying altogether, so as to better serve the purposes of the ascendant Lost Cause propagandists of the era. The second published version appeared in 1949. The editor this time was novelist and short-fiction writer Ben Ames Williams, whose fascination with Chesnut's vibrant personality and determination to enhance the diary's literary appeal led him to make numerous undisclosed emendations, additions, and deletions to the manuscript.[3]

Unaware that Chesnut's published diary was anything other than the original version, literary critic Edmund Wilson hailed it in 1961 as not just an "extraordinary document" but a "work of art" and a "masterpiece" of its genre. And there the general perception of the diary stood in the mid-1970s, when few were aware that what had been published so far differed markedly in many respects from the original 1860s journal. In reality, the massive Chesnut collection at the University of South Carolina's Caroliniana Library amounted to some 40,000 pages, consisting not only of the initial diary but of the several postbellum efforts to revise it in the 1870s and 1880s, along with some unpublished novels and other later writings, none of which had been thoroughly examined by a historian qualified to organize, edit, and contextualize it.[4]

With an eye to remedying this, James Meriwether, a prominent literary scholar at South Carolina, let Woodward know in October 1974 that both he and the Chesnut family were "very much in hopes that you will undertake the responsibility for a new edition of the main diary." Woodward had long been interested in the diary, and when he expressed interest in the project,

Meriwether was quick to make the prospect more enticing, promising that South Carolina's Institute for Southern Studies would be "pleased and proud to offer you all possible assistance" if he came to campus to work on the project in the spring term of 1975, when he would be on leave from Yale. As a senior research fellow at the institute, Woodward would have an office convenient to the building where the Chesnut Collection was housed, in addition to at least one and maybe two grad assistants, who could work ten to twenty hours a week, "depending on your needs." On top of this came free photocopying and clerical support and a stipend of $5,000 for the semester, with "no formal teaching duties involved."[5]

Woodward would benefit enormously from this arrangement, especially from the prodigious contributions of Elisabeth Muhlenfeld, one of Meriwether's PhD students, who not only supervised a squad of student workers soon to be known as "Chesnut-pullers" but devoted a tremendous amount of her time and energy to numerous challenging and tedious tasks. In addition to responding to Woodward's frequent requests for specific information and dates, Muhlenfeld took an active role in transcribing the handwritten content of the original diary into text at the grinding pace of two to three pages an hour, sometimes sitting in a darkroom with an infrared light, trying to reconstruct Chesnut's erasures.[6]

For all the effort put forth by Muhlenfeld and her team at South Carolina, by November 1975 she and Meriwether estimated that an additional 1,500 to 1,700 hours of work would be needed to meet Woodward's rather ambitious expectations for the project, which included at one point not only annotations for all the references to people, place, and events spread across hundreds of pages of text but Chesnut's family tree and "a table of *dramatis personae* with biographical paragraphs for the main characters." Meriwether explained that "even if all of the present crew continued to put all their available time on this project, it would take years to give you this much help."[7]

Woodward responded that he had "no right to expect such a heavy investment of your limited funds" and thought it best to complete the rest of the "annotation and collation" in New Haven. He would continue, however, to receive substantial assistance from Elisabeth Muhlenfeld, who, conveniently enough, abandoned William Faulkner as her dissertation topic in favor of compiling and editing the "non–Civil War" materials from Chesnut's journals, as well as an unpublished Chesnut novel. Since this was such a "straightforward piece of editing," Meriwether saw no reason why Muhlenfeld and "our other Chesnut enthusiasts here should not be able to provide you with what you want—within reason, between now [January 1977] and the end of next summer." If the project continued beyond that point, Meriwether promised that his staff would assist "in any way that we can."[8]

In reality, the more limited scope of the support he would receive from South Carolina going forward proved less of a problem than anticipated because of a grant from the National Historical Publications and Records Commission. Yale also chipped in with significant funding and put a stellar group of graduate assistants at his disposal. Several of these went on to gain distinction in their own careers, including Steven Hahn, Sean Wilentz, and Michael McGerr, whom Woodward singled out for his bravura performance, not only in annotating and checking the manuscript for errors and inconsistencies, but in undertaking the truly daunting task of indexing the completed volume.[9]

Despite Meriwether's and Muhlenfeld's extremely generous, even solicitous, attitude toward Woodward, both objected strongly to his plan to essentially "conflate" the material from Chesnut's original journal of the Civil War years with a version she had reworked in the 1880s. Apparently Chesnut had revisited the manuscript looking to polish its literary style, moderate some of her antislavery rhetoric, and excise certain awkward or potentially embarrassing details that might show her as vain, conceited, or unkind or otherwise cast her in a negative light. Yet Woodward's idea was to use the significantly altered 1880s version as the "basic copy text" while supplementing it with other material, primarily from the original 1860s journal. Instead of placing selected passages from the 1860s in an appendix or in the notes, he planned to insert them directly into the later, expanded text as closely as possible to the point where this material had been cut or dramatically revised from the original. The other material would go in where it was "most relevant."[10]

For her part, Muhlenfeld thought it was too "impressionistic" to simply insert other passages in place of what Chesnut had intended to be in the revised text. Instead, she felt the material from the original wartime journal and elsewhere belonged "in footnotes and parallel columns." Meriwether, meanwhile, argued that because it was clear that there were at least two distinct journals, "each with its own separate identity," they should be published independently, "alone or as part of a set." As it was, Woodward's plan to meld the two into "an eclectic text" struck him as violating "the most basic rule of modern scholarly editing for the entire field."[11]

Woodward was respectful but unmoved by their concerns with the "sacredness of Mary's intentions," particularly if those intentions were "to conceal truth, to misrepresent facts, to cover up, or to lead the reader to believe that she knew or believed things in 1861 when she was writing twenty years later." His own intention, he insisted, was to emphasize rather than minimize the differences between the original and subsequent versions and, in doing so, enhance "the attractiveness of the enterprise to which I invite the reader." In reality, though, he would give reason to suspect that he saw the appeal of the reworked diary depending in greatest measure on the appeal of its author as she came through in the text and notes.[12]

The book eventually went to press in the format Woodward envisioned, only to come under scathing attack in its first major review. Known for deliberately provocative and what struck some as gratuitous ad hominem attacks on fellow historians, Kenneth S. Lynn proved true to his reputation in his assessment of *Mary Chesnut's Civil War*, which appeared in the *New York Times Book Review*. For Lynn, the mere revelation that previously published editions of Chesnut diary were not necessarily based on her actual firsthand reactions to events and experiences during the Civil War itself was more than sufficient cause for working himself into a lather. Rather than celebrated as the author of a literary "masterpiece," he charged, Mary Chesnut should be condemned as the perpetrator of "one of the most audacious frauds in the history of American literature." Though he credited Woodward with exposing the "hoax," he also castigated him for declining "to bestow that label on it." In this, Lynn accused him of adhering to a pattern common to his own and other "distinguished, but rather too anxiously liberal" works, in which "faults of forward-looking citizens are always explained away if they are not simply ignored."[13]

Lynn's accusation was manifestly inaccurate and not a little unfair to Woodward, whether it referred to the corpus of his writing or to the edited volume at hand. In the latter case, he had further exposed Chesnut's racism, snobbery, vanity, and mean-spiritedness at several junctures and juxtaposed at least some of her harsher and less becoming comments from the 1860s with the tamped-down language she had employed in rewriting these passages in the 1880s. Even so, Lynn charged that by excising or scaling back her original attacks on slavery and the southern slavocracy in her revised manuscript from the 1880s, Chesnut had thrown in with Old South romanticizers of that era like Thomas Nelson Page, known for his sappy accounts of benevolent masters and their "adoring" servants. Although Chesnut's references to fears of a postbellum uprising by armed freedmen were changed but little from the original version of the diary, Lynn also likened the revised version to Thomas Dixon's *The Clansman* (1905), with its nightmarish vision of savage blacks "running amok," which was intended to rationalize whatever efforts whites undertook to suppress them. To Lynn, the modifications reflected in her later "simulated diary" showed that Chesnut had embraced "the aims of this disgraceful literary movement."[14]

William Styron offered a much more positive assessment of *Mary Chesnut's Civil War* in the *New York Review of Books*, noting "the extraordinary panorama it presents of a culture being rent asunder." Sensing a rebuke in Styron's praise for the book, Lynn doubled down on his position in a letter to the editor of the *NYRB*, again indicting Chesnut for "fabricating a fake diary of her life during the Civil War" and chiding her most recent editor for his "factually careful but analytically underpowered introduction."[15]

Woodward had known in advance of Lynn's onslaught, reporting to his friend Louis D. Rubin, "Kenneth Lynn is doing it for the *Times* and is attacking me for not using the surviving fragment of the original as copy text. Bastard!" Yet mindful of Henry Nash Smith's appraisal of Lynn as "a psychiatric case and capable of anything," Woodward opted not to respond immediately. He also knew that his friends William R. Taylor and Steven M. Stowe were taking Lynn to task in forthcoming letters to the *New York Times Book Review*, whose editor, he noted, had taken Lynn's side by putting "hoax" in the title of the review and in using an accompanying illustration showing a cut-out depiction of a southern belle holding a book and standing by a damaged architectural column wrapped in the Confederate flag.[16]

Writing jointly, Taylor and Stowe, who were familiar with the content of Chesnut's original journal as well as the later edited and expanded version, corroborated Woodward's contention that the second diary "remained strikingly faithful to her initial perception of war, social class, slavery and, perhaps above all her mixed feelings of anticipation and doom." Since Chesnut herself made no apparent effort to conceal her revision of the original journal, Taylor and Stowe maintained that she "did not even defraud herself, much less us." (As Woodward and several others pointed out, if any fraud was perpetrated, it was by the previous editors of the diary, who removed and inserted text at will without bothering to inform readers.) Taylor and Stowe also believed that "Professor Lynn hardly could be more off the mark" in positing "a literary kinship between Chesnut and the apologias of Thomas Nelson Page and—even more inappropriately—the vicious fantasies of Thomas Dixon." Even if Chesnut had deliberately muted some of her earlier criticism of slavery, the second version of the diary still revealed too many deeply felt, complex, and often contradictory personal feelings about it to be remotely comparable to "the slick fantasies of Page and Dixon."[17]

Taylor and Stowe had rightly challenged Lynn's overcooked indictment of *Mary Chesnut's Civil War*, but while reviewer Michael P. Johnson's reaction was much more measured than Lynn's, he did not conceal his own disappointment with Woodward's decision to publish the revised version of Chesnut's diary without including the original journal in its entirety. Woodward himself had conceded that historians were naturally most interested in Chesnut's "original and immediate reaction, . . . uninfluenced by hindsight . . . and unclouded by fading memory," and he knew that they would have preferred that he use the earlier writings as his basic text, supplemented by passages from the 1880s. He had ultimately decided against putting this admittedly "more candid, personal, spicy, and fresh" material in the foreground, he explained, because he was so thoroughly impressed with Chesnut's "unusual sense of responsibility toward the history she records and a reassuring faithfulness to perceptions of her experience of the period as revealed in her original Journal."[18]

The problem with Woodward's decision, which Johnson demonstrated without quite saying as much, was that by failing to include a full transcription of the original material, he was, in many instances, asking his readers, especially the historically minded ones, simply to take his word for Chesnut's "'reassuring faithfulness' to twenty-year-old perceptions." By Johnson's estimate, the dates covered by Chesnut's entries in her original wartime diary—February through December 1861, and January through February and May through July 1865—accounted for only 40 percent of the pages in *Mary Chesnut's Civil War*. After comparing those pages with the original manuscripts, Johnson clearly did not share Woodward's confidence in Chesnut's fidelity in the 1880s to what she had written more than two decades earlier.[19]

He noted Chesnut's acknowledgment in an unpublished entry from 1861 that, even as a "South Carolina slaveholder" herself, upon seeing a fancily dressed young mulatto woman on the auction block coyly eyeing the bidder, "my very soul sickened—it is too dreadful." She had tried to tell herself at this point that what she saw was no more appalling "than the willing sale most women make of themselves in marriage. . . . Poor women!—poor slaves! Still slavery thou art a bitter draught—disguise it as we will." She would recount a notably more moderate reaction to what she had witnessed that day, however, in the 1880s diary, where she wrote that she had quickly "disciplined" her "wild thoughts" about slavery and what she had seen at the slave auction, which now struck her as little different from "how women sell themselves and are sold in marriage, from queens downward."[20]

Woodward had also failed to restore an 1861 entry that Chesnut deleted from the 1880s draft recounting her horror upon learning of "a Sumter man

The Masterpiece That Became a Hoax

advertising a slave so *white* as to be mistaken for a citizen but on lifting his hat the *brand might* be seen." Regardless of how "sinful" she might be, she could not put herself in the category of "such brutes [who] give me agony—for my country."[21]

Finally, with only the older version of the diary to go on, readers might not discern that, just as Chesnut's position on slavery had softened by the 1880s, her view of blacks had correspondingly hardened. Where, for example, she had originally cast her father-in-law's plantation as a place where "the black man must be kept as dark and unenlightened as his skin," in later versions the black man was now innately "a creature whose mind is as dark and unenlightened as his skin."[22]

For Johnson, these and a number of other discrepancies with the first diary meant that historians looking to Woodward's version of the diary for usable primary source material from the 1860s could safely rely only on content he had identified as coming from the original journal. Otherwise, the only means of assuring that they were seeing Chesnut's initial, unadulterated text was to read that text or whatever transcriptions of it might be housed at Yale or the University of South Carolina's Caroliniana collection or request microfilm copies of the various versions through interlibrary loan. The challenge this posed for scholars looking to identify and authenticate sources was more formidable, but not wholly unlike the consequences of Woodward's decision not to footnote the sources he quoted in *The Strange Career of Jim Crow*. More historians would finally be able to cross-check the published 1880s version of the diary with the original journal after Woodward's and Muhlenfeld's coedited version of the original was published in 1984 as *The Private Mary Chesnut*. Even so, they would clearly have been better served by a single publication offering both versions. As it was, Johnson thought, scholars could only regard the "basic text" of *Mary Chesnut's Civil War* as an "autobiographical memoir about the war years that is sadly but indelibly marked by the author's postwar experiences and perceptions." Johnson's concern was also central to reviews in both the *American Historical Review* and the *Journal of American History*, the former by Carl Degler, which Woodward deemed "hostile," and the other by Catherine Clinton, which he dismissed as "silly."[23]

Reviewer Drew Gilpin Faust was less concerned with discrepancies with the original diary than with her sense that the person who came through in Woodward's edition "is not quite the same woman his introductory remarks describe." Woodward had laid it on a bit thick, she thought, in his opening references to Chesnut's "abolitionist leanings" and "militant feminism," when, throughout the text, Faust saw her struggling "in her own way to preserve the existing southern social order," rather than overturn it. Despite Chesnut's heated critiques of the southern patriarchy, nothing pleased her more than the "attentions of men." Some southern women of her class seemed to seize on the chance to escape the pedestal and play a bigger part in day-to-day affairs during the war, but Chesnut not only passed on the opportunity but actively scorned those who took it. Finally, for all of Chesnut's private harangues against slavery, Faust observed that, "like Thomas Jefferson, she continued to benefit from the system while enjoying the luxury of abhorring it," foregoing none of the privilege of the high society and glittering social interaction made possible only by the coerced labor of enslaved blacks.[24]

Though Woodward was deeply interested in both Chesnut herself and her diary, his work up to that point had devoted little attention to women, who were, as Glenda Gilmore observed, "scarcer than hen's teeth" in *Origins of the New South*, where they accounted for only 16 of 540 index entries. (The same was truer still of *Strange Career*, which, even in its 1974 edition, offered only Mahalia Jackson and Autherine Lucy.) Gilmore suggests that the social thrust of these and other earlier examples of Woodward's writings before and during the Civil Rights movement seemed to reflect a more urgent, overriding concern with overturning the massively evil Jim Crow system once and for all.[25]

In any case, the absence of what Gilmore calls "an explicitly gendered analysis" hardly set *Origins* or *Strange Career* apart from other books of their type published by male historians in the 1950s. The same might be said of Woodward's personal attitudes about women and his behavior toward them in general. His default approach to engaging women in social settings was largely that of a courtly gentleman out to win their favor with his wit and charm rather than draw them into a debate. When polled in 1963 on the matter of admitting women as fellows of Ezra Stiles College at Yale, Woodward replied, "You must list me among the embarrassed *cons*. I say embarrassed because the con position appears so stuffy, so unprogressive. Also it does less than justice to my genuine feelings about the opposite sex whose company I assure you I cherish." Yet New Haven's social life afforded so much opportunity for being in the company of women that "one evening a fortnight [when dinner meetings of the fellows were held] I would gladly absent myself from felicity and put up with monastic company." That said, he allowed that if his "pro-woman" colleagues among the Stiles fellows should carry the day, he would be right in there competing with them for "as much of the new fellow's attention as I can get." (It is worth noting that it would be another year before a woman was granted tenure on the arts and sciences faculty at Yale and six more years before the first female undergraduates were admitted.)[26]

Although Woodward typically showed greater personal interest in outspoken, intellectually challenging women, he clearly considered such women exceptional. Certainly, he felt he had found just such a woman in Mary Chesnut, who stood out to him as the "preeminent writer of the Confederacy." Rather than explore the implications of her diary for the general historiography of southern womanhood in that era, he was more intrigued by it as a testament to her exceptionality as an individual woman "blessed with an unusually rigorous mind . . . trained from birth to be politically astute and socially secure," who was "also intellectually open and aware of the vicissitudes of history." Southern women's history had yet to produce an extensive body of writing in 1981, to be sure, but retrospectively at least, it is hard to overlook the absence in his and Muhlenfeld's editions of the diary of any reference to Anne Firor Scott's pathbreaking study *The Southern Lady*, published more than a decade earlier and manifestly relevant to any appraisal of Mary Chesnut's experience. In fact, Scott, who knew Woodward for over fifty years, recalled waiting in vain for him to say "something, anything" about her book. For that matter, she added, nothing in his writings going forward indicated that he had read any of the contributions to "the flood of southern women's history" that began after her book appeared in 1970.[27]

Glenda Gilmore recounted an incident from an academic conference in the 1990s in which, after listening to a relentless succession of papers and comments, Woodward turned to his Yale colleague Peter Gay, and "in the stage whisper of those who wear hearing aids," asked, "Peter, What is gender?" Still, in the preface of a collection of essays dealing with the interaction of race, politics, and gender written shortly before his death, he praised the contributors for calling attention to the "leadership provided by a race, a gender, or a class [long treated by historians] not as participants but as helpless spectators or victims." Although he may have gained a greater appreciation of the work being done in southern women's history by the end of his life and career, he seemed more than content to keep his distance from the rapidly expanding historiography of that field. Contacted in 1996 by the editor of the *Yale Review* about writing a review essay of two new books dealing with southern women during the Civil War with an eye to surveying "new attitudes—say, by feminist historians—of the role of women during the war," his answer, scrawled at the bottom of the note was "a cowardly 'No.'"[28]

In any case, Woodward's decision to steer clear of any engagement with southern women's historiography in *Mary Chesnut's Civil War* is far more likely to raise eyebrows today than it was forty years ago, when no major reviewer, including Anne Scott, took particular note of it. In the end, the principal concerns about *Mary Chesnut's Civil War* raised in reviews in the principal historical journals came back to Woodward's decision to include material from the original journal only in selective snippets. On the one hand, he had made a wide audience aware for the first time that the contents of the previously published and lavishly praised edition of Chesnut's Civil War diary were not the unadulterated contemporary accounts they were long taken to be. Yet in failing to include the entire text of her original 1860s journals with her revised recollections of the 1880s, he had left readers, scholarly readers especially, still in want of a viable primary account of Chesnut's wartime musings. In the bargain, Woodward came to fear that, having set out to enhance Chesnut's reputation as both a literary and a historical figure, he may have succeeded in doing just the opposite. Although both James Meriwether and Elisabeth Muhlenfeld had counseled sternly against the way he arranged and selected the material in the book, he did not hesitate to ask for their assistance in finding a literary precedent for what Chesnut had done with her diary. The more justifiable her actions seemed, of course, the more legitimate his approach to editing the diary would seem as well, but Woodward seemed entirely sincere in insisting that his principal concern was protecting Chesnut's reputation, rather than his own. He noted to Meriwether that no less an authority than his distinguished fellow southern historian David Donald had observed that "Woodward had destroyed the credibility of Chesnut." If this thinking persisted, Woodward observed, it would not be his scholarship but "Chesnut's integrity or that of her book that is at stake." Alluding to Mark Twain's *Life on the Mississippi* or James Boswell's *Life of Samuel Johnson*, he beseeched Meriwether for other comparable examples of widely accepted and influential diaries or journals that were known to have been significantly revised and expanded from the original, maintaining that "there must be some valid and persuasive way of defending the integrity of this great document."[29]

Perhaps so, but ultimately his effort to rationalize both what Chesnut had done and, by extension, how he had chosen to present it, depended less on any particular literary or scholarly precedent than on his prodigious talent for persuasion. *Mary Chesnut's Civil War* had been in print for three years when Woodward finally undertook to explain his actions in publishing the revised diary of the 1880s unaccompanied by the entire original version, and by that point, he and Muhlenfeld were on the verge of bringing out their own edition of the wartime diary. In a 1984 essay published in the *Yale Review* and later incorporated into his introduction for the original diary, he insisted that Chesnut was not trying to deceive her readers. Instead, the several drafts of the diary revealed that she had spent much of her postbellum life casting about for the "genre" most appropriate for conveying a genuine sense of what she had seen and experienced during the most turbulent time in the South's history. In the end, the search for her true métier, including her flirtation with the novel, had brought her back full circle to her original mode, the diary. Except, Woodward explained, this time around, Chesnut had undertaken not simply to serve up historical truth but "to combine historical with figurative and fictional truth" in order to best "illuminate the great experience she tried to express." In this, he seemed to see Chesnut moving, after a fashion, at least, along the same arc as later southern writers like William Faulkner and Robert Penn Warren who focused on the "truths" of the past rather than the mere facts.[30]

In reality, Woodward argued, "*Mary Chesnut's Civil War* must be understood as a creative work that uses personal experiences, real people, and actual events instead of invented or fictional material." Though she had inserted, altered, and excised considerable text in revising her diary, Chesnut had made no bones about what she was doing to anyone who asked, and what she produced was the result of a conscious choice rather than a "bungled deception." She had not set out to mislead her readers but to introduce them to "real flesh-and-blood people caught in the turmoil and anguish of a great historical crisis and [to] herself as a participant." How well she had succeeded in this, Woodward suggested, could best be discerned, not in the moralistic rhetoric of high dudgeon affected by the likes of Kenneth Lynn, whom he did not identify by name, but rather in the "virtually unanimous" acclaim of "the more reputable, informed and able critics whose opinions command respect" and who variously deemed it "'a masterpiece,' 'a work of art,' [and] 'a classic.'"[31]

Brisk sales suggested that many readers outside the academy found Woodward's *Mary Chesnut's Civil War* artful and thoroughly engaging, notwithstanding the challenge of wading through 881 pages of formal text and expository material. Meanwhile, whatever their misgivings, no other historian came close to echoing Lynn's charge that Woodward was complicit with Chesnut in perpetrating a hoax. On the other hand, most went out of their way to praise the literary grace, not simply of the diary itself, but of Woodward's preface, introduction, and annotations. Even so, given the criticism and controversy stirred by the book, it is hard to imagine that he did not feel an extra measure of personal vindication when he learned that *Mary Chesnut's Civil War* had been awarded the Pulitzer Prize in history for 1982.[32]

Even as the congratulations poured in, however, like the book itself, this decision met with skepticism in some quarters. The history jurors for the 1982 competition were Columbia's Eric Foner, John W. Toland (whose writings typically seemed geared toward a popular audience), and Woodward's friend and Yale colleague John Blum. In ranking the three titles they put forward, the jurors designated *Mary Chesnut's Civil War* as "1a.," calling it "one of the only two outstanding books among the entire group. . . . It is a special work. The jury believes the book fully merits a Pulitzer Prize." Because there were questions about "whether the prize in American history should be awarded for a work of historical editing," they added, should the Pulitzer board decide "that such a work does not conform to the criteria for that prize, . . . the jury strongly urges a special Pulitzer award for this book." Next came book "1b.," George Fredrickson's *White Supremacy: A Comparative Study in American and South African History*, which was "the other of the only two outstanding books among the entire group" and "a work of impeccable scholarship and historical imagination."[33]

John Blum's participation in the jury that recommended his friend and colleague's book for the prize might seem questionable, but Pulitzer juries were consistently drawn from such a tight and select circle that this situation was by no means unprecedented. When Richard Hofstadter's *Age of Reform* received the Pulitzer Prize in history for 1956, the jury consisted of his close friend C. Vann Woodward and Harry Carman, Hofstadter's mentor and colleague at Columbia. For his part, Woodward had already served on several Pulitzer juries at that point and would still be doing so some twenty years later, at age ninety.[34]

Because there was no clear agreement about whether edited works should be considered for the traditional Pulitzer in history, there was some murmuring when, instead of a special citation, the board gave the formal prize to Woodward. The decision bothered some who questioned whether the book itself should been seen as wholly historical, as opposed to partly fictional. According to Woodward, one critic compared the Pulitzer he received to the one for reporting given the year before to the *Washington Post*'s Janet Cooke only to be rescinded when her writing later proved to be based largely on a fabrication.[35]

The only notable charge that cronyism was by any means responsible for Woodward winning the Pulitzer came several years later. Woodward had incurred the wrath of writer and critic Gore Vidal by pointing to the many historical distortions in Vidal's 1984 historical novel about Abraham Lincoln. After a series of heated exchanges between the two, Vidal had pronounced Woodward the "premier conductor of that joyous, glory-bound [academic] gravy train" jealously guarded by him and his fellow "scholar-squirrels." For

The Masterpiece That Became a Hoax

his part, Woodward had simply pronounced Vidal "an unspeakable skunk," his appraisal no doubt reinforced by Vidal's charge that "Comer's own Pulitzer Prize (bestowed for his having edited the perhaps questionable diary of Mary Chesnut)" had actually come courtesy of his connections and was really the fruit of "a lifetime of successful maze-threading," culminating with his friend John Blum "awarding him the prime cheddar for what is hardly history writing in our committee's strict sense." Still, "to be fair," Vidal was prepared to concede that "Comer did deserve an honorable mention back in 1955 for *The Strange Career of Jim Crow*."[36]

Ironically, even if Vidal meant his closing observation as nothing more than a final condescending jab, he may have come as close as anyone to explaining the Pulitzer board's decision in this case. Woodward's earlier, more traditionally researched and written contributions to the field of history, especially *Origins of the New South*, had arguably achieved Pulitzer-worthy stature many years earlier. Meanwhile, his later books were largely composed of insightful, carefully crafted, but previously published and rarely documented essays. Though important, such works thus fell even farther outside the traditional Pulitzer concentration on historical works drawn from the author's research than his edited compilation of Mary Chesnut's diaries.

From a broader perspective, beyond the enormous body and consistently high quality of Woodward's writing lay his likely unsurpassed record of helping fellow historians fine-tune and strengthen their own contributions to the field. On top of that, there were the hundreds of reviews and essay reviews in which Woodward had helped to elucidate the interpretive significance and import of many of the most important books, including Pulitzer winners, written in American history across the last half of the twentieth century. The Pulitzer jurors and board members may well have seen themselves honoring Woodward's far-reaching, cumulative contributions to the field as much as his work on *Mary Chesnut's Civil War*. On the other hand, if this was their primary objective, it still begs the question of why they did not simply present him with a "Special Award or Citation" for overall achievement in a particular area, much like the one later bestowed on his Yale colleague Edmund Morgan for his "creative and deeply influential body of work as an American historian." This option might have struck the board as seeming too much like a "consolation prize" to do full justice to Woodward's contributions, but whatever the rationale for their decision, even his sternest critics would surely have found it difficult to argue that the distinctive recognition the traditional Pulitzer Prize conveyed was wholly unmerited in his case.[37]

The spring of 1982 should have been a season of high celebration for C. Vann Woodward. On March 31, less than two weeks before he got word about the Pulitzer, he had been feted at a huge dinner at Bookbinder's Restaurant in Philadelphia. The occasion marked the publication of a Festschrift titled *Region, Race and Reconstruction*, featuring essays written in his honor by former PhD students from both Johns Hopkins and Yale. The strikingly high quality of so many of these contributions not only made the book one of the relatively few such honorific collections to become a valuable resource in its own right but marked it as a fitting tribute to the effectiveness of Woodward's mentorship. Coming so closely on the heels of this event, the Pulitzer announcement should only have enhanced Woodward's feelings of satisfaction or accomplishment. Yet these emotions were forced to fight what was surely a losing battle with the grief and despair gripping him at that point as he watched cancer, his old tormentor, take its final, agonizing toll on his wife, Glenn, who died less than two months after he learned about the Pulitzer.[38]

Like most pairings that survive well into their fifth decade perhaps, as we have seen, Vann and Glenn Woodward's had begun as a work in progress, and decidedly incremental progress at that. Intense feelings for a partner in a previous relationship are almost certain to prompt comparisons with a new spouse, but in this case, despite her husband's genuine devotion to her, even in death, Glenn Woodward would never quite escape the shadow of his first true love. Nearly two years into their marriage, Vann Woodward was still weighing his interactions with Glenn against what he fancied married life with his beloved "Nina" (Antonina Hansell Jones) might be like: "It has not been a very exciting or stimulating arrangement—and perhaps it should not be. Glenn fell into the feminine and submissive role naturally, and it seems to suit her. I had once fancied that such a fine fierce fellow as myself demanded a mate equally independent and bent on her own high destiny, which would cross mine only tangentially, and perhaps a bit casually. Maybe so. Maybe not. I guess one always wonders about such matters and never really knows."[39] Regardless of what Woodward may have meant by "submissive," Glenn's role could hardly have been more supportive, beginning with the honeymoon, when she urged him to bring along the uncorrected proofs of his Watson book. He readily accepted her offer to index the book and had been "counting on Glenn," he later complained to a friend, but "she had to go and catch the flu and left the index on my hands." Nor did he seem to be wishing that Glenn was off pursuing her own "high destiny" in December 1939 when, caught up in his early research for *Origins*, he reported to Glenn Rainey that he was reading "stack after stack of books" and "running through one periodical after another marking passages for copying while Glenn follows up by typing up the notes. It seems like an endless job." She would also type and retype numerous drafts of chapters for *Origins*, and his research notes for his abortive Reconstruction book are replete with handwritten as well as typed passages supplied by Glenn.[40]

For all the anxieties that Woodward revealed both before and immediately after their wedding, he and Glenn soon settled into a mutually loving and appreciative marriage. Glenn had formed close attachments to his friends Bill Carleton and Manning Dauer in their early days in Florida, and over the years she had seemed comfortable among the friends they had acquired largely through her husband's interactions and affiliations. These included "Red" Warren and his wife, Eleanor Clark, Richard and Bede Hofstadter, and Alex and Joanne Bickel, as well as former students like William McFeely and his wife, Mary, and Willie Lee Rose and her husband, Bill. She was especially close to Vann's longtime friend the fiercely outspoken Alabaman Virginia Durr, who was also the mother-in-law of Vann's student Sheldon Hackney. Glenn was by no means as vocal as Durr, but the two shared a special bond as sufferers from what Woodward called "recurrent depression." Glenn's condition had grown acute enough to require hospitalization at least once, in 1950–51, and remained chronic enough to dog her throughout her adult life.[41]

She seemed notably susceptible to various physical ailments as well. She had apparently struggled with the Florida climate and developed a severe fungal infection on her face while they were in Gainesville. Manning Dauer recalled visiting the Woodwards during their traditional summer stay at Ocean City, Maryland, in August 1963, right before the March on Washington. He had planned to do some research at the Library of Congress and then participate in the march himself. Though "Glenn was not too well" at the time, Vann had been so excited by their conversations about the march that he suddenly announced, "I'm going with you. I can't miss this!" Noticing that Glenn's face was plainly saying "this won't do," Dauer refused to take his friend with him and insisted that "if you go, you can leave Glenn here and take your own car." In the end, Dauer thought, Woodward "really was torn about seeing [the march] in person and devotion to Glenn, who was just not well."[42]

Like Woodward himself, those in the couple's circle of friends spoke guardedly about Glenn's health problems, but they agreed without exception that Peter's death in 1969 had made her emotional difficulties infinitely worse. She grew more reclusive, and it was less common thereafter for her to accompany her husband to conventions or speaking engagements or sometimes even social gatherings. Despite Glenn's great fondness for Virginia

Durr, when the couple was invited to visit with the Durrs at a party given by Lucy and Sheldon Hackney in April 1971, Woodward responded that he would be "delighted" to attend, "but Glenn does not seem to be going along." Just short of a year after Peter's death, she did join her husband on a trip to the Soviet Union, from which they both returned exhausted, but he reported, where a combination of utter fatigue and a dose of Nembutal had afforded him "a big sleep of ten hours . . . poor Glenn abstained from the pills and tossed and turned all night."[43]

There were murmurs that some of Glenn's troubles might be alcohol-related, especially after a September 1979 fire left the Woodwards' house severely damaged, and according to Glenn Rainey, upon returning to discover the blaze, Vann had been unable initially to revive his wife and had to carry her to the window to be treated by the firemen. A few days after the fire, a concerned Red Warren was asking, "How did Glenn manage to take the business?" It is not clear if her lungs were damaged by the smoke from the fire, but at that point Glenn's already frail health was clearly in decline. She was bedridden for more than a month in the summer of 1980, with what Woodward described as a combination of "vertigo, ear infection, and eye trouble." She had recovered sufficiently to travel with him to Portugal the following spring, but upon their return, both came down with bronchitis, which, in Glenn's case, turned into pneumonia, putting her in the hospital and forcing her to rely on an oxygen tank after she returned home.[44]

By the end of March 1982, Woodward would be grimly telling a friend that "Glenn and I are fighting the battle you don't win. Only a matter of how long the fight lasts. It's the one we fought and lost for Peter. It's in her left lung and extensive. Doctors say no surgery, no therapy. She is in some discomfort but no pain. We have, of course, been through the ordeal before, together, and in some way that lends us strength. We will need all we can muster. She will stay at home as long as possible. I will have nurse aid. Old friends here rally." The wives of his "two dearest colleagues" were currently "fighting the same enemy," he added, although "their chances seem somewhat brighter for the time being." Glenn Woodward died sixty days later, on May 30, 1982.[45]

After Glenn's death, more than one of those who wrote to offer condolences cast her as Woodward's faithful helpmate. His own feelings for his wife clearly went well beyond simple gratitude for her years of unconditional devotion and support, however, and the great sense of loss he already felt from Peter's death and those of several of his closest friends grew infinitely more painful with her passing. He had not only grieved sorely for both Glenn's emotional and physical suffering but come to understand the pain of one

The Masterpiece That Became a Hoax

was inseparable from the pain of the other. In keeping with his admiration for strong-minded and independent women like Antonina Hansell and, as he saw her at least, Mary Boykin Chesnut, Woodward was especially fond of the plainspoken Virginia Durr. When he learned in January 1984 that Durr was just emerging from a particularly severe bout with depression after undergoing cataract surgery, he wrote to commiserate. "I went through the cataract ordeal with Glenn—as well as many other physical afflictions—and know how the purely physical can affect the psyche and bring on depression," he assured Durr. Glenn had "fought to keep them apart—not very successfully—but it was cancer that got her in the end. But you have a stronger and more indomitable mind and will not let it be victimized by the inevitable body ailments that will keep on coming. Let the medicine men do what they can about the body but keep them away from the psyche."[46]

Though no one could seriously doubt the depth of his feelings for Glenn and his primary aim was clearly boosting Durr's spirits at this point, it is hard not to sense just a whiff of his wistful vision of Nina in his comparisons of Glenn and Virginia Durr, especially in light of Durr's response, which offered a poignantly empathetic assessment of his late wife's deeply personal feelings. "I am sure one reason Glenn and I got on so well," she explained, "was we had both had Depression. . . . And, of course, Glenn never got over hers after your son died so suddenly. She felt he was the great accomplishment of her life and was so proud of him. She used to sit on my bed and talk to me by the hour, and she always spoke of you with love and trust but felt she had somehow failed while you had succeeded. She did not have anything to turn to that was outside herself and her family." Several months later, Woodward thanked Durr for the "sweet letter to me about Glenn and your talks with her. It moves me very deeply and I am so grateful to you. I still love her."[47]

Five months after Glenn's passing, his old friend Bill Carleton would be dead, and Woodward would have reason to feel even more isolated. Meanwhile his former graduate student and dear friend, the brilliant and feisty Willie Lee Rose, had suffered a debilitating stroke in 1978. Though he would continue a one-way correspondence with Rose, her inability to reply denied him not simply the company of a close and caring friend but the kind of intellectual stimulation that he not only craved but genuinely needed.[48]

Woodward had also cherished the good-natured intellectual jousting and repartee afforded by his friendship with Eugene Genovese, which dated back to the 1960s, but to his great dismay, their relationship went from warm to frigid in the space of a few months, beginning in 1980. Although the generally measured and composed Woodward seemed an unlikely match with the mercurial and combative Genovese, he made no secret of his admiration and affection for the Marxist scholar, despite the latter's pugnacity and penchant for provocation, revealed, for example, in his 1965 declaration at Rutgers that he did not "fear or regret the impending Vietcong victory in Vietnam. I welcome it."[49]

By the time Genovese had moved to the University of Rochester in 1969, the two had become not only friends but confidants. Woodward dutifully offered his highly prized endorsement on the great many occasions when Genovese sought to move on to a variety of more attractive positions elsewhere. In 1973 when Princeton sought Woodward's evaluation of Genovese, his endorsement was emphatic, although he made it a point to disclose that the two of them had "developed a personal friendship that I value very much." He praised Genovese's "impressive command of historical and humane literature" and hailed his forthcoming book, *Roll, Jordan, Roll*, which he had read in manuscript, as "a major work of prime importance, comparable in significance with any work in the field." Confident that his friend's professional stature would only continue to grow, he already ranked him on par with David Brion Davis and believed he had "surpassed Carl Degler," both of whom were highly accomplished contemporaries. All told, he saw Genovese becoming "an asset and an ornament to your department."[50]

Such high praise consistently marked Woodward's many letters in Genovese's behalf as he became not only his most respected and consistent booster but the kind of patient, understanding friend that the famously volatile Genovese found hard to make and even harder to keep. In addition to reading Genovese's work, Woodward lent an indulgent ear to his friend's spectacular rants about the "pig sty" that was the University of Rochester's history department or the "swinish performance" of Herbert Gutman in his book on the black family or the sly machinations of David Donald, who, Genovese declared, "had really become either insane or despicable."[51]

Woodward's unflagging support had not gone entirely unreciprocated, however. With Woodward struggling to remain above the fray when the Radical Caucus took on the American Historical Association establishment in 1969, Genovese did front-line duty as the "bad cop," eager to give such insurgents as Jesse Lemisch and Staughton Lynd a taste of his notoriously brutal rhetorical billy club. Several years later, with the Yale-Aptheker controversy heating up, Genovese had informed Woodward in April 1976 that, although he thought he and his Yale colleagues had "probably made an error in judgment," he felt "the best collection of American historians in the country has the right to be snooty about its appointments, and in any case, errors are not crimes." Even so, he pronounced himself "deeply relieved" when Woodward reported prematurely that Yale's "Ap-Flap" had apparently been resolved by the approval of the seminar for the fall semester in 1976 under the sponsorship of the political science department. The pressure to "attack Yale" had grown so intense, he claimed, that "even my closest friends on the left were warning me that further silence would finish me off in that quarter."[52]

When it turned out that the matter was not settled in the least, the pressures quickly returned for Genovese, who was preparing to assume the presidency of the Organization of American Historians as the joint committee report came up for approval at the group's April 1978 meeting. He had remained uncharacteristically circumspect about his stance on efforts to revise the report's conclusions so that they would reflect more critically on Woodward and his colleagues, and Stanley Katz left the executive board's discussion of it fully persuaded that Genovese had "joined the other side." Presiding later at the business meeting, he had deftly undercut Marvin Gettleman's call for expanding the authority of the joint committee in this and subsequent investigations by assuring the audience that the executive board had already agreed to review the committee's composition and procedures. Sharing her take on the proceedings with Woodward, Willie Lee Rose concluded, "One would think that things would not have gone as they did if Gene had not intervened."[53]

Despite the professional recognition afforded Genovese by his selection as president of the OAH, his reputation for being prickly and combative personally and the lingering fallout from his strident attacks on U.S. military involvement in Vietnam combined to render him generally too radioactive for a politically freighted and typically consensus-seeking academic hiring process that became all the more so when a senior appointment was involved. Though Woodward remained steadfast in supporting his friend's perennially abortive efforts to secure a new position, he was clearly apprehensive when Genovese reported in March 1980 that he had just learned that "I am probably going to get an offer from the Harvard Department of Afro-American Studies." Wary of the situation at Harvard, Woodward warned that "very recent dispatches from my spies on the inside" say that "the Afro-Dept. is an unholy mess, practically insoluble. . . . En garde!" Many black students at Harvard had complained bitterly about the near-stagnant black studies program, which after eleven years had reportedly tenured only one professor. Even so, Woodward sensed that they would not be so enthusiastic about expanding the faculty if it meant bringing in white professors. Still, he assured Genovese, "if you want to risk it, I will swear your grandmother was a full-blooded Bantu and you are a half-breed Gibbon."[54]

Sure enough, black students at Harvard did openly and stridently object to the possible appointment of Genovese and another white scholar, Lawrence W. Levine of Berkeley. Worse yet, some Harvard faculty and administrators outstripped anything seen in Yale's handling of the Aptheker appointment by allowing objections, not only to Genovese's Marxist perspective, but to his reputation as a difficult colleague, to play out in the pages of the *Harvard Crimson* and the *New York Times*. Eventually, the local papers back in Rochester, where Genovese was still teaching, jumped on the story as well. To make matters worse, Genovese had also been pursuing a position at the University of Maryland, where, although Woodward had written in his behalf, he was rejected after much discussion in which search committee chair Louis Harlan revealed that the candidate's Marxist views were not "a negligible issue." Genovese himself claimed that he was "told privately that the Red-baiting was outright, flagrant and undisguised."[55]

In the immediate aftermath of the Harvard debacle, a chastened Genovese conceded that he "should have listened" to Woodward's warning rather than get involved in a situation as "vicious as anything I have seen since Rutgers." He charged Harvard historian David Donald with orchestrating a nationwide smear campaign against him. He also pointed to members of an ad hoc external advisory body to the search, including Harvard PhD and Woodward's Yale colleague David Brion Davis, who had remained silent throughout the abuses he suffered.[56]

Woodward promptly assured Genovese that Davis had made "a strong pitch for your nomination," but his proposal got nowhere because it "ran into such opposition . . . said to be non-ideological but strong." At any rate, Woodward added, "I think you would have been in an unhappy situation there and are well out of it." Like Davis, Woodward had "done what I could" at Maryland, but when he learned from a letter in the *New York Times* that things had fallen through there as well, he wrote again to let Genovese know that he had written a "strong" letter in his behalf for a job at the University of Illinois–Chicago Circle and to encourage him to "use my name as a reference wherever you think it might do any good." Beyond that, he promised to "continue to mention you to places who write for suggestions about senior appointments."[57]

Woodward had offered these reassurances in late June 1980, and it would be nine months before Genovese finally broke what had now become a truly thunderous silence, explaining that he had actually "written you several times but torn every letter up because in the end, I simply could not see the point." After months of alternately brooding and seething with anger over the lumps he had taken in very public fashion, he revealed that it was not simply David Davis's silence about the debacle at Harvard that had upset him so much but Woodward's as well. He conceded that Woodward had offered to speak out about his treatment at Maryland, but the real harms had been done at Harvard, where he had been "indicted, tried, convicted, and publicly pilloried as a bad colleague and God knows what else." Yet despite all the lies about him that had been spread across the country, he noted bitterly, not one protest had been raised about the way he was treated. It was bad enough that his former colleagues among the leadership of the AHA and OAH and various fellow scholars on the left had chosen not to defend him or indict those who had smeared his reputation, but it was worse yet that Woodward, his close friend, who had "gone on record as standing for academic confidentiality at all costs," had remained silent.[58]

Genovese had been diagnosed with heart problems, and Woodward had worried that his "long silence" might be due to illness. Still, he was surely no less dismayed to learn that Genovese had gone incommunicado because of his "faltering faith in a friend." He gently reminded him that, even as he urged him to avoid "the mess at Harvard," he had nonetheless offered to write in his behalf if he pursued the position, only to receive no request for a letter from either Genovese or Harvard. He once again challenged Genovese's suspicions that David Brion Davis and his other friends had sold him out and, citing "a black demonstration . . . against you and Levine," suggested that "the Harvard blacks . . . were responsible for leaking the story to the press."[59]

Woodward's explanation for why he, as a stalwart defender of confidentiality, didn't "speak out" in protest against these leaks at Harvard was that his "recent experience with 'speaking out' at Yale [during the Aptheker affair] did not encourage a follow up." He conceded, "You have had a rough time. But your integrity has not yet been made the subject of an official investigation by the OAH or AHA, nor were their official publications filled for month after month with correspondence, committee reports, and counter-reports about your motives, your principles and your honor. 'Confidentiality' was no protection from that campaign of vilification." Though he would continue to "speak out whenever I think it's justified and will do any good," Woodward confessed to "some doubts" about how Genovese would have benefited from such headlines as "Yale McCarthyite Wants Red for Harvard" or "If One for Harvard, Why Not One for Yale?"[60]

If Woodward's explanation seemed a bit forced, he may have thought it at least more likely to appease Genovese than telling him point-blank that he was expecting quite a bit from someone who had no firsthand involvement in the Harvard search, regardless of how unprofessional it might have seemed at a distance. Nor was the outcome of the search or the damage it had inflicted on Genovese's reputation going to be reversed because of the post hoc comments of a representative of Harvard's primary institutional rival. Still, looking to leave no question of his own continuing allegiance to his friend, he quoted what had become something of a boilerplate passage in his letters of recommendation for Genovese: "His standing in the profession is attested, among other ways, by his election as president of the Organization of American Historians. Primarily this was a tribute to his scholarship, but also I think it was testimony of admiration for a man who has repeatedly shown the courage of his convictions. I suspect that this admiration is shared by many historians who do not share those convictions."[61]

Whatever Genovese's immediate reaction to Woodward's letter, several years passed without evident signs of communication between the two. In 1986 *Radical History Review* published Woodward's interview with former student James Green, in which he insisted yet again that Herbert Aptheker did not meet his department's "standards of scholarship," not simply in his writings on slavery, but in subsequent books defending Soviet actions in Hungary and Czechoslovakia, where "it was perfectly obvious that he was following the party line." Two of the most strident voices in the predictable torrent of protests from the left unloosed by these comments belonged to Eugene and Elizabeth Fox-Genovese, who bluntly condemned the journal's "contemptible editorial silence" in the face of Woodward's "transparent red-baiting." Genovese also noted privately to Aptheker in December 1986 that "many, many people, including Woodward's students are enraged. . . . For myself, I have had enough and want no more to do with him."[62]

Despite this vow to sever all ties with Woodward, the Genoveses did not object when he continued to boost Gene for senior positions in southern history and to dutifully review his and Betsey's books. A few weeks before the Genoveses' rebuke appeared in print, Woodward had enthusiastically recommended Gene for a chaired position at William and Mary, explaining that he had followed Genovese's career since "he first surfaced in the profession, read all his books, and was instrumental in getting him to come to Yale as a visiting professor for a term." Indeed, he thought Genovese belonged "among the top four or five" in any ranking of historians who wrote about the antebellum South. Responding to frequent requests for his ranking of leading figures in the field, Woodward persisted in giving Genovese high marks, even suggesting in one instance that he belonged in a class of his own.[63]

The Masterpiece That Became a Hoax

Woodward was also quite positive when contacted in 1992 about Elizabeth Fox-Genovese's qualifications for a chaired position in the humanities at the University of Kentucky. He had been most impressed with the results of Fox-Genovese's transition from European history to the history of the antebellum South after her marriage to Gene, adding that he thought highly of her major book in the latter field, *Within the Plantation Household,* which he had reviewed most favorably in, "I believe, the *New York Review of Books.*" Woodward professed that, at this point, he was not "fully informed" about Fox-Genovese's recent resignation as director of the Institute for Women's Studies at Emory, but he ventured that the root of the problem seemed to have been "something in the nature of her administrative style."[64]

Though Woodward's studiously vague suggestion about the situation at Emory was broadly accurate, a few weeks earlier he had hastened to correct Sheldon Hackney's impression that Fox-Genovese had been "forced out, or frozen out, by her politically correct colleagues." Though the Genoveses claimed that Betsey was being persecuted for the stunning far left to far right about-face on politics, religion, and other social issues she and Gene had executed in the 1980s, Woodward assured Hackney that "Emory does not deserve the opprobrium it gets in the suspicion of discrimination against Betsey for ideological or other reasons." This perception had thus far gone unchallenged only because "Emory cannot afford to make public the real reason."[65]

How much Woodward knew about the "real reason" at that point is difficult to say, but it soon came to light that some of her female former graduate students had charged Fox-Genovese with bullying them into performing menial personal services, such as cleaning her house, picking up her laundry, and walking her dog, duties that, they insisted, would never have been foisted upon their male colleagues. She and Emory University would soon face a lawsuit filed by one of those former graduate students and staff subordinates charging sexual harassment and discrimination.[66]

The lawsuit was still active when Gene Genovese contacted Woodward in November 1994, ostensibly to ask him to chair a session at the annual meeting of the St. George Tucker Society, which had largely begun as Genovese's brainchild in 1980. (At that time, by Michael O'Brien's recollection, Genovese had scoffed at the notion of inviting a "dishonest, two-timing liberal" like Woodward to be part of the group.) Genovese's letters to Woodward after the Harvard debacle in 1980 were often marked by a biting and accusatory language aimed, if not at him directly, then at his friends and former students.

When his and Betsey's discussions with Duke fell through in 1985, he made John Hope Franklin the culprit. Though still confident in late 1994 that the suit against his wife would come to nothing, Genovese blamed it on political correctness running amok at Emory, much as it had when Woodward's former student Sheldon Hackney "instituted such gangsterism" as president of the University of Pennsylvania. Appearing to laugh off or ignore such barbs, Woodward seemed so intent on recapturing his good standing with Genovese that, whatever his true feelings about the Emory situation, he asked him to "please tell Betsey that I have endlessly admired her cool and calm in the face of the stupid assault upon her. And please give her my love."[67]

At eighty-six, Woodward's earnest, almost desperate efforts to recapture a lost friendship spoke to the loneliness, not simply of old age, but of someone who had by then lost his wife and only child and almost all of a small circle of his closest friends. Their deaths had cost him both convivial, affectionate company and, perhaps just as important, the kind of stimulating intellectual interaction that he so cherished and that Genovese offered in such abundance. Later, even after his once-close friend's death, Genovese could not refrain from insisting that Woodward's "nasty side" and capacity for "petty jealousy" had gone largely unnoticed throughout his career. This was a sobering postscript on the demise of what O'Brien aptly described as "a close intellectual relationship and a warmth of mutual respect that each granted to few others."[68]

Woodward suffered the loss of yet another older and even closer relationship in 1989, when cancer rose up once again to claim his friend, confidant, and fellow southerner Robert Penn Warren. The two had known each other since the 1930s, when Warren's continuing ties to the Nashville Agrarians encouraged a mutual wariness. A reciprocal admiration had blossomed by the 1950s, however, leading Woodward to dedicate *The Burden of Southern History* to Warren in 1960. Warren also played a key role in recruiting him to Yale, where their personal friendship only grew deeper, bolstered by a shared sense of regional and intellectual kinship.

Not only did their families travel together and visit often, but over the course of a quarter century in New Haven, the two men were frequently engaged in sharing both their ideas and their writing for the other's critical scrutiny. In characteristically self-deprecatory fashion, Woodward would insist that he was the greater beneficiary of these recurrent exchanges, but a close reading of their correspondence suggests otherwise, for Warren's interest in history was stronger than his sense of how it had been interpreted. From the

1960s forward, Warren asked Woodward to read practically every piece of nonfiction he wrote on historical or "southern" topics, ranging from the Civil War to his revised version of his 1929 book on John Brown to the transcripts of interviews he had conducted for his 1965 book, *Who Speaks for the Negro?* Woodward made no secret of his admiration for this "poet with history in his bones," but though he seemed to relish every reading assignment, he did not hesitate to rein Warren in a bit if he seemed to be straying too close to historiographical minefields, cautioning, for example, against sweeping, undeveloped allusions such as Warren's reference to the Civil War as a "secret school" for World War I and World War II.[69]

Woodward also knew when his friend needed affirmation more than criticism. Despite his own reservations about Warren's 1963 novel, *Flood*, when the author expressed shock at what he called the "slaughterous reviews" it received in the New York press, Woodward observed that, of all his novels, *Flood* was the "most completely detached from reference to a concrete historical event." He understood Warren's objections to being typecast as "any kind of historical novelist." Yet many of his readers expected this sort of writing from him at a uniformly high standard every time out. This was the price to be paid, he gently explained, for Warren's "unique gift in the history of letters ... the power of lifting the commonplace historical experience, any experience that has enough appeal to penetrate the collective mind, to a plane of universal meaning," and for his part, Woodward simply hoped his friend would "not fight it."[70]

Warren proved perennially awash in unread galleys and never entirely free, it seemed, from the pressure of looming deadlines. Perhaps as a consequence, while pithy enough, his critiques of Woodward's works in progress often lacked the depth, detail, and organization that his friend typically provided after reading something for him. Still, he was a perceptive reader and commentator, especially on "big picture" issues, as he demonstrated in his response to the drafts of Woodward's 1978 Jefferson Lectures on European views of America, which were later incorporated into Woodward's book *The Old World's New World*. In this case, Warren thought that Woodward had given too little attention to American self-criticism in the early stages of the nation's history and focused too narrowly on its early failure to gain international distinction in "intellect and the arts," when, after 1920, New York came quickly to rival, if not supplant, Paris and Rome in this respect. Finally, feeling that Woodward's commentary generally "die[d] away" at the end, he challenged him to at least come up with some "possibilities, threats, [or] promises. Or, better yet, something you'll think up." Still, Warren assured him that what he had done was far too important to simply "hide away," urging him to "put it back on the stove if you must, but keep it cooking."[71]

A badly ailing Warren's brief, scrawled comments on the manuscript for Woodward's 1986 memoir, *Thinking Back*, did not arrive until it was too late to incorporate them into the book, but in acknowledging receipt of the manuscript, he had offered his friend something far more meaningful. Just three years older than Woodward, he felt their "early lives were almost parallel in various ways," as were their relationships "to the worlds in which we grew up: in relation to 'official' Southernism." Warren's suggestion of a spiritual and intellectual kinship, based not simply on a common regional heritage but on a shared ambivalence about that heritage clearly resonated with Woodward, who was fond of referring to the two of them as a pair of "southern exiles." Delivering the eulogy at Warren's memorial service in 1989, he conveyed his profound sadness at losing so special a personal bond based on "this Southern connection," including "the many ties of birth, schooling, and growing up in the South that we shared."[72]

The pain inflicted by each of the many personal losses Woodward endured in the two decades after Peter's death in 1969 simply added to the cumulative toll they would exact over the remaining ten years of his life. While he was never free of its effects, he would resolutely refuse to buckle under what could have been a soul-crushing sense of loss. Instead, he would spend the final chapter of his life, much as he had spent each that preceded it, stressing the importance of the past to understanding the present and assessing the portent of the present for the future.

17

Still More That I Can Do

The Satisfactions of Staying the Course

Woodward's response to Robert Penn Warren's death was virtually the same as it had been not only to the passing of his other dear friends but even to the loss of Peter and Glenn. William McFeely recalled that Woodward seemed more miffed than gratified when he and other junior instructors at Yale offered to cover some of his classes during Peter's last days in 1969, and "we backed off fast." Four days before his son's death, Woodward was apologizing to Norman Pollack for the delay in reading his book manuscript brought on by a "grave illness in the family" and promising to "get to it as soon as I can." As McFeely noted, Woodward sought a respite from his pain in an arduous, disciplined regimen of critiquing manuscripts, which he maintained "no matter what was happening to his family and his friends and in his personal life." In the immediate aftermath of Peter's death, Woodward had thrown himself into preparing for his AHA presidential address and strategizing about how to handle the Radical Caucus challenge to the group's constitution as the annual meeting loomed.[1]

In the months after Glenn's death in 1982, he committed himself to a near-frenetic schedule of speaking and travel, from Columbia to Tuscaloosa, to the SHA meeting in Memphis, and to Philadelphia for a visit with Sheldon Hackney, who had recently been installed as president of the University of Pennsylvania. There had also been an initially apprehensive but ultimately satisfying sojourn to his native Arkansas and then a Thanksgiving stay with Bill and Mary McFeely on Cape Cod. In all of this, he confided to Willie Lee Rose at the end of November 1982, he had been "mostly running away from loneliness instead of settling in with it as my normal way of life. And embracing it as the scholar's way of work." After Christmas, he assured her, he would "indeed settle down to work." And there was plenty to be done. Beyond sparing himself "the abominations of shopping," another reason that he had sought out a caterer to prepare his meals was that it saved precious time with book chapters "pour[ing] in from various quarters," each demanding his scrutiny as the longtime editor of Oxford University Press's History of the United States series.[2]

Woodward had launched this multivolume series back in 1961 with his then coeditor Richard Hofstadter, and a backlog of manuscripts had been a rare concern indeed in an editorial tenure that had been and would continue to be marked more by fits and starts, frustration, and maddening tests of his patience than by the publication of books. Still, over the latter years of his editorship, especially, his involvement with this project sustained a crucial if sometimes vexing connection with a discipline whose capacity to reach a broad popular audience struck him as essential to maintaining its viability and importance going forward.

As outlined in the original prospectus, the Oxford History of the United States was to be modeled, loosely at least, after the multivolume Oxford History of England. At the outset, its core was to consist of six chronological volumes capturing the entire sweep of the nation's experience from the colonial era to the present and "emphasizing political history." (The early plan for both Hofstadter and Woodward to write one of the chronological volumes soon went by the boards.) In addition, there were to be six or so books focused on such topics as economic, intellectual, and diplomatic history. The chief aim was to ensure that, while based on sound scholarship, the volumes, roughly 600 pages each, would also be accessible and engaging to readers outside the academic realm. The editors would collaborate in recruiting authors for the volumes in consultation with the appropriate editorial personnel at Oxford University Press, whose president would also be actively involved in editorial and general discussions related to the series.[3]

Books in the series would be available to sellers at the most favorable trade discount and promoted as "major trade books, both here and abroad" and priced comparably with textbooks. After meeting with Oxford's John Brett-Smith and Byron Hollinshead in February 1961, Woodward foresaw "some exciting possibilities" for the project, primarily because he knew that he and Hofstadter could "agree without so much trouble and . . . disagree without disastrous results." With that, they immediately set their sights on potential authors, and with Oxford's encouragement, they shot for the stars. Along with John Blum and Edmund Morgan, both of whom Woodward would soon join at Yale, they quickly approached David Donald (then at Princeton), Harvard's John Higham, Berkeley's Kenneth Stampp, and Wisconsin's Merrill Jensen, all worthy members of anyone's "Who's Who?" of American historians at that point. Yet a year later, after pursuing what they considered the cream of the crop in U.S. history, they had yet to sign up a single author, having been turned down graciously but flatly by Donald and Higham and effectively put on hold by others such as Stampp and Morgan. Edmund Morgan was still working on a book on the Puritans and wanted to "savor my freedom for a couple of years" after completing it, meaning, Hofstadter explained, that it would be five years before Morgan would even "consider" signing a contract with them. As much as he had hoped to add Morgan to the list of authors, Woodward confided to Hofstadter that he was not willing to wait five years simply for him "to make up his mind." He had been courted recently himself by "*Time Life Ink* [*sic*]," whose representatives "came waving bills of large denominations" in an effort to persuade him to contribute to their own six-volume history of the United States, having already secured the much-sought-after services of Richard Morris and Henry Steele Commager. This initiative, Woodward thought, along with a similar series by Cornell University Press, "should goad us on to desperate decisions."[4]

Not only had they "drawn a really frightful blank so far," Hofstadter agreed in January 1962, but they had already run through all the most distinguished historians they had originally discussed with Oxford. With the demographic of prospective contributors now at an unanticipated "level of juniority," he thought the editors had little choice but to widen the scope of their recruitment. Hofstadter's spirits would brighten, temporarily at least, in March 1962, when Merrill Jensen formally agreed to write volume 1, covering the colonial period. In keeping with what would become an all-too-familiar scenario, Jensen would not be able to work on his volume for at least another two years, but he assured the editors that he had cleared away the 1964–65 academic year for the task and fully expected to complete a draft of the book by the end of that period. Woodward pronounced himself "perfectly content" to wait until Jensen's current project was finished and foresaw that his book for the series "will still, in all probability, be the first volume published. That's what we have hoped for all along."[5]

Not only would Jensen's not be the first volume published in the series, but he would never write it, and his case would prove more the rule than the exception. All of the prospective authors the editors approached were extremely busy and typically overcommitted scholars who had agreed to write books for the series only after their current writing projects were completed, meaning that it would be years, not months, before they would even begin work on the volumes they had promised to Hofstadter and Woodward. Beyond that, their estimates of when they might make good on these promises invariably presumed that their works then in progress truly progressed on schedule, which was rarely if ever the case. Jensen was still struggling to finish a "big book" on the American Revolution for Oxford University Press when he agreed to undertake the volume on the colonial period for the series. Yet upon learning that the editors were pursuing Harvard's Bernard Bailyn, some seventeen years his junior, to write the book on the Revolution, he was soon lobbying to take over that volume himself and pushing Bailyn as the author of the colonial era volume. Hofstadter suspected at that point that Jensen was trying to prevent Oxford from publishing another book on the Revolution that was likely to overlap with, and perhaps steal attention from, his own.[6]

As it turned out, by the time his own book on the Revolution finally appeared in 1968, Jensen had little need to worry. Unable to extract a firm commitment from Bailyn, Woodward and Hofstadter had turned to Virginia's Merrill Petersen, who agreed in 1964 to write the volume on the American Revolution for the series, only to decide in January 1967 that, at his age, "the task is much too formidable." At this news, Woodward quickly ventured to Hofstadter and Oxford's Byron Hollinshead that they should now "let Jensen switch to Volume II [on the Revolution]. . . . I doubt he would ever do Volume I anyway, and he does seem to be keen on proceeding with Volume II."[7]

Keen or not, nearly four years later, in December 1970, when Woodward pressed Jensen for a report on his progress, he had none to report and suggested they might consider "getting a younger man all full of bright new ideas" for the assignment. For once, at least, these words were not unwelcome. Already convinced that Jensen would never finish the book, and looking to avoid any reversal in his thinking, Woodward quickly informed him that "we have set the bicentennial of 1976 for completion of the series." Because this deadline would be impossible for Jensen to meet without compromising his high professional standards, Woodward asked gently, "Would it not be better for you to relieve yourself of this burden?"[8]

Again, the editors' unrequited nine-year investment in Jensen did not prove unusual or even extreme in comparison to other cases. Beyond dealing

Still More That I Can Do

with historians who were in great demand and not lacking for attractive alternatives, Woodward and Hofstadter were constrained in nudging them along because so many of the authors were also their close friends or protégés. They had turned in 1962 to Stanley Elkins and Eric McKittrick—both of whom had studied under Hofstadter at Columbia and been mentored informally by Woodward—to collaborate on the fifth of the six chronological volumes then envisioned. In response, Elkins and McKittrick, whose previous work had concentrated on slavery and the Reconstruction era, proposed instead to write the third volume on the years 1789–1815. At this, Hofstadter pronounced himself "delighted" to have his former students working "in any area they feel they could hold down." He worried only that their focus on this brief period would make "a slightly short book."[9]

Hofstadter's concern about the brevity of the Elkins-McKittrick contribution to the series would seem ironic indeed thirteen years later, in 1975, when the two proposed either dropping out of the series or doing not one but several volumes illuminating the twenty-six-year period they had originally contracted to cover in a single book. Mindful of the time—and money in advances—already invested in the two, Oxford's Sheldon Meyer pulled out the stops to dissuade them from backing out, stressing that, with the project finally seeming to gain momentum, losing them would be not only a "grievous setback for the series" but a "psychological blow" to the other authors. Meyer also reminded Elkins and McKittrick of the "unusual consideration" they had received in being allowed to write about a period in which neither had "specialized" and in receiving an advance "nearly double" that given to any other contributor. Oxford had also gone along with their extended writing schedule, and Meyer assured them of his willingness to continue to be flexible. However, the press was not agreeable to publishing their contribution to the series in multiple volumes or waiting indefinitely on the single volume they had contracted to write. Accordingly, he pressed them for a "projected delivery date, even if that proves to be four or five years off."[10]

Meyer should have been so lucky. Four years later, Woodward would still be pressing them for such a date. When he asked them in April 1979 to "get your heads—or telephones—together" on a time for delivery of the book, they did not reply until September. At that point, McKittrick reported that he and Elkins were in the middle of producing a massive, two-volume work called "The Age of Washington and Jefferson," with a third condensed volume to follow. Their first volume was still two years away from going to press, meaning it would be nine years at least before they even got started on their book for Oxford. Hence, the publication date for that book, McKittrick advised, could not be "much earlier" than 1990. If this date, marking roughly twenty-eight years after they had signed their contract struck Woodward and Meyer as "unreasonable," they should feel free "to find another author who could produce the required volume more quickly." Their considerable patience finally exhausted, Woodward and Meyer turned in 1982 to Gordon S. Wood, who did, in fact "produce the required volume," though not exactly "quickly." More than twenty-five years would pass before his book was published, and neither Meyer nor Woodward would be alive to see it.[11]

The striking turnover among authors fairly mocked Hofstadter's admission in 1966 that he was savoring the anticipated brief "hiatus" between completing the task "of finding these authors and the receipt of the first M.S., which I trust and hope is still a couple of years off!" Had Hofstadter not succumbed to leukemia in 1970, coping with a sudden surge of manuscripts would have been the least of his concerns. In fact, Morton Keller of Harvard, who had agreed in 1964 to take on the 1865–1900 volume, "Reconstruction and Industrial America," which, initially, was to have been Woodward's assignment, was the only author on the series roster at that point to even submit a manuscript, which arrived in 1971, only to be rejected by Woodward and Meyer after several attempted revisions because it did not adhere closely enough to the narrative format and provide detail sufficient to the needs of a general reader.[12]

In addition to Keller, the list of contributors and their respective volumes listed on Oxford University Press's first official announcement of the series in 1970 included: Colonial America (Alden Vaughan); The Revolutionary Era (Merrill Jensen); Early National America, 1789–1815 (Stanley Elkins and Eric McKittrick); Jacksonian America, 1815–1846 (Charles G. Sellers); The Civil War (William Freehling); Early Twentieth-Century America, 1900–1930 (William H. Harbaugh); The New Deal, 1930–1945 (Ernest May); The American Economy (Stuart Bruchey); American Diplomacy (Norman A. Graebner); and The Intellectual History of the United States (John W. Ward).

Of these, not a single author would produce a volume that was accepted for the series, although some did see their efforts yield books published separately by Oxford and other presses. Not until 1982 would *This Glorious Cause, 1763–1789*, written by Robert Middlekauff, who had signed on to cover the Revolutionary era in the wake of Merrill Jensen's departure, become the first volume of the series to appear in print, more than two decades after Woodward and Hofstadter began pursuing scholars whose work met the high standards they had set.[13]

Still More That I Can Do

The list of series authors appearing on the jacket of Middlekauff's book in 1982 bore only three of the names on the 1970 roster, along with several new ones, including Timothy H. Breen, who had replaced Alden Vaughan on the colonial era; Gordon Wood, who had replaced Elkins and McKittrick, on the early national period; James McPherson, who replaced Willie Lee Rose (who had replaced Freehling), on the Civil War; George Fredrickson, who replaced Morton Keller, on the period 1865–1900; David M. Kennedy, who succeeded Ernest May, on the New Deal volume; and finally, the slow progress of the series having made it necessary to extend its chronology forward, William E. Leuchtenburg, who was now slated to cover "Post-War America, 1945–1965." In the end, neither Breen nor Fredrickson nor Leuchtenburg (who would soon give way to James Patterson) would complete their respective volumes as listed. Indeed, after investing nearly forty years in the series, Woodward would live to see only four volumes published: Middlekauff's in 1982, James McPherson's *Battle Cry of Freedom* (1988), Patterson's *Grand Expectations, 1945–1974* (1996), and Kennedy's *Freedom from Fear* (1999). When Woodward died in 1999, it had been some seventeen years since Gordon Wood agreed to write the early national period volume, and it would be another decade before Wood's *Empire of Liberty* became the only other book Woodward had signed to be published as part of the series.

Middlekauff was the third author contracted to write the Revolutionary War volume, and McPherson the fourth one signed for the Civil War book. There was surely no calculating, or perhaps even imagining, how much effort Woodward had invested in prodding authors, first to come onboard, and then to produce the volumes they agreed to write, not to mention reading outlines and even whole manuscripts that were never to work out. Still, the four volumes in the series that he actively edited spoke well of his efforts. McPherson and Kennedy's books received the Pulitzer Prize in history, and despite some criticism, Middlekauff's was a Pulitzer finalist, while Patterson's was awarded the Bancroft Prize. All of these were books written by talented and accomplished historians, of course, but one reason their efforts proved so fruitful while those of numerous predecessors fell short may have been their shared commitment to crafting the clear, straightforward, broadly accessible narrative that Woodward and Hofstadter had established as the veritable sine qua non for books published in the series. Lip service to such a standard might be found in the boilerplate language of other series offered by other publishers, but Hofstadter and Woodward and their colleagues at Oxford truly meant to uphold it—and they did.

Woodward encouraged Columbia's Stuart Bruchey, who had undertaken a volume on American economic history (ultimately deemed unsuitable for the series), to keep discussions of economic theory "down to a minimum" and make sure that his discussions of the work of other economists did not pass "over the heads of your readers." Woodward had also patiently but repeatedly reminded Morton Keller that his primary objective was "to inform an intelligent, well-read, but unspecialized reader of what happened of importance" in the United States between 1865 and 1900. Oxford's Sheldon Meyer explained why this was a bottom-line concern. Noting that Oxford's marketing estimate for books in the series anticipated a minimum sale of 25,000 copies over the first three years, he did not mince words in telling Keller that he did not "think it possible for your book to reach this size of an audience, or even a substantial portion of it." Like the other authors whose manuscripts appeared to fall short of the requisite writing or organizational standards set for the series, Keller's scholarship itself was not in question. His book would soon be in print with Harvard University Press.[14]

In deciding whether to approach William Freehling or Charles Sellers about the Jacksonian era volume, Richard Hofstadter did not have to read much of Sellers's writing to incline him toward Freehling. "See how many sentences you'd care to let stand if it were your own prose," he urged Woodward. Freehling got the nod, initially, but when the withdrawal of Kenneth Stampp prompted him to request the Civil War assignment instead, the Jacksonian era volume fell to Sellers by default. Sellers joined the project in 1969, but not until 1987 did Woodward receive what amounted to a partial draft of the manuscript. To say the least, Sellers's sometimes dense writing and broadly theoretical approach were not much to Woodward's liking either. He saw too much of a "tendency toward abstraction" in Sellers's text when "a bit more flesh and blood" from "your vast store of concrete events and historic figures" would be in order. He took special note of the space Sellers had allotted to the rather unorthodox theories on sexuality espoused by two ministers in particular and suggested that "political, economic and military figures and forces" should figure more prominently in forthcoming chapters to "balance off the pages of Todd and Graham on masturbation." Finally, in 1990, twenty-one years after Sellers signed his contract, with all of Woodward's prodding and cajoling having gone largely for naught, he informed Sellers that both he and Meyer still found enough in the manuscript that was likely to "baffle and turn away [nonacademic] readers" to persuade them that "it would be a mistake to use it here."[15]

Woodward maintained his strong preference for the broad, engaging narrative, even as trends in historical publishing indicated that many of his younger colleagues were gravitating toward a more specialized, tightly focused, and scientifically oriented approach. Mindful of the mounting criticism of narrative history as outdated, in 1982, he marked the appearance of Middlekauff's *Glorious Cause* as the first published volume in the series with an essay defending that approach in the *New York Times Book Review*. There was, he argued, "still . . . a need for narrative history written for the general reader" that relied on "the art of the craft" to report historical findings "however scientific they may be." As academic professionals came to dominate American historical writing after the turn of the twentieth century, he explained, their desire to make their craft more "scientific" had tended over time to make their work less readable for anyone other than their peers, leading them in turn "not so much [to] lose the public as [to] abandon it."[16]

The sweeping syntheses of Charles A. Beard and other reform-minded "Progressive" historians writing in the years between the world wars won back some general readers, as did the subsequent revival of the old "storyteller" tradition in the nationalistic, consensus-oriented World War II era offerings of Samuel Eliot Morison and Allan Nevins. In time, however, growing skepticism of Cold War triumphalism, with its emphasis on the superiority of American institutions, inspired another coterie of scientifically oriented historians. Looking askance at grand, unifying syntheses, they drew on quantifiable data to document the objective realities such sweeping syntheses often passed over. Spurning the elites in order to uncover the history of the masses, they delved into topics like marriage, family, health, and ethnicity once thought too mundane to be of much interest or importance. Relying on computer analyses and sophisticated sampling techniques, they churned out hard data challenging the pronouncements of "Consensus" historians about the peculiar efficacy of American institutions and the popular faith and deference they commanded. If their findings could be jarring, so was the increasingly jargonized insider terminology in which they presented them.[17]

For his part, Woodward objected to the implication that "history has findings and secrets too arcane for the general reader." Such an impression merely reflected the reluctance of many historians to invest the additional effort needed to present and explain the import of their discoveries "to the layman in readable, unspecialized prose he can read and enjoy." The impression that a new generation of scholars were now writing mainly for themselves made it all the more imperative that the "old" narrative historians make the more specialized findings of this group more accessible to a broader audience, hence the need for "periodic syntheses such as the Oxford History of the United States."[18]

Woodward may have genuinely felt that his essay was "conciliatory," as he put it, but UCLA's Eric Monkonen, an ardent practitioner of the social science–oriented "New History," did not seem particularly conciliated in a fiercely overreactive letter to the editor of the *New York Times Book Review*. Monkonen not only attacked Woodward's call for a return to narrative history as "the worst in the recent wave of anti-intellectual Luddism" but likened it to the demand of "Reaganism and the New Right . . . for a return to simpler times and simpler tales, for a world no longer mired in complexity and opacity." In fact, he charged, by trying to "find a plot" in a tumultuous and inconsistent past, historians were simply imposing "a story line best left to the novelist."[19]

Ironically, though, it was not Monkonen but a historian who had recently signed on to contribute to the Oxford History of the United States who put the biggest damper on Woodward's celebration of the appearance of the first volume of the series. Although Gordon Wood had recently agreed to write the 1789–1815 volume abandoned at long last by Elkins and McKittrick, he appeared to question the overall soundness of the narrative approach in a long and sharply critical essay review of Middlekauff's book in the *New York Review of Books*. The most striking aspect of the essay was not Wood's unenthusiastic assessment of Middlekauff's contribution as "narrative history with a vengeance" but his own skeptical view of "the validity of traditional narrative history itself." Such a disclosure was, to say the least, not exactly music to the ears of Woodward and his Oxford editorial colleagues, coming as it did and when it did from someone who had just committed himself to a series dedicated specifically to the genre of historical writing that he now seemed to disparage.[20]

Wood acknowledged legitimate concerns about an increasingly atomized approach to historical writing, but he took little issue with those who dismissed narrative history as hardly more than "storytelling," in which "incidents no longer just pile up on one another" but are "drawn together, connected, and given [their] meaning by the end of the story." Fairly echoing Monkonen, Wood noted that the goal of the traditional narrativists was a story that was straightforward and uncluttered, not just in its conclusion, but in its telling. In Middlekauff's case, Wood ventured, this approach had produced "a narrative history of surface events" in which more subtle, complex, and deep-seated influences such as demographic change or market expansion

Still More That I Can Do

or other "long-range forces" were overshadowed by the motives and deeds of high-profile actors such as William Pitt and Samuel Adams and the "chief events," such as the Stamp Act and the Boston Tea Party, that their actions precipitated.[21]

In Wood's view, Middlekauff had often skirted complex issues in pursuing a smoother, less complicated account of how the quest for independence became the central, defining "Glorious Cause" of the Revolutionary generation. By adopting a narrowly teleological approach in which the way the story ends dictates the selection of events and actors to be emphasized, Middlekauff had simply "played into the hands of all those who . . . argue that historical narrative is just another form of fiction." Wood's take on a narrative history as too much akin to fiction did not go unchallenged, but his critique struck an especially sensitive nerve among historians who had been thoroughly catechized in the old narrative form but now feared that, in clinging to it, they might be consigning themselves and their careers to a premature obsolescence.[22]

Not surprisingly, this concern loomed largest within the ranks of younger scholars, where Woodward and his Oxford colleagues had been forced to seek replacements for the authors who had been their first, second, third, and even fourth choices. Timothy H. Breen, who had been recruited to write the series volume on the colonial period, was among the series authors listed on Middlekauff's book jacket in 1982, but three years later, he informed Woodward that he was withdrawing from the project, explaining that his volume had come to seem too much like a long, if somewhat more sophisticated, version of a textbook and no longer commanded his interest. He also confessed not only to sharing Wood's disappointment with Middlekauff's book but to fearing that it had "cast the entire series in a negative light," to the point that he found himself repeatedly explaining why his own work would be anything other than a glorified textbook.[23]

Instead of trying to change Breen's mind, Sheldon Meyer simply responded that his departure was "undoubtedly best," because his comments about writing something resembling a textbook represented "a complete miscomprehension of what you were supposed to be doing." He bore down harder on Breen's reference to Gordon Wood's critique, not only of Middlekauff's book, but of the philosophy behind it. Meyer felt that Breen had been "too much aware of Wood's criticism" and too ready to embrace the notion that it had rendered the entire series "suspect," and hence his participation in it suspect as well.[24]

Woodward's response, meanwhile, was fairly dripping with irony. It would not have done, he ventured, for Breen "to have persisted and written the book in such a spirit of despair," which could only have "ended in disaster and the probable rejection of a manuscript." Still, he made it clear that the type of "inflated textbooks" to which Breen referred were for the likes of Page Smith and James MacGregor Burns, and not the goal of the Oxford series, which sought to put "our fragmented craft back together again and restore a sense of purpose and mastery." Happily, Woodward reported, he had seen no indication of flagging faith in these principles in the incoming manuscripts he was reviewing.[25]

Perhaps this was true, but two years later he was hearing the same apprehensions from George Fredrickson, who had already wavered in his commitment to the series once and now feared that the best he could do with his volume on the late nineteenth century might still come down to a "glorified textbook." That would not happen, Woodward assured him, if he would re-dedicate himself to his original goal of crafting "a new vision of a period of crucial importance that has long been papered over with faded clichés." He offered an important insight into his own approach to historical writing when he ventured to Fredrickson that historians fell into two types. The first "starts with outlining" and is "willing to waste time in futile and self-fulfilling prophesies." The second is prepared to hold off and "see what he finds & thinks" and "waits with suspense and wonder to read what he writes in order to know what he thinks." Fredrickson, he thought, was "proceeding as if you were Type I when you are really [like Woodward himself] Type II." Still, if Fredrickson felt he could not "rise to the challenge," Woodward advised him to "pull out now and spare us both embarrassment," which he eventually did.[26]

As this and many other such episodes reveal, despite all the time and emotional and intellectual energy his editorial responsibilities consumed, Woodward's dedication to them never faltered. He was enormously pleased after reading several manuscript chapters for David Kennedy's future Pulitzer-winning *Freedom from Fear*, which covered the period 1929 to 1945. Yet in July 1998, just a few months shy of his ninetieth birthday, he pointed out that Kennedy's book, projected to print out at just under 1,000 pages, would be considerably longer than either James McPherson's or James Patterson's recent contributions, "both of them big books" in their own right. Accordingly, he urged Kennedy to do all the cutting possible "without sacrifice of quality," and to demonstrate that this was no mere perfunctory admonition, he cited both chapter and specific page sequences where he thought cuts were feasible.[27]

In addition to the four volumes published during Woodward's nearly thirty-nine-years as coeditor and editor, five more appeared between 1999 and 2018 under the editorship of David Kennedy. Since the series was officially announced in 1970, the list of projected chronological volumes had grown from six to eleven; eight of which, along with a volume on U.S. foreign relations, were in print by 2018. The crisper pace of publication under Kennedy's editorship might raise some questions about the efficacy of his predecessor's approach, although, in fairness, launching any new book series, let alone one as selective and exacting in its editorial standards as this one, was bound to entail initial errors in judgment and meet with unforeseen complications.[28]

We should not minimize the challenges posed by such an ambitious endeavor. Yet there is no escaping the reality that, for all the early buzz over plans for a multivolume history of the United States edited by two of the nation's most prominent historians, the number of volumes in print at Woodward's death nearly forty years later was, at best, disappointing. Truth be told, had he and Meyer not remained so resolute in keeping the project alive in the face of disappointment after disappointment, it might well have expired before it produced a single book. Oxford's costly long-term commitment to an enterprise so tortuously slow in yielding tangible returns on its investment spoke to Meyer's faith in the intrinsic value of the project and his sense of the vital importance of his press's continued support of such a worthy undertaking. As for Woodward, he clearly had alternatives to spending so much of his retirement, even down to the last few years of his life, pleading with fellow historians whose books had been under contract for more than a decade for "your assurance of continued commitment to the Oxford series" and "good news of your progress and prospects of completion."[29]

Moreover, what seemed a somewhat underwhelming record of productivity at that juncture surely reflected in no small measure Woodward's absolute refusal to compromise on the standards of clarity, coherence, and accessibility to general readers to which books published in the series must rise. Had he and Meyer not remained so steadfast on this point, for example, they could easily have had the books by Keller and Sellers in print in the series well before the end of Woodward's editorial tenure. Even as that tenure drew to a close only a few months before his death in 1999, however, he gave no indication that he was second-guessing his willingness to have his editorial legacy judged on the quality rather than the quantity of the books published on his extraordinarily long and challenging watch.

In certain respects, Woodward had seemed to see the assault on narrative history in the 1980s as essentially of a piece with demands on the left for separate facilities and programs of study for blacks, calls for multicultural instruction, and the introduction of speech codes on college campuses. All of these indications of a changing academic mind-set ran counter, not only to his own values and priorities, but to those of a great many white liberals of his intellectual generation. Yet, here again, his unfaltering allegiance to these principles that had marked him as a liberal when they were under assault from the right now cast him as a conservative, even a reactionary, in the eyes of many on the left.

If he felt any need to correct this perception, he gave no indication of it in 1986 when he insisted on a literal interpretation of the principles articulated in the Woodward Report more than a decade before. He had done so at the behest of Wayne Dick, a Yale undergraduate who had been placed on probation for posting flyers that mocked "Gay and Lesbian Awareness Days" by announcing "Bestiality Awareness Days." Dick had cited the Woodward Report in his defense, and his new champion explained, "Certainly I don't agree with his ideas, but they all come under the protection of free speech." Yale's executive committee agreed to a rehearing of his case and cleared Dick after Woodward recruited several influential witnesses to testify in his behalf, including Yale Law School dean Guido Calebrese, who conceded that Dick's actions were "tasteless, even disgusting," but allowed, "That's beside the point. Free expression is more important than civility in a university."" By this time, of course, many at Yale and other universities were openly questioning whether the right to free expression should give sanction to actions that were aggressively uncivil by design.[30]

In the end, the outcome of the Wayne Dick affair amounted more to a triumph of Woodward's will than an affirmation of Yale's unalterable commitment to protecting free speech regardless of the circumstances or costs. The steady erosion of this commitment after Woodward's death culminated in a 2015 incident that would surely have left him aghast. After Professor Nicholas Kristakis, master of Silliman College (along with his wife, Erika, the associate master), declined to formally caution students against choosing Halloween costumes that might offend certain minorities on campus, he found himself facing a mob of angry, expletive-hurling students. Upon hearing one of them declare at the top of her lungs that Kristakis's job was to create not "intellectual space" but "a place of comfort and home," Woodward might have taken her words as all the confirmation he needed that his worst fears about the direction of American universities during the latter years of his life had been realized.[31]

Overtly, at least, Woodward had seemed to take little note of the possibility that absolute, undifferentiated guarantees of free speech might lead to harassment and intimidation of minority students. Incensed by what he saw as efforts to restrict what could be said or taught on campus, Woodward sometimes allowed his outrage to cloud his judgment. This was never more apparent than in his controversial 1991 *New York Review of Books* essay on notorious right-wing provocateur Dinesh D'Souza's *Illiberal Education: The Politics of Race and Sex on Campus*. It became clear at the outset that Woodward's primary aim was not simply to review D'Souza's rather sensationalized account of leftist- and minority-inspired assaults on free speech and traditional curricular canons that were wreaking havoc on American university campuses. Instead, as he later conceded, he was more interested in drawing examples and anecdotes from the book to support what was really his airing of his own "views of the issues [it] addressed." Woodward and D'Souza were hardly soul mates in the traditional political sense. He acknowledged D'Souza's ties to the Reagan White House and the American Enterprise Institute and even his prior role as editor-in chief of the often designedly shocking, ultraright *Dartmouth Review*. If anything, Woodward seemed more worried about the author's politics being "used to dismiss his findings" than about the reliability of some of those findings or even the admittedly "polemical" nature of his book, with its "occasional stretching of evidence and logic to score a point."[32]

Woodward clearly wanted to have his say on the subject, but he would surely have been better advised to do it elsewhere, in another format, where he could be understood as expressing his own views. Instead, he opted for what came across as a largely uncritical paraphrase of D'Souza's views, which drew heavily on the author's sometimes suspect accounts of developments at Stanford, Harvard, Michigan, Duke, and Berkeley. At UC Berkeley, according to D'Souza, racially proportioned (relative to the state's population) admissions policies had thrust academically unprepared blacks and Hispanics into an environment in which they found it "impossible to compete effectively," leading nearly a third of them to drop out during their freshman year. Meanwhile, admitting so many "ill-equipped" minority applicants had only prompted both further stereotyping among white students and "defensive withdrawal and self-segregation" by minority students seeking refuge from their frustrations in their designated dorms and "ethnic theme houses." With these came demands for a curriculum tailored strictly to their views that, rather than doing greater justice to their particular ethnocultural group's contributions to Western civilization, seemed more like a rejection of this heritage altogether. This attitude, it seems, was reflected in "We are tired of your shit," the words of a black student at Stanford shared first by D'Souza, then Woodward.[33]

Woodward also blithely passed on D'Souza's claim that Stanford had abandoned its traditional emphasis on Western civilization in favor of a multicultural curriculum ultimately requiring all freshmen to take a course reputedly focused "on the works of blacks, Hispanics, feminists and homosexuals." Turning to Duke's pursuit of multiculturalism, which entailed a number of marquee faculty appointments, Woodward noted the school's "fine start" on "the black side" with John Hope Franklin, "the best historian in his field." On the other hand, Duke's commitment to having at least one minority faculty member in each of its academic departments by 1993 struck Woodward as neither practical nor wise, because the paucity of black PhDs in so many fields was likely to result in lower standards for hiring and tenure. Here and elsewhere, Woodward cited faculty in the field of literary criticism as the most vocal proponents of hiring more minority professors regardless of costs and qualifications. He linked this move at Duke to the recent appointments of leading proponents of "deconstructionism," whom he charged with leading the assault on even "minimal" designated standards for evaluating either faculty performance or the "content and quality" of the texts they wrote or required students to read.[34]

For Woodward, the overarching concern was the threat to academic freedom lurking within the push to make cultural sensitivity to minorities a primary factor in determining what could be said in classroom lectures and elsewhere. Again drawing heavily on D'Souza, he cited an incident at Harvard in which black students objected to historian Stephen Thernstrom reading aloud from southern plantation journals that allegedly depicted slavery as "benevolent." Campus administrators had reportedly waited a month before announcing that no disciplinary measures would be taken against Thernstrom, though two weeks later Harvard president Derek Bok cautioned professors to guard against actions suggesting "possible insensitivity." Woodward also pointed to restrictive "speech codes" at a wide range of institutions, including Emory, his alma mater, and quoted Yale president Benno Schmidt's lament that many leading universities "have adopted rules which empower groups of faculty and students with roving commissions to punish offensive speech." Finally, rather than offer a summary appraisal of the book ostensibly under review, Woodward concluded his essay by exhorting his fellow scholars to "rally to the defense of free speech" and to "stand up, be counted and speak out."[35]

There were many who chose to "speak out" in response to Woodward's unorthodox essay, but most who did so publicly did not do so approvingly. These included particularly rabid sorts such as the Afrocentrist who assailed

Woodward's "ignorant and lazy article" as just another example of "one white liar quoting another white liar." The literature professor who complained to *New York Review* editor Bob Silvers was more respectful but found it "particularly depressing whenever D'Souza hoodwinks such a truly distinguished scholar" who, instead of an actual book review, had simply "filed on D'Souza's behalf a long amicus brief that largely ignores D'Souza's own work." (As a case in point, Woodward seemed to accept at face value D'Souza's claim that, as an Indian émigré himself, he felt a natural empathy with minorities, even though while he was editor, the *Dartmouth Review* had published "Dis Sho Ain't No Jive Bro," a brutal parody of the speech patterns of African American students, in addition to a lighthearted interview with a Klansman and a staged photo of a black man hanging from a tree on campus.)[36]

Most troubling to Woodward personally were the sharply critical letters to the *New York Review* penned by longtime friends, some of whom had sought and benefited from his assistance in the past. Now teaching at Stanford, George Fredrickson handily refuted D'Souza's claim, recycled by Woodward, that his university required freshmen to take a course centering on works by "blacks, Hispanics, feminists and homosexuals." He, too, was concerned to see Woodward and other rather too credulous academic liberals "playing into the hands of right-wingers who wish to eliminate dissent from mainstream ideas and values from our universities." For Woodward, though, by far the most painful rebuke came in a letter to the editor of the *New York Review* from his old comrade John Hope Franklin. As a fellow pioneer in trying to "'integrate' white and African American history," Franklin bristled at the suggestion that he had been recruited primarily to teach "black studies," when, in fact, he had taught only courses in southern history and American constitutional history since arriving in Durham. Franklin also resented what he saw as Woodward's implication that black scholars simply gravitated toward black studies by choice when, in reality, it was only after being "rebuffed by white scholars in other fields [that] they had retreated to the study of Negroes."[37]

In his published response to several critical letters that appeared in the *NYRB*, Woodward focused most of his attention on Franklin's, suggesting that he "must have got up on the wrong side of the bed on the day he wrote his letter. It does not sound like him." He first reminded "my old friend" of the many nice things he had said and written about him in the course of a relationship spanning almost fifty years. Then, in a painfully awkward and unpersuasive attempt to explain that when he alluded to Franklin as "the best in his field," he insisted he was not referring simply to black history but literally "any field of history he cultivated." He cited a review of a book of Franklin's essays in which he lauded his triumphant refusal "to be segregated by race into black history."[38]

By way of personal fence-mending, Woodward quickly wrote Franklin directly under the guise of congratulating him on an op-ed piece comparing controversial Supreme Court nominee Clarence Thomas to Booker T. Washington. His real purpose quickly became apparent when he assured his old friend that "I can take anything from you in the way of correction and reproval—anything but a break or a cooling in an old and cherished friendship. That, I am not prepared to accept." It would be more than two months before he heard from Franklin, who first let him know that he had "no confidence in [D'Souza] or his findings," not only in his "unfair" report on Duke, but in his version of events at Harvard and Stanford. "My problem was not with you," he maintained, "but with the way in which your honest effort to understand the problem of so-called political correctness lent itself to be exploited and corrupted by D'Souza and his backers," including, "Bush, Reagan, his godfathers at the *Dartmouth Review* and others." At any rate, he insisted, "None of this affects our friendship and my warm affection for you, you can be certain of that."[39]

Though Woodward later noted that Franklin "came forth eventually with assurances of continued friendship," he clearly sensed otherwise, however, and the awkwardness between them was still detectable three years later at a conference honoring Franklin at the National Humanities Center. In his autobiography, Franklin recalled a final conversation, scarcely a year before Woodward's death, where the two reaffirmed "our personal regard and mutual esteem" and "reminisce[ed] about the culture wars and racial wars we had fought together." Yet he also admitted that Woodward's "best in his field" reference had "personally grated" and noted the "patronizing tone" of Woodward's explanation that he had simply meant "any field of history [Franklin] cultivated," when, in fact, "he was talking to the point D'Souza was making about black studies."[40]

A month after his essay appeared, Woodward estimated that he had so far gotten "more than fifty letters—and still they come . . . some pro, some con, some obscene, some to be answered, some definitely not." Two months later, he had received more than ninety letters, with the more recent ones apparently trending in a more positive direction, leading him to suggest to a like-minded friend that "there appears to be more serious concern and support for our point of view in the academy at large than I had expected." That support, however, seemed to come in greatest measure from liberal white scholars of Woodward's own fast-fading generation, including Edmund Morgan and Arthur Schlesinger Jr., whose critical treatment of many of the same themes in his recent book, *The Disuniting of America*, had won high praise from Woodward in the *New Republic*. Schlesinger predicted initially that Woodward's "barrage" in the *New York Review of Books* would "have very considerable impact . . . in rallying those who should be with us" and "even perhaps in persuading some who have been on the other side," only to write back two weeks later professing astonishment at the strikingly negative response it had elicited in other circles.[41]

Schlesinger stood out among his generational peers for having taken a similar public stand, but even his support for Woodward came through private channels. The historic reluctance among academics to speak out publicly and forcefully on controversial issues was well known, and if anything, Woodward may have actually encouraged such reticence in this case by penning what could only be seen as a tacit endorsement of the views of one of the most polarizing—and for many, ethically suspect—representatives of the American right. Had he taken the time to do a little more digging on his own and set forth his own views independently of D'Souza's in the restrained and persuasive prose that had always been his trademark, he might have made an important contribution at a relatively early stage of a controversy that remains very much unresolved more than a quarter century later.[42]

It would not do simply to leave it at that, however, without noting that the man who had charged headlong into the middle of a controversy he once would have approached more deliberately and thoughtfully was only a few months shy of his eighty-third birthday at that point. After spending more than half a century defending free speech and academic freedom, he was understandably concerned that these principles might be trampled underfoot in what struck him as a veritable blitzkrieg of political correctness sweeping across America's campuses. Fueled by identity politics and meeting with little determined resistance, this movement, he feared, would ultimately stifle freedom of thought and expression and compromise the integrity of the academic teaching and learning process, all of which he had devoted the balance of his life to preserving.

In February 1991, he had written to praise Schlesinger's recent criticism of calls to incorporate a "multicultural" requirement, emphasizing the historic roots of Western civilization in sub-Saharan Africa, into the public school curriculum. A month later, he had written again, declaring himself "enormously pleased to hear that you are doing a book [*The Disuniting of America*] on the Afrocentric nonsense. . . . As Anglocentric nonsense diminishes or yields to criticism, the black variety expands and gains immunity from criticism. It is difficult to get white academics, and even more, black ones, to speak out.... While you are at it, I hope it is not too much to suggest that you add a chapter on Gendercentric nonsense and Homophobic nonsense. University curricula are already disgracefully cluttered with such stuff."[43]

Though he was grateful for Woodward's support, Schlesinger confessed a few months later that, henceforth, he would personally steer clear of involvement with groups like the National Association of Scholars that were resisting the encroachments of political correctness and overzealous multiculturalism on campus. "I feel I have spent enough time on this controversy," he explained, "and don't want to get further involved in organizational intrigues." Woodward was not ready to abandon the fight just yet, however, and he found many of his concerns compatible with those voiced by the NAS, which was formed in 1987 with a commitment to promoting "intellectual freedom" and preserving "the tradition of reasoned scholarships and civil debate" on America's college campuses. Still, he surely must have felt more than a twinge of irony, not to mention discomfort, when he received the group's Sidney Hook Memorial Award for 1993. Forty years earlier, after all, as Woodward and other Johns Hopkins faculty were steadfastly defending the academic freedom of their embattled colleague Owen Lattimore, Hook, a philosopher and virulent anticommunist, was warning that Lattimore was not simply another "well-meaning liberal martyrized by McCarthy" but "at the very least . . . a devious and skillful follower of the Communist Party line on Asian affairs." He had accepted the Hook award itself with some "misgivings," Woodward admitted to historian David Burner, but did so "with the hope of helping them shake off the identification as reactionaries and accept liberals who share their view of academic freedom."[44]

Of all the disturbing social developments Woodward had witnessed over the past thirty years, none would continue to agitate him more consistently than what he saw as the attempts of black separatists to forestall fuller integration and interaction with whites, not only on college campuses, but throughout the whole of American society. He gave full vent to his feelings about "the rise of movements for black power and racial separation" in his remarks on "Recent Paradoxes of American Race" at a conference on race and ethnicity in September 1994. Impressed by Woodward's unflinching assessment of race relations and the state of black leadership at that point, W. W. Norton president Donald Lamm asked him a few months later to take a year to explore the prospect of a short book highlighting these paradoxes and the concerns they raised. As an enticement, Lamm promised a $50,000 advance, the first $10,000 of which Woodward could keep even if the project should "lose its appeal" to him.[45]

Woodward set about immediately to gather "great piles of books, stacks of notes, and daily press clippings." He seemed eager to get on with the book in October 1995, when he began a letter to Lamm by reporting that the recent "[O. J.] Simpson and Rev. [Louis] Farrakhan TV melodramas" had helped him to better focus his thoughts on the issue. He even listed some additional "paradoxes" that had occurred to him, such as efforts to achieve "black unity by embracing slaveholders['] 'one-drop' [of black blood] definition of black" and using "Africa, the most disunited of continents, as [a] model for black unity in [the] U.S." Yet just when he had Lamm's hopes up, Woodward noted that presenting any of the paradoxes he raised would inevitably entail "some degree of criticism or reproach for blacks." Some of this might be "welcome," especially a candid discussion of the Simpson trial, with its "use of money and race to subvert justice and [to] disgrace trial by jury," or "plain speaking about Farrakhan . . . and his blatant racism." Yet he imagined that the response to his criticisms from most blacks would be a pained: "This from Woodward . . . one white southerner we have been taught to regard as a friend. But look at what he is saying now!"[46]

In reality, had he followed through with the book, Woodward would have simply been updating or expanding on what he had written in "Clio with Soul," the revised editions of *The Strange Career of Jim Crow*, and his essay on D'Souza's *Illiberal Education*. Moreover, what might be called the "black backlash" against these earlier observations suggested that his estimate of his current standing with black intellectuals—including, perhaps, even his longtime friend John Hope Franklin—might have been somewhat inflated. His long history of involvement in public debates over controversial issues surely justified his claim that he had "never let hostility to my views stop me from putting them into print." Yet he now professed concern that raising these "paradoxes of race" would inevitably mean matching wits with "pundits" and other experienced contemporary analysts. Although he conceded that he had done this many times in the past, in this case, he contended, he would be writing, not as "a historian with command of the evidence," but rather more as a "journalist" or "sociologist," and, he concluded, "to come forth in either or both roles in such times as this would be a poor way to end a long career as a historian."[47]

It was surely understandable that, a month shy of his eighty-seventh birthday, Woodward might have simply decided against closing out so magnificent a career on a sour or combative note. Yet he was still not quite ready to go silent on this issue, and less than two years later, in a conference presentation that would become the last of his formal essays published before his death, he appeared to do precisely what he told Lamm he wanted to avoid. First came what was by now his almost trademark indictment of posturing and manipulative black separatist leaders for inciting the burning, looting, and "carnage" that erupted in major American cities and triggered the white backlash that had seemed to stop the civil rights movement dead in its tracks. Turning then to the intellectually and historically suspect underpinnings of black nationalist ideology, he endorsed Arthur Schlesinger's suggestion that a conniving Klansman intent on creating "a curriculum for the specific purpose of handicapping and disabling black Americans" would be hard-pressed to "come up with anything more diabolically effective than Afrocentrism."[48]

Finally, the master ironist could not resist contrasting the racially diverse group assembled at the Lincoln Memorial in 1963 to hear Reverend King's inspiring dream of an America no longer divided by color with the much larger and entirely black crowd, which gathered on the same spot in 1995, "facing the opposite way—in more than the literal sense," to hear the Reverend Louis Farrakhan "spread his gospel of nationalism, separatism, racism and hatred." In this sobering juxtaposition of images Woodward found all the justification he needed to warn that "ethnic nationalism" now posed a serious threat to "*e pluribus unum*" in a nation that, throughout its history, had promised "assimilation for all."[49]

Despite the sense of alienation he conveyed here and elsewhere, Woodward refused to succumb to feelings of powerlessness or irrelevance, and his last years were not without their comforts and satisfactions. He clearly enjoyed the company of Helen Reeve, a professor of Russian studies at Connecticut College, and there were various club memberships, as well as friends and former colleagues available for lunch at the legendary Mory's near the Yale campus, where he still maintained an office. "I continue in reasonably good health," he reported to John Hope Franklin in October 1994, "good enough to do what I want to do, including managing a big old house and the surrounding woods. I intend to see it out here and would not want to live anywhere else. . . . I still enjoy feeling a part of the university. Still more that I can do in service to our common calling. Besides work of my own, there is the need for keeping up with former students, many of them gray grandfathers by now, and their continuing flow of books and manuscripts they expect me to read at once and write them sooner. And I take genuine pride in some of their work." He also continued to review some of their books and to run interference for them with editors, as he did for Bertram Wyatt-Brown's *House of Percy* in 1995.[50]

In the main, however, Woodward continued to find both purpose and solace in a regimen of work and travel that many half his age would have found taxing. He was off to New Zealand for a series of lectures in 1995. Two years later, after taking the red-eye from New York to Copenhagen on the first leg of a protracted journey to a conference on a remote island off the coast of Denmark, he arrived showing less sign of fatigue than most of the younger fellow Americans attending the meeting.[51]

Nor was there any trailing off in his long record of social and political involvement. As soon as the Walt Disney Corporation announced plans in 1994 for a massive theme park just three and a half miles from the Manassas Battlefield National Historic Park, he threw himself into revving up resistance to the project, assailing it as an "appalling commercialization and vulgarization of the scene of our most tragic history." When the ensuing outcry eventually forced Disney to abandon the plan, he exulted in "our triumph over the Disney invaders," admitting his "satisfaction in the triumph of words over bucks—even bucks by the billions." In October 1998, just a few days shy of turning ninety, he joined Arthur Schlesinger Jr. in lending his name and cachet to a petition signed by more than 400 "Historians in Defense of the Constitution," who condemned what they saw as a nakedly partisan campaign by congressional Republicans to impeach President Bill Clinton. Realizing that their initiative might open them up to charges of partisanship, they had immediately sought the endorsement of the historian widely regarded as the exemplar of professional integrity and objectivity and persuaded him to join them on a C-SPAN press conference and later on *The Charlie Rose Show*.[52]

In this instance, however, the implication that Woodward had joined their effort purely as a matter of professional conscience as opposed to partisan or personal bias might have been something of a stretch. He had empathized with Bill Clinton as a fellow Arkansan even before he knew him personally, and he was positively smitten with Hillary, whom he had met, ironically enough, when she asked him to oversee the preparation of a special report on presidential misconduct for the House committee investigating the Watergate affair in 1974. He was beyond pleased when she told him in the receiving line for a huge White House dinner in May 1994 that she had arranged for him to be seated next to her for the evening. Admitting several weeks later that his head was still reeling from the experience, he could only exclaim, "What a woman! Pres. Bill sent me a photo of me shaking hands with him instead of her, unfortunately."[53]

A few days before his almost giddy report on the dinner, Woodward had chided *New Republic* editor Martin Peretz for running certain pieces he thought were too critical of Bill Clinton's alleged pre-presidential misdeeds after he was named in a sexual harassment lawsuit dating back to his days as governor of Arkansas. Before making such an issue of Clinton's "personal misconduct [in] the past," he cautioned Peretz and other liberal critics "to consider and confront the alternatives, the political alternatives that would follow from such a course." Conservative historian Stephen Thernstrom ventured that if Richard Nixon had been charged with offenses comparable to Bill Clinton's while in office, many of the same historians purportedly defending Clinton on purely constitutional grounds would just as readily have signed a petition demanding Nixon's impeachment. By all appearances, Thernstrom might well have relied on Woodward as "Exhibit A" in this case. In his appearance on *The Charlie Rose Show*, after all, he had charged congressional Republicans clamoring to impeach Clinton with trying to "assert a supremacy [over the presidency] which is denied them by the Constitution," despite defending the impeachment prerogative as "a constitutionally granted authority" back in 1974, when Nixon was the anticipated target. Still, suspect as his objectivity may have been in this instance, even at ninety, Woodward, who would be dead scarcely a year later, had not shied away from stepping into the public arena yet again to support an effort by students of the past to sway the affairs of the present.[54]

As his ninetieth birthday came and went, Woodward was energetically wading through stacks of books as the chair, yet again, of the history jurors panel for the Pulitzer Prize, admitting he "loved" Edward Ball's *Slaves in the Family* but asking his fellow jurors, "Is it history?" Meanwhile, there were fellowship recommendations for friends and former students and a request from one of the latter to intercede with Robert Silvers to get his new book reviewed in the *New York Review of Books*. In the final months of his forty-year editorship of the Oxford History of the United States, he was still critiquing manuscripts, cajoling authors to pick up their pace, and coping with those who decided to withdraw. There was an essay to finish for a collection honoring his longtime editor and friend Sheldon Meyer, who was retiring after more than four decades with Oxford University Press. He also found time in June 1999 for a long letter to the *New York Review of Books* warning that efforts to unionize graduate assistants by reclassifying them as university employees could lead to a "disastrous revolution in basic relations" between them and their faculty mentors.[55]

Despite the spunk and determination demanded by such an active routine, however, Woodward was ninety, and after surviving two earlier brushes with cancer, he was now contending with a seriously ailing heart. He had been diagnosed with atrial fibrillation in 1992. (When a doctor prescribed Coumadin, a blood thinner that he was to take for the rest of his life and strictly forbade the further consumption of his cherished predinner martini in the bargain, Woodward immediately consulted with a second physician, who assented only after what he described as a serious conversation about "the size of the martini.") He confided to Bertram Wyatt-Brown at the end of March 1999 that one of his "famous" physicians had told him he "could prolong my life if I would submit to major surgery," but painfully aware of "old friends who endured years of helpless dependency," he had explained to the doctor "that I preferred to enjoy what remained of a long life rather than face the risks of prolonging it."[56]

He apparently changed his mind, however, undergoing surgery in July 1999 after tests indicating a severe narrowing of his aortic valve led a cardiac specialist to recommend replacing that valve despite his age. Although his daughter-in-law, Susan, could not be in New Haven for extended periods, Woodward's friend and associate dean at Yale, Penelope Laurans, oversaw his care after the operation. Historian Glenda Gilmore, a friend who would go on to hold the Peter V. and C. Vann Woodward Professorship that he had endowed at Yale, was a regular visitor. University of Virginia historian Paul Gaston came to see Woodward in the hospital shortly after the surgery. When their wide-ranging conversation had to be cut short so that Woodward could rest before entertaining the next visitor, rather than convey any sense of finality, he simply urged Gaston to "keep in touch." Former Yale colleagues John Blum and Edmund Morgan also reported that Woodward had sounded strong and in good spirits when they called him in the hospital in late July.[57]

Yet despite a steady stream of well-wishers, who wrote, called, or came by, Woodward's fear of "years of hopeless dependency" were surely closing in on him as his stay in the hospital proved only a prelude to several additional months of convalescence at Whitney Center, a nearby total-care facility for the elderly. He was still there at the end of November, and former Yale colleague Robin Winks admitted that when he first learned that Woodward was in Whitney Center, he was unsure if he should be "relieved or saddened," although he took the news to mean "you emerged from the hospital much better, but wanted now to be surrounded by friends." By all accounts, however,

Woodward made it quite clear throughout his prolonged stay that where he really wanted to be was at home.[58]

To his great relief, on December 16, 1999, roughly a month after his ninety-first birthday, he was finally allowed to return to the house on Rodgers Road in the New Haven suburb of Hamden that he and Glenn had purchased upon coming to Yale in 1962. There is reason to think that by the time his doctors finally acceded to Woodward's fervent pleading to go home, they knew full well that about all they could do for him was to allow him to choose where he died. Sheldon Hackney and his wife, Lucy, stopped by to see him about an hour after he made it back to his house. This was "where he desperately wanted to be," Hackney knew, "but he was mostly asleep and did not really recognize us." Woodward's bed had been situated amid his books in the sunroom, but the next day he asked to be moved to the familiar desk chair from his study, where he quietly passed away after spending scarcely twenty-four hours in the place where he had longed to be for many months. Noting that Woodward died in the same chair where he had spent countless hours working, Bertram Wyatt-Brown thought it was "as if, after a brief nap, he would resume the writing that had given his life its greatest meaning. This time, however, he did not awaken."[59]

Conclusion

America's Historian

Though Woodward understood and accepted that his long life was approaching its end well before he went in for heart surgery in July 1999, other than his 1986 memoir, *Thinking Back*, he left little indication that he had spent much time reflecting on what might be said or written about him after he was gone. When that time came, those charged with assessing his achievements and legacy found it no easy matter to do justice to the importance, let alone the intricacy, of his lengthy and multifaceted career. Not only did that career span some six generations chronologically, but Woodward was a multigenerational figure in the intellectual sense as well.

Though perhaps a bit of a latecomer, he can certainly be read and understood as part of the fabled Generation of 1900, composed of southern writers born around the turn of the twentieth century who subsequently served notice of their intellectual independence by assailing the entrenched historical and literary orthodoxy imposed by the New South creed. At the same time, Woodward was also part of a distinctly accomplished cohort of historians on both sides of the Atlantic who rose to prominence after World War II. They generally set themselves apart from their professional predecessors with what William A. Palmer called their more resolute and unflinching "engagement with the past," aimed at making it more accessible to a contemporary public audience and more relevant to the issues of their own day.[1]

These scholars could hardly have emerged at a time more propitious for establishing their credibility in the public arena. Historians had been heavily involved as staffers and advisers for a variety of New Deal agencies, and either as civilians or in uniform, a great many others, including Woodward, functioned in their capacity as historians in support of the military during World War II. Meanwhile, the universities at which they taught had also contributed to the war effort in a variety of services from training to research. The cumulative effect was a heightened regard for academic expertise, reflected in the postwar expansion of university press publishing and decisions by several major commercial houses (and a few more trade-oriented university presses, such as Oxford) to introduce paperback series featuring readable and engaging academic books likely to appeal to more educated general readers. The stage had thus been set for the debut of a dynamic new cast of scholars turned public intellectuals. Woodward had burst onto that stage in the mid-1950s, to join Arthur Schlesinger Jr. and Richard Hofstadter, both of whom, as Sam Tanenhaus observed, had also "reached maturity as historians at the precise moment when the nation itself was coming into its own, [as] a freshly minted world power blessed with unparalleled wealth and social mobility."[2]

For all its promise, however, this newly ascendant postwar America was also racked by anxiety. The ever-present prospect of communist aggression abroad made the threat of nuclear war seem anything but distant. On the home front, fears of communist subversion posed a serious threat to civil liberties, while mounting pressure to secure and defend the civil rights of black Americans also raised the specter of a race war. This pervading sense of peril afforded a peculiar opportunity for a small group of historians who, having proven themselves quite proficient at their craft, were also confident enough to step outside their academic comfort zone and share their perspectives on the most pressing concerns of the day with a broad popular audience.

There is much to be said for viewing Woodward's work through these generational lenses, but his career was so long and its impact so enduring that it can be fully appreciated only by considering it in longitudinal perspective as well. His writings on the Reconstruction, Redeemer, Populist, and New South eras gave more than a nod to Charles Beard's insistence on the primary importance of prevailing economic interests in determining historical outcomes. Yet Woodward's belief in the importance of human choice in shaping those outcomes and his determination to explore the moral dimensions of human conflicts led him to abjure the strict, soulless economic determinism attributed to Beard and other historians associated with the Progressive school. Their emphasis on persistent conflict arising out of divergent economic interests also met with mounting disfavor as the menacing global context of the Cold War era favored historians who were inclined to emphasize unity over division as the norm in American life.

By the 1950s, Beardianism had largely given way to the Consensus School of historians whose writings subordinated economic, social, and political divisions to a common and enduring faith in the nation's institutions and values. Woodward's realism and innate skepticism would admit of no such tidy metanarrative of America's past. Despite their differences, however, he had formed and maintained close friendships with Richard Hofstadter, David Potter, and Edmund Morgan and a mutually admiring relationship with Daniel Boorstin, all of them exemplars of the Consensus School. His oft-affirmed and generally honored commitment to civil and constructive debate also served him well in maintaining a cordial intellectual coexistence with them as well.

As the 1960s unfolded, a younger and more contentious cohort of radical, New Left historians assailed their Consensus predecessors for glossing over the historic disparities in wealth, power, and opportunity between America's "haves" and its "have nots," who had fought consistently to throw off the shackles of deprivation and powerlessness. Woodward's writing offered little justification for attacking him on these grounds. Though the Radical Caucus insurgents at the 1969 meeting of the American Historical Association knew that he was not sympathetic to their effort to restructure the organization, he commanded enough professional and personal respect within their ranks to earn him a certain benefit of the doubt as he presided over the confrontation and deftly defused it. His stance on the Herbert Aptheker appointment at Yale obviously disappointed and perturbed some of his colleagues on the campus and beyond. The same could be said of his ill-concealed hostility to multiculturalism and what he saw as the intellectually stifling dictates of political correctness. Younger historians seemed most likely to be rankled by these stances, but they appeared to do little damage to his standing with his contemporaries or with a succeeding generation who had entered the profession during his long reign as its ultimate role model.

As we know, Woodward found the calls of some African American leaders in the 1960s for de facto social and cultural distancing from whites especially perturbing because, instead of a valid scientific distinction, he saw race as little more than a repressive social construction imposed on blacks by whites. This concept had become unfashionable and, to some, even subversive of liberal values well before his death. In historical perspective, though, this view of race had once put him at the cutting edge of liberal racial thought, close on the heels of pioneering cultural anthropologists such as Margaret Mead and Zora Neale Hurston. Both were disciples of Franz Boas at Columbia, and their work in the 1920s and 1930s unearthed a common, transcendent humanity hidden beneath layers of man-made distractions such as color, gender, and custom. If, as Charles King noted, their efforts put them "on the front lines of the greatest moral battle of our time," then Woodward would stand alongside them soon enough. Yet by the end of his career, some critics on the left were ready to relegate him to the proverbial "wrong side of history" simply for maintaining the same stance that had once put him squarely on the right one, and well ahead of many of his contemporaries at that.[3]

Woodward dedicated himself to dismantling the historical argument for segregation because, so long as it survived, he saw little hope of achieving not only civil and political equality for blacks, but social and cultural assimilation as well. By the 1960s, though, he was championing racial integration in the face of hostility from black revolutionaries instead of white reactionaries, while simultaneously defending free speech from the censorious political correctness of the left rather than the conformist nationalism of the right. After helping to throw open the floodgates of change, he suddenly found himself helpless to control the flow of the revolutionary currents he had helped to unloose.

This was hardly the only unforeseen consequence of Woodward's earnest efforts to make a revised vision of the past an instrument of change in the present. By way of encouraging challenges to the current order in the South, he had attacked what he saw as the entrenched myths and misconceptions that helped to rationalize that order as historically unavoidable. In his view, human agency had always been the critical element in shaping the realities of the past, and by extension, the impact of those realities on the present. He denied that conditions in the South in the 1950s were inevitable because he envisioned a different set of decisions by southern leaders in generations past that might have resulted ultimately in a different, and decidedly preferable, present. The inevitable is "almost always unpleasant," he liked to observe, and thus "needs all the opposition it can get."[4]

In Woodward's view, the obstacle to change posed by the myth of historical inevitability was all the more reason for historians to dedicate themselves to "purg[ing] the past of myth" lest it succeed in "replacing history" altogether. Hence, he had committed himself to disabusing his readers of the myths of the past while prodding them to acknowledge its realities and their consequences for the present. Yet, in following his own dictate, he sometimes wound up simply replacing an old historical myth with a new one of his own making, as he did whenever he offered, or at least implied, an alternative, essentially conjectural version of the past that could have led to an altered but no less conjectural version of the present. If the Jim Crow laws had not been implemented, for example, then segregation and discrimination might never have become such fixed and formidable barriers to achieving racial justice in the contemporary South. Likewise, if the Redeemers and their New South successors had not invited greedy northern capitalists to ruthlessly exploit their region's plentiful labor and raw materials, then the South might have been spared the egregiously undemocratic political system and tragic extremes of poverty and human blight still plaguing it at the middle of the twentieth century.[5]

In the abstract, at least, major political actors in the New South era could have opted to do certain things differently. Yet, here and elsewhere, Woodward offered readers scant indication of the actual probability of alternative decisions leading to the alternative outcomes he suggested. It is one thing, after all, to entertain the likelihood of a battle turning out differently if a critical set of orders had not been lost or intercepted. It is quite another to envision the seismic shifts in major economic, social, demographic, and political realities within the region and outside it that would have been necessary to set the post-Reconstruction South on a faster track to modernity or to reverse the deterioration of the racial climate that Woodward blamed for the appearance of the segregation statutes.

As Richard Hofstadter grew older, he became increasingly skeptical of historians whose primary objective seemed to be extracting meanings from the past that might be brought directly to bear on current concerns. By 1968, he was warning that the present-mindedness of these "activist historians" put them at risk of losing, not just their respect for the "integrity" of the past, but even their sense of its very "pastness." Though Woodward appeared in certain exchanges with David Potter to question the value of exploring the past without regard for its implications for the present, he certainly never lost sight of the distinctions between them. Every major piece of writing he undertook proved to be a valuable contribution to historical scholarship in its own right, without regard for its relevance to the affairs of his own day.[6]

In fact, despite his misgivings about his friend's approach, Potter credited him for showing "that history can retain its basic scholarly validity even in a context of active presentism," though he was quick to stipulate that this approach could be entrusted only to a scholar of Woodward's rare intellectual maturity and breadth of mind. Woodward was clearly not lacking in either. Still, having grasped early on the cold truth of the Orwellian dictum "Who controls the past, controls the future," he was very much a historian on a mission. His propensity for fashioning alternative historical explanations into challenges to the status quo sometimes led him to play fast and loose with the evidence, as he had done in several instances, from exaggerating racial tolerance within the Populist rank and file to overstating the case for relative fluidity in southern race relations before the Jim Crow laws. Taking such liberties suggests a determination, not simply to make the past speak to the present, but to script its message in accordance with what the writer feels the people of the present need most urgently to hear. In pursuing this aim, the historian, even one so discerning as Woodward, risks becoming less an interpreter than a ventriloquist.[7]

Woodward's brand of presentism harkened back in many respects to the call for a "usable past" with "living value" for the present, issued by literary critic Van Wyck Brooks in 1918 and heartily endorsed by influential Progressive historians such as Carl Becker and Charles Beard. The concept seemed destined to fall into terminal disfavor with the ascent of the Consensus School after World War II and the attendant demise of Beard, who struck Hofstadter as "our supreme tragic example of the activist mind in history."[8]

Hofstadter may have felt justified in penning Beard's historiographical epitaph in 1968, but any implication that historical activism had died with him was decidedly premature. In fact, at that very point, a younger, more aggressively activist cohort of New Left historians were already pursuing a "vision of the past which would enable us to remake the present and the future." Publicly at least, Woodward seemed to empathize with New Left historians' efforts to call attention to the struggles of hitherto marginalized masses and uncover a history of dissent and conflict that had been swept under the "rug of liberal consensus." Professing even to see his earlier self in the young radicals, he urged his own contemporaries to give them a fair hearing because, collectively, their work offered a much-needed antidote to "a complacent and nationalistic reading of our past." Still, even if his personal commitment to activism had lost none of its conviction or vigor, he realized that, by and large, the firebrands of the New Left saw him at this point as a fixture of the liberal establishment they were out to topple. Meanwhile, the limits of his identification with them came through in his low-key but determined defusing of the Radical Caucus insurgency at the 1969 meeting of the AHA. The same might be said of his more forceful denunciation of disruptive student protests and what he saw as the incendiary rhetoric and extremist demands of black separatists on and off campus.[9]

At that point, the debate over writing history with an eye to influencing the affairs of the present remained strikingly one-dimensional. Not only had "activism" become thoroughly conflated with "presentism" in these discussions, but both came across as the peculiar province of historians looking to undermine the legitimacy of the status quo by offering a new, more critical vision of the past on which it rested. Woodward knew better, however, having realized early on that preceding generations of southern historians had practiced their own more implicit brand of presentism in pursuit of precisely the opposite ends. By continually reinforcing a distinct historical narrative that effectively rationalized the abuses and inequities of the current order, they had fashioned the past into a shield against the kind of activist presentism that sought to rectify or eliminate these wrongs. In challenging their consistently recycled (rather than revised) version of the past meant to shore up the defenses of the present, Woodward had essentially inverted the purpose of writing southern history by turning it into a force for change rather than a bulwark against it. He had done much the same in assailing the U.S. historians of the 1950s who uncritically ascribed their nation's material and military success to date to its innate genius and superior virtue, thereby nurturing a smugness and complacency that, if left unchallenged, might well lead to America's undoing. For all the establishment bona fides that would ultimately be his, at a critical moment in the South's and the nation's history, his approach had been as consciously subversive of the professional order of that day as any pursued by the new generation of self-described radical historians.

This is not to say that Woodward was always keen on the activist presentism of other liberal historians. He had decried what struck him as an exaggerated and misleading emphasis on black agency and resistance under slavery, which seemed geared to providing a historical foundation for the emerging Black Power and Afrocentrist movements of the mid- to late 1960s. He made it clear at the time that he saw little good coming of this development. Had he lived to see it, he would surely have seized on the irony of so many of today's U.S. history textbooks devoting more attention to blacks' resistance and resilience in the face of their enslavement than to the horrors inflicted on them, even as Black Lives Matter protests and demands for reparations for the damage inflicted by slavery continued apace.

A more recent trend in historical emphasis and representation might have drawn comment from Woodward as well. In reality, well before his death, it had become almost routine for historians to encourage readers to connect their treatments of historical actors and groups, social and political movements, and other phenomena to what they saw unfolding in their own day. We might even say that presentism rarely invites controversy now, had the sense of the term as used in Woodward's day not been effectively reversed by some historical activists in recent years. Where it once referred to drawing on the past to understand the values and priorities of the present, it is almost as likely today to imply allowing the values and priorities of the present to shape and color our vision of the past. Contemporary outrage over seemingly more frequent and egregious police violence against blacks as well as other racial abuses has helped to fuel a propensity to hold key figures of generations—even centuries—past effectively accountable to the standards of morality and humanity by which we purport to measure ourselves today. Within the popular consciousness, this new historical mind-set has manifested itself in the widespread toppling of monuments, not simply to prominent Confederates, but to some of the fabled Founding Fathers and other high-profile historical actors who had some association with slavery or segregation. The outrage behind these moves has likewise spurred calls for renaming schools or other public buildings on the same grounds.

We may be safe in assuming Woodward's sympathy with the genuine historical grievances behind these moves, but there is less certainty about his broader philosophical take on these developments, were he around to share it. His scholarly treatments reveal an admiration for former slaveholders such as Charles Colcock Jones, Robert Dabney, and other antebellum leaders who "invested their honor and their lives" in defending their society in the Civil War and then went on to take their stand against the greed and materialism propelling the New South effort to resurrect its fortunes. On the other hand, there is no escaping his deep antipathy toward the cynical manipulators of the myths and symbols of Old South grandeur and Lost Cause valor. The countervailing discordance of these sentiments makes him seem an unlikely candidate either to lead a charge to knock down a Confederate monument or to defy a bulldozer to save one. Yet what we know of his approach to his discipline gives reason to suspect that the raw emotionalism that often marks such confrontations might lead him to subtly caution the current generation of historians about allowing what he called "the menace of morals" to creep into their writing. By this, he meant that even the most laudable concern for justice or human brotherhood and the deepest commitment to any number of noble causes could cloud their vision of the past. Not excluding even pressures from powerful political and economic interests, he saw no greater threat to the objectivity and complexity of historical interpretations than the desire of historians themselves to be identified with righteous causes, an impulse that might be called virtue-signaling today. To Thomas Jefferson's remonstrance against construing history as a "moral exercise," because "her lessons would be too infrequent," he added that "the integrity of the art over which Clio presides can be threatened by the just as well as the unjust, the righteous as well as the unrighteous, [and] the moral as well as the immoral."[10]

This was just the kind of unwavering and forthright stance that Arthur Schlesinger had in mind when he lauded his friend for upholding "the standards of the historians' craft against the nostrums of the passing day." Schlesinger offered this and other soaring praise in a remarkable letter written less than two months before Woodward's death that was more than anything a premortem eulogy, and one surely as fitting and elegant as any offered upon Woodward's actual passing. Seizing on what he surely suspected might be his last opportunity to pay tribute to his friend of four decades while he was still alive, Schlesinger wrote, "As I contemplate your life, I hope you will realize how much you have meant to the historical profession. Your preeminence derives partly from the superb quality of your historical writing. But it derives as much from your human presence." Praising Woodward once again as "the conscience of our profession," Schlesinger added, "Like every other guild, the historians' guild is always in need of moral leadership. That, you have provided, unassumingly, effectively and courageously, and you have inspired younger scholars to do their resolute best to grapple with a mysterious past."[11]

Schlesinger's tribute was both genuine and revealing. His pedigree and connections had given him a leg up on becoming a celebrated public intellectual, but he truly admired, and possibly even envied just a bit, the way Woodward had come to his own lofty standing. Woodward's junior by nearly a decade, Schlesinger died in 2007. At eighty-nine, he had more than twenty books and scores upon scores of essays for popular readers to his credit, meaning he was more prolific as a publishing public intellectual than Woodward. Yet, finding the clubby cocktail circuits of Washington and New York more to his taste than graduate seminars and faculty retreats, Schlesinger had effectively cut the cord with academe early on. This, in turn, freed him of the burdensome regimen of teaching and mentoring graduate students, reading manuscripts for his academic peers, and sustained involvement in a variety of professional organizations, all of which had commanded a substantial share of Woodward's time and energy.

There was no denying the profusion of Schlesinger's writings or the critical insights they frequently offered. Yet, despite his repeated claims to professional detachment, he would be remembered in greatest measure for his unflagging loyalty to the Kennedy clan and his instrumental role in crafting and disseminating the family legend. This was entirely in keeping, of course, with his history of active involvement in liberal Democratic politics in general. Hence, the caption for his *New York Times* obituary referred to him rather bluntly as a "partisan historian of power." While Woodward's views and political predilections were similar to Schlesinger's in most respects, he publicly bemoaned the shortcomings of Democratic and Republican administrations alike, and his writing generally conveyed too little hint of whatever partisan preference he might harbor to warrant such an identification. Although he might have found a certain wry amusement in the caption of his own *Times* obituary, with its narrow, understated reference to him as "a historian who wrote extensively about the South," it is fair to surmise that he would have much preferred this overly modest characterization to the one accorded his friend.[12]

Woodward's typical response to glowing tributes like Schlesinger's was to claim that the lionized individual in question was unrecognizable to him. In reality, Schlesinger had exaggerated but little in his portrayal of Woodward, though one qualification might have been in order. Without discounting his stellar reputation for integrity among his fellow historians in the least, strictly speaking, Woodward was more visibly the "social" than the "moral" conscience of his profession, per se. If, in the former capacity, he sometimes seemed less intent on depicting the past accurately than in fashioning it into an instrument for changing the present, there is still a great deal to be said for what he achieved in pursuing this approach. He displayed a rare genius in implying a striking resemblance between the Populists of the 1890s and the tenant organizers of the 1930s. The same could be said of casting the self-serving Redeemers who hastened the demise of the first Reconstruction as virtual stand-ins for the latter-day opportunists vowing to stop a second one dead in its tracks. Such associations might come across as a bit too facile to suit the tastes of some professional historians, but they nonetheless persuaded a broad public readership that the past could help them make better sense of their own times. As Schlesinger observed, this talent was surely not lost on several decades' worth of historians drawn to the profession by the exhilarating prospect of drawing on their craft to make a difference in the here and now.

Edward L. Ayers began his PhD studies at Yale in 1975 and managed to enroll in the last course Woodward offered before he retired. Though he was impressed with his instructor's professional stature and taken with his personal charm, Ayers acknowledged that Woodward's most critical influence on him came via *Origins of the New South*, which, he declared flatly, "changed my life. I was in American studies and interested in literature, but when I read it, I thought, 'If this is what history is, I want to write history.'" It is impossible, of course, to say just how many of Ayers's own or previous generations of historians were similarly affected by Woodward's work, although I certainly know one, and feel entirely confident that Ayers and I are far from alone.[13]

The job market for newly minted PhDs in American history has effectively been on life support for the past half-century, meaning that some of those, myself included, who fell under Woodward's spell may have had occasion to second-guess a decision made on the spur of a Pied Piper moment when his writing inspired them to pursue a career he had once resolutely rejected for himself. At the same time, among those talented, diligent, and just plain fortunate enough to find or make their places in the historical profession, only a precious few would know even a fleeting taste of the fame and influence that was Woodward's for so long. Even so, if they came ultimately to understand and accept that, irrespective of the standing they achieved, the rewards for their accomplishments would always be primarily intrinsic, they likely enjoyed more in common with him than they realized. Why else, after all, would he have devoted so much of his time and energy to improving the work of others? Or how, otherwise, to explain why he soldiered on so dutifully as editor of the Oxford History of the United States despite all the frustration that so frequently marked his efforts and left him with not a single volume to show for them for more than half of his nearly forty-year tenure?

We should not lose sight of the many individual achievements Woodward did register over that span or the succession of severe personal losses that accompanied them. If anything, his already legendary productivity may well have gotten an additional boost from his determination to blunt the pain of these losses by plunging even more energetically into his work. Mental health experts might not have universally endorsed this approach, but Woodward knew full well that, for him, backing away from his writing, professional commitments, and involvement with graduate students meant an existence largely devoid of meaning or satisfaction. Thus it was that, for all his inner turmoil, outwardly Woodward presented as the masterfully composed, unfailingly diligent, and productive scholar so many aspirants to the profession sought to emulate.

In the final summing up, though, C. Vann Woodward's most vital and enduring contribution went well beyond inspiring so many others to make studying and teaching history their life's work. His supreme achievement lies in the untold numbers of Americans—many of whom might have been hard put to make it through even one of his lectures—that his writing awakened to the potential of the past to clarify their understanding of the present and guide them in anticipating and perhaps even influencing what was yet to come. In this, he surely knows no equal among American historians of his own century or any who have come since.

Woodward's father Hugh ("Jack"), *right*, and his uncle
Comer when both were students at Emory, ca. 1900.
*Photographer unknown, courtesy Manuscripts
and Archives, Yale University Library.*

Woodward as a senior at Emory, 1930, age twenty-one.
Photographer unknown, courtesy of Stuart A. Rose Manuscript,
Archives, and Rare Book Library, Emory University.

Woodward's friend and longtime confidant Glenn Rainey.
Photographer unknown, courtesy of Hal G. Rainey.

Ernest Hartsock, poet and editor who nurtured
Woodward's appreciation of literature.
*Photographer unknown, courtesy of Stuart A. Rose Manuscript,
Archives, and Rare Book Library, Emory University.*

Howard K. Beale, Woodward's dissertation adviser
at the University of North Carolina.
*Photographer unknown, courtesy Manuscripts
and Archives, Yale University Library.*

Woodward shortly before his discharge from Naval Intelligence, ca. 1945.
Photographer unknown, courtesy of the John Simon
Guggenheim Memorial Foundation.

Woodward speaking at a Civil War symposium at
Gettysburg College, 1957. His address was later published
as "Equality: The Deferred Commitment."
*Photographer unknown, courtesy Manuscripts
and Archives, Yale University Library.*

Woodward's son Peter, who graduated from Yale
in 1964 and died of cancer in 1969.
Photographer unknown, courtesy of Yale University Alumni Association.

Woodward's portrait in the National Portrait Gallery, 1969.
*Photograph by Pach Brothers Studio, courtesy
of the National Portrait Gallery.*

Woodward in his office at Yale, 1979.
Photograph by William R. Ferris, courtesy of William R. Ferris.

Woodward with fellow southerners and Yale colleagues Robert
Penn Warren, *left*, and Cleanth Brooks, *right*, 1979.
Photograph by William R. Ferris, courtesy of William R. Ferris.

Sketch of Woodward by Randall J. Stephens.
Courtesy of Randall J. Stephens.

Woodward with John Hope Franklin at a celebration of his
ninetieth birthday, Birmingham, Alabama, 1998.
*Photographer unknown, courtesy of Manuscripts
and Archives, Yale University Library.*

Woodward with a group of his former students at his ninetieth
birthday celebration, Birmingham, Alabama, 1998. *Left to right,
front row*: Robert F. Engs, Charles B. Dew, Woodward, Lawrence N.
Powell, Anne Wyatt-Brown, Marc W. Kruman. *Second row*: David
L. Carlton, James M. McPherson, Vincent G. DeSantis, William S.
McFeely. *Third row*: John A. Williams, J. Morgan Kousser, J. Mills
Thornton III, F. Sheldon Hackney, Bertram Wyatt-Brown.
*Photographer unknown, courtesy of Manuscripts
and Archives, Yale University Library.*

Illustration derived from a sketch of Woodward by Charles W. Joyner, 1998.

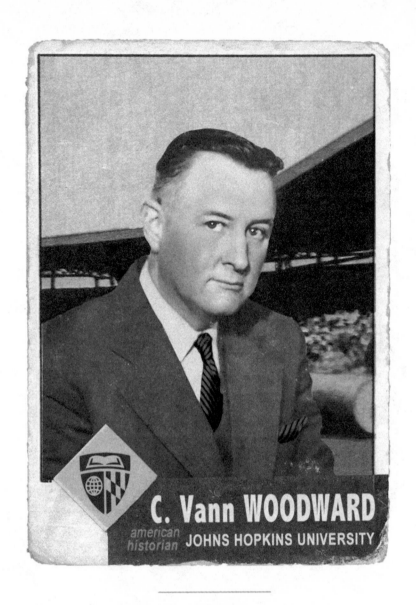

Great Historians Trading Card created by Randall J. Stephens.
Courtesy of Randall J. Stephens.

Notes

ABBREVIATIONS USED IN THE NOTES

Beale Papers   Howard K. Beale Papers, Wisconsin Historical Society, Division of Library, Archives, and Museum Collections, Madison

Carleton Papers   William G. Carleton Papers, Special and Area Studies Collections, George A. Smathers Libraries, University of Florida, Gainesville

C. M. Woodward Papers   Comer McDonald Woodward Papers, Stuart A. Rose Manuscript, Archives, and Rare Book Library, Emory University, Atlanta, Ga.

CVW   C. Vann Woodward

CVWP   C. Vann Woodward Papers, Manuscripts and Archives, Yale University Library, New Haven, Conn.

Looker Papers   Antonina Hansell Looker Papers, 1836–1987, Southern Historical Collection, Wilson Library, University of North Carolina at Chapel Hill

Odum Papers   Howard Washington Odum Papers, Southern Historical Collection, Special Collections, Wilson Library, University of North Carolina at Chapel Hill

Rainey Papers   Glenn Weddington Rainey Papers, Stuart A. Rose Manuscript, Archives, and Rare Book Library, Emory University, Atlanta, Ga.

Ramsdell Papers   Charles William Ramsdell Papers, 1844–1942, Dolph Briscoe Center for American History, University of Texas at Austin

Roper Papers   John Herbert Roper Papers, Southern Historical Collection, Special Collections, Wilson Library, University of North Carolina at Chapel Hill

Stephenson Papers   Wendell Holmes Stephenson Papers, David M. Rubenstein Rare Book and Manuscript Library, Duke University, Durham, N.C.

Vance Papers   Rupert Bayless Vance Papers, Southern Historical
Collection, Special Collections, Wilson Library,
University of North Carolina at Chapel Hill
Warren Papers   Robert Penn Warren Papers, Yale Collection of American
Literature, Beinecke Rare Book and Manuscript
Library, Yale University, New Haven, Conn.
Wiley Papers   Bell Irvin Wiley Papers, Stuart A. Rose Manuscript, Archives,
and Rare Book Library, Emory University, Atlanta, Ga.

Some of the manuscript collections cited here have been reorganized at least once since research for this book began. In cases where it is clear that the original location of material I noted is not up-to-date according to the current finding aids, I have supplied the locations indicated in the finding aids.

INTRODUCTION

1. "Congressional Impeachment Inquiry," C-SPAN, www.c-span.org/video/?114447-1 /congressional-impeachment-inquiry (accessed October 28, 1998).

2. "A History of Impeachment," *Charlie Rose Show*, October 28, 1998, https://charlierose.com/videos/14069 (accessed October 1, 2018).

3. Drew Gilpin Faust, "C. Vann Woodward: Helping to Make History," *Chronicle of Higher Education*, January 14, 2000, www.chronicle.com/article/c-vann-woodward -helping-to-make-history (accessed June 16, 2019).

4. CVW, *Tom Watson: Agrarian Rebel* (New York: Macmillan, 1938).

5. CVW, *Origins of the New South, 1877–1913* (Baton Rouge: Louisiana State University Press, 1951); CVW, *Reunion and Reaction: The Compromise of 1877 and the End of Reconstruction* (Boston: Little, Brown, 1951).

6. CVW, *The Strange Career of Jim Crow* (New York: Oxford University Press, 1955).

7. Richard H. King, *A Southern Renaissance: The Cultural Awakening of the American South, 1930–1955* (New York: Oxford University Press, 1980), 257.

8. Flannery O'Connor is quoted in Sally Fitzgerald, ed., *The Habit of Being: Letters of Flannery O'Connor* (New York: Farrar, Straus and Giroux, 1979), 521–22.

9. CVW to Antonina Jones Hansell, October 16, 1937, Looker Papers.

CHAPTER 1

1. "Col David C. Cross," Find a Grave, www.findagrave.com/memorial/12513536 /david-c_-cross (accessed November 10, 2016); "Col. David C. Cross," in *Biographical and Historical Memoirs of Eastern Arkansas* (Chicago: Goodspeed, 1890), 325, 386; John Herbert Roper, *C. Vann Woodward, Southerner* (Athens: University of Georgia Press, 1987), 8.

2. Dallas Tabor Herndon, *Centennial History of Arkansas*, vol. 3 (Chicago: S. J. Clarke, 1922), 804; "Tennessee Marriages, 1796–1950," database, *FamilySearch*, https://familysearch .org/ark:/61903/1:1:XD9J-PQ8 (accessed July 12, 2014), W. B. Woodward and Elizabeth Lockhart, December 22, 1870, Franklin, Tennessee, reference 2: KVPNC6, FHL microfilm 576,303, *Franklin County, Tennessee: History and Genealogy*, http://genealogytrails.com /tenn/franklin/marr1793.html (accessed November 10, 2016); Comer M. Woodward to Hoyt M. Dobbs, June 7, 1918, Box 90, Folder 8, CVWP.

3. Roper, *C. Vann Woodward*, 18–19; "United States Census, 1870," database with images, FamilySearch, https://familysearch.org/ark:/61903/1:1:MD8Y-F37 (accessed October 17, 2014; Amelia E. Lockhart in household of James Lockhart, Tennessee, United States, citing p. 10, family 64, NARA microfilm publication M593 (Washington, D.C.: National Archives and Records Administration, n.d.); FHL microfilm 553,026; "United States Census, 1860," database with images, *FamilySearch*, https://familysearch.org/ark:/61903/1:1:M8TZ-6P7 (accessed December 30, 2015), James Lockhart, 1860 (accessed November 10, 2016).

4. Herndon, *Centennial History*, 804–5; CVW, "Morrilton Memoir," Box 71, Folder 114, CVWP.

5. Roger Adelson, "Interview with C. Vann Woodward," *Historian* 54 (Autumn 1991): 4; CVW to Hugh A. Woodward, n.d. [Spring 1930?], Box 60, Folder 732, CVWP.

6. CVW, "Morrilton Memoir"; "Books Belonging to C. Vann Woodward, Left for Storage, 8-24-43," Box 92, Folder 44, CVWP.

7. Julia Ann Oxner Hall, "C. Vann Woodward: American Educator" (PhD diss., University of Mississippi, December 1977), 21–25; Howard K. Beale to CVW, October 1, 1940, Box 7, Folder 66, CVWP.

8. "Impressionistic Prose," Box 35, Folder 415, CVWP.

9. "Town astride Pegasus," Box 35, Folder 415, CVWP.

10. Boulware Martin Ohls, John Gladden Hall, and Julia Hall, interviews by John Herbert Roper, March 12, 1984, Roper Papers; Hall, "C. Vann Woodward," 27–28.

11. Ohls, Hall, and Hall interviews; C. R. Huie to John Herbert Roper, September 1, 1983, Roper Papers; Roper, *C. Vann Woodward*, 26.

12. CVW to Boulware Martin, n.d. [1930?], and Martin to CVW, August 4, 1934, Box 35, Folder 415, CVWP.

13. Ohls to CVW, April 18, 1950, Box 35, Folder 415, CVWP.

14. CVW, "Emory Landlubber Goes to Sea," *Atlanta Journal*, September 8, 1929, 7.

15. CVW, interview by John Herbert Roper, October 12, 1980, Roper Papers.

16. CVW interview; CVW, interview by Roper, July 19, 1978, Roper Papers.

17. Comer M. Woodward to Hugh Allison Woodward, February 13, 1926, Box 1, Folder 8, C. M. Woodward Papers.

18. Comer M. Woodward to Hugh Allison Woodward, February 27, 1926, Box 1, Folder 8, C. M. Woodward Papers.

19. Hugh Allison Woodward to Comer M. Woodward, February 28, 1926, Box 1, Folder 8, C. M. Woodward Papers.

20. Comer M. Woodward to Hugh Allison Woodward, March 1926, Box 1, Folder 8, C. M. Woodward Papers.

CHAPTER 2

1. "Emory University," *New Georgia Encyclopedia*, last edited November 5, 2015, www.georgiaencyclopedia.org/articles/education/emory-university (accessed March 18, 2019); "Emory History and Traditions," Emory University, www.emory.edu/home/about/history/index.html (accessed March 18, 2019).

2. "Emory Enrollment 1,008; Grades Better Than 1928: Addition of New Upper Classmen Offsets Loss of Many Deficient Freshmen," *Atlanta Constitution*, January 26, 1930, 3A.

3. CVW, interview by John Herbert Roper, October 12, 1980, Roper Papers; John Herbert Roper, *C. Vann Woodward, Southerner* (Athens: University of Georgia Press, 1987), 46.

4. Leroy E. Loemker, interview by Roper, August 11, 1979, Roper Papers.

5. CVW to David Riesman, March 11, 1962, Box 47, Folder 551, CVWP; Roper, *C. Vann Woodward*, 319, n. 17.

6. Roper, *C. Vann Woodward*, 319, n. 17.

7. Roper, 30–41; "Brief Abandon" is quoted in Minnie Hite Moody, "On the Death of a Young Poet: The Work of Ernest Hartsock," *Sewanee Review* 39 (July–September 1931): 363.

8. Hartsock to Glenn W. Rainey, "Thursday night," Box 6, Folder 6, Rainey Papers.

9. CVW to H. A. Woodward, Sunday evening, n.d. [Spring 1930?], Box 60, Folder 732, CVWP.

10. CVW to Rainey, November 10, 1930, Box 6, Folder 8, Rainey Papers.

11. CVW to Rainey, November 10, 1930, and CVW telegram to Rainey, December 14, 1930, Box 6, Folder 8, Rainey Papers.

12. CVW to Rainey, February 19, 1931, Box 6, Folder 8, Rainey Papers.

13. Rainey to CVW, September 16, 1929, Box 6, Folder 11, Rainey Papers; CVW to Rainey, "Tuesday" [July 1933], Box 6, Folder 9, Rainey Papers.

14. Rainey, interview by Roper, March 25, 27, 1980, Roper Papers; CVW, interview by Roper, April 13, 1979, Roper Papers.

15. CVW to Rainey, February 19, 1931.

16. CVW to Rainey, May 11, 1931, Box 6, Folder 8, Rainey Papers.

17. CVW to Rainey, May 11, 1931.

18. CVW to Rainey, October 20, 1931, Box 6, Folder 8, Rainey Papers.

19. CVW to Rainey, October 20, 1931, and CVW to Comer M. Woodward, n.d. [1931?], Box 1, Folder 8, C. M. Woodward Papers.

20. CVW to Comer M. Woodward, October 20, 1931, Box 1, Folder 8, C. M. Woodward Papers.

21. CVW to Rainey, October 20, 1931, Box 6, Folder 8, Rainey Papers; unknown Rhodes Committee member to CVW, December 14, 1931, Box 46, Folder 534, CVWP.

22. CVW to Rainey, April, n.d. [1932?], Box 6, Folder 9, GWRP; CVW, "J. Thomas Heflin, the Nativist" (MA thesis, Columbia University, 1932), 105–6.

23. CVW, "J. Thomas Heflin," 108, 107, 135.

24. CVW to Rainey, January 28, 1932, Box 6, Folder 8, Rainey Papers; CVW to Rainey, "Tuesday," 1932, Box 6, Folder 9, GWRP.

25. CVW to Rainey, September 17, [1931], Box 6, Folder 9, Rainey Papers; CVW to Rainey, October 20, 1931, Box 6, Folder 8, Rainey Papers.

26. CVW to Rainey, "Tuesday," April 1932 (after April 17, based on Rainey's letter to which CVW was responding), Box 6, Folder 9, Rainey Papers.

27. CVW to Rainey, "Tuesday," April 1932; Michael O'Brien, ed., *The Letters of C. Vann Woodward* (New Haven, Conn.: Yale University Press, 2013), 21, n. 48.

28. CVW to Rainey, August 11, [1932], Box 6, Folder 8, Rainey Papers; "Four Days on the Volga," *Atlanta Journal*, undated clipping, Box 90, Folder 8, CVWP.

29. CVW interview, April 13, 1979.

30. James Green, "Past and Present in Southern History: An Interview with C. Vann Woodward," *Radical History Review* 36 (1986): 85; "Ask Free Speech for Reds," *New York Times*, August 4, 1930, https://timesmachine.nytimes.com/timesmachine/1930/08/04/102142984.html?pageNumber=4 (accessed March 1, 2020).

31. Charles H. Martin, *The Angelo Herndon Case and Southern Justice* (Baton Rouge: Louisiana State University Press, 1976), 7, 196.

32. Green, "Past and Present," 85; CVW, interview by Roper, July 18, 1978, Roper Papers; CVW, interview by John Egerton, January 12, 1991, Interview A-0341, Southern Oral History Program Collection (#4007), https://docsouth.unc.edu/sohp/html_use /A-0341.html/ (accessed March 20, 2019).

33. CVW to Rainey, "Friday night," [1933], Box 6, Folder 9, Rainey Papers.

34. CVW, *Tom Watson: Agrarian Rebel* (New York: Macmillan, 1938), 298.

35. CVW to Rainey, "Tuesday," [July 1933], Box 6, Folder 9, Rainey Papers.

36. "Monday, September," [1933], Box 6, Folder 9, Rainey Papers.

37. CVW to Rainey, [late June 1930], Box 6, Folder 9, Rainey Papers. Though it is un- dated, this letter could not have been written in 1934, because in it CVW asks Rainey to pass on his regards to Ernest Hartsock, who died in December 1930. To further confirm the date of this letter, see Rainey to CVW, July 1, 1930, Box 6, Folder 11, Rainey Papers. CVW placed this meeting in 1934 in his memoir: *Thinking Back: The Perils of Writing History* (Baton Rouge: Louisiana State University Press, 1986), 20. Apparently, based on an inter- view with CVW, John Herbert Roper does the same; see Roper, *C. Vann Woodward*, 77–78.

38. CVW to Rainey, [late June 1930].

39. Howard W. Odum to Will Alexander, October 11, 1933, Folder 331, Odum Papers.

40. Alexander to Odum, October 12, 18, 1933, and Odum to Alexander, October 20, 1933, Folder 331, Odum Papers.

41. CVW to Rainey, "Friday," [October 1933], Box 6, Folder 9, Rainey Papers.

42. CVW to Rainey, "Friday," [October 1933].

43. Odum to Jackson Davis, December 5, 1933, Folder 334, Odum Papers.

44. CVW to Rainey, April 1, May 21, 1934, Box 6, Folder 8, Rainey Papers.

45. Davis to Odum, May 29, 1934, and Odum to Davis, June 8, 1934, Folder 336, Odum Papers; CVW to Rainey, n.d. [early June 1934], Box 6, Folder 9, Rainey Papers; CVW to Rainey, June 17, 1934, Box 6, Folder 8, Rainey Papers.

46. CVW to Rainey, June 17, 1934.

47. Georgia Watson Craven to Roper, July 28, 1978, Roper Papers; CVW to Georgia Watson, October 3, 1933, Roper Papers.

48. CVW to Rainey, "Friday," [October 1933].

49. CVW to Rainey, April 1, May 11, 1934, Box 6, Folder 8, Rainey Papers.

50. CVW, *Thinking Back*, 22.

CHAPTER 3

1. CVW, *Thinking Back: The Perils of Writing History* (Baton Rouge: Louisiana State University Press, 1986), 21.

2. E. Merton Coulter, "What the South Has Done about Its History," in *The Pursuit of Southern History: Presidential Addresses of the Southern Historical Association, 1935–1963*, ed. George B. Tindall (Baton Rouge: Louisiana State University Press, 1964), 14–17.

3. William E. Dodd, "Some Difficulties of the History Teacher in the South," *South Atlantic Quarterly* 3 (April 1904): 119; David W. Blight, *Race and Reunion: The Civil War in American Memory* (Cambridge, Mass.: Harvard University Press, 2001), 296.

4. Peter Novick, *That Noble Dream: The "Objectivity Question" and the American Histori- cal Profession* (Cambridge: Cambridge University Press, 1988), 80.

5. Phillip Alexander Bruce, *The Rise of the New South* (Philadelphia: George Barrie's Sons, 1905), v–vi; Paul M. Gaston, "The New South," in *Writing Southern History: Essays in Historiography in Honor of Fletcher M. Green*, ed. Arthur S. Link and Rembert W. Patrick (Baton Rouge: Louisiana State University Press, 1965), 318–19, 321.

6. Coulter, "What the South Has Done about Its History," 3–22; Frank L. Owsley, "The Fundamental Cause of the Civil War, Egocentric Sectionalism," *Journal of Southern History* 7 (February 1941): 3–18; A. B. Moore, "One Hundred Years of Reconstruction of the South," *Journal of Southern History* 8 (February 1942): 3–22; B. B. Kendrick, "The Colonial Status of the South," *Journal of Southern History* 9 (May 1943): 153–80; H. C. Nixon, "Paths to the Past: The Presidential Addresses of the Southern Historical Association," *Journal of Southern History* 16 (February 1950): 35–38.

7. CVW, *Thinking Back*, 22; Fred Hobson, *Tell about the South: The Southern Rage to Explain* (Baton Rouge: Louisiana State University Press, 1983), 190.

8. Rupert B. Vance, *Human Geography of the South: A Study in Regional Resources and Human Adequacy*, 2nd ed. (Chapel Hill: University of North Carolina Press, 1935), 22; George B. Tindall et al., "Rupert Bayless Vance, March 15, 1899–August 25, 1975," A Memorial Presented to the Faculty Council of the University of North Carolina at Chapel Hill, October 17, 1975 (copy in author's possession).

9. J. Carlyle Sitterson, interview by Dewey Grantham, August 14, 1981, May 24, 1983, Interview L-0087, Southern Oral History Program Collection, Southern Historical Collection, University of North Carolina at Chapel Hill; Bennett H. Wall, interview by John Herbert Roper, April 11, 1979, Roper Papers; CVW, *Tom Watson: Agrarian Rebel* (New York: Macmillan, 1938), ix.

10. Richard H. King, *A Southern Renaissance: The Cultural Awakening of the American South, 1930–1955* (New York: Oxford University Press, 1980), 258–59; CVW, *Thinking Back*, 22–23.

11. CVW, *Thinking Back*, 21–23.

12. CVW to Glenn W. Rainey, October 27, 1934, Box 6, Folder 8, Rainey Papers.

13. CVW to Rainey, October 27, 1934, and CVW to Rainey, "Sunday, Chapel Hill," [1934, after the previous letter], Box 6, Folder 9, Rainey Papers.

14. CVW to Rainey, February 4, 1935 [incorrectly dated as 1934], Box 6, Folder 8, Rainey Papers.

15. CVW to Rainey, September 24, 1934, April 29, 1935, Box 6, Folder 8, Rainey Papers.

16. CVW to Rainey, October 27, 1934, Box 6, Folder 8, Rainey Papers. On their discussions of writing a novel, see Rainey to CVW, March 22, 1931, Box 6, Folder 11, Rainey Papers.

17. CVW to Rainey, October 27, 1934.

18. CVW to Rainey, April 13, 1936, Box 6, Folder 8, Rainey Papers.

19. CVW to Rainey, October 2, 1938, July 12, 1936, Box 6, Folder 8, Rainey Papers; CVW to Rainey, October 27, [1934], Box 6, Folder 9, Rainey Papers.

20. CVW to David Entin, February 25, 1963, Box 17, Folder 185, CVWP; CVW to Rainey, September 24, 1934, Box 6, Folder 7, Rainey Papers.

21. CVW to Rainey, March 3, 1935, and "Speaking the Campus Mind," undated clipping [late February/early March], 1935, *Daily Tar Heel* (UNC), Box 6, Folder 9, Rainey Papers.

22. "Speaking the Campus Mind."

23. CVW to Rainey, March 3, 1935.

24. CVW to Rainey, July 2, 1936, Box 6, Folder 8, GWRP. "STFU" refers to the Southern Tenant Farmers' Union.

25. Wall interview.

26. Sitterson interview.

27. George B. Tindall to Roper, October 24, 1978, Roper Papers.

28. "Food for Thought," typescript, n.d., Roper Papers.

29. CVW to Rainey, May 17, 1936, Box 6, Folder 8, Rainey Papers.

30. "Vann Woodward, written Ph.D. exam, May 1936," Beale Papers; Sitterson, interview by Roper, November 10, 1979, Roper Papers.

31. CVW to Rainey, July 2, 1936.

32. CVW, *Tom Watson*, ix; CVW to Rainey, May 7, 1937, Box 6, Folder 8, Rainey Papers.

33. CVW to "Jack," July 15, 1937, Box 6, Folder 10, Rainey Papers; CVW to Rainey, May 7, September 11, 1937, Box 6, Folder 8, Rainey Papers.

34. CVW to Rainey, [late July] 1937, Box 6, Folder 9, Rainey Papers.

35. Harold S. Latham to CVW, September 7, 1937, Box 35, Folder 411, CVWP; CVW to Rainey, September 11, 1937, Box 6, Folder 8, Rainey Papers.

36. CVW to Rainey, September 11, 1937, and Rupert Vance to CVW, April 13, 1938, Box 57, Folder 684, CVWP; CVW to Howard W. Odum, October 14, 1939, Box 39, Folder 475, CVWP.

37. CVW to Georgia Watson, October 3, 1933, Roper Papers; CVW to Rainey, "Friday" [October 6, 1933], August 24, [1934], Box 6, Folder 9, Rainey Papers; CVW to Rainey, April 13, 1936, November 8, 1937, Box 6, Folder 8, Rainey Papers; Beale to CVW, October 8, 1937, Box 3, Folder 1, Department of History of the University of North Carolina at Chapel Hill Records, University Archives, Wilson Library, University of North Carolina at Chapel Hill.

38. CVW to Rainey, October 27, 1937, Box 6, Folder 8, Rainey Papers.

39. CVW to Rainey, October 27, 1937, January 10, 1938, Box 6, Folder 8, Rainey Papers.

40. CVW to Antonina Jones Hansell, September 2, 1934, April 7, 1935, Looker Papers.

41. CVW to Hansell, September 25, 1935, Looker Papers.

42. CVW to Hansell, August 29, 1936, n.d. [December 1936?], Looker Papers.

43. CVW to Hansell, May 6, 1936, Looker Papers.

44. CVW to Hansell, November 7, 1937, Looker Papers; CVW, interviews by Roper, April 13, 1979, October 12, 1980, Roper Papers.

45. CVW to Rainey, January 10, 1938, Box 6, Folder 8, Rainey Papers.

CHAPTER 4

1. CVW to Glenn W. Rainey, "Tuesday" [July 1933], Box 6, Folder 9, Rainey Papers.

2. Thomas E. Watson, *Bethany: A Story of the Old South* (New York: D. Appleton, 1905).

3. Columbia County, Georgia, largest slaveholders from 1860 slave census schedules and surname matches for African Americans on 1870 census, transcribed by Tom Blake, February 2002, http://freepages.genealogy.rootsweb.ancestry.com/~ajac/gacolumbia.htm/ (accessed January 16, 2018); CVW has him owning only forty-five slaves.

4. CVW, *Tom Watson: Agrarian Rebel* (New York: Macmillan, 1938), 5–6, 13; Watson, *Bethany*, 10–19, is quoted on p. 6.

5. Julie Beck, "When Nostalgia Was a Disease," *Atlantic*, August 14, 2013, www.theatlantic.com/health/archive/2013/08/when-nostalgia-was-a-disease/278648/ (accessed April 2, 2019).

6. CVW, *Tom Watson*, 27, 42–43, 98.

7. CVW, *Tom Watson*, 17–18; Bertram Wyatt-Brown, "Tom Watson Revisited," *Journal of Southern History* 68 (February 2002): 3–30.

8. CVW, *Tom Watson*, 218, 404, 402, 348; Staughton Lynd, "Beard, Jefferson and the Tree of Liberty," *Midcontinent American Studies Journal* 9 (Spring 1968): 9.

9. Howard K. Beale, *The Critical Year: A Study of Andrew Johnson and Reconstruction* (New York: Harcourt, Brace, 1930), 2; CVW, *Tom Watson*, 53, 217–18.

10. CVW, *Tom Watson*, 39.

11. CVW, *Tom Watson*, 69, 124–25, 348.

12. Charles Crowe, "Tom Watson, Populists, and Blacks Reconsidered," *Journal of Negro History* 55 (April 1970): 103, 166, 219; CVW to Rainey, November 9, 1938, Box 6, Folder 8, Rainey Papers.

13. Rainey to CVW, January 30, 1935, Box 6, Folder 11, Rainey Papers; CVW to Rainey, February 5, 1935, Box 6, Folder 8, Rainey Papers.

14. CVW to Boulware Martin, July 19, [1931], Box 35, Folder 415, CVWP.

15. CVW to Rainey, October 27, 1939, Box 6, Folder 8, Rainey Papers; CVW to Rainey, "Friday," [early October 1933], Box 6, Folder 9, Rainey Papers.

16. CVW, *Tom Watson*, 221; Beale to Woodward, December 14, 1937, Box 7, Folder 65, CVWP.

17. CVW, *Tom Watson*, 221, 231, 220; CVW to Rainey, March 9, 1938, Box 6, Folder 8, Rainey Papers.

18. CVW, *Tom Watson*, 222, 239.

19. CVW, *Tom Watson*, 239–41. See also "Watson Rebuked," *Atlanta Constitution*, October 31, 1892, 4.

20. CVW, *Tom Watson*, 241–42; *Contested Election of Thomas E. Watson vs. J. C. C. Black: From the Tenth Congressional District of Georgia, United States Congress, House* (Washington, D.C.: Government Printing Office, 1896), 781, 793, https://catalog.hathitrust.org/Record/008679524 (accessed December 9, 2016).

21. *Contested Election*, 683–84.

22. Barton C. Shaw, *The Wool-Hat Boys: Georgia's Populist Party* (Baton Rouge: Louisiana State University Press, 1984), 84–87; CVW, *Tom Watson*, 241; *Contested Election*, 264, 286–87.

23. Wyatt-Brown, "Tom Watson Revisited," 9.

24. CVW, *Tom Watson*, 402, quoting Thomas E. Watson, "The Negro Question," *Watson's Jeffersonian Magazine* 1 (November 1907): 1032–40. In the original text, Watson actually described "the Negro" as the "menace" rather than "Negro domination." See also Thomas E. Watson, "The Hearst Paper, the Egyptian Sphinx, and the Negro," *Watson's Jeffersonian Magazine*, February 3, 1909, 97.

25. CVW, *Tom Watson*, 371, 221, 432.

26. Rainey to CVW, February 12, 1938, Box 6, Folder 11, Rainey Papers.

27. CVW to Rainey, March 9, 1938 [dated incorrectly as 1937], Box 6, Folder 8, Rainey Papers.

28. Watson is quoted in Robert M. Saunders, "The Transformation of Tom Watson, 1894–1895," *Georgia Historical Quarterly* 54 (Fall 1970): 352, 356, n. 93; CVW, *Tom Watson*,

371; Charles Postel, *The Populist Vision* (New York: Oxford University Press, 2007), 19. See also Shaw, *Wool-Hat Boys*, 87.

29. CVW, *Tom Watson*, 371–72, 220; Watson, "Negro Question," 1035–36. See also Corey J. Cantrell, "A Man of His Time: Tom Watson's New South Bigotry" (MA thesis, Georgia State University, 2014), 24–25, http://scholarworks.gsu.edu/history_theses /79/ (accessed January 9, 2017).

30. CVW, *Tom Watson*, 384.

31. CVW, *Tom Watson*, 395.

32. CVW, *Tom Watson*, 425, 433–34.

33. Wyatt-Brown, "Tom Watson," 27; Shaw, *Wool-Hat Boys*, 198; CVW, *Tom Watson*, 433–34.

34. CVW, *Tom Watson*, 335–42.

35. CVW, *Tom Watson*, 403, 417–18, 433, 431.

36. CVW, *Tom Watson*, 418–23.

37. CVW, *Tom Watson*, 419–20, 423–24. See also Shaw, *Wool-Hat Boys*, 121–22; Justin Nordstrom, *Danger on the Doorstep: Anti-Catholicism and American Print Culture in the Progressive Era* (Notre Dame, Ind.: University of Notre Dame Press, 2006), 56–57; CVW, *Tom Watson*, 420; and Watson to John N. Taylor, October 5, 1910, Folder 111, Thomas E. Watson Papers, Digital Collection, Southern Historical Collection, Wilson Library, University of North Carolina at Chapel Hill (available online at https://docsouth.unc.edu /watson/).

38. Nordstrom, *Danger on the Doorstep*, 56–57; CVW, *Tom Watson*, 424–25, 434.

39. CVW, *Tom Watson*, 436–38.

40. CVW, *Tom Watson*, 438.

41. CVW, *Tom Watson*, 443, 439.

42. CVW, *Tom Watson*, 446, 450. Woodward mistakenly placed this ceremonial rebirth "on a summer night in 1915."

43. CVW, *Tom Watson*, 442; Thomas Loyless, "Editorial," *Augusta Chronicle*, September 12, 1915, quoted in CVW, *Tom Watson*, 442.

44. CVW, *Tom Watson*, 442.

45. CVW, *Tom Watson*, 449.

46. CVW, *Tom Watson*, 473.

47. CVW, *Tom Watson*, 483–85, 485.

48. CVW, *Tom Watson*, vii; Beale to Woodward, October 8, 1937, Box 3, Folder 1, Department of History of the University of North Carolina at Chapel Hill Records, University Archives, Wilson Library, University of North Carolina at Chapel Hill.

49. CVW, *Tom Watson*, 18, 344–45.

50. CVW, *Tom Watson*, 346, 395, 444.

51. "'Tom' Watson," *New York Times*, September 27, 1922, 13, https://timesmachine .nytimes.com/timesmachine/1922/09/27/99080335.html?pageNumber=13; CVW, *Tom Watson*, 486, viii.

52. CVW, *Tom Watson*, vii, viii.

53. CVW to F. M. Reeves, April 22, 1940, CVWP.

54. "Song Memorial in Honor of Thomas E. Watson," Folder 569, Thomas E. Watson Papers, https://docsouth.unc.edu/watson/ (accessed June 24, 2019); Wendell Holmes Stephenson to CVW, January 5, 1938, Box 29, Folder 339, CVWP; CVW, "Tom Watson and the Negro in Agrarian Politics," *Journal of Southern History* 4 (February 1938): 33.

55. Woodward, *Thinking Back*, 34; CVW to Rainey, "Friday" [October 1933], Box 6, Folder 9, Rainey Papers; CVW to Rainey, October 27, 1937, Box 6, Folder 8, Rainey Papers.

56. CVW to Rainey, "Friday," [Fall 1937], Box 6, Folder 9, Rainey Papers; CVW to Rainey, October 27, 1937, Box 6, Folder 8, Rainey Papers; William Doerflinger to CVW, October 23, 1937, Box 35, Folder 411, CVWP; John D. Hicks, review of *Tom Watson: Agrarian Rebel*, by CVW, *Journal of Southern History* 4 (November 1938): 539.

57. CVW to Rainey, December 4, 1942, November 8, 1937, Box 6, Folder 8, Rainey Papers.

58. Gerald W. Johnson, "Vinegar Tree," *New Republic*, April 20, 1938, 338. See the review of *Tom Watson: Agrarian Rebel* by Alex Mathews Arnett in *American Historical Review* 44 (April 1939): 661–62; and Hicks, review of *Tom Watson*, 539. See also John D. Hicks, *The Populist Revolt: A History of the Farmers' Alliance and the People's Party* (Minneapolis: University of Minnesota Press, 1931).

59. CVW to Rainey, January 10, 1938, Box 6, Folder 8, Rainey Papers; Allan Nevins, *Grover Cleveland: A Study in Courage* (New York: Dodd, Mead, 1933), 594; CVW, *Tom Watson*, 157, n. 32; Nevins, "Tom Watson and the New South: Crucial Economic, Social and Political History Is Reflected in His Career," *New York Times Book Review*, April 3, 1938, 1, 26.

60. Frank L. Owsley, review of *Tom Watson: Agrarian Rebel*, by CVW, *Mississippi Valley Historical Review* 25 (December 1938): 431–32. See also Shaw, *Wool-Hat Boys*, 209.

61. CVW, *Thinking Back*, 29–30.

62. CVW, *Thinking Back*, 42.

63. CVW to Antonina Jones Hansell, April 11, 1938, Looker Papers.

CHAPTER 5

1. Howard K. Beale to CVW, December 14, 1937, January 8, November 11, 1938, Box 7, Folder 65, CVWP.

2. Glenn W. Rainey to CVW, October 11, 1938, Box 6, Folder 11, Rainey Papers; Beale to CVW, December 6, 1938, Box 7, Folder 65, CVWP.

3. CVW to Rainey, February 13, 1938, March 26, 1939, Box 6, Folder 8, Rainey Papers; CVW to Henry Steele Commager, March 4, 1939, Box 12, Folder 136, CVWP.

4. H. G. Askew, J. M. Brown, and W. B. Walker to George W. Littlefield, May 3, 1913, Box 3A93, George W. Littlefield Papers, Center for American History, University of Texas at Austin.

5. "Schedule I, Quotations of Terms of Gift or Bequest of Certain Trust Funds Given to or Handled by the University of Texas," Box 2, Folder 104, "Correspondence, Classified, 1945–1952 and undated," Eugene C. Barker Papers, Dolph Briscoe Center for American History, University of Texas at Austin.

6. "Editor's Preface," Box 45, Folder "A History of the South Series, 1942–1951, undated," Stephenson Papers.

7. Helen F. Coleman to Wendell H. Stephenson, October 19, 1939, Box 3N04, Ramsdell Papers.

8. Thomas Abernethy is quoted in Fred Arthur Bailey, "Thomas Perkins Abernethy: Defender of Aristocratic Virtue," *Alabama Review* 45 (April 1992): 89.

9. Stephenson to Charles William Ramsdell, January 3, May 20, 1938, Box 3N292, Ramsdell Papers.

10. Ramsdell to Stephenson, May 25, 1938, Box 3N292, Ramsdell Papers.

11. B. B. Kendrick to Ramsdell, February 11, 1939, and Stephenson to Ramsdell, January 23, 1939, Box 3No3, Ramsdell Papers; Francis B. Simkins, "New Viewpoints of Southern Reconstruction," *Journal of Southern History* 5 (February 1938): 58.

12. "Editor's Preface"; Stephenson to Ramsdell, January 3, 1938, Box 3N292, Ramsdell Papers.

13. Ramsdell to Stephenson, January 29, 1930, Ramsdell to Kendrick, January 30, 1939, and Stephenson to Ramsdell, January 23, 1939, Box 3N303, Ramsdell Papers.

14. Kendrick to Ramsdell, January 16, 23, 1939, Ramsdell to Kendrick, January 20, 1939, Albert R. Newsome to Ramsdell, February 15, 1939, Ramsdell to Stephenson, January 20, 1939, and Stephenson to Ramsdell, January 23, 1939, Box 3N303, Ramsdell Papers.

15. Ramsdell to Kendrick, February 7, 1939, Kendrick to Ramsdell, February 11, 1939, and Ramsdell to Stephenson, January 31, 1939, Box 3No3, Ramsdell Papers; Stephenson to E. Merton Coulter, February 12, 1939, and Coulter to Stephenson, February 15, 1939, Box 55, Folder "Coulter, E. Merton, 1934–1941, undated," Stephenson Papers.

16. Holland Thompson, *The New South: A Chronicle of Social and Industrial Evolution* (New Haven, Conn.: Yale University Press, 1921), 25; Ramsdell to Stephenson, February 20, March 8, 1939, Box 3No3, Ramsdell Papers.

17. "Statement of Royalty Account," H. S. Latham to CVW, March 24, 1939, Box 35, Folder 411, CVWP; B. Ramsdell to CVW, March 6, 1939, and CVW to Ramsdell, March 11, 1939, Box 3N303, Ramsdell Papers; CVW to Rainey, March 26, 1939, Box 6, Folder 8, Rainey Papers.

18. CVW, *Thinking Back: The Perils of Writing History* (Baton Rouge: Louisiana State University Press, 1986), 38; CVW, "The South in Search of a Philosophy," in *Phi Beta Kappa Addresses at the University of Florida*, vol. 1 (1938), 10–11, 17, 16, 18–20. For Woodward's almost solicitous attitude toward the Agrarians, see his letter to Donald Davidson after Davidson took him to task for mischaracterizing their perspective. CVW to Donald Davidson, November 15, 1939, Box 14, Folder 153, CVWP.

19. Herman Clarence Nixon, *Forty Acres and Steel Mules* (Chapel Hill: University of North Carolina Press, 1938), 9, 31–32; CVW, "Hillbilly Realism," *Southern Review* 4 (Spring 1939): 676.

20. CVW to Howard Beale, February 18, 1941, Box 26, Folder 5, Beale Papers; CVW to William G. Carleton, n.d. ["Sunday, March ?, 1940"], Carleton Papers.

21. CVW to Rainey, March 26, May 25, 1939, Box 6, Folder 8, Rainey Papers.

22. CVW to Ramsdell, August 30, 1939; "Origins of the New South, 1880–1913," typescript, Box 70, Folder 102, CVWP.

23. CVW to Rainey, December 10, 1939, Box 6, Folder 8, Rainey Papers; CVW, "Statement in Favor of Abolishing Poll Taxes," *Congressional Digest* 20 (1941): 309–10.

24. CVW to Beale, April 28, 1938, and Beale to CVW, January 8, March 31, April 22, June 8, 1938, Box 7, Folder 65, CVWP; CVW to Rainey, June 12, 1938, Box 6, Folder 8, Rainey Papers.

25. Beale to CVW, November 11, 1938, Box 7, Folder 65, CVWP.

26. CVW to Beale, April 1, 1940, Box 7, Folder 66, CVWP.

27. CVW to Beale, April 1, May 2, 30, 1940, Box 7, Folder 66, CVWP.

28. Howard W. Odum to CVW, October 16, 1939, April 12, 1940, and CVW to Odum, May 30, 1940, Box 39, Folder 475, CVWP.

29. CVW to Beale, November 16, December 15, 1940, Box 7, Folder 66, CVWP.

30. Beale to CVW, November 28, 1940, Box 7, Folder 66, CVWP.

31. "A History of Scripps College Presidents: Ernest J. Jaqua, 1926–1942," Scripps, www .scrippscollege.edu/president/history/ernest-jaqua/ (accessed April 15, 2019); CVW to Beale, February 12, 18, 1941, Box 26, Folder 5, Beale Papers; Beale to CVW, January 26, 1942, Box 7, Folder 67, CVWP.

32. CVW to Rainey, October 28, 1941, Box 6, Folder 8, Rainey Papers; CVW to Beale, December 15, 1940, Box 7, Folder 66, CVWP; CVW to Beale, March 15, May 9, October 20, 1941, Box 26, Folder 5, Beale Papers.

33. CVW to Beale, December 6, 1941, Box 26, Folder 5, Beale Papers.

34. CVW to Beale, December 24, 1941, Box 26, Folder 5, Beale Papers.

35. U.S. Naval Intelligence Service, 11th Naval District, investigation report, March 7, 1944, Woodward, Comer Vann, Lieutenant j.g., A-V(s), copy acquired under the Freedom of Information Act, in author's possession; Philipp Gassert, "Between Political Reconnaissance Work and Democratizing Science: American Studies in Germany, 1917–1953," *Bulletin of the German Historical Institute* 32 (Spring 2003): 34, www.ghidc .org/fileadmin/publications/Bulletin/bu32.pdf (accessed April 15, 2019).

36. "Keith Powell Post No. 78 to the Parents of Scripps College Students, April 10, 1942," is quoted in Sebastian Liebold, "Arnold Bergstraesser und Fritz Caspari in Amerika," in *Intellektuelle Emigration: Zur Aktualität eines historischen Phänomens*, ed. Frank Schale, Ellen Thümmler, and Michael Vollmer (Wiesbaden: Springer VS, 2012), https://link .springer.com/chapter/10.1007/978-3-531-19658-9_4/ (accessed October 12, 2018).

37. CVW to Rainey, June 27, 1942, Box 6, Folder 8, Rainey Papers.

38. CVW to Rainey, June 27, 1942; CVW to Beale, June 7, 1942, Box 26, Folder 5, Beale Papers; "Dr. Ernest J. Jaqua of Scripps College," *New York Times*, July 28, 1972, 35, https://timesmachine.nytimes.com/timesmachine/1972/07/28/83450269.html (accessed November 10, 2017).

39. CVW to Rainey, October 19, 1942, Box 6, Folder 8, Rainey Papers.

40. CVW to Stephenson, October 13, 1942, Box 61, Folder "History of the South Series, 1937–1943, undated," Stephenson Papers.

41. CVW to Stephenson, October 13, 1942; CVW to Rainey, June 27, 1942; Beale to CVW, February 13, 1942, Box 7, Folder 67, CVWP.

42. CVW to Rainey, April 4, 1943, Box 6, Folder 8, Rainey Papers.

43. CVW to Rainey, April 4, 1943.

44. CVW to Rainey, July 13, 1943, Box 6, Folder 8, Rainey Papers; CVW, *Thinking Back*, 46.

45. CVW to Rainey, May 7, 1944, Box 6, Folder 8, Rainey Papers; CVW, *The Battle for Leyte Gulf* (New York: Macmillan, 1947).

46. CVW to E. Merton Coulter, December 24, 1944, Box 7, Folder 1, "Coulter, E. Merton, 1942–1967," Stephenson Papers.

47. CVW to Stephenson, January 23, 1945, January 23, September 14, November 27, 1946, and Stephenson to CVW, January 18, 1946, Box 36, Folder "C. Vann Woodward (1944–1956)," Stephenson Papers.

48. CVW, *Thinking Back*, 47; Stephenson to CVW, June 23, 1947, and CVW to Stephenson, July 2, 1947, October 20, 1947, Box 36, Folder "C. Vann Woodward, 1944–1956," Stephenson Papers.

49. CVW to Stephenson, July 8, 1949, Box 36, Folder "C. Vann Woodward (1944–1956)," Stephenson Papers.

50. CVW to Stephenson, July 8, 23, 1949, Box 36, Folder "C. Vann Woodward (1944–1956)," Stephenson Papers.

51. Stephenson to CVW, August 3, 1949, Box 36, Folder "C. Vann Woodward (1944–1956)," Stephenson Papers.

52. CVW to Stephenson, August 23, 1949, Box 36, Folder "C. Vann Woodward (1944–1956)," Stephenson Papers.

CHAPTER 6

1. CVW to Stanley Salmen, May 19, 1950, Box 71, Folder 109, CVWP.

2. CVW to Salmen, May 19, 1950.

3. CVW to Salmen, May 19, 1950; CVW to Manning J. Dauer, July 11, 1950, Box 71, Folder 109, CVWP.

4. CVW to Angus Cameron, July 4, 1950, Box 71, Folder 109, CVWP; CVW, *Reunion and Reaction: The Compromise of 1877 and the End of Reconstruction and the Compromise of 1877* (Boston: Little, Brown, 1951); CVW, *Origins of the New South, 1877–1913* (Baton Rouge: Louisiana State University Press, 1951).

5. CVW, *Reunion*, 215. See Charles A. and Mary R. Beard, *The Rise of American Civilization*, 2 vols. (New York: Macmillan, 1927).

6. Charles A. Beard to CVW, September 20, 1938, Box 7, Folder 70, CVWP. The Watson book was also noted favorably in Charles A. Beard and Mary Beard, *America in Midpassage* (New York: Macmillan, 1939), 917; James P. Philbin, "Charles Austen Beard: Liberal Foe of American Internationalism," *Humanitas* 13, no. 2 (2000): 95, 99, https://css.cua.edu /wp-content/uploads/2018/01/philbin13-2.pdf (accessed April 22, 2019); Peter Novick, *That Noble Dream: The "Objectivity Question" and the American Historical Profession* (Cambridge: Cambridge University Press, 1988), 291–92; CVW, *Reunion*, ix.

7. CVW, *Thinking Back: The Perils of Writing History* (Baton Rouge: Louisiana State University Press, 1986), 55–56.

8. CVW to Glenn W. Rainey, December 4, 1942, Box 6, Folder 8, Rainey Papers. See Samuel Eliot Morison and Henry Steele Commager, *The Growth of the American Republic*, vol. 1 (New York: Oxford University Press, 1942), 277.

9. Rainey to CVW, November 14, 1942, Box 6, Folder 11, Rainey Papers.

10. CVW, *Reunion*, 3–4; Howard K. Beale, *The Critical Year: A Study of Andrew Johnson and Reconstruction* (New York: Harcourt, Brace, 1930), 1, 225.

11. CVW, *Reunion*, 12–15, 240.

12. CVW to Cameron, July 14, 1950, Box 71, Folder 109, CVWP; CVW, *Reunion*, 53.

13. Michael Les Benedict, "Southern Democrats in the Crisis of 1876–1877: A Reconsideration of Reunion and Reaction," *Journal of Southern History* 46 (November 1980): 490.

14. Dumas Malone, "The Deal That Restored the South," *New York Times Book Review*, May 13, 1951, sec. 7, pp. 1, 22; E. Merton Coulter, "The Great Barbecue," *Saturday Review of Literature*, May 19, 1951, 14.

15. Wallace E. Davies, review of *Reunion and Reaction: The Compromise of 1877 and the End of Reconstruction*, by CVW, *Pennsylvania Magazine of History and Biography* 75 (October 1951): 471; Dan M. Robison, review of *Reunion and Reaction: The Compromise of 1877 and the End of Reconstruction*, by CVW, *Journal of Southern History* 18 (February 1952): 94–95.

16. CVW, *Reunion*, 62, 127; Benedict, "Southern Democrats," 515; *Congressional Record*, 44th Cong., 1st Sess., December 15, 1875 (Washington, D.C.: Government Printing Office,

1875), 227. See also Carl V. Harris, "Right Fork or Left Fork? The Section-Party Alignments of Southern Democrats in Congress, 1873–1897," *Journal of Southern History* 42 (November 1976): 471–506 (note that Harris included Kentucky, Maryland, and West Virginia in the South, whereas CVW used the old Confederacy, plus Kentucky); Terry L. Seip, *The South Returns to Congress: Men, Economic Measures, and Intersectional Relationships, 1868–1879* (Baton Rouge: Louisiana State University Press, 1983), 260, n. 51.

17. Irwin Unger, *These United States: The Questions of Our Past*, vol. 2 (Boston: Little, Brown, 1978), 491. See John Morton Blum et al., *The National Experience, Part Two: A History of the United States since 1865*, 5th ed. (New York: Harcourt, Brace, Jovanovich, 1981), 412–16; and CVW, *Thinking Back*, 52.

18. Allan Peskin, "Was There a Compromise of 1877?," *Journal of American History* 60 (June 1973): 65, 72; Keith Ian Polakoff, *The Politics of Inertia: The Election of 1876 and the End of Reconstruction* (Baton Rouge: Louisiana State University Press, 1973), ix–x.

19. Benedict, "Southern Democrats," 515. See also Harris, "Right Fork or Left Fork," 471–506; and Terry L. Seip, *The South Returns to Congress: Men, Economic Measures, and Intersectional Relationships, 1868–1879* (Baton Rouge: Louisiana State University Press, 1983), 260, n. 51. Beale to CVW, October 14, 1950, CVW to Cameron, October 23, 1950, and CVW to Dauer, July 10, 1950 (see Dauer's notes in the margins), Box 71, Folder 109, CVWP; Polakoff, *Politics of Inertia*, 247, 319, 246, n. 49.

20. Benedict, "Southern Democrats," 490, n. 3, 520; Seip, *South Returns*, 262, n. 53; CVW, "Yes, There Was a Compromise of 1877," *Journal of American History* 60, no. 1 (June 1973): 215–23. See also CVW, *Thinking Back*, 53–56.

21. CVW, *Origins*, 20 (emphasis added); CVW, *Thinking Back*, 63.

22. CVW, *Origins*, 172–74.

23. William G. Carleton, interview by John Herbert Roper, July 21, 1979, Roper Papers; Lewis D. Rubin Jr., "W. J. Cash after Fifty Years," *Virginia Quarterly Review* 67 (Spring 1991), www.vqronline.org/essay/wj-cash-after-fifty-years/ (accessed July 24, 2017).

24. CVW, "The Southern Ethic in a Puritan World," *William and Mary Quarterly*, 3rd ser., 25 (July 1968): 363–64.

25. CVW, *Tom Watson*, 56, 62–63; CVW, *Reunion and Reaction*, 13, 40.

26. CVW, *Origins*, 153.

27. CVW, *Origins*, 14; CVW to Carleton, February 17, 1952, Carleton Papers.

28. H. L. Mencken, "The Sahara of the Bozart," in Mencken, *Prejudices: Second Series* (New York: Alfred A. Knopf, 1920), 136–54.

29. H. L. Mencken, "The Calamity of Appomattox," *American Mercury* 21 (September 1930): 29–31; CVW, "New South Fraud Is Papered by Old South Myth," *Washington Post*, July 9, 1961, E3.

30. CVW, *Origins*, 59, 65.

31. CVW, *Origins*, 188, 176–77.

32. CVW, *Origins*, 180, 183.

33. CVW, *Origins*, 180.

34. CVW to Carleton, February 17, 1952, Carleton Papers; CVW, *Origins*, 291.

35. Benjamin B. Kendrick, "The Colonial Status of the South," *Journal of Southern History* 8 (February 1942): 17–18.

36. CVW, *Origins*, 311, 318–19.

37. Gavin Wright, *Old South, New South: Revolutions in the Southern Economy since the Civil War* (New York: Basic Books, 1986), 61–63.

38. CVW to Virginia Durr, June 8, 1951, as quoted in Morton Sosna, *In Search of the Silent South: Southern Liberals and the Race Issue* (New York: Columbia University Press, 1977), 11; Edward L. Ayers, "Narrating the New South," *Journal of Southern History* 61 (August 1995): 564; Karl Marx, "The Eighteenth Brumaire of Louis Bonaparte," *Liberty, Equality, Fraternity*, http://chnm.gmu.edu/revolution/d/580/ (accessed April 25, 2019); David L. Carlton, "The Revolution from Above: The National Market and the Beginnings of Industrialization in North Carolina," *Journal of American History* 77 (September 1990): 449, 474.

39. Ayers, *Narrating the New South*, 564; William N. Parker, "The South in the National Economy, 1865–1970," *Southern Economic Journal* 46 (April 1980): 1045–46.

40. CVW, *Origins*, 22; Bell Irvin Wiley, "A New Dixie for the Few," *New York Times*, December 23, 1951, BR2, https://timesmachine.nytimes.com/timesmachine /1951/12/23/121637515.html?pageNumber=28.

41. CVW to Rainey, December 8, 1942, Box 6, Folder 8, Rainey Papers; Rainey to CVW, November 14, 1942, Box 6, Folder 11, Rainey Papers; Beale to CVW, December 3, 1942, Box 26, Folder 1, Beale Papers.

42. CVW, "New South Fraud"; David Donald, "After Reconstruction," *Nation*, May 17, 1952, 484.

43. CVW, "New South Fraud."

44. CVW, "New South Fraud."

45. CVW to Rainey, July 12, 1936, Box 6, Folder 8, Rainey Papers; James Tice Moore, "Redeemers Reconsidered: Change and Continuity in the Democratic South, 1870–1900," *Journal of Southern History* 44 (August 1978): 357–78. See also Moore, "The Historical Context for 'Redeemers Reconsidered,'" in *Origins of the New South Fifty Years Later: The Continuing Influence of Historical Classic*, ed. John B. Boles and Bethany L. Johnson (Baton Rouge: Louisiana State University Press, 2003), 135.

46. Rupert B. Vance to CVW, August 1, 1949, and Harriet L. Herring to CVW, September 17, 1949, Box 1, Folder 12, Vance Papers; Avery O. Craven, "The South in Critical Days after the Civil War—Debunking Some Legends," *Chicago Tribune*, January 20, 1952, pt. 4, p. 5.

47. Daniel J. Singal, *The War Within: From Victorian to Modernist Thought in the South* (Chapel Hill: University of North Carolina Press, 1982), 374; CVW, *Thinking Back*, 64.

48. Jonathan M. Wiener, *Social Origins of the New South: Alabama, 1865–1885* (Baton Rouge: Louisiana State University Press, 1978); Dwight B. Billings Jr., *Planters and the Making of a "New South": Class, Politics, and Development in North Carolina, 1865–1900* (Chapel Hill: University of North Carolina Press, 1979).

49. Michael O'Brien, "The Nineteenth-Century American South," *Historical Journal* 24 (September 1981): 762; James C. Cobb, "Beyond Planters and Industrialists: A New Perspective on the New South," *Journal of Southern History* 54 (February 1988): 45–68.

50. An example of considering southern development in a global context is Peter A. Coclanis, "Globalization before Globalization: The South and the World to 1950," in *Globalization and the American South*, ed. James C. Cobb and William Stueck (Athens: University of Georgia Press, 2005), 19–35.

51. CVW to Richard L. Wentworth, February 18, 1969, Box 33, Folder 394, CVWP.

52. J. Fred Rippy to E. Merton Coulter, October 24, 1961, Box 34, Folder 5, and Coulter to Rippy, October 25, 1961, Box 48, Folder 5, E. Merton Coulter Manuscripts, Hargrett Rare Book and Manuscript Library, University of Georgia Libraries, Athens.

53. Roger W. Shugg, review of *Origins of the New South, 1877–1913*, by CVW, *Mississippi Valley Historical Review* 39 (June 1952): 142; Dumas Malone, "An Unflinching Picture of the South, from Reconstruction to Wilson," *New York Herald Tribune Book Review*, December 23, 1951, 3; Avery O. Craven, "The South and the Critical Days after the Civil War—Debunking Some Legends," *Chicago Sunday Tribune Magazine of Books*, January 20, 1952, 5; Allen W. Moger, review of *Origins of the New South, 1877–1913*, by CVW, *Journal of Southern History* 18 (November 1952): 519. See also Wiley, "New Dixie," 142; and William B. Hesseltine, review of *Origins of the New South, 1877–1913*, by CVW, *American Historical Review* 57 (July 1952): 994.

CHAPTER 7

1. CVW to the Board of Governors of the Johns Hopkins Club, December 18, 1947, Box 28, Folder 327, CVWP.

2. CVW to William B. Hesseltine, December 8, 1948, Box 51, Folder 603, CVWP.

3. David M. Potter, "An Appraisal of Fifteen Years of the *Journal of Southern History*, 1935–1949," *Journal of Southern History* 16 (February 1950): 27, 31.

4. CVW to H. C. Nixon, February 4, 1949, and H. C. Nixon to CVW, February 9, 1949, Box 51, Folder 604, CVWP.

5. H. C. Nixon, "Paths to the Past: The Presidential Addresses of the Southern Historical Association," *Journal of Southern History* 16 (February 1950): 37, 35.

6. CVW is quoted in Sarah Newman Shouse, *Hillbilly Realist: Herman Clarence Nixon of Possum Trot* (Tuscaloosa: University of Alabama Press, 1986), 164–66. See also Bethany Leigh Johnson, "Regionalism, Race, and the Meaning of the Southern Past: Professional History in the American South, 1896–1961" (PhD diss., Rice University, 2001), 427.

7. Frank Owsley and Benjamin Kendrick are quoted in Johnson, "Regionalism," 394, 401.

8. W. E. B. Du Bois is quoted in Johnson, "Regionalism," 402–3, 405; see also 455–56, nn. 18–22.

9. John Hope Franklin, *Mirror to America: The Autobiography of John Hope Franklin* (New York: Farrar, Straus and Giroux, 2005), 140.

10. Hesseltine to CVW, January 5, 1949, Box 51, Folder 604, CVWP; Vernon Wharton to CVW, December 24, 1948, and Gerald M. Capers to CVW, December 18, 1948, Box 51, Folder 603, CVWP.

11. Lester J. Cappon to CVW, January 28, 1949, Box 51, Folder 604, CVWP.

12. CVW to Cappon, draft of telegram, January 31, 1949, Box 51, Folder 604, CVWP.

13. Cappon to CVW, January 31, 1949, Box 51, Folder 104, CVWP.

14. CVW to John Hope Franklin, February 4, 1949, Box 51, Folder 604, CVWP.

15. Franklin to CVW, February 17, 1949, Box 51, Folder 604, CVWP.

16. CVW to Franklin, February 23, 1949, Box 51, Folder 604, CVWP.

17. Cappon to CVW, February 16, 1949, Box 51, Folder 104, CVWP.

18. CVW to Cappon, February 23, 1949, and CVW to Franklin, February 23, 1949, Box 51, Folder 604, CVWP.

19. Franklin to CVW, February 26, 1949, Box 51, Folder 604, CVWP.

20. Cappon to CVW, May 12, June 8, 1949, and CVW to Cappon, May 20, 1949, Box 51, Folder 604, CVWP.

21. CVW to Franklin, June 2, 1949, Franklin to CVW, June 19, 1949, and Carl Bridenbaugh to CVW, June 15, September 29, 1949, Box 51, Folder 604, CVWP.

22. Bridenbaugh to CVW, October 4, 6, 1949, Box 51, Folder 604, CVWP.

23. Franklin to CVW, October 10, 11, 1949, and Bridenbaugh to CVW, October 17, 1949, Box 51, Folder 604, CVWP.

24. Bridenbaugh to CVW, June 15, 27, 1949, Box 51, Folder 604, CVWP.

25. CVW to Howard K. Beale, May 18, 1949, Box 26, Folder 3, Beale Papers.

26. CVW to Beale, July 18, 1949, Box 26, Folder 3, Beale Papers.

27. CVW to Beale, July 18, 1949.

28. Beale to Cappon, October 15, 1949, Box 28, Folder 25, Beale Papers.

29. Bridenbaugh to CVW, October 4, 1949, Box 51, Folder 604, CVWP.

30. *Program of Southern Historical Association Annual Meeting*, Williamsburg, Va., November 10–12, 1949, copy in author's possession.

31. Franklin, interview by John Egerton, July 27, 1990, Interview A-0339, Southern Oral History Program Collection, University of North Carolina, Chapel Hill; "Descendants of Edmund Ruffin," www.wikitree.com/genealogy/Ruffin-Descendants-22 (accessed May 4, 2019).

32. *Richmond (Va.) Times-Dispatch* clipping, November 11, 1949, Box 9, Folder 2, Wiley Papers; Johnson, "Regionalism," 428, 424.

33. Beale to Cappon, October 15, 1949, Box 28, Folder 30, Beale Papers; Johnson, "Regionalism," 419, 428, 422.

34. CVW is quoted in Johnson, "Regionalism," 465, n. 82.

35. Gordon T. Chappell to Bell I. Wiley, February 16, 1951, Box 186, Folder 10, Wiley Papers; Thomas P. Govan to CVW, November 25, 1951, Box 51, Folder 605, CVWP.

36. CVW to Govan, November 30, 1951, Box 51, Folder 605, CVWP.

37. CVW to Franklin, January 15, 1952, CVW to J. Wesley Hoffman, February 5, 1952, Govan to CVW, January 24, 1952, Box 51, Folder 605, CVWP.

38. Govan to CVW, February 18, 1952, CVW to Govan, February 28, 1952, CVW to Hoffman, February 26, 1952, "Tentative Draft, Southern Historical Association Program, Knoxville, Tennessee, November 6, 7, and 8," Hoffman to CVW, March 13, 1952, and CVW to LeRoy P. Graf, March 17, 1952, Box 51, Folder 605, CVWP.

39. CVW to Govan, October 29, 1952, Box 21, Folder 253, CVWP; Graf, interview by John Herbert Roper, April 12, 1979, Roper Papers; Bennett H. Wall, interview by Roper, April 11, 1979, Roper Papers; CVW, "The Irony of Southern History," *Journal of Southern History* 19 (February 1953): 3–19.

40. Francis B. Simkins, "Tolerating the South's Past," *Journal of Southern History* 21 (February 1955): 3–16.

41. Franklin to Beale, December 6, 1954, Box 9, Folder 8, Beale Papers.

42. Johnson, "Regionalism," 450.

43. Franklin to Robert L. Carter, August 19, 1952, Box 9, Folder 139 (as indicated by Richard Kluger's notes on NAACP Legal Defense Fund Correspondence), *Brown v. Board of Education* Collection, Manuscripts and Archives, Yale University Library.

44. Richard Kluger, *Simple Justice: The History of Brown v. Board of Education and Black America's Struggle for Equality* (New York: Alfred A. Knopf, 1976), 615.

45. John A. Davis to CVW, July 8, and CVW to Davis, July 21, 1953, Box 78, Folder 39, CVWP.

46. Davis to CVW, August 7, 1953, Box 78, Folder 39, CVWP.

47. "The Background of the Abandonment of Reconstruction," typescript, Box 78, Folder 39, CVWP.

48. "Background of the Abandonment of Reconstruction."

49. "Background of the Abandonment of Reconstruction."

50. "Background of the Abandonment of Reconstruction."

51. Jack Greenberg, *Crusaders in the Courts: How a Dedicated Band of Lawyers Fought for the Civil Rights Revolution* (New York: Basic Books, 1994), 187; Rayford W. Logan, "The Political Aspects of the Compromise of 1877," Box 9, Folder 140, *Brown v. Board of Education* Collection.

52. *Brief for Appellants in Nos. 1, 2, and 4 and for Respondents in No. 10 on Reargument*, Supreme Court of the United States, October Term, 1953, 57, n. 19.

53. CVW, *Origins of the New South, 1877–1913* (Baton Rouge: Louisiana State University Press, 1951), 212, quoted in *Brief*, 64–65.

54. *Brief*, 64, 42, 43, 65.

55. CVW to Thurgood Marshall, November 5, 1953, Box 9, Folder 140, *Brown v. Board of Education* Collection.

56. CVW, "Equality: The Deferred Commitment," in *The Burden of Southern History*, 3rd ed. (Baton Rouge: Louisiana State University Press, 1993), 87. This essay was first delivered as an address at Gettysburg College and published in the *American Scholar* in 1958.

57. Alfred H. Kelly, "An Inside Story: When the Supreme Court Ordered Desegregation," *U.S. News and World Report*, February 5, 1962, 88. This article was lifted from a paper Kelly delivered to the American Historical Association, December 28, 1961, reprinted in *Congressional Record*, 87th Cong., 2nd Sess., September 11, 1962, 19023–25.

58. Kelly, "Inside Story"; Alfred H. Kelly, "Clio and the Court: An Illicit Love Affair," *Supreme Court Review* (1965): 144; John Hope Franklin, "The Dilemma of the American Negro Scholar," in *Soon One Morning: New Writing by American Negroes 1940–1962*, ed. Herbert Hill (New York: Alfred A. Knopf, 1975), 74.

CHAPTER 8

1. CVW, *Thinking Back: The Perils of Writing History* (Baton Rouge: Louisiana State University Press, 1986), 89.

2. S. V. McCasland to CVW, May 20, 1953, Box 3, Folder "University of Virginia Lectures, 1953–1954," CVWP.

3. John Hope Franklin, interview by John Herbert Roper, November 10, 1978, Roper Papers; CVW to Rupert B. Vance, June 21, 1954, Box 57, Folder 684, CVWP; Franklin to Howard K. Beale, December 6, 1954, Box 9, Folder 8, Beale Papers.

4. CVW to Edward Younger, August 23, 1954, Box 62, Folder 753, CVWP.

5. Younger to CVW, September 13, 1954, Box 62, Folder 753, CVWP.

6. CVW to Younger, September 16, 1954, Box 62, Folder 753, CVWP; "Segregation in Historical Perspective," typescript, Box 73, Folder 130, CVWP; "Editorial," *Cavalier Daily* (UVA), May 18, 1954.

7. CVW, "Segregation."

8. Barrington Moore Jr., *Social Origins of Dictatorship and Democracy: Lord and Peasant in the Making of the Modern World* (Boston: Beacon Press, 1967), 486.

9. CVW, *The Strange Career of Jim Crow* (New York: Oxford University Press, 1955), ix; Howard W. Odum, *The Way of the South* (New York: Macmillan, 1947), 38; CVW to Daniel Rodgers, April 12, 1982, Box 31, Folder 366, CVWP.

10. CVW, *Strange Career*, 88. Howard Odum is quoted in John Egerton, *Speak Now against the Day: The Generation before the Civil Rights Movement in the South* (Chapel Hill: University of North Carolina Press, 1995), 595; James Reston, "A Sociological Decision," *New York Times*, May 18, 1954, 14, www.nytimes.com/1954/05/18/archives/a-sociological -decision-court-founded-its-segregation-ruling-on.html/ (accessed May 5, 2019); "All God's Chillun,'" *New York Times*, May 18, 1954, 28, https://timesmachine.nytimes.com /timesmachine/1954/05/18/issue.html (accessed January 15, 2018).

11. Both Adlai Stevenson and Dwight D. Eisenhower are quoted in CVW, *The Strange Career of Jim Crow*, 2nd rev. ed. (New York: Oxford University Press, 1966), 164, 163.

12. CVW, *Strange Career* (1955), vii–viii. A Google Ngram sampling of books published in "American English" shows references to "segregation" increasing gradually after 1920 before spiking by 77 percent between 1940 and 1947, http://books.google.com/ngrams /graph?content=+racial+segregation%2C+Negro+segregation%2C+segregation&year _start=1900&year_end=1960&corpus=17&smoothing=3&share=/ (accessed May 3, 2019).

13. CVW, *Strange Career* (1955), 47; CVW, "Segregation."

14. "Jim Crow Not Dead Yet—Woodward," *Cavalier Daily* (UVA), October 1, 1954, 1; CVW to Beale, September 30, October 22, 1954, Box 26, Folder 8, Beale Papers.

15. CVW, *Thinking Back*, 93; Franklin to Beale, December 6, 1954, Box 9, Folder 8, Beale Papers; John Hope Franklin, *Mirror to America: The Autobiography of John Hope Franklin* (New York: Farrar, Straus and Giroux, 2005), 328; Manning J. Dauer to CVW, September 27, 1954, Box 15, Folder 165, CVWP.

16. Lee E. Grove to CVW, October 19, 1954, Box 40, Folder 484, CVWP; CVW, "Journal, kept while at Queens College, Oxford," November 8, 1954, Box 92, Folder 17, CVWP.

17. CVW, "Journal," January 24, 1955; CVW to William G. Carleton, Box 7, Folder "Woodward, C. Vann. 1940–1971," Carleton Papers.

18. Grove to CVW, June 17, 1955, Box 40, Folder 484, CVWP.

19. CVW, *Origins of the New South, 1877–1913* (Baton Rouge: Louisiana State University Press, 1951), 210, 212.

20. CVW, *Origins*, 212; CVW, "The Strange Career of a Historical Controversy," in *American Counterpoint: Slavery and Racism in the North-South Dialogue* (Boston: Little, Brown, 1971), 237.

21. Howard Rabinowitz, "More Than the Jim Crow Thesis: Assessing *The Strange Career of Jim Crow*," *Journal of American History* 75 (December 1988): 847.

22. David M. Potter, "C. Vann Woodward," in *Pastmasters: Some Essays on American Historians*, ed. Marcus Cunliffe and Robin W. Winks (New York: Harper and Row, 1969), 395.

23. Dauer to CVW, September 27, 1954, Box 15, Folder 165, CVWP; Alfred A. Knopf to CVW, March 5, 1956, Box 30, Folder 362, CVWP.

24. Sir George Campbell, M.P., *White and Black: The Outcome of a Visit to the United States* (New York: R. Worthington, 1879), 194–95.

25. CVW, *Strange Career* (1955), 18; Campbell, *White and Black*, 194–95.

26. CVW, *Strange Career* (1955), 18; A South Carolinian [pseud. Belton O. Townshend], "South Carolina Society," *Atlantic Monthly* 391 (June 1877): 676.

27. CVW, *Strange Career* (1955), 19, 30; George W. Cable, *The Silent South: Together with the Freedman's Case in Equity and the Convict Lease System* (New York: Charles Scribner's Sons, 1885), 5–86.

28. CVW, *Strange Career* (1955), 23, 16; Vernon Lane Wharton, *The Negro in Mississippi, 1865–1890* (reprint, New York: Harper and Row, 1965), 230.

29. CVW, *Strange Career* (1955), 23; Wharton, *Negro in Mississippi*, 231–32.

30. CVW, *Strange Career* (1955), 24; Charles Dudley Warner, "Impressions of the South," *Harper's New Monthly Magazine* 71 (September 1885): 550.

31. CVW to Younger, September 21, 1956, Box 62, Folder 753, CVWP; CVW to Charles E. Wynes, August 13, 1956, and Wynes to CVW, August 19, 1956, Box 61, Folder 741, CVWP.

32. CVW, *Strange Career* (1955), 16, 17; T. W. Higginson, "Some War Scenes Revisited," *Atlantic Monthly* 42 (July 1878): 9, 8.

33. The first quotation of Thomas Wentworth Higginson is from Howard N. Meyer, ed., *The Magnificent Activist: The Writings of Thomas Wentworth Higginson, 1823–1911* (Boston: Da Capo, 2000), 33. CVW, *Strange Career* (1966), 35; CVW, *Origins*, 167–68; the second Higginson quote is from W. Scott Poole, "Thomas Wentworth Higginson and the Uncertain Meaning of the Civil War," *Civil War History* 51 (June 2005): 202–3.

34. CVW, *Strange Career*, 20–21; Charles E. Wynes, *Race Relations in Virginia, 1870–1902* (Charlottesville: University of Virginia Press, 1961), 77.

35. CVW, *Strange Career*, 22.

36. CVW, *Strange Career*, 22.

37. Stewart is quoted in George B. Tindall, *South Carolina Negroes, 1877–1900* (Columbia: University of South Carolina Press, 1952), 305.

38. Stewart is quoted in Charles E. Wynes, "T. McCants Stewart: Peripatetic Black South Carolinian," *South Carolina Historical Magazine* 80 (October 1979): 316; CVW, *Strange Career* (1966), 38.

39. Tindall, *South Carolina Negroes*, 300.

40. CVW, *Strange Career*, 16; Higginson, "Some War Scenes," 8.

41. Potter, "C. Vann Woodward," 474, n. 22; Stephen J. Riegel, "The Persistent Career of Jim Crow: Lower Federal Courts and the 'Separate but Equal' Doctrine, 1865–1896," *American Journal of Legal History* 28 (January 1984): 23; CVW, *Strange Career* (1966), 28.

42. Riegel, "Persistent Career," 30, n. 61, 23; Barbara Young Welke, *Recasting American Liberty: Gender, Race, Law, and the Railroad Revolution, 1865–1920* (New York: Cambridge University Press, 2001), 287–88; Wynes, *Race Relations in Virginia*, 68.

43. Louisville, New Orleans, and Texas Railway Co. v. Mississippi, 133 U.S. 587 (1890); Roger A. Fischer, *The Segregation Struggle in Louisiana, 1862–1877* (Urbana: University of Illinois Press, 1974), 151.

44. CVW, *Origins*, 210–11.

45. CVW, *Strange Career*, 30, 31.

46. *Charleston News and Courier*, February 25, 1897, is quoted in Tindall, *South Carolina Negroes*, 301; see also 295, 300. CVW, *Strange Career*, 18–19; CVW, *Origins*, 19.

47. CVW, *Origins*, 163–64; CVW, *Strange Career*, 26.

48. CVW, *Strange Career*, 51, 63–65.

49. CVW, *Strange Career*, 53, 152; Douglass is quoted in David W. Blight, *Frederick Douglass: Prophet of Freedom* (New York: Simon and Schuster, 2018), 557; W. E. B. Du Bois, *Black Reconstruction in America: An Essay toward a History of the Part Which Black Folk Played in the Attempt to Reconstruct Democracy in America, 1860–1880* (New York: Harcourt and Brace, 1935), 626.

50. CVW to Vance, September 14, 1954, and Vance to CVW, September 21, 1954, Series 1, Folder 28, "1954," Vance Papers.

51. CVW to Eric L. McKittrick and Stanley M. Elkins, June 10, 1955, Box 75, Folder 10, CVWP.

52. CVW, *Strange Career*, 7, 87.

53. Rabinowitz, "More Than the Jim Crow Thesis," 844; Tindall, *South Carolina Negroes, 1877–1900* (Columbia: University of South Carolina Press, 1952), 294, 291, 293.

54. Gunnar Myrdal is quoted in CVW, *Strange Career*, 91; see also 93. For a firsthand account of the impact of Jim Crow statutes in Charleston, see Mamie Garvin Fields and Karen E. Fields, *Lemon Swamps and Other Places: A Carolina Memoir* (New York: Free Press, 1983), 48.

55. CVW, *Strange Career*, 93.

56. CVW, "Strange Career of a Historical Controversy," 237; Rufus E. Clement, review of *The Strange Career of Jim Crow*, by CVW, *Journal of Southern History* 21 (November 1955): 557.

57. Grove to CVW, May 9, July 7, 1956, and CVW to Grove, June 21, 1956, Box 40, Folder 484, CVWP; Sheldon Meyer to CVW, February 26, April 6, 11, 1960, Box 71, Folder 113, CVWP; CVW, *Thinking Back*, 93.

58. CVW, "Young Jim Crow," *Nation*, July 7, 1956, 10; CVW, "The Disturbed Southerners," *Current History* 32 (1957): 279. See also CVW, "The New Reconstruction in the South," *Commentary* 21 (1956): 501–8; and CVW, "The South and the Law of the Land," *Commentary* 26 (1958): 369–74.

59. CVW, *Strange Career* (1955), 91–92; CVW, *The Strange Career of Jim Crow*, 3rd rev. ed. (New York: Oxford University Press, 1974), 105–6.

60. CVW, *Strange Career*, 148–49.

61. Virginia Durr to CVW, December 5, 1955, and CVW to Durr, December 9, 1955, Box 16, Folder 183, CVWP.

62. Rayford W. Logan, review of *The Strange Career of Jim Crow*, by CVW, *American Historical Review* 61 (1955): 212; E. Franklin Frazier, review of *The Strange Career of Jim Crow*, by CVW, *Saturday Review*, June 11, 1955, 13.

63. Martin Luther King Jr., "Our God Is Marching On," speech at Stanford University, March 25, 1965, Martin Luther King Jr. Research and Education Institute, Stanford University, Stanford, Calif., http://mlkkpp01.stanford.edu/index.php/kingpapers/article /our_god_is_marching_on/ (accessed May 19, 2019). See also "Our God Is Marching On!" (March 25, 1965), pt. 3, https://youtu.be/FiGZUtgjLwc (accessed June 26, 2021).

CHAPTER 9

1. Brown v. Board of Education of Topeka, 349 U.S. 294 (1955); "The Hound of Heaven —Poem by Francis Thompson," PoemHunter.com, www.poemhunter.com/poem/the -hound-of-heaven/comments/ (accessed May 31, 2019). See also CVW to Lee E. Grove, August 27, 1956, Box 40, Folder 484, CVWP.

2. CVW, *The Strange Career of Jim Crow*, new and rev. ed. (New York: Oxford University Press, 1957), 131, 157, 169.

3. CVW, *Strange Career*, 175, 179, 176, 179.

4. Virginia Durr to CVW, February 25, 1963, Box 16, Folder 183, CVWP.

5. CVW, *The Strange Career of Jim Crow*, 2nd rev. ed. (New York: Oxford University Press, 1966), 163–64, 168–69.

6. CVW, *Strange Career* (1966), 181–90.

7. CVW, *Strange Career* (1966), 190–91.

8. CVW to Robert Penn Warren, September 22, 1966, Box 82, Folder 1610, Warren Papers. See also CVW to Glenn W. Rainey, October 4, 1966, Box 6, Folder 8, Rainey Papers.

9. CVW, "What Happened to the Civil Rights Movement?," *Harper's Magazine*, January 1967, 32.

10. CVW, *The Burden of Southern History*, 3rd ed. (Baton Rouge: Louisiana State University Press, 1993), 186.

11. CVW, *Burden*, 184; Alfred A. Knopf to CVW, January 3, 1967 (misdated "1966"), Box 30, Folder 364, CVWP; "Investigations: Adam and Yvette," *Time*, February 24, 1967, http://content.time.com/time/magazine/article/0,9171,899407,00.html/ (accessed May 17, 2019).

12. CVW to Knopf, January 8, 1967, Box 30, Folder 364, CVWP; CVW, "Powell as Symbol," letter to the editor, *New York Times*, January 18, 1967, 34, https://timesmachine.nytimes.com/timesmachine/1967/01/18/issue.html (accessed March 12, 2020).

13. CVW, *The Strange Career of Jim Crow*, 3rd rev. ed. (New York: Oxford University Press, 1974), 188, vi–vii.

14. CVW, *Strange Career* (1974), 197–98, 190, 202.

15. Laura M. Miller, "'Black Power' Speech (July 28, 1966, by Stokely Carmichael)," *Dictionary of American History*, 2003, Encyclopedia.com, www.encyclopedia.com/history/dictionaries-thesauruses-pictures-and-press-releases/black-power-speech-28-july-1966-stokely-carmichael (accessed September 30, 2015); CVW to Linda Moses, August 10, 1966, Box 52, Folder 623, CVWP; CVW, *Strange Career* (1974), 209–10.

16. CVW, *Strange Career* (1974), 216.

17. CVW, *Strange Career* (1974), 217, 215; Milliken v. Bradley, 418 U.S. 717 (1974).

18. Fon W. Boardman to CVW, January 17, 1956, Lee E. Grove to CVW, March 1, July 7, 1956, and CVW to Grove, June 21, 1956, Box 40, Folder 484, CVWP.

19. CVW to George B. Tindall, March 8, 1955, and Tindall to CVW, March 20, 1955, Box 53, Folder 632, CVWP.

20. CVW, *The Strange Career of Jim Crow*, new and rev. ed. (New York: Oxford University Press, 1957), xii, xiv–xv; Tindall to CVW, June 16, August 30, 1956, Box 53, Folder 632, CVWP.

21. Sheldon Meyer to CVW, February 26, April 6, 11, 1960, Box 71, Folder 113, CVWP.

22. Kenneth M. Stampp, *The Peculiar Institution: Slavery in the Ante-Bellum South* (New York, Alfred A. Knopf, 1956), vii.

23. CVW, *The Strange Career of Jim Crow* (New York: Oxford University Press, 1955), ix; CVW, "The Strange Career of a Historical Controversy," in *American Counterpoint: Slavery and Racism in the North-South Dialogue* (Boston: Little, Brown, 1971), 237.

24. Charles E. Wynes, *Race Relations in Virginia, 1870–1902* (Charlottesville: University of Virginia Press, 1961), 149, 68, 150, 149.

25. Joel Williamson, *After Slavery: The Negro in South Carolina during Reconstruction, 1861–1877* (Chapel Hill: University of North Carolina Press, 1965), 298, 275, 298.

26. Richard C. Wade, *Slavery in the Cities: The South, 1820–1860* (New York: Oxford University Press, 1964).

27. CVW, *Strange Career* (1966), ix, 13, 34.

28. CVW, *Strange Career* (1966), 13, 24.

29. CVW, *Strange Career* (1966), 22–29.

30. CVW, "Strange Career of a Historical Controversy," 242.

31. Potter, "C. Vann Woodward," 398. Though I disagree with certain inferences Howard Rabinowitz draws from some of them, he offers a comprehensive list of the works that might be seen as testing CVW's Jim Crow thesis in some way. See Rabinowitz, "More Than the Jim Crow Thesis: Assessing *The Strange Career of Jim Crow*," *Journal of American History* 75 (December 1988): 845, n. 10.

32. Forrest McDonald, *Recovering the Past: A Historian's Memoir* (Lawrence: University Press of Kansas, 2004), 105; CVW to John Herbert Roper, September 6, 1977, Roper Papers; Potter, "C. Vann Woodward," 398.

33. Potter, "C. Vann Woodward," 397–99; CVW to Potter, November 13, 1960, Box 3, Folder "Letters Answered, 1960–63," David Morris Potter Papers (SC0088), Department of Special Collections and University Archives, Stanford University Libraries, Stanford, Calif.

34. David Hackett Fischer, *Historians' Fallacies: Toward a Logic of Historical Thought* (New York: Harper and Row, 1970), 147–49, n. 38.

35. John W. Cell, *The Highest Stage of White Supremacy: The Origins of Segregation in South Africa and the American South* (Cambridge: Cambridge University Press, 1982), 92; CVW, *Thinking Back: The Perils of Writing History* (Baton Rouge: Louisiana State University Press, 1986), 97–98; Joel R. Williamson, *The Crucible of Race: Black-White Relations in the American South since Emancipation* (New York: Oxford University Press, 1984), ix.

36. Howard Rabinowitz, *Race, Ethnicity and Urbanization: Selected Essays by Howard N. Rabinowitz* (Columbia: University of Missouri Press, 1994), 138; CVW, *Thinking Back*, 97.

37. CVW, *Thinking Back*, 97.

38. Cell, *Highest Stage of White Supremacy*, x.

39. Edward L. Ayers, *The Promise of the New South: Life after Reconstruction* (New York: Oxford University Press, 1992), 142, 145; Welke, *Recasting Liberty*, 351–52.

40. Williamson, *Crucible of Race*, 212; Michael McGerr, *A Fierce Discontent: The Rise and Fall of the Progressive Movement in America, 1870–1920* (New York: Free Press, 2003), 188, 186; CVW, "Strange Career of a Historical Controversy," 259, 257.

41. CVW, "Strange Career of a Historical Controversy," 257–58; Jennifer Roback, "The Political Economy of Segregation: The Case of Segregated Streetcars," *Journal of Economic History* 46 (December 1986): 899, 906, 910, 916. See also Walter E. Campbell, "Profit, Prejudice, and Protest: Utility Competition and the Generation of Jim Crow Streetcars in Savannah, 1905–1907," *Georgia Historical Quarterly* 70 (Summer 1986): 197–231.

42. Williamson, *After Slavery*, 298; Steven Hahn, *A Nation under Our Feet: Black Political Struggles in the Rural South from Slavery to the Great Migration* (Cambridge, Mass.: Harvard University Press, 2003), 566, n. 6.

43. David Donald is quoted on the jacket of CVW, *The Strange Career of Jim Crow*, 3rd rev. ed. (New York: Oxford University Press, 1974).

44. Joel Williamson, *A Rage for Order: Black-White Relations in the American South since Emancipation* (New York: Oxford University Press, 1986), 262; Rabinowitz, "More Than the Jim Crow Thesis," 849.

45. Rabinowitz, "More Than the Jim Crow Thesis," 856.

46. Woodward to Edward Younger, September 21, 1956, Box 62, Folder 753, CVWP; Woodward to Byron Hollingshead, February 19, 1965, and Hollingshead to CVW, February 26, 1965, Box 40, Folder 485, CVWP.

47. Catherine C. Linnet to CVW, December 1, 1965, January 25, 1966, Box 40, Folder 485; CVW to Arthur Thornhill, January 5, 1967, CVW to Ned Bradford, September 20, 1954, February 12, 1969, and Bradford to CVW, September 21, 1954, Box 32, Folders 386–87, CVWP.

48. Edgar F. Shannon to Sheldon Meyer, January 14, 1974, Meyer to CVW, January 25, 1974, and CVW to Meyer, February 6, 1974, Box 56, Folder 678, CVWP.

49. Meyer to CVW, February 13, 1974, Box 56, Folder 678, CVWP; Yale Corporation to Professor C. Vann Woodward," May 1974, Everett M. Sims to CVW, October 23, 1974, Box 24, Folder 279, CVWP; "Inflation Calculator," www.in2013dollars.com/us/inflation/ (accessed November 5, 2021). See also John Morton Blum, *A Life with History* (Lawrence: University Press of Kansas, 2004), 162–63.

50. See William S. McFeely, "Afterword," in CVW, *Strange Career of Jim Crow*, commemorative ed. (New York: Oxford University Press, 2001), 229; Potter, "C. Vann Woodward," 397.

CHAPTER 10

1. "Historical News and Notices," *Journal of Southern History* 17 (August 1951): 426; CVW to Donald R. Ellegood, September 16, 1954, Box 37, Folder 392, CVWP.

2. CVW to Ellegood, November 30, 1958, Ellegood to CVW, December 5, 1958, and Ellegood to Charles G. Sellers, December 4, 1958, Box 68, Folder 81, CVWP.

3. CVW to Ellegood, December 11, 1958, Box 68, Folder 81, CVWP; Tindall to CVW, February 26, 1959, Box 53, Folder 632, CVWP.

4. CVW to Tindall, March 3, 1959, Box 53, Folder 632, CVWP; CVW to Richard Wentworth, November 8, 1960, Box 68, Folder 81, CVWP.

5. CVW to Ellegood, July 29, 1959, and Ellegood to CVW, August 13, 1959, Box 68, Folder 81, CVWP.

6. David M. Potter to Ellegood, January 4, 1960, Louis D. Rubin to Ellegood, August 18, 1959, and Daniel Boorstin to Ellegood, November 6, 1959, Box 68, Folder 81, CVWP.

7. "Title Alternatives," typescript, Box 68, Folder 81, CVWP; CVW to David H. Donald, April 8, 1960, Box 16, Folder 175, CVWP; "What Burden? Whose Burden?," typescript, Box 64, Folder 32, CVWP; CVW, *Thinking Back: The Perils of Writing History* (Baton Rouge: Louisiana State University Press, 1986), 109; CVW, *The Burden of Southern History*, 3rd ed. (Baton Rouge: Louisiana State University Press, 1993), x.

8. CVW to Ellegood, May 17, 1960, Box 68, Folder 81, CVWP.

9. CVW, "The Irony of Southern History," *Journal of Southern History* 19 (February 1953): 3–19.

10. Reinhold Niebuhr, *The Irony of American History* (New York: Charles Scribner's Sons, 1952); CVW, "Irony," in *Burden*, 191.

11. CVW, "Irony," 191–93.

12. CVW, "Irony," 188–89.

13. CVW, "Irony," 188, 191–92, 188, 191–92.

14. CVW, "Irony," 200–202, 204–5.

15. CVW, "Irony," 205, 209.

16. CVW, "Irony," 188, 210, 208–9.

17. CVW, "The Search for Southern Identity," in *Burden*, 19, 12–13.

18. CVW, "Search for Southern Identity," 22.

19. CVW, "Search for Southern Identity," 9–10; Ulrich B. Phillips "The Central Theme of Southern History," *American Historical Review* 34 (October 1928): 30–43.

20. CVW, "Search for Southern Identity," 4, 11–13.

21. CVW to John Herbert Roper, September 6, 1977, Folder 30, Roper Papers.

22. Potter, "C. Vann Woodward," 397–98, 393.

23. Potter, 9; Walker Percy, "Red, White and Blue-Gray," in *Signposts in a Strange Land*, ed. Patrick Samway (New York: Farrar, Straus and Giroux, 1991), 80, 21. On segregation as the foundation for white southerners' "modern sense of themselves," see Grace Elizabeth Hale, *Making Whiteness: The Culture of Segregation in the South, 1890–1940* (New York: Pantheon Books, 1998), 9.

24. CVW, "Search for Southern Identity," 13–14, 16.

25. Donald to CVW, July 10, 1958, Box 16, Folder 175, CVWP.

26. Ellegood to CVW, August 31, 1960, March 21, 1961, Box 68, Folder 81, CVWP; Richard Wentworth to CVW, February 3, September 11, 1969, May 29, 1968, Box 34, Folder 394, CVWP.

27. CVW, "The South in Search of a Philosophy," in *Phi Beta Kappa Addresses Delivered at the University of Florida*, vol. 1 (1938), 15; CVW to Rainey, October 19, 1942, Box 16, Folder 8, Rainey Papers; CVW to Donald, June 17, 1984, Box 16, Folder 176, CVWP.

28. CVW, "The Historical Dimension," in *Burden*, 39.

29. CVW, "Historical Dimension," 37.

30. CVW to Henry F. May, December 15, 1953, Box 68, Folder 81, CVWP; "What Burden? Whose Burden?" This essay became the basis for chapter 6, "Shifting the Burdens," in *Thinking Back*, 101–19.

31. CVW, "A Southern Critique for the Gilded Age," in *Burden*, 137, 116, 124–25.

32. CVW, "John Brown's Private War," in *Burden*, 41–42.

33. CVW, "John Brown's Private War," 50–51.

34. CVW, "John Brown's Private War," 53, 68; CVW, *Thinking Back*, 112.

35. Robert Penn Warren to CVW, September 21, 1960, Box 59, Folder 703, CVWP; CVW to William G. Carleton, October 9, 1945, Carleton Papers.

36. CVW, *Thinking Back*, 92.

37. CVW, "Equality: The Deferred Commitment," in *Burden*, 87.

38. CVW, "Equality," 71–72.

39. CVW, "Equality," 83–86.

40. CVW, "Equality," 105, 106.

41. CVW, "The Anti-Slavery Myth," in *The Future of the Past* (New York: Oxford University Press, 1989), 273, 277. The essay first appeared in *American Scholar* 31 (1962): 316–27.

42. CVW, "Anti-Slavery Myth," 277.

43. CVW, "Anti-Slavery Myth," 278–79; Brooks D. Simpson, "C. Vann Woodward and the Dilemma of White Southern Liberalism," Crossroads (blog), March 14, 2011,

http://cwcrossroads.wordpress.com/2011/03/14/c-vann-woodward-and-the-dilemma-of
-white-southern-liberalism/ (accessed January 21, 2019).

44. Potter, "The Historian's Use of Nationalism and Vice Versa," *American Historical Review* 671 (July 1962): 924–50; Fawn M. Brodie, *Thaddeus Stevens: Scourge of the South* (New York: W. W. Norton, 1959), 373; Fawn M. Brodie, "Who Won the Civil War Anyway? Some Recent Interpretations Are Protested by a Historian," *New York Times Book Review,* August 5, 1962, 1, 22; CVW to Potter, August 21, 1962, Box 44, Folder 520, CVWP.

45. CVW to Potter, August 21, 1962.

46. Merrill Jensen to CVW, July 18, 1947, Box 56, Folder 680, CVWP; John Wuorinen to CVW, December 12, 1951, and Richard Morris to CVW, Box 12, Folder 134, CVWP; Jensen to CVW, July 18, 1947, Box 56, Folder 680, CVWP; Sydney Painter to CVW, n.d., Box 28, Folder 330, CVWP; CVW to Walter Johnson, September 16, 1954, Box 28, Folder 526, CVWP; CVW to Carl Bridenbaugh, October 19, November 1, 1955, Box 65, Folder 755, CVWP.

47. CVW to Joseph R. Strayer, February 24, 1959, Strayer to CVW, February 27, 1959, and CVW to Strayer, March 12, 1959, Box 92, Folder 22, CVWP; CVW to Arthur Thornhill Jr., March 31, 1959, and Lilly Foundation, Statement of a Project submitted by CVW, draft, n.d., Box 80, Folder 3, CVWP.

48. Bridenbaugh to CVW, October 16, 1955, Box 65, Folder 755, CVWP; CVW to Bridenbaugh, October 19, November 1, 1955; CVW to Strayer, March 12, 1959.

CHAPTER 11

1. Randy Kennedy, "George Pierson, 88, a Professor at Yale and Its Historian," *New York Times,* October 15, 1993, www.nytimes.com/1993/10/15/obituaries/george-pierson-88-a
-professor-at-yale-and-its-historian.html/ (accessed January 22, 2019); John Morton Blum, *A Life with History* (Lawrence: University of Kansas Press, 2004), 157; William Palmer, *From Gentleman's Club to Professional Body: The Evolution of the History Department in the United States, 1940–1980* (Lexington: University Press of Kentucky, 2009), 55–56.

2. "Table of Organization (confidential)," RWW, "Department of History [Yale] 1960–1961, Master List, Ph.D.'s Granted, 1947–November 1960," and "Harvard University, History Department Newsletter, May 1960," Box 86, Folder 12, CVWP.

3. J. H. Hexter, "Call Me Ishmael, or a Rose by Any Other Name," *American Scholar* 52 (Summer 1983): 339–40; Edmund Morgan is quoted in Palmer, *Gentleman's Club,* 57.

4. George Pierson to CVW, July 7, October 10, November 3, 1960, Box 86, Folder 12, CVWP.

5. CVW to Pierson, May 5, 1959, and Pierson to CVW, November 3, 1960, Box 86, Folder 12, CVWP.

6. Pierson to CVW, November 3, 1960, Box 86, Folder 12, CVWP.

7. Pierson to CVW, November 3, 1960.

8. CVW to Pierson, November 7, 1960, Box 86, Folder 12, CVWP.

9. Pierson to A. Whitney Griswold, "Report of the History Department for 1956–1957, 15 July 1957," quoted in Peter Novick, *That Noble Dream: The "Objectivity Question" and the American Historical Profession* (Cambridge: Cambridge University Press, 1988), 366.

10. CVW to David M. Potter, November 13, 1960, Box 86, Folder 12, CVWP; John M. Blum, interview by John Herbert Roper, December 13, 1984, Roper Papers.

11. George W. Pierson, *A Yale Book of Numbers: Historical Statistics of the College and University, 1701–1976* (New Haven, Conn.: Yale University Press, 1983), 88, 368–70; CVW to Potter, November 13, 1960.

12. William Palmer, *Engagement with the Past: The Lives and Works of the World War II Generation of Historians* (Lexington: University of Kentucky Press, 2001), 142; Potter to CVW, November 15, 1960, Box 86, Folder 12, CVWP.

13. Morgan to CVW, November 15, 1960, and Pierson to CVW, November 3, 1960, Box 86, Folder 12, CVWP.

14. Morgan to CVW, November 15, 1960.

15. Blum to CVW, November 15, 1960, Box 86, Folder 12, CVWP.

16. CVW to Robin Winks, October 26, 1960, Box 60, Folder 728, CVWP.

17. Winks to CVW, November 11, 1960, Box 60, Folder 728, CVWP.

18. Winks to CVW, November 11, 1960; CVW to Winks, November 18, 1960, Box 60, Folder 728, CVWP.

19. CVW to Arthur Thornhill, February 21, 1961, Box 71, Folder 108, CVWP; CVW to Pierson, November 20, 1960, and Pierson to CVW, December 2, 1960, Box 86, Folder 12, CVWP.

20. CVW to Pierson, November 18, 1960, Box 86, Folder 12, CVWP; Pierson to CVW, December 2, 1960.

21. Alvin Kernan, *In Plato's Cave* (New Haven, Conn.: Yale University Press, 1999), 91; Palmer, *Gentleman's Club*, 51.

22. Pierson to CVW, November 23, 1960, and CVW to Pierson, November 26, December 5, 1960, Box 86, Folder 12, CVWP.

23. CVW to Pierson, December 12, 1960, handwritten note for a telegram, Box 86, Folder 12, CVWP.

24. CVW, "Exile at Yale," in *The Legacy of Robert Penn Warren*, ed. David Madden (Baton Rouge: Louisiana State University Press, 2000), 28; CVW to Robert Penn Warren, December 17, 1960, Box 82, Folder 1609, Warren Papers.

25. CVW to Morgan, December 17, 1960, Box 86, Folder 12, CVWP; CVW to William G. Carleton, December 15, 1960, Carleton Papers.

26. Pierson to CVW, December 14, 1960, Blum to CVW, December 13, 1960, and Arthur Wright to CVW, December 15, 1960, Box 86, Folder 12, CVWP.

27. CVW to Glenn W. Rainey, December 4, 1963, Box 6, Folder 8, Rainey Papers.

28. Pierson to CVW, February 7, 1961, and CVW to Pierson, April 11, 1961, Box 86, Folder 12, CVWP.

29. Pierson to CVW, February 7, 15, April 12, 1961, March 1, March 15, 1962, Box 86, Folder 12, CVWP.

30. Pierson to CVW, March 15, 1962; CVW to Pierson, March 19, 1962, Box 86, Folder 12, CVWP; CVW, interview by Roper, December 14, 1984, Roper Papers.

31. "The Faculty Raiders," *Time*, January 12, 1962, 36.

32. CVW to Pierson, March 26, 1962, Box 86, Folder 12, CVWP; Fred M. Hechinger, "Colleges Step Up Faculty Raids for 'Name' Professors," *New York Times*, June 10, 1962, 1, 68, https://timesmachine.nytimes.com/timesmachine/1962/06/10/issue.html (accessed April 1, 2020).

33. Hechinger, "Colleges Step Up," 68.

34. Pierson to CVW, July 20, 1962, Kingman Brewster Jr. to CVW, June 15, 1962, and CVW to Brewster, June 19, 1962, Box 86, Folder 12, CVWP.

35. CVW to Morgan, July 6, 1964, Box 62, Folder 746, CVWP.

36. CVW to Morgan, July 6, 1964; Palmer, *Engagement with the Past*, 125.

37. Roger Adelson, "Interview with Woodward," *Historian* 54 (Autumn 1991): 1–18; Alexander E. Sharp, "C. Vann Woodward: Dignity with a Southern Accent," *Yale Daily News*, April 3, 1963, 1; Palmer, *Engagement with the Past*, 125.

38. Louis R. Harlan, "My Rough Ride as One of Woodward's Graduate Students," Box 92, Folder 21, CVWP; Joseph W. Pearson, "Making Sense of Patterns: A Conversation with J. Mills Thornton III," in *The Historian behind the History: Conversations with Southern Historians*, ed. Megan L. Bever and Scott A. Suarez (Tuscaloosa: University of Alabama Press, 2014), 111–12.

39. David Walsh, "American Historian C. Vann Woodward Dies: An Interview with Civil War Historian James McPherson on Woodward's Contribution," December 24, 1999, World Socialist Web Site, www.wsws.org/en/articles/1999/12/cvw-d24.html/ (accessed October 29, 2018); Sheldon Hackney, Anne Firor Scott, Bertram Wyatt-Brown, William S. McFeely, and Lawrence N. Powell, "C. Vann Woodward, 1908–1999: In Memoriam," *Journal of Southern History* 66 (May 2000): 218; Steven Hahn, *The Roots of Southern Populism: Yeoman Farmers and the Transformation of the Georgia Upcountry, 1850–1890* (New York: Oxford University Press, 1983), ix.

40. Hackney et al., "Woodward, 1908–1999," 215, 218.

41. William S. McFeely, *Grant: A Biography* (New York: W. W. Norton, 1981); James M. McPherson, *Battle Cry of Freedom: The Civil War Era* (New York: Oxford University Press, 1988); Louis R. Harlan, *Booker T. Washington: The Wizard of Tuskegee, 1901–1915* (New York: Oxford University Press, 1983). My count of Woodward's PhD students differs slightly from the list provided by John Herbert Roper, who lists Steven Hahn as one of his advisees, although Howard Lamar formally took over as Hahn's dissertation director of record when Woodward retired in 1977. See Glenn Feldman, ed., *Reading Southern History: Essays on Interpreters and Interpretations* (Tuscaloosa: University of Alabama Press, 2001), 287–88.

42. Donald to CVW, September 5, 1962, and CVW to Donald, September 5, 1962, Box 16, Folder 175, CVWP.

43. CVW to James McPherson, September 10, 1962, Box 36, Folder 421, CVWP.

44. McPherson to CVW, September 13, 24, December 4, 1962, Box 36, Folder 421, CVWP; see also Willie Lee Rose to CVW, August 23, 1962, Box 47, Folder 557, CVWP.

45. CVW to McPherson, January 23, 1963, Box 36, Folder 421, CVWP; James M. McPherson, *The Struggle for Equality: Abolitionists and the Negro in the Civil War and Reconstruction* (Princeton, N.J.: Princeton University Press, 1964).

46. CVW to McPherson, November 4, 1963, Box 36, Folder 421, CVWP.

47. James McPherson, "Deconstructing Affirmative Action," *Perspectives*, American Historical Association, April 1, 2003, www.historians.org/publications-and-directories /perspectives-on-history/april-2003/deconstructing-affirmative-action/ (accessed July 13, 2018).

48. Sheldon Hackney to CVW, November 19, 1965, and CVW to Hackney, January 14, February 7, May 9, 1966, Box 24, Folder 272, CVWP.

49. CVW, "Notes on LNP dissertation," copy provided to the author by Lawrence N. Powell. CVW also suggested the title for Powell's dissertation and the book it became. See Lawrence N. Powell, *New Masters: Northern Planters during the Civil War and Reconstruction* (New Haven, Conn.: Yale University Press, 1980).

50. CVW to John W. Blassingame, July 23, 1970, Box 8, Folder 79, CVWP.

51. CVW to Blassingame, September 18, 1972, Box 8, Folder 79, CVWP.

52. Blassingame's dissertation was published as *Black New Orleans, 1860–1880* (Chicago: University of Chicago Press, 1973).

53. Kenneth M. Stampp to CVW, January 10, November 16, 1972, and CVW to Stampp, November 21, 1972, Box 52, Folder 614, CVWP.

54. Winthrop D. Jordan to CVW, December 27, 1972, Box 28, Folder 334, CVWP.

55. Stampp to CVW, January 29, 1973, Box 52, Folder 614, CVWP.

56. CVW to Stampp, February 5, 1973, Box 52, Folder 614, CVWP.

57. CVW to Blassingame, February 5, 1973, Box 8, Folder 79, CVWP.

58. Blassingame to CVW, February 7, 1973, Box 8, Folder 79, CVWP.

CHAPTER 12

1. Lee E. Grove to CVW, July 17, 1957, Box 40, Folder 484, CVWP; Jesse Stein to CVW, November 19, 1958, Box 46, Folder 543, CVWP.

2. CVW to Arthur Thornhill Sr., September 27, 1958, Box 71, Folder 108, CVWP.

3. Thornhill to CVW, October 7, 1958, and CVW to Thornhill, March 2, 1959, Box 71, Folder 108, CVWP.

4. Thornhill to CVW, March 23, 1959, Box 71, Folder 108, CVWP.

5. CVW to Thornhill, March 31, 1959, and Thornhill to CVW, April 17, 1959, Box 71, Folder 108, CVWP.

6. "Statement of Project for Lilly Foundation," Box 80, Folder 3, CVWP.

7. "Questions of Approach" (for Reconstruction book), Box 71, Folder 108, CVWP.

8. See his comments on the letter of a Unionist who wrote Thaddeus Stephens to complain of Virginia's "stay" laws, which prevented him from collecting from white debtors in the state. See also his notes on Hugh McCulloch to Elihu Washburne, September 14, 1866, Box 80, Folder 7, CVWP; J. R. Sybbes to Thaddeus Stevens, n.d., and [unknown] to Stevens, February 27, 1866, Box 80, Folder 5, CVWP. See also "disfranchisement figures from Georgia," in "registration" file and "the number of disfranchised whites" file, "S.C," Box 84 (note cards), CVWP.

9. "Statement of Project for Lilly Foundation"; CVW to Henry Allen Moe, n.d., Box 22, Folder 26, CVWP; CVW to David M. Potter, April 25, 1960, Box 44, Folder 520, CVWP. Generally, CVW's notes from this northern research may be found in Box 71, Folder 108, and Box 80, Folders 5–10, CVWP. A few may also be found in Box 84.

10. CVW to John Hope Franklin, February 13, 1962, and CVW to George W. Pierson, March 11, 1962, Box 86, Folder 12, CVWP; Thomas B. Alexander to CVW, March 30, 1962, Box 71, Folder 108, CVWP.

11. Michael O'Brien, ed., *The Letters of C. Vann Woodward* (New Haven, Conn.: Yale University Press, 2013), xxx.

12. CVW to Thornhill, September 27, 1958, February 21, 1961, Box 71, Folder 108, CVWP; Willie Lee Rose to CVW, January 17, 1963, Box 47, Folder 557, CVWP; CVW to Carleton, December 24, 1961, December 25, 1964, February 17, 1965, Carleton Papers.

13. Bernard A. Weisberger, "The Dark and Bloody Ground of Reconstruction Historiography," *Journal of Southern History* 25 (November 1959): 434, 429.

14. John Hope Franklin, *Reconstruction after the Civil War* (Chicago: University of Chicago Press, 1961); John Hope Franklin, *Mirror to America: The Autobiography of John*

Hope Franklin (New York: Farrar, Straus and Giroux, 2005), 194–95; Kenneth M. Stampp, *The Era of Reconstruction, 1865–1877* (New York: Random House, 1965).

15. James G. Randall and David Donald, *The Civil War and Reconstruction*, 2nd rev. ed. (Boston: D. C. Heath, 1961); David Donald, *The Politics of Reconstruction, 1863–1877* (Cambridge, Mass.: Harvard University Press, 1965); Eric L. McKittrick, *Andrew Johnson and Reconstruction* (Chicago: University of Chicago Press, 1960); Lawanda F. Cox and John H. Cox, *Politics, Principle, and Prejudice: Dilemma of Reconstruction America* (New York: Macmillan, 1963); Rembert W. Patrick, *Reconstruction of the Nation* (New York: Oxford University Press, 1967); CVW to Byron S. Hollinshead, May 24, 1966, Box 41, Folder 490, CVWP.

16. Thornhill to CVW, May 17, June 22, 1965, CVW to A. L. Hart Jr., June 17, 1965, and CVW to Thornhill, June 17, 1965, Box 71, Folder 108, CVWP.

17. Rose to CVW, September 8, 1965, Box 47, Folder 557, CVWP.

18. CVW to Thornhill, October 25, 1965, July 19, 1966, January 5, 1967, CVW to Ned Bradford, November 18, 1968, and Bradford to CVW, February 4, 1969, Box 32, Folder 387, CVWP; "Messenger Lectures," 1964, Cornell University, Box 64, Folder 23, CVWP; Natalie J. Ring and Sarah E. Gardner, eds., *The Lost Lectures of C. Vann Woodward* (New York: Oxford University Press, 2020); CVW, "Seeds of Failure in Radical Race Policy," *Proceedings of the American Philosophical Society* 110 (1966): 1–9.

19. CVW to Stanley Elkins, January 26, 1958, Box 75, Folder 10, CVWP.

20. CVW to Richard Hofstadter, May 11, 1962, Box 26, Folder 302, CVWP; Richard Hofstadter, *Anti-Intellectualism in American Life* (New York: Alfred A. Knopf, 1962).

21. CVW to Franklin, February 13, August 15, 1962, Box 19, Folder 222, CVWP; Franklin, *Mirror to America*, 197.

22. CVW to James W. Silver, September 25, 1963, Box 50, Folder 590, CVWP; James W. Silver, *Mississippi: The Closed Society* (New York: Harcourt, Brace, and World, 1964).

23. These numbers are derived from a bibliography of CVW's writings provided in John Herbert Roper, *C. Vann Woodward, Southerner* (Athens: University of Georgia Press, 1987), 352–62.

24. CVW to William P. Fidler, May 30, 1963, Box 2, Folder 13, CVWP.

25. CVW to Glenn Woodward, May 15, 1960, Box 60, Folder 731, CVWP; John M. Blum et al., *The National Experience: A History of the United States* (New York: Harcourt, Brace, and World, 1963).

26. CVW to Fidler, May 30, 1963.

27. CVW to Esmond Wright, December 1, 1940, Box 60, Folder 736, CVWP; CVW to William G. Carleton, January 17, 1956, Carleton Papers.

28. CVW, *Thinking Back: The Perils of Writing History* (Baton Rouge: Louisiana State University Press, 1986), 63.

29. O'Brien, *Letters of C. Vann Woodward*, xxiii; "Questions of Approach," Box 71, Folder 108, CVWP.

30. Donald to CVW, January 7, 1957, Box 16, Folder 175, CVWP; CVW to Carleton, December 24, 1961, Carleton Papers.

31. CVW to Carleton, December 23, 1958, Carleton Papers.

32. CVW to Carleton, December 24, 1961.

33. CVW to Carleton, December 24, 1961.

34. CVW to Howard K. Beale, October 22, 1954, Box 26, Folder 8, Beale Papers.

35. O'Brien, *Letters of C. Vann Woodward*, xxx; CVW to Bertram Wyatt-Brown, October 25, 1994, Box 61, Folder 740, CVWP.

36. O'Brien, *Letters of C. Vann Woodward*, xxx. Woodward did provide documentation for *The Old World's New World* (New York: Oxford University Press, 1991). This was the published version of lectures sponsored by the New York Public Library in 1990.

37. C. Vann Woodward, "The Fate of the Union: Kennedy and After," *New York Review of Books*, December 26, 1963, 8–9, https://www.nybooks.com/articles/1963/12/26/the -fate-of-the-union-kennedy-and-after-10/ (accessed June 10, 2019).

38. CVW, "After Watts—Where Is the Negro Revolution Headed?," *New York Times Magazine*, August 29, 1965, 84; Felix Gilbert, Richard Hofstadter, H. Stuart Hughes, Leonard Krieger, William E. Leuchtenberg, C. Vann Woodward, and Gordon Wright, letter to the editor, *New York Times*, May 10, 1970, 17E, https://timesmachine.nytimes.com /timesmachine/1970/05/10/354920102.html?pageNumber=173 (accessed April 3, 2019).

39. William E. Leuchtenburg, "The Historian and the Public Realm," *American Historical Review* 97 (February 1992): 9; CVW, ed., *Responses of the Presidents to Charges of Misconduct* (New York: Dell, 1974), xxvi.

40. CVW, "That Other Impeachment," *New York Times*, August 11, 1974, 215, www .nytimes.com/1974/08/11/archives/that-other-impeachment-a-convulsive-past-that -haunts-a-tormented.html/ (accessed October 11, 2017).

41. CVW, "That Other Impeachment."

42. CVW to James Morton Smith, November 5, 1973, Box 1, Folder 2, CVWP; CVW, "The Graying of America," *New York Times*, December 29, 1976, 25, https://timesmachine .nytimes.com/timesmachine/1976/12/29/140544312.html (accessed January 8, 2018).

43. CVW, "The Fall of the American Adam," *American Academy of Arts and Sciences Bulletin* 35 (November 1981): 33; CVW et al., "The Election and the Future: A Symposium," *New York Review of Books*, December 22, 1988, 35, www.nybooks.com/articles/1988/12/22 /the-election-and-the-future-a-symposium/ (accessed January 8, 2018).

44. Paul Lieberman, "Historians Warn House Panel on Diluting Voting Rights Act," *Atlanta Constitution*, June 25, 1981, clipping, Roper Papers; Roper, *C. Vann Woodward*, 290.

CHAPTER 13

1. CVW, "Success That Failed," *New York Times Book Review*, January 3, 1965, 6; James McPherson to CVW, January 9, 1965, and CVW to McPherson, January 5, 1965, Box 36, Folder 422, CVWP.

2. CVW to Bertram Wyatt-Brown, October 25, 1994, Box 61, Folder 740, CVWP; CVW to Robert Silvers, June 15, 1995, Box 43, Folder 513, CVWP; "We Unhappy Few," review of *The House of Percy: Honor, Melancholy, and Imagination in a Southern Family* and *The Literary Percys: Family History, Gender and the Literary Imagination*, by Bertram Wyatt Brown, *New York Review of Books*, June 22, 1995, 32–36, https://www.nybooks.com /articles/1995/06/22/we-unhappy-few (accessed October 22, 2018). For more examples of CVW's reviews of books by former students, see CVW, "Homegrown Radicals," review of *Grass-Roots Socialism: Radical Movements in the Southwest, 1895–1943*, by James R. Green, *New York Review of Books*, April 5, 1979, www.nybooks.com /articles/1979/04/05/home-grown-radicals/ (accessed October 22, 2018); CVW, "Role Player," review of *The Wizard of Tuskegee, 1901–1915*, by Louis R. Harlan, *New York Times*,

May 22, 1983, www.nytimes.com/1983/05/22/books/role-player.html/ (accessed October 22, 2018); CVW, "The Enigma of U.S. Grant," review of *Grant: A Biography*, by William S. McFeely, *New York Review of Books*, March 19, 1981, www.nybooks.com /articles/1981/03/19/the-enigma-of-us-grant/ (accessed October 22, 2018).

3. Stephen J. Whitfield, "Understanding Backward," *Virginia Quarterly Review* 63 (Spring 1987): 352.

4. CVW to Joel Williamson, April 7, 1971, Box 60, Folder 726, CVWP; CVW to Sheldon Hackney, March 29, 1971, and Hackney to CVW, March 14, April 8, 1971, Box 24, Folder 272, CVWP; Organization of American Historians, "Program of the Annual Meeting," 1971, 33, copy in author's possession; Hackney, "Origins of the New South in Retrospect," *Journal of Southern History* 38 (May 1972): 213; CVW, *Thinking Back: The Perils of Writing History* (Baton Rouge: Louisiana State University Press, 1986), 67. For reviews of CVW's books by former students, see Vincent P. Desantis, "Politics and Segregation in the Gilded Age," review of *The Strange Career of Jim Crow*, by CVW, *Review of Politics* 18, no. 1 (1956): 122–25; J. Morgan Kousser, review of *Thinking Back: The Perils of Writing History*, by CVW, *Journal of Economic History* 47, no. 2 (1987): 591–92; Bertram Wyatt-Brown, "The Sound and the Fury," review of *Thinking Back: The Perils of Writing History*, by CVW, *New York Review of Books*, March 13, 1986, http://www.nybooks.com/articles/1986/03/13/the -sound-and-the-fury/ (accessed February 9, 2018).

5. CVW to McPherson, February 15, 1965, Box 36, Folder 422, CVWP; CVW to Winkler, December 17, 1966, April 25, 1967, Winkler to CVW, n.d., [1967] (in response to CVW's report), and Winkler to CVW, April 14, 1967, Box 4, Folder 26, CVWP; CVW to Hackney, December 18, 1966, Box 87, Folder 22, CVWP.

6. See Sheldon Hackney, "Southern Violence," *American Historical Review* 74 (February 1969): 906–25. Scarcely a year after this article appeared, CVW was positively "glowing with admiration" for another provocative Hackney essay on "The South as Counterculture." He pronounced it "too elegant to waste" on a lesser publication and advised Hackney that he had told the editor of the *American Scholar* "that I am urging you to submit the essay." Hackney of course complied, and as Woodward predicted, his piece went on to "grace the pages of that journal." CVW to Hackney, July 9, 1970, Box 24, Folder 272, CVWP; Sheldon Hackney, "The South as a Counterculture," *American Scholar* 42 (Spring 1973): 283–93.

7. CVW to Sheldon Meyer, June 1, September 5, 1962, Box 40, Folder 484, CVWP; Willie Lee Rose, *Rehearsal for Reconstruction: The Port Royal Experiment* (New York: Bobbs-Merrill, 1964).

8. CVW to J. Morgan Kousser, November 20, 1988, Box 31, Folder 366, CVWP.

9. CVW to Jean H. Quataert, December 16, 1982, and CVW to David Hollinger, November 16, 1981, Box 62, Folder 758, CVWP. See also Bruce Palmer, *Man over Money: The Southern Populist Critique of American Capitalism* (Chapel Hill: University of North Carolina Press, 1980).

10. CVW to Susan Garfield, December 22, 1992, and CVW to National Humanities Center Fellowship Application Committee, October 9, 1986, Box 62, Folder 758, CVWP.

11. CVW to McPherson, July 1, 1968, Box 86, Folder 18, CVWP.

12. "To: Students writing dissertations under my supervision," February 2, 1977, Box 61, Folder 745, CVWP.

13. CVW to Kent Roberts Greenfield, January 19, 1951, Box 22, Folder 261, CVWP; CVW to R. S. Walters, February 3, 1981, Box 86, Folder 19, CVWP; "Draft of Guggenheim Recommendation," November 24, 1981, Box 87, Folder 38, CVWP.

14. CVW to Robert Fogel, February 6, 1973, Box 18, Folder 216, CVWP; CVW to Eugene D. Genovese, April 2, 1973, Box 21, Folder 214, CVWP; CVW to Robert Silvers, March 17, 1964, October 24, 1972, Box 38, Folder 459, CVWP; CVW, "A Southern Conscience," *New York Review of Books*, August 20, 1964, www.nybooks.com /articles/1964/08/20/a-southern-conscience/ (accessed January 22, 2018); CVW, "The Jolly Institution," *New York Review of Books*, May 2, 1974, www.nybooks.com /articles/1974/05/02/the-jolly-institution/ (accessed January 22, 2018); CVW, "Seeing Slavery Whole," *New York Review of Books*, October 3, 1974, www.nybooks.com /articles/1974/10/03/seeing-slavery-whole/ (accessed January 22, 2018).

15. CVW to Committee of Applications of the National Humanities Center, October 9, 1986, Box 62, Folder 758, CVWP; Howard Rabinowitz to CVW, December 8, 1979, July 25, 1983, Box 46, Folder 539, CVWP.

16. CVW to Mills Thornton, September 30, 1975, Box 88, Folder 43, CVWP; "John Simon Guggenheim Memorial Foundation: Confidential Report on Candidate for Fellowship," December 8, 1983, Box 22, Folder 263, CVWP. See Jonathan M. Wiener, *Social Origins of the New South: Alabama, 1865–1885* (Baton Rouge: Louisiana State University Press, 1978).

17. CVW to Scott A. Samson, August 25, 1993, and CVW to Mary Ann Worklan, April 11, 1988, Box 62, Folder 758, CVWP.

18. Gordon S. Wood, "Star-Spangled History," *New York Review of Books*, August 12, 1982, www.nybooks.com/articles/1982/08/12/star-spangled-history (accessed June 19, 2018).

19. CVW to Bernard Bailyn, October 14, 1963, and "Recommendation for Bailyn," n.d., Box 7, Folder 57, CVWP; CVW to Barry D. Karl, January 22, 1991, Box 62, Folder 758, CVWP.

20. CVW to Morton Keller, Department of History, February 11, 1985, Box 62, Folder 758, CVWP.

21. CVW to Robert L. Tignor, September 1, 1986, Box 62, Folder 758, CVWP.

22. George M. Fredrickson, letter to the editor, *New York Times Book Review*, July 20, 1971; Fredrickson to CVW, July 21, August 2, 1971, Box 19, Folder 224, CVWP; J. Morgan Kousser to CVW, April 13, 1999, Box 31, Folder 366, CVWP; CVW, "Our Own Herrenvolk," *New York Review of Books*, August 12, 1971, www.nybooks.com/articles/1971/08/12 /our-own-herrenvolk/ (accessed February 15, 2018); George M. Fredrickson, *The Black Image in the White Mind* (New York: Harper and Row, 1971).

23. CVW to William Styron, April 11, 1967, Box 52, Folder 726, CVWP.

24. CVW to Raymond Walters, October 4, 1967, Box 38, Folder 361, CVWP; CVW, "Confessions of a Rebel: 1831," *New Republic*, October 7, 1967, 28; Wilfred Sheed, "The Slave Who Became a Man," *New York Times Book Review*, October 8, 1967, 2.

25. CVW to Lee Benson, March 16, 1973, Box 8, Folder 73, CVWP; CVW to David Donald, July 11, 1966, Box 16, Folder 176, CVWP; CVW to Robert B. Silvers, April 14, 1969, Box 38, Folder 459, CVWP.

26. CVW, "W. J. Cash Reconsidered," *New York Review of Books*, December 4, 1969, www.nybooks.com/articles/1969/12/04/wj-cash-reconsidered/ (accessed August 11, 2019).

27. CVW, "W. J. Cash Reconsidered"; "David Donald Comments on 1969 SHA Session," Box 181, Folder 38, Wiley Papers.

28. Hackney to CVW, February 23, 1970, Box 65, Folder 54, CVWP.

29. Joseph L. Morrison to Silvers, December 5, 1969, Folder 62, Joseph L. Morrison Papers, Southern Historical Collections, University of North Carolina, Chapel Hill (collection arranged by folder); Silvers to CVW, January 12, 1971, April 21, 1990, Box 38, Folder 459, CVWP; David Brion Davis, "The Rebel," *New York Review of Books*, May 17, 1990, www.nybooks.com/articles/1990/05/17/the-rebel/ (accessed October 22, 2018).

30. CVW to Glenn W. Rainey, April, n.d. [1932], Box 6, Folder 9, Rainey Papers; Mrs. H. A. Woodward to Dr. and Mrs. Vann Woodward, June 3, 1955, and CVW to Hugh A. Woodward, n.d. [Spring 1930], Box 60, Folder 732, CVWP.

31. Bess Woodward to CVW, n.d. [1949], and Hugh A. Woodward to CVW, September 4, 1952, Box 60, Folder 732, CVWP.

32. Peter V. Woodward to CVW, February 10, 1966, Box 60, Folder 374, CVWP.

33. CVW to Peter V. Woodward, June 8, 1967, Box 60, Folder 734, CVWP.

34. CVW to Peter V. Woodward, January 3, 1969, September 27, 1968, and Peter V. Woodward to CVW, January 17, 1969, Box 60, Folder 734, CVWP.

35. John Herbert Roper, *C. Vann Woodward, Southerner* (Athens: University of Georgia Press, 1987), 237–38; CVW to Virginia Durr, October 16, 1969, Box 16, Folder 183, CVWP.

36. Jesse Lemisch to Arthur Waskow, September 13, 1969, Box 75, Folder 2, CVWP.

37. Jesse Lemisch, "Higham, Hofstadter, and Woodward: Three Liberal Historians?," U.S. Society for Intellectual History (USSIH), March 15, 2014, https://s-usih.org /2014/03/higham-hofstadter-and-woodward-three-liberal-historians-guest-post-by-jesse -lemisch/ (accessed February 23, 2019); CVW to Susan L. Woodward, January 1, 1970, Box 60, Folder 735, CVWP; Paul Ward to CVW, n.d. [Fall 1969?], Box 75, Folder 2, CVWP.

38. CVW to Susan L. Woodward, January 1, 1970.

39. Ronald Radosh, "A Historian Taught by History: Eugene Genovese, 1930–2012," *Weekly Standard*, October 15, 2012, www.weeklystandard.com/a-historian-taught-by -history/article/653811/ (accessed February 23, 2018); CVW to Susan L. Woodward, January 1, 1970.

40. Carl Mirra, "Forty Years on: Looking Back at the 1969 Annual Meeting," *Perspectives on History: The News Magazine of the American Historical Association*, February 1910, www.historians.org/publications-and-directories/perspectives-on-history/february-2010 /forty-years-on-looking-back-at-the-1969-annual-meeting#note4/ (accessed February 23, 2018); CVW to Susan L. Woodward, January 1, 1970.

41. "Minutes of the Annual Business Meeting, December 28–29, 1969," *AHA Perspectives*, February 1970, www.historians.org/about-aha-and-membership/aha -history-and-archives/historical-archives/minutes-of-the-annual-business-meeting -december-28-29-1969/ (accessed February 23, 2018); CVW to Susan L. Woodward, January 1, 1970.

42. CVW to Susan L. Woodward, January 1, 1970.

43. William S. McFeely, interview by Roper, December 4–5, 1984, Roper Papers; CVW to McFeely, September 26, 1975, Box 35, Folder 416, CVWP.

44. William G. Carleton, interview by Roper, July 21, 1979, Roper Papers.

45. John M. Blum, interview by Roper, December 13, 1984, Roper Papers.

46. Martin Ridge to CVW, March 6, 1973, and CVW to Ridge, March 14, 16, 1973, Box 28, Folder 336, CVWP; CVW to Otto Pflanze, June 5, 1979, Box 4, Folder 26, CVWP.

CHAPTER 14

1. John Herbert Roper, *C. Vann Woodward, Southerner* (Athens: University of Georgia Press, 1987), 198; David Moltke-Hansen, "Turn Signals: Shifts in Values in Southern Life Writing," in *Dixie Redux: Essays in Honor of Sheldon Hackney,* ed. Raymond Arsenault and Orville Vernon Burton (Montgomery, Ala.: New South Books, 2013), 172.

2. CVW to Kingman Brewster, March 4, April 22, 1969, Box 62, Folder 749, CVWP.

3. Clark Kerr was the former president of the University of California, whom California governor Ronald Reagan assailed for treating student protestors too indulgently. CVW to Gerald W. Johnson, March 2, 1969, Box 27, Folder 323, CVWP.

4. Alexander Bickel et al. to Kingman Brewster, April 25, 1970, Box 62, Folder 749, CVWP.

5. CVW to Brewster, February 19, 1968, Box 62, Folder 749, CVWP.

6. Robert F. Engs to CVW, September 1, 1970, and CVW to Engs, September 8, 1970, Box 86, Folder 8, CVWP.

7. John White, "The Novelist as Historian: William Styron and American Negro Slavery," *American Studies* 4 (1971): 233; Randall Kennedy, "On Judging Nat Turner," in Arsenault and Burton, *Dixie Redux,* 22.

8. See Charles V. Hamilton, "Our Nat Turner and William Styron's Creation," in *William Styron's Nat Turner: Ten Black Writers Respond,* ed. John Henrik Clarke (Boston: Beacon Books, 1968), 73–78.

9. Sam Tanenhaus, "The Literary Battle for Nat Turner's Legacy," *Vanity Fair,* September 2016, www.vanityfair.com/culture/2016/08/the-literary-battle-for-nat-turners -legacy/ (accessed March 14, 2018); Lerone Bennett Jr., "The Case against William Styron's Nat Turner," *Ebony,* October 23, 1968, 151. See also John Oliver Killens, "The Confessions of Willie Styron," in Clarke, *William Styron's Nat Turner,* 28; and Ernest Kaiser, "The Failing of William Styron," in Clarke, *William Styron's Nat Turner,* 57.

10. CVW to Wilma Dykeman Stokely, June 3, 1968, Box 52, Folder 620, CVWP; CVW to William Styron, July 8, 1968, Box 52, Folder 626, CVWP. See also Eugene D. Genovese, "The Nat Turner Case," *New York Review of Books,* September 12, 1968, www.nybooks .com/articles/1968/09/12/the-nat-turner-case/ (accessed August 21, 2019).

11. CVW to Ralph Ellison, March 18, 1968, Box 17, Folder 194, CVWP; typescript copy of the SHA session transcript in the author's possession. The edited transcript was later published as Ralph Ellison, William Styron, Robert Penn Warren, and C. Vann Woodward, "A Discussion: The Uses of History in Fiction," *Southern Literary Journal* 1 (Spring 1969): 57–90.

12. Bennett H. Wall to CVW, Box 51, Folder 607, CVWP; James L. West, *William Styron: A Life* (New York: Random House, 1998), 393–94; Robert Penn Warren to Robert Heilman, January 19, 1969, in *Selected Letters of Robert Penn Warren,* vol. 5, *Backward Glances and New Visions: 1969–1979,* ed. Randy Hendricks and James A. Perkins (Baton Rouge: Louisiana State University Press, 2011), 205.

13. CVW to Tilden G. Edelstein, May 14, 1968, Box 17, Folder 189, CVWP; CVW, "Clio with Soul," *Journal of American History* 56 (June 1969): 9, 16.

14. CVW, "Clio with Soul," 16–17.

15. CVW, "Clio with Soul," 14, 17, 19–20.

16. CVW, "Clio with Soul," 18–19.

17. CVW, "American History (White Man's Version) Needs an Infusion of Soul," *New York Times Magazine*, April 20, 1969, 32–33, 108–14, https://timesmachine.nytimes.com/timesmachine/1969/04/20/170473802.html?pageNumber=102 (accessed August 21, 2019); CVW to Harvey Shapiro, January 28, 1969, Box 38, Folder 460, CVWP.

18. LeRoi Jones, "Letter to the Editor 2, No Title," *New York Times Magazine*, May 11, 1969, https://timesmachine.nytimes.com/timesmachine/1969/05/11/88996393.html?pageNumber=425/ (accessed August 21, 2019).

19. Sterling Stuckey, "Twilight of Our Past: Reflections on the Origins of Black History," in *Amistad 2*, ed. John A. Williams and Charles A. Harris (New York: Vintage, 1971), 280–83, 286.

20. CVW to Sterling Stuckey, February 17, May 25, 1971, and Stuckey to CVW, March 31, 1971, Box 40, Folder 574, CVWP; CVW, introduction to "Clio with Soul," as reprinted in *The Future of the Past* (New York: Oxford University Press, 1989), 29; J. Mills Thornton III, "C. Vann Woodward: November 13, 1908–December 17, 1999," *Civil War History* 46 (2000): 337–40.

21. CVW, *The Strange Career of Jim Crow*, 3rd rev. ed. (New York: Oxford University Press, 1974), 199–200.

22. Eric Pace, "Owen Lattimore, Far East Scholar Accused by McCarthy, Dies at 88," *New York Times*, June 1, 1989, www.nytimes.com/1989/06/01/obituaries/owen-lattimore-far-east-scholar-accused-by-mccarthy-dies-at-88.html/ (accessed August 15, 2019); Sidney Painter to CVW, August 2, 1955, Box 28, Folder 238, CVWP.

23. All of the information noted for both 1951 investigations and one in 1944 clearing CVW to serve in Naval Intelligence is attached to "Department of the Navy, Office of the Chief of Naval Operations, Memorandum for Mr. J. Edgar Hoover, Director, Federal Bureau of Investigation, March 8, 1954, Attention: Liaison Section, Subject: Woodward, Lt. Comer Vann, USNR, 276102/1105." See Enclosures 1–9, for February–April 1944, and Enclosures 10–14, for June–November 1951. A copy is in the author's possession.

24. Glenda Elizabeth Gilmore, *Defying Dixie: The Radical Roots of Civil Rights, 1919–1950* (New York: W. W. Norton, 2008), 227, 269.

25. "Memorandum for Mr. J. Edgar Hoover," Enclosure 12, July 27, 1951.

26. "Memorandum for Mr. J. Edgar Hoover," Enclosure 10, June 25, 1951; CVW to Colonel Thomas G. Dobyns, January 14, 1952, Box 54, Folder 640, CVWP; CVW to Thomas A. Krueger, June 19, 1963, Box 29, Folder 345, CVWP.

27. CVW to Lord Halifax, September 3, 1954, Box 40, Folder 483, CVWP.

28. CVW to Frank Freidel, November 28, 1954, Box 19, Folder 277, CVWP; CVW to Merle C. Curti, June 3, 1955, Box 13, Folder 151, CVWP; CVW to Boyd Shafer, November 16, 1954, Box 40, Folder 482, CVWP. See entries for October 30, November 2, 9, 1954, in CVW, "Journal while at Queens College, Oxford, 1954–1955," Box 92, Folder 17, CVWP.

29. CVW to Cushing Strout, July 6, 1992, Box 52, Folder 62, CVWP.

30. CVW to *Yale Daily News*, January 29, 1974, clipping, Box 61, Folder 745, CVWP; Brewster to CVW, August 5, 1974, Box 62, Folder 749, CVWP; Nathaniel Zelinsky, "Challenging the Unchallengeable (Sort of)," *Yale Alumni Magazine*, January/February 2015, https://yalealumnimagazine.com/articles/4017-woodward-report/ (accessed March 16, 2018).

31. Zelinsky, "Challenging the Unchallengeable"; "Report of the Committee on Freedom of Expression at Yale: II. Of Trials and Errors," December 23, 1974, https://yalecollege.yale.edu/deans-office/reports/report-committee-freedom-expression-yale#Of Trials and Errors/ (accessed March 19, 2018).

32. "Report of the Committee on Freedom of Expression at Yale: I. Of Values and Priorities," December 23, 1974, https://yalecollege.yale.edu/deans-office/reports/report-committee-freedom-expression-yale#Of%20Values%20and%20Priorities/ (accessed September 19, 2018); Nat Hentoff, "It's Still a Star Chamber at Yale," *Washington Post*, October 25, 1986, www.washingtonpost.com/archive/opinions/1986/10/25/its-still-a-star-chamber-at-yale/d070ca1a-9cd9-4969-aaba-c2b8fe94a107/ (accessed September 16, 2019).

33. CVW to Strout, November 1, 1991, July 6, 1992, Box 52, Folder 62, CVWP.

34. Herbert Aptheker, *American Negro Slave Revolts* (reprint ed., New York: International Publishers, 1963), 162–63, 373.

35. Aptheker, 162–63, 373; Hoover is quoted in Gary Murrell, *The Most Dangerous Communist in the United States: A Biography of Herbert Aptheker* (Amherst: University of Massachusetts Press, 2015), 167.

36. Schlesinger is quoted in Murrell, *Most Dangerous Communist*, 85; Herbert Aptheker, *The Truth about Hungary* (New York: Mainstream, 1957).

37. CVW to John Hall, October 14, 1975, Box 62, Folder 746, CVWP.

38. David Horowitz, "Bettina Aptheker: A Critique of Her Memoir by Conservative David Horowitz," History News Network, November 10, 2006, historynewsnetwork.org/article/31687/ (accessed September 4, 2019).

39. CVW to Editor, *New Statesman and Nation*, November 14, 1954, Box 37, Folder 444, CVWP; James Green, "Past and Present in Southern History: An Interview with C. Vann Woodward," *Radical History Review* 36 (1986): 84; Angus Cameron to CVW, October 27, November 9, 1961, Box 30, Folder 363, CVWP. CVW did join a few others for an informal private conversation with Alger Hiss in 1959. The former State Department official was convicted of perjury in 1950 after denying charges that he had been a communist in the 1930s and a Soviet spy, though it is hard to say whether CVW was moved to do so more by sympathy or by curiosity. "Alger Hiss Memorandum," as dictated on May 3, 1959, Box 75, Folder 17, CVWP.

40. CVW to Staughton Lynd, April 19, 1965, Box 33, Folder 397, CVWP.

41. CVW, *Thinking Back: The Perils of Writing History* (Baton Rouge: Louisiana State University Press, 1986), 86; CVW to Glenn W. Rainey, March 9, 1938, Box 6, Folder 7, Rainey Papers; CVW to W. E. B. Du Bois, April 3, 1938, Box 85, Folder 2, CVWP; Du Bois to CVW, April 8, 1938, Box 16, Folder 180, CVWP.

42. CVW to Herbert Aptheker, February 16, 1971, Box 85, Folder 2, CVWP; CVW to Bernard Bailyn, May 6, 1967, Box 7, Folder 57, CVWP.

43. CVW, "W. E. B. Du Bois," n.d., Box 63, Folder 17, CVWP. Though this document was written as an introduction to a proposed collection of Du Bois's writings, the author has found no evidence that the introduction was published, and it is cataloged in the CVWP under "Short Writings," which includes unpublished as well as published work.

44. CVW, "W. E. B. Du Bois."

45. CVW, "W. E. B. Du Bois"; see also David Levering Lewis, *W. E. B. Du Bois: A Biography, 1868–1963* (New York: Henry Holt, 2009), 696.

46. Roper, *C. Vann Woodward*, 284; Rayford W. Logan, ed., *W. E. B. Du Bois: A Profile* (New York: Hill and Wang, 1971), xiv; see also Clarence Contee, review of *The Correspondence of W. E. B. Du Bois*, vol. 1, *Selections, 1877–1934*, edited by Herbert Aptheker, *Journal of Southern History* 40 (August 1974): 498–99.

47. Herbert Aptheker, ed., *Correspondence of W. E. B. Du Bois*, vol. 1, *Selections, 1877–1934* (Amherst: University of Massachusetts Press, 1973), 223, 465.

48. Aptheker, 82, 467–69. Woodward was by no means alone in suspecting Aptheker's motives. See Logan, *W. E. B. DuBois*, xiv; and Rayford W. Logan, ed., *What the Negro Wants* (Chapel Hill: University of North Carolina Press, 1944), 61.

49. Aptheker to Du Bois, November 24, 1961, quoted in Murrell, *Most Dangerous Communist*, 200.

CHAPTER 15

1. W. E. B. Du Bois to Charles F. Kellogg, July 21, 1950, Box 16, Folder 180, CVWP.

2. CVW to Herbert Aptheker, April 21, 1964, and Aptheker to CVW, April 28, December 12, 1964, Box 5, Folder 40, CVWP.

3. Aptheker to CVW, May 6, 1954, December 15, 1969, and CVW to Aptheker, January 14, 1970, Box 5, Folder 40, CVWP; CVW to Virginius Dabney, n.d., Box 14, Folder 160, CVWP. CVW to Robert Penn Warren, September 22, 1966, Box 82, Folder 1610, Warren Papers.

4. CVW to Aptheker, January 26, 1971, and Aptheker to CVW, January 15, 1971, Box 85, Folder 2, CVWP.

5. Aptheker to CVW, February 2, 1971, "Application Summary, National Endowment for the Humanities, NEH application H-7708, October 1970," Box 85, Folder 2, CVWP; Gary Murrell, *The Most Dangerous Communist in the United States: A Biography of Herbert Aptheker* (Amherst: University of Massachusetts Press, 2015), 217.

6. CVW to Aptheker, February 16, 1971, Aptheker to CVW, February 25, 1971, CVW to Aptheker, March 17, 1971, and Aptheker to CVW, March 31, 1971, Box 85, Folder 2, CVWP.

7. Aptheker to William R. Emerson, August 2, 1973, and CVW to Emerson, August 21, 1973, Box 85, Folder 2, CVWP. CVW's response likely caused Emerson no great dismay, judging at least from University of Massachusetts Press director Leone Stein's account of being accosted in a restaurant by Emerson, who railed at the "effrontery" and "stupidity" of "America's Number 1 Communist" applying for an NEH grant in the first place. Stein is quoted in Murrell, *Most Dangerous Communist*, 220.

8. CVW to Aptheker, August 21, 1973, and Aptheker to CVW, August 28, 1973, Box 85, Folder 2, CVWP.

9. CVW to Stein, January 28, 1974, CVW to John Hope Franklin and Louis Harlan, September 24, 1973, Aptheker to CVW, February 20, 1974, CVW to Aptheker, February 27, 1974, and Aptheker to CVW, March 1, 1974, Box 85, Folder 2, CVWP.

10. CVW to National Endowment for the Humanities, Division of Research Grants, February 26, 1976, Box 85, Folder 2, CVWP.

11. Ramsay MacMullen to CVW, n.d. [January 1976], CVWP.

12. Jonathan Mandell, "Poli Sci Sponsors Aptheker Seminar," *Yale Daily News*, October 24, 1975, 1; Paul A. Rahe, "Appointment for Aptheker," *Yale Revue*, clipping, n.d. [October 1975], Box 85, Folder 1, CVWP.

13. Horace Taft to CVW, November 17, 1975, Box 85, Folder 4, CVWP.

14. CVW to Taft, November 20, 1975, Box 85, Folder 4, CVWP; Clarence Contee, review of *The Correspondence of W. E. B. Du Bois*, vol. 1, *Selections, 1877–1934*, edited by Herbert Aptheker, *Journal of Southern History* 40 (August 1974): 498–99; Robert A. Blecker, "Aptheker and Power," *Yale Daily News*, February 4, 1977, 2, 9.

15. Taft to CVW, December 2, 1975, Box 85, Folder 4, CVWP.

16. Minutes of the Joint Board of Permanent Officers, December 4, 1975, Box 85, Folder 1, CVWP.

17. Minutes of the Joint Board of Permanent Officers, December 4, 1975.

18. CVW to Taft, December 8, 1975, and Taft to CVW, December 10, 1975, Box 85, Folder 4, CVWP.

19. CVW to Taft, December 8, 1975.

20. "We the Undersigned Faculty to Horace Taft," n.d., Box 85, Folder 2, CVWP; Joseph LaPalombara, "Aptheker: Academic Overkill," *Yale Daily News*, December 17, 1975, 2, 4.

21. CVW to Joseph LaPalombara, January 27, 1976, Box 85, Folder 1, CVWP.

22. Herbert Aptheker, "Aptheker Speaks: 'I Need No Protection,'" *Yale Daily News*, January 30, 1976, clipping, Box 85, Folder 1, CVWP.

23. CVW, letter to *Yale Daily News*, February 2, 1976, clipping, Box 85, Folder 1, CVWP.

24. CVW, letter to *Yale Daily News*, February 2, 1976.

25. Murrell, *Most Dangerous Communist*, 231; William S. McFeely, interview by John Herbert Roper, December 4, 1984, Roper Papers; John Blum, interview by Roper, December 13, 1984, Roper Papers. Lemisch is quoted in Murrell, *Most Dangerous Communist*, 244.

26. Aptheker to Mack Thompson, February 12, 1976, John H. Bracey Jr. to John Blassingame, February 4, 1976, and Blassingame to Bracey, February 23, 1976, Box 85, Folder 1, CVWP.

27. CVW to National Endowment for the Humanities, Division of Research Grants, February 26, 1976, Box 85, Folder 2, CVWP.

28. Letter from the Committee to Support the Du Bois Seminar, *Yale Daily News*, March 24, 1976, Box 85, Folder 1, CVWP.

29. MacMullen is quoted in Murrell, *Most Dangerous Communist*, 231–32.

30. Ruth Marcus, "Aptheker Addresses 300 at Cross Campus Rally," *Yale Daily News*, March 30, 1976, 1, 7.

31. CVW to Marvin Gettleman, March 15, 1976, Box 85, Folder 1, CVWP.

32. Richard H. Kirkendall to CVW, March 1, 1976, and CVW to Kirkendall, March 15, 1976, Box 85, Folder 1, CVWP.

33. Gettleman to CVW, February 12, March 4, April 7, 14, 1976, and CVW to Gettleman, February 23, 1976, Box 85, Folder 1, CVWP.

34. CVW to Genovese, April 16, 1976, Genovese to CVW, April 22, 1976, and CVW to Alden Whitman, March 31, 1976, Box 85, Folder 1, CVWP.

35. Lemisch and Gettleman are quoted in Murrell, *Most Dangerous Communist*, 234; CVW to John W. Hall, May 11, 1976, and Hall to Richard S. Kirkendall, May 12, 1976, Box 85, Folder 1, CVWP.

36. Jesse Lemisch, "If Howard Cosell Can Teach at Yale, Why Can't Herbert Aptheker," copy in Box 85, Folder 1, CVWP.

37. Hall to Kirkendall, June 23, 1976, Box 85, Folder 1, CVWP.

38. See "A Statement in Support of the Resolution" and "Reply to the Statement by Professor Jesse Lemisch and Associates," *Organization of American Historians Newsletter*,

4 (July 1976): 4–6; Richard Kirkendall telegram to John Hall, October 11, 1976, Box 85, Folder 1, CVWP.

39. Murrell, *Most Dangerous Communist*, 237.

40. CVW to Charles Gibson and Kenneth M. Stampp, July 20, 1977, Box 43, Folder 12, CVWP.

41. CVW to Gibson and Stampp, July 20, 1977.

42. Gibson and Stampp to CVW, June 28, 1977, CVWP; "Draft of reply to Kirkendall by José Cabranes," n.d., Box 85, Folder 4, CVWP; "Yale-Aptheker Inquiry Concluded," *AHA Newsletter*, February 16, 1978, 1.

43. CVW to Charles Gibson and Kenneth M. Stampp, July 20, 1977, Box 43, Folder 12, CVWP; CVW, "The Erosion of Academic Privileges and Immunities," *Daedalus* 103 (Fall 1974): 33–37.

44. "Yale University and Dr. Herbert Aptheker, A Report of the American Historical Association-Organization of American Historians Committee on the Defense of the Rights of Historians under the First Amendment," *OAH Newsletter*, 5 (January 1978), 9–14.

45. John Weltman, "Historians Finish Aptheker Inquiry," *Yale Daily News*, November 8, 1977, 1.

46. "Yale University and Dr. Herbert Aptheker"; "The Debate over the Report on Yale University and Dr. Herbert Aptheker," *OAH Newsletter* 6 (July 1978), 11–18; Murrell, *Most Dangerous Communist*, 240–41.

47. Murrell, *Most Dangerous Communist*, 241–42; Kenneth M. Stampp, "Historian of Slavery, the Civil War and Reconstruction, Berkeley, 1946–1983," an oral history conducted in 1996 by Ann Lage, Regional History Office, Bancroft Library, University of California Berkeley, 1998, https://oac.cdlib.org/view?docId=kt258001zq&brand=oac4&doc .view=entire_text (accessed September 1, 2016); "The Debate over the Report"; Stampp to CVW, February 2, 1977, Box 52, Folder 614, CVWP; Frank Freidel to CVW, April 12, 1976, Box 85, Folder 1, CVWP.

48. "The Debate over the Report"; Murrell, *Most Dangerous Communist*, 241–43.

49. "The Debate over the Report"; *OAH Newsletter*, vol. 6, no. 2, January 1979.

50. "Voting Results," *OAH Newsletter*, vol. 6, no. 2, January 1979.

51. Roper, *C. Vann Woodward*, 284.

52. Leone Stein and John H. Bracey to George Farr, June 30, 1976, quoted in Murrell, *Most Dangerous Communist*, 223.

53. CVW to Eileen Kraditor, December 12, 1976, Box 31, Folder 367, CVWP; CVW, interview by Roper, November 4–5, 1982, Roper Papers.

54. Paul Rahe, "Listen to History," *Yale Daily News*, January 24, 1977, 2; David Lauter, "Shaky Scholarship," *Yale Daily News*, January 24, 1977, 2; "A letter from members of the Du Bois seminar," *Yale Daily News*, February 18, 1977, 2; Robert A. Blecker, "Aptheker and Power," *Yale Daily News*, February 4, 1977, 2, 11.

55. David Lempert, "Fraud Case Settled," *Yale Daily News*, November 8, 1977, 1, 3; CVW to Paul H. Partington, September 14, November 14, 1977, Box 43, Folder 507, CVWP; Kenneth Stampp to CVW, February 9, 1978, Box 52, Folder 614, CVWP. See also Partington to Roper, August 13, 1989, Roper Papers. The materials Partington deposited were added to the Beinecke Library's W. E. B. Du Bois Collection, https://archives.yale.edu /repositories/11/archival_objects/362188.

56. "Legal Complaint," Box 43, Folder 507, CVWP; Herbert Gstalder to Henry A. Turner, March 2, 1978, Roper Papers; "Correction," *Yale Daily News*, January 19, 1978, 2; "Historians Absolve Yale in Aptheker Dispute," *Yale Alumni Magazine*, February 1978, 52–53. See also Partington to Roper, August 13, 1989, Roper Papers.

57. James Lebovitz, "Retirements Weaken History Department," *Yale Daily News*, April 13, 1977, 1, 7.

CHAPTER 16

1. CVW, ed., *Mary Chesnut's Civil War* (New Haven, Conn.: Yale University Press, 1981).

2. CVW, *Mary Chesnut's Civil War*, xx, xvi, xlix, 32, 59, 508.

3. Isabella D. Martin and Myrta Lockett, eds., *A Diary from Dixie, as Written by Mary Boykin Chesnut, Wife of James Chesnut, Jr., United States Senator from South Carolina, 1859–1861, and Afterward an Aide to Jefferson Davis and a Brigadier General in the Confederate Army* (New York: D. Appleton, 1905); Hans Skei, "Review Essay: Mary Chesnut's Civil War," *American Studies in Scandinavia*, 15, 37, https://rauli.cbs.dk/index.php/assc/article/view/1203/1202/ (accessed May 8, 2018).

4. Wilson is quoted in Kenneth S. Lynn, "The Masterpiece That Became a Hoax," *New York Times Book Review*, April 26, 1981, www.nytimes.com/1981/04/26/books/the-masterpiece-that-became-a-hoax.html/ (accessed May 3, 2018).

5. James B. Meriwether to CVW, October 14, November 11, 1974, Box 36, Folder 426, CVWP.

6. Elisabeth Muhlenfeld to CVW, May 16, September 25, 1975, Box 69, Folder 87, CVWP.

7. CVW to Muhlenfeld, November 17, 1975, Box 69, Folder 89; Meriwether to CVW, November 29, 1975, Box 36, Folder 426, CVWP.

8. CVW to Meriwether, December 15, 1975, Meriwether to CVW, January 11, 1977, Box 36, Folder 426, CVWP.

9. CVW, *Mary Chesnut's Civil War*, xii.

10. CVW, *Mary Chesnut's Civil War*, lvii; Muhlenfeld to CVW, November 24, 1975, Box 69, Folder 87, CVWP; Meriwether to CVW, November 29, 1975, Box 36, Folder 426, CVWP.

11. Muhlenfeld to CVW, November 24, 1975, Box 69, Folder 87, CVWP; Meriwether to CVW, November 29, 1975, Box 36, Folder 426, CVWP.

12. CVW to Muhlenfeld, December 2, 1975, Box 69, Folder 87, CVWP.

13. Lynn, "Masterpiece."

14. Lynn.

15. William Styron, "In the Southern Camp," *New York Review of Books*, August 13, 1981, www.nybooks.com/articles/1981/08/13/in-the-southern-camp/ (accessed May 3, 2018); Kenneth S. Lynn, letter to the editors, and reply by William Styron, *New York Review of Books*, October 8, 1981, www.nybooks.com/articles/1981/10/08/mrs-chesnuts-affair/ (accessed May 3, 2018).

16. CVW to Louis D. Rubin Jr., March 8, 1981, quoted in Michael O'Brien, ed., *The Letters of C. Vann Woodward* (New Haven, Conn.: Yale University Press, 2013), 343; CVW to Elisabeth Muhlenfeld, April 7, 1981, Box 69, Folder 89, CVWP.

17. William R. Taylor and Steven M. Stowe, letter to the editor, *New York Times*, May 17, 1981, www.nytimes.com/1981/05/17/books/l-mary-chesnut-s-diary-124664.html (accessed May 2, 2018).

18. CVW is quoted in Michael P. Johnson, "Mary Boykin Chesnut's Autobiography and Biography: A Review Essay," *Journal of Southern History* 47 (November 1981): 587.

19. Johnson, "Mary Boykin Chesnut's Autobiography," 587–88.

20. Johnson, "Mary Boykin Chesnut's Autobiography," 588.

21. Johnson, "Mary Boykin Chesnut's Autobiography," 589.

22. Johnson, "Mary Boykin Chesnut's Autobiography," 588–89.

23. Johnson, "Mary Boykin Chesnut's Autobiography," 590; CVW to Elisabeth Muhlenfeld, March 31, 1982, Box 37, Folder 440, CVWP. See Carl N. Degler, review of *Mary Chesnut's Civil War*, edited by CVW, *American Historical Review* 87 (February 1982): 261–62; Catherine Clinton, review of *Mary Chesnut's Civil War*, edited by CVW, *Journal of American History* 68 (March 1982): 939–41; CVW and Elisabeth Muhlenfeld, eds., *The Private Mary Chesnut: The Unpublished Civil War Diaries* (New York: Oxford University Press, 1984).

24. CVW, *Mary Chesnut's Civil War*, xxvii, 549; Drew Gilpin Faust, "In Search of the Real Mary Chesnut," *Reviews in American History* 10 (March 1982): 55–57.

25. Glenda E. Gilmore, "Gender and *Origins of the New South*," in John B. Boles and Bethany L. Johnson, eds., *Origins of the New South: Fifty Years Later: The Continuing Influence of a Historical Classic* (Baton Route: Louisiana State University Press, 2003), 221–22.

26. CVW to Richard B. Sewall, December 19, 1963, Box 61, Folder 720, CVWP.

27. Gilmore, "Gender and *Origins of the New South*," 221; CVW, *Private Mary Chesnut*, xviii; Anne Firor Scott, *The Southern Lady: From Pedestal to Policies, 1830–1930* (Chicago: University of Chicago Press, 1970); Anne Firor Scott, "Gender and Vann Woodward," in Boles and Johnson, eds., *Origins of the New South: Fifty Years Later*, 291.

28. Gilmore, "Gender and *Origins*," 232; J. D. [Sandy] McClatchy to CVW, n.d. [probably 1996], Box 61, Folder 745, CVWP; CVW, "Preface," in *Jumpin' Jim Crow: Southern Politics from Civil War to Civil Rights*, ed. Jane Daily, Glenda Elizabeth Gilmore, and Bryant Simon (Princeton, N.J.: Princeton University Press, 2000), xi.

29. CVW to James B. Meriwether, July 5, 1981, Box 70, Folder 100, CVWP. Donald actually wrote that he found it "ironical" that, in this case, "the publication of an authoritative text has undermined the credibility of what has been a basic source in southern history." See David Herbert Donald, "Word from the Old South," *New York Times Book Review*, June 28, 1981, 3, 23.

30. "Mary Chesnut in Search of Her Genre," as reprinted in CVW, *The Future of the Past* (New York: Oxford University Press, 1989), 260.

31. "Mary Chesnut in Search of Her Genre," 260–61, 254–55.

32. Robert C. Christopher to CVW, April 12, 1982, Box 42, Folder 416, CVWP.

33. Heinz-Dietrich Fischer et al., ed., *American History Awards, 1917–1991*, The Pulitzer Prize Archive, vol. 7 (Munich: K. G. Saur, 1994), lix–lx.

34. Fischer et al., *American History Awards*, lx, lxv. See also David S. Brown, *Richard Hofstadter: An Intellectual Biography* (Chicago: University of Chicago Press, 2006), 112.

35. CVW, "Chesnut in Search," 256.

36. Letter to the Editor, Gore Vidal, Reply by CVW, "Gore Vidal's 'Lincoln'?: An Exchange," *New York Review of Books*, September 28, 1988, www.nybooks.com/articles /1988/04/28/gore-vidals-lincoln-an-exchange/ (accessed October 7, 2019); CVW to John

Updike, May 25, 1996, Box 53, Folder 638, CVWP; Gore Vidal, *The Last Empire: Essays, 1992–2000* (New York: Knopf-Doubleday, 2002), 292.

37. "The Pulitzer Prizes: Special Awards and Citations," www.pulitzer.org/prize-winners-by-category/260/ (accessed May 15, 2018).

38. CVW to Sheldon Meyer, April 5, 1982, Box 40, Folder 486, CVWP; J. Morgan Kousser and James M. McPherson, eds., *Region, Race and Reconstruction: Essays in Honor of C, Vann Woodward* (New York: Oxford University Press, 1982).

39. CVW to Hansell, October 15, 1939, Looker Papers.

40. CVW to Andrew J. Walker, January 30, 1938, Box 6, Folder 10, Rainey Papers; CVW to Rainey, December 10, 1939, Box 6, Folder 8, Rainey Papers.

41. On Glenn's illness in 1950–51, see Howard K. Beale to CVW, November 21, 1950, Box 7, Folder 66, CVWP; and Lester J. Cappon to CVW, April 25, 1951, Box 61, Folder 605, CVWP. See also CVW to John Hope Franklin, October 11, 1994, Box 19, Folder 222, CVWP.

42. William G. Carleton and Manning J. Daver, interviews by John Herbert Roper, July 21, 1979, Roper Papers.

43. CVW to Hackney, March 25, 1971, Box 24, Folder 272, CVWP; CVW to Susan L. Woodward, September 3, 1970, Box 60, Folder 735, CVWP.

44. Rainey, interview by Roper, Roper Papers; Robert Penn Warren to CVW, September 13, 1979, and CVW to Warren, August 13, 1980, Box 59, Folder 703, CVWP; CVW to David Riesman, June 15, 1981, Box 47, Folder 551, CVWP.

45. CVW to Elisabeth Muhlenfeld, March 31, 1982, Box 37, Folder 440, CVWP.

46. See Ruth Claus to CVW, June 3, 1982, Box 86, Folder 16, CVWP; CVW to Virginia Durr, January 23, 1984, quoted in Michael O'Brien, ed., *The Letters of C. Vann Woodward* (New Haven, Conn.: Yale University Press, 2013), 357.

47. Virginia Durr to CVW, February 4, 1984, Box 16, Folder 183, CVWP; CVW to Virginia Durr, June 2, 1984, O'Brien, *Letters*, 357.

48. Carleton interview.

49. Kelly Heyboer, "Why a Rutgers Prof's Two Sentences about Vietnam Went Viral in 1965," www.nj.com/education/2015/04/rutgers_genovese_vietnam_anniversary_how_a_marxist.html/ (accessed April 17, 2018).

50. CVW to James M. McPherson, October 5, 1973, Box 36, Folder 423, CVWP.

51. Eugene Genovese to CVW, August 17, 1970, Box 21, Folder 240, CVWP; Genovese to CVW, October 17, 1979, January 20, 1977, Box 21, Folder 241, CVWP.

52. Genovese to CVW, April 7, 22, May 11, 1976, CVW to Genovese, May 7, 1976, Box 21, Folder 241, CVWP.

53. Murrell, *Most Dangerous Communist*, 240, 242; Willie Lee Rose to CVW, April 25, 1978, Box 47, Folder 558, CVWP.

54. Genovese to CVW, March 6, 1980, CVW to Genovese, March 20, 1980, Box 21, Folder 241, CVWP. Though he was joking in any case, Woodward may have mistakenly believed that "Gibbon" referred to an African tribe rather than a species of ape that actually is indigenous to Asia.

55. "Controversial Character," *Harvard Crimson*, April 30, 1980, www.thecrimson.com/article/1980/4/30/controversial-character-pbwbhen-the-afro-american-studies/ (accessed December 5, 2018). See also, "Problems Plague Harvard's Black Studies Program," *New York Times*, April 20, 1980, 23, https://timesmachine.nytimes.com/timesmachine/1980/04/20/issue.html (accessed December 5, 2018); Judith Cummings

and Albin Krebs, "Prof. Genovese Rejected," *New York Times*, June 13, 1980, B5, https://timesmachine.nytimes.com/timesmachine/1980/06/13/issue.html/ (accessed December 5, 2018).

56. Genovese to CVW, April 25, 1980, Box 21, Folder 241, CVWP.

57. CVW to Genovese, May 2, June 23, 1980, Box 21, Folder 241, CVWP.

58. Genovese to CVW, March 21, 1981, Box 21, Folder 241, CVWP.

59. CVW to Genovese, April 6, 1981, Box 21, Folder 241, CVWP.

60. CVW to Genovese, April 6, 1981.

61. CVW to Genovese, April 6, 1981.

62. James Green, "Past and Present in Southern History: An Interview with C. Vann Woodward," *Radical History Review* 36 (1986): 96; Elizabeth Fox-Genovese and Eugene D. Genovese, Letter to Editors, *Radical History Review* 38 (1987):144–45; Genovese is quoted in Murrell, *Most Dangerous Communist*, 321.

63. CVW to Thomas M. Finn, November 24, 1986, CVW to Morton Keller, February 11, 1985, Box 62, Folder 758, CVWP.

64. CVW to Roger Anderson, April 6, 1992, Box 62, Folder 758, CVWP.

65. Hackney to CVW, March 3, 1992, CVW to Hackney, March 23, 1992, Box 24, Folder 272, CVWP.

66. Jonathan Wiener, *Historians in Trouble: Plagiarism, Fraud, and Politics in the Ivory Tower* (New York: New Press, 2005), 13–21.

67. Michael O'Brien, "A Retrospective on the Southern Intellectual History Circle, 1988–2013," Society for U.S. Intellectual History, U.S. Intellectual History Blog, January 29, 2014, https://s-usih.org/2014/01/a-retrospective-on-the-southern-intellectual-circle-1988-2013/ (accessed January 26, 2018); Genovese to CVW, November 19, 1994, January 31, 1985, Box 21, Folder 241, CVWP; CVW to Genovese, December 3, 1994, Box 21, Folder 241, CVWP. Genovese had actually asked Woodward to join the Tucker Society in May 1994. See CVW to Genovese, May 11, 1994, Box 21, Folder 241, CVWP.

68. Genovese is quoted in Murrell, *Most Dangerous Communist*, 219; O'Brien, "Retrospective."

69. CVW to Robert Penn Warren, April 26, 1983, September 4, 1960, Box 82, Folder 1609, Warren Papers.

70. Warren to CVW, July 14, 1964, Box 79, Folder 703, CVWP; CVW to Warren, July 24, 1964, Box 82, Folder 1609, Warren Papers.

71. Warren to CVW, August 6, 1978, Box 59, Folder 703, CVWP.

72. Warren to CVW, July 28, 1985, Box 59, Folder 703, CVWP; CVW, "Robert Penn Warren 1905–1989," Yale Memorial Service, October 26, 1989, Box 66, Folder 71, CVWP.

CHAPTER 17

1. William S. McFeely, interview by John Herbert Roper, December 4, 1984; CVW to Norman Pollack, September 16, 1969, Box 44, Folder 518, CVWP.

2. CVW to Willie Lee Rose, November 30, 1982, Box 47, Folder 558, CVWP.

3. "Preliminary Prospectus: Oxford History of the United States," n.d., Box 41, Folder 487, CVWP.

4. Richard Hofstadter to CVW, June 2, 1961, Box 21, Folder 241, CVWP; CVW to Hofstadter, December 2, 1961, Box 41, Folder 487, CVWP.

5. CVW to Merrill Jensen, March 19, 1962, Box 75, Folder 3, CVWP.

6. Hofstadter to CVW, January 14, 1963, Box 41, Folder 488, CVWP.

7. Merrill Petersen to CVW, January 31, 1967, and CVW to Hofstadter, February 6, 1967, Box 41, Folder 487, CVWP.

8. Jensen to Byron S. Hollinshead, February 16, 1970, Jensen to CVW, December 14, 1970, and CVW to Jensen, February 17, 1971, Box 41, Folder 490, CVWP.

9. Hofstadter to CVW, October 30, 1962, Box 41, Folder 488, CVWP; Hofstadter to CVW, n.d., Box 42, Folder 499, CVWP.

10. Sheldon Meyer to Stanley Elkins and Eric McKittrick, September 18, 1975, Box 41, Folder 492, CVWP.

11. CVW to Elkins and McKittrick, August 18, 1975, Box 41, Folder 491, CVWP; CVW to Elkins and McKittrick, September 9, 1979, Box 41, Folder 492, CVWP; McKittrick to CVW, September 9, 1979, Box 11, Folder 492, CVWP.

12. Hofstadter to CVW, undated, 1966, Box 45, Folder 499, CVWP; Morton Keller to Meyer, September 23, 1975, Box 41, Folder 492, CVWP.

13. "Announcing the Oxford History of the United States, edited by Richard Hofstadter and C. Vann Woodward," printer's galley, February 1970, and CVW to Robert Middlekauff, August 29, 1971, Box 41, Folder 490, CVWP.

14. CVW to Stuart Bruchey, October 6, 1975, Box 41, Folder 492, CVWP; CVW to Keller, August 18, 1975, Box 41, Folder 491, CVWP; Meyer to Keller, draft letter, Box 41, Folder 490, CVWP.

15. Hofstadter to CVW, n.d., Box 42, Folder 499, CVWP; CVW to Sellers, May 19, 1969, Box 41, Folder 489, CVWP; CVW to Sellers, April 16, 1987, Box 42, Folder 496, CVWP; CVW to Sellers, August 17, 1990, Box 42, Folder 497, CVWP. Sellers's book was later published separately by Oxford as *The Market Revolution: Jacksonian America, 1815–1846* (New York: Oxford University Press, 1991).

16. CVW, "A Short History of American History," *New York Times Book Review*, August 8, 1982, cited here as reprinted in CVW, *The Future of the Past* (New York: Oxford University Press, 1989), 315–17, quotation on 315.

17. CVW, "Short History," 318–19.

18. CVW, "Short History," 318–19.

19. Eric Monkonen, "The Resurgence of Narrative History," *New York Times Book Review*, September 5, 1982, www.nytimes.com/1982/09/05/books/l-resurgence-of -narrative-history-125637.html/ (accessed June 18, 2018).

20. Gordon S. Wood, "Star Spangled History," *New York Review of Books*, August 12, 1982, www.nybooks.com/articles/1982/08/12/star-spangled-history (accessed March 4, 2019).

21. Wood, "Star Spangled History."

22. Wood, "Star Spangled History." See "Writing History: An Exchange," *New York Review of Books*, December 16, 1982, www.nybooks.com/articles/1982/12/16/writing -history-an-exchange/ (accessed March 4, 2019).

23. T. H. Breen to CVW, October 1, 1985, Box 42, Folder 495, CVWP.

24. Meyer to Breen, October 16, 1985, Box 42, Folder 495, CVWP.

25. CVW to Breen, October 16, 1985, Box 42, Folder 495, CVWP.

26. CVW to George Fredrickson, May 3, 1987, Box 42, Folder 496, CVWP.

27. CVW to David M. Kennedy, July 11, 1998, Box 42, Folder 429, CVWP.

28. Christopher Shea, "The Rejection Bin of History," *Boston.com*, December 24, 2006, http://archive.boston.com/news/education/higher/articles/2006/12/24/the _rejection_bin_of_history/ (accessed December 12, 2018).

29. CVW to Gordon S. Wood, November 16, 1995, Box 42, Folder 498, CVWP.

30. Barbara Vobeda, "Punishment Rescinded in Yale Free-Speech Case," *Washington Post*, October 2, 1986, www.washingtonpost.com/archive/politics/1986/10/02 /punishment-rescinded-in-yale-free-speech-case/99c6efe6-3628-4b18-8ce0-4de82d6cfaa9/ (accessed March 20, 2018); "Professors Back Yale Student on Free Speech," *New York Times*, September 28, 1986, www.nytimes.com/1986/09/28/nyregion/professors-back -yale-student-on-free-speech.html/ (accessed March 20, 2018).

31. Conor Friedersdorf, "The Perils of Writing a Provocative Email at Yale," *Atlantic*, May 26, 2016, www.theatlantic.com/politics/archive/2016/05/the-peril-of-writing-a -provocative-email-at-yale/484418/ (accessed October 22, 2019). Kristakis remained on the faculty and was ultimately awarded a Sterling Professorship on the strength of his scholarship, but after months of student protests demanding the couple's removal and what seemed, at best, muted support from many of their faculty colleagues, the two resigned their positions with Silliman College in May 2016.

32. CVW, "Freedom & the University," *New York Review of Books*, July 18, 1991, 32–37; https://www.nybooks.com/articles/1991/07/18/freedom-the-universities/ (accessed October 22, 2019); CVW to Steven Hahn, August 2, 1991, Box 72, Folder 123, CVWP.

33. CVW, "Freedom and the University," 32–37.

34. CVW, "Freedom and the University."

35. CVW, "Freedom and the University"; D'Souza, *Illiberal Education*, 194–97.

36. Abu Kathara to CVW, July 5, 1991, Box 72, Folder 122, CVWP; Michael Bérubé to Robert Silvers, July 16, 1991, Box 72, Folder 123, CVWP. The July 18 edition of the *New York Review of Books* was actually available in early July; Chuck Lane, "Crying Out in Igno-rance," *Harvard Review*, June 7, 1982, www.thecrimson.com/article/1982/6/7/crying-out -in-ignorance-pbwhat-did/ (accessed October 23, 2019).

37. Letters from John Hope Franklin and George Fredrickson, as well as CVW's response, appeared in "Illiberal Education: An Exchange," *New York Review of Books*, September 26, 1991, 74–76, https://www.nybooks.com/articles/1991/09/26/illiberal -education-an-exchange/ (accessed, October 22, 2019). In the same issue, see also the letters from Jon Wiener, Ernst Benjamin, Barbara Bergman (in behalf of the AAUP), Clyde D. Ryals, and Gene H. Bell-Villada.

38. "Illiberal Education."

39. CVW to Franklin, August 2, 1991, and Franklin to CVW, October 8, 1991, Box 72, Folder 123, CVWP.

40. The author was a participant in this conference. See "The Future of the South," *American Issues Forum 1*, National Humanities Center, Research Triangle Park, N.C., 1995; CVW to Cushing Strout, November 1, 1991, Box 52, Folder 62, CVWP; and John Hope Franklin, *Mirror to America: The Autobiography of John Hope Franklin* (New York: Farrar, Straus, and Giroux, 2005), 312 (note: Franklin mistakenly places his conversation with Woodward at the 1999 meeting of the Southern Historical Association, which Wood-ward, within weeks of his death, did not attend. If the conversation took place at an SHA meeting, it was likely the previous year, when the group celebrated Woodward's ninetieth birthday).

41. CVW to Hahn, August 2, 1991; CVW to Strout, November 1, 1991; Edmund Morgan to CVW, July 1, 1991, Box 72, Folder 122, CVWP; Arthur Schlesinger Jr. to CVW, July 4, 17, 1991, Box 72, Folder 123, CVWP; CVW, "Equal but Separate," *New Republic*, July 15, 1991, 41–42.

42. D'Souza pled guilty in 2014 to felony charges of making illegal campaign contributions in a 2012 Senate race and was pardoned in 2018 by President Donald Trump. Inhae Oh, "Trump Pardoning of Dinesh D'Souza May Be Another Signal for Loyalists in Russia Probe," *Mother Jones*, May 31, 2018, www.motherjones.com/politics/2018/05 /trump-dinesh-dsouza-pardon-announcement/ (accessed October 24, 2019).

43. CVW to Schlesinger, February 1, March 1, 1991, Box 49, Folder 577, CVWP.

44. Schlesinger to CVW, July 17, 1991; CVW to David Burner, May 17, 1993, Box 9, Folder 97, CVWP; Ronald Radosh, "Sidney Hook Was Right, Arthur Schlesinger Is Wrong," *History News Network*, December 16, 2002, https://historynewsnetwork.org /article/1154/ (accessed August 18, 2018). See also CVW, "Where the Unthinkable Can Be Thought," *Academic Questions* 6 (December 1993): 69–71, https://link.springer.com /article/10.1007%2FBF02682863/ (accessed June 18, 2018).

45. CVW, "Recent Paradoxes of American Race," unpublished manuscript, Box 70, Folder 105, CVWP; Donald S. Lamm to CVW, January 27, 1995, Box 70, Folder 104, CVWP.

46. CVW to Lamm, October 21, 1995, Box 70, Folder 104, CVWP.

47. CVW to Lamm, October 21, 1995.

48. CVW, "Post-Reconstruction Periods Compared: 1890s and 1990s," in *The Southern State of Mind*, ed. Jan Nordby Gretlund (Columbia: University of South Carolina Press, 1999), 220–21.

49. CVW, "Post-Reconstruction Periods Compared," 222.

50. CVW to John Hope Franklin, October 11, 1994, Box 19, Folder 252, CVWP; CVW to Robert Silvers, June 15, 1995, Box 43, Folder 513, CVWP; CVW, "We Unhappy Few," *New York Review of Books*, June 22, 1995, www.nybooks.com/articles/1995/06/22/we-unhappy -few/ (accessed March 11, 2019).

51. CVW to Bertram Wyatt-Brown, June 14, 1995, Box 43, Folder 513, CVWP. The author was also a participant in the 1997 meeting in Denmark.

52. Joan M. Zenzen, *Battling for Manassas: The Fifty-Year Preservation Struggle at Manassas National Battlefield Park* (University Park: Pennsylvania State University Press, 1998), 162, 177; CVW to Franklin, October 11, 1994. See also CVW, "Virginia's Rich Historic Region Can Do without the Disney Park," *Philadelphia Inquirer*, June 20, 1994, 11A; and John F. Harris, "400 Historians Denounce Impeachment," *Washington Post*, October 29, 1998, www.washingtonpost.com/wp-srv/politics/special/clinton/stories/president102998 .htm/ (accessed January 13, 2021).

53. CVW to Elizabeth Muhlenfeld, May 24, 1994, Box 37, Folder 440, CVWP.

54. CVW to Martin Peretz, May 19, 1994, Box 43, Folder 501, CVWP; David Greenberg, "All the President's Men," *Lingua Franca*, April 1999, http://linguafranca.mirror.theinfo .org/9904/fn.html/ (accessed January 10, 2018); Peter Charles Hoffer, *Past Imperfect: Facts, Fictions, Fraud—American History from Bancroft and Parkman to Ambrose, Bellesiles, Ellis, and Goodwin* (New York: Public Affairs, 2004), 124; C. Vann Woodward, Arthur Schlesinger Jr., and Sean Wilentz, "A History of Impeachment," *Charlie Rose Show*, October 28, 1998, https://charlierose.com/videos/14069 (accessed October 1, 2018).

55. CVW to William H. Goetzmann, September 26, 1998, Box 45, Folder 528; Morgan Kousser to CVW, April 13, 1999, Box 31, Folder 366; "Comments on Sheldon Hackney as a Fellowship Candidate," June 10, 1998, and draft of a fellowship recommendation for Joel Williamson, May 1, 1999, Box 62, Folder 758, CVWP; CVW to Michael McGerr, October 13, 1998, Box 42, Folder 499, CVWP; James H. Merrell to CVW, March 23, 1999, Box 42, Folder 498, CVWP; CVW to J. Mills Thornton, June 14, 1999, Box 53, Folder 630, CVWP; CVW with reply by Andrew Hacker, "Sticking to the Union," *New York Review of Books*, June 10, 1999, www.nybooks.com/articles/1999/06/10/sticking-to-the-union/ (accessed October 25, 2019).

56. Laurence S. Cohen to Charles D. Sabatino, November 11, 1992, Box 14, Folder 158, CVWP; CVW to Bertram Wyatt-Brown, March 31, 1999, Box 61, Folder 740, CVWP.

57. Cohen to Sabatino, June 7, 1999, Box 14, Folder 158, CVWP; John Blum to Helen Reeve, July 29, 1999, Box 47, Folder 547, CVWP; Paul Gaston, "Remembering C. Vann Woodward (1908–1999)," *Southern Changes* 12 (Winter 1999), http://southernchanges .digitalscholarship.emory.edu/sc21-4_1204/sc21-4_008/ (accessed March 10, 2019).

58. Schlesinger to Reeve, October 24, 1999, and Robin Winks to CVW, November 30, 1999, Box 47, Folder 547, CVWP.

59. Sheldon Hackney is quoted in Gaston, "Remembering C. Vann Woodward"; Bertram Wyatt-Brown, "In Memoriam: C. Vann Woodward (1908–99)," American Historical Association, *Perspectives on History*, March 1, 2000, www.historians.org/publications -and-directories/perspectives-on-history/march-2000/in-memoriam-c-vann-woodward / (accessed March 7, 2019).

CONCLUSION

1. William Palmer, *Engagement with the Past: The Lives and Works of the World War II Generation of Historians* (Lexington: University of Kentucky Press, 2001)

2. Sam Tanenhaus, "History, Written in the Present Tense," *New York Times*, March 4, 2007, www.nytimes.com/2007/03/04/weekinreview/04tanenhaus.html/ (accessed March 16, 2020).

3. Charles King, *Gods of the Upper Air: How a Circle of Renegade Anthropologists Reinvented Race, Sex, and Gender in the Twentieth Century* (New York: Doubleday, 2019), 4.

4. CVW is quoted in Barbara J. Fields, "Dysplacement and Southern History," *Journal of Southern History* 82 (February 2016): 26.

5. CVW, "Behind the Myths," in *The Future of the Past* (New York: Oxford University Press, 1989), 263.

6. Richard Hofstadter is quoted in William E. Leuchtenburg, "The Historian and the Public Realm," *American Historical Review* 97 (February 1992): 8.

7. David M. Potter, "C. Vann Woodward," in *Pastmasters: Some Essays on American Historians*, ed. Marcus Cunliffe and Robin W. Winks (New York: Harper and Row, 1969), 406–7; George Orwell, *1984* (reprint ed., New York: Penguin, 1977), 248.

8. Van Wyck Brooks, "On Creating a Usable Past," *Dial*, April 11, 1918, 337–41; Leuchtenburg, "Historian and the Public Realm," 9.

9. Warren I. Susman, "History and the American Intellectual: Uses of a Usable Past," *American Quarterly* 16 (Summer 1964): 262. CVW is quoted in Michael O'Brien, "C. Vann Woodward and the Burden of Southern Liberalism," *American Historical Review* 78 (June 1973): 600; CVW, "Wild in the Stacks," *New York Review of Books*, August 1, 1968, 8–12,

https://www.nybooks.com/articles/1968/08/01/wild-in-the-stacks (accessed November 12, 2019). For a New Left perspective on Woodward, see Jesse Lemisch, "Higham, Hofstadter and Woodward: Three Liberal Historians?," Society for U.S. Intellectual History (blog), March 15, 2014, https://s-usih.org/2014/03/higham-hofstadter-and -woodward-three-liberal-historians-guest-post-by-jesse-lemisch/ (accessed March 19, 2021).

10. CVW, "Behind the Myths," 309, 311.

11. Arthur Schlesinger Jr. to CVW, October 24, 1999, Box 47, Folder 547, CVWP.

12. Douglas Martin, "Arthur M. Schlesinger Jr., a Partisan Historian of Power, Is Dead at 89," *New York Times*, March 2, 2007, www.nytimes.com/2007/03/02/obituaries /02schlesinger.html/ (accessed June 21, 2020); Richard Severo, "C. Vann Woodward, Historian Who Wrote Extensively about the South, Dies at 91," *New York Times*, December 19, 1999, www.nytimes.com/1999/12/19/us/c-vann-woodward-historian-who-wrote -extensively-about-the-south-dies-at-91.html/ (accessed June 21, 2020).

13. Edward Ayers is quoted in Mark Alden Branch, "History for Everyone," *Yale Alumni Magazine*, March/April 2015, https://yalealumnimagazine.com/articles/4070-historian -edward-ayers/ (accessed March 20, 2021).

Index

Page numbers in italics refer to illustrations.

Abernethy, Milton, 46, 56
Abernethy, Thomas P., 86, 266
Ab's Intimate Bookshop, 46, 307
academic confidentiality, 332, 334, 335, 337, 363
academic freedom: political correctness and, 384, 387–88; Woodward disputes over, 306, 308–9, 318, 335–36; at Yale, 236
ACLS (American Council of Learned Societies), 265, 284
Adair, Douglas, 137
Adams, Henry, 221
African states, 175–76, 304
Afrocentrism, 304, 305, 384–85, 387–88, 401
Age of Reform (Hofstadter), 354
"Age of Washington and Jefferson, The" (Elkins and McKittrick), 373
agrarianism, 61–62, 78, 90–91, 114, 217
AHA (American Historical Association). *See* American Historical Association
Aldrich, Winthrop W., 308
Alexander, Will, 23, 24, 29–30, 32–34, 46–47
Alfred A. Knopf, 164, 179, 189
Alpha Tau Omega, 18

America in Midpassage (Beard), 108
American Communist Party, 29, 46–47, 312, 313, 315–18, 329, 388
American Council of Learned Societies (ACLS), 265, 284
American Dilemma (Myrdal), 177
American Historical Association (AHA): and Aptheker dispute, 328, 330, 332–33, 334–35; and Harmsworth Professorship, 308; Radical Caucus of, 292–95, 330, 397, 400; Woodward's presidential address to, 291–92, 369
American Historical Review, 265, 271, 278–79, 349
American Legion, 76, 98
American Negro Slave Revolts (Aptheker), 312
American Philosophical Society, 261, 265
American Scholar, 454n6
Andrews, Matthew Page, 86
anticommunism, 213–14, 268, 306, 332
Anti-Intellectualism in American Life (Hofstadter), 262
anti-interventionism, 96–97
anti-Semitism, 28, 31, 73–74

Antislavery (Dumond), 225–26, 227–28
Aptheker, Herbert: about, 313–14;
    American Negro Slave Revolts, 312;
    Blassingame and, 251; Du Bois and, 312,
    316–17, 319–22; lawsuit against, 339–40.
    See also Aptheker seminar dispute
Aptheker seminar dispute: AHA complaint
    and, 328; background and overview of,
    8, 312–13; classroom effectiveness of
    Aptheker and, 339; conclusions on, 338–
    39, 341, 364, 397; Genovese and, 320,
    325, 337, 360–61; history department
    requests and, 313, 314–15, 317–18, 323–24,
    328–29; OAH investigation of, 330–38,
    339; political science department
    sponsorship and, 323–27, 329–30;
    Woodward on, 326–28, 331
Arnett, Alex M., 80
assimilation, 390, 398
Atlanta Constitution, 18
Atlanta Journal, 28, 73
Atlantic Monthly, 73, 165–66
Augusta Chronicle, 74
Avary, Myrta L., 343
Ayers, Edward L., 121, 202, 404–5

Bailyn, Bernard, 284, 372
Ball, Edward, 392
Bancroft Prizes, 127, 246, 247,
    284, 375
Barker, Eugene C., 85
Basic Books, 261
Battle Cry of Freedom (McPherson),
    375, 376
Battle of Leyte Gulf, 101–2
Beale, Howard K., *411*; assistance to
    Woodward in finding jobs, 93–94, 95–
    96, 100; Beard and, 61, 108; *The Critical
    Year*, 51; "Fallacies of the Interventionist
    View," 97; *Origins* and, 123; *Reunion and
    Reaction* and, 113; SHA and, 138–40,
    141; *The Strange Career of Jim Crow*
    and, 176; as Woodward's dissertation
    adviser, 12, 34, 49–51, 53–54, 63, 76, 79,
    83; Woodward's Richard Lectures and,
    160–61

Beard, Charles A.: *America in Midpassage*,
    108; Beale and, 51, 61, 108; falling out
    of fashion of, 108–9; influence of, on
    Woodward works, 107–9, 110; views of,
    96–97, 396–97, 400
Becker, Carl, 400
Benedict, Michael Les, 110–11
Bennington College lecture series, 222
Benson, Lee, 286–87, 291
Bergstraesser, Arnold, 97–98
Bethany (Watson), 58–59, 70
Bicentennial, American, 274
Bickel, Alexander, 295–96, 300, 357
Billings, Dwight B., Jr., 126
Biltmore Hotel, 131
Black, J. C. C., 64
Black Codes, 151, 166–67, 193, 196–97
black Divinity students (Yale), 299
black history, 132, 303–4, 305, 306, 385–86
Black Image in the White Mind, The
    (Fredrickson), 285–86
black militants, 188, 299, 300, 305
black nationalism, 302, 304, 305, 390
Black Panthers, 294, 300
Black Power movement, 189, 190–92, 258,
    302–3, 388, 401
Black Rage (Grier and Cobbs), 190
Black Reconstruction (Du Bois), 175, 315
black separatism, 7, 190–92, 299–300, 305,
    306, 326, 388–90, 397
Black Student Alliance (Yale), 300, 323
black studies, 300–301, 304, 306, 361,
    385, 386
"Black Ulysses" (Odum), 33
Blair, Lewis Harvie, 175
Blassingame, John: Aptheker dispute
    and, 313, 325, 328, 333, 339; Frederick
    Douglass Papers and, 320; *The Slave
    Community*, 250–53; Woodward and,
    249–50, 281, 301
Blum, John Morton: about, 230, 238;
    Aptheker dispute and, 313, 321, 325,
    328, 332, 339; *Mary Chesnut's Civil War*
    and, 354; Oxford History of the United
    States series and, 371; Woodward and,
    230, 235–36, 240, 243, 296, 393

Boas, Franz, 398
Bobbs-Merrill (publisher), 280
Bok, Derek, 384
Booker T. Washington Papers, 320
Boorstin, Daniel, 210–11, 240, 397
Bourbons, 116, 183
boycotts, 181–82, 202
Bozart (magazine), 20
Bracey, John H., Jr., 328, 338
Bradford, Larned G. ("Ned"), 205, 261
Brandeis University, 265, 285
Breen, Timothy H., 375, 379–80
Brett-Smith, John, 370
Brewster, Kingman, 241, 242, 243, 299–300,
    309, 310, 329
Bridenbaugh, Carl, 133, 135–40,
    229, 266
"Brief Abandon" (Hartsock), 20
Brinton, Crane, 155
Brisbane, Robert H., 278
Brockway, George P., 255–56
Brodie, Fawn M., 227
Brooks, Cleanth, 239, 417
Brooks, Van Wyck, 400
Brown, Georgia Lee Watson, 36–37
Brown, Henry Billings, 157
Brown, H. Rap, 190
Brown, John, 168, 222–23
Brown, Joseph E., 116
Brown, Joseph M., 69
Brown v. Board of Education:
    implementation of, 184–85, 186–87;
    NAACP Legal Defense Fund and,
    147, 151–53; reaction to, 156, 162, 181;
    Woodward and, 147–50, 151–52, 296
Bruchey, Stuart, 374, 376
Bryan, William Jennings, 31
Buck, Paul H., 87
Bulldozer Revolution, 180, 217
Burden of Southern History, The: about, 4–5,
    6, 218–19, 220–21, 224; "Equality: The
    Deferred Commitment" in, 224–25;
    "The Historical Dimension" in, 219–20;
    "The Irony of Southern History" in,
    211–14, 216, 218–19, 221, 227, 271; "John
    Brown's Private War" in, 222–23; "The

Political Legacy of Reconstruction"
    in, 225; "The Search for Southern
    Identity" in, 208, 209–10, 215–19, 227;
    second edition of, 188–89; "A Southern
    Critique for the Gilded Age" in, 221;
    success of, 261
Butler, Nicholas Murray, 28
Byrd, Harry F., 156

Cable, George Washington, 166, 173, 174–75
Cabranes, José, 334
Caldwell, Joseph R. "Spec," 49
Calebrese, Guido, 382
Cameron, Angus, 107, 110, 314
Campbell, George, 165
Candler, Asa Griggs, 17, 62
Candler family, 62–63
Capers, Gerald M., 132
capital investment in southern states, 121
capitalism, 61–63, 115–16, 117, 119, 213
Cappon, Lester J., 128–29, 133–34, 135–36,
    137, 138–40
Carleton, Bill, 115, 117, 258, 268–69, 296,
    357, 359
Carlton, David L., 420
Carman, Harry, 354
Carmichael, Stokely, 190–92
carpetbaggers, 91, 110
Carter, Jimmy, 274
Cash, W. J., 115, 287–88, 320
Caspari, Fritz, 98
Cavalier Daily, 156, 158, 160
Cell, John, 175–76, 199–200, 201–2
Central High School, integration of, 182
Channing, Edward, 84–85
Charleston News and Courier, 174
Charlie Rose Show, 1–2, 391, 392
Chesnut, Mary Boykin, 342–43, 346, 347,
    348–49, 350. See also *Mary Chesnut's
    Civil War; Private Mary Chesnut, The*
Chesnut Collection, 343, 344
Chesnut, James, 342
Chronicles of America series, 43
Civil Rights Act of 1964, 186
Civil Rights Acts of the Reconstruction
    era, 148–49, 152, 172, 175

civil rights movement, 182–83, 187, 188–93, 254–55, 272, 299

Civil War and Reconstruction (Randall), 259

Clansman, The (Dixon), 346

Clark, Thomas D., 141–42

Clement, Rufus E., 178–79

Cleveland, Grover, 68, 170

Clinton, Bill, 1, 391–92

Clinton, Catherine, 349

Clinton, Hillary Rodham, 272, 391

Cold War, 213–14, 377, 396–97

Coleman, Mrs. William A., 85–86

colonization of the South, northern, 119–21

Colquitt, A. H., 116

Columbia Sentinel, 75

Columbia University: Bancroft Prize of, 127, 246, 247, 284, 375; Woodward at, 24–26, 27–28

Commager, Henry Steele, 109, 140, 371

Commission on Interracial Cooperation, 23, 33

committee on junior appointments at Yale University, 323–24

"Committee to Support the Aptheker Seminar," 323, 328–29

communism: Aptheker and, 312–13, 317–18, 324, 329; Cold War and, 212, 213, 214, 396; Du Bois and, 315–17, 324; Lattimore and, 289, 306, 313, 388

Communist Party, 29, 46–47, 312, 313, 315–18, 329, 388

"Comparability of American History," 261

Compromise of 1877, 3, 103, 106–14, 120, 149–50, 188, 297

Confessions of Nat Turner, The (Styron), 286, 301–2

confidentiality, academic, 332, 334, 335, 337, 363

congressional voting records, 111–12, 113–14

Conkin, Paul, 333, 334

Consensus School of American history, 108–9, 397, 400

Conservatives: and civil rights movement, 191–92; and race after Reconstruction, 174–75

Constitutional Convention of 1787, 109

Contee, Clarence, 317, 324

Cooke, Janet, 354

Cornell University, 261, 306

Couch, William T., 52, 104

Coulter, E. Merton: on defense of South's past, 39–40; and History of the South series, 104, 132, 256; and *Origins of the New South*, 86–87, 89, 127; on *Reunion and Reaction*, 111; and SHA, 41, 86–87, 132, 138–39

Council of the American Association of University Professors, 265

Cox, John and Lawanda, 259

Craven, Avery O., 44–45, 87, 125, 126–27

Craven, Wesley Frank, 86, 87

Critical Year, The (Beale), 51

crop-lien system, 114, 119, 120

Cross, David C., 9

Cross, Nancy, 9

Crowe, Charles, 62

Curti, Merle, 308

Cutler, Lloyd, 310

Dabney, Robert L., 115, 402

Dabney, Virginius, 320

Daedalus, 335

Dahl, Robert, 310, 311

Daily Tar Heel, 47–48

Daily Worker, 30, 47

Darden, Colgate, 156

"Dark and Bloody Ground of Reconstruction Historiography, The" (Weisberger), 259

Dartmouth Review, 383, 385

Dauer, Manning, 113, 160–61, 357

Davidson, Donald, 90–91

Davidson, Philip, 87

Davies, Wallace E., 111

Davis, David, 106

Davis, David Brion, 288, 341, 360, 362, 363

Davis, Jackson, 34

Davis, Jefferson, 40

Davis, John A., 147–49, 153

Davis, Lambert, 209

Debs, Eugene V., 84

de facto segregation, 187, 191

Degler, Carl, 349, 360
"deliberate speed," 185
"Deliberate Speed vs. Majestic Instancy,"
    184–86
Democracy (Adams), 221
Democrats, 68, 105–7, 109–10, 112, 113
DeSantis, Vincent G., 420
desegregation, 158, 181, 185. See also *Brown
    v. Board of Education*; segregation
Dew, Charles B., 420
Dick, Wayne, 382
discrimination, racial, 172–73, 303–4.
    See also segregation
disfranchisement, 27, 68–69, 171
Dissolution of the Virginia Company
    (Craven), 86
Disuniting of America, The
    (Schlesinger), 387
Dixiecrat Party, 111
Dixon, Thomas, 346, 347
Doar, John, 272
Dobbs, Samuel Candler, 62
Dodd, William E., 40
Donald, David: *Civil War and
    Reconstruction* revision by, 259, 260;
    Genovese and, 360, 362; McPherson
    dissertation and, 246–47; Oxford
    History of the United States series
    and, 371; *Politics of Reconstruction*, 259;
    rebuke of Woodward's critique of Cash,
    287–88; Sumner and, 223; on works of
    Woodward, 123, 203, 218–19, 352, 464n29
Douglass, Frederick, 68, 175
Doyle, H. S. "Seb," 64–65
D'Souza, Dinesh, 8, 383–85, 386, 469n42
Duberman, Martin, 247, 248
Du Bois, Shirley Graham, 319, 321
Du Bois, W. E. B.: Aptheker and, 312,
    313; *Black Reconstruction*, 175, 315;
    communism and, 315–17, 324; Harlem
    Experimental Theater and, 27; SHA
    and, 131; *Souls of Black Folk*, 315;
    Woodward and, 315, 319
Du Bois Papers, 319–22, 328, 333
Duke, James B., 63
Duke University, 63, 384

Dumond, Dwight, 225–26, 227–28
Dunning, William A., 40–41, 86
Dunning School, 87, 256, 259
Durr, Clifford, 181, 248
Durr, Virginia, 181–82, 186, 248, 357–58, 359

Eisenhower, Dwight D., 158, 186
election of 1876, presidential, 105–7
Electoral Commission of 1876, 106
Elkins, Stanley, 176, 250, 262, 373, 374, 375
Ellegood, Donald, 208, 209
Ellison, Ralph, 215, 302–3
emancipation, 159, 224
Emerson, Ralph Waldo, 223
Emerson, William, 321–22
Emory Junior College, 16
Emory University, 2, 10, 14, 16, 17–19, 63,
    365–66
Empire of Liberty (Wood), 374, 375, 378–79
Engerman, Stanley, 282
Engs, Robert, 281, 300–301, 420
Era of Reconstruction (Stampp), 259, 260
Erikson, Erik, 279

faculty raiding, 241–42
faculty recruitment, 240–41, 242, 384
Fairbank, John K., 294
"Fallacies of the Interventionist View"
    (Beale), 97
farmers, 30–31, 61–62, 119
Farmers' Alliance, 30–31
Farragut Hotel, 144, 145
Farrakhan, Louis, 389, 390
Faulkner, William, 6, 46, 117, 118, 146, 220,
    282, 353
Faust, Drew Gilpin, 2, 285, 349–50
FBI, 98
Felton, William H., 62
Ferguson, Charles, 23
fiction, southern, 46, 58, 118
Fifteenth Amendment, 150, 151, 259
First Amendment, 334
Fischer, David Hackett, 199
Fischer, Roger A., 173
Fleming Lectures, 207–8, 209
Flood (Warren), 367

Florida, 106, 146, 163, 166, 167

Fogel, Robert, 282

folkways, 157–58, 160, 179–80

Foner, Eric, 354

Fortune, T. Thomas, 170

Forty Acres and Steel Mules (Nixon), 91

Forum Lectures, 261

Fourteenth Amendment, 50, 147, 148–50, 151, 152

Fox-Genovese, Elizabeth, 364–66

Frank, Leo, 31, 73–75, 81

Franklin, John Hope: about, 132, *419*; civil rights history manuscript of, 263; Genovese and, 366; *The Militant South*, 133; NAACP Legal Defense Fund and, 147, 151, 153; Powell and, 189; *Reconstruction after the Civil War*, 259; *Romanticism and Nationalism in the Old South* review by, 141–42; SHA and, 132–41, 142, 143, 146; *From Slavery to Freedom*, 132; Woodward's D'Souza essay and, 384, 385–86; Woodward's Richard Lectures and, 155, 160

Frazier, E. Franklin, 182

Frederick Douglass Papers, 320

Fredrickson, George, 175–76, 285–86, 354, 375, 380, 385

Freedom from Fear (Kennedy), 375, 380

Freehling, William, 374, 375, 376

free speech, 309–11, 382–88, 398

Freidel, Frank, 336

From Slavery to Freedom (Franklin), 132

fundamentalists, 262–63

Galaxy Paperback series, 179, 184

Garland Literary Society, 12

Garrison, William Lloyd, 225

Gaston, Paul M., 278, 393

General Education Board, 32

Generation of 1900, 6, 395–97

Genovese, Eugene: AHA and, 292–93, 294; *Roll, Jordon, Roll*, 282, 360; Woodward and, 115, 285, 302, 318, 338, 359–64, 365–66

Georgia State College for Women at Milledgeville, 93

Georgia Tech, 19, 20, 21, 28, 30, 289

Gettleman, Marvin, 330–31, 337, 361

Gibson, Charles, 333, 334

Giddings, Franklin, 157–58

Gilman School, 290

Gilmore, Glenda, 350, 351, 393

Glorious Cause, The (Middlekauff), 284, 374, 375, 377–79

Goldwater, Barry, 191

Gordon, John B., 107, 116, 123

Govan, Thomas P., 142–44

Grady, Henry W., 41, 61, 92, 170

Graebner, Norman A., 374

Graf, LeRoy, 144–45

Graham, Frank Porter, 47–48, 83, 307, 308

Graham, Howard J., 151

Grand Expectations (Patterson), 375

Green, James, 364

Greenberg, Jack, 150

Griswold, A. Whitney, 231

Grove, Lee, 161, 162, 179, 192

Guggenheim Foundation, 94, 102, 257, 282, 283

Gutman, Herbert, 360

Hackney, Sheldon: about, 369, *420*; Genoveses and, 365, 366; on *Origins*, 125, 277–78; "Populism and Progressivism in Alabama," 248–49; "The South as Counterculture," 454n6; "Southern Violence," 278–79; Woodward and, 248–49, 288, 298, 394

Hahn, Steven, 203, 244–45, 345, 450n41

Haiti, 304

Hall, John, 326, 329, 331–32, 333, 335

Hamilton, J. G. de Roulhac, 44

Hampton, Wade, 173, 174

Hanna, Kathryn A., 145

Hansell, Antonina Jones "Nina," 55–56, 265, 356

Harbaugh, William H., 374

Hardwick, Thomas, 69, 70

Hare, Ida, 9

Harlan, Louis, 244, 246, 281, 320, 322, 362

Harlem Experimental Theater, 27

Harpers Ferry, 222

Harper's Magazine, 4, 73, 188–89

Harrison, Benjamin, 170

Hart, A. L., Jr., 260

Hartsock, Ernest, 19–22, *410*

Hartz, Louis, 115

Harvard Crimson, 362

Harvard University, 231, 310, 361–63, 384

Harvard University Press, 376

Hayes, Rutherford B., 105–7, 112–13

Hechinger, Fred, 242

Heflin, J. Thomas, 25–26, 37

Henderson-Brown College, 2, 12–13, 14

Hentoff, Nat, 311

Herndon, Angelo, 29–30, 307

Herring, Harriet L., 125

Hesseltine, William B., 132

Hexter, J. H., 231, 244

Hicks, John D., 80, 88

Higginson, Thomas Wentworth, 168–69, 172, 222

Higham, John, 371

Historian's Fallacies (Fischer), 199

"Historians in Defense of the Constitution," 391

historians of Woodward's generation, 395–97

"Historian's Use of Nationalism and Vice Versa, The" (Potter), 227

historical activism, 399–402

historical creed of the South, 4, 39–42, 85

historical myth, 224, 398–99

History of the South series: Coulter's volume of, 132, 256; finding writers for, 85–90; origins of, 42, 84–85; Thompson as prospective contributor to, 89–90. See also *Origins of the New South, 1877–1913*

Hoffman, J. Wesley, 143–44

Hofstadter, Richard: about, 272, 295, 396; on activist historians, 399; *Age of Reform*, 354; *Anti-Intellectualism in American Life*, 262; on Beard, 400; Elkins and, 262; Oxford History of the United States and, 264, 284, 370, 371, 372–73, 374, 375, 376; Woodward and, 266, 295–96, 357, 397

Hollinshead, Byron, 193, 370, 372

Holt Mills plant bombing, 47

homosexuality, 20, 23, 27, 277, 301, 382, 384

Hook, Sydney, 388

Hoover, J. Edgar, 312

Hope, John, 23

Hornaday, Clifford L., 13

hotels and black lodgers, 131, 136–37, 139, 144–46, 168

Houck, Lola, 172

"Hound of Heaven" (Thompson), 185

House of Percy (Wyatt-Brown), 277, 391

Hudson, John H., 307

Huntington, Collis P., 106–7, 116

Huntington Library, 94, 95

Hurston, Zora Neale, 398

identity, racial, 190

identity, southern, 213, 215–19, 220

"If Howard Cosell Can Teach at Yale, Why Can't Herbert Aptheker?" (Lemisch), 332

Illiberal Education (D'Souza), 383–85

I'll Take My Stand, 90, 217

Impressionism, 12

Independents, 62

industrial development of the South, 120–21

Innis, Roy, 310

Institute for Research in Social Science, 32, 42

integration, 181, 191–92, 300. See also *Brown v. Board of Education*; segregation

irony, 211–13, 216

Irony of American History (Niebuhr), 210, 211–12

Jack, Theodore, 19

Jackson, Blyden, 321

James, Henry, 11, 221

James, William, 18, 55

James W. Richard Lectures, 154–56, 158–61, 162, 204, 269–70

Jaqua, Ernest, 93–95, 96, 98–99

Jefferson, Thomas, 403

Jeffersonian Magazine, 71, 72, 73

Jefferson Lectures on European views of America, 367–68

Jensen, Merrill, 371–72, 374

Jim Crow laws: challenges to Woodward's thesis on, 193, 195–200, 297; civil rights movement and, 186, 187, 192–93; conclusions on, 202–3, 399; SHA and, 128, 131, 137, 142, 146; Woodward on, 151–52, 158–59, 163–64, 167–68, 173, 176–81, 206. *See also* segregation

John Harvard Library pamphlet series, 284

Johns Hopkins Club, 128

Johns Hopkins University: Woodward at, 102, 128, 228–29, 244, 245, 253, 261; Woodward's Yale offer and, 233–34, 237

Johnson, Andrew, 257, 273

Johnson, Bethany, 141

Johnson, Gerald W., 80, 299

Johnson, James Weldon, 320

Johnson, Lyman, 147

Johnson, Lyndon B., 187, 271–72

Johnson, Michael P., 347–48, 349

Joint Board of Permanent Officers, 323, 324–25, 329

Joint Chiefs of Staff security clearance, 306–8, 313–14

Joint Committee on the Defense of the Rights of Historians under the First Amendment, 330, 332–38, 340, 361

Jones, Charles Colcock, 61–62, 115, 223, 402

Jones, LeRoi, 305

Jordan, Winthrop, 250, 251

Journal of American History, 271, 278, 297, 303, 349

Journal of Southern History, 88, 129, 130, 141–42, 211, 259, 271, 278

Katz, Stanley, 335–36, 361

Keller, Morton, 374, 375, 376

Kelly, Alfred H., 151, 153

Kendrick, Benjamin B., 87–90, 120, 131

Kennan, George F., 241

Kennedy, David M., 375, 380–81

Kennedy, John F., 271–72

Kernan, Alvin, 238

Kerr, Clark, 299, 457n3

Key, V. O., 129

Key Reporter, 264

King, Charles, 398

King, Martin Luther, Jr., 182–83, 188–89, 190, 223

King, Richard H., 4

Kirkendall, Richard S., 330, 331–33, 334

Knopf, Alfred A., 164, 179, 189

Knoxville, Tenn., 142–44

Kousser, J. Morgan, 280, 285, 420

Kristakis, Nicholas, 382, 468n31

Kruman, Marc W., 420

Ku Klux Klan, 15, 26, 74, 76

laissez-faire principle, 118–19

Lamar, L. Q. C., 107, 173

Lamm, Donald, 388–89

Lampland, Susan, 290–91

Landes, David, 241

LaPalombara, Joseph, 326

Latham, H. S., 90

Lattimore, Owen, 289, 306, 314, 388

Laurans, Penelope, 393

law: as reflection of historical reality, 176–77

Legal Defense Fund of NAACP, 147–53, 154

Lemisch, Jesse, 292–93, 328, 330, 331, 332, 333

Leuchtenburg, William E., 272, 375

Levine, Lawrence W., 362

Levy, Eugene, 319–20

Lewis, Elsie, 144

Liberia, 304

Lilly Endowment, 232, 238, 241, 256, 257

Lincoln, Abraham, 224

Lincoln National Life Insurance Company, 289

literary conscience, 54

litigation on "separate but equal," 172–73. See also *Brown v. Board of Education*

Little, Brown (publisher), 92, 105, 107, 205, 254–56, 260–61

Littlefield, George W., 84–85

Lockhart, Elizabeth, 10

Lockhart, Sir John, 10

Lockhart, Walter, 10

Loemker, Leroy, 18–19

Logan, Frenise, 197–98
Logan, Rayford W., 144, 150, 182
Lost Cause, 40–41, 58, 117, 130, 343, 402
Louisiana, 106, 151, 173
Louisiana State University, 207–8
Louisiana State University Press, 42, 85, 127, 207–9, 219
Loyless, Thomas W., 74, 75
lynch law, 67
Lynd, Staughton, 61, 292, 293–94, 314
Lynn, Kenneth S., 346–48, 353

MacArthur Foundation, 283, 284
Macleod, Glenn Boyd, 54–56, 231, 293, 356–59
Macmillan, 52–53, 54, 71, 80, 102, 307
MacMullen, Ramsay, 323, 325, 329
Macon Telegraph, 158
Maget, Emily, 9
"majestic instancy," 185
Malone, Dumas, 111, 127
Manassas Battlefield National Historic Park, 391
"Marse Chan" (Page), 169
Marshall, Thurgood, 147, 151, 152–53
Martin, Boulware, 13–14
Martin, Isabella D., 343
Marx, Karl, 121–22
Mary Chesnut's Civil War: compiling of, 343–46; historiography of southern women and, 351; Pulitzer Prize for, 353–56; reviews of, 346--52; Woodward's defense of Chesnut and, 352–53
Maverick, Maury, 83–84
May, Ernest, 374, 375
May Day rally, 300
Mays, Benjamin E., 146
McCarthyism, 214, 268, 306, 332
McCasland, S. V., 154–55
McDonald, Forrest, 198
McFeely, William S., 246, 280–81, 296, 298, 327–28, 357, 369, 420
McGerr, Michael, 345
McKittrick, Eric, 176, 259, 373, 374, 375

McPherson, James, 244, 246–48, 276, 278, 281, 375, 376, 420
Mead, Margaret, 398
Melville, Herman, 221
Memphis, Tenn., 146
"menace of morals," 402–3
Mencken, Henry Louis, 20, 33, 118
Meriwether, James B., 343–45, 352
Messenger Lectures, 261
Methodist Episcopal Church, 13, 17
Meyer, Sheldon, 193, 205, 279–80, 373–74, 376, 379, 381, 392
Middlekauff, Robert, 284, 374, 375, 377–79
Militant South, The (Franklin), 133
Miller, Stephen Decatur, 342
Millis, Mary Raoul, 29
Mind of the South (Cash), 287–88, 320
Mississippi, 167, 173, 193, 263
Mississippi: The Closed Society (Silver), 263–64, 282
Mississippi Valley Historical Association, 138
Mitchell, Margaret, 46
Moltke-Hansen, David, 298
Monkonen, Eric, 378
Montgomery, Ala., boycott, 181
Moore, Barrington, Jr., 157, 287
Moore, James Tice, 124–25
Morgan, Edmund: Aptheker dispute and, 339; award of, 355; Oxford History of the United States series and, 371; Pulitzer citation and, 355; Woodward and, 284, 387, 393, 397; Woodward's decision on Yale and, 230, 231, 235, 243, 244
Morison, Samuel Eliot, 109, 306, 308, 377
Morris, Richard B., 226, 228, 371
Morrison, Joseph L., 287, 288
Muhlenfeld, Elisabeth, 344–45, 349, 351, 352
multiculturalism, 7, 384, 387, 388, 397
Murphy, Edgar Gardner, 202
Murphy, Paul L., 333
Musser, Benjamin, 22
Myrdal, Gunnar, 127, 177

NAACP (National Association for the Advancement of Colored People), 146, 147–53, 154
narrative vs. scientific history, 377–80, 381
Nashville Agrarians, 90–91, 366
Nation (magazine), 77, 179, 270
National Association of Scholars, 388
National Book Award, 284
National Endowment for the Humanities (NEH), 321–23, 328, 338
National Historical Publications and Records Commission grant, 345
National Humanities Center, 282
Nazism, 28, 98
Negro in Mississippi, The (Wharton), 167, 177, 195
Nevins, Allan, 80–81, 82, 110, 226, 377
New American Library, 219
New Deal, 97, 111, 122, 396
New Haven, 235
New Left, 397, 400
New Masses, 320
New Republic, 264, 270, 277, 286, 387
Newsome, Albert R., 89
New South: ascent of, 41, 59; investment in, 120–22; Mencken and, 118; Toombs and, 61–62; Woodward and, 81, 115–18, 122–24, 399, 402. See also *Origins of the New South, 1877–1913*
New South, The (Thompson), 89
New York Review of Books: about, 270; Oxford History of the United States series and, 378–79; review of *Mary Chesnut's Civil War* in, 347; Woodward letter on unionizing teaching assistants to, 392
New York Times: Aptheker dispute and, 331, 337; on *Brown v. Board of Education*, 158; on faculty raiding, 242; on Genovese, 362; Nixon and, 272, 273; on *Reunion and Reaction*, 111; on Schlesinger, 404; on Watson, 77; Woodward and, 189, 274, 277, 404
New York Times Book Review: Brodie in, 227; Oxford History of the United

States series and, 377–78; on works by Woodward, 80–81, 346, 347
New York Times Magazine, 304–5
Niebuhr, Reinhold, 210, 211–12
Nixon, Herman Clarence, 41, 91, 129–30, 142, 306
Nixon, Richard, 191, 272–73, 291, 392
Nordstrom, Justin, 72
Northen, W. J., 65
North-South reconciliation: and blacks, 175; and whites, 175–76;
nostalgia, 59–60, 117
Novick, Peter, 40
nuclear weapons, 212

O'Brien, Michael, ix, 126, 258, 285, 365, 366
O'Connor, Flannery, 6
Odum, Howard W.: about, 32; as adviser to Woodward, 32–36, 42, 50–52, 53, 95, 307; "Black Ulysses," 33; segregation and, 157–58; *Social Forces* and, 26; *The Strange Career of Jim Crow* and, 157–58
O'Ferrall, Charles, 68
Old South: aristocracy and, 6, 114–18, 183; Chesnut and, 343, 346; Mencken and, 118; race and, 215; southern fiction and, 58, 117; southern historians and, 40–41; Watson and, 58–59, 61
Oracle (Henderson-Brown College), 12, 13
Organization of American Historians (OAH), 138, 264, 277–78, 292, 303, 330–38, 339, 364
Origins of the New South, 1877–1913: about, 3; Beard influence on, 107–9; capitalism and, 117; Compromise of 1877 and, 114; conclusions on, 126–27; Glenn Woodward and, 356–57; Higginson and, 169; planter class paternalism and, 173, 174; publication of, 63, 107, 255; Redeemers and, 114–15, 122; reviews of, 123, 124–26, 127, 277, 405; segregation and, 162–63; *The Strange Career of Jim Crow* and, 164, 165; women in, 350; Woodward NAACP report and, 150–51; writing of, 92, 99, 102–4, 267
Osterweiss, Rollin G., 141–42

Owsley, Frank L., 41, 81, 91, 130–31
Oxford History of the United States series: background and overview of, 5, 370–71; finding authors for, 283–84, 371–75, 376; Kennedy as editor of, 380–81; narrative vs. scientific history and, 376–80, 381–82; publication of, 377, 381; writing standards for, 375–76, 381. *See also specific volumes of*
Oxford University, 25, 155, 290, 308–9
Oxford University Press, 3, 161–62, 164, 179, 204–5, 254, 260, 279. *See also* Oxford History of the United States series

Page, Thomas Nelson, 169, 346, 347
Painter, Sidney, 228
Palmer, Bruce, 280
Palmer, Robert, 292, 294, 341
Palmer, William A., 395
Parker, Theodore, 222, 223
Parker, William N., 122
Partington, Paul, 339–40
Patrick, Rembert, 259–60
Patterson, James, 375, 380
Peabody Hotel, 146
Peculiar Institution, The (Stampp), 194, 252, 262
People's Party Paper, 68, 71, 80
Percy, Walker, 218, 277
Percy, William Alexander, 277
Percy, William Armstrong, III, 277
Peretz, Martin, 392
Peskin, Allan, 112–13, 297
Petersen, Merrill D., 272, 372
Phagan, Mary, 73–74
Phi Beta Kappa Address, 90
Phillips, Ulrich Bonnell, 86, 115–16, 216, 217, 227, 295
Phoenix (magazine), 18, 19, 20
Pierson, George W., 230–35, 237–38, 240–41, 242, 293
Pipkin, Charles W., 24–25, 27
planter class, 117, 125–26, 173, 215, 221
Plessy v. Ferguson, 50, 151, 152, 157
Polakoff, Keith Ian, 113

political correctness, 8, 366, 387, 388, 397, 398
Politics of Reconstruction (Donald), 259
Pollack, Norman, 369
poll tax, 93, 269
Pomfret, John E., 133, 134, 136, 140
Poole, Scott, 169
"Populism and Progressivism in Alabama" (Hackney), 248–49
Populist Revolt, The (Hicks), 80
Populism: attitudes toward, 80, 81, 124; black voters and, 65–66, 68–69; capitalism and, 62; race and, 68–69, 174–75; southern poverty and, 122; Wallace and, 291; Watson and, 64, 67, 70; Woodward and, 91, 295, 404
Postel, Charles, 68
Potter, David: death of, 295; "The Historian's Use of Nationalism and Vice Versa," 227; "Search for Southern Identity" and, 210; SHA and, 129; as southerner, 227; *The Strange Career of Jim Crow* and, 164, 197, 198, 206; Woodward and, 18, 217, 235, 296, 397, 399
Powell, Adam Clayton, Jr., 189
Powell, Lawrence N., 244, 245, 249, 282, 420, 450n49
presentism, 399–402, 404, 406
presidential abuse of power, 272–73
presidential election of 1876, 105–7
Princeton University, 228–29, 239, 248
Princeton University Press, 247
Private Mary Chesnut, The (Muhlenfeld and Woodward), 349, 350
Proceedings of the American Philosophical Society, 261
Progressive school, 51, 111, 396
Proust, Marcel, 22
Pulitzer Prizes, 87, 246, 284, 301; *Mary Chesnut's Civil War* and, 353–56; Oxford History of the United States series and, 375, 380; Woodward and, 5, 162, 265, 392

quantification methods, 285, 286–87, 377
Quarles, Benjamin, 321

Rabinowitz, Howard, 200, 202, 204, 282–83
Rabinowitz Foundation, 314
Race Relations in Virginia (Wynes), 168, 195, 196, 197
Radcliffe College, 231
"Radical Caucus" at 1969 American Historical Association meeting, 292–95, 330, 397, 400
Radical History Review, 364
Radical Republicans, 51, 61, 110, 148–49, 221–22, 257, 259
railroads, 106–7; segregation and, 166–67, 172–75, 177–78, 180, 193, 195–97, 202, 203
Rainey, Glenn: about, 19, 30, 96, *409*; capitalism and, 62; criticism of Woodward's work by, 67–68, 109, 123; Hartsock and, 20–22; Woodward advice from, 83–84
Ramsdell, Charles, 85–90, 92
Randall, James G., 259
Randolph, A. Phillip, 189, 191
Randolph, John, 83
Random House, 219, 254
Reagan, Ronald, 274–75, 457n3
"Recent Paradoxes of American Race" (speech), 388–89
Reconstruction: books on, 259–60 (*see also specific books*); Compromise of 1877 and, 3, 109, 112; ending of, 109, 159, 404; segregation during, 163; southern historians and, 40–41; Woodward's Legal Defense Fund report and, 148–51
Reconstruction after the Civil War (Franklin), 259
Reconstruction book (Woodward): background and overview of, 256–57; cancellation of, 260–61; editor meetings on, 260; Glenn Woodward and, 357; loss of interest in, 258, 266, 268–69; origins of, 254–56; other Reconstruction books and, 259–60; research for, 257–58, 261, 267
Redeemers: about, 41; Brodie on, 227; Nixon and, 91; *Origins of the New South* and, 114–15

Reeve, Helen, 390
Reeves, F. M., 78
Region, Race and Reconstruction (Kousser and McPherson), 356
Rehearsal for Reconstruction (Rose), 279
Republicans, 106–7, 109, 112, 113; Radical Republicans, 51, 61, 110, 148–49, 221–22, 257, 259
Reston, James, 158
Reunion and Reaction: about, 3, 105–7; argument and evidence for, 111–12; Beard and, 107–9, 110; historians' challenges to, 112–13; Legal Defense Fund report and, 148–49, 150, 162; origins of, 103–4, 105; publishing of, 107, 255, 261; reviews of, 110–11; rise of capitalism and, 116–17; Woodward's Beardian perspective in, 109–10
Richard Lectures (University of Virginia), 154–56, 158–61, 162, 204, 269–70
Richmond Times-Dispatch, 141
Ridge, Martin, 297
riots, 187, 190
Road to Reunion (Buck), 87
Robison, Dan M., 111
Rockefeller, John D., 32, 35
Rockefeller Foundation, 36, 42, 46
Rodham, Hillary, 272, 391
Roll, Jordon, Roll (Genovese), 282, 360
roll call votes, 111–12, 113–14
Roman Catholicism: and Tom Watson, 31, 71–73, 75, 76, 12
Romanticism and Nationalism in the Old South (Osterweiss), 141–42
Roosevelt, Franklin D., 97, 108
Roots of Southern Populism, The (Hahn), 244–45
Roper, John Herbert, 18
Rose, Charlie, 1–2
Rose, Willie Lee, 247, 249, 260, 279, 357, 359, 361, 375
Rosenwald Fund, 23–24, 63, 84, 94
royalties, book, 155, 204, 205–6, 255
Rubin, Louis D., Jr., 115, 210, 321
Ruffin, Edmund, 141

Rusher, William, 310
Russell, Joe, 96

"Sahara of the Bozart, The"
    (Mencken), 20, 118
Salmen, Stanley, 105
Saturday Review, 46, 111, 270
Schapiro, Leonard, 241
Schlesinger, Arthur, Jr.: about, 396, 403–4;
    on Afrocentrism, 390; Aptheker and,
    313, 338; Clinton impeachment and,
    1, 391; *The Disuniting of America*, 387;
    Oxford University and, 308; SHA and,
    129; Woodward and, 1, 2, 387–88, 403
Schmidt, Benno, 384
Schmitt, Bernadotte, 97
scientific vs. narrative history,
    377–80, 381
Scott, Anne Firor, 351
Scott, Sir Walter, 10, 130
Scott, Tom, 106–7
Scottsboro case, 28–29
Scripps College, 93–96, 97–99
Seale, Bobby, 300
Second Reconstruction, The, 185–86, 188,
    191, 254–55, 257, 259
sectionalism, 41, 130, 227
security clearance, Joint Chiefs of Staff,
    306–8, 313–14
segregation: *Brown v. Board of Education*
    and, 147–53, 154; Darden and, 156; as
    improvement in black circumstances,
    201; in North, 187, 191; origins of, 163,
    194, 201–2; Second Reconstruction
    and, 185–86; separate railroad cars
    laws and, 166–67, 172–75, 177–78, 180,
    195–97, 202, 203; *The Strange Career
    of Jim Crow* and, 3–4, 156–60, 162–68,
    192–93, 194–95, 200–201; Tindall and,
    192–93; Woodward's works of 1950s
    and, 179–81, 398
Sellers, Charles G., 208, 374, 376
"separate but equal," 151, 173
separatism, black, 7, 190–92, 299–300, 305,
    306, 326, 388–90, 397

"Seven for Demos" (Woodward's planned
    book), 26, 32
Sewall, Arthur, 31
Shannon, Edgar F., 205
sharecropper strike, Arkansas, 48
sharecropping, 114, 119, 120
Shaw, Barton, 65, 70
Sheed, Wilfred, 286
Shockley, William A., 310
Shugg, Roger. W., 127
Sidney Hook Memorial Award, 388
Silent South, The (Cable), 166, 173,
    174–75
Silver, James W., 263–64, 282
Silvers, Robert, 277, 282, 287, 288
Simkins, Francis Butler, 88, 146
Simpson, Brooks, 226
Simpson, O. J., 389
Singal, Daniel J., 125
Sitterson, J. Carlyle, 45, 50, 142
Slaton, John M., 73–74
Slave Community, The (Blassingame),
    250–53
slavery: Chesnut and, 343, 346, 347, 348–49,
    350; Dumond on, 225–26; economics
    of, 119, 122; *The Peculiar Institution* and,
    194, 252, 262; segregation and, 156, 159,
    165, 167, 193, 194, 196; Styron on, 286, 301
Slavery (Elkins), 262
Slaves in the Family (Ball), 392
Smith, Gerritt, 222
Smith, Henry Nash, 240, 347
Smith, Hoke, 67, 69, 70, 71, 73, 74, 75
Smith, Lillian, 19
SNCC (Student Nonviolent Coordinating
    Committee), 189, 190, 191, 314
Social Forces, 26, 32, 42
Social Science Research Council, 84
Sons of Confederate Veterans, 86
Souls of Black Folk (Du Bois), 315
South Africa, 175–76, 201
"South as Counterculture, The" (Hackney),
    454n6
South Carolina, 106, 170, 171, 174, 177,
    195–96, 197

South Carolina Negroes (Tindall), 164, 174, 177, 195

South during Reconstruction (History of the South series), Coulter, 104, 132, 256

Southern Conference for Human Welfare, 19, 308

"Southerner as an American" collection, 208–9

southerners, blacks as, 215; as referring to whites, 215–17

Southern Historical Association (SHA): 1949 meeting of (*see* Southern Historical Association [SHA] 1949 meeting); 1951 meeting of, 142; 1952 meeting of, 142–45; 1953 meeting of, 145; 1968 meeting of, 302–3; 1969 meeting of, 287–88; about, 41; black member participation in, 130–32, 143–44, 145–46; Woodward and, 8, 207, 211, 271; "Yankee take-over" of, 134

Southern Historical Association (SHA) 1949 meeting: Beale and, 138–40; Franklin and, 132–41; Nixon and, 129–30, 132; Potter and, 129; Woodward invitation to chair program of, 128–29

Southern Historical Society, 40

southern history: as a field before Woodward, 39–42; Woodward's impact on, 3–5, 401

Southern Honor (Wyatt-Brown), 277

Southern Lady, The (Scott), 351

Southern Tenant Farmers' Union, 48

"Southern Violence" (Hackney), 278–79

speech codes, 382, 384

Spencer, Herbert, 157

Stalin, Joseph, 316

Stampp, Kenneth M.: Aptheker dispute and, 333, 334, 335–37, 340; *Era of Reconstruction*, 259, 260; Oxford History of the United States series and, 371; *The Peculiar Institution*, 194, 252, 262; *The Slave Community* and, 250–52

Stanford University, 383–84

stateways, 157, 180

Stein, Leone, 338

Stephens, Randall J., *418*, 422

Stephenson, Wendell Holmes, 78, 85–89, 99, 102–4

Stevens, Thaddeus, 149, 257

Stevenson, Adlai, 158

Stewart, T. McCants, 169–71

St. George Tucker Society, 365, 466n67

Stiles, Ezra, 211, 350

Stowe, Steven M., 347

Strange Career of Jim Crow, The: 1957 edition of, 181, 184–86, 192–93, 194, 197, 204, 216; 1966 edition of, 186, 187–88, 193, 196, 204, 389; 1974 edition of, 190, 205, 306, 389; "careers" of, 184; conclusions on, 202–4, 206, 261; demise of Jim Crow and, 218; Higginson and, 168–69, 222; King and, 182–83; legislation and, 172–74, 176–80; notes and sources for, 164–65, 168, 171; *Origins of the New South* and, 162–63; Potter and, 197, 198–99; public's "misreading" of, 179, 182; research for, 271; reviews of, 164, 168, 182, 195, 198–99; as Richard lectures, 154–61, 179, 204, 270; sales and proceeds from, 204–6; on segregation, 3–4, 156–60, 162–68, 192–93, 194–95, 200–201; Stewart and, 169–71; women in, 350; Woodward's defense of, 199–200

Strange Splendor (Hartsock), 21

"Strange Splendor" (Hartsock), 20

Strayer, Joseph, 228

Stuckey, Sterling, 305

Student Nonviolent Coordinating Committee (SNCC), 189, 190, 191, 314

Student's History of the United States (Channing), 84–85

Styron, William, 239, 286, 301–2, 347

Summer, William Graham, 157

Sumner, Charles, 149, 158, 223, 257

Sydnor, Charles S., 87

Taft, Horace, 323–25, 333

Tanenhaus, Sam, 396

Taylor, William R., 347

Texas and Pacific Railroad, 107

textile strike of 1934, 47

Thermidorian reaction, 109

Thernstrom, Stephen, 384, 392

These United States (Unger), 112

Thirteenth Amendment, 148, 151

Thomas, Norman, 47

Thompson, Francis, 185

Thompson, Holland, 89

Thompson, Mack, 333

Thoreau, Henry David, 223

Thornhill, Arthur, 205, 254–56, 258, 260–61

Thornton, J. Mills, III, 244, 280, 305, 420

Tilden, Samuel J., 105–7

Tillich, Paul, 155

Tillman, Benjamin R., 26, 171–72, 202

Time, 4, 241

Time Life, 371

Time on the Cross (Fogel and Engerman), 282

Tindall, George B., 49–50, 164, 174, 177, 192–93, 195, 209

tokenism, 188

Toland, John W., 354

Tom Watson: Agrarian Rebel: about, 3, 56–57; Bourbon Triumvirate and, 116; compared to dissertation, 76–77, 78; photos in, 79–80; Redeemer–New South regimes in, 91; research for, 32, 36–37, 266–67; reviews of, 80–81, 91; sales of, 90; Vance and, 42; Watson agrarianism in, 60–61; Watson and Catholicism in, 71–73; Watson and Doyle incident in, 64–65; Watson and Frank in, 73–75; Watson and race in, 63–65, 66–69; Watson as senator in, 75–76; Watson's boyhood in, 58–60; Watson's death in, 76, 77; Watson's dysfunctional behavior and psychosis in, 60, 66, 70, 75, 76, 78; Watson's political support in, 69–70; Watson's writings and publications in, 70–73, 74, 75; Woodward on, 81–82; Woodward's personal feelings on Watson and, 76–79, 115

"Tom Watson and the Negro in Agrarian Politics" (Woodward), 78

Tom Watson's Magazine, 71

Toombs, Robert, 61–62, 223

Townshend, Belton O., 165–66

"Triumph of Tokenism, The" (Woodward envisioned book), 188

troop withdrawal from the South, 1877, 106, 172

Truman, Harry S., 181, 316

Trumbull, Lyman, 257

Turner, Henry, 340

Turner, Nat, 286, 301

Twain, Mark, 117, 352

Tyler, Lyon G., 141

Tyler, Susan Ruffin, 141

Underground (play), 27

Underwood, Oscar, 83

Unger, Irwin, 112

United Confederate Veterans (UCV), 84–85

United Daughters of the Confederacy (UDC), 85–86

United States Commission on Civil Rights, 263

University of California, Berkeley, 228, 383

University of Chicago, 10, 14, 228, 284

University of Chicago Press, 262

University of Florida, 40, 52, 92, 93

University of Kentucky, 147

University of Maryland, 362

University of North Carolina, 3, 36–37, 39–42. *See also* Woodward, C. Vann— education of

University of North Carolina Press, 52, 209

University of South Carolina, Institute for Southern Studies, 344

University of Tennessee, 145

University of Texas, 84–85

University of Tokyo, 147, 207

University of Virginia: black students at, 156; *Brown v. Board of Education* and, 156, 160; *Cavalier Daily* and, 156, 158, 160; Richard Lectures at, 154–55,

204; royalties from *Strange Career of Jim Crow* and, 204, 205; Woodward's teaching at, 63, 92, 266

University of Wisconsin, 96, 228

U.S. House of Representatives Committee on the Judiciary, 93

U.S. Supreme Court, 147, 151, 152, 181, 191

Vance, Rupert: *Origins of the New South* and, 89, 125; southern history and, 42; *The Strange Career of Jim Crow* and, 176; Woodward and, 34, 52, 53, 95, 155, 160–61

Vann, Emily "Bess" Branch, 9, 11, 16, 288–90

Vann, John, 9

Vann, John Maget, 9

Vann, Renselear, 9

Vardaman, James K., 26, 202

Vaughan, Alden, 374, 375

Vidal, Gore, 354–55

Vietnam War, 272, 274, 292, 294, 360

Virginia, the Old Dominion (Andrews), 86

Virginia Quarterly Review, 208, 219

Voting Rights Act of 1965, 186, 187, 275

Wade, Richard C., 196, 199

Wall, Bennet H., 45–46, 48, 142, 144–45, 146, 302

Wallace, George, 191, 291, 309

Walt Disney Corporation, 391

Walter Lynwood Fleming Lectures, 207–8, 209

Walters, Raymond, 286

Ward, John W., 374

Ward, Paul, 292, 293

Warner, Charles Dudley, 167–68

Warren, Robert Penn: about, 6, 368, 417; *Flood*, 367; SHA and, 142, 302–3; *Who Speaks for the Negro?*, 367; Woodward and, 143, 210, 220, 223, 239, 357, 366–68

Washington, Booker T., 170–71

Washington Post, 124, 354

Washington University (Saint Louis), 231

Waskow, Arthur, 283, 293

Watergate scandal, 5, 272–73, 274

Watson, Georgia Doremus, 36–37

Watson, Georgia Durham, 77, 79

Watson, John Smith, 59

Watson, Thomas E. (Tom): about, 30–31; Bethany, 58–59, 70; Roman Catholicism and, 31, 71–73, 75, 76. See also *Tom Watson: Agrarian Rebel*

Watson, Thomas Miles, 59

Watson Papers, 37, 266–67

Watson's Magazine, 71, 72–73

Watts riots, 187

Webb, Walter Prescott, 124

Weekly Jeffersonian, 71, 74

Weisberger, Bernard A., 259

Welke, Barbara Young, 202

Wentworth, Richard L., 127

West, Don, 47, 307, 314

Westerner, S.S., 14

Westmoreland, William, 309

Wharton, Vernon Lane, 132, 167, 177, 195

Whigs, 109, 112, 113, 278

white supremacy: Jim Crow laws and, 151, 163, 173, 201, 203, 216; Populists and, 68; Reconstruction and, 225; southern identity and, 217–18, 225; Watson and, 67

White Supremacy (Fredrickson), 354

Whitfield, Stephen J., 277

Whitman, Alden, 331

Whitney Center, 393–94

Whittle Springs, 145

Who Speaks for the Negro? (Warren), 367

Wiebe, Robert, 335–36

Wiener, Jonathan, 126, 283

Wilentz, Sean, 1, 345

Wiley, Bell Irvin, 123, 140, 142, 144, 146

William and Mary College, 133, 135, 139, 140, 141, 364

Williams, Ben Ames, 343

Williams, John A., 420

Williamsburg Inn, 136–37

Williamsburg Lodge, 136

Williamson, Joel, 195–96, 197, 199, 200, 201, 203, 282, 285

Wilson, Edmund, 343

Wilson, Woodrow, 71, 75

Winkler, Henry R., 278–79

Winks, Robin, 236–37, 393

Within the Plantation Household
(Fox-Genovese), 365
Wolfe, Thomas, 6, 46, 79, 117, 220
Wood, Gordon S., 283–84, 374, 375, 378–79
Woodward, Comer McDonald (uncle), 10,
14–16, 23, 25, 290, 407
Woodward, C. Vann: activism of,
29–30, 128–30, 399–401, *408*, *413*,
415–22; address to American Historical
Association, 291–92, 369; alleged tilt
to conservatism, 298–99, 311–12, 382;
on Aptheker seminar dispute, 326–28,
331; background and overview of, 1–8;
on blacks prior to segregation, 165, 168,
200–201; as book reviewer, 264, 266,
270, 276–77, 282, 285–88 (*see also specific
books*); and *Brown v. Board of Education*,
147–50, 151–52, 296; childhood of,
2, 10–11, 15; and communism, 28, 29,
46–47, 306–7, 308, 313–14, 459n39;
death of, 394; deaths of friends and
family of, 288–91, 295–96, 358–59, 366,
368, 369; as debater, 12, 18; disputes of,
over academic freedom, 306, 308–9, 318,
335–36; as dissertation adviser, 244–49,
261–62, 279, 281; European trip (1932),
28; family of, 9–11; Festschrift for, 356;
fire at home, 358; grant and fellowship
proposal reviews of, 283–84; health of,
393–94; on ideas over facts, 135, 266;
impact of, on southern history, 3–5,
401; on impeachment, 272–73, 391–92;
on Jim Crow laws, 151–52, 158–59,
163–64, 167–68, 173, 176–81, 206; as
instructor, 5, 244–53, 450n41 (*see also
under specific universities*); job dodging
by, 52; last years of, 390–94; legacy
of, 395, 405–6; literary interests of, 11,
46; literature preferred to history by,
28; manuscript evaluation by, 262–64,
390–91 (*see also specific books*); marriage
of, 56; as mentor for students, 276–77,
279–82 (*see also specific protégés*);
Naval Intelligence service of, 101–2,
412; on Old South, 402; organizational
commitments of, 264–66; papers

of, 271; PhD exams of, 49–50; on
racial segregation, exceptions to, 163,
198, 199; and realism, 91, 198, 397; on
Redeemers, 116–18, 120, 121–22, 124–25,
399, 404; research and use of sources
by, 164–65, 168, 171, 209, 266–68, 271,
349, 453n36; retirement from Yale, 341;
scholar rankings by, 284–85; southern
roots of, 226–28; as speaker, 12, 268;
visits to Soviet Union, 28, 314, 358;
women in writing of, 350–51; writing
of, for public vs. academia, 269–71; and
Yale professorship decision, 233–40;
and Yale Sterling Professorship offer,
230–33, 237–39
—education: at Columbia University,
24–26, 27–28; at Emory, 2–3, 14, 16,
17–19; at Henderson-Brown College,
12–14; at Morillton, 11–12; PhD exams
at UNC and, 49–50; Rosenwald
scholarship and, 23–24; at UNC, 3, 39;
UNC dissertation and, 32, 44, 51, 52,
53–55; UNC faculty and, 42–43, 44–45,
50–52
—works: "Age of Reinterpretation," 265;
American Counterpoint, 441n20, 444n23;
"The Background of the Abandonment
of Reconstruction," 147–49, 152, 154,
162; *The Burden of Southern History*
(*See Burden of Southern History, The*);
"Clio with Soul," 303, 389; "Equality:
The Deferred Commitment," 224–25;
essay on D'Souza, 383–87, 389; *The
Future of the Past*, 188; "The Historical
Dimension," 219–20; "Impressionistic
Prose," 12; "The Irony of Southern
History," 145, 210–14, 216, 218–19, 221,
227, 271; "John Brown's Private War,"
222–23; *Mary Chesnut's Civil War*
(*see Mary Chesnut's Civil War*); NAACP
LDF report, 147–49, 152, 154, 162; *The
National Experience*, 112, 205–6, 336;
New York Review of Books, essays in, 270,
271, 277, 282, 285–86, 287–88, 383–87;
New York Times Book Review, essays in,
270, 276, 285–86; *The Old World's New*

World, 367–68, 453n36; *Origins of the New South, 1877–1913* (*see Origins of the New South, 1877–1913*); "The Outlawry of War" (speech), 12; "The Political and Literary Career of Thomas E. Watson," 44, 51, 52–55, 76–77, 78 (see also *Tom Watson: Agrarian Rebel*); "The Political Legacy of Reconstruction," 225; *The Private Mary Chesnut*, 349, 350; "Recent Paradoxes of American Race" (speech), 388–89; *Reunion and Reaction* (see *Reunion and Reaction*); Reconstruction book, unpublished (*see* Reconstruction book); "Romance and Realities" (speech), 12; "The Search for Southern Identity," 208, 209–10, 215–19, 227; "Seeds of Failure in Radical Race Policy," 261; "The South in Search of a Philosophy," 433n18, 447n27; "A Southern Critique for the Gilded Age," 221; *The Strange Career of Jim Crow* (see *Strange Career of Jim Crow, The*); *Thinking Back*, 81, 199–200, 210, 368; *Tom Watson: Agrarian Rebel* (*see Tom Watson: Agrarian Rebel*); "What Happened to the Civil Rights Movement?," 188–89

Woodward, Emily "Bess" Branch Vann (mother), 9, 11, 16, 288–90

Woodward, Glenn Boyd Macleod (wife), 54–56, 231, 290, 356–59

Woodward, Hugh Alison "Jack" (father), 10, 15–16, 289–90, 407

Woodward, Peter Vincent (son), 100, 232, 288, 290–91, 295, 357, 414

Woodward, Susan Lampland (daughter-in-law), 290–91, 295

Woodward, William Benjamin (grandfather), 10

"Woodward Report" (Yale), 310–12, 382

Works Progress Administration (WPA), 35

World War II, 96–98, 100–101, 108, 122, 180, 396

Wright, Arthur, 240

Wright, Gavin, 120

W. W. Norton, 255–56, 388–89

Wyatt-Brown, Anne, 420

Wyatt-Brown, Bertram, 60, 420; *House of Percy*, 277, 391; *Southern Honor*, 277; on Watson, 70; Woodward and, 245, 285, 394

Wynes, Charles E., 168, 172–73, 195, 196, 197

Yale Alumni Magazine, 340

Yale Daily News, 310, 326, 327, 335, 337, 339–40, 341

Yale Review, 351, 352

Yale University, 5; Aptheker dispute at (*see* Aptheker seminar dispute); black student unrest at, 299–301; and Chesnut diary, 345; history department in 1960, 230–31; faculty recruitment at, 240–41, 242; and free speech, 309, 310–11, 382; reputation of, 230; rules of confidentiality at, 332, 334, 335, 337; and Wayne Dick affair, 382; and women, 350; Woodward and, 233–40, 341

Yale University Press, 321

Younger, Edward, 155–56, 168

youth movement, southern, 141–42

Zinn, Howard, 293, 294–95